June 23–26, 2014
Bloomington, IN, USA.

I0047544

Association for Computing Machinery

Advancing Computing as a Science & Profession

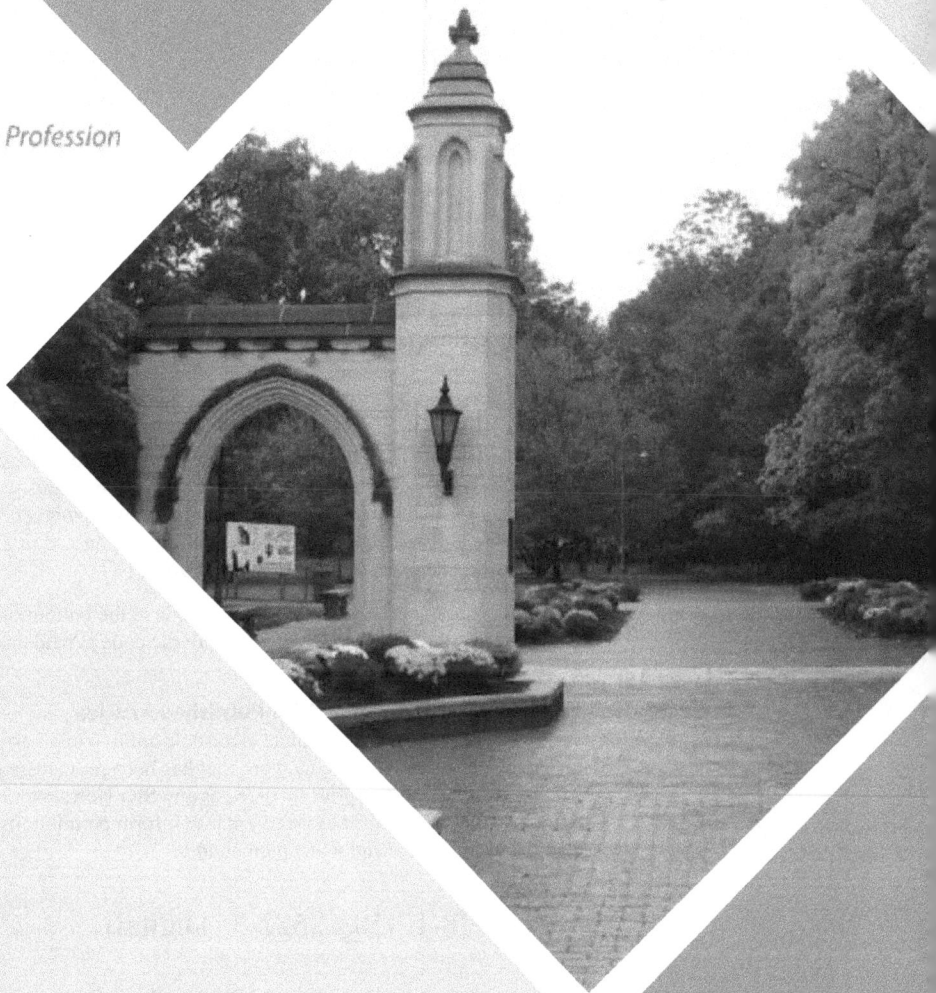

WebSci'14

Proceedings of the 2014 ACM

Web Science Conference

Sponsored by:

ACM SIGWEB

Supporters:

IU School of Informatics and Computing, Center for Complex Networks and Systems Research, IU Pervasive Technology Institute, Google, IUB Office of the Vice Provost for Research, IUB Office of the Provost, Microsoft, Facebook, RPI Tetherless World Constellation, IUB Graduate School, NOW Publishers, Continuum Analytics, GESIS, Morgan & Claypool Publishers, IU Department of Sociology, and Kelley School of Business

**Association for
Computing Machinery**

Advancing Computing as a Science & Profession

The Association for Computing Machinery
2 Penn Plaza, Suite 701
New York, New York 10121-0701

ISBN: 978-1-4503-2622-3 (Digital)

ISBN: 978-1-4503-3112-8 (Print)

Additional copies may be ordered prepaid from:

ACM Order Department
PO Box 30777
New York, NY 10087-0777, USA

Phone: 1-800-342-6626 (USA and Canada)
+1-212-626-0500 (Global)
Fax: +1-212-944-1318
E-mail: acmhelp@acm.org
Hours of Operation: 8:30 am – 4:30 pm ET

Printed in the USA

Web Science 2014 Chairs' Welcome

Welcome to the ACM Web Science 2014 Conference. This is the 6th conference of the series and the 3rd to be sponsored by ACM through the Special Interest Group on Hypertext, Hypermedia and the Web (SIGWEB). The Conference continues to acknowledge the centrality of the Web as a socially constructed artifact, focusing on the study of information networks, social communities, organizations, applications, and policies that shape and are shaped by the Web. The conference provides a unique forum for researchers from different disciplines, including computer, social, and related sciences, with the goal of fostering and supporting a thriving interdisciplinary community of Web Science.

This year we were very pleased to receive 144 valid full and short paper submissions and 33 poster submissions. The largest number of contributions was from the US followed by the UK and Germany. Almost all submissions received 3 reviews, for a total of over 500 reviews from around 100 reviewers. Based on the reviews, on discussions among the reviewers, and on a meta-review phase by the Program Chairs, 20 submissions were accepted as full papers, 9 submissions were accepted as short papers and 35 submissions were accepted as posters in total (some accepted posters were originally submitted as full/short papers). The overall acceptance rate for full/short papers was 20.14% (29 papers accepted out of 144 submissions).

The highly selective program allowed us to maintain Web Science 2014 as a single track conference, to expose all participants to the high-quality contributions we accepted, give their authors high visibility, and help foster a cohesive Web Science community. This year we decided to also have three "lightning talk" sessions for posters on the first day of the conference, so that all the authors of accepted posters will have a chance to make their work visible in an incisive format that, we believe, will better engage conference participants with the poster contributions and the poster sessions.

We thank all the authors who have contributed to Web Science: we are confident that the papers, posters and conference program will provide a platform of insight, evidence and methods that will support the community in taking this exciting and important discipline forward. We also thank the PC members and reviewers who delivered detailed and helpful comments during the review process. We take this opportunity to express our gratitude to all the conference organizers, and especially the general co-chairs (Jim Hendler and Bill Dutton), the workshop chairs (Sandra González-Bailón, Alessandro Flammini, Daniela Paolotti), the data challenge chair (David Crandall), the publicity chair (Giovanni Luca Ciampaglia), the local chair (Emilio Ferrara), and the proceedings chair (Filippo Radicchi). Last, but not least, we acknowledge the generous university and corporate sponsors who are allowing us to keep Web Science very affordable for all participants.

The conference program is accompanied by a number of exciting keynote talks given by Dame Wendy Hall (U. of Southampton), JP Rangaswami (Salesforce.com), Laura DeNardis (American University) and Daniel Tunkelang (LinkedIn). In addition, a series of workshops are held to give the community a forum to present and discuss work-in-progress:

- Altmetrics'14 - Expanding Impacts and Metrics
- Computational Approaches to Social Modeling (ChASM)
- Massive Data Flow: Understanding the Complex Dynamics of the Web
- The Web of Scientific Knowledge: Current Trends & Future Perspectives in the Big Data Era
- Interdisciplinary Coups to Calamities
- Web Science Education: Sharing Experiences and Developing Community

- 2nd International Workshop on Building Web Observatories (B-WOW2014)
- Research Methodologies for Analyzing Cybercrime and Cyberwar

The program also includes a doctoral consortium to provide PhD students in the later stages of their research with a supportive and critical learning opportunity to discuss their work in progress and to receive feedback and guidance from senior Web and information science scholars. Conference attendees will have an opportunity to enjoy the exhibit *Places & Spaces: Mapping Science,* meant to inspire cross-disciplinary discussion on how to best track and communicate human activity and scientific progress on a global scale. Finally, we will award prizes for the most innovative visualizations of Web data. For this data challenge, we are providing four large datasets that will remain publicly available to web scientists.

WebSci14 is hosted on the beautiful campus of Indiana University (IU) in Bloomington, Indiana. In fact, Thomas Gaines in his 1991 book *The Campus as a Work of Art* cited IU's limestone campus as one of the five most beautiful in the U.S. Established in 1820, Indiana University is a leading public institution of higher learning with particularly notable strengths related to this conference: the social sciences, informatics, information science, computer science, and network science. The location of the meeting in the Indiana Memorial Union is one of the largest student union buildings in the world. The university and the town of Bloomington have many cultural, architectural, and culinary attractions that we hope participants will be able to take advantage of during their time in the rolling hills of southern Indiana.

We are pleased to welcome you to *WebSci14*, and look forward to a stimulating conference.

The Web Science 2014 Program Chairs,
Markus Strohmaier
Eric T. Meyer
Ciro Cattuto

The Web Science 2014 General Chairs,
Filippo Menczer
Jim Hendler
William Dutton

Table of Contents

Keynote Addresses

Session 1: Methods (Full papers)
Session Chair: Daniela Paolotti *(ISI Foundation)*

Session 2: Geographies (Full papers)
Session Chair: Giovanni L. Ciampaglia *(Indiana University)*

Session 3: Engagements (Full papers)

Session Chair: Filippo Menczer *(Indiana University)*

Session 4: Networks (Full papers)

Session Chair: Emilio Ferrara *(Indiana University)*

Session 5: Interactions (Short papers)

Session Chair: Eric T. Meyer *(University of Oxford)*

Session 6: Activities (Short papers)

Session Chair: Alessandro Flammini *(Indiana University)*

Session 7: Content (Full papers)
Session Chair: Filippo Radicchi *(Indiana University)*

Pecha Kucha 1: Quick poster presentations
Session Chair: Ciro Cattuto *(ISI Foundation)*

Pecha Kucha 2: Quick poster presentations

Session Chair: Markus Strohmaier *(Koblenz-Landau)*

Pecha Kucha 3: Quick poster presentations

Session Chair: Eric T. Meyer *(University of Oxford)*

Web Science 2014 Conference Organization

General Chairs: Filippo Menczer *(Indiana University, USA)*
Jim Hendler *(Rensselaer Polytechnic Institute, USA)*
William Dutton *(University of Oxford, UK)*

Program Chairs: Markus Strohmaier *(GESIS & University of Koblenz-Landau, Germany)*
Ciro Cattuto *(ISI Foundation, Italy)*
Eric T. Meyer *(University of Oxford, UK)*

Proceedings Chair: Filippo Radicchi *(Indiana University, USA)*

Local Arrangements Chair: Emilio Ferrara *(Indiana University, USA)*

Local Arrangements Committee: Judy Warner *(Indiana University, USA)*
Tara Holbrook *(Indiana University, USA)*

Publicity Chair: Giovanni Luca Ciampaglia *(Indiana University, USA)*

Publicity Committee: Clayton Davis *(Indiana University, USA)*
Rachael Fulper *(Indiana University, USA)*
Jared Lorince *(Indiana University, USA)*

Treasurer & Registration Chair: Ying Ding *(Indiana University, USA)*

Workshop Chairs: Sandra González-Bailón *(University of Pennsylvania, USA)*
Alessandro Flammini *(Indiana University, USA)*
Daniela Paolotti *(ISI Foundation, Italy)*

Data Challenge Chair: David Crandall *(Indiana University, USA)*

Steering Committee Chair Wendy Hall *(University of Southampton, UK)*

Program committee: Yong-Yeol Ahn *(Indiana University, USA)*
Luca Maria Aiello *(Yahoo! Research, Spain)*
Harith Alani *(Open University, UK)*
William Allen *(University of Oxford, UK)*
Sitaram Asur *(HP Labs, USA)*
Alain Barrat *(CNRS, France)*
Fabricio Benevenuto *(Federal University of Minas Gerais, Brazil)*
Mark Bernstein *(Eastgate Systems, Inc., USA)*
Paolo Boldi *(Università degli Studi di Milano, Italy)*
Ian Brown *(Oxford Internet Institute, UK)*
Niels Brügger *(Aarhus Universitet, Denmark)*
Licia Capra *(University College London, UK)*
Carlos Castillo *(Qatar Computing Research Institute, Qatar)*
Lu Chen *(Wright State University, USA)*
Cristobal Cobo *(Oxford Internet Institute, UK)*

Program committee (continued):   David Crandall *(Indiana University, USA)*
Pasquale De Meo *(Vrije Universiteit, Netherlands)*
David De Roure *(Oxford e-Research Centre, UK)*
Grace Eden *(University of Oxford, UK)*
Kevin Feeney *(Trinity College Dublin, Ireland)*
Pnina Fichman *(Indiana University, USA)*
Alessandro Flammini *(Indiana University, USA)*
Fabian Flöck *(KIT Karlsruhe, Germany)*
Matteo Gagliolo *(Université libre de Bruxelles, Belgium)*
Laetitia Gauvin *(ISI Foundation, Italy)*
Daniel Gayo Avello *(University of Oviedo, Spain)*
Florian Geigl *(TU-Graz, Austria)*
Scott Golder *(Cornell University, USA)*
Bruno Gonçalves *(Aix-Marseille Université, France)*
Andrew Gordon *(University of Southern California, USA)*
Scott Hale *(University of Oxford, UK)*
Noriko Hara *(Indiana University, USA)*
Bernhard Haslhofer *(University of Vienna, Austria)*
Denis Helic *(KMI, TU-Graz, Austria)*
Andreas Hotho *(University of Wuerzburg, Germany)*
Geert-Jan Houben *(TU Delft, Netherlands)*
Jeremy Hunsinger *(Wilfrid Laurier University, Canada)*
Robert Jäschke *(L3S Research Center, Germany)*
Marina Jirotka *(University of Oxford, UK)*
Ajita John *(Avaya Labs, USA)*
Andreas Jungherr *(University of Bamberg, Germany)*
Jérôme Kunegis *(University of Koblenz-Landau, Germany)*
Haewoon Kwak *(Telefonica Research, Spain)*
Renaud Lambiotte *(University of Namur, Belgium)*
Daniel Lamprecht *(Graz University of Technology, Austria)*
Matthieu Latapy *(CNRS, France)*
Silvio Lattanzi *(Google, USA)*
Vili Lehdonvirta *(University of Oxford, UK)*
Sune Lehmann *(TU Denmark, Denmark)*
Kristina Lerman *(University of Southern California, USA)*
Q. Vera Liao *(University of Illinois at Urbana Champaign, USA)*
David Liben-Nowell *(Carleton College, USA)*
Haiko Lietz *(GESIS Leibniz Institute for the Social Sciences, Germany)*
Yu-Ru Lin *(University of Pittsburgh, USA)*
Huan Liu *(Arizona State University, USA)*
Jared Lorince *(Indiana University, USA)*
Mathias Lux *(Klagenfurt University, Austria)*
Massimo Marchiori *(Università di Padova, Italy)*
Yutaka Matsuo *(University of Tokyo, Japan)*
Jaimie Murdock *(Indiana University, USA)*

Program committee (continued): Mirco Musolesi *(University of Birmingham, UK)*

Eni Mustafaraj *(Wellesley College, USA)*

Wolfgang Nejdl *(L3S and University of Hannover, Germany)*

André Panisson *(ISI Foundation, Italy)*

Hanwoo Park *(YeungNam University, South Korea)*

Fernando Pedone *(University of Lugano, Switzerland)*

Leto Peel *(University of Colorado at Boulder, USA)*

Orion Penner *(IMT Lucca, Italy)*

Nicola Perra *(Northeastern University, Italy)*

Isabella Peters *(ZBW, Germany)*

Brian Pickering *(University of Southampton IT Innovation Centre, UK)*

Rob Procter *(University of Warwick, UK)*

Cornelius Puschmann *(Humboldt-University of Berlin, Germany)*

Daniele Quercia *(Yahoo Labs, Spain)*

Carlos P. Roca *(Universitat Rovira i Virgili, Spain)*

Richard Rogers *(University of Amsterdam, Netherlands)*

Daniel Romero *(Northwestern University, USA)*

Matthew Rowe *(Lancaster University, UK)*

Giancarlo Ruffo *(Università di Torino, Italy)*

Derek Ruths *(McGill University, Canada)*

Rossano Schifanella *(Università di Torino, Italy)*

Ralph Schroeder *(Oxford Internet Institute, UK)*

Kalpana Shankar *(University College Dublin, Ireland)*

Xiaolin Shi *(Microsoft Corporation, USA)*

Elena Simperl *(University of Southampton, UK)*

Philipp Singer *(Knowledge Management Institute, USA)*

Marc Smith *(Connected Action Consulting Group, USA)*

Steffen Staab *(University of Koblenz-Landau, Germany)*

Burkhard Stiller *(University of Zurich, Switzerland)*

Gerd Stumme *(Uiniversity of Kassel, Germany)*

Lei Tang *(@WalmartLabs, USA)*

Loren Terveen *(University of Minnesota, USA)*

Sebastiano Vigna *(Università degli Studi di Milano, Italy)*

Claudia Wagner *(GESIS-Leibniz Institute for the Social Sciences, Germany)*

Simon Walk *(Technical University Graz, Austria)*

Jillian Wallis *(CENS - UCLA, USA)*

Stan Wasserman *(Indiana University, USA)*

Matthew Weber *(Rutgers University, USA)*

Ingmar Weber *(Qatar Computing Research Institute, Qatar)*

Katrin Weller *(GESIS Leibniz Institute for the Social Sciences, Germany)*

Lilian Weng *(Indiana University, USA)*

Christopher Wienberg *(University of Southern California, USA)*

Joss Wright *(Oxford Internet Institute, UK)*

Ben Zhao *(UC Santa Barbara, USA)*

Arkaitz Zubiaga *(Dublin Institute of Technology, Ireland)*

Additional reviewers:

Mohammad Ali Abbasi

Amparo E. Cano

Giovanni Luca Ciampaglia

Elena Demidova

Martina Deplano

Emilio Ferrara

Rachael Fulper

Costas Gabrielatos

Mihai Georgescu

Cesar Gonzalez-Perez

Eelco Herder

Muhammad Imran

Jasleen Kaur

Fabrizio Messina

Azadeh Nematzadeh

Ashwin Rajadesingan

Miriam Redi

Michael Riegler

Domenico Rosaci

Giuseppe Sarnè

Claudio Schifanella

Christoph Scholz

Emilio Sulis

Marcella Tambuscio

Jiliang Tang

Asmelash Teka Hadgu

Onur Varol

Greg Ver Steeg

Sarah Vieweg

Gianluigi Viscusi

Suhang Wang

Xiangjun Wang

Taha Yasseri

Reza Zafarani

Web Science 2014 Sponsor & Supporters

Sponsor: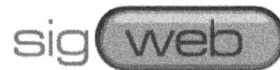

Supporters:

Microsoft

 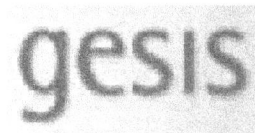

Observing the Web

Wendy Hall

Professor Dame, DBE FRS FREng
Dean, Faculty of Physical Sciences and Engineering
University of Southampton
Southampton SO17 1BJ UK
wh@ecs.soton.ac.uk

Abstract

It is ten years since the concept of Web Science was conceived against a backdrop of a dramatically evolving Web. At the time social networks were in their infancy and linked data was only talked about in the research labs. Today as we celebrate the 25th anniversary of the birth of the Web and we become increasingly aware of the pressures on it going forwards, I see Web Science as more significant to the evolution of the Web than ever. It is so important we can present real evidence to the major stakeholders in the development of the Web to demonstrate the likely consequences of decisions they might take. It is my hypothesis that we cannot achieve this without establishing an international project to observe what is happening on the Web and to set this in the wider social context and what has happened before. This means developing mechanisms to share data and data analytics across different projects and cultures over time – including the creation of "safe harbours" in which private and public data can be integrated with out compromising privacy, confidentiality, or data security issues. This thinking has led to the establishment of the Web Observatory project, the latest incarnation of which will be presented in this talk. There are many such observatories in existence. The grand challenge is to create a distributed framework to facilitate the virtual integration of the data that resides in the various repositories and the sharing of data analysis tools as well as the results of the research that such international collaboration will engender.

Categories and Subject Descriptors: K.4.0

Keywords: Keynote Talk; Computers and Society

Short Bio

Wendy Hall is a Professor of Computer Science at the University of Southampton, UK, and Dean of the Faculty of Physical and Applied Sciences. She has been a pioneer in the development of research on multimedia and hypermedia, digital libraries, Semantic Web, and the emerging discipline of Web Science. Her current research includes applications of the Semantic Web and exploring the interface between the life sciences and the physical sciences. In addition to her PhD from Southampton, Hall has honorary degrees from Oxford Brookes University, Glamorgan University, Cardiff University, the University of Pretoria, and the University of Sussex. She has served as Head of the School of Electronics and Computer Science at Southampton, Senior Vice President of the Royal Academy of Engineering, member of the UK Prime Minister's Council for Science and Technology, founding member of the Scientific Council of the European Research Council, President of the British Computer Society, and President of the ACM. She is a Fellow of the ACM, the Royal Society, the British Computer Society, the Institution of Engineering and Technology, the City and Guilds, and a Dame Commander of the Order of the British Empire. Through these UK and international leadership roles, Dame Wendy Hall has played a prominent role in shaping science and engineering policy and education. Various news organizations have listed her among the most influential women in IT and in the UK. Among her many honors we note the Anita Borg Award for Technical Leadership. Hall is a Founder and the Managing Director of the Web Science Trust.

WebSci'14, June 23–26, 2014, Bloomington, IN, USA.
ACM 978-1-4503-2622-3/14/06.
http://dx.doi.org/10.1145/2615569.2618143

Web Science: How is it Different?

Daniel Tunkelang

LinkedIn

Mountain View, CA

dtunkelang@linkedin.com

ABSTRACT

The scientific method of observation, measurement, and experiment may be our greatest achievement as a species. The technological innovation we enjoy today is the product of a culture of systematized scientific experimentation.

But historically scientific experimentation has been expensive. Experiments consumed natural resources, took a long time to conduct, and required even more time and labor to analyze. In order to be productive, scientists have had to factor these costs into their work and to optimize accordingly.

Web science is different. Not, as some have speciously argued, because big data has made the scientific method obsolete. The key difference is that web science has changed the economics of scientific experimentation. Thus, even as web scientists apply the traditional scientific method, they optimize based on very different economics.

In this talk, I'll survey how web science has changed our approach to experimentation, for better and for worse. Specifically, I'll talk about differences in hypothesis generation, offline analysis, and online testing.

Categories and Subject Descriptors

G.3 [Probability and Statistics]: Experimental design.

General Terms

Measurement, Economics, Experimentation.

Keywords

Scientific Method, Web Science.

BIOGRAPHY

Daniel Tunkelang is Head of Query Understanding at LinkedIn, where he previously formed and led the product data science team. LinkedIn search allows members to find people, companies, jobs, groups and other content. His team aims to provide users with the best possible results that satisfy their information needs and help to get insights from professional data. Tunkelang has BS and MS degrees in computer science and math from MIT, and a PhD in computer science from CMU. He co-founded the annual symposium on human-computer interaction and information retrieval (HCIR) and wrote the first book on Faceted Search (Morgan and Claypool 2009). Prior to joining LinkedIn, Tunkelang was Chief Scientist of Endeca (acquired by Oracle in 2011 for $1.1B) and leader of the local search quality team at Google, mapping local businesses to their home pages. He is the co-inventor of 20 patents.

WebSci'14, June 23–26, 2014, Bloomington, IN, USA.
ACM 978-1-4503-2622-3/14/06.

The Global War for Internet Governance

Laura DeNardis
American University
Washington, DC, USA

Abstract

Internet governance conflicts are the new spaces where political and economic power is unfolding in the 21st century. Technologies of Internet governance increasingly mediate freedom of expression and individual privacy. They are entangled with national security and global commerce. The distributed nature of Internet governance technologies is shifting historic control over these public interest areas from sovereign nation-states to private ordering and new global institutions. The term "Internet governance" conjures up a host of global controversies such as the prolonged Internet outage in Syria during political turmoil or Google's decision not to acquiesce to U.S. government requests to remove an incendiary political video from YouTube. It invokes narratives about the United Nations "taking over" the Internet, NSA surveillance revelations, cybersecurity concerns about denial of service attacks, and the mercurial privacy policies of social media companies. These issues exist only at the surface of a technologically concealed and institutionally complex ecosystem of governance that is generally out of public view. This talk explains how the Internet is currently governed, particularly through the sinews of power that exist in technical architecture and new global institutions, and presents several brewing Internet governance controversies that will affect the future of economic and expressive liberty..

Categories and Subject Descriptors

H.5 Miscellaneous

Keywords

Internet governance; Internet protocols; domain name system; interconnection

Short Bio

Laura DeNardis is a scholar of Internet architecture and governance and a Professor of Communication at American University in Washington, D.C. She is an affiliated fellow of the Yale Information Society Project and served as its Executive Director from 2008-2011. She is a co-founder and co-series editor of the MIT Press Information Society book series and currently serves as the Vice-Chair of the Global Internet Governance Academic Network. She has previously taught at New York University, in the Volgenau School of Engineering at George Mason University, and at Yale Law School. With a background in information engineering (Cornell University) and doctoral training in Science and Technology Studies (Virginia Tech), DeNardis is an expert consultant in Internet governance and architecture to Fortune 500 companies, foundations, and government agencies. In the 1990s she was the President of Internet strategy consultancy Atlantic Consulting Group (Falls Church, VA) and previously worked as a computer networking management consultant for Ernst & Young's global information technology practice. Her books include The Global War for Internet Governance (Yale University Press, in press); Opening Standards: The Global Politics of Interoperability (MIT Press 2011); Protocol Politics: The Globalization of Internet Governance (MIT Press 2009); and Information Technology in Theory (2007).

Permission to make digital or hard copies of part or all of this work for personal or classroom use is granted without fee provided that copies are not made or distributed for profit or commercial advantage, and that copies bear this notice and the full citation on the first page. Copyrights for third-party components of this work must be honored. For all other uses, contact the owner/author(s). Copyright is held by the author/owner(s).
WebSci'14, June 23–26, 2014, Bloomington, IN, USA.
ACM 978-1-4503-2622-3/14/06.
http://dx.doi.org/10.1145/2615569.2618146

Translating Surveys to Surveillance on Social Media: Methodological Challenges & Solutions

Chao Yang
Department of Computer Science
The University of Iowa
Iowa City, IA, USA
chao-yang@uiowa.edu

Padmini Srinivasan
Department of Computer Science
The University of Iowa
Iowa City, IA, USA
padmini-srinivasan@uiowa.edu

ABSTRACT

Passive surveillance of preferences, opinions and behaviors on social media is becoming increasingly common. The general goal is to make inferences from observations collected from the numerous posts publicly available in blogs, microblogs, and other social forums. A traditional approach for collecting observations is by querying a random (or convenience) sample of individuals with surveys. A wide variety of well respected survey instruments have been developed over many decades especially in social sciences. The question addressed here is: how does one 'translate' a survey of interest into surveillance strategies on social media? Specifically, how does one find the posts that could be interpreted as valid responses to the survey? Developing a general methodology for translating a survey into social medial surveillance might further the inclusion of social media research into traditional social science research. We propose a translation methodology using a well-reputed survey (the Satisfaction with Life Scale) as an example. A second methodological contribution that goes beyond the survey translation focus is a crowdsourcing approach, which we claim with reasonable confidence, finds close to all the relevant items in a dataset. This is different from the standard approach of asking workers to annotate all items in a small dataset. Our method supports more accurate evaluations (i.e., more precise recall calculations) as well as the development of larger training datasets. Finally the resulting surveillance method derived from the life satisfaction survey achieves recall, precision and F scores between 0.59 and 0.65. This is considerably better than standard methods using lexicons (precision around 0.16) or classifiers (precision, recall and F scores between 0.32 and 0.38).

Categories and Subject Descriptors

H.4 [**Information Systems Applications**]: Miscellaneous; D.2.8 [**Software Engineering**]: Metrics—*complexity measures, performance measures*

General Terms

Algorithms, Human Factors, Measurement

Keywords

Life Satisfaction, Information Retrieval, Crowdsourcing

1. INTRODUCTION

The question we address is: what is the appropriate methodology for finding social media posts related to a survey. To the best of our knowledge this has not been addressed in prior research. The particular social media of interest to us is Twitter and the survey we use as a case is the Satisfaction With Life Scale [6]. Despite these specific interests, our question is important in the larger context of strengthening connections between research in domains such as sociology and psychology where surveys are common and social media research.

Surveillance is a standard approach in many areas of human enterprise where it is important to collect opinions, beliefs, preferences, etc., in populations. Surveillance is active when individuals are contacted and their responses solicited through surveys for example. Surveillance may also be passive when one relies on observations (of behavior and choice for example); these may be collected from reports, databases, etc [13]. Social media surveillance is of increasing interest. We see for example surveillance of flu posts [5, 18], of health beliefs [1], and of happiness [7]. Our larger goal is to design methods that support surveillance on social media for goals related to surveys of interest.

Consider a simple survey asking questions on jogging frequency and distance. Translated to surveillance on Twitter one would want to find tweets about individual jogging practices (e.g., "*I hate having to jog everyday at 5.am.*" and "*I can now run 3 miles at a stretch*"). However, the tweet "*the store is a short jog away from my home*" is not relevant. The challenge is to find tweets conveying information that is essentially synonymous with valid survey responses.

We propose a survey translation methodology that results in a set of template-driven, tweet retrieval strategies. Surveillance may be done by running these queries on daily data or at the frequency desired. Periodically, as with any other surveillance tool, the strategies will need update to accommodate evolution in language etc. We show that our method provides superior results compared to results from conventional tweet finding methods using classifiers or lexicons.

Our second contribution, that is relevant beyond the survey focus, relates to evaluation strategies for tweet finding methods. A well-known limitation concerns the calculation of recall; one seldom knows how much relevant information is present in a realistically sized dataset. Typically one uses a hand annotated gold standard subset for evaluation, with crowdsourcing becoming popular for annotation. This dataset is usually limited in size because of annotation costs and time. Unfortunately a good portion of the annotation effort is spent in marking negatives - this is especially true when the positives appear at low to very low frequencies. The value of the gold standard dataset also depends crucially on how it is identified; through randomization, randomization combined with stratification etc. Moreover, social media is characterized by linguistic liberties and diverse ways of expressing making any statement. This compounds the challenge of appropriate sampling for gold standard annotation. To counter these problems we propose a method that uses crowdsourcing *not to annotate but to find the positives*. Further as we use humans to search for data generated by humans our approach is better equipped to handle the variety of linguistic expressions in social media. In general, our method may be used to build gold standard datasets where recall is important. We use it here as proof-of-concept to build the gold standard dataset for the evaluation of our life satisfaction surveillance strategies.

In sum we make two novel contributions in this paper. First we propose a novel translation method that can be used to derive a social media surveillance method from a survey of interest. We apply this to the well reputed Satisfaction With Life Scale. Second we propose a novel method to find close to all positive examples of a class of interest in a dataset. We use this to find tweets that express information related to individual satisfaction with life.

2. RELATED WORK

2.1 Finding Tweets

A fundamental step in much of social media research is to first find posts that are on a topic or that convey a particular sentiment. For example in flu prediction with Twitter [5, 18] the starting step is to find tweets talking about the occurrence of flu in individuals. In political sentiment research a typical approach is to find tweets about a politician, party or event and then identify the sentiment expressed, positive, negative or neutral [22]. In belief surveillance one first has to find the tweets discussing the belief of interest [1]. In all of these we start with a topic (flu, politician, product) and optionally a sentiment class (positive, negative, neutral) and aim to find relevant posts.

If one were looking for posts on a narrow topic such as a specific person or product then a reasonable approach is to search on all referents of the entity (e.g., Obama, Barack Obama, U.S. President etc.). This would of course be followed by a disambiguation step.

More sophisticated methods are needed when the topics are complex. Thus we see lexicon-based methods to find posts expressing some sentiment [10, 4, 21]. We also see machine learning algorithms used for sentiment analysis [15, 22]. When starting with a survey it is difficult to see how a lexicon might sufficiently represent the survey's themes and sub-themes. The problem with classifiers is that the data we are looking for can be extremely sparse and diverse especially given social media.

There is also related work in the TREC microblog initiative which has been running for a few years [14, 19]. Participants are given a set of topics and asked to find relevant tweets in a collection that is provided to them. The difference in the current work is that unlike their topics (e.g., *identify theft protection; Haiti Aristide return*), our 'topic' is a survey of interest. We have to retrieve statements that are possible responses to the survey, paying attention to aspects such as tense, whether it is written in first person singular form or not, and whether the statement includes a negation or not.

2.2 Life Satisfaction Social Media Research

We choose Life Satisfaction as our example survey in this study. Life Satisfaction is easily confused with happiness. A good discussion of differences is provided in the following FAQ written by Ed Diener, a leading researcher in the field[1]. In general, there is this notion of subjective well-being which has 3 components: 1) the presence of positive emotions 2) the absence of negative emotions and 3) life satisfaction [11]. The first two are influenced by daily events (good company, bad weather etc.). The third is a longer-term cognitive assessment of one's own life. This assessment is done using whatever criteria that individual considers important. Social media research by Dodds et al., [7] (discussed next) refer to components 1 and 2 as 'happiness'. The tweets 'I enjoyed the movie' and 'I hate this rainy day' reflect positive and negative affect respectively while 'I've achieved all I wish' is life satisfaction. As the FAQ says the three components are somewhat independent (FAQ question: 'Is happiness really a single thing?') and are also studied independently.

Dodds et al. [7] designed a lexicon driven 'hedonometer' to gauge the level of happiness (positive and negative affect) conveyed in texts including in tweets. Their approach is described later in this paper. They use their hedonometer to estimate the overall happiness score in Twitter for a 2-year-period, computing daily and weekly cycles of happiness. They also show how happiness is influenced by specific events. Researchers have also found that happiness is assortative in Twitter networks, both reciprocal-reply [2] and friend networks [3]. In 2013, Mitchell et al. [12] showed that the happiness levels of states and cities (estimated with Twitter using the same hedonometer) correlates with several well-being measures such as: Behavioral risk factor survey score (BRFSS)[2], 2013 Gallup Healthways Well-Being Index[3], 2012 United States Peace Index[4] and 2011 United Health Foundations Americas health ranking (AHR)[5]. Quercia et al. [17] found that Gross Community Happiness as measure via tweets relates to socio-economic wellbeing in London communities.

Unlike these happiness studies (that focus on affect), life satisfaction has not received much attention in social media research. Additionally the prior works are limited in that they do not consider tense (was the person happy earlier

---

[1]http://internal.psychology.illinois.edu/~ediener/faq.html#LS
[2]http://www.cdc.gov/brfss/
[3]http://info.healthways.com/wbi2013
[4]http://www.visionofhumanity.org/sites/default/files/2012-United-States-Peace-Index-Report_1.pdf
[5]http://www.americashealthrankings.org/Reports

versus being happy now or in the future?) or the difference between expressions in first person, singular and expressions in other forms (second and third person for example). These are crucial in terms of finding posts that match the survey emphasis which is on current, self assessments of life satisfaction.

3. SATISFACTION WITH LIFE SCALE

This widely cited survey is used in psychology for rating ones satisfaction with life [6, 16]. It has 5 statements shown below; respondents are expected to rate them-selves on the applicability of each statement to their own lives. A 7-point scale is used from 1 to 7 (1 = Strongly Disagree; Disagree; Slightly Disagree; Neither Agree nor Disagree; Slightly Agree; Agree; 7 = Strongly Agree).

1. In most ways my life is close to my ideal.
2. The conditions of my life are excellent.
3. I am satisfied with life.
4. So far I have gotten the important things I want in life.
5. If I could live my life over, I would change almost nothing.

The survey deliberately avoids focus on particular criteria for satisfaction such as family, career, health and wealth. This allows the respondent to consider any criteria that he/she thinks important. Life satisfaction refers to a cognitive and some-what stable (temporally) assessment of one's life.

Our goal is to find tweets expressing content and sentiment related to the 5 items of the scale. At this point we do not differentiate between levels of satisfaction, rather we look for tweets expressing satisfaction (Class S) and tweets expressing dissatisfaction (Class D) with their own lives. Tweets not in Class S or Class D, are regarded as irrelevant (Class I). Refinement into levels is left for further research.

4. CHALLENGES IN FINDING RELEVANT TWEETS

A tweet stating *"I am satisfied with my life"* is an obvious match to the scale. The same is true of *"I am dissatisfied with life"*. But the linguistic challenges are immediately apparent when we consider the many synonymous expressions possible. To illustrate, the expressions *"I have gotten all my goals"* and *"Haleluya I'm soooo content with my existence"* share no non-trivial words with the scale statements. Yet both communicate satisfaction with life and are synonymous to statements 4 and 3 respectively. Thus we need a process that allows us to find the many different expressions related to life satisfaction. As indicated earlier, given the linguistic liberties taken in social media, we can expect to find a wide variety of expressions.

We propose a method to build retrieval strategies for the life satisfaction scale as follows. For each statement we find a set of synonymous expressions. Next we generalize these into relevant statement templates. We do with this with the help of a lexicon that is developed in parallel with the generalization step. Each template is then transformed into a set of Indri [20] search queries. Finally we apply a set of filters to remove non-relevant tweets. This method is general enough to be applicable to other scales of interest. Figure 1 shows the flowchart of our method.

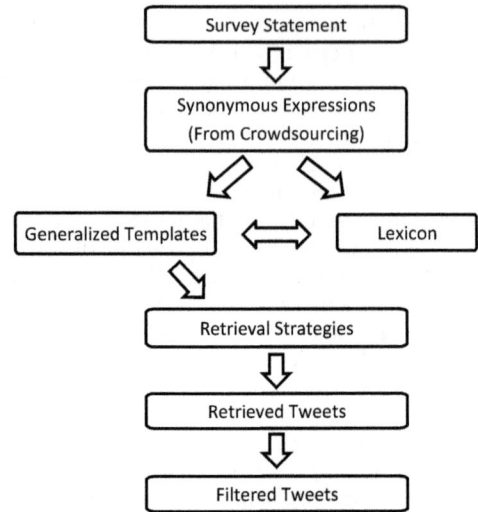

Figure 1: Flowchart

4.1 Synonymous Statements

We obtained an initial set of synonymous statements through crowdsourcing with Amazon Mechanical Turk[6] (MTurk). Ten workers were each asked to provide 20 alternate sentences for each statement. They were given a few examples such as for statement 3: *"I am very happy with my life"*, *"I have a satisfying life"* and *"My life is the way I want it to be"*. Thus we obtained around 1,000 synonymous statements for the 5. It took less than 5 days to obtain this set and cost less than 10 dollars.

4.2 Statement Templates

The set of 1,000 statements were manually augmented and then generalized into templates. A template is a relevant sentence with optional variables referring to entries in a lexicon of functionally synonymous terms. Two students from linguistics were mostly responsible for this work[7]. The work took roughly five weeks of effort but was spread over an 8-month period because of work schedules. The templates and the lexicon were developed simultaneously. Our lexicon has 70 sets of functionally synonymous terms. The total number of templates developed is 778. Table 1 gives examples of synonym sets and illustrates their use in 3 sample templates. The lexicon and template set may be obtained by contacting the authors. Note that the dissatisfaction sentences include both negations for satisfaction sentences (e.g., *"I do not like my life"*) and statements directly conveying dissatisfaction (e.g., *"I am tired of my life"* and *"My life is terrible"*).

A key point to note is that we kept the exercise of building templates and the lexicon as simple as possible. For instance it does not matter if a tweet is retrieved by more than 1 template. It also does not matter if a template allows nonsensical sentences. The template in example 3 allows: *"I am having loving life"*. Chances of this statement occurring are low, however, if it does occur then one might reasonably conclude that the writer is conveying satisfaction but

---

[6]https://www.mturk.com/mturk/
[7]We also conducted one informal exercise with 10 undergrads soliciting tweets on life satisfaction. These added around 30 statements to our collection.

Table 1: Sample Sentence Templates and Lexicon Entries

Phrase entries are in parenthesis. Lexicon variable names carry no meaning.
Example 1: Sentence: My life is perfect. Sentence Template: my X Y
Lexicon entry X: {life's (life is) (life has) (life has been) (life's been) (life has always been) (life's always been) etc...}
Lexicon entry Y: {amazing adorable awesome beautiful best (the best) blessed bliss blissful brilliant comfortable comfy contended delightful desired dream enjoyable exemplary excellent exciting fabulous fantastic fine flawless fulfilled fulfilling (full of joy) glorious good gorgeous grand gratifying great greatest happy heavenly ideal idyllic incredible joyous love (full of love) lovable lovely magical outstanding peaceful (picture perfect) perfect perfection pleasing super superb splendid etc...}
Example 2: Sentence: I live a perfect life. Sentence Template: A Y B
Lexicon entry A: {(I have been living) (I've been living) (I am living) (I'm living) (I live) (I have been having) (I've been having) (I am having) (I'm having) (I have) (I have been leading) (I've been leading) (I am leading) (I'm leading) (I lead) (I have been getting) (I've been getting) (I am getting) (I'm getting) (I get) (I have got) (I've got) (I have gotten) (I've gotten) etc., ..}
Lexicon entry Y: {Shown Above.}
Lexicon entry B: {life existence}
Example 3. Sentence: I love my life. Sentence Template: D E F
Lexicon entry D: {(I've (I have) (I have been) (I've been) (I've been having) (I have been having) (I am) I'm Im (I'm having) (I am having) I...}
Lexicon entry E: {like liking love loving adore adoring enjoy enjoying etc.. }
Lexicon entry F: {life existence (my life) (this life) myself (my existence) (this existence) etc...}

with grammatically weak English. We feel it is important to include such posts as well.

4.3 Retrieval Strategies

Our next step is to build a set of retrieval strategies (search queries) from the sentence templates. We use the Indri retrieval system to index the tweet collection and to run queries. Table 2 illustrates the 12 kinds of queries we build from each template. The columns indicate word gap, which is the number of other words allowed between the words of a template. The rows indicate the number of words (W) allowed before or after the text segment satisfying the template. Limiting W is a conservative strategy designed to limit the length of the retrieved tweets.

These 12 strategies are designed as a 'cascading' set. That is if a tweet is retrieved by multiple strategies then it is considered retrieved by the most restrictive query. The strategies are less restrictive (increase recall but potentially risk precision) as one moves down a column or to the right on a row. To compensate for possible losses in precision we apply a set of quality filters to the retrieved set as explained next.

4.4 Filtering Strategies

We need to filter out irrelevant tweets that are retrieved. For example strategy A-W3 will also retrieve "*My life is amazing because of you*" which is not relevant. As said earlier the life satisfaction survey deliberately steers away from specifying causes for happiness such as pets, home, travel, spouse etc. We are also not interested in tweets that refer to the future or the past ("*I so used to be happy*"). Table 3 shows the filters used. Also our dataset is limited to tweets in the first person in order to find statements about the tweeter's life satisfaction.

5. PERFORMANCE OF METHODOLOGY

5.1 Evaluating Precision

Our first evaluation is a standard one. We apply our retrieval strategies on a corpus and have two judges annotate the tweets retrieved with differences resolved by a third judge. We use this data to calculate precision. We randomly selected 1 day from our tweet corpus: December 30th, 2012 (close to 4 million tweets). Table 4 and Table 5 show the results for each strategy for the satisfied and dissatisfied classes respectively.

Table 4: Precision with Dec. 30th, 2012 data (Class Satisfied Tweets)

#Retrieved (Precision)	A	B	C	D
W1	404 (0.93)	463 (0.68)	245 (0.34)	167 (0.3)
W2	266 (0.83)	320 (0.77)	180 (0.57)	99 (0.34)
W3	202 (0.73)	494 (0.89)	151 (0.48)	54 (0.17)
Total: 3045 (0.69)				

Table 5: Precision with Dec. 30th, 2012 data (Class Dissatisfied Tweets)

#Retrieved (Precision)	A	B	C	D
W1	419 (0.98)	208 (0.89)	184 (0.67)	123 (0.55)
W2	260 (0.95)	166 (0.66)	139 (0.57)	107 (0.33)
W3	112 (0.69)	132 (0.75)	76 (0.63)	78 (0.13)
Total: 2004 (0.74)				

We can see that with one exception precision scores are generally highest for column A and decrease along a row

Table 2: 12 retrieval strategies derived from a statement template. Entries in [] and {} may be substituted by lexicon entries for set X and set Y respectively.

Template: My [X] {Y} Statement: [My life is] {perfect}.	A (word gap = 0) [My life is] {perfect}.	B (word gap = 1) [My life is] really {perfect}.	C (word gap = 2) [My life is] really quite {perfect}.	D (word gap = 3) [My life is] completely and truly {perfect}.
W1 (1 word allowed before and after)	Absolutely [my life is] {perfect}!	[My life is] really {perfect}, truly.	Happily [my life is] really quite {perfect}.	See [my life is] completely and truly {perfect}!
W2 (2 words allowed before and after)	I feel [my life is] {perfect}!	[My life is] really {perfect} so far.	For sure [my life is] really quite {perfect}.	See [my life is] completely and truly {perfect} for good.
W3 (3 words allowed before and after)	I can say [my life is] {perfect} and no less.	No one doubts [my life is] really {perfect}.	[My life is] really quite {perfect} since my childhood.	[My life is] completely and truly {perfect} that's the truth!

Table 3: Filters

Filter	Method	Example Tweets Filtered
Remove tweets ending with irrelevant words	Words referring to pets, and other objects are in a stoplist	Words referring to pets, and other objects are in a stoplist
Remove tweets referring to past or future tense.	Words referring to specific times such as "will", "was", "now", … are in a tense stoplist	party! I am happy now
Don't cross sentence boundaries when filling a template	Check for sentence boundaries	I am happy! Sure.
Remove tweets referring to 3rd person.	"you", "his", "her", … are in a stoplist	I think you are a happy person
Remove tweets asking a question	Check for question mark	I am happy?

towards column D. Moving down columns there is less consistency. For column A in both tables precision decreases. In the first table the middle row seems to have a bump up in precision.

We also evaluated precision of each filter using the same data. Results shown in Table 6 indicate that our filters are effective.

Table 6: Precision of Filters on Dec. 30th, 2012 data

Filter	# Tweets Filtered Out	Precision
Includes past or future tense	3222	0.95
Has End Punctuation	2138	0.95
Is not 1st Person	518	0.98
Is a question	384	0.99

5.2 Evaluating Recall

As mentioned in the introduction evaluating recall is challenging, as we do not know how many relevant tweets are in the collection. Thus we propose a method for finding as many relevant items as possible, again using crowd workers.

We randomly selected an additional day Jan 11, 2013 and added those tweets to our Dec. 30th dataset. The total number of tweets for the two days is about 8 million.

First we deleted duplicate tweets keeping a record of the duplicates. We then removed the tweets for which we already had judgments from our precision evaluation (section 5.1). Then we indexed the remaining tweets with Indri. Next we asked MTurk workers to search this collection through a web interface that we built. They were asked to use whatever queries they thought appropriate. The top 10 queries they used shown in Table 7. As an aside we note that these queries did not retrieve any results as our template set had already included them.

Table 7: Most Frequent Queries

Frequency	Query
112	Life
102	Life is good
64	My life sucks
62	Life sucks
56	Happy with my life
56	Happy
50	Life is great
43	Happy life
42	My life is great
39	I love my life

They were asked to submit retrieved tweets after labeling them as belonging to class S, class D or class I. Submitted tweets were re-evaluated by our team. Workers were paid $0.05 for every correct class S or D tweet. The submitted tweets were then deleted from the index; thus the next round of workers would find new relevant tweets. A tweet was considered labeled only if it had at least 2 votes supporting a label. Accepted labels were then propagated to all identical tweets in our two-day collection.

This process for finding relevant tweets started May 12th, 2013, and still continues. By the end of 2013, 327 workers had participated in this effort and they found 1954 and 2801 class S and class D tweets respectively (total cost $237). This indicates that recall for our methods are 0.46 and 0.43 respectively for the satisfied and dissatisfied classes.

We miss more than 50% of life satisfaction tweets. A reason for a large portion of the misses is tweet length; we had deliberately avoided retrieving long tweets (using $W <= 3$) hoping to keep precision reasonable. But we missed for example, *"I have a perfect life, well its perfect in my eyes. I'm not complaining by any means"*. We will focus on long tweets in the future work.

Figure 2 shows the number of relevant tweets found each week. (We had a minor technical glitch between weeks 15 and 20). Figure 3 shows the cumulative number of relevant tweets found. This number includes the ones found in our evaluation of precision (section 5.1).

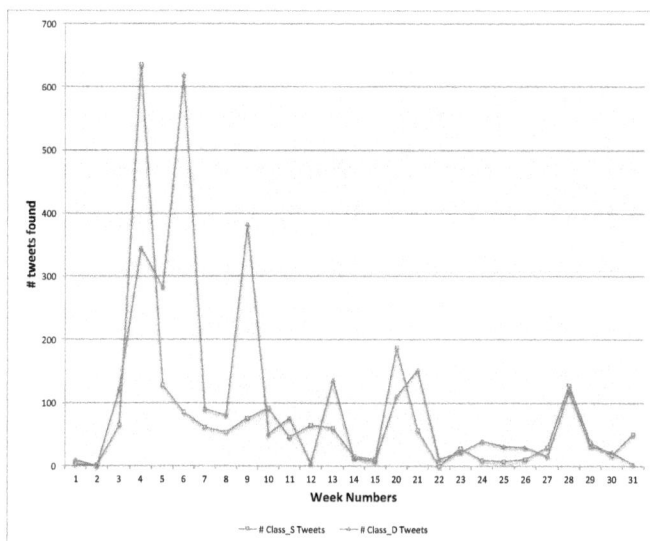

Figure 3: Cumulative # of relevant tweets found by week

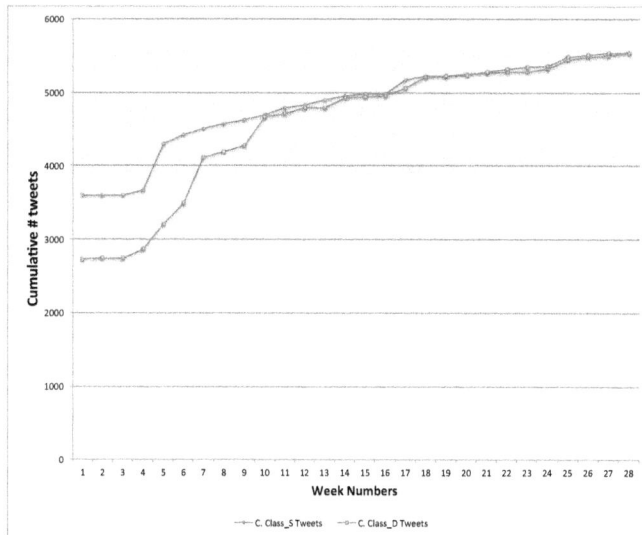

Figure 2: # of relevant tweets found each week

We can see that over the first 10 weeks, the MTurk workers found the majority of the tweets. Then the number of tweets dropped dramatically. We remind the reader that the task gets harder over time as we remove the tweets found in a given round. At present the workers are still submitting tweets, but only a tiny fraction are relevant.

To the best of our knowledge this strategy of using humans directly to *find* class members in a collection (rather than annotate a *pre-defined* collection) has not been explored before. Although we cannot say with certainty that we have found all tweets making posts about personal life satisfaction we can reasonably claim that we have found most of them. This makes our dataset fairly unique amongst current Twitter research. Table 8 summarizes the statistics related to our process. We suggest this process may be used with success in other research especially when there are many ways of writing posts belonging to the class of interest.

6. COMPARISONS WITH OTHER METHODS

Our template-based tweet finding strategy differs considerably from lexicon and classifier strategies. Certainly we have spent effort (though we think still at a feasible level) towards finding synonymous statements, building templates and deriving retrieval strategies. We claim that this effort is necessary in order to obtain reasonable precision especially in social media research. Here we offer some comparisons with methods using lexicons and classifiers.

6.1 Lexicons

There is no lexicon built specifically for "life satisfaction". But there is a related lexicon, labMT, built to identify tweets that reflect 'happiness' [7]. This lexicon contains more than 10,000 words. Each has an average score of 50 ratings made by MTurk workers, on a scale from 1 to 9. 1 is the lowest happiness rating (i.e., the word conveys the most unhappiness) while 9 represent is the highest happiness rating. For example, *laughter* has happiness score of 8.50 while for *suicide* it is 1.30. Using this lexicon Dodds et al. calculate the happiness score for a tweet by averaging the scores for its words. Their method has been adopted in several papers [2, 3].

We sampled 100,000 tweets from our Dec. 30th, 2012 twitter data. Dodd's strategy identified 56,150 tweets as 'happy' (tweet score $>= 6.0$). We manually evaluated the top 100 ranked tweets containing the word "life". Only 16 correctly indicate the tweeter's life satisfaction (precision at 100 = 0.16). Table 9 shows the top 10 "happy" tweets. The key point is that even if we use the lexicon just for the intended goal: i.e., to identify 'happy' tweets the top ranked tweet and the ones ranked 3 and 7 indicate the precision challenge faced. This underlines our point that lexicon based strategies face a big risk with precision.

6.2 Classifiers

Another popular method for finding relevant tweets is to use classifiers from machine learning. We test this approach

9

Table 8: Summary Statistics

Total Two Days' Tweets	8,640,007
Total Two Days' Tweets Without Duplicates	7,437,551
Start Date of Labeling experiment	May 12th, 2013
Running Time	More than half a year so far
# MTurk Workers Participated	327 (by the end of 2013)
# tweets labeled by us initially	Class S: 3594 Class D: 2735
# tweets submitted by MTurk Workers	Class S: 6001 Class D: 6557
# correct submissions by MTurk Workers	Class S: 1954 Class D: 2801
Accuracy of MTurk Workers	0.38 (0.34)
Final Unique Tweets in Labeled Set	Class S: 5547 Class D: 5536 Class I: 7,426,468
Final Tweets (considering duplicates) in Labeled Set	Class S: 8181 Class D: 6250 Class I: 8,625,576
Class Distribution in Labeled Set	Class S: 0.095% Class D: 0.072% Class I: 99.833%

Table 9: Top 10 "happy" tweets (with the word life) ranked by Dodds' method

Rank	Tweet	Happiness Score	Indicates life satisfaction?
1	So funny"@iam dheji: The love of ur life"@Teh mi: Sule"@iam dheji: @Teh mi @dacutest me u that mouth that u are usin to hiss, I destr	8.42	No
2	@Louis Tomlinson I love your zest for life <;3 Xx	7.87	No
3	@babblingbrat But do I have a life? *laughs*	7.75	No
4	RT @MeekMill: I ain't tripping life Is great!	7.6	Yes
5	@DaniCim Dani you're super! when you smile at me your smile forces also smile ! your life is Paradise:) you're the best	7.47	No
6	RT @phamBAAAM: a haiku about my love life: hahahahaha. hahaha-hahahaha. hahahahaha	7.46	No
7	RT @DLdemons: I find it hard to trust, hard to love, hard to determine what's real in this life. Some days it just gets too hard.	7.44	No
8	RT so true @MeekMill: I ain't tripping life Is great!	7.43	Yes
9	@postsofagirl: I'll look back on this and smile, because it was life and I decided to live it. #postsofagirl	7.42	No
10	I'm back in the relationship life And I must say it's great...	7.41	No

with two sets of experiments using SVM (SMO in Weka) [9]. In each we use 1, 2 and 3-gram word features to build a 3-class classifier distinguishing between tweets expressing satisfaction with life, tweets expressing dissatisfaction and tweets that are not relevant.

First we conducted three 10-fold cross validation experiments using data from our Dec. 30th, 2012 collection. The experiments differed in class balance. In the first experiment all 3 classes were roughly equal in size. We added close to a million non-relevant tweets for our second experiment. In the third experiment, the most natural one, we used all of the data (close to 4 million) for that date. Table 10 provides a summary description of the three experiments including the results.

In experiment 1 with the balanced dataset we have the best classifier performance. F scores are more than 0.83 for each class. In experiment 2 where the dataset is more challenging classifier performance drops considerably, F scores are less than 0.5 for the two classes of interest. But this performance is far far better than when using classifiers with the full dataset in experiment 3.

In a second set of experiments we use January 11, 2013 data as test data. There are 2900 tweets in class S, 2496 in class D and the remaining 3,685,815 are not relevant (class I). The classifier models are trained using the Dec. 30th dataset. As expected we find that the balanced dataset classifier (of experiment 1) has very poor performance for the classes of interest. In comparison the model built with data containing close to a million non-relevant tweets performs reasonably well with F scores equal to 0.35 for classes S and D. This is not bad given the highly skewed nature of the data. Building a classifier from all of the Dec 30th data was computationally prohibitive for us. Compared to these classifier results our strategy, built using Dec. 30th data, achieved superior results; for class S: 0.6 precision, 0.65 recall, 0.62 F score and for class D: 0.59 precision, 0.6 recall, 0.59 F score. We will develop our methods further using the annotations in this dataset.

7. CONCLUSION

We have shown that it is possible to translate a survey into a surveillance strategy on Twitter. We have presented a general methodology for this translation that involves using crowdsourcing and student expertise to find statements that could be survey responses. These were then converted into retrieval strategies. Applying this translation method to Diener's Satisfaction with Life Scale yields results that are consistently better than approaches using lexicons and classifiers built from training data. Although our approach requires some investment in terms of money and effort these are affordable and reasonable and the returns definitely are rewarding. Our translation methodology may be used with other surveys such as the Entrapment Scale [8] and Peace of Mind Scale [11].

There are a few limitations in our work. For example did not consider the different levels of satisfaction in the SWLS survey. Instead we handled only the binary case. We consider a single survey and a single social medium. Clearly more combinations need to be tested. Also more sophisticated machine learning methods may be used although we did test a widely used classifier. We face a limitation common to most surveillance research on social media, which is that the populations participating may not represent the general population. However because of the scale of social media these are recognized as significant, additional, sources of signals that cannot be ignored.

Our second significant contribution is a method for building a gold standard dataset (several millions large) where the members of classes of interest have been almost completely identified. Instead of asking humans to annotate a given dataset, we have asked them to find the positives in a dataset. This seemingly simple change in strategy is powerful in that we are confident that we have found close to all the positives in the data. We also suggest that given the diversity in language usage in social media (even just in English), using humans to find relevant items amongst the writings of humans may be the most appropriate way for building gold standard datasets. We will study this point further in future research.

8. REFERENCES

[1] S. Bhattacharya, H. Tran, P. Srinivasan, and J. Suls. Belief surveillance with twitter. In *Proceedings of the 3rd Annual ACM Web Science Conference*, pages 43–46. ACM, 2012.

[2] C. A. Bliss, I. M. Kloumann, K. D. Harris, C. M. Danforth, and P. S. Dodds. Twitter reciprocal reply networks exhibit assortativity with respect to happiness. *Journal of Computational Science*, 3(5):388–397, 2012.

[3] J. Bollen, B. Gonçalves, G. Ruan, and H. Mao. Happiness is assortative in online social networks. *Artificial life*, 17(3):237–251, 2011.

[4] J. E. Chung and E. Mustafaraj. Can collective sentiment expressed on twitter predict political elections? In *Proceedings of the twenty-fifth AAAI conference on artificial intelligence*, pages 1768–1769, 2011.

[5] A. Culotta. Towards detecting influenza epidemics by analyzing twitter messages. In *Proceedings of the first workshop on social media analytics*, pages 115–122. ACM, 2010.

[6] E. Diener, R. A. Emmons, R. J. Larsen, and S. Griffin. The satisfaction with life scale. *Journal of personality assessment*, 49(1):71–75, 1985.

[7] P. S. Dodds, K. D. Harris, I. M. Kloumann, C. A. Bliss, and C. M. Danforth. Temporal patterns of happiness and information in a global social network: Hedonometrics and twitter. *PloS one*, 6(12):e26752, 2011.

[8] P. Gilbert and S. Allan. The role of defeat and entrapment (arrested flight) in depression: an exploration of an evolutionary view. *Psychological medicine*, 28(3):585–598, 1998.

[9] M. Hall, E. Frank, G. Holmes, B. Pfahringer, P. Reutemann, and I. H. Witten. The weka data mining software: an update. *ACM SIGKDD explorations newsletter*, 11(1):10–18, 2009.

[10] J. Kim and J. Yoo. Role of sentiment in message propagation: Reply vs. retweet behavior in political communication. In *Proceedings of the International Conference on Social Informatics*, pages 131–136. IEEE, 2012.

[11] Y.-C. Lee, Y.-C. Lin, C.-L. Huang, and B. L. Fredrickson. The construct and measurement of peace

Table 10: Experiments with Classifiers: Descriptive details and Results

	Experiment,1: Balanced Dataset			Experiment,2: Un-balanced Dataset 1			Experiment,3: Un-balanced Dataset 2		
Total # Tweets	4,901			1,000,001			3,746,340		
# Tweets in Class_S	1,559			1,559			1,559		
# Tweets in Class_D	1,744			1,744			1,744		
# Tweets in Class_I	1,598			996,698			3,743,036		
Time taken to run 10 fold cross,validation	30 secs			1.6 days			8.6 days		
Accuracy	86.65%			99.73%			99.91%		
Precision|Recall|Fscore,for Class S	0.853	0.899	0.875	0.669	0.313	0.427	0.923	0.023	0.045
Precision|Recall|Fscore for Class D	0.866	0.917	0.891	0.72	0.334	0.457	0	0	0
Precision|Recall|Fscore for Class I	0.884	0.78	0.828	0.998	1	0.999	0.999	1	1
Below are the results using Jan 11 test set									
Time taken to classify Jan 11 test set	16,minutes			12,minutes			N/A		
Accuracy in Jan 11 test set	89.69%			99.91%			N/A		
Precision|Recall|Fscore for Class S in,Jan 11 test set	0.0054	0.9104	0.0108	0.34	0.35	0.35	N/A		
Precision|Recall|Fscore for Class D in,Jan 11 test set	0.0066	0.9061	0.0131	0.38	0.32	0.35	N/A		
Precision|Recall|Fscore for Class I in,Jan 11 test set	0.9999	0.8969	0.9456	0.99	0.99	0.99	N/A		

of mind. *Journal of Happiness studies*, 14(2):571–590, 2013.

[12] L. Mitchell, M. R. Frank, K. D. Harris, P. S. Dodds, and C. M. Danforth. The geography of happiness: Connecting twitter sentiment and expression, demographics, and objective characteristics of place. *PloS one*, 8(5):e64417, 2013.

[13] P. Nsubuga, M. White, S. Thacker, M. Anderson, S. Blount, C. Broome, T. Chiller, V. Espitia, R. Imtiaz, D. Sosin, et al. Public health surveillance: a tool for targeting and monitoring interventions. *Disease Control Priorities in Developing Countries. 2nd edition.*, 2006.

[14] I. Ounis, C. Macdonald, J. Lin, and I. Soboroff. Overview of the trec-2011 microblog track. In *Proceedings of the 20th Text REtrieval Conference (TREC 2011)*, 2011.

[15] B. Pang, L. Lee, and S. Vaithyanathan. Thumbs up?: sentiment classification using machine learning techniques. In *Proceedings of the ACL conference on Empirical methods in natural language processing*, pages 79–86. Association for Computational Linguistics, 2002.

[16] W. Pavot and E. Diener. Review of the satisfaction with life scale. *Psychological assessment*, 5(2):164, 1993.

[17] D. Quercia, J. Ellis, L. Capra, and J. Crowcroft. Tracking gross community happiness from tweets. In *Proceedings of the ACM 2012 conference on Computer Supported Cooperative Work*, pages 965–968. ACM, 2012.

[18] A. Signorini, A. M. Segre, and P. M. Polgreen. The use of twitter to track levels of disease activity and public concern in the us during the influenza a h1n1 pandemic. *PloS one*, 6(5):e19467, 2011.

[19] I. Soboroff, I. Ounis, J. Lin, and I. Soboroff. Overview of the trec-2012 microblog track. In *Proceedings of the 21st Text REtrieval Conference (TREC 2012)*, 2012.

[20] T. Strohman, D. Metzler, H. Turtle, and W. B. Croft. Indri: A language model-based search engine for complex queries. In *Proceedings of the International Conference on Intelligent Analysis*, volume 2, pages 2–6, 2005.

[21] A. Tumasjan, T. O. Sprenger, P. G. Sandner, and I. M. Welpe. Predicting elections with twitter: What 140 characters reveal about political sentiment. *Proceedings of the Fourth International AAAI Conference on Weblogs and Social Media (ICWSM)*, 10:178–185, 2010.

[22] H. Wang, D. Can, A. Kazemzadeh, F. Bar, and S. Narayanan. A system for real-time twitter sentiment analysis of 2012 us presidential election cycle. In *Proceedings of the ACL 2012 System Demonstrations*, pages 115–120. Association for Computational Linguistics, 2012.

Rolling through Tumblr: Characterizing Behavioral Patterns of the Microblogging Platform

Jiejun Xu, Ryan Compton, Tsai-Ching Lu, David Allen
HRL Laboratories
3011 Malibu Canyon Road
Malibu, CA 90265
{jxu, rfcompton, tlu, dallen}@hrl.com

ABSTRACT

Tumblr, a microblogging platform and social media website, has been gaining popularity over the past few years. Despite its success, little has been studied on the human behavior and interaction on this platform. This is important as it sheds light on the driving force behind Tumblr's growth. In this work, we present a quantitative study of Tumblr based on the complete data coverage for four consecutive months consisting of 23.2 million users and 10.2 billion posts. We first explore various attributes of users, posts, and tags in detail and extract behavioral patterns based on the user generated content. We then construct a massive *reblog* network based on the primary user interactions on Tumblr and present findings on analyzing its topological structure and properties. Finally, we show substantial results on providing location-specific usage patterns from Tumblr, despite no built-in support for geo-tagging or user location functionality. Essentially this is done by conducting a large-scale user alignment with a different social media platform (e.g., Twitter) and subsequently propagating geo-information across platforms. To the best of our knowledge, this work is the first attempt to carry out large-scale measurement-driven analysis on Tumblr.

Categories and Subject Descriptors

H.4 [**Information Systems Applications**]: Miscellaneous; J.4 [**Computer Applications**]: Social And Behavioral Sciences; C.2 [**Computer-Communication Networks**]: General

General Terms

Measurement, Human Behavior

Keywords

Tumblr, Online Social Network, Quantitative Methods, Location-based Patterns

1. INTRODUCTION

Microblogging has become one of the most popular mediums for users to create and share information. Some of the most well-known microblogging platforms include Twitter[TM], Tumblr[TM], and Sina Weibo[TM][1]. Generally these platforms allow users to generate short-form, mixed-media (e.g., text, image) posts on any topics that are of interest to the users. These posts are then exchanged and propagated either through public broadcast or within a social network based on the connected users. While much research has been carried out to study user behaviors and social networks on different platforms, such as Twitter [20, 19, 36, 23] and Sina Weibo [13, 15, 33], little work has been done for Tumblr despite its rapid growth and popularity. As of the writing of this article, there are a total of 171.7 million blogs and 76.9 billion posts on Tumblr [1]. According to the data from the web traffic analysis company Alexa[2], Tumblr is ranked 17 in United States and 32 globally based on a combination of average daily visitors and pageviews to the site over the past 3 month. On average, a user spends six and a half minutes on Tumblr daily. An online user study [12] shows that Tumblr is ranked second (after Facebook[TM]) in terms of average time US visitors spent on all social media sites in a month, and it is four times more than Twitter. A survey of American internet users [28] also reveals that Tumblr is the favorite social network site for younger social media users in the age groups of 13-18 (teens) and 19-25 (young adults). One of the main design goals of Tumblr is to let everyone create and share anything effortlessly. It allows users to publish short text, photos, and other form of posts to the platform similar to other microblogging platforms. At the same time, it allows longer posts and provides extensive support for users to customize HTML page as in more traditional blogs. In a way, Tumblr is considered as a hybrid of Twitter and Wordpress[TM] as it combines parts from both [25]. The content-rich nature of Tumblr attracted not only individuals but also organizations to participate with different intentions ranging from business marketing [3] to government campaigns. The sheer volume of users and activities makes Tumblr an appealing platform to study human behavior of using social media as well as web-based large-scale social interaction. To this end, we conducted an in-depth measurement-driven analysis on Tumblr with 100% data covering four consecutive months

---

[1]The most popular microblogging platform in China.
[2]www.alexa.com/siteinfo/tumblr.com
[3]http://moz.com/blog/how-to-use-tumblr-for-seo-and-social-media-marketing

(between June 1st 2013 to September 30th 2013). To our knowledge, this is the first attempt to conduct such a large-scale study on Tumblr. The main contributions of our work are as follows:

- We explore different attributes on Tumblr (e.g., users, posts, tags) in detail and characterize their patterns based on the user generated content.

- We construct a massive *reblog* network based on the primary user interaction on Tumblr and present findings on analyzing its topological structure and properties.

- We introduce a practical solution to extract location-specific usage patterns from Tumblr by conducting a large-scale user alignment between Tumblr and Twitter.

The paper is organized as follows. Section 2 reviews related work on different microblogging and social media platforms. Section 3 provides background information about Tumblr as well as details of the data set. Section 4 describes the findings of human behavioral and usage patterns from the data. In Section 5, the Tumblr *reblog* network is discussed in-depth. In Section 6, we present the detail of obtaining location information for Tumblr users. Finally, Section 7 concludes the paper with insights and discussions.

2. RELATED WORK

Prior studies on human behavior and social interaction have been carried out quite extensively on existing microblogging platforms. Java et al. [20] analyzed the topological and geographical properties of the Twitter social network to determine individual user's intention in using such a platform. They found people predominantly use microblogging service to talk about their daily activities and to seek or share information. Kwak et al. [23] conducted an analysis on the follower-following topology of the Twitter social network, and found a significant deviation from known characteristics of human social networks in terms of the non-power-law follower distribution, a short effective diameter, and low reciprocity. Furthermore, the authors proposed three measures to rank influential users. Similar study on influential users was carried out in [5]. The authors compared users with different set of measures, and they found that the most followed users were not necessary the highest in other measures. Wu et al. [31] studied a few longstanding questions in media communication in the context of Twitter. They first developed a mechanism to distinguish between elite users versus ordinary users. Subsequently they found that a strong concentration of attention, in that half of the URLs consumed are generated by a small percentage of elite users. In addition, a significant homophily was observed in their work, which means contact between similar people occurs at a higher rate than among dissimilar people. Yu et al. [33] examined the key topics that trend on Sina Wiebo, and compared them with the observations on Twitter. They found a vast contrast between the two, in that trends in China are more centered around content such as jokes, images and video. Hutto et al. [18] conducted a longitudinal study on Twitter to an attempt to understand what factors lead to more followers. They concluded that variables for message content, social behavior, and network structure should all be given equal consideration when attempting to predict followers. Park et al. [27] took an unique angle by studying the emoticons on Twitter communication. They found that emoticons not only convey specific emotions, but also reflect socio-culture norms which vary depending on the identity of the speaker.

Besides typical microblogging platforms, behavioral studies have been carried out in more general social media platforms. Cha et al. [7] collected and analyzed large-scale traces of information dissemination in the Flickr^{TM} social network. They found that even the most popular photos do not spread widely and quickly, which is contrary to common marketing belief. Ugander et al. [29] studied the structure of social graph of active Facebook users. The authors observed a clear degree assortativity patterns in the graph by studying the demographic and network property of users. They also observed a strong effect of age on friendship preferences as well as a globally modular community structure driven by nationality. A followup study on the Facebook social graph [4] reported a 4.74 degree of separation (i.e., average number of intermediaries on the path) between active users. Hochman et al. [17] applied Cultural Analytic techniques on large collection of Instagram^{TM} photos to identify collective recurring visual patterns that provide insights into the study of different cultural practices. A more recent behavioral study on photo-sharing websites was conducted in [8]. The authors performed analysis of a large Flickr user logs to examine the navigation patterns between photo streams. Based on the observation, a stream transition graph was constructed to analyze common stream topic transitions. The graph was later incorporated in a collaborative filtering scheme for photo recommendations. Lately, less prevalent social medias platforms have also been explored. Coscia et al.[11] performed an empirical approach to study the behavior of internet memes, which are defined as specific fundamental cultural traits. The authors proved that in Quickmeme.com there are actual memes as they compete and collaborate, and sometimes cluster in large ensembles. Their work differed from main stream studies, in that they proposed a perspective without the use of network effects. Wang et al. [30] described findings of a detailed analysis on a social media-based question and answer site Quora^{TM}, based on three connection networks derived from the site. Their results showed a diversity in the user and question graphs are significant contributors to the quality of Quora's knowledge base. Finally, Mitta et al. [24] analyzed the Pinterest^{TM} social network to extract general user behavior and common characteristics of different attributes in that platform. Two recent works which focused more on specific aspects of Pinterest can be found in [35] and [26]. Our work on Tumblr marks the latest addition to the large-scale social media analytic domain.

3. BACKGROUND

Tumblr is a content-rich microblogging and social media platform, where users create and share posts that are of interest to them. Each Tumblr user owns a *blog*, which contains all the posts from the user, and serves as the gateway to follow others. Tumblr primarily works with seven types of post: *text, photo, quote, link, chat, audio* and *video*. Note that there is another less common post type known as *answer*. Basically this allows a Tumblr user to add a box

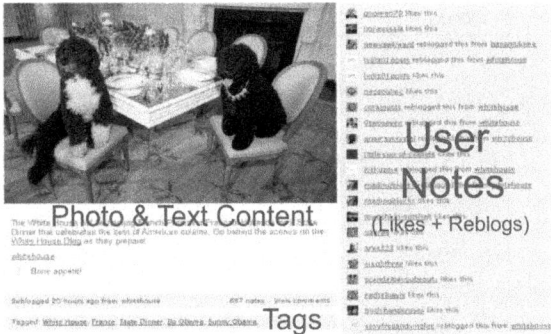

Figure 1: An example of a Tumblr *photo* post with caption. User activities (*Notes*) include both *likes* and *reblogs*

Photo	8,147,730,433	Answer	81,898,088
Text	1,406,432,506	Chat	73,191,208
Quote	246,930,034	Audio	63,099,299
Video	88,097,336	Link	45,397,589

Table 1: Number of Tumblr posts for each post type.

section on his *blog* for visitors to ask questions. Once the question is answered, it will turn into a regular post and displayed on the owner's Tumblr *blog*. Once a post is created, it could be published to Tumblr using one of the privacy control options. Unless the post is set to private, it is visible to other users. There are two types of actions (*like* and *reblog*), which can be applied on the post. The former is similar to Twitter *favorites* and marks what a user likes. The latter is similar to Twitter *retweet* and will clone the post to the *blog* of the acting user. The two actions are commonly referred as *notes* on Tumblr. Figure 1 shows an example of a Tumblr post. Users who "liked" and "rebloged" this post are displayed on the right pane.

As can be seen from Figure 1, Tumblr users can also assign tags to their posts. These tags make it easier for other users to find posts about a specific topic. In fact, the original search mechanism on Tumblr only applies to tags, which means there is no way to retrieve a post from the Tumblr search engine if it is not tagged. This search function was improved in late 2013 to provide more comprehensive search results by checking other textual information in post contents and image captions.

The *follow* functionality in Tumblr provides a convenient way for users to get the latest updates (e.g., new posts) from other users. Similar to Twitter, the *follow* relation here is directional. This means a user U_a can follow user U_b without explicit permission, and U_b's updates will automatically appear in U_a's activity feeds (known as *dashboard* in Tumblr). By default, *follow* is considered as private data, thus not displayed publicly.

3.1 Tumblr Dataset

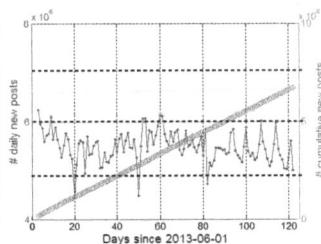

Time Period	2013-06-01 to 2013-09-30
# Posts	10,152,776,493
# Unique Posts	694,999,518
# Unique Users	23,228,627
# Unique Tags	230,898,675

(a)   (b)

Figure 2: (a) Statistics for the four-month data. (b) Number of original posts growing per day.

We obtain the Tumblr corpus over a 122 day period between June 1st, 2013 to September 30th, 2013 via GNIP[4] "firehose" (the complete stream of all posts). During the period, every public activity on Tumblr posts (including *publish*, *like* and *reblog*) is delivered to our system in real time encapsulated as a JSON record. Besides a record id, there is also a special identifier known as the *reblogkey* associated with each record. This is to indicate the origin of the post. For instance, if a new post is "liked" and "rebloged" after it is "published", we will receive a total of three records indicating the three activities, and these records all share the same *reblogkey*. The total size of data collected is roughly 10.6 TB with bzip2 compression. Data is stored via Hadoop Distributed File System (version 0.20.2-cdh3u3) deployed across a multi-node multi-core cluster.

The basic statistics of our dataset is summarized in Figure 2(a). As can be seen, the total number of posts collected over the four-month period is over 10 billion. However, the number of unique posts (i.e., excluding *reblog* posts) is only about 695 million. This suggests that large portion of Tumblr posts are simply duplicates of a small percentage of original contents (6.8%). Figure 2(b) shows the number of original posts observed on each day, as well as the cumulative number of posts observed during the same period. On average, there are $5,696,717$ original posts and $77,522,762$ *reblogs* generated everyday on Tumblr. Over the period of the four months, the total number of posts appears to grow linearly. We also analyze the distribution of different types of Tumblr posts (see Table 1). As can be seen, *photo* content dominates the microblogging platform by contributing 80% of the total posts. During our investigation, we also found that motion gif images are particularly popular on Tumblr. Finally, we have observed more than 23 million unique users and 230 millions unique tags in the data corpus. All the experiments in this work are implemented using a combination of standard Java MapReduce code and Apache Pig [5].

4. BEHAVORAL PATTERNS

We begin by exploring various Tumblr attributes in detail and extracting their associated patterns.

Posts and Users: We first analyze the relationship between posts and users. Figure 3 plots the distribution of number of posts per users over the four months period in a log-log grid. As *photo* posts consist of the primary content in Tumblr, we first focus our attention on its corresponding distribution (plotted in the top-left). This curve mirrors a typical heavy-tailed distribution, which occurs commonly in the social media domain. If a power law distribution is fitted to the curve, the parameter of α is found to be 2.17. It shows that for large majority of the users, each user publishes only a small number of posts during the period, while a small

---

[4]http://gnip.com/sources/tumblr/
[5]http://pig.apache.org

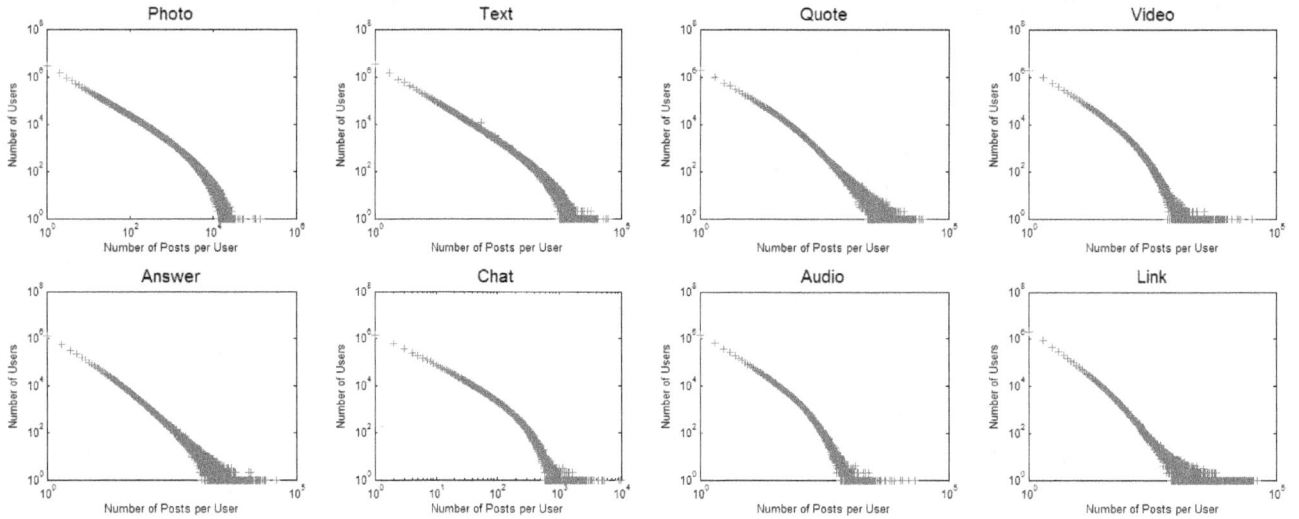

Figure 3: Number of posts per users (for different types of Tumblr posts). Plots are ordered based on the popularity of the corresponding post types from top-left to bottom right.

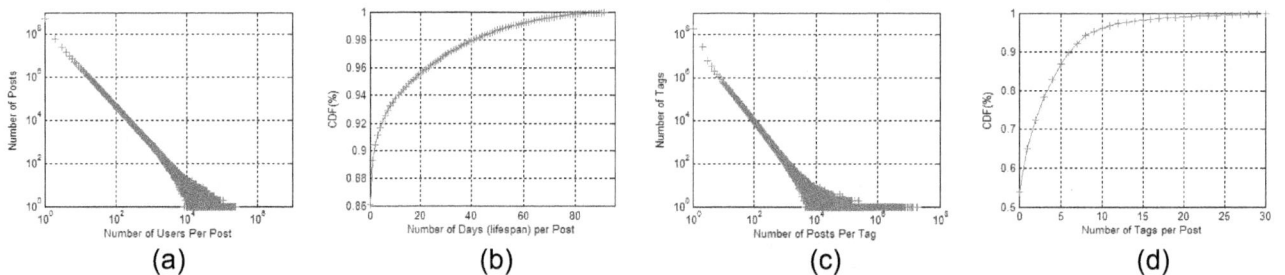

Figure 4: Various distributions of posts, users, and tags.

portion of users publish much more than the average. Similar distribution can be observed from the rest of the plots in Figure 3. The heavy-tail distribution in these plots indicate a high variability in user posting patterns. Note that longer tails are observed for less popular post types.

Next we study how users interact with posts. Specifically we compute the number of users who have "liked" or "rebloged" particular Tumblr posts. This computation can be conveniently implemented in a MapReduce paradigm, where the (key, value) pair consists of Tumblr *reblogkey* and user ID (or *uid*). The *Map* procedure takes in the data corpus and extract the specified (*reblogkey, uid*) pairs. Then the *Reduce* procedure takes in the collected pairs and combines them by counting the number of distinct *uids* for each key. In order to see the overall distribution, we invoke a final grouping step to sum up the number of keys at a each count level. Figure 4(a) plots the resulting distribution. This suggests that large majority of the original contents only attract a small percentage of users, while a small portion of popular contents are responsible for attracting most of the user interactions.

We are also interested in knowing the lifespan of original posts on Tumblr. We consider a post "alive" as long as it is still being "liked" or "rebloged". Since each original post in Tumblr is identified by a *reblogkey*, we can simply compute the lifespan of an original post by finding the first and last occurrence of its *reblogkey* in our data corpus. In order

to compensate posts which are generated in late September and stayed "alive" beyond the coverage of our dataset, we only consider original posts which are first published between June and August 2013. The distribution of number of days a Tumblr post stays "alive" is shown in Figure 4(b). We observe that 90% of original posts has lifespan less than 2 days since its first creation. On the other hand, there is about 5% of original posts stay "alive" even 20 days after its creation, and about half of those goes beyond 40 days. The average lifespan of Tumblr posts appears to be longer than their counterparts in other micorblogging or social media platforms. Similar finding was reported in an online article regarding to Tumblr content[6].

Tags and Posts: Tags generally indicate specific topics, here we study the relation between tags and posts. Figure 4(c) shows the distribution of number of posts per tag. We observe a heavy-tail distribution: millions of user-defined tags are used in less than 10 posts, while a small set of tags are responsible for annotating the majority of the posts. Data points that lie on the right end of the curve correspond to most commonly used tags, and data points that lie on the left end of the curve correspond to rare tags. The long tail typically results from unconstrained tagging, where a user can put in any arbitrary text.

---

[6]http://unionmetrics.tumblr.com/post/45919888558/

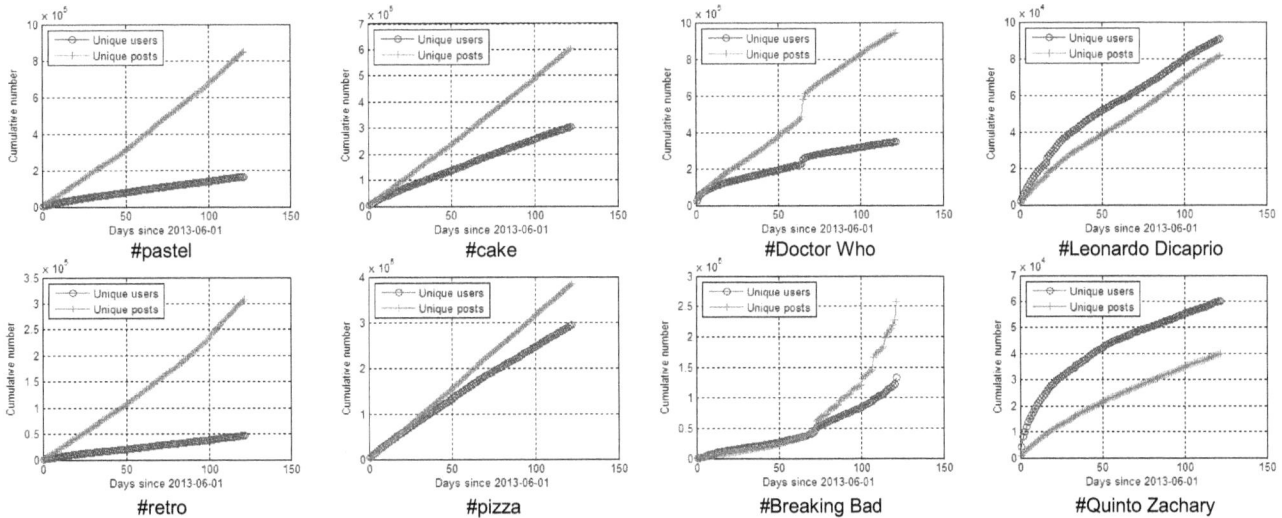

Figure 6: Cumulative numbers of unique users and posts (with mentions of specific tag) over time. Plots in the same column are considered to be in the same category.

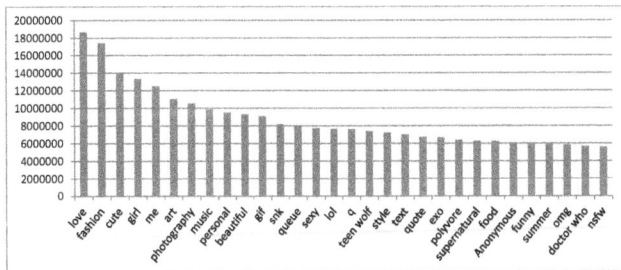

Figure 5: Most mentioned tags in Tumblr.

Knowing that a small number of tags are responsible for most posts, it is interesting to see what exactly the top tags are in Tumblr. Figure 5 shows the most frequently used tags in the platform. Clearly, Tumblr posts are highly biased towards certain topics. For example, "love" is used in more than 18 million Tumblr posts (about 1% of all), followed by "fashion" which is used in a similar magnitude. Based on the observation of the top-10 used tags, it again hints that Tumblr is largely visual-driven and the platform is centered around user hobbies and interests.

Next we study the average number of tags associated with Tumblr posts. We focus the study with respect to original contents, because by default *reblogs* do not include the tags from the original posts and *reblog* users are not likely to add them back. In our implementation, we first identify the list of original posts. Then for each post, we compute the maximum number to tags occurred in the *reblog* chain. The resulting distribution is plotted in Figure 4(d). It shows that more than 53% of the posts contain zero tags. On the other hand, there are about 4% posts which have more than 10 tags. We expect the curve to shift upward if we were to include all *reblog* posts.

Tags and Users: Here we investigate the popularities of different topics on Tumblr by examining the aggregated growth patterns of new users and posts for each topic. In particular, we focus on the following categories: fashion, food, TV show and celebrity. As topics are not explicitly defined in Tumblr, we carry out the experiment based on the representative tags from each topic. Similar method has been shown to be effective in existing literature [31, 32]. For each topic, we select two frequently used tags according to the summaries in the official Tumblr Year-in-Review webpage[7]. The final selections of tags are "pastel", "retro", "cake", "pizza", "Doctor Who", "Breaking Bad", "Leonardo Dicaprio" and "Quinto Zachary". Figure 6 shows the growth patterns for each tag. Plots located on the same column are from the same topic.

We make a few key observations from Figure 6 above. First, all topics do show steady rise in terms of number of users and posts over the four months period. However, the growth patterns appear to be rather different across topics. For instance, there are noticeble "jumps" in popularity for the TV show category. We suspect that they were triggered by real life events. In fact, the big jump in the number of users and posts for "Doctor who" was related to the announcement regarding to the actor of the show in June 2013. Similarly the continuous jumps for "Breaking Bad" correspond to the weekly broadcast dates. The correlations to real-world events may suggest that Tumblr is another effective social media for TV and movie box office predictions [3]. Another observation is that the large increase in the number of posts do not seem to bring in many new users for the fashion topic. We suspect that the active user group who drives the growth of the topic is highly focused and specialized. In this case, users are likely to be advocates of the particular fashion trends. Similar number of posts was accumulated for the food category as for fashion. However, this appears to be a more general topic as the growth in the number of posts is more aligned with the number of new users. Finally, the growth pattern is most different for the celebrity category, in that there are more users than the number of posts. The large number of users most likely consist of fans of the

---

[7]http://yearinreview.tumblr.com/2013

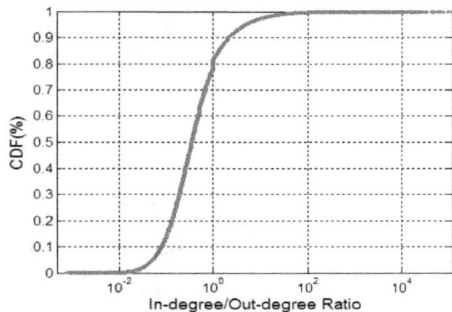

Figure 7: CDF(%) of the user in-degree and out-degree ratio.

Model	In-dgree	Out-degree
Power law	$\alpha = 1.26$	$\alpha = 1.13$
Truncated power law	$\alpha = 1.18, \lambda = 1.23 \times 10^{-4}$	$\alpha = 1.00, \lambda = 2.78 \times 10^{-4}$
Lognormal	$\mu = 2.40, \sigma = 2.90$	$\mu = 3.35, \sigma = 2.85$
Stretched exponential	$c = 0.248, \lambda = 0.092$	$c = 0.319, \lambda = 0.016$

Table 2: Fitted parameters for degree distributions of the Tumblr *reblog* network

celebrities. The sharp increase for "Quinto Zachary" at the beginning of the curve happens to align with the release of the latest "Star Trek" movie.

5. REBLOG NETWORK

Numerous network can be derived from Tumblr based on different user attributes. In this section, we study the *reblog* network as it is the primary online interaction on Tumblr.

5.1 Reciprocity

We build a social network, the *reblog* network, with users as vertices and weighted directed edges corresponding to *reblogs*. That is, if user i "reblogs" user j for w_{ij} times, then we have a directed edge from i to j with weight w_{ij}. Note that in our network users who generate popular content will have a high in-degree while users who primarily share content will have a high out-degree.

Our data contains $7,062,528,912$ *reblogs*. From these we build a network consisting of $18,367,173$ users with $999,548,135$ directed edges between them. Based on the constructed network, we observe that only $87,832,337$ (8.8%) of the edges were reciprocated (i.e. user i "reblogged" user j and user j "reblogged" user i).

The low reciprocation rates happen elsewhere in the social media platform Twitter [23]. In addition to the popular *retweet* phenomenon, Twitter users often "@mention" each other by appending an "@" symbol to the mentioned user's name. This two activities are often used as the mediums to study reciprocity. To put in perspective the network structure of Tumblr, we directly compare it with the network structure of Twitter. We use the same Twitter data as we used in [10], which consists of 10% sample of public tweets from April 2012 to January 2014 obtained through the GNIP Decahose[8]. The same Twitter corpus is also used for large-scale user alignment and it will be discussed in Section 6.1. The full dataset amounted to 67.2TB of uncompressed JSON data and a total of $22,455,584,506$ @mentions of any type. From *retweets* only, we built a weighted and directed network of $137,269,098$ users with $4,493,285,385$ edges. Filtering edges for reciprocation left us with in $248,104,403$ edges, i.e. a 5.5% chance of *retweet* reciprocation. From nonretweet @mentions only, we built a weighted and directed network of $198,755,741$ users and $3,954,866,992$ edges. Here, we found $738,295,950$ reciprocated edges, i.e. an 18.6% chance of nonretweet @mention reciprocation. Our results suggest that *reblogs* on Tumblr are stronger indicators of social ties

---

[8]http://gnip.com/sources/twitter/

than their Twitter counterpart of *retweets*, but weaker indicators than Twitter @mentions.

We also investigate the distribution of the ratio of a user's incoming and outgoing degrees in the *reblog* network. Results are shown in Figure 7. In our dataset, only $11,259,743$ users have both nonzero in-degree and out-degree, and our experiment is carried out among these users. Overall, $2,486,406$ (22%) users have higher in-degree than out-degree. If we loosely assume that the number of in-degree is proportional to the number of "follower", these users have higher "follower-followee" ratios. A very small portion (2.76%) have 10 times more in-degree than out-degree.

5.2 Activity vs Degree

We observe that node degree distributions of the Tumblr *reblog* network do not closely follow standard power laws. A similar result was obtained for other blogging platforms in [16]. To be precise, we fit degree distributions to the following models:

- Power law: $x^{-\alpha}$

- Exponentially truncated power law: $x^{-\alpha}e^{-\lambda x}$

- Lognormal: $\frac{1}{x}e^{-\frac{(\ln x - \mu)^2}{2\sigma^2}}$

- Stretched exponential: $x^{c-1}e^{-\lambda x^c}$

We utilized the software package provided by [2] for precise model fittings, and the parameters are obtained via the method of [9]. The complete networks for both degree cases are used in the fitting process. For computational efficiency, we only fit once over the full degree range (i.e., $x_{min} = 1$ and $x_{max} = $ the max weighted node degree in each network). Results are summarized in Table 2, plots of the data with various fits are shown in Figure 8.

Pairwise comparison of different models is achieved via the loglikelihood-ratio test. Truncated power laws fit better than standard power laws in both situations (for in-degrees: loglikelihood ratio 46461.17, $p < 0.0001$; for out-degrees: loglikelihood ratio 2103152.75, $p < 0.0001$). On the in-degree network, a lognormal model outperforms the truncated power law (loglikelihood ratio 19800.16, $p < 0.0001$) and appears to outperform the stretched exponential in the tail. Overall fit, however, shows that the difference between the lognormal and stretched exponential fits is not statistically significant (loglikelihood ratio 31.91, $p = 0.96$). Similarly, for out-degrees, the truncated power law models the tail well, but this result is not statistically significant when compared against the stretched exponential over the full range (loglikelihood ratio 0.92, $p = 0.99$). Ultimately, understanding the true underlying processes of Tumblr network formation requires a detailed sociological model (such as the work found in [6]) which is outside the scope of this work.

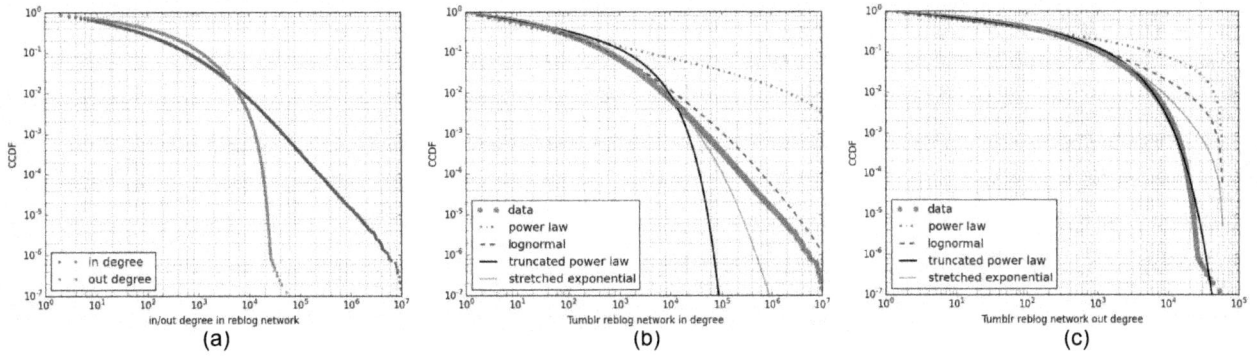

Figure 8: (a) Log-scale plots of in/out-degree distributions of the Tumblr *reblog* network. (b)-(c) Log-scale plots of in/out-degree distributions of the *reblog* network with various statistical fits.

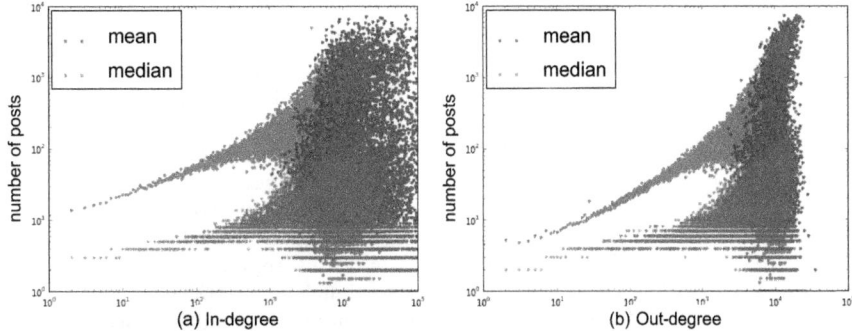

Figure 9: (a) Activity level v.s. in-degree. (b) Activity level v.s. out-degree.

In order to investigate the correlation between user node degrees (unweighted) and that of user activities (i.e.,published posts), we plot the number posts against the number of in/out-degree a user has in Figure 9(a) and Figure 9(b). As can be seen, user activity is an increasing function of both degree types when $x \leq 100$. This suggests that high-degree users are more apt to post often. In addition, we observe that the average number of posts again the number of degrees per user is above the median in most degree range. Towards larger degrees, extremely active outlying users are becoming more prevalent as evidenced by the discrepancy between mean and median in both degree cases.

5.3 Ranking Tumblr Blogs

The popularity of Tumblr users (or their corresponding blogs) can be estimated by various measures. Here we consider two aspects: the total number of *reblogs* of a user and the (unweighted) in-degree of the user in the *reblog* network. We compute and compare the results of the top-20 users from both measures in a side-by-side manner. For privacy concern, we don't explicitly disclose the details of individual users. Based on our observation, 14 out of 20 users are common in both rankings, and the top-4 users are identical in both cases. The top-ranked user according to *reblog* counts has a total of 26,030,925 *reblogs*, which is an order of magnitude more than the next top-ranked user. The rest of the 19 users in the list have *reblog* counts ranging between 4 million to 9 millions during the four months period. In terms of ranking by in-degree, the top-ranked user has more than 500,000 in-coming nodes, and the rest of the users have

between 250,000 to 470,000 in-coming nodes. A closer look on each blog reveals that majority of the blogs belong to individuals. This is radically different from the top-ranked users (with the same measures) in Twitter, as most of them come from news organizations or celebrities [23]. The majority contents from the top-ranked Tumblr blogs consist of fashion images, jokes and other topics that are most popular among younger social media users.

6. USER LOCATIONS

Another interesting study is to dissect the Tumblr social network based on users' geolocations and investigating how users' geolocation impacts their participation in the platform. However, Tumblr does not support any forms of geo-taggging or provide any user location information in its native platform. Inspired by the success of our prior work on geocoding Twitter users [21, 10], we propose a practical solution to obtain geolocation for Tumblr users by first conducting a large-scale user alignment with the Twitter platform and subsequently propagating user geolocations across.

6.1 User Alignment

User alignment across social media has been a topic of growing interest [34, 22]. However, most existing approaches rely on complicated correlation analysis and modeling, which impose strong constraints on scalability. In this work, we take a simpler extractive-based approach to align social media users by utilizing the additional Twitter data we obtained (see Section 5.1). Specifically, we search for two types of user linkages from Twitter as follows.

Explicit Self-reported Links: Due to the increasing popularity of social media, many active social media users have their virtual identities in multiple social media platforms. For instance, it is common for Twitter users to provide alternative social media accounts in their profile in order to promote their online presence. For our case, we are interested in detecting explicit mentions of the Tumblr user accounts. To do that, we simply search for every user profiles in our Twitter corpus with the regular expression "http://[www.]*[a-zA-Z0-9-_].tumblr.com". This gives us a total of $5,672,374$ pairs of aligned users between Twitter and Tumblr.

Implicit Cross-Links: Many existing social media sites support content synchronization in order to reduce end user effort. Basically, this allows users to submit a post from one platform, and the content of the post will be automatically published to all other social media platforms under the same user. For the case of Twitter, there is usually a URL appended at the end of a tweet to indicate its origin. For example, the top image in Figure 10 shows a sample tweet which encodes a link to the Tumblr platform (e.g., http://tmblr.co/ZVxw1y15H_Go3). In other words, the tweet content was original published in Tumblr, and it was automatically synchronized to Twitter. Bottom image in Figure 10 shows the referenced original Tumblr post.

This kind of cross-referencing turns out to be very useful in terms of identifying the same user across the two platforms. The key here is the shorten URL with the prefix pattern of "tmblr.co". This shorten URL is automatically generated by the Tumblr server, and it would only be triggered by the synchronization process between Tumblr and Twitter. Since synchronization only happens when a user owns both accounts, this should be reliable way to identify same users across platforms. Thus we scan our entire Twitter corpus for URL mentions in the form of "http://tmblr.co/(\\S{4,20})" We detect a total of $35,907,479$ such cross-linking instances. By a post processing step to resolve the shorten URLs, we are able to identify a total of $1,444,447$ unique pairs of aligned Twitter and Tumber user accounts. Figure 11(a) shows the raw cross-linking frequencies from the identified users. Note that users are ordered based on the frequencies in the x-axis. Figure 11(b) plots the same data in a log-log scale. The curve shows typical characteristic of a Zipf curve.

Figure 10: An example of implicit cross-linking between Twitter and Tumblr.

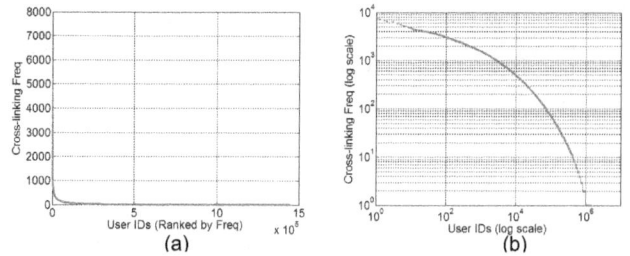

Figure 11: (a) Implicit Twitter-Tumblr cross-linking distribution by users. (b) log-log plot of the same distribution.

We perform an preliminary evaluation on the aligned users in order to verify the accuracy of the implicit cross-linking approach. Basically we sample at random 40 aligned users at different cross-linking frequency range for manual inspection. That is 40 users with at most one cross-linking instance, 40 with between 1 and 10, 40 with between 10 and 100, 40 with between 100 and 1000, and finally 40 with over 1000 cross-linking instances. This is essentially sampling at different spectrum of the log-log curve in Figure 11(b). During visual inspection, a human user determines if the linked pair is correct based on various heuristics such as user names, profile images, and others. Figure 12 summarizes the accuracy of this approach. As can be seen, the alignment accuracy remains at 100% as long as the cross-linking frequency between two accounts is greater than 1. Error only occurs in the lowest cross-linking frequency range. We suspect these rare cases are due to direct "copy-and-paste" of tweets. In order to maintain the good accuracy, we use the frequency value as a threshold and discard all aligned pairs with less than 5 cross-linking instances.

	Ture	False	N/A (Account deactivated)	Unsure
>1000	36	0	3	1
>100, <1000	36	0	4	0
>10, <100	32	0	8	0
>1, <10	35	0	5	0
=1	23	9	3	5
Overall	162	9	23	6
	94.74%	5.26%		

Figure 12: Evaluation on implicit cross-linking.

To summarize, we have obtained a total of $6,549,937$ unique pairs of aligned users with both explicit self-report links and implicit cross-links.

6.2 Geocoding

The basic idea of our prior works [21, 10] is to formulate the Twitter user geocoding problem as a graph-based optimization problem. Nodes in the network represent users, and edges represent geodesic distances between users weighted by their number of reciprocated @mentions. Given a small set of initial nodes (users) with geolocation information, the goal is to propagate this information to the rest of the network through the intrinsic structure of the network. Essentially the optimization is to seek a stable state of the network such that the sum over all geographic distances between connected users is minimized. The intuition behind

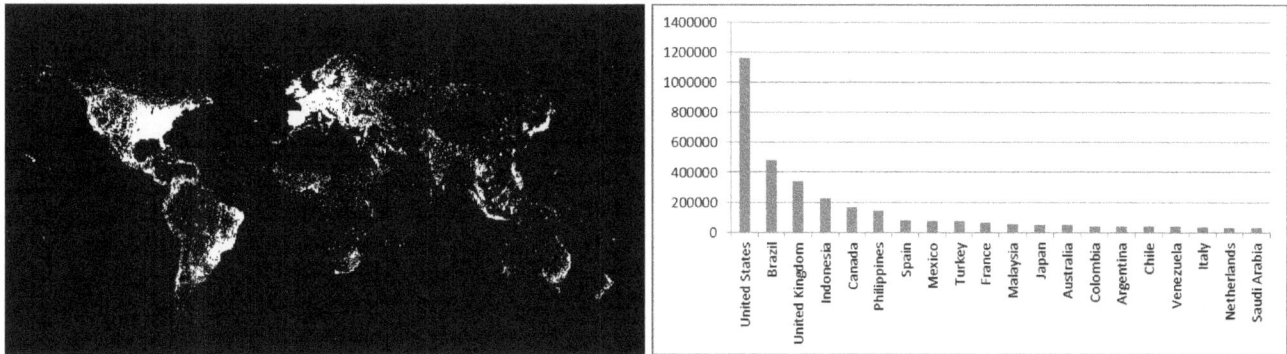

Figure 13: (Left) Distribution of geocoded Tumblr users. (Right) Top-20 countries with most geocoded users.

such an approach is that users who have strong social ties in online community are likely to live in a nearby proximity.

The works in [21, 10] successfully inferred the locations for 89% of the users in our Twitter corpus with a median error of 6.65 km. Subsequently, based on the overlapping users identified from the Twitter and Tumblr alignment, we are able to provide geolocation information for a total of 4,449,990 Tumblr users. Figure 13 shows the global distribution of geocoded Tumblr users, as well as the top-20 countries. Substantial coverage is obtained in north and south American, Europe, and south-east Asia.

Figure 14 shows the total number of posting activities from different countries based on geocoded users. For simplicity, only countries fall into one timezone are selected. As can be seen from the figure, clear daily recurring patterns are observed in all countries. However, each country does exhibit a distinct posting characteristics in a finer hourly scale. For instance, Japan has more activities during the day, and Colombia has more activities later in the evening. While detailed country-level analysis is beyond the scope of this work, user localization on Tumblr makes it possible to conduct similar study as in [14].

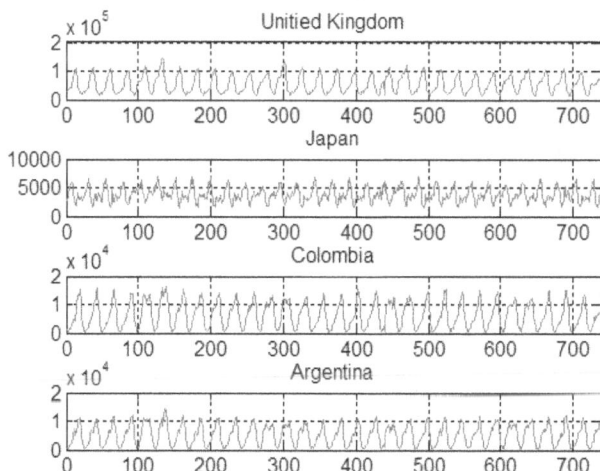

Figure 14: Country-specific hourly activity (# post) since 2013-09-01T07:00. Hours are normalized with respect to GMT+00:00.

7. CONCLUSIONS

In this paper, we presented a large-scale quantitative study to analyze the collective microblogging patterns on Tumblr. We found that 1) The contents in Tumblr are mostly centered around users' interests and hobbies, and the majority of users appear to fall in the younger demographic group; 2) Most of the Tumblr posts are essentially relogs, and original contents consist of less than 10% of the overall posts; 3) Tumblr posts typically have longer lifespan, however, the popularity growth of posts in different topics varies significantly; 4) Social ties derived from the Tumblr *reblog* network is weaker than the @mention network in Twitter. Furthermore, we provided substantial results on localizing Tumblr users based on a large-scale user alignment with the Twitter platform. We believe that our work is the first step towards better understanding and exploring the full potential of Tumblr.

In the future, we are interested in extending our work to several directions. First, we would like to study the patterns of information dissemination on Tumblr in a fine scale under different topics or categories. Second, we would like to extend our user alignment work to cover different social media platforms. Third, given the user linkages across platforms, we are interested in constructing large-scale multiplex networks and study their structures as well as the corresponding cascading behaviors.

8. ACKNOWLEDGMENTS AND DISCLAIMER

Supported by the Intelligence Advanced Research Projects Activity (IARPA) via Department of Interior National Business Center (DoI / NBC) Contract Number D12PC00285. The U.S. Government is authorized to reproduce and distribute reprints for Governmental purposes notwithstanding any copyright annotation thereon. The views and conclusions contained herein are those of the author(s) and should not be interpreted as necessarily representing the official policies or endorsements, either expressed or implied, of IARPA, DoI/NBC, or the U.S. Government.

9. REFERENCES

[1] Tumblr official page. http://www.tumblr.com/about. Accessed: 2014-02-20.

[2] J. Alstott, E. Bullmore, and D. Plenz. powerlaw: a python package for analysis of heavy-tailed distributions. *PLoS ONE 9(1): e85777*, 2013.

[3] S. Asur and B. A. Huberman. Predicting the future with social media. *CoRR*, abs/1003.5699, 2010.

[4] L. Backstrom, P. Boldi, M. Rosa, J. Ugander, and S. Vigna. Four degrees of separation. In *WebSci*, pages 33–42, 2012.

[5] M. Cha, H. Haddadi, F. Benevenuto, and K. Gummadi. Measuring user influence in twitter: The million follower fallacy. In *4th International Conference on Weblogs and Social Media*, 2010.

[6] M. Cha, H. Kwak, P. Rodriguez, Y.-Y. Ahn, and S. Moon. I tube, you tube, everybody tubes: Analyzing the world's largest user generated content video system. In *Proceedings of the 7th ACM SIGCOMM Conference on Internet Measurement*, New York, NY, USA, 2007.

[7] M. Cha, A. Mislove, and K. P. Gummadi. A measurement-driven analysis of information propagation in the flickr social network. In *Proceedings of the 18th International Conference on World Wide Web*, WWW '09, pages 721–730, New York, NY, USA, 2009. ACM.

[8] L. Chiarandini, P. A. Grabowicz, M. Trevisiol, and A. Jaimes. Leveraging browsing patterns for topic discovery and photostream recommendation. In *ICWSM*, 2013.

[9] A. Clauset, C. R. Shalizi, and M. E. J. Newman. Power-law distributions in empirical data. *SIAM Rev.*, 51(4):661–703, Nov. 2009.

[10] R. Compton, D. Jurgens, and D. Allen. Geotagging one hundred million twitter accounts with total variation minimization. *arXiv:1404.7152*, 2014.

[11] M. Coscia. Competition and success in the meme pool: A case study on quickmeme.com. In *ICWSM*, 2013.

[12] J. Delaney, N. Salminen, and E. Lee. Infographic: The growing impact of social media. *http://www.sociallyawareblog.com*, Nov. 2012.

[13] Q. Gao, F. Abel, G.-J. Houben, and Y. Yu. A comparative study of users' microblogging behavior on sina weibo and twitter. In *Proceedings of the 20th International Conference on User Modeling, Adaptation, and Personalization*, pages 88–101, Berlin, Heidelberg, 2012.

[14] S. A. Golder and M. W. Macy. Diurnal and seasonal mood vary with work, sleep, and daylength across diverse cultures. *Science*, 333:1878–1881, 2009.

[15] W. Guan, H. Gao, M. Yang, Y. Li, H. Ma, W. Qian, Z. Cao, and X. Yang. Analyzing user behavior of the micro-blogging website sinaweibo during hot social events. *CoRR*, abs/1304.3898, 2013.

[16] L. Guo, E. Tan, S. Chen, X. Zhang, and Y. E. Zhao. Analyzing patterns of user content generation in online social networks. In *Proceedings of the 15th ACM SIGKDD International Conference on Knowledge Discovery and Data Mining*, KDD '09, pages 369–378, New York, NY, USA, 2009. ACM.

[17] N. Hochman and R. Schwartz. Visualizing instagram: Tracing cultural visual rhythms. In *ICWSM*, 2012.

[18] C. Hutto, S. Yardi, and E. Gilbert. A longitudinal study of follow predictors on twitter. In *Proceedings of the SIGCHI Conference on Human Factors in Computing Systems*, pages 821–830, 2013.

[19] B. J. Jansen, M. Zhang, K. Sobel, and A. Chowdury. Twitter power: Tweets as electronic word of mouth. *J. Am. Soc. Inf. Sci. Technol.*, 60(11), Nov. 2009.

[20] A. Java, X. Song, T. Finin, and B. Tseng. Why we twitter: Understanding microblogging usage and communities. In *Workshop on Web Mining and Social Network Analysis*, pages 56–65, 2007.

[21] D. Jurgens. That's what friends are for: Inferring location in online social media platforms based on social relationships. In *ICWSM*, 2013.

[22] M. Korayem and D. J. Crandall. De-anonymizing users across heterogeneous social computing platforms. In *ICWSM*, 2013.

[23] H. Kwak, C. Lee, H. Park, and S. Moon. What is twitter, a social network or a news media? In *Proceedings of the 19th International Conference on World Wide Web*, pages 591–600, 2010.

[24] S. Mittal, N. Gupta, P. Dewan, and P. Kumaraguru. The pin-bang theory: Discovering the pinterest world. *CoRR*, abs/1307.4952, 2013.

[25] M. Novak. Unwrapping tumblr. *http://www.slideshare.net/myklnovak*, Jan. 2013.

[26] R. Ottoni, J. P. Pesce, D. B. L. Casas, G. F. Jr., W. M. Jr., P. Kumaraguru, and V. Almeida. Ladies first: Analyzing gender roles and behaviors in pinterest. In *ICWSM*, 2013.

[27] J. Park, V. Barash, C. Fink, and M. Cha. Emoticon style: Interpreting differences in emoticons across cultures. In *ICWSM*, 2013.

[28] C. Smith. Tumblr offers advertisers a major advantage: Young users, who spend tons of time on the site. *http://www.businessinsider.com/tumblr-and-social-media-demographics-2013-12*.

[29] J. Ugander, B. Karrer, L. Backstrom, and C. Marlow. The anatomy of the facebook social graph. *CoRR*, 2011.

[30] G. Wang, K. Gill, M. Mohanlal, H. Zheng, and B. Y. Zhao. Wisdom in the social crowd: an analysis of quora. In *WWW*, 2013.

[31] S. Wu, J. M. Hofman, W. A. Mason, and D. J. Watts. Who says what to whom on twitter. In *Proceedings of the 20th International Conference on World Wide Web*, pages 705–714, New York, NY, USA, 2011.

[32] J. Yang and J. Leskovec. Patterns of temporal variation in online media. In *Proceedings of the Fourth ACM International Conference on Web Search and Data Mining*, pages 177–186, 2011.

[33] L. L. Yu, S. Asur, and B. A. Huberman. What trends in chinese social media. *CoRR*, abs/1107.3522, 2011.

[34] R. Zafarani and H. Liu. Connecting users across social media sites: A behavioral-modeling approach. In *SIGKDD*, pages 41–49, 2013.

[35] M. A. Zarro, C. Hall, and A. Forte. Wedding dresses and wanted criminals: Pinterest.com as an infrastructure for repository building. In *ICWSM*, 2013.

[36] D. Zhao and M. B. Rosson. How and why people twitter: The role that micro-blogging plays in informal communication at work. In *Proceedings of the ACM 2009 International Conference on Supporting Group Work*, 2009.

Identifying and Analyzing Researchers on Twitter

Asmelash Teka Hadgu
L3S Research Center
Appelstraße 4, 30167 Hannover, Germany
teka@l3s.de

Robert Jäschke
L3S Research Center
Appelstraße 4, 30167 Hannover, Germany
jaeschke@l3s.de

ABSTRACT

For millions of users Twitter is an important communication platform, a social network, and a system for resource sharing. Likewise, scientists use Twitter to connect with other researchers, announce calls for papers, or share their thoughts. Filtering tweets, discovering other researchers, or finding relevant information on a topic of interest, however, is difficult since no directory of researchers on Twitter exists.

In this paper we present an approach to identify Twitter accounts of researchers and demonstrate its utility for the discipline of computer science. Based on a seed set of computer science conferences we collect relevant Twitter users which we can partially map to ground-truth data. The mapping is leveraged to learn a model for classifying the remaining. To gain first insights into how researchers use Twitter, we empirically analyze the identified users and compare their age, popularity, influence, and social network.

Categories and Subject Descriptors

H.4 [**Information Systems Applications**]: Miscellaneous; H.3.7 [**Information Storage and Retrieval**]: Digital Libraries; H.2.8 [**Database Management**]: Database Applications—*Data mining*

Keywords

Twitter; Computer Science; Classification; Social Network

1. INTRODUCTION

Twitter is a communication platform, a social network, and a system for resource sharing [8]. For scientists, it offers an opportunity to connect with other researchers, announce calls for papers and the like, communicate and discuss – basically: stay up-to-date. However, the exponential growth of information in society [7] does not exclude social media like Twitter: an abundant number of users court on one's attention which leads to the question of how (young) researchers can focus on the essential users and tweets?

The classical approach in science to filter information is peer review: only information that is considered to be novel, sound, and significant by experts in the respective field is published. Currently, such a process is at most implemented manually: researchers can subscribe individually to other researcher's feeds by following them. However, there is no 'directory' of scientists on Twitter and finding feeds of experts in a specific discipline or area of interest is cumbersome.

Furthermore, the trend to consider visibility of scientific articles in the social web as a possible (and immediate) alternative or complement to citation counts [13] (with services like Altmetric[1] that provide counts for how often a scientific article has been mentioned on Twitter and other social networks) necessitates the need for peer-review-like mechanisms for the social web. Simple approaches purely based on the popularity of users, tweets, or URLs do not work as a tool for scientists to discover relevant research(ers), since popularity on the social web is fundamentally a matter of the crowd of non-scientists. Articles that are popularized by the media – often independent of their scientific significance – get superior attention compared to other, more important works. Consider the Ig Nobel Prizes,[2] whose winning (scientific) publications get quite some attention on the social web, e.g., the URL[3] of the winner of the 2012 physics prize [5] has been mentioned in more than 230 tweets.[4] Enabling users (and in particular researchers) to access the scientists' perspective in the social web and considering only tweets from physicists would provide a different and likely better picture.

Existing Twitter directories like Wefollow[5] rely on users' initiative to register and reveal their interests. This clearly limits the set of available profiles, since professionals have limited time and there is no immediate benefit for registration. Therefore, providing an automatically curated directory of scientists would simplify expert finding and the provision of topic-relevant feeds authored by peers. This approach requires to first identify scientists on Twitter and then classify their discipline, topics of interest, and expertise. Since only little is known about scientists on Twitter, such an endeavor should be accompanied by further steps to understand how Twitter is used by them.

In this work, we present an approach for the identification and classification of scientists on Twitter together with

---

[1] http://www.altmetric.com/
[2] http://www.improbable.com/ig/
[3] http://prl.aps.org/abstract/PRL/v108/i7/e078101
[4] http://topsy.com/trackback?url=http%3A%2F%2Fprl.aps.org%2Fabstract%2FPRL%2Fv108%2Fi7%2Fe078101
[5] http://wefollow.com/

an empirical analysis of researchers from computer science found on Twitter. We take a pragmatic approach on which users we regard as 'scientists': users being interested in the topics of the target discipline and having similar, Twitter-based features like users that have published scientific papers. We start with a list of seeds that are highly-relevant for the discipline of interest and use it to build and augment a set of candidate users that are likely scientists. For a subset of the candidates that we can match to ground-truth data from a digital library, we build a model for the classification of scientists. We can show that the model is very accurate and use it to classify all of our candidates. Both sets of users (matched and classified) allow us to perform an empirical analysis of scientists on Twitter.

The main contributions of this work are

- a complete framework for discipline-specific researcher classification on Twitter using a small set of seeds only,
- an automatic approach for the generation of ground-truth data by combining different data sources,
- an empirical analysis of computer scientists that are actively using Twitter, and
- the provision of the used datasets.

To the best of our knowledge, such an analysis has not been performed before. In addition, we publish the datasets of the different sets of users to foster research in the areas of expert finding and scientometrics.[6]

This paper is organized as follows: In Section 2 we review related work and in Section 3 we describe our classification approach and its concrete implementation. The results are presented in Section 4, accompanied by an empirical analysis of computer scientists on Twitter in Section 5. We draw conclusions about our approach in Section 6.

2. RELATED WORK

Several Twitter directories like Wefollow, Twellow, and JustTweetIt[7] list Twitter users by different areas of interest. There also exist more specific directories which, for example, list emergency physicians[8] or top Canadian politicians and keep track of what they and other citizens have to say on Twitter (and other social media) about politics.[9] In Wefollow, users provide their interests upon registration and are then ranked according to a prominence score that is computed similar to PageRank, restricted to the respective interest groups.[10] Even though the user interest is very accurate, because the users themselves provide the information, this approach is not scalable as it requires users to register at the web site and explicitly state their interests. Unlike Wefollow, our approach automatically builds profiles of Twitter users. In Twellow, user categorization is determined automatically using keyword/phrase matching on the users' Twitter profiles.[11] Our approach incorporates more features to get more accurate user classification. To the best of our knowledge, there is no directory that curates a list of scientists on Twitter. In this paper we present a general

approach for generating a Twitter user directory and show its validity for computer scientists.

A good overview and one of the first comprehensive analyses of Twitter is [8] with findings on the distribution of followers and followees, tweets, trending topics and users, and retweet dynamics. The results suggest that Twitter, due to the speed of retweets, is a good medium for information diffusion from which scientists can benefit.

User classification in Twitter has been studied in [11] and [14]. Pennacchiotti and Popescu [11] propose a machine learning framework to perform large-scale user classification. They extract features from profile, content, and network connections of users and apply their framework to classify users by their political affiliation, ethnicity and affinity for a particular business. Similarly, Rao et al. [14] automatically infer users' latent attributes such as gender, age, regional origin, and political orientation on Twitter using features derived from tweet messages only. They use a focused crawling approach to build separate datasets for each attribute learning task. Starting from seed accounts of the target class, they gather more users by looking at their followers to manually build ground-truth data. They train an SVM model to perform the prediction. Another closely related work to our task of user classification deals with researcher home page classification. Gollapalli et al. [6] use URL-based features in addition to the content of a web page in a co-training scheme to classify web pages as academic or otherwise. In our approach, we use features that have been reported to work well in these three works.

Another line of research related to our work deals with measuring user influence in Twitter [1, 2]. In [1] Bakshy et al. study the characteristics and influence of a large set of Twitter users by examining information cascades, more specifically the diffusion trees associated with tweets containing URLs. They found that predicting influential users or tweets with URLs in terms of generating large diffusion trees is unreliable. They conclude that to harness word-of-mouth in Twitter it is necessary to target a large number of potential influencers instead of just the top influencers. Cha et al. [2] study user influence by comparing directed links among users. They regard the three influence measures number of followers, retweets, and mentions. Among others, they found that the number of followers alone is not a good indicator of influence, i.e., popular users who have a large number of followers are not necessarily the most influential users when considering the number of retweets or mentions. We use these different influence metrics to identify prominent computer scientists on Twitter.

Closely related to our work is also research that studies the use of Twitter for academic activities and analyzes the spread of scientific tweets as an instrument for citation analysis [12, 4, 16, 9]. Priem and Hemminger [12] study whether and how scholars cite on Twitter by analyzing tweets from 28 scholars. They define a citation as a tweet that contains a URL to a peer-reviewed scholarly article. They find that scholars use Twitter to cite articles and suggest to use this information to augment traditional scientometric methods. Weller et al. [16] propose a methodology to analyze citations in Twitter during scientific conferences. They manually inspect and classify URLs and retweets of users to conclude that citations on Twitter are different from classical citations. Another example is the work by Eysenbach [4], who explores which metrics could enable the prediction of cita-

[6] https://github.com/L3S/twitter-researcher
[7] cf. http://www.twellow.com/, http://justtweetit.com/
[8] http://emergencytwitter.ivor-kovic.com/
[9] http://politwitter.ca/
[10] http://wefollow.com/about/score
[11] http://www.twellow.com/faq

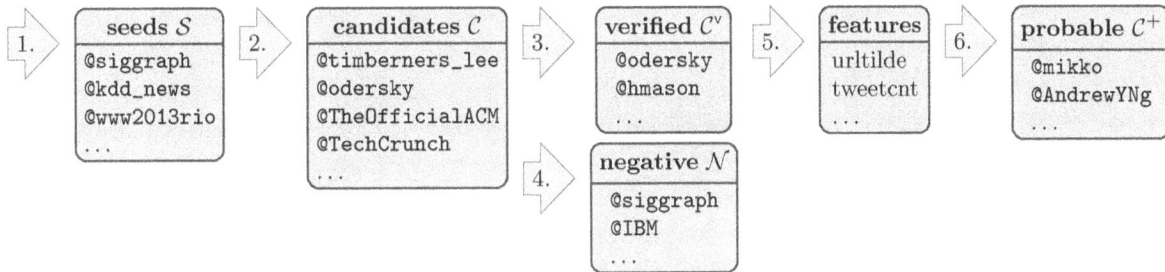

Figure 1: Overview of the processing pipeline.

tion counts based on tweets. Eysenbach computes metrics for 1 573 tweets that contain links to 55 articles of the Journal of Medical Internet Research and compares them with the citation counts. Letierce et al. [9] present the result of a survey to understand how Twitter is used for spreading scientific messages by semantic web researchers. These approaches can be seen as further motivation for our work, since we try to bridge the gap between Twitter and science by providing an automatic approach to identify scientists on Twitter. This task is not addressed by existing approaches, since the users and their (scientific) background is not considered. Furthermore, by focusing only on tweets that are linked to peer-reviewed articles, other forms of scientific discourse are ignored. Our approach to identify scientists, on the contrary, enables the analysis of a much larger share of academic content and its reception in Twitter.

3. APPROACH

In this section we describe our approach. We start with an overview of the processing pipeline and then explain the components in detail. The processing pipeline (cf. Figure 1) comprises the following six steps:

1. We start by building a *seed set* $\mathcal{S}$ of Twitter accounts for which we assume that they are typically followed by researchers. This set should be easy to obtain and should fulfill our assumption. By starting with a small set of seeds instead of (focused) crawling we favor precision over recall.

2. By collecting all users that follow the seeds or are otherwise related to them, we obtain an initial set $\mathcal{C}$ of *candidates*. This set can be further expanded by repeating the process several times with the candidates in place of the seeds.

3. We now match the candidates against ground-truth data $\mathcal{G}$. The subset $\mathcal{C}^v \subseteq \mathcal{C}$ of candidates for which we find a match with high confidence (*verified* candidates) allows us already to empirically analyze researchers on Twitter and will act as training data for Step 6.

4. The other part of the training data consists of *negative* examples $\mathcal{N}$, i.e., users that are not researchers. Basically, we are facing a one-class classification problem for which it is difficult to obtain ground truth data for the negative (outlier) class.

5. We identify and extract *features* for all users.

6. Based on the verified users $\mathcal{C}^v$ and negative examples $\mathcal{N}$ we train a model to classify the remaining candidates, which partitions them into users $\mathcal{C}^+$ that are

probably researchers and users $\mathcal{C}^-$ that are *probably not* researchers.

Each step is a basic building block of our approach whose implementation could differ from the one we chose. In the following, we motivate and describe each step in more detail and present our implementation.

3.1 Generating a Seed Set of Twitter Accounts

The first step of our approach is the collection of Twitter users that serve as the seed set $\mathcal{S}$ for crawling further users in the next step by retrieving their friends, followers and retweeters. Our requirements to the seed set are similar to that of a focussed web crawl, where the crawling efficiency can be significantly influenced by the selection of seed URLs [17]: We want to ensure that the friends, followers and retweeters of the seeds have a high probability of being the target class, i.e., researchers, and that they are representative examples, e.g., have a good coverage over different sub-topics. Furthermore, the seed set should be small such that it could be curated manually.

In our implementation we chose Twitter accounts of *scientific conferences* as seeds, since we expect that these are typically followed or retweeted by computer scientists. Conferences are quite important and accepted in computer science, compared to other disciplines. To the best of our knowledge, such a list of accounts is not readily available. However, there exist some sources for lists of conferences, e.g., in Microsoft Academic Search,[12] or in Wikipedia.[13] Such lists can be taken as input for a subsequent manual or automatic collection of corresponding Twitter screen names. We decided to use the Wikipedia list, since it is maintained by the community and with 268 conferences it is quite comprehensive. Although the selection and completeness of this list could be questioned (as that of any list), it fulfills the initially stated requirements of being representative for computer science and of being small enough to acquire the corresponding seed set of Twitter accounts with high confidence. The choice of Wikipedia also makes our approach easily adaptable, since similar lists exist for other disciplines.

Once we have a list of seed conferences, we want to link them to their Twitter accounts, if they have any. Rather than identifying these accounts manually, which requires a lot of effort and restrains reproducibility, we combine two search approaches:

1) Twitter Search. Motivated by the observation that many conferences have Twitter screen names that corre-

---

[12] http://academic.research.microsoft.com/ ?SearchDomain=2&entitytype=3

[13] http://en.wikipedia.org/wiki/List_of_computer_ science_conferences

spond to their acronyms and are possibly followed by the year of the conference, we construct potential screen names for the years 2008 to 2014 by appending two and four digit numbers to each acronym, e.g., WWW is extended to @www09, ... and @www2009, ... Including the plain conference acronyms we issued in total 3 960 such queries from 264 acronyms[14] against the Twitter API[15] which returned detailed information for 1 652 valid Twitter screen names.

2) Web Search. We try to find links to Twitter from the web pages of the conferences. Therefore, for each seed conference, we perform a search with Microsoft Bing[16] to find its corresponding web site. We issue the conference's full name together with the years 2008 to 2014, e.g., for the WWW conference in 2009 we query for *World-Wide Web Conference 2009*. For each of the top three results of each query, we parse the web page for any link pointing to Twitter. From these links, we extract potential screen names for which we query the Twitter API to verify if they indeed represent Twitter accounts. Using this approach we could identify 260 accounts, some of which could not be found using the first approach, e.g., @www2012lyon or @www2013rio for the WWW conference.

The merged list of Twitter accounts from both approaches contained some noise which we removed by restricting to accounts that (a) contained one of the strings 'conference', 'symposium', 'workshop', or 'forum' in their profile description or (b) contained at least one of the phrases 'call for (papers|demos|tutorials|workshops)', '(paper|workshop) deadline', '(full|short|accepted) papers' and 'camera-ready' in their original (i.e., not retweeted) tweets. The resulting conference accounts were then validated by experts and only correct accounts were retained for the next step. A comparison of both approaches to generate seeds is given in Sections 4.1.

3.2 Generating Candidates

Having built a high-quality seed set, we gather candidate users C that follow the seeds or are otherwise related to them. In practice, there are other relationships we can leverage, e.g., users are followed by one of the seeds, or re-tweeted a seed's tweet. Other, more indirect relationships include the mention of a seed's name in a user's tweet or vice versa, the usage of mutual hash tags, or the following of common users. Our assumption is that the more direct and closer the relationship of the users to the seeds is, the more likely they are of our target class. Note that this expansion process can be repeated several times with the current set of candidates as input instead of the seeds. However, with every expansion round the distance to the seed set grows and thereby the likelihood that the users are researchers decreases.

In our implementation we follow an approach that is inspired by [15], where the retweet signal is used to collect politically interested Twitter users starting from a seed set of users. However, we also add users that follow or are followed by (i.e., are *friends* with) the users in the seed set – the latter because we observed that most conferences follow fellow researchers. In our initial experiments we expanded the candidate set once. However, we considered the expanded set as both too large (more than 30 million users) and too broad to be useful and therefore omitted the expansion step in our implementation to favor precision instead of recall.

3.3 Matching Candidates With Ground-Truth

The preceding step generated a set of candidate users that are likely from our target class, i.e., researchers. To classify these users, training data for machine learning is required, i.e., a set C^v of Twitter screen names known to be scientists. Since such a list does not exist and manually building it is tedious and error prone, we use an automatic method to generate the training data for classification. Therefore, we leverage the fact that a common goal of researchers is the publication of their results in journals or at conferences, and that meta data about publications and hence authors is often readily available from *digital libraries* (e.g., PubMed for medicine, or arXiv.org for physics). Thus, given a list G of authors in the discipline of interest, we can match their names against the real names from the Twitter profiles of the candidate users C. Of course, using the real name to match persons has some drawbacks: people might use false names in their profile and many names are not unique. On the other hand, the real name is the best indicator which we have, since in our setup all of the candidates have specified their name.[17] Choosing both the seeds and the ground-truth data from the particular scientific discipline of interest we minimize the chance of mismatches. To further reduce errors, we omit candidates and authors whose names appear more than once in the respective set and match the names without any normalization (e.g., without abbreviating first names). Given these measures, we are confident that the matching provides high-accuracy ground-truth data.

In our implementation the candidates are matched against authors from DBLP [10], a computer science bibliography hosted at the University of Trier. We downloaded the XML dump of DBLP[18], parsed it and extracted 1 304 283 author names from all publications.

DBLP disambiguates authors with the same name by appending a number to their name, e.g., *Abbas Mohammadi*, *Abbas Mohammadi 0001*, and *Abbas Mohammadi 0002*. Furthermore, author names in DBLP are case sensitive. For instance, *BorMin Huang* and *Bormin Huang* represent distinct authors. We regard both cases as duplicates. After removal of duplicate names (13 688 in DBLP and 2 686 in our candidate set) we performed exact string matching (ignoring case) on the full names. We do not conduct more complicated matching operations as we want to collect matches with high confidence. This way, we could match 9 191 DBLP authors ($= C^v$) against Twitter users in our candidate set C. The result of validating this mapping is given in Section 4.2.

3.4 Generating Negative Examples

Since we can identify and describe the positive examples and regard everything else as negative examples, we are basically dealing with a one-class classification problem. However, regardless of whether we apply a binary or unary clas-

---

[14] Four acronyms appeared twice, because they referred to different conferences (ISWC for *International Semantic Web Conference* and *International Symposium on Wearable Computers*) or the same conference appeared under different names but with the same acronym (USENIX, FSE, CHES).

[15] http://dev.twitter.com/docs/api/1.1/get/users/lookup

[16] http://datamarket.azure.com/dataset/bing/search

[17] In contrast, only 55% of the candidates have specified a web site which could be used for identification, though this would then require ground-truth data that includes researchers' web sites.

[18] http://dblp.uni-trier.de/xml/dblp.xml

sification approach, we still need negative examples to test and compare the performance of the learned model and the different algorithms. Since $\mathcal{C}$ is a biased sample of Twitter users mostly from our target class, it is not a good source for generating a representative sample of negative examples. Instead, we crawl users with Twitter's streaming API. From this set we remove all users contained in $\mathcal{C}$ and then create $\mathcal{N}$ as a randomly sampled subset.

In our implementation we crawled $1\,000\,000$ users with the Twitter streaming API and removed all users from $\mathcal{C}$ and all their followers and friends. Therefrom, we sampled $1\,500$ users which serve as the set $\mathcal{N}$ of negative examples. In addition to these $1\,500$ users, we added the seeds $\mathcal{S}$ to $\mathcal{N}$, since they are on the one hand closely related to our target class (by the topics of their tweets and their relationships with other users) and on the other hand not our target. We observed that our candidate set contained quite some technology companies. Thus, we identified companies from the Forbes Global 2000 list[19] whose names matched with our candidates after filtering duplicates. We found 24 such companies and added them to $\mathcal{N}$.

3.5 Feature Generation

Building upon ideas from [11] and [14], we generate features from *profile* and *content* information. These groups mimic semantically the steps a human surfer would normally perform, if asked to determine whether a given Twitter account corresponds to a researcher or not: The *profile* features are derived from the top information that is displayed on the web page of a user's Twitter account. These include name, location, URL, description and global counts like the number of tweets, followers, and friends. Ideally, these are the fields that represent the identity of a user and should be sufficient to determine who is who. In reality, the profile information is not enough since some fields are missing or they are not specific enough. With the *content* features, we consider the user's tweets. They provide information about the topics the user is interested in which allows us to decide whether an account belongs to a researcher or not.

In our implementation we use different features for each group which we explain in the following.

Profile Features. The *number of tweets, number of followers, number of friends*, and the *ratio of followers and friends* can be regarded as global indicators that capture how active the user is in the social media platform. Researchers are professionals and hence we capture how well organized the profile is with the boolean features *location, profile picture, description* which indicate whether the corresponding fields have been set. Inspired by [6] we constructed features that capture if a website is given in the profile and if it likely points to a researcher's web page (*website exists, website contains tilde character, website contains academic top-level domain .edu or country code second-level domain .ac (e.g., .ac.uk)*). Keywords such as *phd, researcher,* or *scientist* are a strong signal that the user is a researcher. We build a set of keywords that can be found in the bio of our verified users $\mathcal{C}^v$ but not in the negative examples $\mathcal{N}$ by employing the following steps: 1) we generate a list of top $k\%$ terms from the bio fields of users in $\mathcal{C}^v$, 2) we generate a list of top $l\%$ terms from the bio fields of users in $\mathcal{N}$ that serve as our 'stop words', and 3) we remove these stop words from the terms generated in the first step. The thresholds $k = 5\%$ and $l = 5\%$ were

determined experimentally during the learning phase of the classification using cross-validation. The final terms are *architect, assistant, associate, author, candidate, co-founder, cs, designer, developer, director, engineer, fellow, founder, geek, graduate, lecturer, manager, phd, ph.d, prof, professor, programmer, researcher, scientist, senior.* These result in a boolean feature which indicates if the *bio contains keywords* from the above list.

Content Features. We include features that quantify the activity and topical interests of the users, such as the number of *original tweets, retweets, retweets to tweets ratio, tweets containing URL(s), fraction of tweets with URL(s), tweets containing hashtags, distinct hashtags* and *fraction of distinct hashtags used.* A good signal to distinguish researchers from other users is the fraction of tweets that are related to science. Since hashtags are often used to define the topic of a message, we can use them as an approximation of the topics a user is interested in. Therefore, we bootstrap the top hashtags used by the seeds $\mathcal{S}$ to gather similar scientific hashtags. These are typically conference acronyms or scientific terms preceded by the hash symbol, e.g., #siggraph2013, #machinelearning, ... In a political context, Conover et al. [3] showed that it is possible to extend seed political hashtags using co-occurence patterns to gather more political hashtags. Unfortunately, this method does not work for scientific hashtags. Whereas it is usual to use similar and conflicting political hashtags such as #obama #romney in a single tweet like "How could Watson and Big data help pick a better US president http://bit.ly/PFo3me #obama #debate #romney", it is unlikely that researchers use different conference acronyms as hashtags (e.g., #www2013, #siggraph2013) in the same tweet. Instead, we consider terms that occur most often with the seed hashtags and collect other hashtags that occur in a similar context. More precisely, we implemented the following approach to gather more scientific hashtags from a small seed of hashtags:

1. We build a set of seed hashtags by collecting the most frequent hashtag of each seed conference.

2. We identify the unigrams in tweets that contain one of the seed hashtags and remove the most frequent unigrams we can find in random tweets – these act as stop words. This way, we generate a set of terms that frequently co-occur with the hashtags from Step 1, e.g., *papers, workshop, keynote, poster, etc.*

3. We gather all hashtags that co-occur with these terms. (e.g., #wsdm2011, #websci13, #machinelearning, ...)

4. We remove the most common hashtags from random tweets which again act as stop words. This removes very general hashtags such as #ff, #followfriday.

With the final set of $1\,872$ hashtags, we can leverage the *number of tweets containing scientific hashtags* as feature for classification. Finally, we count *how often a user mentions other users that have used one of these hashtags.*

In preliminary experiments we also considered *network features* like the *number of seeds* that have been *mentioned*, are *followed*, or whose tweets have been *retweeted*, and the *number of candidates* that have been *retweeted* or *mentioned*, or are *followers* or *followees.* Although these would allow us to capture the notion that our target users more likely connect to the conferences in $\mathcal{S}$ and to each other, the features are biased towards our approach to gather the candidates

---

[19] http://www.forbes.com/global2000/list/

Table 1: Overview on the used datasets.

dataset	date	#users	#tweets
seeds $\mathcal{S}$	Nov 2013	170	23 843
candidates $\mathcal{C}$	Nov/Dec 2013	52 678	54 146 027
ground-truth $\mathcal{G}$	Dec 2013	1 304 283	–
verified $\mathcal{C}^v$	Jan 2014	9 191	7 726 905
negative $\mathcal{N}$	Jan 2014	1 694	3 639 650

Table 2: Results of the automatic seed generation.

	Twitter Search	Web Search	Inter-section	Union
queries	3 960	1 869	–	–
screen names	1 652 (90%)	260 (14%)	69 (4%)	1 843 (100%)
filtered screen n.	135 (63%)	139 (65%)	60 (28%)	214 (100%)
valid screen n.	122 (72%)	107 (63%)	59 (35%)	170 (100%)
conferences	74 (76%)	75 (77%)	51 (52%)	98 (100%)

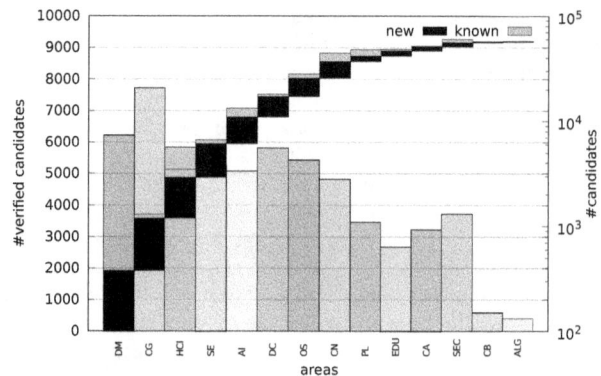

Figure 2: Distribution of the number of (verified) candidates over the different computer science areas.

and the negative examples. Since the examples were randomly sampled, their chance to be well-connected with the seeds or the candidates is very low, though for the candidates necessarily the opposite is true.

3.6 Classification

The target for the classification are the candidates that could not be matched against ground-truth data, i.e., $\mathcal{C} \setminus \mathcal{C}^v$, where we expect that many of them are also researchers. Having identified verified candidates $\mathcal{C}^v$ and some negative cases $\mathcal{N}$, we use these users to train a machine learning algorithm to classify the remaining unknown users in our candidate set. Any binary classification algorithm can be used, alternatively, one-class classification could be performed.

In our implementation we chose the classification algorithms Support Vector Machines (SVM), Random Forest (RF), Classification and Regression Trees (CART), and Logistic Regression (LR) using the implementations *e1071, rpart, randomForest and glm* available in R, the free software for statistical computing. We performed a stratified 10-fold cross-validation to train the models on 2 000 random users from $\mathcal{C}^v$ and all users from $\mathcal{N}$, results are given in Sec. 4.5. Finally, the best performing algorithm is selected and trained on the complete training set to classify the remaining users.

4. RESULTS

In this section we analyze the implementation of our approach and present the results of the classification step. An overview of the datasets used is given in Table 1.

4.1 Seeds

In total, we found 170 Twitter screen names for 98 conferences (37% of the 268 conferences) using either Twitter Search or Web Search, cf. Table 2. The number of accounts found by both methods is 60. This shows that the methods are complementary in that we find Twitter accounts for conferences with one approach that we can not find with the other. On the other hand, in the intersection of both approaches (after filtering) almost all seeds are valid screen names of conferences, since only one of the 60 screen names was judged to be a false positive. Thus, if the effort of manual validation is too high and one can accept a smaller seed set, the process can be automated by using the screen names

that are returned by both approaches only. We also note that Twitter Search has much more false positives before filtering which is caused by users that have screen names that resemble conference acronyms, e.g., @cikm, @www, etc. For Web Search the experts judged more of the filtered screen names to be false positives. One reason is that it yielded some accounts of research databases and conference organizers, e.g., @msftacademic, @ieeeorg, or @globaleventlist that can not be easily filtered by keyword matching on profiles and tweets. Overall, both approaches have a similar performance, although Web Search covers slightly more conferences with less screen names.

Since on the list from Wikipedia the conferences are partitioned into sub-areas of computer science[20] we can plot the contribution of each area to the sets $\mathcal{C}$ and $\mathcal{C}^v$ in Figure 2. Sorted by the number of verified candidates that each area contributes, the black bars indicate the contribution relative to the previous area in the list (e.g., *DM* contributes most, followed by *CG*). The grey bars extend the black bars and thereby show the overal number of verified candidates from each area. We shifted the bars up such that they reach the sum of 9 191 in $\mathcal{C}^v$ to the very right. The colored bars in the background show the (logarithmic) number of users each area contributes to $\mathcal{C}$.

Figure 3 shows a similar plot for each of the 98 seed conferences where the color of each conference matches the areas in Figure 2. The conference with by far the most followers is SIGGRAPH with 19 394 followers, followed by SC (5 229) and CHI (4 016). While following a conference clearly shows interest in it, retweeting one of its tweets is an even stronger signal.[21] Ranked by retweeters to followers ratio the order of conferences is: ICAC (38%), I3D (36%), ECOOP (33%), and AOSD (32%). Though ICAC has only 8 followers, the other conferences have more than 75 followers. On average, a user follows or retweets 1.1 conferences. Broken down by conference, ECCOP, ICDE and UIST have the most diverse users that follow or retweet on average 3.9, 3.5, and 3.0 con-

---

[20] namely, Data Management (DM), Computer Graphics (CG), Human-Computer Interaction (HCI), Software Engineering (SE), Artificial Intelligence (AI), Concurrent, Distributed and Parallel Computing (DC), Operating Systems (OS), Computer Networking and Networked Systems (CN), Programming Languages (PL), Education (EDU), Computer Architecture (CA), Security and Privacy (SEC), Computational Biology (CB), and Algorithms and Theory (ALG)

[21] Due to scarcity of space, we present only selected results.

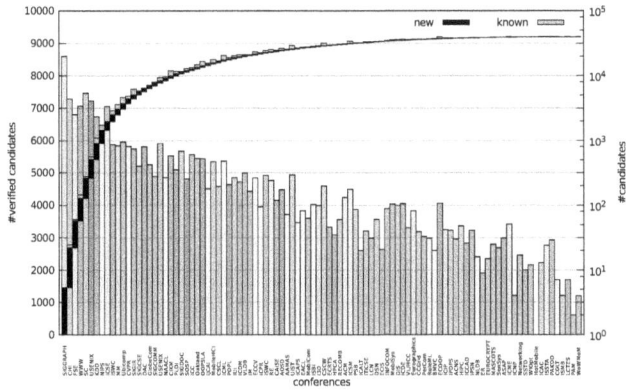

Figure 3: Distribution of the number of (verified) candidates over the conferences.

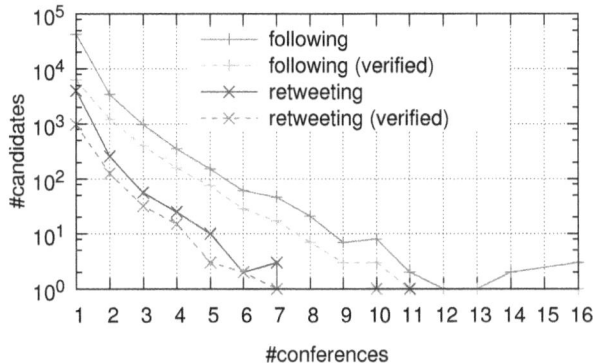

Figure 4: Distribution of the number of (verified) candidates that follow/retweeted one or more conferences.

ferences. SIGGRAPH and DAC have the most homogeneous users that, on average, follow 1.08 and 1.13 conferences, respectively. If we restrict the followers and retweeters to the verified candidates $\mathcal{C}^v$, SIGGRAPH still leads with 1 408 followers but is then followed by CHI (1 182) and SC (649). The retweeter/follower ratio is lead by I3D (77%), followed by RULEML (44%) and AOSD (40%).

4.2 Candidates

In the candidate generation step, we found 52 678 candidates, of which 47 870 follow at least one of the seed conferences. An additional 1 180 users retweeted at least one of the seeds' tweets but did not follow them at the time of our crawl, and 3 741 users were followed by one of the seeds (but the users neither followed nor retweeted the seeds). Most candidates are interested in one conference only (around 83% for both following and retweeting), though some are interested in five or more conferences (cf. Figure 4). Since we are interested in the researchers among the candidates, we present more insights in Sections 4.5 and 5.

4.3 Training Data

The training data consists of verified candidates $\mathcal{C}^v$ and negative examples $\mathcal{N}$. Overall, we could find 9 191 users (17.46%) in $\mathcal{C}$ whose names match with those in our ground-truth data from DBLP. They form the set $\mathcal{C}^v$. The fraction

Table 3: Performance of the feature groups using Random Forest.

feature group	P	R	F1	Acc	TNR
profile	0.91	0.89	0.90	0.91	0.92
content	0.94	0.88	0.91	0.92	0.95
profile + content	**0.96**	**0.92**	**0.94**	**0.95**	**0.97**

of them that follow more than one conference is 10% higher than for the whole candidate set (cf. also Figure 4).

The fraction of candidates of a conference that we could verify using DBLP varies strongly, as can be seen in Figure 3. SIGGRAPH is very popular among non-computer scientists, since only 7% of its candidates are in $\mathcal{C}^v$, but still 1 449 are verified – the largest absolute value of all conferences. On the other extreme are HOTMOBILE with 1 of 1 verified candidate, ICNP which has 75% verified candidates (3 of 4) and COLT, where 7 of the 13 users could be verified. Of the conference accounts with more than 100 candidates, ECOOP (53/107 $\triangleq$ 50%), ICSM (85/173 $\triangleq$ 49%), CSCW, (91/196 $\triangleq$ 46%), and SOSP (110/240 $\triangleq$ 46%) have a ratio of at least 45% verified candidates.

We evaluated the quality of our mapping by randomly selecting 150 users from $\mathcal{C}^v$ and asking three experts to verify if each candidate Twitter account (e.g., `https://twitter.com/odersky`) belongs to the identified DBLP author (e.g., `http://dblp.uni-trier.de/pers/hd/o/Odersky:Martin.html`). For 87 of the 150 users the experts came to the same decision (76 correct match, 4 wrong, 7 unknown) which underlines the difficulty of the matching task. For the 63 remaining cases, the experts jointly re-performed the task and reached an agreement (33 correct match, 17 wrong, 13 unknown). In summary, 109 (73%) of the matches were identified to be correct, 21 (14%) wrong, and 20 (13%) unknown. Many of the wrong and unknown matches either had different DBLP pages, or there was not enough evidence to confidently link their Twitter and DBLP accounts. However, most of these users were still researchers in computer science.

4.4 Features

We study the importance of features and feature groups for the classification. Using cross-validation as described in Section 3.6 to train and test the models, we restrict the features to single feature groups and the combination of both groups. For each set of features we learn models using 10-fold cross-validation (with stratified sampling). The classification accuracy of the feature groups for the best algorithm Random Forest is shown in Table 3. We can observe that *profile* and *content* alone yield a comparable good performance while their combination yields even better results. To gain more insights into the importance of individual features, we investigate the feature ranking as provided by Random Forest. The top ten important features are given in Table 4. The mean decrease accuracy (MDA) shows how much using the feature in the classifier reduces the classification error. Most important is the *number of tweets*, followed by more specific features targeted towards researchers.

4.5 Classification

The performance of the different classification algorithms during cross-validation is shown in Table 5. Random Forest is the best algorithm in all performance measures (precision (P), recall (R), F1-measure (F1), accuracy (Acc) and

Table 4: Individual features in order of importance by their mean decrease accuracy (MDA).

rank	feature	MDA	group
1	#tweets	54.57	profile
2	#tweets with scientific hashtags	49.35	content
3	friend/follower ratio	40.86	profile
4	bio contains keywords	40.33	profile
5	#conference mentions	39.53	content
6	#original tweets	34.14	content
7	#friends	34.04	profile
8	fraction of distinct hashtags	30.90	content
9	fraction of tweets with a URL	30.89	content
10	#tweets with a URL	27.57	content

Table 5: Performance comparison of the algorithms.

algorithm	P	R	F1	Acc	TNR
SVM	0.90	0.89	0.90	0.91	0.92
Random Forest	**0.96**	**0.92**	**0.94**	**0.95**	**0.97**
CART	0.88	0.90	0.89	0.90	0.90
Logistic Regression	0.88	0.87	0.88	0.89	0.90

true negative rate (TNR)). As a baseline, we trained an SVM classifier with a simple bag-of-words model and TF-IDF weighting. It yielded an F1-measure of 0.93. Given that 94% of all candidates have tweets, this approach is a viable alternative due to its simplicity and good performance. Finally, we retrained Random Forest on all the training data and used the model to score the remaining candidates. From a total of 43 383 unverified users in our candidate set, it classified 38 368 as researchers ($\mathcal{C}^+$) and the remaining 5 015 as non-researchers ($\mathcal{C}^-$).

5. RESEARCHERS ON TWITTER

In this section we empirically analyze computer scientists on Twitter. We consider this as a first important step towards a better understanding of how Twitter is used by researchers and how science can benefit from it. More specifically, we answer the following research questions:

- What kind of computer scientists use Twitter? We explore this from two perspectives namely, age and productivity.
- Which of Twitter's activities are used most frequently between researchers?
- Who are the most influential researchers on Twitter? Can we characterize these users?
- What are the most important scientific topics treated by computer scientists on Twitter?

5.1 Demographics

We start with the question *whether there is a bias of Twitter usage towards young researchers*. Although we do not have the birth dates of the researchers, we can leverage the fact that we mapped a portion of them to DBLP and use the year of their first publication as a proxy for their age. Let us first have a look at the corresponding distribution for *all* authors from DBLP, i.e., the set $\mathcal{G}$ (+): Figure 5 shows for each year between 1960 and 2013 the number of authors whose first publication was published in that year. We can see that the number of authors increases over the years with

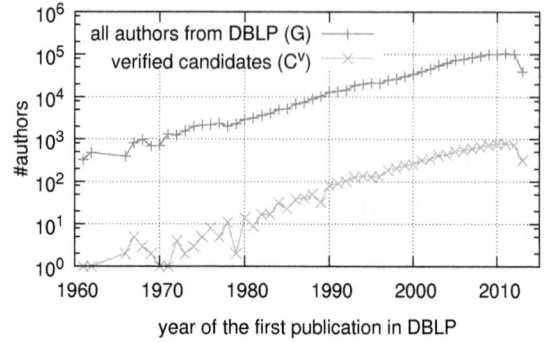

Figure 5: Distribution of the no. of authors per year.

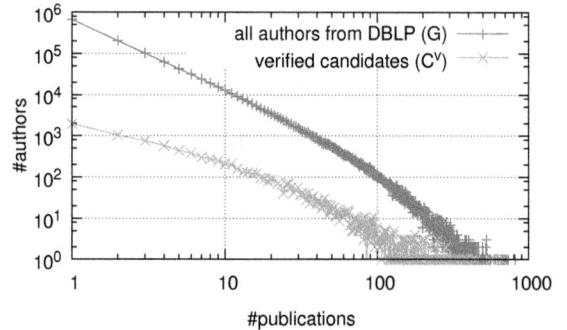

Figure 6: Distribution of the no. of publications per author.

a peak in 2011 and then a drop in 2013 which is caused by the yet incomplete data for this year. On the one hand, the increase reflects the real growth of the number of computer scientists (and publications) over the last decades, and on the other hand, it is possibly also influenced by the coverage of DBLP. When we compare this to the distribution of users from $\mathcal{C}^v$ ($\times$) we can see that both distributions are very similar. This means that the subset of authors from DBLP that can be found in our sample of Twitter users has a similar distribution of first publication years as that of the average computer scientist from DBLP. We conclude that – at least for computer science – we can not find a difference in Twitter use between younger and older researchers.

As a measure for productivity we consider the number of publications an author has written. The plot in Figure 6 shows the long-tail distribution of the number of publications for the ground-truth authors from DBLP (+). It indicates that most authors (665 949 or 51%) have written only one paper and that only very few authors have written 100 or more. This can largely be explained by the large portion of young authors who just started to publish and probably by other cases like keynote speakers from industry, co-authors from other disciplines, etc. We get a different picture for the verified candidates ($\times$): the curve is less steep and only 21% (1 949) of the candidates have published just one article. Although at first sight this might raise the idea that scientists on Twitter are more productive, another explanation could be that many of the 'one-paper-authors' in DBLP indeed are researchers from other disciplines. They are less likely related to our seeds and therefore under-represented in our candidate set – which would support our assumption that conferences are good seeds for computer science.

5.2 Relationships

How are computer scientists connected with each other on Twitter? Analyzing the different ways people connect through the follow, mention, or retweet relation lays the foundation for understanding how the different connections on social media could correspond to traditional citations on peer-reviewed publications. Therefore, we quantify which fraction of positive and verified candidates follows, mentions, or retweets which fraction of the same or the other set (cf. Figure 7). From the relative values, follow and mention are very similar. The values for follow are much higher than for mention (at least 10 percentage points), except for the followed verified candidates that are followed by verified candidates (69.4%). The amount of users following one of the positive candidates is very high (91.8% and 93.3%) although the conferences are not contained in $\mathcal{C}^+$. In general, the order of activity is follow, mention, retweet.

5.3 Popularity

Who are the most influential computer scientists on Twitter? We apply some commonly used and intuitive influence measures used in [2]. These measures are the number of followers, the number of retweets and the number of times the user is mentioned in other users' tweets. However, unlike in [2] our use of the measures is contextualized to the community of interest (i.e., computer scientists). Thus, the numbers are restricted to $\mathcal{C}^v \cup \mathcal{C}^+$, e.g., 'retweet' is the number of retweets by users in $\mathcal{C}^v \cup \mathcal{C}^+$. Table 6 shows the ranking positions for the top 20 users from $\mathcal{C}^v$ by the number of retweets, followers, and mentions. As was previously found in [2], we observe that the number of followers alone is not a good indicator of the popularity of users. We can see that users with a top ranking by followers are not necessarily among those with a top ranking by retweets or mentions. The fact that many users with a rather low number of publications on DBLP appear among the top indicates on the one hand that people from industry are relevant for researchers and on the other hand that the number of publications in DBLP could be used to further adjust the focus to scientists, though without considering the age of publications it would mean that most younger researchers would be omitted.

Next, we inspect the 'bio' field in the profiles of the top influential users in $\mathcal{C}^v \cup \mathcal{C}^+$ to understand how they differ from the rest. Figure 8(a) shows the words for the top 200 influential researchers by all three measures, and Figure 8(b) the top words in the profiles of the remaining users. Influential researchers tend to be *professors*, *scientists*, and *researchers*. The remaining users are *PhD* students in *computer science*, *software developers*, *engineers*, *designers*, and *artists*.

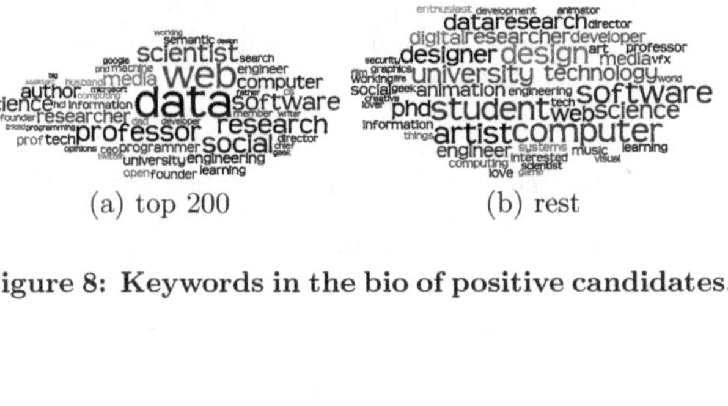

(a) top 200   (b) rest

Figure 8: Keywords in the bio of positive candidates.

Table 6: Popularity of researchers in $\mathcal{C}^v$ ranked by the number of researchers ($\mathcal{C}^v \cup \mathcal{C}^+$) who retweet (r), follow (f) and mention (m) them, and the number of publications (p) in DBLP.

screen name	name	r	f	m	p
@timoreilly	Tim O'Reilly	1	2	1	16
@billgates	Bill Gates	2	1	2	1
@hmason	Hilary Mason	3	9	3	2
@zephoria	Danah Boyd	4	7	6	24
@csoghoian	Christopher Soghoian	5	51	12	5
@doctorow	Cory Doctorow	6	16	4	2
@ioerror	Jacob Appelbaum	7	30	7	5
@mattmight	Matthew Might	8	47	16	34
@kentbeck	Kent Beck	9	18	17	35
@mattcutts	Matt Cutts	10	15	9	2
@timberners_lee	Tim Berners-Lee	11	3	5	35
@codepo8	Christian Heilmann	12	87	14	1
@mattblaze	Matt Blaze	13	60	25	72
@digiphile	Alex Howard	14	42	13	1
@paulg	Paul Graham	16	11	10	23
@migueldeicaza	Miguel de Icaza	15	32	21	1
@mralancooper	Alan Cooper	17	80	27	5
@werner	Werner Vogels	18	14	19	36
@timbray	Tim Bray	19	37	18	7
@pogue	David Pogue	20	8	8	8

Table 7: Most retweeted tweets – scientific above, non-scientific below.

@jimmy_wales	Student warning! Do your homework early. Wikipedia protesting bad law on Wednesday! #sopa
@timberners_lee	The Web Index launched just now http://t.co/CyJH7gRb @webfoundation well done! #opendata #oneweb
@kapravel	probably the saddest graph ever shown in a CS conference. #Linux #tshirtsize pic.twitter.com/RWBnTSJ2ip
@josh_wills	Data Scientist (n.): Person who is better at statistics than any software engineer and better at software engineering than any statistician.
@timberners_lee	Aaron dead. World wanderers, we have lost a wise elder. Hackers for right, we are one down. Parents all, we have lost a child. Let us weep.
@jaykreps	Trick for productionizing research: read current 3-5 pubs and note the stupid simple thing they all claim to beat, implement that.

5.4 Topics

One interesting question to address is what the popular tweets are among computer scientists. Broadly, we can classify the content as being scientific and non-scientific. We define a scientific tweet as one that contains at least one scientific hashtag or mention (as described in Section 3.5). Table 7 shows popular tweets ranked by the number of retweets from $\mathcal{C}^v \cup \mathcal{C}^+$. The scientific talk mostly concerns top events, e.g., #sopa and the dissemination of scientific articles from conferences, whereas the non-scientific talk is mostly humor and private life (e.g., *death*) of researchers.

6. CONCLUSION & FUTURE WORK

In this work we presented a framework for the generation of discipline-specific directories of researchers using Twitter. We proposed automatic methods for assisting the tedious task of finding seeds by searching for conference accounts using Twitter and web search. We also showed ways to au-

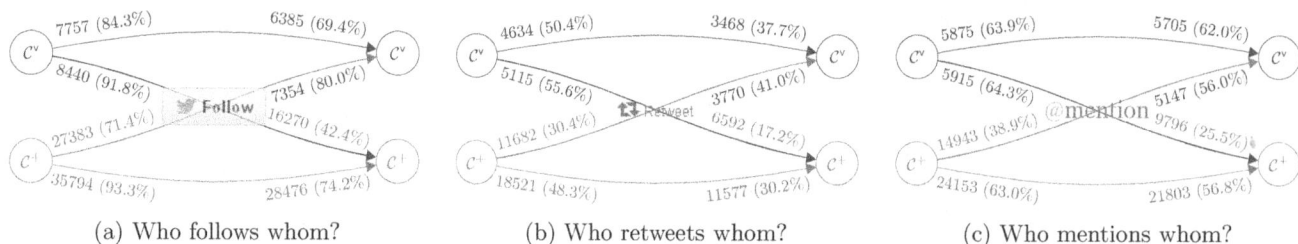

(a) Who follows whom?   (b) Who retweets whom?   (c) Who mentions whom?

Figure 7: Relationships between computer scientists on Twitter.

tomatically leverage ground-truth data by matching against author names in digital libraries. Using machine learning we were then able to build a set of probable computer scientists' Twitter accounts. Our approach lays a foundation for more detailed analyses and understanding of researchers and science in social media at a large scale.

As next steps, we plan to investigate the impact of the seed selection process and of different numbers of expansion rounds in Step 2 on our findings. Likewise, we want to verify the negative examples and improve the matching accuracy in Step 3. A grouping of researchers by their areas of interest (e.g., artificial intelligence, databases, etc.) would help us to answer questions such as *Which differences in the activity of the different research areas are there on Twitter?, How diverse or homogeneous are users in a given area?,* or *Which relations exist between the communities of interest?* For the verified users, the publications they have written are a good source to identify their expertise and interests. Another resource to identify expertise are Twitter's *lists.* A first analysis revealed that the 9 191 verified candidates maintain 12 826 lists with 45 270 unique users. Since only 1 150 (3 369) of those users are contained in C^v (C), the coverage will be lower than our approach. We further want to investigate if our approach can be transferred to other disciplines such as the humanities. This would help us to investigate the connections between different disciplines. Finally, we want to build a web application – a directory of researchers – which features different disciplines and the recommendation of tweets, users, and posted URLs.

7. ACKNOWLEDGEMENTS

This work was performed in the context of the Leibniz Research Alliance 'Science 2.0'.[22]

8. REFERENCES

[1] E. Bakshy, J. M. Hofman, W. A. Mason, and D. J. Watts. Everyone's an influencer: quantifying influence on Twitter. In *Proc. 4th Int. Conf. on Web Search and Data Mining*, WSDM '11, pages 65–74. ACM, 2011.

[2] M. Cha, H. Haddadi, F. Benevenuto, and K. P. Gummadi. Measuring user influence in Twitter: The million follower fallacy. In *Proc. 4th Int. Conf. on Weblogs and Social Media*, pages 10–17. AAAI, 2010.

[3] M. Conover, J. Ratkiewicz, M. Francisco, B. Gonçalves, A. Flammini, and F. Menczer. Political polarization on Twitter. In *Proc. 5th Int. Conf. on Weblogs and Social Media*, pages 89–96. AAAI, 2011.

[4] G. Eysenbach. Can tweets predict citations? Metrics of social impact based on Twitter and correlation with traditional metrics of scientific impact. *Journal of Medical Internet Research*, 13(4), 2011.

[5] R. E. Goldstein, P. B. Warren, and R. C. Ball. Shape of a ponytail and the statistical physics of hair fiber bundles. *Phys. Rev. Lett.*, 108(7):078101, Feb. 2012.

[6] S. D. Gollapalli, C. Caragea, P. Mitra, and C. L. Giles. Researcher homepage classification using unlabeled data. In *Proc. 22nd Int. Conf. on World Wide Web*, WWW '13, pages 471–482. International World Wide Web Conferences Steering Committee, 2013.

[7] M. Hilbert and P. López. The world's technological capacity to store, communicate, and compute information. *Science*, 332(6025):60–65, 2011.

[8] H. Kwak, C. Lee, H. Park, and S. Moon. What is Twitter, a social network or a news media? In *Proc. Int. Conf. on World Wide Web*, pages 591–600, 2010.

[9] J. Letierce, A. Passant, J. Breslin, and S. Decker. Understanding how Twitter is used to widely spread scientific messages. In *Proc. Web Science Conf.*, 2010.

[10] M. Ley. DBLP: some lessons learned. *Proc. VLDB Endow.*, 2(2):1493–1500, Aug. 2009.

[11] M. Pennacchiotti and A.-M. Popescu. Democrats, republicans and starbucks afficionados: user classification in Twitter. In *Proc. Int. Conf. on Knowl. Discovery and Data Mining*, pages 430–438, 2011.

[12] J. Priem and K. L. Costello. How and why scholars cite on Twitter. *Proceedings of the American Society for Information Science and Technology*, 47(1):1–4, 2010.

[13] J. Priem and B. Hemminger. Scientometrics 2.0: New metrics of scholarly impact on the social web. *First Monday*, 15(7), 2010.

[14] D. Rao, D. Yarowsky, A. Shreevats, and M. Gupta. Classifying latent user attributes in Twitter. In *Proc. 2nd Int. Workshop on Search and Mining User-Generated Contents*, pages 37–44. ACM, 2010.

[15] I. Weber, V. R. K. Garimella, and A. Teka. Political hashtag trends. In *Proc. European Conf. on Information Retrieval Research*, pages 857–860, 2013.

[16] K. Weller, E. Dröge, and C. Puschmann. Citation analysis in Twitter: Approaches for defining and measuring information flows within tweets during scientific conferences. In *Proc. ESWC 2011 Workshop on 'Making Sense of Microposts'*, pages 1–12, 2011.

[17] J. Wu, P. Teregowda, J. P. F. Ramírez, P. Mitra, S. Zheng, and C. L. Giles. The evolution of a crawling strategy for an academic document search engine: whitelists and blacklists. In *Proc. 3rd Annual Web Science Conf.*, pages 340–343. ACM, 2012.

---

[22]http://www.leibniz-science20.de/

Twitter: Who gets Caught?

Observed Trends in Social Micro-blogging Spam

Abdullah Almaatouq
Center for Complex
Engineering Systems at
KACST and MIT
amaatouq@mit.edu

Ahmad Alabdulkareem
Center for Complex
Engineering Systems at
KACST and MIT
kareem@mit.edu

Mariam Nouh
Center for Complex
Engineering Systems at
KACST and MIT
mnouh@kacst.edu.sa

Erez Shmueli
Massachusetts Institute of
Technology (MIT) Media Lab
shmueli@mit.edu

Mansour Alsaleh
King Abdulaziz City for
Science and Technology
maalsaleh@kacst.edu.sa

Vivek K. Singh
Massachusetts Institute of
Technology (MIT) Media Lab
singhv@mit.edu

ABSTRACT

Spam in Online Social Networks (OSNs) is a systemic problem that imposes a threat to these services in terms of undermining their value to advertisers and potential investors, as well as negatively affecting users' engagement. In this work, we present a unique analysis of spam accounts in OSNs viewed through the lens of their behavioral characteristics (i.e., profile properties and social interactions). Our analysis includes over 100 million tweets collected over the course of one month, generated by approximately 30 million distinct user accounts, of which over 7% are suspended or removed due to abusive behaviors and other violations. We show that there exist two behaviorally distinct categories of twitter spammers and that they employ different spamming strategies. The users in these two categories demonstrate different individual properties as well as social interaction patterns. As the Twitter spammers continuously keep creating newer accounts upon being caught, a behavioral understanding of their spamming behavior will be vital in the design of future social media defense mechanisms.

Categories and Subject Descriptors

H.0 [**Information systems**]: General; K.4.2 [**Social issues**]: Abuse and crime involving computers; H.2.8 [**Database Applications**]: Data mining

Keywords

Spam; Online Social Networks; Microblogging; Account Abuse

1. INTRODUCTION

Spam exists across many types of electronic communication platforms, including email, web discussion forums, text messages (SMS),

and social media. Today, as social media continues to grow in popularity, spammers are increasingly abusing such media for spamming purposes. According to a recent study [21], there was a 355% growth in social spam during the first half of 2013. Twitter company's initial public offering (IPO) filing indicates spam as a major threat in terms of undermining their value to advertisers and potential investors, as well as negatively affecting users' engagement [32].

While there is a growing literature on social media in terms of developing tools for spam detection (e.g., [18, 24, 33]) and analyzing spam trends (e.g., [27, 37, 38]), spammers continue to evolve and change their penetration techniques. Therefore, there is a continuous need for understanding the evolving and diverse properties of malicious accounts in order to combat them properly [21, 32].

In this paper, we present an empirical analysis of spam accounts on Twitter, in terms of profile properties and social interactions. The analysis includes identifying categories (sub-populations) of spam accounts (see Section 4). Through profile analysis we identify distinct characteristics and patterns that pertain to different identified categories of Twitter accounts (see Section 5). We also examine the network properties of several social interactions (namely, follow relationship and mention) to improve our understanding of the methods used by spammers for reaching spam victims (see Section 6).

To perform the study, we collected over 100 million tweets over the course of one month (from March 5, 2013 to April 2, 2013) generated by approximately 30 million distinct user accounts (see Section 3). In total, over 7% of our dataset accounts are suspended or removed accounts due in part to abusive behaviors and other violations. The summary and future work of our study discussed in Section 8.

In summary, we frame our contributions as follows:

- We categorize spam accounts based on their behavioral activities and find that Twitter spammers belong to two broad behavioral categories. We observe that these categories of spam accounts exhibit different spamming patterns and employ distinct strategies for reaching their victims, and should therefore be analyzed separately and treated differently by future social media defense mechanisms.

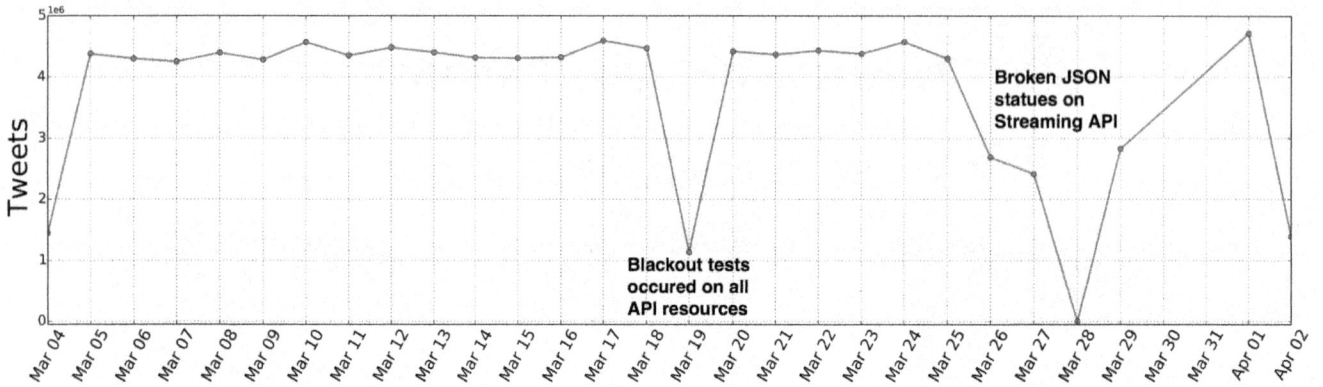

Figure 1: Tweets received per day. On average, we receive 4 million tweets per day

- We analyze the different properties of spam accounts in terms of their profile attributes and use the attributes of legitimate accounts as a baseline. From this, we identify a cluster of malicious accounts that seems to be originally created and customized by legitimate users, whereas the other cluster deviates from the baseline significantly.

- Through network analysis of multiple social interactions, we reveal a set of diverse strategies employed by spammers for reaching audiences. We focus on the mention function as it is one of the most common ways in which spammers engage with users, bypassing any requirement of sharing a social connection (i.e., follow/following relationship) with a victim.

2. BACKGROUND

Twitter is a micro-blogging platform and an Online Social Network (OSN), where users are able to send *tweets* (i.e., short text messages limited to 140 characters). According to a recent study, Twitter is the fastest growing social platform in the world [12]. In 2013, Twitter estimated the number of active users at over 200 million, generating 500 million tweets per day [32].

Twitter spam is a systemic problem [27]. While traditional email spam usually consists of spreading bulks of unsolicited messages to numerous recipients, spam on Twitter does not necessarily comply to the volume constraint, as a single spam message on Twitter is capable of propagating through social interaction functions and reach a wide audience. In addition, previous studies showed that the largest suspended Twitter accounts campaigns directed users via affiliate links to some reputable websites that generate income on a purchase, such as Amazon [27]. Such findings blur the line about what constitutes as OSN spam. According to the "Twitter Rules", what constitutes *spamming* will evolve as a response to new tactics employed by spammers [31]. Some of the suspicious activities that Twitter considers as indications for spam [31] include: (1) aggressive friending; (2) creating false or misleading content; (3) spreading malicious links; and (4) trading followers.

Spam content can reach legitimate users through the following functions: i) *home timeline*: a stream showing all tweets from those being followed by the user or posts that contain @*mention* requiring no prior follow relationship; ii) *search timeline*: a stream of messages that matches a search query; iii) *hashtags*: tags used to mark tweets with keywords or topics by incorporating the symbol # prior to the relevant phrase (very popular hashtags are called *trending topics*); iv) *profile bio*: spam accounts generate large amounts of relationships and favorite random tweets from legitimate users

with the hope that victims would view the spammer account profile which often contains a URL embedded in its bio or description; and v) *direct messages*: private tweets that are sent between two users.

Accounts distributing spam are usually in the form of: i) *fraudulent accounts* that are created solely for the purpose of sending spam; ii) *compromised accounts* created by legitimate users whose credentials have been stolen by spammers; and iii) legitimate users posting spam content. While, multiple previous studies focused on fraudulent accounts(e.g., [27, 28]), the compromised accounts are more valuable to spammers as they are relatively harder to detect due to their associated history and network relationships. On the other hand, fraudulent accounts exhibit a higher anomalous behavior at the account level, and hence are easier for detection [9].

3. DATASETS

Our Twitter dataset consists of 113,609,247 tweets, generated by 30,391,083 distinct users, collected during a one month period from March 5th, 2013 to April 2nd, 2013 using the Twitter public stream APIs [30]. For each tweet, we retrieve its associated attributes (e.g., tweet text, creation date, client used, etc.) as well as information tied to the account who posted the tweet (e.g., the account's number of following, followers, date created, etc.). On average, we receive over 4 million tweets per day. We lack data for some days due to network outages, updates to Twitter's API, and instability of the collection infrastructure (using Amazon EC2 instances). A summary of tweets collected each day and outage periods is shown in Figure 1.

In order to label spammer accounts in our dataset, we rely on Twitter's account suspension algorithm described in [27]. Given that the implementation of the suspension algorithm is not publicly available, we verify whether an account has been flagged as spam by checking the user's profile page. In case an account has been suspended or removed, the crawler request will be redirected to a page describing the user statues (i.e., suspended or does not exist). While all of the removed/suspended user's information is no longer available through the Twitter's API, we were able to reconstruct their information based on the collected sample. In total, over 7% of our dataset are suspended/removed accounts. Although the primary cause for suspension or deletion of Twitter accounts is spam-activity, Twitter's policy page states that other activities such as publishing malicious links, selling usernames and using obscene or pornographic images may also result in suspension or deletion [31]. Removed accounts may include users that deactivated their accounts during the data collection period.

4. IDENTIFYING SUB-POPULATIONS

The results of the initial analysis to compare the collective tweeting patterns and social behavior of normal and malicious users showed tendency for bi-modality in the case of spam accounts. This was less evident in the case of legitimate users (see Figure 2). This pattern occurs across multiple attributes (i.e., tweets count, favorites count, followers count, etc.). The bi-modal distributions commonly arises as a mixture of uni-modal distributions corresponding to mixture of populations. Accordingly, we separated the sub-populations within spammers, using Gaussian Mixture Models (GMM), in order to reveal distinct spamming strategies and behaviors.

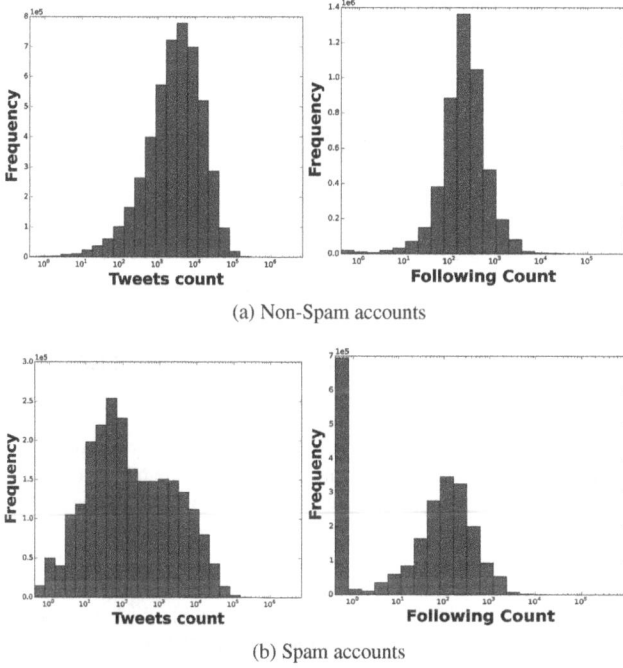

(a) Non-Spam accounts

(b) Spam accounts

Figure 2: An illustration of different tweeting patterns and following behaviors for normal and spam accounts.

In order to identify subsets of malicious accounts, we use Gaussian Mixture Models (GMM). GMM is a probabilistic model that assumes that data points are generated from a mixture of a finite number of Gaussian distributions with unknown parameters. To determine the number of components (i.e., sub-populations or clusters) we fit multiple GMMs with different numbers of Gaussians and then calculate the Bayesian Information Criteria (BIC) score for each fit. The use of BIC penalizes models in terms of the number of parameters or complexity. Hence, complex models (i.e., high number of free parameters) will have to compensate with how well they describe the data. This can be denoted as follows:

$$BIC(M_c) = -2 \cdot \ln P(x|M_c) + \ln N \cdot k \qquad (1)$$

where x is the observed data, N is the number of observations, k is the number of free parameters to be estimated and $P(x|M_c)$ is the marginal likelihood of the observed data given the model M with c number of components.

A GMM with two components and spherical covariance gives the lowest BIC score (see Figure 3). The results of the clustering exhibit two classes of spam accounts $C_1 \subset C$ and $C_2 \subset C$, where C is the set of all accounts. We refer to the normal class (i.e., legitimate

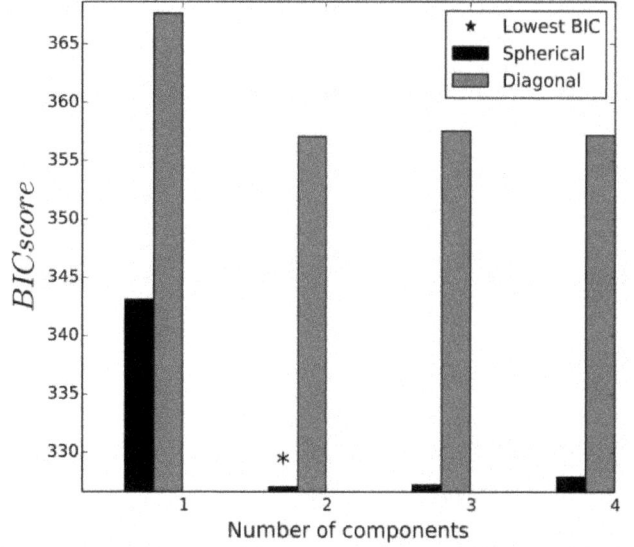

Figure 3: BIC scores for different numbers of components & covariance constraints

accounts) as C_{normal}. The results of the separation in one dimension (i.e., tweets count) is shown in Figure 4.

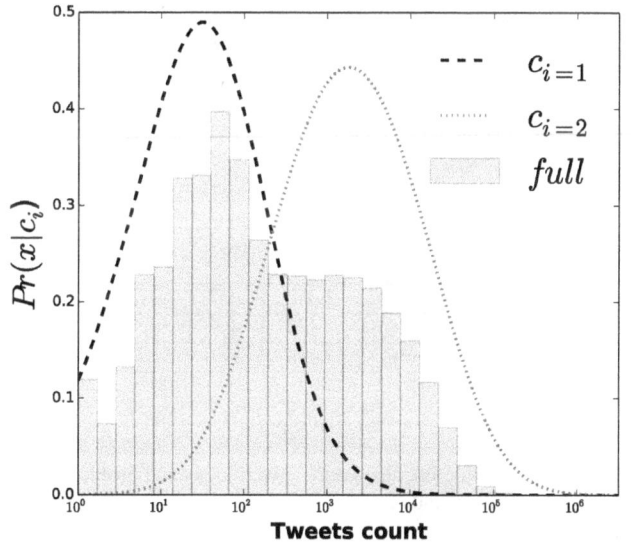

Figure 4: The identified clusters in 1-d (tweets count) for the spam accounts

Based on the separation, we can further investigate the properties and activity patterns of the different identified classes. This separation aids in developing taxonomies and exploit meaningful structures within the spam accounts communities.

5. PROFILE PROPERTIES

In order to further investigate the different identified classes, we examine the Empirical Cumulative Distribution Functions (ECDF) of different attributes for each class (see Figure 5). We find that 50% of the accounts in C_1 have less than 29 tweets, however, for C_{normal} and C_2, 50% of the accounts have tweeted around 2000 times. Furthermore, we find that almost 90% of the accounts in C_1 have no favorites (i.e., tweets added to their favorites list), whereas

(a) Tweets count Empirical Cumulative Distribution Function

(b) Favorites count Empirical Cumulative Distribution Function

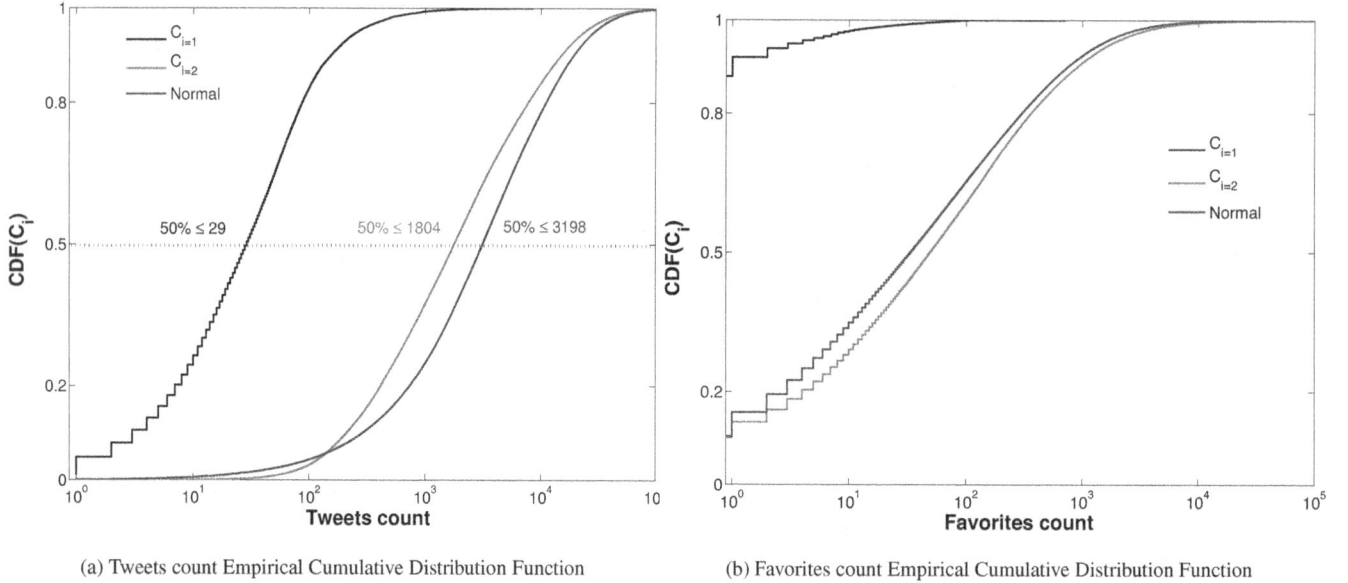

Figure 5: Comparison between the three classes C_1, C_2 and C_{normal} in terms of tweeting and following behaviors after the GMM clustering

C_2 and C_{normal} show closely matching patterns, with 50% of the accounts having less than 50 favorite tweets.

We continue to observe similar patterns across multiple attributes, where C_2 and C_{normal} have similar distributions and C_1 deviates from the baseline. We explain this observation through the hypothesis that C_2 mainly consists of *compromised accounts*, while C_1 consists of *fraudulent accounts* as defined in Section 2.

Table 1: Summary of basic profile attributes

	Default profile	Default image	URL	Bio
C_{normal}	22%	1.3%	29%	83.6%
C_1	76%	14%	4%	60%
C_2	36%	1.5%	20%	84.7%

The similarity between C_{normal} and C_2 in the basic profile attributes, such as the percentage of accounts with default profile settings, default profile images, profile descriptions and profile URLs (see Table 1) might indicate that C_2 accounts were originally created and customized by *legitimate users*. For example, we notice that only 22% of C_{normal} and 36% of C_2 accounts kept their default profile settings unchanged, in comparison to 76% in the case of C_1.

6. SOCIAL INTERACTIONS

In this section we analyze users behavior in terms of the follow relationship and mention functions, from the topological point of view. We approach this by incorporating multiple measures that are known to signify network characteristics (differences and similarity). Through this analysis, we reveal sets of behavioral properties and diverse strategies employed by spammers for engaging with victims and reaching audiences.

6.1 Preliminaries

Let $G = (V, E)$ be the graph that represents the topological structure of a given function (i.e., follow or mention), where V is the set of nodes and E is the set of edges. An edge in the graph is denoted by $e = (v, u) \in E$ where $v, u \in V$. Note that in the follow and men-

tion networks, a node v corresponds to a Twitter user and an edge corresponds to an interaction between a pair of users. If two nodes have an edge between them, they are adjacent and we refer to them as neighbors.

We define the neighborhood of node v as the sub-graph $H = (V', E') \mid V' \subset V$ and $E' \subset E$ that consists of all the nodes adjacent to v (alters) excluding v (we refer to v as ego) and all the edges connecting two such nodes. The 1.5 egocentric network $E_{1.5}(v)$ of node v is defined as the neighborhood sub-graph including v itself. Therefore, the neighborhood can be denoted as $N(v) := \{u \mid (u, v) \in E \text{ or } (v, u) \in E\}$ and the 1.5 ego network as $E_{1.5}(v) := \{N(v) \cup \{v\}\}$.

Focusing on the egocentric networks around the nodes allows for studying the local graphical structure of a given user and signifies the types of interactions that develop within their social partners. Figure 6 shows an illustration of different levels of egocentric networks. From this we can define node properties and measure the relative importance of a node within its egocentric network such as node degree $d(v)$, node out-degree $d_{out}(v)$, in-degree $d_{in}(v)$, and reciprocal relationship $d_{bi}(v)$.

$$
\begin{aligned}
d_{out}(v) &= |\{u \mid (v, u) \in E_{1.5}(v)\}| \\
d_{in}(v) &= |\{u \mid (u, v) \in E_{1.5}(v)\}| \\
d(v) &= d_{in} + d_{out} \\
d_{bi}(v) &= |\{u \mid (u, v) \in E_{1.5}(v) \wedge (v, u) \in E_{1.5}(v)\}|
\end{aligned}
\tag{2}
$$

From the properties defined in equation 2 we can derive the in-degree density $density_{in}(v)$, out-degree density $density_{out}(v)$, and the density of reciprocal relationships $density_{bi}(v)$.

$$
\begin{aligned}
density_{in}(v) &= \frac{d_{in}(v)}{d(v)} \\
density_{out}(v) &= \frac{d_{out}(v)}{d(v)} \\
density_{bi}(v) &= \frac{d_{bi}(v)}{d(v)}
\end{aligned}
\tag{3}
$$

In addition, we calculate the betweenness centrality for each ego node in order to quantify the control of such node on the communication between other nodes in the social network [10]. The measure computes the fraction of the shortest paths that pass through the node in a question v within its egocentric network $E_{1.5}(v)$. Therefore, the betweenness centrality $C_B(v)$ can be computed as [5]:

$$C_B(v) = \sum_{u \neq w \in N(v)} \frac{\sigma_{uw}(v)}{\sigma_{uw}} \qquad (4)$$

where σ_{uw} is the total number of shortest paths from node u to node w and $\sigma_{uw}(v)$ is the number of those paths that pass through the node v. Therefore, $C_B(v) = 0$ in the case where all the alters are directly connected to each other and $C_B(v) = 1$ when the alters are only connected to each other through the ego node.

We also compute the closeness centrality $C_C(v)$ which measures the inverse of the sum of the shortest path distances between a node v and all other nodes $u_0, u_1, .., u_n \in N(v)$ normalized by the sum of minimum possible distances. This can be formulated as follows:

$$C_C(v) = \frac{n-1}{\sum_{u \in N(v)} \sigma(v, u)} \qquad (5)$$

where $\sigma(u, v)$ is the shortest path distance between v and u, and n is the number of nodes in the egocentric graph.

A network is strongly connected if there is a path between every node to every other node in a directed graph. We define the number of strongly connected components in the egocentric networks $E_{1.5}(v)$ and open neighborhood $N(v)$ to be $SCC_{E_{1.5}}(v)$ and $SCC_N(v)$ respectively. By replacing all of the directed edges with undirected edges, we compute the number of weakly connected components for the egocentric network and open neighborhood as $WCC_{E_{1.5}}(v)$ and $WCC_N(v)$ respectively. The SCC and WCC are used to measure the connectivity of a graph.

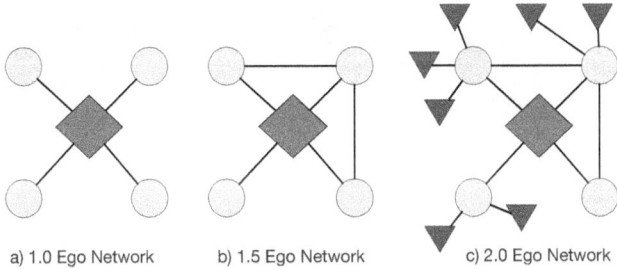

(a) Followers d_{in} vs. following d_{out} for C_1 and C_2 accounts.

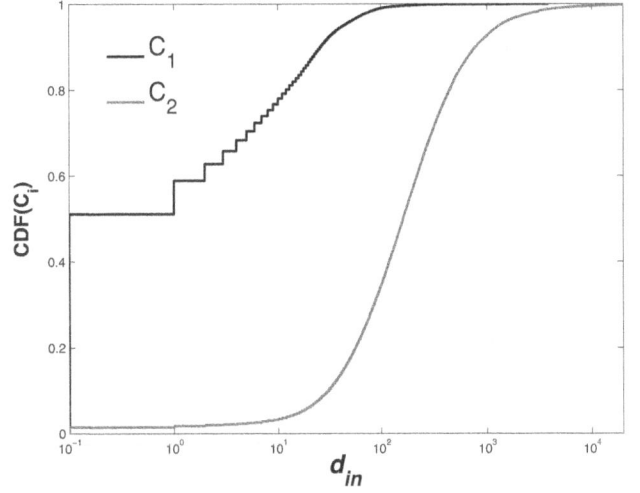

(b) Followers count Empirical Cumulative Distribution Function.

Figure 7: Illustration of the different relationship behaviors for C_1 and C_2. We find that spam accounts that belong to C_1 are heavily skewed towards following rather than followers or the identity line. The effect of the number of following limit (i.e., 2000 d_{out}) is apparent/observed in both classes.

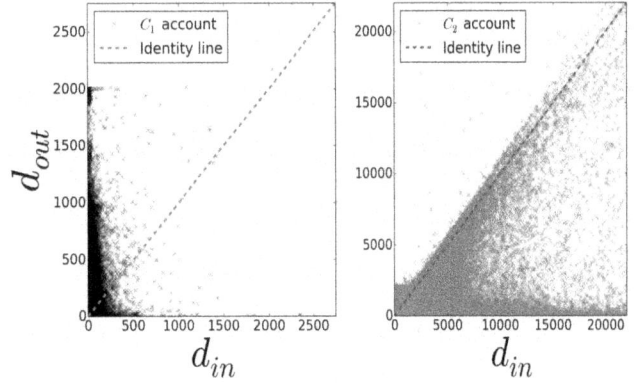

a) 1.0 Ego Network   b) 1.5 Ego Network   c) 2.0 Ego Network

Figure 6: An illustration of the a) 1.0 egocentric network; b) the 1.5 egocentric network; and c) the 2.0 egocentric network. The Ego node is marked in red (diamond) and its connections (alters) are marked in yellow (circles) and the alters' connections are marked in blue (triangles).

6.2 Relationship Graph

Twitter follow relationship is modeled as a directed graph, where an edge between two nodes $e = (v, u) \in E$ means that v is following u. For the follow relationship, we only have the number of followers and following for each account, and not the actual relationship list. Therefore, in order to compare relationships formed by both C_1 and C_2, we aggregate following and follower data from both classes.

Figure 7 shows the number of followers and following represented by the in-degree d_{in} (follower) and out-degree d_{out} (following) for each class. We find that spam accounts that belong to C_1

are heavily skewed towards following rather than followers, which could indicate a difficulty in forming reciprocal relationships. Furthermore, we observe a low $density_{in}$ for C_1 with an average of 0.16 and high $density_{out}$ with an average of 0.4. On the other hand, C_2 has more balanced densities with approximately 0.5 for both.

While Twitter does not constrain the number of followers a user could have, the number of following (i.e., d_{out}) is limited [29]. Every user is allowed to follow 2000 accounts in total; once an account reaches this limit, they require more followers in order to follow more users [29]. This limit is based on the followers to following ratio.

Furthermore, as shown in Figure 7b, almost 50% of C_1 accounts have no followers (i.e., they did not embed themselves within the social graph) and almost 75% of these accounts have less than ten followers. We find that C_2 accounts are more connected in terms of social relationships, which makes them harder to detect and hence contribute more content. These findings adhere to a known phenomenon observed in multiple security contexts. For example, Altshuler et al. [2] showed that in many cases (especially in social networks), optimal attack strategies (i.e., causing greater damage or spreading more spam content) exhibit slow spreading patterns rather than spreading aggressively.

Table 2: Market prices for followers

Provider	$-per-follower
Socialkik	$0.024
BuyTwitterFriends	$0.003
UnlimitedTwitterFollowers	$0.02

The compromised account population that exists within C_2 can utilize the associated history and network relationships of the original account owner to aid them in increasing the visibility of their spam content. It is also possible that fraudulent and compromised accounts can gain more followers by purchasing them from online services (see Table 2 for recent market prices) to evade detection [36, 37].

6.3 Mention Graph

The mention function is one of the most common ways in which spammers engage with users, unlike the *Direct Messages (DM)*, it bypasses any requirement of prior social connection with a victim.

The mention network is constructed as a simple, weighted, and directed graph, such that an edge between two nodes $e = (v, u) \in E$ means that user v mentioned user u during our collection period. We extract the 1.5 egocentric network $E_{1.5}(v)$, where v are the accounts in C_1 and C_2.

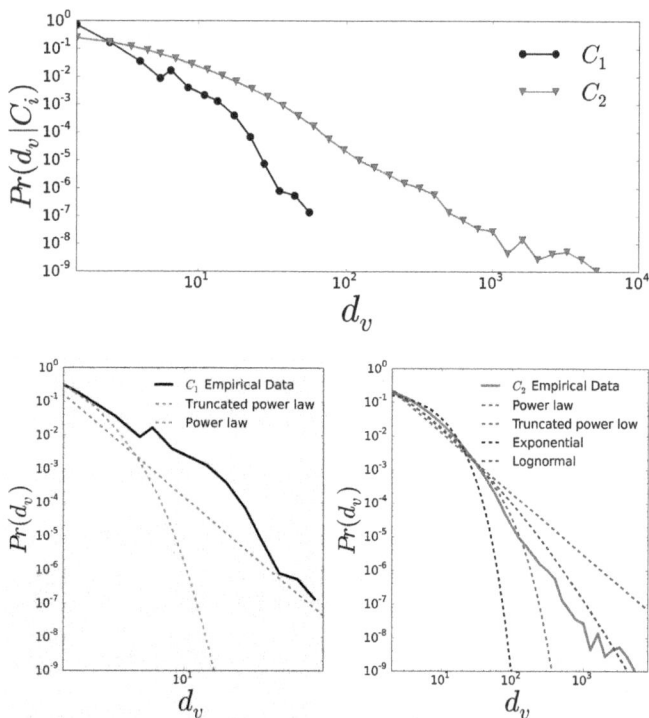

Figure 8: The top figure shows the distribution of the frequency of mentions $d(v)$ for C_1 (black circles) and C_2 (red triangles). The bottom figures compare the empirical distribution obtained with best fits of other heavy-tailed distributions (see Appendix A).

Figure 8 shows the degree distribution of the mention network. Although multiple studies observed that the degree for the mention network follows heavy-tailed distributions (e.g., [15]), in order to understand the topological structure, we further investigate the concrete goodness of fit (see Appendix A). The scale-free nature of the

mention network (i.e., degree distribution that follows a power law) implies a very high heterogeneity level in user behavior, which is expected for human activity phenomena [4, 20]. In addition, the figure shows a clear difference between the length of the tail of the distributions between the two classes C_1 and C_2.

Table 3: Comparing different centrality measures for the mention network for C_1 and C_2 accounts

Class	Betweenness (C_B)		Closeness (C_C)	
	μ	σ	μ	σ
C_1	0.014	0.08	0.97	0.12
C_2	0.096	0.14	0.77	0.25

Table 3 compares two centrality measures for the mention network, namely the betweenness C_B and closeness C_C centralities. We observe that the average betweenness centrality for C_2 is significantly higher than C_1, which indicates that C_1 accounts target users that mention each other (i.e., communities and clusters of users). This is somewhat a surprising outcome, as we expect C_2 accounts to utilize the associated relationships of the original account owner, where the nodes in the neighborhood are real friends and are more likely to mention one another. The relatively low betweenness in C_1 can be explained by at least three possibilities:

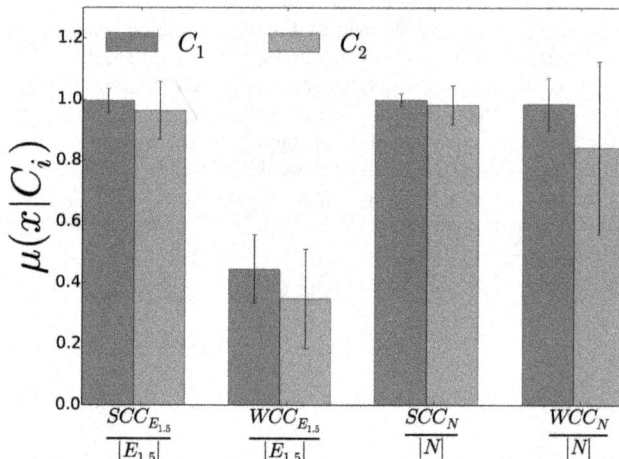

Figure 9: The density of connected components in the mention network for C_1 and C_2

- *Conversations hijacking.* We observe that 51.5% of the tweets captured by C_1 contain mentions, and 43.3% of these mentions are replies. In addition, only 1.2% of their mentions were reciprocated ($density_{bi} = 0.0127$), which arouses suspicion that C_1 accounts intrude on on-going conversations between legitimate users, and thus have resulted in a low betweenness centrality.

- *Targeting hubs.* Due to the scale-free nature (i.e., degree distribution that follows a power law) of the mention network, mentioning or replying to hubs (nodes that are highly connected to other nodes in the network) increase the chance that the alters will be connected, and hence the low betweenness score.

- *Crawling profiles.* It is also possible that C_1 accounts target communities and connected users in the mention graph by crawling profiles (i.e., visiting the followers/following lists or users' *timeline* of the seed targeted profile).

Figure 9 shows high average densities of strongly connected components for both the egocentric network and the neighborhood network in classes C_1 and C_2 (i.e., $\frac{SCC_N}{|N|}$ and $\frac{SCC_{E_{1.5}}}{|E_{1.5}|}$). This observation indicates a difficulty in forming reciprocal mention relationships as discussed earlier. Also, a higher score in the densities of weakly connected components ($\frac{WCC_N}{|N|}$ and $\frac{WCC_{E_{1.5}}}{|E_{1.5}|}$) for C_1 explains the lower betweenness centrality score observed in Table 3.

The discrepancy in network measures (i.e., degree distribution, centralities, and connectivity) between C_1 and C_2 indicates the existence of different strategies for reaching audiences employed by each class accounts.

7. RELATED WORK

We discuss prior related work on OSNs' spam and network analysis using the following categories: i) OSN organized spam campaigns; ii) OSN spam accounts analysis; and iii) spam detection in OSNs. Although we focus on spam accounts analysis, our first in its kind approach of spam behavioral categorization (i.e., identifying sub-populations), analyzing the different classes of spam accounts, and analyzing the mention interactions, all provide a unique view in looking at spam trends in OSNs.

7.1 Spam in Social Networks

With the rapid growth of OSNs popularity, we are witnessing an increased usage of these services to discuss issues of public interest and hence shape public opinions [8]. This model of users as an information contributors has provided researchers, news organizations, and governments with a tool to measure (to some degree) representative samples of populations in real time [1, 13, 17, 25]. However, Lumezanue et al. [16] identified *propagandists* Twitter accounts that exhibit opinions or ideologies to either sway public opinion, disseminate false information, or disrupt the conversations of legitimate users. The study focused on accounts connected to two political events: i) the 2010 Nevada senate race; and ii) the 2011 debt-ceiling debate. A similar campaign has been analyzed [26], in which spam accounts flood out political messages following the announcement of Russia's parliamentary election results. In addition, classical forms of abuse such as spam and criminal monetization exist in Twitter including phishing scams [6], spreading malware [22], and redirecting victims to reputable websites via affiliate links [27] to generate income.

7.2 Social Network Spam Analysis

Due to the popularity of social media services, several studies measured and analyzed spam in OSNs. Yang et al. [36] provided an analysis of some of the evasive techniques utilized by spammers, and discussed several detection features. In addition, Yang et al. [37] performed an empirical analysis of the social relationship in Twitter (i.e., following relationship) in the spam community. The study showed that spam accounts follow each other and form small-world networks. Stringhini et al. [23] examined *Twitter account markets*, and investigated their association to abusive behaviors and compromised profiles. Thomas et al. [28] performed a study in collaboration with Twitter to investigate the *fraudulent accounts* marketplace. The study discussed prices, availability, and fraud perpetrated by 27 merchants generating 127 to 459K US dollars for their efforts over the course of ten months. In another study [27], Thomas et al. examined tools, techniques, and support infrastructure spam accounts rely upon to sustain their campaigns. Surprisingly, the study showed that three of the largest spam campaigns in Twitter direct users to legitimate products appearing on reputable websites via affiliate links that generate income on a pur-

chase (e.g., *Amazon.com*). However, the authors considered only tweets that contained URLs, and thus overlook malicious accounts that employ other spamming strategies, such as: i) embedding *non-hyperlink URL* by encoding the ASCII code for the dot; ii) *follow spam accounts* that generate large amounts of relationships for the hope the victim account would reciprocate the relationship or at least view the criminal's account profile which often has a URL embedded in its bio. Ghosh et al. [11] investigated the spammers' mechanism of forming social relationship (link framing) in Twitter, and found that vast majority of spam accounts are followed by legitimate users who reciprocate relationships automatically (social capitalists). The dataset used in this study contained 41,352 suspended Twitter accounts that posted a blacklisted URL. However, Grier et al. [14] discussed the ineffectiveness of blacklisting at detecting social network spam in a timely fashion.

7.3 Social Network Spam Detection

A number of detection and combating techniques proposed in the literature rely on machine learning. Benevenuto et al. [3] manually labeled 8,207 Twitter accounts, and developed a classifier to detect spammers based on the URL and hashtag densities, followers to following ratio, account-age, and other profile-based features. The account-age and number of URLs sent were the most discriminating features. Stringhini et al. [24] created a diverse set of "honey-profiles", and monitored activities across three different social networks (Facebook, Twitter, and MySpace) for approximately one year. They also built a tool to detect spammers on Twitter and successfully detected and deleted 15,857 spam accounts in collaboration with Twitter.

Another approach is presented by Xie et al. [35], where they designed and implemented a system that recognizes legitimate users early in OSNs. They utilized an implicit vouching process, where legitimate users help in identifying other legitimate users. Finally, Wanga et al. [34] investigated the feasibility of utilizing crowd-sourcing as the enabling methodology for the detection of *fraudulent accounts*. This study analyzed the detection accuracy by both "experts" and "turkers" (i.e., workers from Amazon Mechanical Turk under a variety of conditions.

8. SUMMARY AND FUTURE WORK

This paper presents a unique look at spam accounts in OSNs through the lens of the behavioral characteristics, and spammers' techniques for reaching victims. We find that there exist two main classes of spam accounts that exhibit different spamming patterns and employ distinct strategies for spreading spam content and reaching victims. We found that C_2 (i.e. category 2 of spammers) and C_{normal} (i.e. legitimate users) manifest similar patterns across multiple attributes. We attempt to explain this observation through the hypothesis that C_2 mainly consists of compromised accounts, while the accounts in C_1 (i.e. category 1 of spammers) are fraudulent accounts, as we find support for the hypothesis throughout our analysis of profile properties. In terms of the relationship graph, we find that spam accounts that belong to C_1 are heavily skewed towards following rather than followers, which indicates difficulty in forming reciprocal relationships. Furthermore, we observe a low in-degree density for C_1, while C_2 has a more balanced in/out degree densities. We show that the betweenness centrality for C_1 in the mention graph is significantly lower than C_2, which might be a result of hijacking conversations, targeting hubs, or crawling profiles.

We acknowledge that our analysis may contain some bias. We have a partial view of the activities occurring during the data collection period due to the at most 1% sampling limit imposed by

Twitter. However, the work of Morstatter et al. [19] showed that the implications of using the Twitter Streaming API depend on the coverage and type of analysis. Generally, the streaming API can be sufficient to provide representative samples, that gets better with higher coverage, for certain types of analysis (i.e., top hashtags, topics, retweet network measures). Furthermore, we lack the absolute ground truth labels for the accounts presented in the dataset and primarily rely on Twitter's suspension algorithm. This might impose a lower bound on the number of spam accounts in our dataset (i.e., uncaught spam accounts are treated as legitimate users). In addition, there might be a fraction of legitimate users who deactivated their accounts during the collection period, and hence would be labeled as removed. We also lack the appropriate resolution for important attributes used in the analysis; for example, we only have the number of followers and following for each user, and not the actual relationships list. We also acknowledge that some of the explanations proposed in this work might lack rigorous validations, due to the difficulties in thoroughly obtaining the motivations and social actions of spam accounts. However, we believe that our first in its kind analysis of twitter functions and spam behavioral categorization describe well the current trends and phenomenon of OSN's spam and can be leveraged in designing OSN spam detectors and resilient architectures.

In our future work, we will design and test alternative labeling and validation mechanisms for the analyzed accounts. In addition, we plan to further investigate the differences between the spam accounts utilizing other interactions functions (e.g., hashtag, retweet, and favorite). We also intend to quantify the success of spam campaigns and explore the tools, techniques, and spam underground markets utilized by spam accounts to spread their content and evade many of the known detection mechanisms.

Acknowledgments

The authors would like to thank King Abdulaziz City for Science and Technology (KACST) for funding this work. In addition, the authors thank the Center for Complex Engineering Systems (CCES) at KACST and MIT for their support.

9. ADDITIONAL AUTHORS

Additional authors: Abdulrahman Alarifi (King Abdulaziz City for Science and Technology, email: aarifi@kacst.edu.sa), Anas Alfaris (Center for Complex Engineering Systems, email: anas@mit.edu), and Alex (Sandy) Pentland (MIT - Media Lab, email: pentland@mit.edu).

10. REFERENCES

[1] A. Almaatouq, F. Alhasoun, R. Campari, and A. Alfaris. The influence of social norms on synchronous versus asynchronous communication technologies. In *Proceedings of the 1st ACM International Workshop on Personal Data Meets Distributed Multimedia*, PDM '13, pages 39–42, New York, NY, USA, 2013. ACM.

[2] Y. Altshuler, N. Aharony, A. Pentland, Y. Elovici, and M. Cebrian. Stealing reality: When criminals become data scientists (or vice versa). *IEEE Intelligent Systems*, 26(6):22–30, 2011.

[3] F. Benevenuto, G. Magno, T. Rodrigues, and V. Almeida. Detecting spammers on Twitter. In *Proceedings of the Seventh Annual Collaboration, Electronic messaging, Anti-Abuse and Spam Conference (CEAS)*, July 2010.

[4] J. Borondo, A. J. Morales, J. C. Losada, and R. M. Benito. Characterizing and modeling an electoral campaign in the context of Twitter: 2011 Spanish Presidential election as a case study. *Chaos: An Interdisciplinary Journal of Nonlinear Science*, 22(2), 2012.

[5] U. Brandes. A faster algorithm for betweenness centrality. *Journal of Mathematical Sociology*, 25:163–177, 2001.

[6] S. Chhabra, A. Aggarwal, F. Benevenuto, and P. Kumaraguru. Phi.sh/$ocial: The phishing landscape through short urls. In *Proceedings of the 8th Annual Collaboration, Electronic Messaging, Anti-Abuse and Spam Conference*, CEAS '11, pages 92–101, New York, NY, USA, 2011. ACM.

[7] A. Clauset, C. R. Shalizi, and M. E. J. Newman. Power-law distributions in empirical data. *SIAM Rev.*, 51(4):661–703, Nov. 2009.

[8] M. Conover, J. Ratkiewicz, M. Francisco, B. Gonçalves, A. Flammini, and F. Menczer. Political polarization on twitter. In *Proc. 5th International AAAI Conference on Weblogs and Social Media (ICWSM)*, 2011.

[9] M. Egele, G. Stringhini, C. Kruegel, and G. Vigna. COMPA: Detecting Compromised Accounts on Social Networks. In *ISOC Network and Distributed System Security Symposium (NDSS)*, 2013.

[10] L. C. Freeman. A Set of Measures of Centrality Based on Betweenness. *Sociometry*, 40(1):35–41, Mar. 1977.

[11] S. Ghosh, B. Viswanath, F. Kooti, N. K. Sharma, G. Korlam, F. Benevenuto, N. Ganguly, and K. P. Gummadi. Understanding and combating link farming in the twitter social network. In *Proceedings of the 21st International Conference on World Wide Web*, WWW '12, pages 61–70, New York, NY, USA, 2012. ACM.

[12] GlobalWebIndex. Global web index: Q4 2012, 2013.

[13] S. González-Bailón, J. Borge-Holthoefer, A. Rivero, and Y. Moreno. The dynamics of protest recruitment through an online network.

[14] C. Grier, K. Thomas, V. Paxson, and M. Zhang. @spam: The underground on 140 characters or less. In *Proceedings of the 17th ACM Conference on Computer and Communications Security*, CCS '10, pages 27–37, New York, NY, USA, 2010. ACM.

[15] S. Kato, A. Koide, T. Fushimi, K. Saito, and H. Motoda. Network analysis of three twitter functions: Favorite, follow and mention. In D. Richards and B. Kang, editors, *Knowledge Management and Acquisition for Intelligent Systems*, volume 7457 of *Lecture Notes in Computer Science*, pages 298–312. Springer Berlin Heidelberg, 2012.

[16] C. Lumezanu, N. Feamster, and H. Klein. bias: Measuring the tweeting behavior of propagandists. In *ICWSM*, 2012.

[17] A. Marcus, M. S. Bernstein, O. Badar, D. R. Karger, S. Madden, and R. C. Miller. Twitinfo: Aggregating and visualizing microblogs for event exploration. In *Proceedings of the SIGCHI Conference on Human Factors in Computing Systems*, CHI '11, pages 227–236, New York, NY, USA, 2011. ACM.

[18] M. McCord and M. Chuah. Spam detection on twitter using traditional classifiers. In *Proceedings of the 8th international conference on Autonomic and trusted computing*, ATC'11, pages 175–186, Berlin, Heidelberg, 2011. Springer-Verlag.

[19] F. Morstatter, J. Pfeffer, H. Liu, and K. M. Carley. Is the sample good enough? comparing data from Twitter's streaming API with Twitter's Firehose. *Proceedings of ICWSM*, 2013.

[20] M. E. J. Newman. Power laws, pareto distributions and zipf's law. *Contemporary Physics*, 46:323–351, December 2005.

[21] H. Nguyen. 2013 state of social media spam. Technical report, Nexgate, 2013.

[22] A. Sanzgiri, A. Hughes, and S. Upadhyaya. Analysis of malware propagation in twitter. *Reliable Distributed Systems, IEEE Symposium on*, 0:195–204, 2013.

[23] G. Stringhini, M. Egele, C. Kruegel, and G. Vigna. Poultry markets: On the underground economy of twitter followers. In *Proceedings of the 2012 ACM Workshop on Workshop on Online Social Networks*, WOSN '12, pages 1–6, New York, NY, USA, 2012. ACM.

[24] G. Stringhini, C. Kruegel, and G. Vigna. Detecting spammers on social networks. *Proceedings of the 26th Annual Computer Security Applications Conference on - ACSAC '10*, page 1, 2010.

[25] M. Thelwall, K. Buckley, and G. Paltoglou. Sentiment in twitter events. *J. Am. Soc. Inf. Sci. Technol.*, 62(2):406–418, Feb. 2011.

[26] K. Thomas, C. Grier, and V. Paxson. Adapting Social Spam Infrastructure for Political Censorship. In *Proceedings of the 5th USENIX Workshop on Large-Scale Exploits and Emergent Threats (LEET)*, Apr. 2012.

[27] K. Thomas, C. Grier, D. Song, and V. Paxson. Suspended accounts in retrospect: an analysis of twitter spam. In *Proceedings of the 2011 ACM SIGCOMM conference on Internet measurement conference*, IMC '11, pages 243–258, New York, NY, USA, 2011. ACM.

[28] K. Thomas, D. McCoy, C. Grier, A. Kolcz, and V. Paxson. Trafficking fraudulent accounts: The role of the underground market in twitter spam and abuse. In *Proceedings of the 22nd Usenix Security Symposium*, 2013.

[29] Twitter. Following rules and best practices. https://support.twitter.com/articles/68916-following-rules-and-best-practices, 2012. [Online; accessed 22-October-2013].

[30] Twitter. Public stream. https://dev.twitter.com/docs/streaming-apis/, 2012. [Online; accessed 1-October-2013].

[31] Twitter. Rules. https://support.twitter.com/articles/18311-the-twitter-rules, 2012. [Online; accessed 1-October-2013].

[32] Twitter. Initial public offering of shares of common stock of twitter, inc. http://www.sec.gov/Archives/edgar/data/1418091/000119312513390321/d564001ds1.htm, 2013. [Online; accessed 5-October-2013].

[33] A. H. Wang. Don't follow me: Spam detection in twitter. In *Security and Cryptography (SECRYPT), Proceedings of the 2010 International Conference on*, pages 1–10, 2010.

[34] G. Wang, M. Mohanlal, C. Wilson, X. Wang, M. J. Metzger, H. Zheng, and B. Y. Zhao. Social turing tests: Crowdsourcing sybil detection. In *NDSS*. The Internet Society, 2013.

[35] Y. Xie, F. Yu, Q. Ke, M. Abadi, E. Gillum, K. Vitaldevaria, J. Walter, J. Huang, and Z. M. Mao. Innocent by association: Early recognition of legitimate users. In *Proceedings of the 2012 ACM Conference on Computer and Communications Security*, CCS '12, pages 353–364, New York, NY, USA, 2012. ACM.

[36] C. Yang, R. Harkreader, and G. Gu. Die free or live hard? empirical evaluation and new design for fighting evolving twitter spammers. In R. Sommer, D. Balzarotti, and G. Maier, editors, *Recent Advances in Intrusion Detection*, volume 6961 of *Lecture Notes in Computer Science*, pages 318–337. Springer Berlin Heidelberg, 2011.

[37] C. Yang, R. Harkreader, J. Zhang, S. Shin, and G. Gu. Analyzing spammers' social networks for fun and profit: a case study of cyber criminal ecosystem on twitter. In *Proceedings of the 21st international conference on World Wide Web*, WWW '12, pages 71–80, New York, NY, USA, 2012. ACM.

[38] C. M. Zhang and V. Paxson. Detecting and analyzing automated activity on twitter. In *Proceedings of the 12th international conference on Passive and active measurement*, PAM'11, pages 102–111, Berlin, Heidelberg, 2011. Springer-Verlag.

APPENDIX

A. THE SCALE-FREE NATURE OF THE MENTION NETWORK

We investigate the scale free nature of the mention network by examining whether power law is the best description for our data's degree distribution. We achieved this by comparing the power law fit to fits of other distributions using log-likelihood ratios R and generating p-value p (the significance for this ratio) to specify which fit is better [7] (see Table 4 and Figure 8). Generally, the first distribution is a better fit when $R > 0$, alternatively the second distribution should be preferred when $R < 0$. We find for C_2 is significantly (with $p = 1.8^{-173}$) best described as a truncated power law distribution. As for the case of C_1 power law is insignificantly better describer than truncated power ($p = 0.9$).

Table 4: Comparing different heavy-tailed distributions for the degree distribution of the mention network.

Candidates	Class	R	p
Power law vs Exponential	C_1	193.8	$< 10^{-10}$
Power law vs Trunc. power law	C_1	0.03	0.9
Power law vs Exponential	C_2	45.7	$< 10^{-10}$
Power law vs Trunc. power law	C_2	-68.2	$< 10^{-10}$
Power law vs Lognormal	C_2	-111	$< 10^{-10}$
Trunc. power law vs Lognormal	C_2	28.1	1.8^{-173}

The Impact of Visual Attributes on Online Image Diffusion

Luam Totti
Federal University of
Minas Gerais (UFMG)
Belo Horizonte, MG, Brazil
luamct@dcc.ufmg.br

Felipe Costa
Federal University of
Minas Gerais (UFMG)
Belo Horizonte, MG, Brazil
felipealco@dcc.ufmg.br

Sandra Avila
RECOD Lab., DCA / FEEC /
UNICAMP
Campinas, SP, Brazil
sandra@dca.fee.unicamp.br

Eduardo Valle
RECOD Lab., DCA / FEEC /
UNICAMP
Campinas, SP, Brazil
dovalle@dca.fee.unicamp.br

Wagner Meira Jr.
Federal University of
Minas Gerais (UFMG)
Belo Horizonte, MG, Brazil
meira@dcc.ufmg.br

Virgílio Almeida
Federal University of
Minas Gerais (UFMG)
Belo Horizonte, MG, Brazil
virgilio@dcc.ufmg.br

ABSTRACT

Little is known on how visual content affects the popularity on social networks, despite images being now ubiquitous on the Web, and currently accounting for a considerable fraction of all content shared. Existing art on image sharing focuses mainly on non-visual attributes. In this work we take a complementary approach, and investigate resharing from a mainly visual perspective. Two sets of visual features are proposed, encoding both aesthetical properties (brightness, contrast, sharpness, etc.), and semantic content (concepts represented by the images). We collected data from a large image-sharing service (Pinterest) and evaluated the predictive power of different features on popularity (number of reshares). We found that visual properties have low predictive power compared that of social cues. However, after factoring-out social influence, visual features show considerable predictive power, especially for images with higher exposure, with over 3:1 accuracy odds when classifying highly exposed images between very popular and unpopular.

Categories and Subject Descriptors

H.2.8 [**Database Management**]: Database applications—*Data mining*

General Terms

Content diffusion, popularity prediction, image popularity.

1. INTRODUCTION

Online social networks have evolved from textual blogging tools to complex real-time systems of creation, consumption and diffusion of different media. More recently, the ubiquity of digital cameras has contributed to a rapid growth of image-sharing services such as Instagram, Tumblr

and Pinterest. Image sharing is not restricted to dedicated services: Facebook, for example, reports visual information corresponding to the majority of reshared content [15], with more than 300 million images processed every day [41].

Therefore, image-sharing services have recently drawn the attention of researchers from many disciplines. The ability to predict image popularity (amount of views and reshares) has impact on advertising, viral marketing, and infrastructure capacity planning. Most works, however, approach prediction exclusively from a social perspective, focusing on the network structure, influence propagation, and temporal analysis [20, 1, 4, 42].

In this work, we take a complementary approach and evaluate the impact of visual attributes on image popularity. We define two sets of visual features, aesthetic and semantic, and analyze their impact on popularity (measured by the number of reshares) of images on Pinterest, a social network of large and increasing audience.

Image aesthetics is the perception of beauty by viewers [13]. It is challenging to extract features representing beauty, due to its abstract and subjective nature, but existing works show some consensus on what makes images more visually appealing [23]. Guided by that prior art, we have carefully choosen image features that encode important aesthetics properties. Our methodology comprises the design, implementation and evaluation of several of those features.

The semantic of images, understood as the identification of concepts represented in the image, stands on the other side of the spectrum of image analysis. Semantic analysis is a challenging open problem of Computer Vision, since visually similar images may portrait completely distinct concepts, and, conversely, similar concepts have much visual variability. The concepts to identify may be the concrete presence of certain classes of objects (e.g., people, cars), the nature of the image (e.g., landscape, interior scene), and even abstract notions (e.g., entertainment, violence). Perhaps due to the challenges of automatically identifying those concepts, semantic analysis is rarely employed on the study of image-sharing social networks. In this work, we have employed semantic features extracted with a state-of-the-art technique [38]. Each image receives a semantic feature vector of 85 dimensions, each quantifying the confidence on the presence of a concept the system was trained to recognize.

We also take into account social-network aspects, like number of followers, category tags, etc. The social attributes are both used as predictors, allowing to compare their predictive power to those of the image features, and also as a nuisance factor for the latter.

The original contributions of this work are:

- One of the first efforts to employ visual analysis in popularity and diffusion on online social networks from a mainly visual perspective;

- A compilation of aesthetics and semantics features, selected and implemented for the task. Those features are useful *per se*, and may be applied to other visual analysis tasks, such as recommendation, or retrieval. Social-network features were also selected and implemented;

- Collection of Pinterest resharing data, that we made publicly available[1]. Pinterest has a large and fast increasing popularity, presenting an interesting case for research.

2. RELATED WORK

Information diffusion on online services is a vastly researched topic [3, 4, 8, 9, 27]. Most of those works focus on designing metrics and models to quantify observable patterns of information diffusion.

Fewer researchers have looked into the users' motivations behind content endorsement actions such as 'retwetting', 'repinning' or 'liking'. Macskassy and Michelson proposed several models for explaining resharing behavior on Twitter, showing that users tend to retweet content on topics different to those of their own tweets, a behavior the authors called anti-homophily [33]. Suh et al. presented a large-scale analysis on how context features are associated to retweetability [43], concluding, among other findings, that the presence of URLs and hashtags correlate positively with retweeting. Stieglitz and Dang-Xuan extended that work by investigating how sentiment alignment affects retweetability on politically engaged content [42]. They found that neutral tweets are less likely to be reshared than polarized tweets (positive or negative), although no significant distinction could be found between those two alignments. Zarella [48], in a series of blog posts, presents practical advice for content creators. Analysing his data, he suggests the inclusion of hashtags, images, and URLs on tweets to increase resharing.

Existing art on image-sharing services tends to focus on social-network aspects, such as user influence, and social ties. Anagnostopoulos et al. developed a statistical test to distinguish causal social influence from simple correlation by examining the spread of picture tags in Flickr [1]. Lerman and Jones investigated photo propagation on Flickr, concluding that the social environment of users plays a significant role on the diffusion of the images [26]. Cha et al. support and extend those results by considering multiple hops on the social network around each user [10]. This paper, by focusing on image visual content, is complementary to all those works that focus on social aspects and user interaction.

Two very recent works have taken into account visual information. Khosla et al. [25] analyzed the predictive power of both visual and social features in the resharing of images on Flickr. Their prediction models successfully predicted, to some extent, image popularity on different settings, such as *one-image-per-user* or *user-specific*. Important differences from our work are the service studied (Flickr vs. Pinterest), and our analysis of visual features accross the spectrum of strong predictive social-features, like number of followers, an approach in which we use social properties as a nuisance factor. Cheng et al. [11] aimed at predicting cascades of reshares for images on Facebook, modeling resharing as a temporal process, and using the past to predict the future, in a scheme that reveals interesting insights on resharing process. They were able to predict well, for images that were reshared k times in the past, whether or not they would be reshared $2k$ times in the future. Our work is different both in the metric of popularity we are trying to predict, and in the visual features evaluated, since their work does not explore the aesthetic features. Remark that those works were unpublished at the time we completed our experiments, we came in contact with preprints as we were finishing the writing of the paper. As we will show, our work supports the conclusion of both works, that visual features are less predictive of popularity than user and network features.

The aesthetic features we evaluate were proposed on works focused on aesthetics assessment. Early works employed low-level features explicitly designed to quantify perceptual quality. Such features vary from simple channel statistics to complex blur estimation and region segmentation techniques. The works of Datta et al. [13] and Ke et al. [24] stand as the first efforts to infer aesthetic quality by applying Machine Learning techniques on those features, showing that aesthetics can be successfully inferred to some extent. Later works extended and improved the features [14, 22, 31], offered insights for the handling of images in specific corpora (e.g., paintings [28], images with faces [29]), and integrated image-enhancing systems [5]. Although those works yield good and interpretable results, custom-designed features cannot be exhaustive due to the diversity of both perceptual attributes and image corpora. Therefore, recent works have introduced more general visual features as an alternative to the hand-crafted ones. Marchesotti et al. [35] employ GIST and SIFT low-level descriptors, with a bag-of-visual-words and Fisher Vector mid-level descriptors, to infer aesthetic quality more accurately at the cost of less interpretable results. Attempting to achieve both accuracy and interpretability, Marchesotti and Perronnin [34] employed Machine Learning on images and associated textual comments to automatically discover and learn visual attributes.

3. DATA COLLECTION

The data used in this work was entirely collected from Pinterest[2], a recent image-sharing web service, brought to prominence as the fastest-growing large commercial social network [40]. In 2011 alone, the service grew 4000% in number of visits. At the end of 2013, Pinterest had the highest growth rate among all sharing channels, including Facebook, and, as of March 2014, it stands as the fourth most popular social network in number of unique accesses per month [16].

Despite Pinterest drawing much attention from mass media, few academic works aimed at understanding its dynamics [37, 17]. We believe to be the first work to study image

---

[1]https://github.com/luamct/WebSci14

[2]http://www.pinterest.com

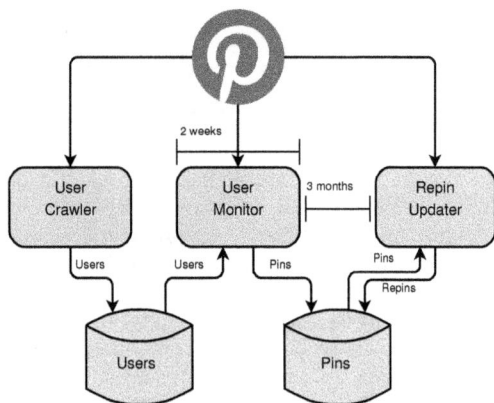

Figure 1: Flowchart of the data collection process. Because Pinterests has no data collection API, a scheme was created to obtain a measure of repins over a certain time span.

popularity on Pinterest. By making the collected data available, we hope to incite researchers to further investigate that network and its dynamics.

3.1 Pinterest Platform

Pinterest uses the metaphor of a pin-board as a collection of images (pins) within some topic of interest. Users can post on their boards by 'pinning' images from the Internet, uploading local content or 'repinning' existing pins (much like retweeting in Twitter). Users follow specific boards and may comment, like, or repin any posted pin. Although users have a followers and followees count on their profile, those values are a simplification, given that users do not follow other users directly, but individual boards. Both counts are calculated using an "at least one" logic, i.e., if a user A follows at least one board from user B, then A is counted as a follower of B , and B is counted as a followeee of A.

Pinterest adopted unusual strategies to estimulate the sharing of higher-quality content. From its conception, the service was promoted for "people with good taste", with sign-up available at invitation only. Designers intentionally avoided providing ranks of popular users, or even recent trends, to discourage competition among users, or the usage of Pinterest as a news media. Those strategies, along with a clean and elegant interface design, successfully enforced the importance of visually-appealing content above personal or informational content. That also makes Pinterest fairly agnostic to external events or trends when compared to other services [36]. Those characteristics make Pinterest particularly suited for this work, since our main goal is to investigate how visual properties affect image popularity.

In this work we consider the number of repins an image has received as an assessment of its popularity. Although the reasons driving resharing actions are numerous [7], it is vastly accepted in literature that resharing can be seen as an endorsement action, and, therefore, is a reasonable candidate for quantifying popularity [43, 7, 20].

3.2 Data Acquisition

Having no official available public API, the data was collected with HTTP requests over the publicly available information, emulating a regular user browsing the service. Each request was able to retrieve at most 50 pins, due to the lay-

out of the pages returned by Pinterest. Such restrictions imposed some limitations on the collection process, both in terms of volume and completeness of the final dataset. Since our goal is to investigate image popularity, we required repin information about each pin. However it would be unfair to claim that a pin is more popular (has more repins) than other if each has been been exposed for a different duration. At the same time, Pinterest web interface does not provide the precise date the pin was posted, making impossible for us to select pins posted in a given time span. For that reason we performed our collection as a multiple step process:

1. Collected Pinterest user handlers through a breadth-first search starting with a few manually selected users.

2. Monitored the collected users over a span of time for collecting timestamped content.

3. Collected the number of repins of the pins collected on step 2, by later revisiting their Pinterest pages.

Figure 1 summarizes those steps. That process allowed us to collect data with proper timestamps and repin information after the same exposure time on the network. The process started with the collection of approximately 210K user identifiers through a breadth-first search, starting from a small group of manually selected popular users (since no user rank is provided). We understand the limitations of BFS sampling over large networks [18], however due to the lack of a public API, or even numerical identifiers for users and pins, we were left with no better alternative. We then monitored the collected users' activities during the course of two weeks (19th April to 2nd May of 2013) and collected all posted content (around 2 million pins). From that set we randomly selected 10,000 users and their corresponding pins, consisting of 473,665 pins, to make processing manageable. To collect repin information we revisied the Pinterest pages for the selected 473,665 pins after approximately 3 months (July 27), ensuring that the images had roughly the same exposure time in the network.

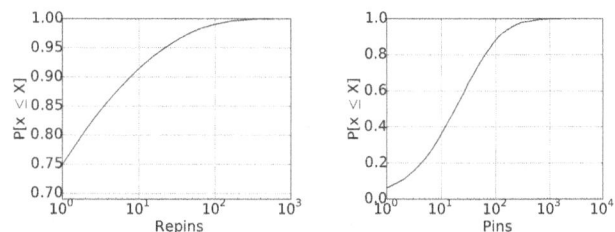

Figure 2: Cumulative distributions for (a) repins per pin and (b) pins per user in the dataset.

To give an overview of the characteristics of the collected data, we show the cumulative distribution of the repins each pin received in Figure 2(a) and of the number of pins posted by each user in Figure 2(b). Figure 2(a) shows a heavy-tailed distribution with 75% of the pins having 1 or less repins and less than 2% of the pins having more than 100 repins. Figure 2(b) shows a less skewed distribution of pins across users, with 50% of the users posting at least 20 pins during the monitored period, but with less than 10% posting more than 100 pins. Given the highly skewed repins-per-pin distribution (nearly 60% of the pins have 0 repins), and the main objectives of this work, we performed all analyses only with the pins repinned at least once, which reduced the count of pins to $187,796$.

4. IMAGE FEATURES

We divided our features into three major groups according to what they encode: visual aesthetics properties, semantic information, and social-network properties. The features employed are summarized on Table 1 and detailed below.

4.1 Aesthetic Features

The development of informative and interpretable visual features for assessing aesthetics properties remains a challenging problem. Even where there is a consensus on what makes images beautiful, efficient features must be designed to properly encode the intended visual notion. The feature selection and design in this work was based upon photography techniques, viewers' intuition, and results from previous works. Features used in different applications, like image retrieval and visual memorability tasks, were also considered [21, 47].

The images were first scaled down to approximately 200,000 pixels while keeping their original aspect ratio. They were then converted to a cylindrical color space (IHSL), which represents color in a more human-friendly way [19].

Channel Statistics: The Hue channel encodes color tonality (i.e., where in the spectrum the color is). Saturation encodes chromatic purity (pure full colors vs. diluted or "pastel" colors). Luminance encodes brightness, the amount of light energy in the color. We compute the mean and standard deviation on pixel values for those three channels. Circular statistics were employed for Hue, since it is an angular measure.

Basic Colors: Colors are one of major components on images. Colors evoke different sentiments and feels on viewers and are deliberately exploited by artists, designers, and photographers. We count the basic colors of each image using the method of Weiber et al. [45].

Dominant Colors: We consider dominant colors as the smallest set of basic colors that occupy 60% of all pixels. The threshold 60% was empirically found to maximize the distance between images with few repins from those with many repins.

Colorfulness: We implement Datta et al. [13] colorfulness metric as an additional quantification of the diversity of colors in the images. This metric divides the RGB color space into 64 equal cubes and computes an histogram over the pixels with those cubes as bins. A hypothetical perfectly colorful image is encoded as a histogram in the same manner and the colorfulness of the target image is taken as the Earth Mover's distance between the two histograms.

Contrast: Proper use of contrast is another important property. Images presenting wider ranges of luminance values are usually perceived as having better contrast. We quantify that by computing a normalized luminance histogram of the image, and taking as metric the size of the minimum contiguous interval of luminance values that concentrates at least 98% of total image luminance (i.e., we count the smallest number of contiguous bins that sum to 0.98).

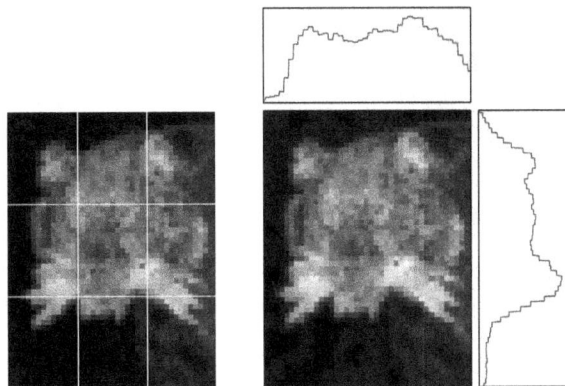

Figure 3: Sharpness-based features. (Left:) Sharpness map superimposed with the 'thirds' grid : region focus is extracted as the mean sharpness of each of those 9 regions. (Right:) The sum of sharpness over rows and columns is employed to measure focus centrality, focus density, and agreement with the 'rule of thirds'.

Aspect Ratio and Resolution: Aspect ratio is given by the ratio between the width w and heigh h of the image, while resolution is given by $w \times h$.

Complexity: Image complexity gives cues about aesthetic value, because simple compositions tend to have more appeal. We quantify that effect by using the number of regions obtained by a segmentation algorithm [12]. Cluttered images tend to segment into many small regions, simpler images tend to generate few large regions.

Texture: Texture, which encodes the perceptual qualities of graininess, smoothness, and directionality, is an important aesthetic cue. Following a similar procedure from previous works [13, 32], we apply a three-level wavelet transform on all three color channels, and summarize information into three features.

Art theory and professional photography rely on rules of spatial composition. Studies show that different compositions trigger different stimuli on observers, also affecting the perceived image quality. The features below explore that.

Region Focus: A widely used technique on artistic photography is to limit the depth of field, i.e., to deliberately blur some regions so as to bring focus and attention to the objects of interest. On the other hand, unintentional blur is perceived as poor technique, degrading aesthetic value. We implemented Vu et al. [46] S_3 algorithm for mapping sharpness levels. Although the concept of sharpness can be subjective, the S_3 algorithm achieves good results by combining both spectral analysis and local contrasts to create a sharpness map, quantifying the sharpness of each pixel. We take $Z(x, y)$ as the normalized sharpness of pixel x, y, i.e., Z as the ℓ_1 normalization of the sharpness map. We define nine spatial features as the mean pixel sharpness for each region of a 3×3 grid over the image, as shown in Figure 3. High quality images are expected to concentrate sharpness on inner regions, while poor images are expected to scatter sharpness across more regions.

Focus Centrality: We measure the centrality metric of the sharpness map (explained above). We compute the sum of normalized sharpness for each row $(Z_{row}(y))$ and each column $(Z_{col}(x))$ of the image, as shown in Figure 3. Rows (columns) centrality is obtained by summing over the sharpness sum of each row (column), attenuated by the squared normalized distance of each row (column) to the center of the image, i.e. $c_{row} = \sum_y Z_{row} \times \left(1 - |y - (h-1)/2| \times (h/2)^{-1}\right)^2$ (analogously for c_{col}). Image sharpness centrality value is the product of the two centralities $c_{row} \times c_{col}$.

Focus Density: From the sharpness map we extract the sharpness density of the image. We measure row (column) spread as the minimum contiguous number of rows (columns) whose total normalized sharpness corresponds to 80% of total image sharpness. For rows, the spread ρ_{row} is $\min_{y_e, y_s} [y_e - y_s]$ subjected to $\sum_{y=y_s}^{y_e} Z_{row}(y) \geq 0.8$ (ρ_{col} is defined analogously). The density measure is given by $1 - \rho_{row} \times \rho_{col}$.

Background Area: Noting that the foreground and background regions of images are mainly defined by boundaries of color and sharpness, we derived a simple but effective background detection algorithm from the sharpness map and segmented image. For each region Q of the segmented image we calculate a vector of four averages $(\bar{Q}_Z, \bar{Q}_L, \bar{Q}_a, \bar{Q}_b)$, corresponding, respectively, to the mean pixel value for the sharpness Z, and for each one of the channels of a La*b* color space. We then employ a 2-means clustering on the regions over the vectors $(\bar{Q}_Z, \bar{Q}_L, \bar{Q}_a, \bar{Q}_b)$ in order to find the two major regions. Finally, we take the region with lower mean sharpness as the background. Figure 4 illustrates the steps of the algorithm. The final metric is the fraction of the image occupied by the background.

Rule of Thirds: is a commonly guideline for good composition, stating that objects of interest should be placed near to one of the four intersections of the 'thirds' of the image (Figure 5). Agreement to the rule of thirds is measured by the density of sharpness around the 'thirds', i.e., as the sum of normalized sharpness of pixels ponderated by a Gaussian window centralized on the 'thirds'. More formally, the agreement for each horizontal axis ($y_a = h/3$, $y_a = 2h/3$) is given by $\sum_y Z_{row}(y) \, N_{y_a, \beta^{-1}}(y)$, where $N_{\mu, \sigma^2}(y)$ is the value at y of a Gaussian distribution with mean μ and variance σ^2 (the contribution of horizontal axes $x_a = w/3$ and $x_a = 2w/3$ is defined analogously). The final metric is the sum of the contributions of the four axes. The concentration parameter $\beta = (\sigma^2)^{-1}$ controls the spread of the Gaussian, the bigger it is, the more strict the metric is in terms of proximity to the axes. We set $\beta = 160$ in our experiments. Figure 5 illustrates the process.

4.2 Semantic Features

For our semantic features, we employ one supervised image classification for each concept, and use the confidence scores given by the concept classifiers as a feature vector. Image classification is a challenging, and highly active research topic, with an extended range of applications. A typical classification scheme consists mainly of three steps: (i) low-level local features extraction, (ii) mid-level global feature extraction, and (iii) supervised classification. Those steps are explained below.

4.2.1 Low-level Features

The low-level local features are extracted directly from the image pixels, sampling different regions of the image. Although purely perceptual, the local descriptors provide invariance properties that make them good building blocks for

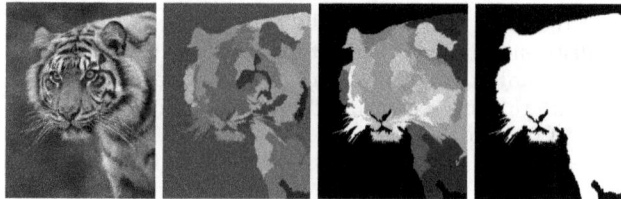

Figure 4: Background detection algorithm. From left to right: (1) Original image; (2) After image segmentation, the mean color $(\bar{Q}_L, \bar{Q}_a, \bar{Q}_b)$ on each region Q is computed on the La*b* color space; (3) After image segmentation, the mean sharpness $\bar{Q}_Z$ is computed using the sharpness map Z; (4) Regions are clustered with a 2-means over the vectors $(\bar{Q}_Z, \bar{Q}_L, \bar{Q}_a, \bar{Q}_b)$, the region with lesser overall sharpness is chosen as background.

more complex representations. The regions may be densely sampled on a grid of overlapping windows of different scales, or they may be sparsely sampled by a detector of regions of interest.

In this work we adopt the widely used SIFT local descriptor [30], which has consistently shown good results on image classification tasks. It is invariant to scale and rotation, besides being invariant to affine illumination changes. We extract the descriptors on a dense spatial grid with a step-size of half the patch-size, over 8 scales separated by a factor of 1.2, with the smallest patch-size set to 16 pixels. As a result, roughly 8000 descriptors are extracted from each image in the dataset. Each SIFT descriptor had its dimension reduced from 128 to 64 by applying Principal Component Analysis (PCA).

4.2.2 Mid-level Features

Even with a highly robust and comprehensive extraction of low-level features, bridging the semantic gap between pixel values and real concepts and entities requires substantially more complex representations. Mid-level features play that role by aggregating low-level descriptors into a global and richer image representation, in a scheme known as Bags of visual Words (BoW). In the BoW model, unsupervised learning is employed to quantize the low-level feature space, establishing a codebook of representative visual appearances. Then, the feature vector of an image is created by encoding its low-level features in relation to the codebook, and pooling over all codes, in order to create a single feature vector. The BoW model and its extensions are active research areas [6, 2, 38].

In this work, we employ as mid-level representation the state-of-the-art Fisher Vectors [38], an extension to the BoW model that encodes how much the first and second moments of the low-level descriptors present in the image deviate from the global distribution found on the dataset. In Fisher Vectors, the codebook is learned with an Expectation–Maximization algorithm to estimate a Gaussian mixture model (GMM) over one million low-level descriptors sampled from the training set. The mid-level feature vector is the sum of the Fisher scores, over the learned GMM, of each low-level feature. The details of the representation go beyond the scope of this work and can be found in [39].

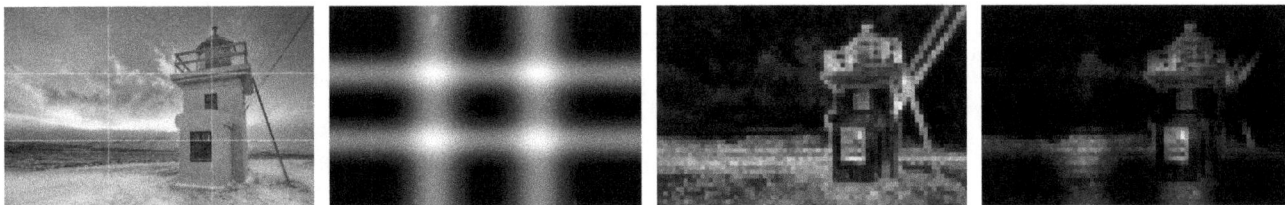

Figure 5: The 'rule of thirds' metric. From left to right: (1) Original image with the axes drawn; (2) Attenuation map corresponding to the contributions of the four axis, each axis contribution being ponderated by a Gaussian window around it; (3) Sharpness map Z generated using the S_3 algorithm; (4) Pixel-wise product of sharpness map and attenuation map. The final accordance metric is the sum of all pixels in the product map.

4.2.3 Supervised Learning

Finally, supervised learning is applied over the mid-level representation, in order to learn a statistical model for each concept, using a training set of annotated images. In this work we adopt the ImageCLEF 2012 Photo Annotation dataset [44] as our training set. The dataset consists of $25,000$ images, of which we employ the training set of $15,000$ instances. The dataset contains 94 concepts including natural elements (e.g., day, snow, fire), environment (e.g., coast, plant, bird), people (e.g., baby, female, small group), and human elements (e.g., car, bicycle, air vehicle). We excluded 9 concepts that we considered to be too related to aesthetics properties (e.g., quality_noblur, style_overlay, etc), leaving us with 85 semantic concepts.

When employing the BoW model, Support Vector Machines (SVM) are often the classifier of choice, due to its ability to learn in very high-dimensional spaces. We use it to perform one-versus-all classification using a linear kernel, since previous works show that Fisher Vectors do not benefit from the slower non-linear kernels [38]. A different classification model is learned for each concept.

The final semantic feature vector for an image is the concatenation of the z-score normalized confidences output by the trained model for that image.

4.3 Social Features

To better understand the predictive power of visual features, we also employ features extracted from metadata about users, images and the social network. We call them social features, since they are mainly derived from the users information and interaction with the service. For each pin P posted by user U on the pinboard B we define the features shown on Table 1.

The category of a pin is defined as the category of the board B in which it is pinned. Pinterest offers 33 different categories (e.g., Architecture, Cars, Food and Drink, Women's Fashion, etc.). Previous versions of the service allowed users to leave boards uncategorized, so around 43% of the boards on the dataset still have no category. For the pins in those uncategorized boards we assign an extra empty value.

Users may post pins in different ways, such as uploading images, pinning an image from an external domain, or repinning an image already in Pinterest. Binary feature is_repin is true only for repins. We also measure, for each user U, the fraction of pins that are repins.

We include two more pin-specific features: the length in characters of the description provided by the creator, and the day of the week the pin was posted. We also include the total number of pins in the board B where the pin was posted.

Given the important role creators play in the diffusion of their messages [1], we employ many user and social features. User profile gives Gender, which can be empty if is not provided by the user (often the case for institutional and commercial accounts). The binary feature has_website is true for users that list an website in their profile (also indicates commercial accounts that use Pinterest as a visual display for products on sale) [37]. Pinterest deals with products by adding a dollar sign ($) in the description of pins that represent products on sale, an information we encode in the binary feature is_product.

Feature #user_followees is the number of users the pin creator U follows. Since users follow specific boards, that number refers to all users that have at least some board followed by user U. Although the service offers board granularity for following, in practice users tend to follow either all or no boards of the followees [37].

Feature category_entropy encodes how general users are regarding the categories of their posted content. Users may specialize in posting on a few categories, or they may post content on many categories. We quantify this by calculating the Shannon entropy of the distribution of categories used on all pins posted by user U. As mentioned, pins that belong to uncategorized boards are also considered uncategorized. The feature uncategorized calculates the percentage of uncategorized pins posted by user U.

Finally, the features #boards and #pins hold the total number of boards user U has created, and the number of pins U has posted.

5. EVALUATION

To evalute the impact of the different features on image diffusion, we employ a classification scheme (using supervised learning) to discriminate between two classes of very popular and very unpopular pins (excluding from the analysis the middle ground of average popular images). The experimental design divides the dataset into a training and testing sets. Accuracy on testing is used as a measure of the features predictive power. A 5-fold cross validation is employed to partition the training and data sets on the experiments, and the average accuracy is reported.

5.1 Popularity Prediction

When dealing with popularity on social networks, precise predictions are extremely difficult to obtain due to a multitude of factors. Fortunately, for most purposes it's suffi-

	Name	#	Brief Description
Aesthetics	*Channel Statistics*	6	Mean and standard deviation of each channel: Hue, Saturation and Brightness.
	Colorfulness	1	Image's distance (EMD) from a hypothetical perfectly colored image.
	Basic Colors	11	Amount of pixels of each basic color: black, blue, brown, green, gray, orange, pink, purple, red, white, yellow.
	Dominant Colors	1	Minimum number of basic colors that cover 60% of the image.
	Aspect Ratio	1	Width divided by height.
	Resolution	1	Width multiplied by height.
	Contrast	1	Measure of the dispersion of histogram of Luminance pixels.
	Texture	3	Roughness and smoothness of the image texture measured by the Wavelet transformation of each channel.
	Complexity	1	Number of regions after *mean-shift* segmentation.
	Region Focus	9	Mean sharpness value in each region on a 3×3 grid over the image.
	Focus Centrality	1	Concentration of sharpness values around the center of the image.
	Focus Density	1	Dispersion of values on the histograms of sharpness on each dimension.
	Background Area	1	Percentage of background area.
	Rule of Thirds	1	Accordance to the rule of thirds.
Semantics	*Concepts*	85	SVM detection confidence for: *view, celestial: (sun, moon, stars), (portrait, closeupmacro, indoor, outdoor), style: (pictureinpicture, circularwarp, graycolor, overlay), combustion: (flames, smoke, fireworks), sentiment: (happy, calm, inactive, melancholic, unpleasant, scary, active, euphoric, funny), gender: (male, female), age: (baby, child, teenager, adult, elderly), flora: (tree, plant, flower, grass), water: (underwater, seaocean, lake, riverstream, other), weather: (clearsky, overcastsky, cloudysky, rainbow, lighting, fogmist, snowice), lighting: (shadow, reflection, silhouette, lenseffect), scape: (mountainhill, desert, forestpark, coast, rural, city, graffiti), relation: (familyfriends, coworkers, strangers), fauna: (cat, dog, horse, fish, bird, insect, spider, amphibianreptile, rodent), timeofday: (day, night, sunrisesunset), quality: (noblur, partialblur, completeblur, motionblur, artifacts), setting: (citylife, partylife, homelife, sportsrecreation, fooddrink), transport: (cycle, car, truckbus, rail, water, air), quantity: (none, one, two, three, smallgroup, biggroup).*
Social	*Category*	(34)	Pin's category defined as the pin's board category.
	Is Repin	(2)	Whether the pin was itself a repin from another pin already in Pinterest.
	Is Product	(2)	Whether the pin is depicts a product for sale.
	Desc. length	1	The size in number of character of the pin's description.
	Day of the Week	(7)	Day of the week the pin P was posted.
	#Board pins	1	Number of pins posted on board B.
	Gender	(3)	The gender of user U as registered in the profile.
	Has Website	(2)	Whether the user U has a website registered in his profile.
	#User Followees	1	Number of followees of user U.
	Category Entropy	1	Entropy of the categories of all of user U's pins.
	Uncategorized	1	Percentage of uncategorized pins of user U.
	Repined	1	Percentage of repins within all pins of user U.
	#Boards	1	Number of boards created by user U.
	#Pins	1	Number of pins posted by user U.

Table 1: Extracted features for a given pin P posted by a user U on a board B. The columns # refers to the dimensionality of the feature vector. The values between parenthesis indicate categorical variables that can assume the number of values shown (*Gender* and *Category* can be unknown, explaining the extra possible value). The *Concepts* employed in semantic analysis are listed hierarchically for readability and contextualization: the detection algorithm actually employs a flat labeling using the concatenation of category and subcategory (e.g.: celestial_sun, celestial_moon, celestial_stars).

cient to foresee whether an image will be *highly popular* or *unpopular*. Therefore, we reduce the problem to a binary classification task into *unpopular* and *popular* pins. More exactly, letting r_i be the number of repins a pin i has received, we define threshold values λ_- and λ_+, and label a pin i as *unpopular* if $r_i < \lambda_-$, and as *popular* if $r > \lambda_+$. The pins between the thresholds are excluded from the analysis. To balance the classes, we set λ_- and λ_+ according to a sep-

aration parameter Δ that represents the percentage of the data discarded in the middle section. For example, $\Delta = 0.7$ means that the pins in the top and bottom 15%-rank of repins were used respectively as the popular and unpopular classes, while the remaining 70% of the pins were ignored.

For all classification results we employed a Random-Forest ensemble of 200 tree estimators with strong randomization on both attribute and cut-off choices. Since the task is a

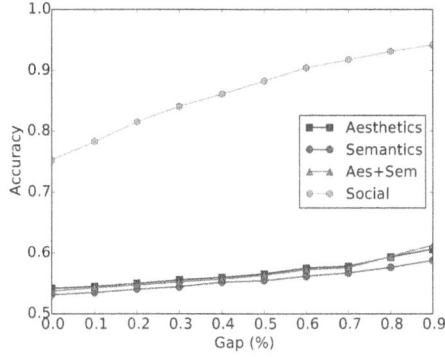

Figure 6: Accuracy of classification into *very popular* and *unpopular* for varying values of the gap Δ separating those two classes, and for different feature sets.

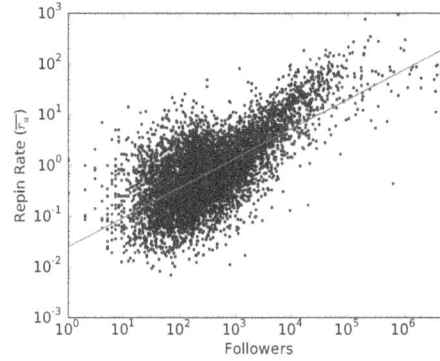

Figure 8: Linear Regression on the log of the mean repin rate given the log of the number of followers of the user.

balanced binary classification, we used accuracy as the evaluation metric, and performed a 5-fold cross-validation over the dataset, in order to obtain the averages and standard deviations of accuracy over the 5 runs.

Figure 6 shows the accuracy for increasing values of the gap Δ. The *Aes+Sem* employs early fusion of both semantical and aesthetical features, concatenating the respective features. Not surprisingly, the social parameters are much more informative in the prediction of popularity than the visual features. This is probably because some social features implicitly encode user popularity, an important factor to predict future posted pin popularity. The aggregated effect of visual features performs a little better than random, but their impact varies widely for different classes of users as we will show later in this section (see Fig. 9).

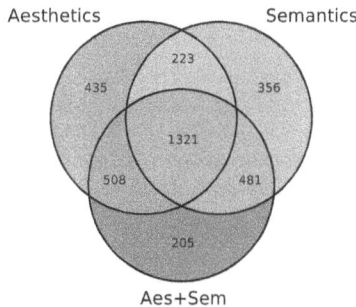

Figure 7: Venn diagram for the correctly classified images using different sets of features.

A particularly intriguing result is the similarity of the curves for aesthetics and for semantics features. Given their very distinct nature and derivation, that result is unexpected. To understand this behavior, Figure 7 shows a Venn diagram of the correctly classified images for all combinations of feature groups (separation $\Delta = 0.7$). We sampled a test set of 4,500 images for that analysis and trained the classifier with the remaining images. The numeric values labeling each region represent the number of images correctly classified using the corresponding set of features. Although there are 1,321 images correctly classified by all sets of features, 435 images were only correctly classified by the aesthetics features and 356 images were only correctly clas-

sified by the semantics features. Furthermore, by merging the two sets of features the classifier is able to identify correctly 205 new images but at the same time misclassify 223 images that were properly identified by the two sets of features separately. That suggests an interesting feature complementarity that could be leveraged in future works. It is still unknown why the classifier was unable to exploit that, given that we employed ensemble techniques with randomized choice of features for the composing tree estimators. Further investigation is required to illuminate that point.

5.2 Factoring-out Social Influence

To better understand the impact of visual features throughout the spectrum of users, we proposed to treat the user popularity (measured as their average number of repins per pin) as a *nuisance factor* and check whether we could improve popularity classification after removing the effects of that variable.

Let f_u be the number of followers user u has and $\bar{r}_u$ be the repin rate of user u, i.e., the average number of repins each pin of user u received. In order to treat f_u as a nuisance parameter we use part of the training set to fit a standard linear least squares model on $log(\bar{r}_u) \sim log(f_u)$ (see Figure 8). By doing this we obtain a regression function $h(f_u)$ that estimates the average number of repins/pin for a user u given their number of followers. Although the function was fitted to user data, we can transfer what we learned to each pin i by providing f_i as argument, which is the number of followers of the board pin i was posted. The predicted value $h(f_i)$ represents the expected number of repins pin i should have received considering only its exposure level.

We then apply a data transformation $\delta_i = r_i - h(f_i)$ for each pin i in order to remove the influence of the number of followers over the number of repins. Basically we are taking the repin residue in log scale of the regression prediction. Finally, we perform the binary classification task as before, but using the residues δ_i instead of r_i. By doing this we are attempting to explain the deviation of the observed number of repins from the expected number of repin given a number of followers.

Figure 8 shows the regressed linear function with each point being a user in the data and the coordinates given by the number of followers and the repin rate (average repins per pin). Figure 9 shows the classification performance of visual features for the transformed variable δ_i. Compared

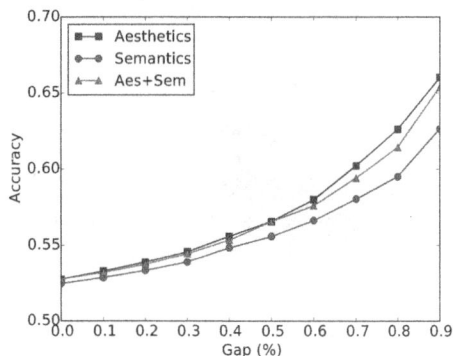

Figure 9: Factoring-out social influences: for different feature sets, accuracy of classification into *very popular* and *unpopular* for varying values of the gap Δ separating those two classes. The classes are defined on the the residue δ_i obtained by subtracting the influence of number of *user* followers, and indicate the deviation from the expected number of repins given the number of followers.

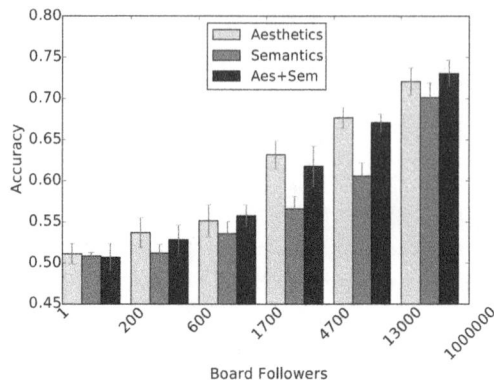

Figure 10: Blocking by number of *board* followers, for different feature sets. The bars plot the accuracy of binary classification for a gap $\Delta = 80$. The classes are defined on the residue δ_i obtained by subtracting the influence of number of board followers, and indicate the deviation from the expected number of repins for that amount of board followers. Error bars are standard deviations.

to Figure 6 the improvement is considerable, with the visual features attaining near 3:1 accuracy odds for the larger gaps.

5.3 Controlling for the Number of Followers

The fact that popularity indeed acts as a nuisance factor for the prediction ability of visual features is further confirmed in Figure 10, where we investigate the impact of the visual features for pins from boards with different number of followers. Each group of bars represent the classification accuracies of only pins from boards with followers within the values in the x axis. The followers intervals were chosen to be as logarithmically separated as possible while maintaining roughly the same number of pins within each interval. The error bars represent the standard deviation within the 5 cross-validation folds. The results show that visual features predict popularity better for pins with higher exposure. It is currently unknown in which direction the causality goes: are visually minded boards more likely to become popular? Or do visually-minded users gravitate towards popular boards, where they are prone to find visually appealing content?

Another interesting question is what explains diffusion of the less-exposed pins, since the visual attributes seem less important in this case. Those are still open questions. Given Pinterest's unusually high regards for visually appealing content, performing those same analyses on a different online service would probably bring interesting insights on those questions.

6. CONCLUSION

In this work we investigated content popularity on Pinterest, a relatively recent online image-sharing service that has a large and growing audience. As expected, social parameters, containing important hints about the popularity of *users*, have the most predictive power over the popularity of *pins*. At first, the aggregated effect of visual features seemed a little better than random, but a finer investigation revealed that the predictive power of visual features is considerable over the pins that have greater exposition (those pinned on boards with more followers) reaching over 3:1 ac-

curacy odds for the pins with larger exposition. Although that does not seem much, when compared to the 4:1 to 20:1 accuracy odds of social features, one has to keep in mind that visual features operate at a much lower level and are intrinsically very imprecise, due to the fact they are the result of automated algorithms. Therefore the predictive power we obtained hints at a lower bound on what could be obtained with future advanced visual features either designed or learned for the task.

As an aditional contribution, we proposed and implemented several features that we made available for the scientific community. Visual recomendation and other image tasks may take advantage of the visual properties extracted in this work.

As future works we would like to uncover the user behavior that explains the correlation between image exposure and visual features predictive power. Exploring our results with different social networks, like Instagram and Vine, would also be very valuable in order to understand different content-sharing behaviors across those services.

7. ACKNOWLEDGEMENTS

This work is partially supported by CAPES, CNPq, FAPEMIG, FAPESP and InWeb - the National Institute of Science and Technology for the Web. Sandra Avila is supported by a grant from Brazilian Samsung Research Institute.

8. REFERENCES

[1] A. Anagnostopoulos, R. Kumar, and M. Mahdian. Influence and correlation in social networks. KDD '08.

[2] S. Avila, N. Thome, M. Cord, E. Valle, and A. de A. Araújo. Pooling in image representation: the visual codeword point of view. *CVIU*, 2013.

[3] E. Bakshy, J. M. Hofman, W. A. Mason, and D. J. Watts. Everyone's an influencer: Quantifying influence on twitter. WSDM '11, 2011.

[4] E. Bakshy, I. Rosenn, C. Marlow, and L. Adamic. The role of social networks in information diffusion. WWW '12. ACM, 2012.

[5] S. Bhattacharya, R. Sukthankar, and M. Shah. A framework for photo-quality assessment and enhancement based on visual aesthetics. In *Proc. of the International Conference on Multimedia*, MM '10.

[6] Y.-L. Boureau, F. Bach, Y. LeCun, and J. Ponce. Learning mid-level features for recognition. CVPR'10.

[7] D. Boyd, S. Golder, and G. Lotan. Tweet, tweet, retweet: Conversational aspects of retweeting on twitter. In *Proc. of HICSS*, 2010.

[8] M. Cha, F. Benevenuto, H. Haddadi, and P. K. Gummadi. The world of connections and information flow in twitter. *Trans. on Systems, Man, and Cybernetics, Part A*, 42(4), 2012.

[9] M. Cha, H. Haddadi, F. Benevenuto, and K. Gummadi. Measuring user influence in twitter: The million follower fallacy. In *ICWSM*, 2010.

[10] M. Cha, A. Mislove, and K. P. Gummadi. A measurement-driven analysis of information propagation in the flickr social network. WWW '09.

[11] J. Cheng, L. Adamic, A. Dow, J. Kleinberg, and J. Leskovec. Can cascades be predicted? In *WWW'14*.

[12] D. Comaniciu, P. Meer, and S. Member. Mean shift: A robust approach toward feature space analysis. *Trans. on Pattern Analysis and Machine Intelligence*, 2002.

[13] R. Datta, D. Joshi, J. Li, and J. Z. Wang. Studying aesthetics in photographic images using a computational approach. ECCV, 2006.

[14] S. Dhar, V. Ordonez, and T. Berg. High level describable attributes for predicting aesthetics and interestingness. In *CVPR*, 2011.

[15] A. Dow, L. Adamic, and A. Friggeri. The Anatomy of Large Facebook Cascades. In *ICWSM*, 2013.

[16] eBiz MBA. http://www.ebizmba.com/articles/social-networking-websites, Mar. 2014.

[17] E. Gilbert, S. Bakhshi, S. Chang, and L. Terveen. "i need to try this"?: A statistical overview of pinterest. In *Proceedings of SIGCHI*, 2013.

[18] M. Gjoka, M. Kurant, and C. T. Butts. A Walk in Facebook: Uniform Sampling of Users in Online Social Networks. *CoRR*, 2009.

[19] A. Hanbury. Constructing cylindrical coordinate colour spaces. *Pattern Recogn. Lett.*, Mar. 2008.

[20] L. Hong, O. Dan, and B. D. Davison. Predicting popular messages in twitter. In *Proc. WWW*, 2011.

[21] P. Isola, J. Xiao, A. Torralba, and A. Oliva. What makes an image memorable? In *CVPR*, 2011.

[22] W. Jiang, A. Loui, and C. Cerosaletti. Automatic aesthetic value assessment in photographic images. In *ICME*, 2010.

[23] D. Joshi, R. Datta, Q.-T. Luong, E. Fedorovskaya, J. Z. Wang, J. Li, and J. Luo. Aesthetics and emotions in images: A computational perspective. In *IEEE Signal Processing Magazine*, 2011.

[24] Y. Ke, X. Tang, and F. Jing. The design of high-level features for photo quality assessment. In *CVPR*, 2006.

[25] A. Khosla, A. D. Sarma, and R. Hamid. What makes an image popular? In *WWW*, April 2014.

[26] K. Lerman and L. Jones. Social browsing on flickr. *CoRR*, abs/cs/0612047, 2006.

[27] J. Leskovec, L. Backstrom, and J. Kleinberg. Meme-tracking and the dynamics of the news cycle. KDD '09.

[28] C. Li and T. Chen. Aesthetic visual quality assessment of paintings. *J. Sel. Topics Signal Processing*, 2009.

[29] C. Li, A. C. Gallagher, A. C. Loui, and T. Chen. Aesthetic quality assessment of consumer photos with faces. In *ICIP*, 2010.

[30] D. G. Lowe. Object recognition from local scale-invariant features. In *Proc. of ICCV*, 1999.

[31] Y. Luo and X. Tang. Photo and video quality evaluation: Focusing on the subject. Proc. ECCV'08.

[32] J. Machajdik and A. Hanbury. Affective image classification using features inspired by psychology and art theory. In *ACM Multimedia*, 2010.

[33] S. A. Macskassy and M. Michelson. Why do people retweet? anti-homophily wins the day! In *ICWSM'11*.

[34] L. Marchesotti and F. Perronnin. Learning beautiful (and ugly) attributes. In *BMVC*. IEEE, 2013.

[35] L. Marchesotti, F. Perronnin, D. Larlus, and G. Csurka. Assessing the aesthetic quality of photographs using generic image descriptors. ICCV'11.

[36] S. A. Myers, C. Zhu, and J. Leskovec. Information diffusion and external influence in networks. In *Proc. of SIGKDD*, 2012.

[37] R. Ottoni, J. P. Pesce, D. B. L. Casas, G. F. Jr., W. M. Jr., P. Kumaraguru, and V. Almeida. Ladies first: Analyzing gender roles and behaviors in pinterest. In *ICWSM*, 2013.

[38] F. Perronnin, J. Sánchez, and T. Mensink. Improving the fisher kernel for large-scale image classification. In *Proceedings of ECCV*, 2010.

[39] J. Sánchez, F. Perronnin, T. Mensink, and J. J. Verbeek. Image classification with the fisher vector: Theory and practice. *IJCV*, 105, 2013.

[40] P. Sloan. www.cnet.com/news/pinterest-crazy-growth-lands-it-as-top-10-social-site, Jan. 2012.

[41] C. Smith. http://www.businessinsider.com/facebook-350-million-photos-each-day-2013-9, Sept. 2013.

[42] S. Stieglitz and L. Dang-Xuan. Political communication and influence through microblogging: An empirical analysis of sentiment in twitter messages and retweet behavior. In *Proc. of HICSS*, 2012.

[43] B. Suh, L. Hong, P. Pirolli, and E. H. Chi. Want to be retweeted? large scale analytics on factors impacting retweet in twitter network. In *Proc. SOCIALCOM'10*.

[44] B. Thomee and A. Popescu. Overview of the imageclef 2012 flickr photo annotation and retrieval task. In *CLEF*, 2012.

[45] J. van de Weijer, C. Schmid, and J. Verbeek. Learning color names from real-world images. In *CVPR*, 2007.

[46] C. Vu and D. M. Chandler. S3: A spectral and spatial sharpness measure. In *2009 First International Conference on Advances in Multimedia*, 2009.

[47] W.-N. Wang, Y.-L. Yu, and S.-M. Jiang. Image retrieval by emotional semantics: A study of emotional space and feature extraction. In *SMC*, 2006.

[48] D. Zarella. The social media scientist. http://danzarrella.com/, June 2013.

The New Blocs on the Block:
Using Community Forums to Foster New Neighbourhoods

Elizabeth M. Daly, Dominik Dahlem
Smarter Cities Technology Centre
IBM Research - Ireland
{dalyeliz,ddahle}@ie.ibm.com

Daniele Quercia
Yahoo Labs
Barcelona, Spain
dquercia@acm.org

ABSTRACT

Research has consistently shown that online tools increase social capital. In the context of neighbourhoods Hampton and Wellman have shown that in newly developed areas residents effectively used mailing lists to connect with each other, circulate information, and ask for help. The research question of whether similar findings would hold in the larger context of a city for a long period of time is still open. To tackle this research question, we have gathered the complete dataset of the most popular neighbourhood online forum in Dublin. In this dataset, we have people sharing a common purpose (blocs) who live in the same neighbourhood and interact online to ask for help, engage in local activities, and, more generally, have a better understanding of their physical community. Our analysis highlights the particularly concentrated usage in newly established developments where a pre-existing community may be absent. Additionally, these communications provide a valuable resource to understand local issues relevant to the community.

Categories and Subject Descriptors

H.1.2 [**User/Machine Systems**]: Human factors

Keywords

Online Communities; Social Capital; Citizen Engagement

1. INTRODUCTION

Settling in a new neighbourhood often poses the challenge of getting acquainted with the surroundings and establishing a community feeling that provides a comfortable and safe place to live. People living in physical communities often turn to existing residents to learn about their area and neighbourhood. Wellman and Wortley found neighbourhood ties play an important role for people concerning specific support such as home improvements and assistance in emergencies [32]. However what happens when all neighbours are new? What happens if the sense of community has yet to be established?

A community that is better connected helps establish social norms, provides a source of information about local issues and enables

the residents to mobilise around community-specific issues. Online communities have emerged to ease the transition into a new neighbourhood and to strengthen the ties with the local communities. A great deal of discussion has emerged around the transformation of local community in the internet age, however much research suggests that online communication can play a key role in supporting local communities instead of supplanting the physical one [30, 24, 14]. From assistance in home repairs to private yoga classes and complaints about noise, people increasingly carry out elements of their lives online.

This paper focuses on data collected on a website designed to support neighbours build a community. Our main research contribution is to study whether and, if so, how the newly established neighbourhoods are linked with four main forum features that might increase social capital – activity, geography, topics, and emotions. We find that, compared to well-established residential areas, newly-developed ones...

- ... use the forum more often;

- ... connect with geographically closer neighbours;

- ... talk about their real-world needs (e.g., DIY);

- ... express themselves using positive and negative emotion words.

These findings suggest that this neighbourhood-based online forum has been a valuable source of social capital, particularly in the absence of an established physical one and highlight that there is much higher activity in newly established residential areas. We employ social network analysis metrics in order to understand the connectivity between community members. Understanding the different engagement levels across counties can assist policy makers wishing to use social media to improve communication with citizens and foster a sense of community. Topic analysis and sentiment analysis are used to gather evidence as to which issues are discussed by the members and identify the general feelings expressed online. As a result, the online forum can be a key tool for policy makers to have a finger on the pulse of the community, identifying the needs of residents such as requirements for schools and transportation infrastructure. In order to analyse the points above, we utilise the three main methodologies of social network analysis, topic analysis, and sentiment analysis to gain a deeper and principled understanding of the posts associated with residential areas.

2. LITERATURE REVIEW

Social capital refers to features of social organisations such as networks, norms and trust that facilitate co-ordination, and co-operation for mutual benefit [22]. Online communities can provide a mechanism to foster social capital. In this section we review related work in the areas of online communities, the study of neighbourhoods and the study of technology and its potential role in neighbourhoods.

2.1 Online Communities

An online community can be defined as an Internet-connected collective of people who interact over time around a shared purpose, interest, or need [23]. Butler *et al.* examined what motivates users to invest in online communities focusing primarily on Listservs [2]. Though a large amount of social interaction on the web sustains pre-existing social ties between friends and family, a great deal of online interaction also occurs among people with no pre-existing relationships. They propose that people can benefit from online relationships as they create trust and provide a credible source of information, a form of social capital [22]. For example, people can now turn to online communities for important issues such as dealing with illness [5].

Online communities, however, only provides a technical infrastructure where social activity *may* take place [13]. As a result, it is important to understand what drives users to engage in a community. Ren, Kraut and Kiesler differentiate between identity and bond based online communities [23]. Identity-based communities are focused on the group identity as a whole where topics discussed are generally on-topic, and members feel a stronger association with the group rather than specific individuals. By contrast, bond-based communities tend to have more off-topic discussions and relationships are therefore more focused on ties between specific individuals.

Ellison *et al.* studied the use of Facebook in the context of a university campus. The study explored how it was used to build social capital, and was most useful to those with low self-esteem [7]. One could imagine a new neighbourhood community establishing itself could also benefit from online support networks.

2.2 The Study of Neighbourhoods

The study of neighbourhoods is not a recent phenomenon. Sociologists and urban planners have long studied the impact of social relationships, homogeneity, and group cohesion to understand the neighbourhood effect in the off-line world. Policy makers have begun to consider "local communities" and their interactions and evolution as a mechanism to tackle and gain insights into social issues such as crime, deprivation and social exclusion [8]. Lang and Hornburg examined how social capital affects housing and community development and found efforts to promote regeneration of disadvantaged neighbourhoods are more effective in areas where social capital is high [19]. Neighbourhoods play a strong role in promoting a sense of community and social cohesion [8]. Sampson *et al.* defined the term "collective efficacy" as a combination of social cohesion of a group and people's ability to collectively intervene and act upon a common interest [25]. They found that collective efficacy is negatively associated with violence. Helliwell found that the ability to easily meet and interact with neighbours in friendly ways and a feeling of belonging to one's community has an impact on trust in neighbours, which in turn has an impact on wellbeing [18].

2.3 The Study of Technology and Neighbourhoods

Hampton and Wellman ask "What is the Internet doing to local community?" [30]. Online communities and technology can be seen as a mechanism to foster social capital. Their research focused on studying a new housing development of Netville where many households were equipped with high speed internet access. Additionally, the community had its own mailing list where members circulated local information and asked for help. The authors found that the combination of online and off-line interactions enabled discussion around local issues and enhanced the sense of community. Resnick and Shah explored the impact of creating shared neighbourhood photo directories and found similarly positive results [24].

Hampton went on in 2007 to expand his study of communities in the e-Neighbourhoods project by examining four neighbourhoods (an apartment, a gated community and two suburban communities), three of which had mailing lists and the other had a neighbourhood website [14]. He found participation levels in online interventions varied depending on neighbourhood characteristics, especially depending on residential stability. The participation level of people living in the apartment block were low compared to the other communities. Through interviews the authors found agreement that there was not a strong existing sense of community. However, when queried residents expressed their desire to engage in additional social contact.

More recently, Harris and Flouch found that online communication through neighbourhood forums stimulates face-to-face connection, supports reciprocal assistance and favours [15, 16]. Both this study and Hampton's found that lurkers do not benefit as much as active participants in the local online community and therefore understanding active participation in these networks plays an important role [15, 14, 14].

To sum up, previous work has not quantified the extent to which neighbourhood online forums are used by newcomers to "get started" in the context of an entire city. Our main research question is to study whether and, if so, how engagement with neighbourhood online forums in new developments differ from that in established areas. As opposed to current qualitative literature on the subject, we will conduct a quantitative study on how these forums are used differently across a variety of dimensions. To address this, we set out to study geographic-based communities that evolve around specific neighbourhoods in Dublin.

3. DATA DESCRIPTION

Neighbours.ie is an online community focusing around physical ones. The site started in 2006 as an Irish community based online forum organised around specific neighbourhoods and residential developments. The site had peak usage of over 3k posts a month in 2007 and has since declined somewhat in activity. Yet this data provides great insight into people's concerns and how these are a reflection of the local urban setting.

3.1 Dublin Property Scene

In order to understand the importance of activity levels on forums surrounding one's local neighbourhood, we need to shed some light around the economic climate of Ireland and Dublin, in particular in recent years. Financial innovation and liberalisation of the Irish market lead to a significant increase in available mortgage credit, even by international standards. The supply of credit had the consequence of pronounced activities in developing residential areas. As people moved into their new homes the sense of a local community was mainly absent. Online forums provided a means of coordinating on a multitude of issues that may arise with new buildings/developments and related infrastructural problems. This paper very much represents a social study to investigate concerns that are publicly discussed and to show how physical neighbourhoods and online communities augment each other.

3.2 Neighbours.ie

Our data consists of a crawl of the Neighbours.ie website for all County Dublin based forums from the start of the online forum in February 2006 until December 2011. This amounts to 20773 threads and 110317 posts contributed by 8801 authors[1]. The forums are organised in a loose hierarchy of 20 root forums representing different post codes in Dublin and 5 forums related to the site in general. As a result, each forum can be linked to a geographic region and forums vary in terms of granularity. Some forums represent entire areas, others are sub-forums to reflect specific apartment blocks or developments. There are 718 unique forums, but only 474 of these have more than one thread which is typically the welcome thread created by the moderators. Generally, users posting on the respective forums are members of the site but they may also post as guests selecting a new user name every time. Over 98% of the posts are contributed by members.

We manually classified each neighbourhood into the following categories: area, street, mature development and new development. The date when a development became active was manually assigned with the help of data from newspapers articles, property websites and online forums. The neighbourhood categories are defined as follows:

- *Area:* An area is defined as a region where there is no singular residential development and the region goes beyond a single street or road. This includes areas defined by a posts code, town, suburb or village area. For example, Dublin 2 or South Docklands Area.

- *Street:* A street is defined as a forum where there is no clear association with a specific development and the title of the forum suggests it reflects a specific street. For example, Baggot Street or Mountjoy Square.

- *Mature Development*: A mature development is defined as a neighbourhood where the dwellings were built by a specific developer creating a collection of homes. This can include housing estates, gated communities and apartment blocks. For example, Wedgewood Estate or Pembroke Square Apartments.

- *New Development*: We define a new development as one that was built within the last 10 years, using the same criteria for a mature development where it refers to well defined collection of homes built at approximately the same time by the same developer. For example, Shelbourne Park Apartment or Bloomfield Park.

Though a large proportion of the forums were created by the website administrations, any user could create and add a new neighbourhood discussion forum. Figure 1 a) shows the break down based on the four different categories: 35% of the forums are centred around new developments, however mature developments are also present making up 25% of the forums. Therefore both types of neighbourhoods are relatively well captured on the basis of forum

---

[1]For access to the data please contact the authors.

Distribution	Mean in mature	Mean in new	p-value
#posts	1.82	3.51	< 0.001
#posters	1.49	2.63	< 0.001
#threads	1.65	2.83	< 0.001
$\frac{\#posts}{\#threads}$	0.73	1.14	< 0.001

Table 1: Mann-Whitney test for the log of the means of our activity metrics: mature vs. new developments.

presence. The forums were manually geocoded and the author locations were inferred based on the weighted average of the location of forums they post to.

4. THE STUDY

We explore the relationship between online forums and the physical communities they represent. In particular, we now study how the presence of city newcomers is linked with four main forum features that might increase social capital – activity, geography, topics, and emotions.

4.1 New Neighbourhoods and Online Activity

Activity levels of an online community can be seen as indications of health of the community, how many people engaged in the forums and what the levels of engagement are. Prior work has shown that people turn to their social connections as sources of information and support [32]. Social capital researchers have found social ties with friends and neighbours are related to indices of psychological well-being, such as self-esteem and satisfaction with life [17]. Given new developments are less likely to have an established sense of community we propose that users turn to online communities in the absence of a physically established one.

We analyse the activity levels based on the type of community and the city regions. Figure 1 b) shows a boxplot of the number of posts in each forum for each neighbourhood type. The engagement levels for new developments is significantly higher than in mature developments with the least amount of engagement for forums that represent streets.

In order to further demonstrate statistical significance of variance in the numbers of posts, posters, and threads in mature developments and new developments we perform the Mann-Whitney test on the log of the means and obtain the results reported in Table 1. We confirm our hypothesis that the true differences in the means for all our activity metrics in mature developments are lower than those in new developments.

We find that forums associated with newly developed neighbourhoods tend to be more active than old neighbourhoods – they have higher number of posts, posters, and threads.

4.2 Newcomers and Their Social Network

Small densely connected networks are often associated with high levels of social and emotional support [22, 2]. In the context of neighbourhoods Sampson *et al.* defined "collective efficacy" as a combination of social cohesion of a group and people's ability to collectively intervene and act upon a common interest [25]. In relation to neighbourhood forums this could range from coordinating around local issues such as the requirement for new schools to mobilizing and coordinating with management companies.

We investigate the topological relationship of users with respect to the forums they post to. The social network graph of the communities is generated to highlight clustered communities where en-

(a) Degree distribution (in log)

(b) Cluster coefficient distribution (in log)

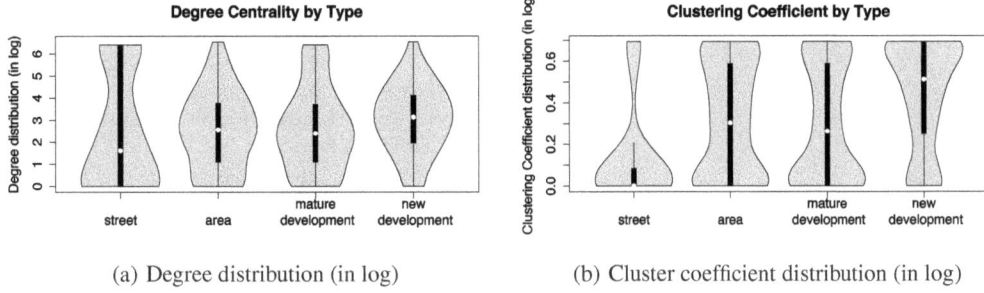

Figure 2: Network Statistics

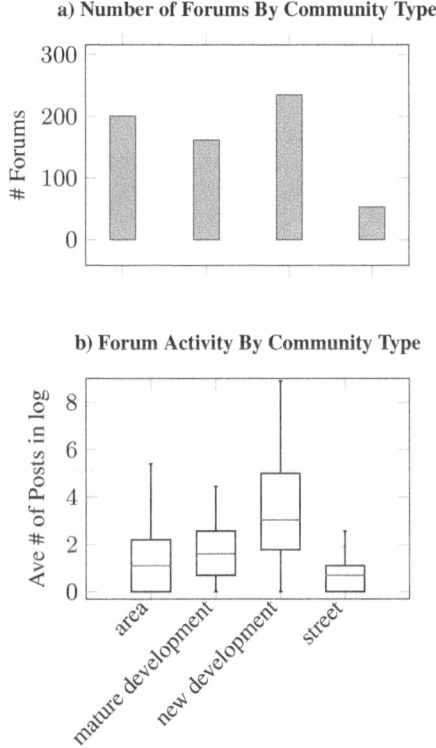

a) Number of Forums By Community Type

b) Forum Activity By Community Type

Figure 1: Forum Statistics

gagement is strong. Given residents in new developments may need to organise themselves in order to coordinate with management companies and start to form a residential community we test the following hypothesis:

In order to explore the different topological social network across the different community types the online interactions are used to generate a social graph.

Each vertex in this graph represents a member if the website and users may post to multiple forums. A directed edge e_{ij} exists from user v_i to user v_j, if user v_i has posted to a thread to which also member v_j posted. More formally, this process of constructing the graph corresponds to the projection of the bipartite graph model of users and their relationship to existing threads onto the user-to-user graph. We also associate the number of overlapping threads between two users as the edge weight. Nearly 90% of the authors only posted to a single forum meaning their social links are only with those in the same neighbourhood forum. 4% of the users

showed no real affinity with a single forum and though it could be assumed these users are spammers, when examining these users we identified only 5 of these as members posting advertising services such as cleaning and painting. The remainder were outreach messages such as highlighting Fingal community services and surveys, seeking volunteers, youth club notices and education programs[2].

- *Degree Centrality* captures the total number of unique other members a person has engaged with by contributing to the same thread. The degree of a vertex v_i is the number of edges e_{ij} that are connected to the vertex [10].

$$C_D(i) = \sum_{k=1}^{N} a(i,k) \qquad (1)$$

where $a(i,k) = 1$ if a direct link exists between v_i and v_k and $i \neq k$.

- *Node Clustering Coefficient* is a measure of how complete/connected the neighbourhood of a node is, where the neighbourhood of a vertex is defined as the set of vertices that are immediately adjacent to vertex v_i [29]. The clustering coefficient for v_i in an undirected graph is given by:

$$C_C(i) = \frac{2|e_{jk}|}{k_i(k_i - 1)} : v_j, v_k \in N_i, e_{jk} \in E \qquad (2)$$

Figure 2 shows the distribution of degree centrality and node clustering coefficient. Forums representing new developments have the highest mean logarithm of the degree centrality however mature developments do show a number of members with a high degree centrality giving evidence to users contributing to a wide variety of threads. Forums representing streets have the highest variance with some highly connected users but a large number of users interacting with relatively few other members. However, figure 2 b) shows the clustering coefficient and cohesiveness of the street communities is very low. New developments on the other hand show the highest clustering of all the development types. It could be assumed that this is due to residents coming together on a small number of welcome threads, however, we found welcome threads tended to have very little engagement. Mature developments are bi-modal with a higher density around low and high clustering coefficients.

The Mann-Whitney test on the logarithm of degree and clustering coefficient shows a significant difference of the means for property types area and new development (p-value < 0.001), mature

---

[2]It should be noted these forums are moderated and therefore spamming posts have more than likely been removed meaning those that remain and are posted to many different forums are more likely to be genuine.

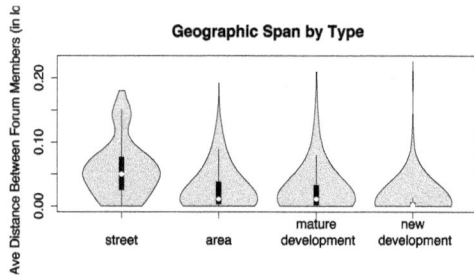

Figure 3: Distribution of average Spatial Distance Between Forum Members by Type

and new developments (p-value < 0.001), new development and street (only for the logarithm of the degree with a p-value < 0.001), and finally area and street (only for the logarithm of the clustering coefficient with a p-value < 0.001).

4.3 Newcomers and Geography of their Communication

Castells states that "people identify themselves primarily with their locality" [3]. Studies show that people communicate more through the Internet, and collaborate more effectively, when they are in closer proximity [31]. Liben-Nowell et al. supported this finding in the context of the popular blogging platform of Live-Journal [20]. Ren, Kraut ad Kiesler differentiate between identity-based online communities where members feel a stronger association with the group and topic as a whole rather than focusing on individual connections in the case of a bond-based community [23]. Newcomers tend to be more welcomed in identity-based communities since the bond is between the community as a whole rather than specific members. Online communities based on neighbourhoods can be seen as identity-based communities where people socialise around local issues.

In order to explore how neighbourhood community types differ in their geographic property we examine the spatial distribution of the members actively engaged in the community. Each member is assigned a geographic location as a weighted average of the forum location the member posts to. Using this inferred location the average distance between posting members and the forum location may be used to calculated the geographic span of the forum. Figure 3 shows distribution of the average distance between the users who post to that community. New developments tend to have a lower geographic span compared to the other developments. Forums representing streets are associated with a relatively large geographically clustered.

Population change and geographic span in new developments do not correlate, but the average geographic span of the posters for forums in new developments is *lower* than that for forums in old developments (Mann-Whitney test, p-value < 0.01) – so indeed "people identify themselves primarily with their locality", which is more pronounced if those people are newcomers.

4.4 Newcomers and Topics

When studying the new housing development of Netville, Hampton and Wellman found that the neighbourhood mailing list enabled discussion around local issues [30]. More recently, the study commissioned by the Ford Foundation found similar patterns on community forums where discussions revolved around issues of local interest [9]. We propose that online neighbourhood communities are identity-based where members connect around local issues and

that members turn to the online community as a source of information and support around these issues.

Topic modelling is used to infer a topic associated with a set of words that co-occur significantly in a given text [26]. In our analysis we use Latent Dirichlet Allocation (LDA) to infer topics from our forum posts [1] [3].

We aggregated all posts from a given thread into a single document and applied Porter's Stemming Algorithm to the text. This text was then used to generate a topic model, selecting a topic number of 20. Table 2 shows a list of stemmed key words associated with each topic with a manually assigned label. As can be seen, the threads include residents discussing a variety of topics ranging from build related issues, management company discussions and community outreach posts. When looking at the key words associated with "Plumbing" it is interesting to note that along with words like "water", "pump" and "boiler" is the word "anyon" which is the stemmed version of "anyone" which suggests this topic primarily arises in the form of a question asking "does anyone know how to..." or "does anyone know a good plumber?" supporting our premise that users are potentially turning to this online community to assist in problem solving or to find recommendations for these kinds of services when moving to a new area. We can also see evidence of local community posts around libraries, social tea events and education.

We focused our analysis on forums with a minimum of 20 posts, which yields 20567 threads to analyse. These threads were assigned a probability distribution over the individual topics. Each thread is then assigned the topic that is most represented in the thread. The topic probability distribution captures how strongly the posts in the thread reflect a given topic, some threads may possibly include a number of different topics and as a result some threads do not exhibit a strong relationship to one specific topic.

Figure 4 shows a heat map of the different thread topics for the different types of communities. Topics most prevalent to new developments are clustered to the left, while those most present in mature developments are clustered towards the right. The topic of plumbing, services, security issues and new build issues are the most discussed topics for new developments showing members are turning to the forum to gain information and potentially support around these issues. Services are an area of concern as they tend to be slow at coming online for new residential areas and members are seeking advice on service providers. Management companies are also actively discussed, as it is common practise for management companies to be hired to handle the administration of the new developments. Active topics for forums representing areas are community events and residents committee. Although forums representing areas are less active, those that are active are related to community engagement and organisation. Community events, home repairs and residential communities are active topics for mature developments as they maintain their more established neighbourhood.

4.5 Newcomers and Emotions

Members of neighbourhood forums share more than information only. They share norms and values within a culture of support and self help [28]. When connecting with companions in fortune and misfortune or in the organisation of bottom-up local activities, forum users connect with each other at an emotional level. This practically translates in the use of emotion words. Kivran-Swaine and Naaman found a link between the number of followers on twitter and the expression of emotions. They propose this could be due to

---

[3] We used the MALLET software to infer the topic models [21].

56

Topic ID	Label	Key Words
1	Plumbing	water, problem, heat, work, turn, pump, boiler, anyon, switch, time
2	Community Engagement	communiti, fingal, inform, pleas, group, librari, support, contact, local, partnership
3	Waste Management	bin, rubbish, clean, collect, estat, area, dump, green, day, garden
4	New Build	snag, week, block, move, anyon, told, builder, complet, hous, hope
5	Services	sky, dish, servic, ntl, broadband, phone, month, channel, connect, instal
6	Moderator/Welcome	forum, post, moder, ani, pleas, free, privat, send, neighbour, feel
7	Residents Committee	resid, meet, committe, issu, ani, post, pleas, contact, associ, peopl
8	Property Prices	price, year, properti, bank, market, interest, cours, hous, ireland, local
9	Reflective	peopl, don't, i'm, time, good, onli, live, realli, thing, ani
10	Family Area	kid, hous, dog, estat, car, area, road, live, children, peopl
11	Community Outreach	tea, event, fingal, contact, network, ticket, danc, citizen, pleas, parent
12	Community Events	school, club, educ, area, pleas, interest, class, gym, communiti, year
13	Security Issues	door, secur, block, night, car, alarm, gate, lock, nois, time
14	Management Company	manag, compani, pay, fee, year, charg, resid, servic, develop, agm
15	Volunteer	befriend, dublin, volunt, fundrais, servic, north, support, someon, experienc, train
16	Local	good, shop, open, great, food, veri, http, night, pub, nice
17	Home Repairs	floor, window, door, wall, hous, anyon, room, ani, paint, problem
18	Transport	road, bus, dublin, traffic, rout, servic, citi, stop, station, area
19	Parking	park, car, space, clamp, peopl, road, resid, visitor, spot, underground
20	Planning Permission	plan, develop, area, site, road, build, dublin, permiss, unit, propos

Table 2: Forum Thread Topic Keywords

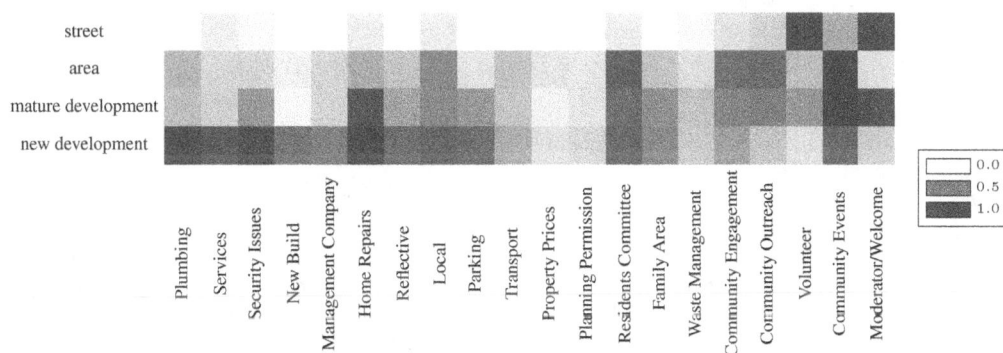

Figure 4: Thread Topic Heat Map By Neighbourhood Category

shared emotional experiences creating more engaging content for people to consume [27]. Moving into a new area can be a combination of highs and lows and given many residents are experiencing this change at the same time.

In this section we assess the sentiment associated with a body of text. Global sentiment can be assessed and their temporal periods quantified using the micro-blogging platform Twitter [11]. Golder *et al.*˙ used the Linguistic Inquiry and Word Count (LIWC) lexicon that provides measures of positive and negative affect. In our analysis we quantify sentiment according to [6] who measure societal-level happiness in Twitter streams according to numerical estimates of happiness of over 10,000 words. The happiness values associated with those words were collected through Amazon's Mechanical Turk and does not rely on word stemming. The important aspect of their approach is two-fold. First, the word list is based on the most frequent words appearing in Twitter, Google Books, music lyrics, and the New York Times. Second, each word has been evaluated 50 times independently on a 9 point integer scale with respect to happiness where 5 represents a neutral value. Utilising this association of happiness to given words allows us to filter the neighbours.ie forum accordingly in order to assign a happiness value to each known word. The sentiment of each post on the forum is then independently quantified as the weighted average with respect to the frequency f_i of a word w_i given the estimated happiness value $h_{avg}(w_i)$ is set to:

$$h_{avg} = \frac{\sum_1^N h_{avg}(w_i) f_i}{\sum_i^N f_i}. \qquad (3)$$

In the same fashion as in [6] we only consider words falling in the range of $5 - \Delta h_{avg} < h_{avg} < 5 + \Delta h_{avg}$, where $\Delta h_{avg} = 1.0$ to remove some high-frequency behaviour. Absolute measures of happiness as defined above, however, do not capture local differences in sentiment. To overcome this, we normalise the happiness score of a pool of texts by subtracting the global happiness score including all texts. This allows us to evaluate the sentiment of a particular forum with respect to the average overall sentiment of all texts. We analyse the sentiment on forums containing at least 20 posts, using the methodology discussed in [6]. It is important to note there were no forums focused around streets that contained more than 20 posts and therefore this category is omitted from this analysis. For the entire collection of posts, we calculated an average happiness measure based on the sentiment of the text and calculated an overall happiness value of 5.9 (where a value of 1 is completely negative and 9 is completely positive). We also compute a happiness value for each forum compared to the average. For a given forum, and a given pool of posts, we first find all posts from that forum and measure the average happiness of the subset of posts within the forum. The average happiness is then subtracted from that value. In this way, we see which forums diverge from the average.

There is little difference in the average sentiment across the different neighbourhood types, however, the true difference is seen in figure 5 which shows the distribution of thread post sentiment. New developments exhibit the widest range of emotions, fluctuating between negative and positive. This is partly due to the initial excitement of new residents and the expressed desire to form a positive new community contrasting with problems associated with new builds and management companies expressing frustration. A more positive sentiment is associated with developments focused around areas. This is mainly due to the prevalence of topics such as community engagement and community events being advertised as we have seen in our topic analysis.

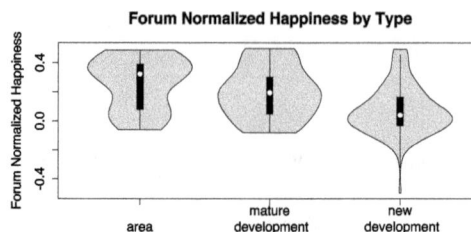

Figure 5: Forum Normalised Happiness Distribution

The Mann-Whitney test shows a significant difference of the means of the sentiment shown in figure 5 between the property types of area and new development (p-value < 0.001) and mature and new developments (p-value < 0.01).

5. CASE STUDY: CELTIC HALL

During the Irish building boom of 2000s, a number of the property developments suffered building-related issues following completion. Our data set includes one that hit the media in October 2011. We use the forum of this development as a case study in evaluating the sentiment and topic analysis of the community and understanding what role the forum plays in connecting residents.

In August 2006, the forum was created and interestingly the development had not even been completed yet. The forum was used by people who had purchased property and were reaching out to their new community for assistance.

> Hi, I was just wondering if anyone who bought in the
> first phase got follow up calls from the estate agent/builders.
> - bigchicken. 22-08-2006

We notice that, the sentiment of the interactions for the first 4 months is positive in figure 6. Residents begin to discuss their communications with the management company and this topic is highly present in the first year. The forum also included threads related to the topic of community outreach aiming building a new local community.

> SO whats gonna be the new local ??? I think we need
> a better booozer than the —– inn ! me thinks the ——
> residents bar. any better suggestions ? :-)
> - namelock. 11-11-2006

In December 2006, there is a drop in sentiment because on December 12th a television show aired discussing building development and their lack of regulation. This resulted in much concern amongst the residents and also sparked the first discussion to mobilise the newly forming community.

> Hi all, Perhaps it is time to organise the first Celtic
> Hall face to face Residents meeting and start making
> some real decisions on the issues so far experienced by
> those snagging, and the rather alarming issues raised
> by Prime Time last night.
> - Harry. 12-12-2006

Not only did the members turn to the forum to coordinate, but they also expressed that the forum was a source of comfort.

> hey all im feeling a little bit better then before i don't
> know why but earlier dismorning i was just in the height
> of it but this forum really helps....
> -celtichall_audrey 12-12-2006

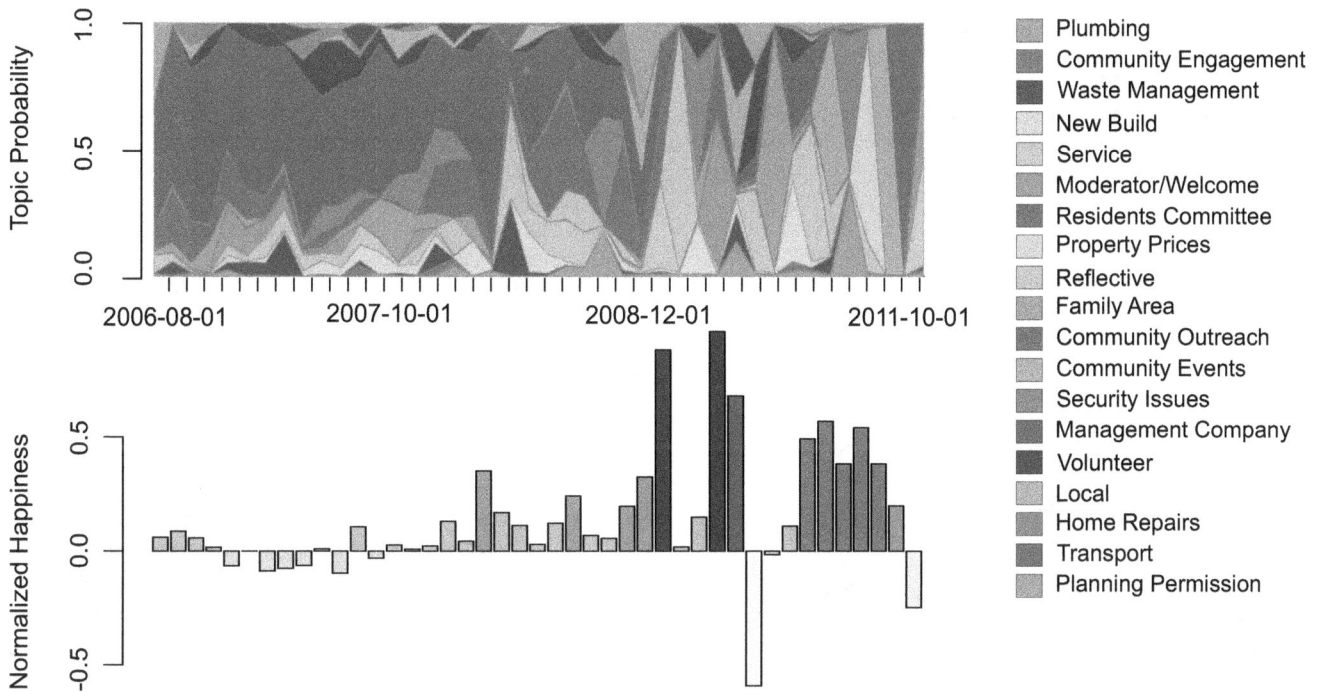

Figure 6: Celtic Hall - Sentiment versus Topic Distribution

The negative sentiment continues for the next few months as the completion date continues to be pushed back while residents use the forum to update each other with any new information. The sentiment returns to positive around May 2007 as residents start to take ownership and topics such as "new build", "services" and "home repairs" start to be discussed and reducing the intense discussion on the topic of the "management company".

> Hey all Just back from my apartment for which I am now the key holder...I am absolutely delighted...To everybody who is still waiting to snag etc.. dont worry it will happen and soon we all will be neighbours. Best of Luck to you all and Im looking forward to meeting you soon !!!
> -Macker. 23-04-2007

During this time, residents turn to the forum to ask questions about their apartment such as how to manage the heating or asking for advice on services. The community reduced in activity after residents had started to settle in. As can be seen the final month of December 2011 has a negative sentiment and it coincides with when residents had to be evacuated due to health and safety concerns. Though usage was less frequent following the move in, members returned to the forum to voice their concerns with the final postings in the dataset below:

> I am posting a note regarding last weeks meeting with the Dublin City Council (15.09.11) and getting legal representation for owners as a joint effort, as this issue is of immense importance and one that will leave our properties unsell-able and unlivable but yet still mortgaged. We have less than 3 weeks to take action and create our own representation. Please reply to this if interested in meeting in the Hilton with a recommended solicitor who is willing to take this case. -R2D2 19-09-2011

As can be seen from this final posting, residents turned to the online community to share their concerns and offer members the chance to meet off-line and coordinate their actions. Though this case study provides primarily anecdotal evidence of forum use, it gives a sample of a number of real world interactions where the forum played an important role for neighbourhood members.

6. DISCUSSION AND CONCLUSION

Theoretical Implications. We have explored the online use of neighbourhood forums representing physical neighbourhoods. We have shown that even though the number of forums are relatively evenly represented by new and mature developments, activity levels and use are higher for new neighbourhoods. This finding supports the proposition that new residents may be turning to online forums in order to assist in establishing a community in the absence of a pre-existing physical one. Our findings suggest that given a digital forum of communication, residents of new developments are more likely to engage as an online community. Forums representing streets and areas are used significantly less. We propose this may be due to a lack of key topics that engage users such as interaction with management companies, shared experiences with build problems and fewer new residents arriving around a similar time frame. However, further investigation and analysis needs to be explored to support this hypothesis. Of the active forums representing areas, figure 4 shows the most popular topics included residents committees and community based discussions. This suggests a need to seed communities of more mature areas, streets and developments with topics and issues relevant to members in order to promote user engagement.

Practical Implications. Encouraging residents to interact through online forums that focus around local issues could have significant benefits for citizens and policy makers alike. Many social problems go beyond the control of government policy makers. However, enabling and supporting neighbourhoods to connect and foster a sense of community can aid in shaping attitudes and social norms. Additionally, strong social networks have been linked to access to jobs [12], influencing health [4], and a source for help in times of need [32]. Online communities may also provide a valuable source of information when understanding the needs of citizens. For example, this work has highlighted the need for services and transportation in newly developed regions.

Limitations. This study has a number of limitations. The age profile of the members were not available to us and, given the preference for a younger generation to voice their concerns online, the results may disproportionally represent some citizens than others. Likewise internet access in the home may have levels of income bias. We also found a number of posts discouraging members to publicly discuss issues related to their community for fear of gaining a bad reputation and of negative effect on house prices. Use of the forums have declined somewhat in recent years. One potential avenue for investigation is to explore whether once the connection to the physical community has become more established and new issues arise less frequently, members may turn less to the online community. Further, we may find indications of reduced activity levels linked to a reduction in volatility of member sentiment over time. Another limitation is that our results do not speak to causality. Though we have found that engagement levels are higher for new developments we cannot necessarily conclude that these interactions lead to active support communities. One avenue for future work can include examining in more depth the text and content of member interactions seeking examples on supportive communication, which can also be followed up with surveys and interviews. Harris and Flouch found that online communication through neighbourhood forums did indeed stimulate face-to-face connection and support reciprocal assistance and favours [15, 16].

We have addressed the research question of understanding the online interactions of neighbourhood forums which work towards a 'connected community'. For the first time, we have been able to conduct a *quantitative* study on an *entire* medium-sized city, and that has shown new insights on the geographic properties of these communities. Researchers have long been studying online communities in relation to physical neighborhoods, but the relationship between these two types of communities has been rarely investigated in a quantitative way (mainly because of lack of data). To answer the question asked by Hampton and Wellman of "what is the Internet doing to local community?" [30], we believe it is playing an important role in encouraging residents to come together around local issues, thus, building a new bloc.

7. ACKNOWLEDGMENTS

We wish to thank Gary Mc Ginty and Marco Capacchietti from the neighbours.ie team for technical assistance while crawling the site and providing permission to collect the data.

8. REFERENCES

[1] D. M. Blei, A. Y. Ng, and M. I. Jordan. Latent dirichlet allocation. *J. Mach. Learn. Res.*, 3:993–1022, Mar. 2003.

[2] B. Butler, L. Sproull, S. Kiesler, and R. Kraut. Community Effort in Online Groups: Who Does the Work and Why? 2001.

[3] M. Castells. *The power of identity : second edition with a new preface.* Wiley-Blackwell, 2010.

[4] N. A. Christakis and J. H. Fowler. The Spread of Obesity in a Large Social Network over 32 Years. *N Engl J Med*, 357(4):370–379, July 2007.

[5] K. P. Davison, J. W. Pennebaker, and S. S. Dickerson. Who talks? The social psychology of illness support groups. *The American psychologist*, 55(2):205–217, Feb. 2000.

[6] P. S. Dodds, K. D. Harris, I. M. Kloumann, C. A. Bliss, and C. M. Danforth. Temporal patterns of happiness and information in a global social network: Hedonometrics and Twitter. Dec. 2011.

[7] N. Ellison, C. Steinfield, and C. Lampe. Spatially Bounded Online Social Networks and Social Capital: The Role of Facebook. In *Annual Conference of the International Communication Association*, 2006.

[8] R. Forrest and A. Kearns. Social Cohesion, Social Capital and the Neighbourhood. *Urban Studies*, 38(12):2125–2143, Nov. 2001.

[9] T. F. Foundation. Inclusive Social Media Project: Participatory Evaluation. Technical report, 2010.

[10] L. C. Freeman. Centrality in Social Networks Conceptual Clarification. *Social networks*, 1(3):215–239, 1978-1979.

[11] S. A. Golder and M. W. Macy. Diurnal and seasonal mood vary with work, sleep, and daylength across diverse cultures. *Science*, 333(6051):1878–1881, Sept. 2011.

[12] M. S. Granovetter. The Strength of Weak Ties. *American Journal of Sociology*, 78(6):1360–1380, May 1973.

[13] J. Hagel and A. G. Armstrong. *Net gain: expanding markets through virtual communities*. Harvard Business School Press, Boston, MA, USA, 1997.

[14] K. N. Hampton. Neighborhoods in the Network Society the e-Neighbors study. *Information, Communication & Society*, 10(5):714–748, Oct. 2007.

[15] K. Harris and H. Flouch. Social Capital and Cohesion. Technical report, Online neighbourhood networks study, 2010.

[16] K. Harris and H. Flouch. The research context. Technical report, Online neighbourhood networks study, 2010.

[17] J. F. Helliwell and R. D. Putnam. The social context of well-being. *PHILOSOPHICAL TRANSACTIONS-ROYAL SOCIETY OF LONDON SERIES B BIOLOGICAL SCIENCES*, pages 1435–1446, 2004.

[18] J. F. Helliwell and S. Wang. Trust and Well-Being. *International Journal of Wellbeing*, 1(1):42–78, 2011.

[19] R. E. Lang and S. P. Hornburg. What is social capital and why is it important to public policy? *Housing Policy Debate*, 9(1):1–16, Jan. 1998.

[20] D. Liben-Nowell, J. Novak, R. Kumar, P. Raghavan, and A. Tomkins. Geographic routing in social networks. *Proceedings of the National Academy of Sciences of the United States of America*, 102(33):11623–11628, Aug. 2005.

[21] A. K. McCallum. MALLET: A Machine Learning for Language Toolkit., 2002.

[22] R. D. Putnam. *Bowling Alone: The Collapse and Revival of American Community*. Simon & Schuster, June 2000.

[23] Y. Ren, R. Kraut, and S. Kiesler. Applying Common Identity and Bond Theory to Design of Online Communities. *Organization Studies*, 28(3):377–408, Mar. 2007.

[24] P. Resnick and V. Shah. Photo Directories: A Tool for Organizing Sociability in Neighborhoods and Organizations. Sept. 2002.

[25] R. J. Sampson, S. W. Raudenbush, and F. Earls. Neighborhoods and Violent Crime: A Multilevel Study of Collective Efficacy. *Science*, 277(5328):918–924, Aug. 1997.

[26] M. Steyvers and T. Griffiths. *Probabilistic Topic Models*. Lawrence Erlbaum Associates, 2007.

[27] F. K. Swaine and M. Naaman. Network properties and social sharing of emotions in social awareness streams. In *Proceedings of the ACM 2011 conference on Computer supported cooperative work*, CSCW '11, pages 379–382, New York, NY, USA, 2011. ACM.

[28] M. Van den Boomen. Leven op het Net. De sociale betekenis van virtuele gemeenschappen. Technical report, 2000.

[29] D. J. Watts and S. H. Strogatz. Collective dynamics of 'small-world' networks. *Nature*, 393(6684):440–442, June 1998.

[30] B. Wellman and C. A. Haythornthwaite, editors. *The Internet in Everyday Life*. Blackwell Publishers, 1 edition, Dec. 2002.

[31] B. Wellman, B. Hogan, K. Berg, J. Boase, J.-A. Carrasco, R. Côté, J. Kayahara, T. L. M. Kennedy, and P. Tran. *Connected Lives: The Project*, chapter 8. Springer, 2006.

[32] B. Wellman and S. Wortley. Different Strokes from Different Folks: Community Ties and Social Support. *The American Journal of Sociology*, 96(3):558–588, 1990.

Mapping the UK Webspace:
Fifteen Years of British Universities on the Web

Scott A. Hale
Oxford Internet Institute
University of Oxford
1 St Giles, Oxford UK
scott.hale@oii.ox.ac.uk

Taha Yasseri
Oxford Internet Institute
University of Oxford
1 St Giles, Oxford UK
taha.yasseri@...

Josh Cowls
Oxford Internet Institute
University of Oxford
1 St Giles, Oxford UK
josh.cowls@...

Eric T. Meyer
Oxford Internet Institute
University of Oxford
1 St Giles, Oxford UK
eric.meyer@...

Ralph Schroeder
Oxford Internet Institute
University of Oxford
1 St Giles, Oxford UK
ralph.schroeder@...

Helen Margetts
Oxford Internet Institute
University of Oxford
1 St Giles, Oxford UK
helen.margetts@...

ABSTRACT

This paper maps the national UK web presence on the basis of an analysis of the .uk domain from 1996 to 2010. It reviews previous attempts to use web archives to understand national web domains and describes the dataset. Next, it presents an analysis of the .uk domain, including the overall number of links in the archive and changes in the link density of different second-level domains over time. We then explore changes over time within a particular second-level domain, the academic subdomain .ac.uk, and compare linking practices with variables, including institutional affiliation, league table ranking, and geographic location. We do not detect institutional affiliation affecting linking practices and find only partial evidence of league table ranking affecting network centrality, but find a clear inverse relationship between the density of links and the geographical distance between universities. This echoes prior findings regarding offline academic activity, which allows us to argue that real-world factors like geography continue to shape academic relationships even in the Internet age. We conclude with directions for future uses of web archive resources in this emerging area of research.

Categories and Subject Descriptors

H.5.4 [**Information Interfaces and Presentation (e.g. HCI)**]: Hypertext/Hypermedia; H.5.3 [**Information Systems**]: Group and Organization Interfaces—Web-based interaction

Keywords

Web Archives; World Wide Web; Network Analysis; Hyperlink Analysis; Big Data; Academic Web

WebSci'14, June 23–26, 2014, Bloomington, IN, USA.
Copyright is held by the owner/author(s). Publication rights licensed to ACM.
ACM 978-1-4503-2622-3/14/06 ...$15.00.
http://dx.doi.org/10.1145/2615569.2615691.

1. INTRODUCTION

The World Wide Web is enormous and is in constant flux, with more web content lost to time than is currently accessible via the live web. The growing body of archived web material available to researchers is thus potentially immensely valuable as a record of important aspects of modern society, but there have previously been few tools available to facilitate research using archived web materials [6]. Nevertheless, with the development of new tools and techniques such as those used in this paper, the use of web archives both to understand the history of the web itself as well as to shed light on broader changes in society is emerging as a promising research area [7]. The web is likely to provide insight into social changes just as other historical artifacts, such as newspapers and books, have done for scholars interested in the pre-digital world. As the web becomes increasingly embedded in all spheres of everyday life and the number of webpages continues to grow, there is a compelling case to be made for examining changes in both the structure and content of the web. However, while interfaces such as the Wayback Machine[1] allow access to individual webpages one at a time, there have been relatively few attempts to work with large collections of web archive data using computational approaches across the corpus. This paper provides a longitudinal analysis of the UK national web domain, .uk, and the academic second-level domain, .ac.uk, in order to demonstrate the benefits and challenges of this type of analysis.

2. BACKGROUND

2.1 Archiving national web domains

National web domains represent one approach to web archive analysis for researchers seeking an overview of a single country's web presence. A particular national web domain offers the potential of both diversity and completeness in its coverage [2], although there are limitations in terms of generalizability beyond the country in question and frequently in terms of the completeness of the analysis based on technical factors (see below). At the same time, however, limiting

---
[1] http://web.archive.org/

the focus to a single country also has the potential to introduce fewer contextual differences (such as language, Internet penetration rates, broadband penetration rates, political openness, economic differences, and so forth), and thus is a sound strategy for demonstrating the potential of this type of analysis, which has not previously been done.

Research in this area is at an early stage, and there are conceptual challenges associated with analyzing national web domains. The content and structure of country-code top-level domains (ccTLDs) such as .uk for the United Kingdom and .fr for France are governed more by traditions than rules [14], complicating efforts to reach a comprehensive definition of what they represent. Brügger [5] discusses the difficulty, for example, of deciding how national presences should be delimited. In the case presented here, the domain name .uk is used, but this does not cover all the webpages originating in the United Kingdom as several British companies, organizations, and individuals operate domains in generic top-level domains (.com, .org, etc.) or elsewhere. Moreover webpages ending with .uk are also used for websites which arguably belong to a different country, as when multinational companies headquartered outside the UK have affiliates within the UK with a .uk address. Finally, it might be contended that not only webpages with a .uk address be examined, but also those that link to and from these webpages. However, for the purposes of this research, these limitations can mostly be noted for future research and do not seriously limit the ability to understand the broad patterns within the UK national web presence.

Another issue that must be decided when undertaking analysis of web domains is the appropriate level of detail. This includes the temporal resolution to use for analysis (since while the web is constantly changing, the number of snapshots available in Internet Archive data vary over time based on the crawl settings in place when the data were gathered) and what level of detail to extract from webpages (i.e., determining the appropriate level of resolution of page content, link information, page metadata, and so forth). Previous research on the .uk ccTLD has examined monthly snapshots over a one year period finding page-level hyperlinks change frequently month to month [3]. As Brügger [4] notes, there are several reasons why archived websites are different from other archived material in respect to these details: choices must be made not just about what to capture but also technical issues about what can be archived and how the archiving process itself shapes the later availability of the archived materials.

2.2 UK web domain

For the .uk domain that will be examined here, the source of the data is the archive files of the UK domain that were obtained from the Internet Archive by the British Library with the specific purpose of creating the basis of a national archive of the web in the UK. This data is currently being expanded via ongoing web archiving activities being performed by the British Library under the terms of the 2003 UK legal deposit law,[2] which was implemented via new regulations that went into effect in April 2013.[3]

[2]Legal Deposit Libraries Act 2003, http://www.legislation.gov.uk/ukpga/2003/28/contents
[3]The Legal Deposit Libraries (Non-Print Works) Regulations, http://www.legislation.gov.uk/uksi/2013/777/contents/made

The .uk country-code top-level domain is managed by the Internet registrar Nominet.[4] Below the .uk top-level domain are several second-level domains (SLDs), the largest of which are .co.uk (commercial enterprises), .org.uk (non-commercial organizations), .gov.uk (government bodies), and .ac.uk (academic establishments).[5] This paper examines the data aggregated to the level of third-level domains such as nominet.org.uk (Nominet), fco.gov.uk (the Foreign and Commonwealth Office of the UK government), or ox.ac.uk (the University of Oxford).

In the case of web archives (or indeed of other archived material which takes the approach of archiving all that can be archived, without a particular topic in mind), it is not scholarly interest that sets the agenda, but rather the goal of the archiving institution. This means that the scope of the archived material and the level of detail available, as with other historical materials, is a function of the archiving processes used to gather and store the data. Thus, unlike web archive research done on the live web using researcher-implemented data collection mechanisms [e.g., 8, 9], for the purpose of this study the dataset itself should be seen as a given. However, it can be mentioned that the Internet Archive's data comprises the most comprehensive archive of the web available [1].

3. DATA

3.1 Data preparation

The data for this study originally comes from the Internet Archive, which began crawling pages from all domains in 1996 [12]. Copies of the approximately 30 terabytes of compressed data relating to the .uk country-code top-level domain (ccTLD) was provided to the British Library and forms the "JISC UK Web Domain Dataset."[6]

Hale et al. [11] cleaned the data by removing error pages (e.g. 404 Not Found pages) as well as pages not within the .uk ccTLD. They produced a plain-text list of all page urls remaining in the collection and the date and times they were crawled, and an additional plain-text list of all outgoing hyperlinks starting from pages within the dataset.

For this study, we started with this list of hyperlinks and filtered it to only include links between different third-level domains. We further grouped pages crawled at similar times (within 1,000 seconds) together and assigned the hyperlink pair a weight based on the number of hyperlinks between the two third-level domains in that time period. For each year, we take the crawl with the largest number of captured hyperlinks between any two domains. We also formed one list of all third-level domains present in the dataset each year and the number of pages crawled within each third-level domain. We loaded these lists into Apache Hive for further analysis.

3.2 Data analysis

In what follows, we undertake a longitudinal network analysis, charting the .uk domain and its core second-level domains over time. As Brügger [4] points out, this type of

[4]http://www.nominet.org.uk/
[5]http://www.nominet.org.uk/uk-domain-names/about-domain-names/uk-domain-subdomains/second-level-domains
[6]http://data.webarchive.org.uk/opendata/ukwa.ds.2/

analysis is not concerned with who produced what, nor with how the web content was used, but rather with what was created and thus "the web which is"—or rather was—"actually available to users."

First, we present an overall longitudinal view of the second-level domains within the .uk domain. We investigate the growth of the entire domain between 1996 and 2010, broken down into its four largest constituent parts, .co.uk, .org.uk, .gov.uk, and .ac.uk. Analysis of these SLDs allows us to investigate the role of different sectors of British society in the growth of the UK web presence.

The second section looks at the linking practices between these SLDs. It asks about the internal link density of each SLD, and analyses how they interact with each other: whether, for example, there are more links between certain subdomains, and whether linking is reciprocal between domains or imbalanced.

The third and final section of the findings takes a closer look at the SLD .ac.uk. It builds on earlier longitudinal analyses of academic webpages, which have investigated, for example, the stability of outlinks [18, 20]. Our findings update earlier studies by extending the period of analysis to the end of 2010 and assessing the effects of new variables, including institutional affiliation, league table ranking, and geographic location on link practices between different universities.

4. RESULTS

4.1 Overview of .uk

Figure 1 displays the overall growth of the .uk ccTLD, showing the total number of nodes (on a logarithmic scale) within each SLD from 1996 to 2010. It also shows the size of the entire .uk domain space (on a linear scale). There is a clear change in the trend of the growth around 2001 for .co.uk and .org.uk. Furthermore, .ac.uk and .gov.uk seem to almost stabilize in size at around the same time.

Figure 2 shows the relative size of the second-level domains .co.uk, .org.uk, .ac.uk, and .gov.uk across the fifteen year period, standardized as each SLD's proportion of the total nodes (i.e., domains/websites, not webpages) in the collection in each year. While these are not the only second-level domains in use within the .uk domain, they are the four largest in terms of number of nodes across the whole period.

As Figure 2 shows, .co.uk is the predominant second-level domain throughout the entire period, with .co.uk sites never accounting for less than 85% of the total. However, also apparent is the large proportion of governmental and, especially, academic sites in the early recorded history of the UK web. This is consistent with the role that universities played in the early establishment, adoption, and development of the web [13]. Over time, however, this early presence was greatly overshadowed in terms of absolute numbers of nodes when compared to the continued growth of the .co.uk and .org.uk domains.

4.2 Link density among and between second-level domains

Up to this point the analysis has drawn only on node data; that is, the number of websites making up each domain. However, link analysis can offer insight into how well integrated each SLD is with itself and with other domains.

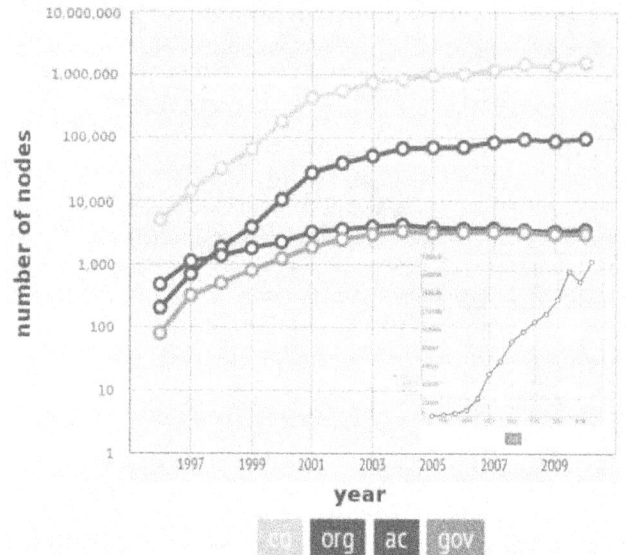

Figure 1: Number of nodes (third-level domains) within each second-level domain over time. The inset shows the sum over all second-level domains.

A link from one site to another has been used as an indicator of awareness between blogs [10] and recognition between academic sites [20]. Figure 3 shows, for each subdomain, how many links there are for every node over time, where a fluctuating relationship between the number of nodes and links to other nodes for each second-level domain is visible. Over the whole period, the .ac.uk academic SLD and, from 1997 onwards, the .gov.uk governmental SLD are the most internally dense SLDs. This observation may reflect the fact that registration for the .ac.uk and .gov.uk subdomains is restricted, whereas .org.uk and .co.uk sites can be registered easily by any party. In addition, the .ac.uk and .gov.uk subdomains are likely constituted by a narrower and more cohesive set of institutions, creating, on average, a stronger basis for linking within the SLDs. Furthermore, there is likely more competition and thus less reason to

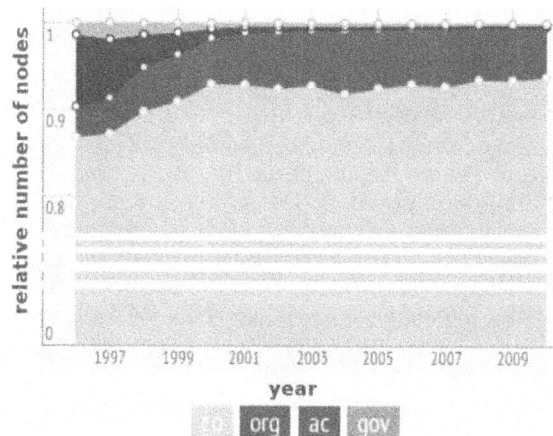

Figure 2: Relative size of second-level domains in the .uk top-level domain over time.

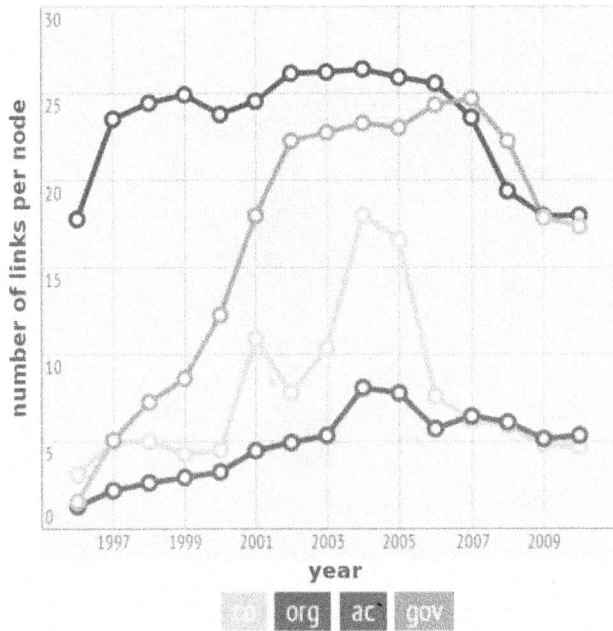

Figure 3: Number of within-SLD links per node in four .uk SLDs, 1996–2010.

link within the .co.uk commercial subdomain compared to .ac.uk or .gov.uk. Higher link density within the .org and .gov domains in comparison to the .com domain has previously been observed in a smaller scale, topical study about climate change [19].

Also of note is the general rise of links in the middle of the period, particularly in the substantial .co.uk subdomain. This peaks sharply in 2004 before falling sharply back to around pre-2001 levels by 2009. This trend has no easy explanation, suggesting that further research is required to explain this pattern. Possible explanations include the norm of including lists of links on webpages such as blogs fell out of favor in the middle of this period or that more websites increasingly linked outside of the .uk ccTLD.

Not only can web domain data tell us how well integrated an SLD is internally, but we can also investigate how well SLDs are connected to each other. Figures 4a and 4b show the quantity of links between SLDs for 2010, the last year in the dataset, where the size of an arc relates to the volume of links from one SLD to another. The color of each arc relates to links sent in one direction, from the host SLD outwards. For example green arcs show links from the .co.uk domain to others. Figure 4a shows the absolute volume of links, while the size of the arcs in Figure 4b are normalized in relation to the number of nodes in the target subdomain. (Note that Figure 4a does not display links within a single SLD, as the volume of links between .co.uk sites dwarfs all other relationships. As Figure 4b controls for the number of nodes in each SLD, the adjusted .co.uk arc is much smaller and links within a single SLD are therefore included.)

Figure 4a shows that the largest volume of links between SLDs in 2010 flowed from .co.uk sites to .org.uk sites, and this relationship is fairly reciprocal, with .org.uk sites sending almost as many links back. Links between other domains are much lower in terms of absolute volume. When controlling for the size of the target subdomain, however,

the picture changes somewhat. As Figure 2 above showed, by 2010 the number of nodes in the .org.uk subdomain far outweighed those in the .ac.uk and .gov.uk subdomains. Figure 4b, adjusting for this, shows that the .gov.uk and, to a lesser extent, the .ac.uk subdomains punch above their weight, receiving proportionally more links from .co.uk and .org.uk sites. Once again, the more restrictive registration policies for these SLDs may be a factor here, driving up the average quality and 'linkworthiness' of sites in these subdomains as compared to .co.uk and .org.uk sites although it may also be related to other factors such as the comparative homogeneity of these SLDs, the perception of objectivity or balance on academic or government websites as opposed to sites oriented towards sales or persuasion, or even the international standing of many UK universities, although understanding these factors would require further investigation.

For the .gov.uk subdomain, the finding that sites link out less than they are linked to suggests a lack of 'outward-lookingness,' compared to the other sectors. In contrast, Escher et al. [8] found the UK Foreign and Commonwealth Office to be relatively more outward-looking than its equivalents in Australia and the US. However, foreign offices, with their outward facing role could easily be an exception to more general government-wide propensity not to link out.

In addition, it is worth noting the relatively heavy proportion of links within the .ac.uk SLD shown in Figure 4b. This propensity of academic institutions to link heavily to other academic institutions (more so than the other domains) reflects (taking a positive view) a strong network among academic institutions, but also potentially (taking a negative view) a tendency towards inward-looking, within-domain links. We examine these links in more depth in the next section.

4.3 The case of the academic subdomain

At this stage we turn our attention to one particular subdomain, the .ac.uk academic subdomain of the UK web. To be eligible for a third-level domain within .ac.uk, an organization must have a permanent physical presence in the UK and either have the majority of its activities publicly funded by UK government funding bodies or be a Learned Society. In addition, the organization must satisfy at least one of the following criteria: the organization must provide tertiary-level education with central government funding, conduct publicly funded academic research, have a primary purpose of supporting tertiary-level educational establishments, or have the status of a Learned Society ("a society that exists to promote an academic discipline or group of disciplines").[7]

The academy was at the forefront of the development of the web, and, as Figure 2 shows, .ac.uk sites constituted a sizeable minority of .uk sites in 1996. Over time, this proportion waned, even as more British universities established a substantial web presence. In this subsection we use the longitudinal data collected to examine the relationship between universities' linking practices and three variables: institutional affiliation, league table ranking, and geographic location. Our hypothesis in doing so was that higher status academic institutions would be more strongly linked to than lower status institutions and would also be more strongly interconnected with their peer institutions.

---

[7]https://community.ja.net/library/
janet-services-documentation/
eligibility-guidelines

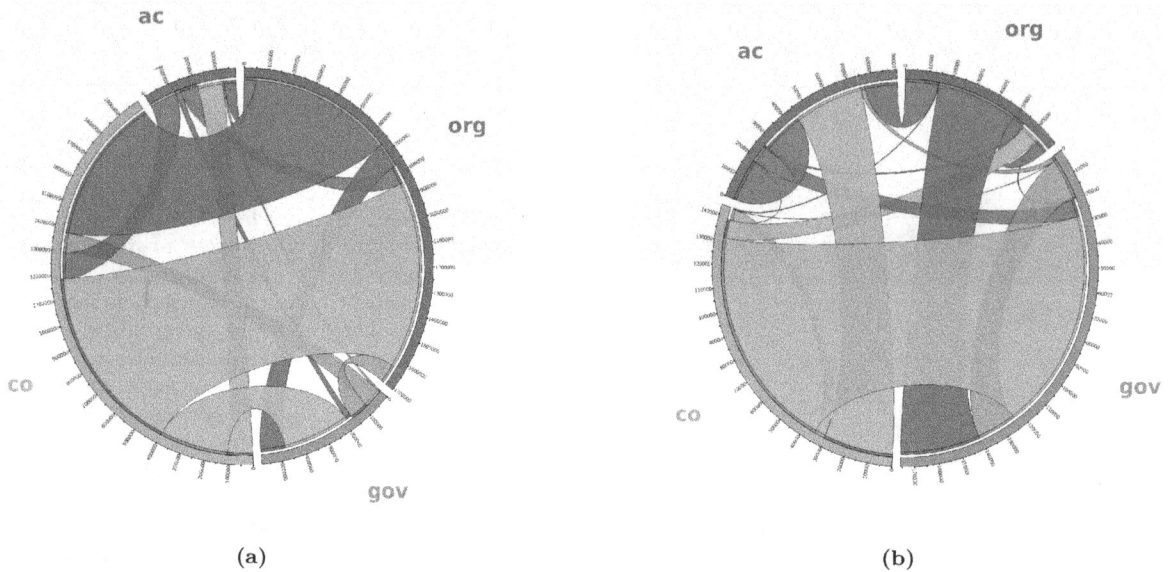

(a)   (b)

Figure 4: Links between four second-level domains. Panel *a* **shows the absolute number of links between different SLDs (self-loops are excluded), and panel** *b* **shows the relative number of links normalized by the size of target subdomain.**

For the analysis, we built a list of the 121 universities listed in the most recent Sunday Times University Guide.[8] Each of these universities has a website, all of which use the `.ac.uk` suffix. We obtained the third-level domain (e.g., `ox.ac.uk`) for each. Further data collection as necessary is described in the respective subsections that follow.

4.3.1 Group affiliation

Many British universities belong to associations, formed to represent their interests and facilitate collaboration. The groups are neither mutually exclusive nor exhaustive, meaning that universities can belong to none, one, or more than one group, but for practical and political reasons most universities belong to only one. We collected data on the memberships of five groups, the Russell Group,[9] the 1994 Group,[10] the University Alliance,[11] the Million+ Group,[12] and the Cathedrals Group.[13]

The best known of these is perhaps the Russell Group, formed in 1994 and now constituted of 24 members. The 1994 Group, which represented smaller research institutions, was formed in response to the Russell Group, but disbanded in 2013; given the time frame of the dataset we include the 11 final members of the group in our analysis. Of the final three groups, the University Alliance is formed of 22 business-oriented UK universities, the Million+ Group is made up of 17 mostly 'new' (post-1992) institutions, and the Cathedrals

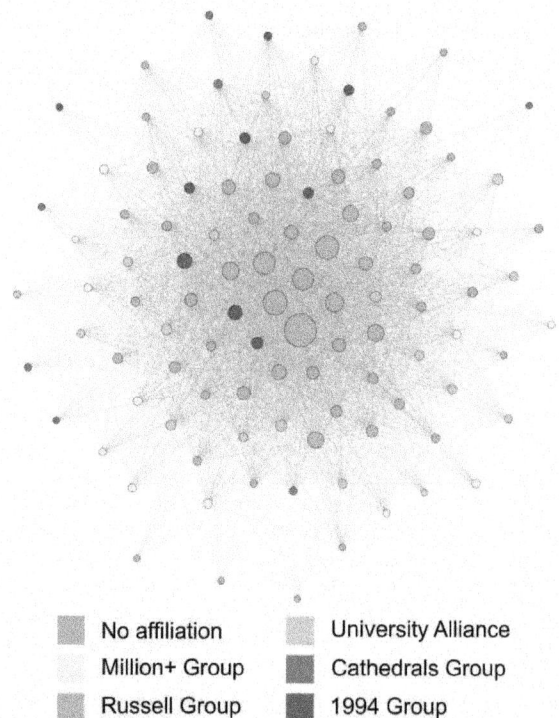

	No affiliation		University Alliance
	Million+ Group		Cathedrals Group
	Russell Group		1994 Group

Figure 5: Network diagram of hyperlinks between universities. Different colors indicate different university affiliations.

[8]http://www.thesundaytimes.co.uk/sto/University_Guide/

[9]http://www.russellgroup.ac.uk/our-universities/

[10]http://www.timeshighereducation.co.uk/news/was-1994-groups-demise-triggered-by-relaunch-delays/2008999.article

[11]http://www.unialliance.ac.uk/member/

[12]http://www.millionplus.ac.uk/who-we-are/our-affiliates/

[13]http://cathedralsgroup.org.uk/Members.aspx

66

Group is made up of 16 universities originally instituted as church-led teacher training colleges. The stated purposes of these groups differ somewhat, but each are constituted broadly to serve the research interests of their members.

In comparing group membership to the density of links between different universities, we sought to discover whether academic affiliation was associated with the density of links between institutions. To do this, we performed a network analysis, investigating whether the universities clustered on the basis of group affiliation. Figure 5 shows a network diagram, with different affiliations marked by different colors.

To the naked eye, Figure 5 shows no discernible clustering on the basis of group affiliation, and network analysis bears this out. The division of the network by affiliations has a modularity score [16] of -0.003, indicating that the division of the network into clusters based on university affiliation is no better than dividing the network into five random clusters. On an individual basis, only one group, the Russell Group, has many internal links and comparatively fewer links to institutions outside the group. It is the most strongly connected group with an internal hyperlink density of 0.71. The Russell Group, which includes 24 of the leading international UK universities with some of the highest levels of research funding, arguably represents most if not all of the elite universities in the UK. It contains 9 of the 10 top-ranked UK universities, including both Oxford and Cambridge. That these universities are more strongly linked to each other is likely related at least in part to their active research cultures, with many collaborations between researchers at these top institutions. The lack of strong web connections in the other associations, however, suggests that while these institutions may or may not have strong connections among their members by other measures, there is no evidence that universities strongly link to the websites of institutions with which they share group affiliation over other institutions.

4.3.2 League table ranking

University league tables are an important if imperfect indicator of a university's prominence. Modern league tables incorporate a whole range of measures, including factors related to teaching, research, and student satisfaction. As such, we wanted to investigate whether a university's league table ranking is associated with its web presence, and whether the relationship has changed over time, in terms of both increasing adoption and development of an institution's web presence and its changes in league table ranking over time. For this analysis, we collected the rankings of British universities published in The Times Good University Guide for three years, 2000, 2005 and 2010, and compared these rankings with data from crawls conducted in the same three years.

In conducting the analysis, we used ten common measures of network centrality for each of the three different years to gauge the relationship between each university's league ranking and its position in the network of hyperlinks flowing between university third-level domains. We then produced lists ranking the universities for each year by each centrality measure and computed Spearman's rank correlation coefficient for each centrality ranking and league table ranking combination. These correlation coefficients are shown in Figure 6.

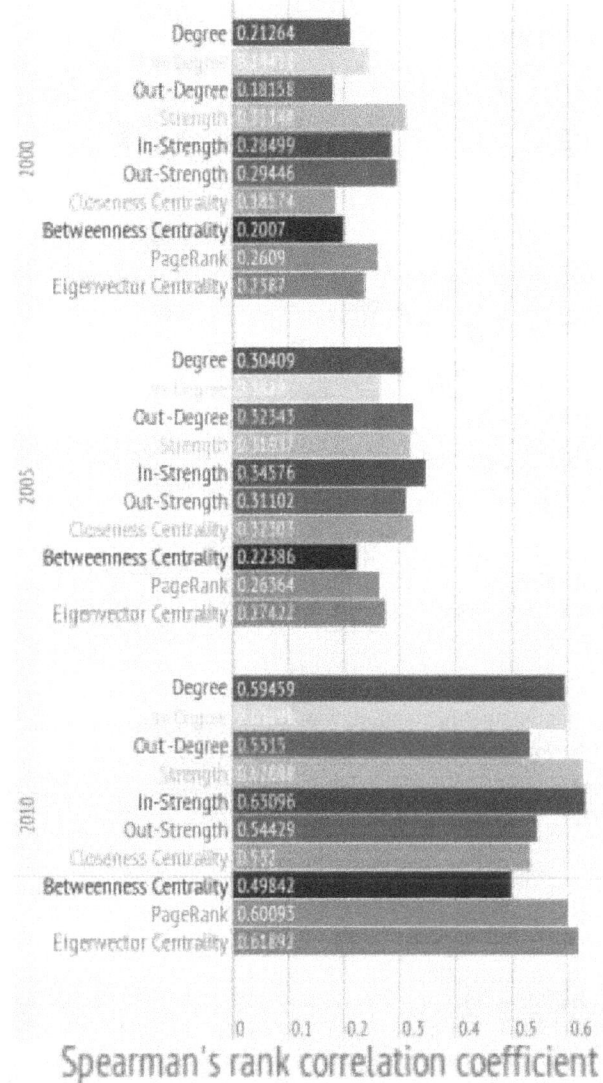

Figure 6: Spearman's rank correlation coefficients between university league table rankings and ten different network centrality measures for three years.

For most measures of centrality used, a pattern emerges: the data for 2010 shows the strongest correlation between league table ranking and centrality, while the relationship is less evident for 2000 and 2005. The most strongly correlated correlation measure is in-strength, a sum of all the hyperlinks linking to a given web domain. This measure uses the weight of each edge, which corresponds to the number of hyperlinks between any two third-level domains. This differs from in-degree which measures the number of other domains that link to a given web domain. Figure 7 shows the fairly strong correlation between universities' league table rankings and their network positions as measured by in-strength. What Figure 6 and Figure 7 suggest is two-fold: first, that university prominence, as measured by league table position, is an increasingly stronger predictor of the number of links to that institution over the 2000–2010 period. Whether this is an example of the Matthew Effect ("the rich get richer") [15]

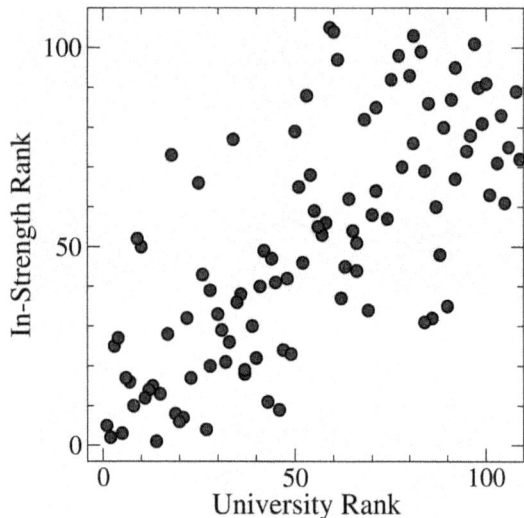

Figure 7: University in-strength rankings compared to university league table rankings for 2010. Spearman's rank correlation is 0.63.

whereby highly prominent institutions become well-linked institutions largely as a result of their prominence (and conversely, marginal institutions become more marginalized as a result of their lack of prominence), or whether there is another independent factor at play here cannot be determined from these data. However, the second conclusion is clear: the hyperlink patterns within the UK academic subdomain support the notion that the web does not inherently challenge existing power structures. Instead, the saturation of the .ac.uk subdomain, in terms of the presence of essentially all possible academic institutions by 2003 (Figure 1), has resulted by 2010 in a subdomain in which network centrality closely mirrors prominence as measured by league tables.

4.3.3 Role of geography

Finally, we investigated whether any association exists between the geographic proximity of British universities and the density of hyperlinks between them. This analysis builds upon work by Pan et al. [17] who found, at a global scale, that rates of academic citations and collaborations between two cities diminish as the distance between them increases, following gravity laws. We conduct a similar analysis, replacing citations and collaborations with hyperlinks collected in the web domain data.

We collected geographic coordinates for each of the British universities in the list using a simple Google Maps search. Universities can be spatially complex, sometimes having multiple campuses and satellite sites; so, some discretion was occasionally required in identifying the center of each university.

The standard, naïve gravity law approach would suggest that the number of hyperlinks, or the strength of the connection, between two given universities is inversely proportional to the square of the distance between the two universities. We let S_{ij} denote the strength from university i to university j. Focusing on the data from 2010, the left frame of Figure 8, shows that the relationship between this measure and the geographical distance between the two universities is very

noisy. To correct for the different sizes of universities and their different linking practices (some universities may just link more than others), we normalize these strengths. We divide S_{ij} by the sum of the weights of all edges coming from university i (S_i^{out}) multiplied by the sum of the weights of all edges linking to university j (S_j^{in}). We denote this normalized measure σ_{ij} and plot it against physical distance in the right frame of Figure 8. With this normalization, the relationship between distance the number of hyperlinks (strength) between universities is very clear. In both frames, we use a moving average window with a length of 500 data points and therefore a lower bound of 20km is introduced. An upper bound is induced by considering only the universities within the UK in this study. However, the gravity law holds significantly within a distance range of almost two decades.

Letting d_{ij} denote the geographical distance between two universities, we then seek the exponent a, which best fits the observed data following $\sigma_{ij} \propto d_{ij}^{-a}$. Using the least squares methods, we fit a linear function to the logarithmically transformed data and find $a = 0.28 \pm 0.02$, which closely matches the findings of Pan et al. [17] for citation and collaboration networks. In that study, Pan et al. found an exponent of $a = 0.30$ for the citation network before any normalization, while finding an even stronger role for geographical distance ($a = 0.77$) after applying a similar normalization to the one we apply here.

Figure 9 maps the universities in the sample along with the connections between them colored according to σ. It is evident, specially in the map of 2010, that the longer connections generally have weaker strength. It is worth nothing that the size limit of the dataset and the geographical constraints, such as the dense region of London extended to Oxford and Cambridge, which includes a large number of universities in our dataset, could partially drive the strong geographical dependency we observed. This dense region is particularly visible in the map of 2005 in Figure 9.

5. CONCLUSION

In this paper, we have reported some of the first findings based on longitudinal analysis of the entire recorded history of the UK web domain. While this current analysis is by necessity at a macro-level in terms of detail, it nevertheless demonstrates the potential of these data for detecting changes in patterns in web linking behavior over time, evidence related to the growth and expansion of the web, and uneven patterns of linking within subdomains, such as the academic .ac.uk subdomain discussed here. We have shown that even though the growth of the commercial side of the web has resulted in increasing commercial dominance of the UK web space in terms of absolute number of nodes, the academic and government subdomains receive proportionally more inlinks per domain. In examining the academic subdomain in particular, we have shown that while there is no generalized clustering based on the affiliation of academic institutions, there are clear patterns in terms of higher inlinks to the highest status academic institutions and stronger connections between geographically-closer institutions.

This analysis also suggests many future possibilities for research with these web archive data, including more detailed micro-level analysis of linking behavior within various subdomains over time, discovery of networks of collaboration between subunits of institutions, comparison between

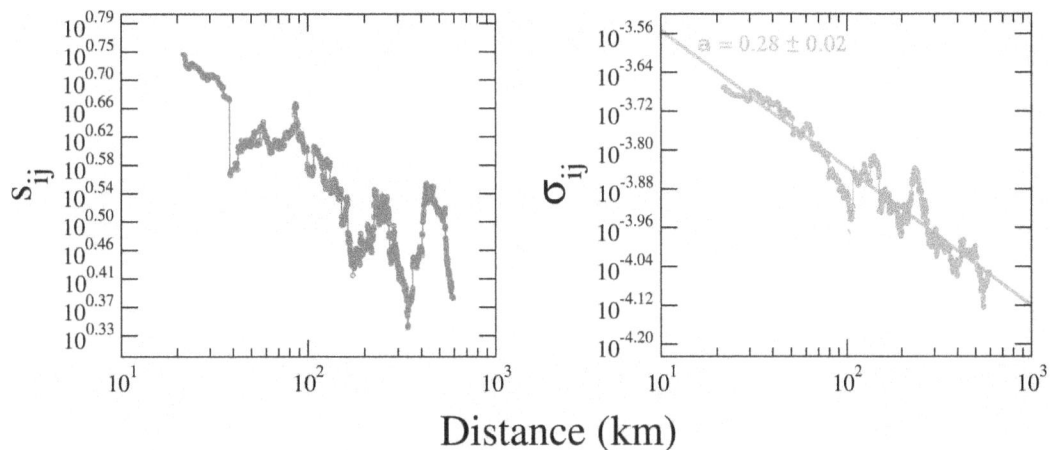

Figure 8: Left: Raw hyperlink strength (S_{ij}) between universities versus geographical distance, and Right: Normalized hyperlink strength ($\sigma_{ij} = \frac{S_{ij}}{S_i^{out} S_j^{in}}$) between universities versus geographical distance. The normalized measure follows a gravity-law model with an exponent of $a = 0.28 \pm 0.02$.

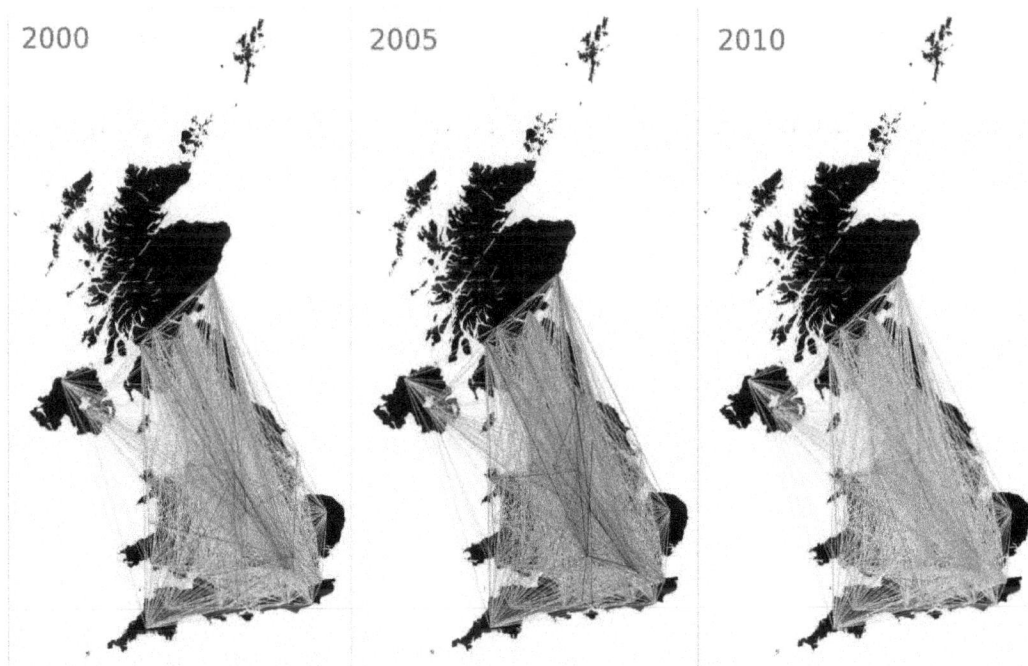

Figure 9: Maps of the UK universities under study for three years: 2000, 2005, and 2010. The connections are the hyperlinks, and color corresponds to the normalized strength of each link (σ_{ij}). The reddest links correspond to the strongest connections.

link measures and other measures of prominence such as citation networks, and analysis of other subdomains besides `.ac.uk`. In addition, there are ongoing efforts to prepare the full-text corpus extracted from the web archive for research (rather than the link corpus used here), which will be able to be combined with these data to answer more detailed questions about the content of the web, the context for links, and discourses on the web.

6. ACKNOWLEDGMENTS

The authors would like to thank Ning Wang for his advice and support on data cleaning and Andreas Kaltenbrunner for his help with creating the geographic visualizations. The authors are also grateful for funding from UK Jisc for the "Big Data: Demonstrating the Value of the UK Web Domain Dataset for Social Science Research" grant (16/11 Enhancing the Sustainability of Digital Collections) that supported the data extraction and early analysis, and further funding for analysis from the UK Arts and Humanities Research Council for the "Big UK Domain Data for the Arts and Humanities (BUDDAH)" grant (AH/L009854/1). Finally, the authors would like to thank our anonymous reviewers for their helpful comments on an earlier version of this paper.

7. REFERENCES

[1] S. G. Ainsworth, A. Alsum, H. SalahEldeen, M. C. Weigle, and M. L. Nelson. How much of the web is archived? In *Proceedings of the 11th Annual International ACM/IEEE Joint Conference on Digital Libraries*, pages 133–136. ACM, 2011.

[2] R. Baeza-Yates, C. Castillo, and E. N. Efthimiadis. Characterization of national web domains. *ACM Transactions on Internet Technology (TOIT)*, 7(2):9, 2007.

[3] I. Bordino, P. Boldi, D. Donato, M. Santini, and S. Vigna. Temporal evolution of the UK web. In *Data Mining Workshops, 2008. ICDMW '08. IEEE International Conference on*, pages 909–918, Dec 2008.

[4] N. Brügger. Historical network analysis of the Web. *Social Science Computer Review*, 31(3):306–321, 2013.

[5] N. Brügger. Probing a nation's web sphere: A new approach to web history and a new kind of historical source. 2014.

[6] M. Dougherty and E. T. Meyer. Community, tools, and practices in web archiving: The state of the art in relation to social science and humanities research needs. *Journal of the American Society of Information Science & Technology*, 2014.

[7] M. Dougherty, E. T. Meyer, C. Madsen, C. V. den Heuvel, A. Thomas, and S. Wyatt. Researcher engagement with web archives: State of the art. Technical report, 2010.

[8] T. Escher, H. Margetts, V. Petricek, and I. Cox. Governing from the centre? Comparing the nodality of digital governments. In *Annual Meeting of the American Political Science Association*, 2006.

[9] K. A. Foot and S. M. Schneider. *Web Campaigning*. The MIT Press, 2006.

[10] S. A. Hale. Net increase? Cross-lingual linking in the blogosphere. *Journal of Computer-Mediated Communication*, 17(2):135–151, 2012.

[11] S. A. Hale, T. Yasseri, and H. Margetts. Extracting clean hyperlink and website data from the JISC UK Web Domain Dataset. Technical report, 2014.

[12] B. Kahle. Preserving the Internet. *Scientific American*, 276(3):82–83, 1997.

[13] B. M. Leiner, V. G. Cerf, D. D. Clark, R. E. Kahn, L. Kleinrock, D. C. Lynch, J. Postel, L. G. Roberts, and S. Wolff. A brief history of the Internet. *ACM SIGCOMM Computer Communication Review*, 39(5):22–31, 2009.

[14] J. Masanès. Web archiving: Issues and methods. In J. Masanès, editor, *Web Archiving*, pages 1–54. Springer, 2006.

[15] R. K. Merton. The Matthew effect in science. *Science*, 159(3810):56–63, 1968.

[16] M. E. J. Newman. Modularity and community structure in networks. *Proceedings of the National Academy of Sciences*, 103(23):8577–8582, 2006.

[17] R. K. Pan, K. Kaski, and S. Fortunato. World citation and collaboration networks: Uncovering the role of geography in science. *Scientific Reports*, 2, 2012.

[18] N. Payne and M. Thelwall. Longitudinal trends in academic Web links. *Journal of Information Science*, 34(1):3–14, 2008.

[19] R. Rogers and N. Marres. Landscaping climate change: A mapping technique for understanding science and technology debates on the World Wide Web. *Public Understanding of Science*, 9(2):141–163, 2000.

[20] M. Thelwall, R. Tang, and L. Price. Linguistic patterns of academic Web use in Western Europe. *Scientometrics*, 56(3):417–432, 2003.

Country-Level Spatial Dynamics of User Activity: A Case Study in Location-Based Social Networks

Anh Le
School of Information
Sciences
University of Pittsburgh
Pennsylvania, USA
atl13@pitt.edu

Konstantinos Pelechrinis
School of Information
Sciences
University of Pittsburgh
Pennsylvania, USA
kpele@pitt.edu

Prashant Krishnamurthy
School of Information
Sciences
University of Pittsburgh
Pennsylvania, USA
prashk@pitt.edu

ABSTRACT

Identifying and understanding the emerging patterns in user activity is an important step in designing and developing features for online social networks. With the explosive growth of user-generated data in such networks, the recorded user activities are no more sparse snapshots but are close to a live reflection of real life. This allows us to extract patterns which are tied to the time and space context of real life activity from such recorded data. In this work, we analyze two rich datasets obtained from two major location-based social networks (Foursquare and Gowalla) and show how users change their activity patterns depending on the *country* they currently reside on. We also compare activity patterns between foreign users from different countries and local users. The detailed results may not automatically generalize but this kind of analysis can be repeated on different datasets and the outcomes of such analyses can benefit social and behavioral scientists as well as designers of online social media.

Categories and Subject Descriptors

H.2.8 [**Database Applications**]: Data mining

Keywords

Spatial dynamics; Location-based social networks

1. INTRODUCTION

The penetration of on-line social media in human lives has facilitated the recording of a large amount of data for studying various human activities. The recorded data form a proxy for traditional sociology studies on topics such as the structure of social networks that have been based on time-consuming interviews with human subjects, which limit their scale. Scale is not a problem with on-line social networks (e.g., MySpace, Facebook etc.) that have generated an abundant source of data that can be used to study the formation and structure of friendships. This information, while

WebSci'14, June 23–26, 2014, Bloomington, IN, USA.
Copyright 2014 ACM 978-1-4503-2622-3/14/06 ...$15.00.
http://dx.doi.org/10.1145/2615569.2615689.

massive, can however include various sources of bias, since actions in the on-line and real world can differ dramatically [23, 25]. As an example, one could argue that generating friendships on-line is much easier (or harder, depending on one's point of view) as compared to real life. Along similar lines, but in a different context, Sproull and Kiesler [22] have found that a lot of the information conveyed through electronic communication would not have been diffused through face-to-face interactions. Hence, in general, on-line, virtual activities may not necessarily be representative of real-world interactions between people, and this can significantly reduce the value of studies that involve data from digital social networks. During the last years a new class of social media, namely location-based social networks (LBSN for short) has emerged. The main interaction of users in these systems is "location sharing" (i.e., voluntary posting of one's whereabout). LBSNs are generating huge datasets of real-world human mobility and activity through user "check-ins" at venues[1]. These data, although generated on-line, do incorporate information on actions of people in real life.

In this work, we utilize two datasets obtained from two commercial LBSNs (Foursquare and Gowalla), to study the spatial dynamics of human activities. Specifically, we examine the dynamics of people's activities with respect to their location. While "location" can be defined at various levels of granularity (e.g., latitude-longitude, specific venue, city, country etc.) our main focus in this work is at the *country-level*. In particular, we ask whether there are similarities or differences in how people act in their home country and how they act when they are abroad. What types of places do they visit in their home country and what types in foreign countries? Can any observable differences be attributed to cultural differences?

We make the following hypotheses which we examine in our study:

H1. Users change their check-in patterns when they travel abroad.

H2. Foreign visitors have their own check-in patterns but can also be aligned with domestic users.

We are aware that our dataset may contain bias from various causes as we will discuss later (e.g., not all users have data roaming or WiFi access when they are abroad, and even if they do, they may not make check-ins at *all* venues visited).

---

[1] We will use the terms venue, location, place and spot interchangeable for the rest of the paper.

However, with the filtering process (see details in Section 3.1) we believe that the final dataset, although not of very large scale, is appropriate for analysis. Furthermore, our method is still applicable to other datasets in the future.

Our work records and provides an understanding of the geographical properties of human behavior. We believe that it can stimulate further research and facilitate related studies in social and behavioral science disciplines. Moreover, services such as recommendations and trip planning may significantly benefit by leveraging the knowledge of these spatial dynamics as we briefly discuss later.

2. RELATED WORK

While our work is novel in the sense of examining the activities of people in the context of their home and foreign locations, spatial dynamics and the effects/role of physical distance has been studied over the last few years in a variety of other contexts. For instance, a large volume of existing literature examines the effects of geographical distance on *social network structure* and the communication patterns emerging in such networks. Specifically (with the list being non-exhaustive), Mok *et al.* [17] suggest that different types of communications are preferred depending on the *distance* between two people, while Lambiotte *et al.* [15] examine the history of mobile phone users to discover the relation between distance and the number of interactions between users. Given that a friendship is already established, Kaltenbrunner *et al.* [13] showed that the level of interaction is almost not affected by distance between two friends. Crandall *et al.* [5] further proposed a way to infer friendship probability from location coincidences, while authors in [1] and [21] studied how the probability of friendship is affected by the distance between users. Scellato *et al.* [20] study the relation between social and geographical properties of connected clusters of users. Their main finding suggests that this relation changes depending on the nature and the objective of the social network at hand.

The socio-spatio-temporal dynamics of LBSN users have been studied under efforts for (social or spatial) link prediction. In particular, Cranshaw *et al.* [6] proposed a set of metrics/features to quantify spatial and temporal dynamics of user activity. These features are then used to predict the *future* social ties of users. Cho *et al.* [3] developed a mobility model that takes into account temporal, spatial and social aspects of user activity and were able to predict the future check-ins of a user. Noulas *et al.* [18] further showed how inter check-in distances correlate with inter check-in times and further examined whether the category of the next check-in location depends on the distance and the category of the last check-in as well as on time elapsed. Similarly, Preotiuc-Pietro and Cohn [19] studied the check-in patterns in Foursquare and used the category of the previous check-ins in conjunction with the time elapsed to predict the category of a possible check-in at current time.

While the above studies analyze data from LBSNs towards a specific application (e.g., link prediction), literature analyzing the spatial properties of some behavioral aspects of online LBSN users exist as well. For example, Cheng *et al.* [2] using data crawled from Foursquare, highlight the differences between the check-in patterns of users from different cities (with different population density, average income). Very recently, Garcia-Gavilanes *et al.* [12] identified correlation between the activity of Twitter users and cultural properties

of their home country. Even closer to our study are efforts from the field of tourism. In particular, Field [9] compared the traveling behavior of domestic and foreign students from Clemson university. He *surveyed* 509 international students and 1501 domestic students with regards to their activities when traveling during summer and spring breaks and compared the responses of the different groups. For example, the study found that domestic students are far more interested in going to the beach, while foreign students are more interested in sightseeing. Our study falls under this broader category of literature. We do not only examine the behavior of different groups of people but also we examine the behavioral change of the same group of people as a function of their location. To reiterate, *our main objective is to examine the behavioral change of location-based social media users - as captured through check-ins - as a function of their location at the country level (i.e., distinguishing between domestic and foreign activity).* Towards this objective we examine the hypotheses stated in Section 1.

3. DATA AND PRE-PROCESSING

In this work, we use two datasets captured from two popular location-based social networks, namely, Gowalla[2] and Foursquare.

Gowalla Dataset: The dataset [3] consists of 6,442,892 public check-ins performed by 196,591 Gowalla users in 1,280,810 distinct places, between February 2009 and October 2010. Every check-in is a tuple in the form <User ID, Time, Latitude, Longitude, Venue ID>.

Foursquare Dataset: This dataset was provided to us by Cheng *et al.* [2]. It includes geo-tagged user generated content originating from a variety of social media that was pushed to Twitter's public feed between September 2010 and January 2011. Each tweet includes location information in the following format: <UserID, TweetID, Latitude, Longitude, Time, Text, VenueID>. There are 22,506,721 tweets in total, from which we filter out those that have not originated from Foursquare, and eventually we get our final dataset of 6,699,516 check-ins.

The original datasets do not include information related to the actual type of venue for every check-in. Given that we are especially interested in characterizing the dynamics of users activity, *we added category information for every venue in the datasets by using our own web crawler.* Gowalla uses a flat list of 283 different categories, while Foursquare uses a hierarchical category classification with nine top-level category groups. In order to have consistent classification, we manually classified Gowalla venues into the same nine top-level categories used by Foursquare (Table 1).

Table 1: Category groups

Category	Description
1	Arts and Entertainment
2	College and University
3	Food
4	Professional and Other Places
5	Nightlife Spot
6	Great Outdoors
7	Shop and Service
8	Travel and Transport
9	Residence

[2]Gowalla has been acquired by Facebook and is currently offline.

We further pre-processed the data and added the following information to facilitate our work:

- *Country of each check-in:* We use a set of GIS maps of countries [24] and examine whether the check-in location under consideration is inside the boundary line of a country. Due to the maps' and/or the check-ins' latitude/longitude resolution, 10% of locations do not fall inside any map. We associate such check-ins with the closest country.

- *Timezone information for each check-in location.* The original datasets include a timestamp based on the UTC timezone. Using GIS maps of timezones [7] we associate locations with timezones and then convert check-in times from UTC to local times.

- *Country information for each user.* Based on the number of check-ins made in each country by each user, we refer to the most frequently checked-in country as the **home country**[3] of a user. However, care needs to be taken in cases where there is not a single, dominant country in a users check-in history. We address this in a later section. Based on the country information for every user u we label his check-ins as **domestic** if they happened within his home country, and **foreign** if they correspond to a location outside the latter. (See Section 4.2 for complete definitions.)

3.1 Data Filtering and Merging

Our focus is to examine in fine-grained detail, the spatial dynamics of LBSN users at the country level. However, the original datasets, as described above, include entries that might not be useful for our purposes (e.g., users that check-in at only one - home - country are not of interest for our study). Hence, we apply the following set of filters on the original data to acquire a relevant subset for our work.

Filter 1: We keep only users who

- Visit at least two countries (home + 1)
- Have at least 30 check-ins in foreign countries

Filter 2: If c_1 is the country where user u has his most check-ins and c_2 is his second ranked country in terms of check-in count, we define :

$$r_{u,c_1,c_2} = \frac{\# \ check\text{-}ins \ in \ c_2}{\# \ check\text{-}ins \ in \ c_1} \quad (1)$$

We only keep users u who have $r_{u,c_1,c_2} \leq 0.90$. With this filter, we want to have more accurate estimation of the home country.

Filter 3: For every pair of consecutive check-ins of a user, we calculate the average speed required in order to be able to perform this pair of check-ins based on the geographical distance and time difference between them. We then remove users who have check-in pairs that correspond to speeds greater than 900km/h (maximum speed of a typical airplane). With this filter we try to apply a basic sanity check to remove users that generate fake check-ins. We recognize that this works only for consecutive check-ins that take place in physically widely separated locations (i.e., not within the same city). Designing algorithms for identifying all possible fake check-ins is beyond the scope of our work.

---

[3]For the rest of the paper we will not make a distinction between home country and country of residence, and we will use the terms interchangeably.

The numbers of remaining users after each filter are shown in Table 2. The number of check-ins, users, venues and countries from the two filtered datasets are further summarized in Table 3. Number of countries of users is different from number of countries of locations because there are some small countries from which there are no (filtered) users, but users from other countries do visit and make check-ins there.

Table 2: Number of users after applying each filter

Dataset	Without filter	Filter 1	Filter 2	Filter 3
Gowalla	105,071	1,029	992	813
Foursquare	186,083	632	604	405

Table 3: Size of filtered datasets

Dataset	Check-ins	Users	Countries of users	Locations	Countries of locations
Gowalla	228,038	813	53	94,969	123
Foursquare	66,219	405	43	18,141	83
Both	294,257	1,218	62	113,110	127

Given that our study is essentially a behavioral analysis of users as captured from their check-in activities, we integrate our two datasets to a single, larger one. While there might be users that have accounts and use both systems, we expect this number to be small. Moreover, the overlapping of the time periods the two datasets span is only one month, which further reduces any impact the above phenomenon might have. This integration of the two dataset will increase the statistical robustness of the results obtained, as compared to analyzing the two datasets individually.

4. RESULTS

In this section we present our results. We begin with some basic analyses of our dataset and then we move on to studying our hypotheses.

4.1 Data Overview

We first examine some basic statistics of our final dataset. For each user u, denote $n_u^{Chk}, n_u^L, n_u^{Ct}$ and n_u^{FT} the numbers of his/her check-ins, visited locations, visited countries and foreign trips[4] respectively. Figure 1 shows activities of users sorted by number of check-ins. From the top three panels we see that number of locations visited n^L strongly correlates with number of check-ins n^{Chk} while number of countries visited n^{Ct} does not (Pearson correlation coefficients equal to 0.86 and 0.02 respectively, p-value $< 10^{-5}$). In an extreme case, there are two users with not so many check-ins but visited more than 20 countries. The fourth panel of Figure 1 shows the number of foreign trips for each user. Again, there is no correlation between n^{FT} and n^{Chk}. The fifth panel shows the ratio of the check-in count divided by the location count, $\frac{n_u^{Chk}}{n_u^L}$. We can see that some users check in a lot at a few locations thus, having this ratio high. However, for 75% of users this ratio is less than 2. The last panel shows the ratio of foreign trip count divided by number of foreign countries visited, $\frac{n_u^{FT}}{n_u^{Ct}-1}$. The CDF tells us that 92% of users have this ratio less than or equal to 5. Usually users may visit

---

[4]A foreign trip is determined as a sequence of all *consecutive* check-ins in one foreign country.

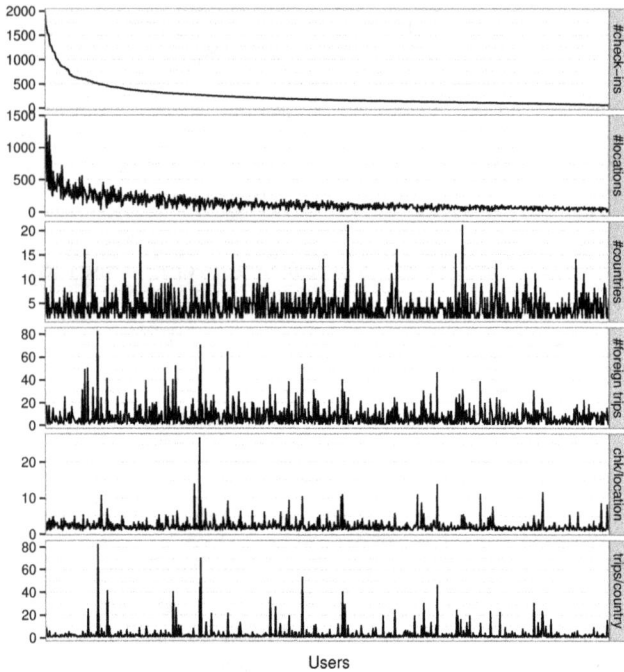

Figure 1: **User activity statistics, where users are sorted by check-in count. Number of visited locations correlate with number of check-ins, while number of visited countries and number of foreign trips do not. The average of check-in count per location is less than 2 for 75% of the users. The average of trips per country is less than 5 for 92% users.**

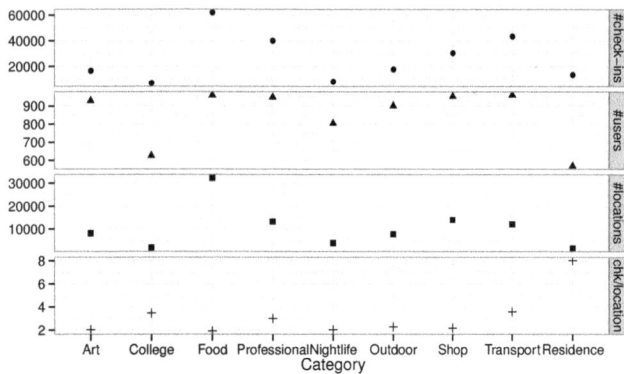

Figure 2: **Statistics by category. Food, Professional, Shop and Transport account for 74% of total check-ins. Food category has the highest number of locations but has on average less than 2 check-ins per location. Residence category attracts not many users but has high average check-ins per location.**

many countries but only once or twice each. However, a few users do keep visiting a small set of countries many times.

Next, we are interested in how check-ins are distributed among the nine different high level *categories* of locations. In Figure 2, for each category we show the number of check-ins, the number of users generating those check-ins, and the number of locations belonging to that category. We also show the average number of check-ins per location for each category. We observe that there are four *favorite* categories

across users which account for 74% of total check-ins: Food, Professional, Shop and Transport.

Furthermore, with regard to the number of locations (irrespective of actual check-ins), Food includes the vast majority of them. From the bottom panel, we see that although there are only a few users checking in to (a small number of) Residence locations, they make frequent check-ins there, so the average check-ins per location makes Residence the top category with an average of 8 check-ins. Transport is the next category, with 3.6 check-ins. Despite the large numbers of check-ins and locations that belong in the Food category, on average, users only check in at each Food spot less than two times (average 1.9).

Summarizing the above basic statistics, we learn that users' behaviors are quite diverse with respect to the number of check-ins or the number of visited locations and countries. There are four main categories Food, Professional, Shop and Transport, which account for a significant portion of the total check-ins. On average, users do not check in at the same location many times, especially for Food locations, while they rarely check-in at home (even though when they do so, they do it often). Simply put, people return to their homes every day, but they want to try different food establishments. While it is not clear why people do or do not generate check-ins at locations, there exist studies that further support the observed check-in patterns. For instance, people, when *surveyed* have reported that they check in at *interesting* places and so they do not check-in at home [16]. Similar reasons can also explain why people check-in at a restaurant only once; check-ins are a type of location bookmark, so once a venue is "saved" there is no need for additional check-ins at the same spot [4].

4.2 Definitions

So far, we have not examined the fine-grained details of check-ins or users. We next define some terms for tagging these details in the paper.

Definition 1. A check-in from a user is called *domestic* (or *foreign*) if it is made inside (or outside of) the home country of that user.

Definition 2. Domestic (or foreign) *feature vector* of user u, denoted by $\mathbf{d}_u$ (or $\mathbf{f}_u$), is a vector whose i-th component ($i \in \{1, \ldots, 9\}$) equals the percentage of check-ins in the i-th category among all domestic (or foreign) check-ins made by user u.

Definition 3. Domestic (or foreign) *feature matrix*, denoted $\mathbf{D}$ (or $\mathbf{F}$), is a matrix where each row is the domestic (or foreign) feature vector of one user.

Definition 4. Domestic (or foreign) *check-in (temporal) distribution matrix* of a country c, denoted $\mathbf{P}_c^d$ (or $\mathbf{P}_c^f$), is a matrix of size 24×9, where the element at i-th column ($i \in \{1, \ldots, 9\}$) and j-th row ($j \in \{1, \ldots, 24\}$) equals the percentage of check-ins made in the i-th category during the j-th hour of the day among the total check-ins made in country c by domestic (or foreign) users.

4.3 Users change their check-in patterns when they travel abroad

We study the hypothesis that users change behavior while traveling, by examining the check-in patterns in different ways (e.g., time and category of check-ins). We drill into users at different aggregate levels (i.e., dataset as a whole, grouping by home country, or individually). To preview our results, our hypothesis is supported when we consider the following features of check-in patterns: (a) time of check-ins, (b) time between two consecutive check-ins, (c) returning frequency to a location, (d) category of repeated checked-in locations, (e) category of check-ins. We also examine: (f) trends among users from the same home country, and (g) trends among all individuals.

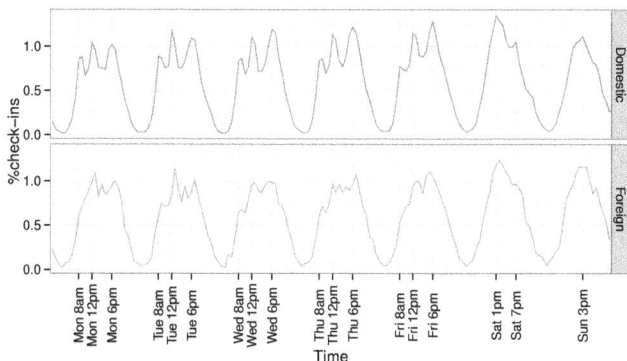

Figure 3: Domestic and foreign check-ins distribution over a cycle of one week. Domestic check-ins exhibit a clear pattern of three peaks in weekdays.

Check-in Time: We start by asking if foreign visitors make check-ins at times of the day that are different compared to domestic users. Specifically, we compare the distribution over *local* time of the number of domestic and foreign check-ins considering all users in aggregate. Note that here we use the *local time* of check-in, not the original UTC timestamp. Figure 3 plots the percentage of check-ins made in one-hour bins during the cycle of a week. Clearly, domestic check-ins exhibit three peaks, Monday through Friday (corresponding to a typical working weekday): at 8am (before work), 12pm (lunch time) and 6pm (after work). On Saturdays we see two peaks around 1pm and 7pm. On Sundays there is only one peak around 3pm. The data analysis indicates that users generate fewer check-ins at the beginning of the week and more towards the weekend. Foreign check-ins do not have *the consistent pattern of three peaks* through weekdays, although we still see an increase in the weekend check-in activity.

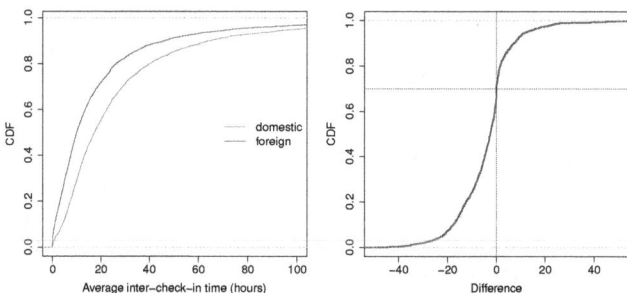

Figure 4: Comparing inter-check-in times. Left: CDF of foreign inter-check-in times is shifted to the left compared to the CDF of domestic inter-check-in times. Right: CDF of differences between average foreign inter-check-in time and average domestic inter-check-in time of users. More than 70% of users have shorter average foreign inter-check-in time.

Inter-check-in Time: We have seen above that in foreign countries, users (in aggregate), do not follow the "three peaks" check-in time patterns as they do in their home country. But how about the check-in frequency, (i.e., do they generate check-in more or less often) ? We next compare the distribution of inter-check-in times of domestic and foreign check-ins. We calculate the empirical CDF of the domestic and foreign inter-check-in times from all users. In Figure 4 (left) we see that the CDF for foreign check-ins (blue line) has a similar shape but it is located entirely on the left (and above) of the CDF for domestic check-ins (red line). A one-sided Kolmogorov-Smirnov test also confirms these CDFs are different (with p-value less than 10^{-10}). Further, for each user we calculate the mean of his domestic inter-check-in times as well as the mean of his foreign inter-check-in times, and the difference between the latter and the former. Figure 4 (right) plots the distribution of such differences. We can see that 70% of users have negative difference. The two plots together confirm that *users tend to check in more frequently during foreign trips.*

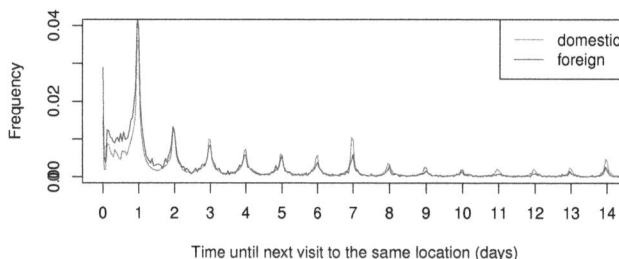

Figure 5: Frequency of returning to visited locations. Both domestic and foreign users exhibit multiple days/weeks returning pattern. However, revisits of foreign users are more likely to happen within one day. The raise at 0 day is caused by multiple check-ins at the same location within an hour.

Returning Frequency: So far we have seen that in foreign countries users tend to generate check-ins more frequently and not regularly at the same times of the day as they do at home (e.g., 8am, 12pm, 6pm). We now examine if users tend to generate check-ins regularly at the same places. In other words, we are interested in the time interval of returning visits, i.e., how long will it take for users to return to locations visited previously. While individuals might not return often to previously visited locations, collectively they provide a large number of such returns to obtain some useful insights. For each (*user, location*) pair, we measure the time differences between check-ins of that user at that location. We then group all those time differences (from all pairs) into one-hour bins. The count in bin k shows how many revisits happens after k hours (k is essentially the elapsed time from the last visit to the same location). Finally we normalize the count in bins to get the frequency of revisiting after k hours. Figure 5 plots the returning frequency for domestic and foreign check-ins. There are clear peaks that occur at "multiple of days" with a decreasing trend in the height of the peaks mixed with a little boost at 7 days and 14 days. This means that for both domestic and foreign trips, users collectively exhibit daily and weekly patterns in their activities. The peaks of returning frequency at 7 days and 14 days are less clear for foreign check-ins because 86% of foreign trips are shorter than 7 days. There is also a crest at time 0, which corresponds to multiple check-ins at the same place within an hour (for example at subway stations during a single trip). Except for the period from 0 to 1 day, the red (domestic) line is very close to the blue (foreign) line. In the range from 0 to 1 day, foreign visitors have higher returning frequency compared to domestic users. This can be a bias caused by the short duration of trips to foreign countries. In particular, during short trips, if users do return to visited locations, then the elapsed time is more probable to be short as well. A closer look at the data shows that Transport category accounts for 36% of the number of foreign revisits to the same locations within an hour, while Food and Professional categories account for 10% and 19% respectively.

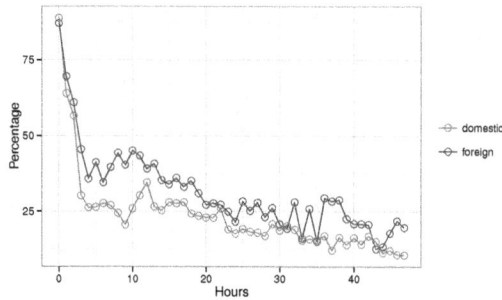

Figure 6: Fraction of back-to-back check-ins at the same locations over all revisits within 48 hours. In foreign countries users are more likely to make multiple check-ins at the same location in a row.

We next count how many of the revisits are consecutive, i.e., there is no other check-in between them. Figure 6 shows that during 48 hours, in foreign countries users have a higher chance to perform back-to-back check-ins at the same place.

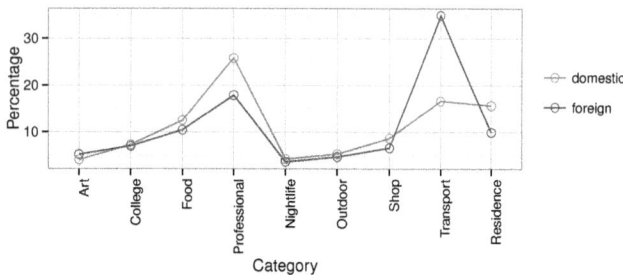

Figure 7: Percentage of repeated check-ins by category. Here we consider all repeated (consecutive) check-ins, regardless of the time between them. As expected, in foreign countries users tend to make more repeated check-ins in Transport locations.

Repeated Check-ins: A natural follow-up question to ask is "Where do users make repeated check-ins (in the same trip)?". We have seen before that while traveling in foreign countries users make more check-ins in Transport. Also, it is common that travelers usually spend time waiting in transits (e.g., airports and train stations), so we expect that foreign repeated check-ins are likely concentrated in the Transport category. Figure 7 confirms our intuition with 33% revisits in Transport spots for foreign check-ins as compared to 16% for domestic check-ins. A closer look reveals that 15% of those repeated foreign Transport check-ins are within 30 minutes,

45% are within 12 hours, 75% are within 24 hours and 89% are within 2 days. The rest (11%) are repeated check-ins that are more than two days apart. We delve further into the details of this result and examine who made that 11% check-ins and if they are users who have check-ins only in Transport spots. The data shows that those users made 9% of total users and Transport takes only a proportion of 52% in their total check-ins. Figure 7 also shows that the percentage of repeated check-ins in Professional and Residence venues is higher in home countries as compared to foreign countries.

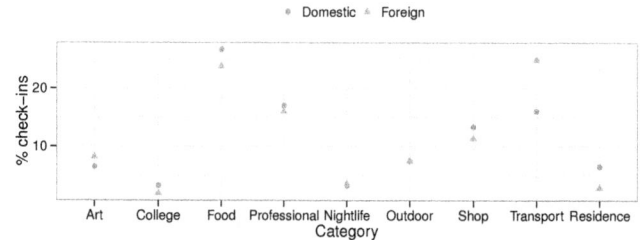

Figure 8: Distribution of domestic and foreign check-ins by category. Proportion of Transport and Art categories are higher for foreign check-ins. Transport accounts for 25% of foreign check-ins, but only 16% of domestic check-ins. Food, Shop and Residence categories hold a lower proportion in foreign check-ins.

Check-in Categories: The data show that while traveling to foreign countries, users change not only the temporal aspects of their check-ins (i.e., when and how often they check in) but also the contextual dimension (i.e., what kinds of locations they check in at) of their check-in patterns. Figure 8 compares the distribution of domestic and foreign check-ins (from all users) over the nine categories. We see that Transport accounts for 25% of foreign check-ins, but only 16% of domestic check-ins. The corresponding numbers for Art are 8% (foreign) and 6.5% (domestic) – slightly different. This can be attributed to the fact that when people travel abroad, they have more chances to generate check-ins in Transport (e.g., in airports) and Art (e.g., in museums) venues. However, when we consider fractions of the total check-ins the increased numbers in the foreign check-ins might signal the "priorities" of users. On the other hand, with foreign check-ins, the percentages in Food, Shop and Residence venues are lower. However the general shape of the two distributions is quite similar. In particular, we still see four main categories: Food, Professional, Shop and Transport.

Trends by Country: As we have seen in the previous paragraph users (as a whole) check in more in Transport and Art categories in foreign countries. We further investigate the trends of users from the same country and compare with users from other countries. In particular, we look at the differences in domestic and foreign feature vectors of users from the same home country (see definitions in Section 4.2). In particular, for each user u we calculate the vector of difference $\mathbf{h}_u = \mathbf{f}_u - \mathbf{d}_u$. A positive value of its i-th component $h_{u,i}$ may indicate that user u is more *interested* in category i when he is abroad. For each category i, we are interested in the distribution of $h_{u,i}$ from all users with the same home country. To maintain a statistically meaningful comparison, we focus on the top-5 countries with *the highest number of domestic*

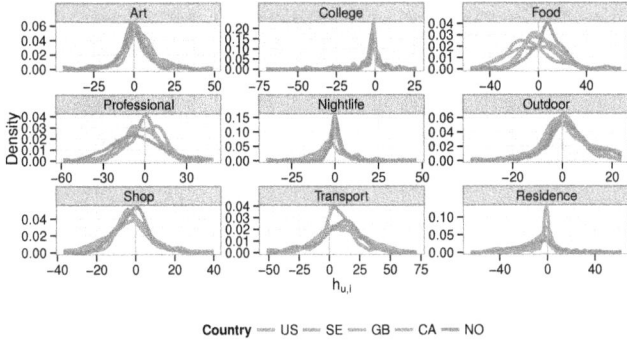

Figure 9: Changes in check-in percentage in categories when users travel abroad. We focus on the top-five countries with the highest number of users: United States (US), Sweden (SE), United Kingdom (GB), Canada (CA), Norway (NO). The mass of the distributions is clearly shifted to the positive side for Transport and Art categories, and to the negative side for Food, Professional and Shop spots. Norwegian users check in more in foreign Food locations but less in foreign Professional locations.

users: United States (US), Sweden (SE), United Kingdom (GB), Canada (CA), Norway (NO). Figure 9 shows the five curves (of five countries) for each category. In Transport and Art categories, as expected, all the distributions have their mass concentrated in the positive values (e.g., users tend to more often use public transportation and visit museums in foreign countries). With the Food category, looking at the US users (red lines), we can see that the mass of the distribution is concentrated in the negative values, which roughly means that US users tend to check in less (percentage-wise) in Food spots in foreign countries. On the other hand, Norwegian users (pink lines) exhibit the opposite behavior. In Professional category Norwegian users tend to check in less in foreign countries, which might be a sign that users from Norway travel mainly for recreational purposes. In the Shop category the distributions are similar among countries with a slight shift to negative direction. While other categories do not show a clear difference in the distribution between countries, we notice the long left tail in the case of College category, caused by users who have a lot of check-ins at school in home country but not in foreign countries.

Trends among Users: Instead of looking for the trends between users from the same country as above, we now try to classify all users (regardless of home country) by their check-in category preferences as captured in the domestic and foreign feature matrices (**D** and **F**) defined above.

To find the groups of users with similar check-in trend, we apply affinity propagation clustering [11] on users using as feature vectors either $\mathbf{d}_u$ or $\mathbf{f}_u$. In Figure 10 the clusters found by using domestic features are denoted from D1 to D7 and shown in rows, while the clusters identified when using foreign features are denoted F1 to F7 and shown in columns. Note that each user belongs to one D cluster and one F cluster. The color dots and foreground numbers show the cluster centroids, i.e., the mean values of features of users in the corresponding clusters. The number at the intersection of a row and a column of the table shows the number of common users between the corresponding D (row) and F

(column) clusters. The numbers in the parentheses capture the cluster sizes.

Examining the clusters we make some interesting observations. In particular, cluster D3 contains 150 users (12% of total) who have a high percentage of domestic Transport check-ins (cluster average in Transport is 50.04%)! We also observe cluster F2 with 303 users (25% of the total population) who have high percentage of foreign Transport check-ins (cluster average in Transport is 51.69%). These two clusters D3 and F2 share 65 common users (5% of total). Thus, from 150 users of D3, only 65 users keep their Transport-high checking pattern, while 28 users merge into cluster F4 (large percentage in Professional category), 27 users merge into F5 (large percentage in Food venues) and the rest 30 users are spread into other F clusters.

Furthermore, all three clusters D1, D2 and D6 contain 711 users (58% of the total population) with large fraction of domestic check-ins in Food (the absolute values are different). However, the number of users from these domestic clusters that appear in F5, which also has a large concentration of check-ins in Food venues, is only 282.

While among D clusters, there is no clear concentration on Shop category, cluster F3 contains 113 users (9% of the total) who show high interest in check-ins at Shop locations. Similarly, there are 64 users forming cluster F1 with high interest in Art.

In summary, assuming that the D clusters represent users' interest in home country and F clusters represent their interest in foreign countries, we see that *only a small part of users retain the same interests.*

4.4 Foreign visitors have their own check-in patterns but can also be aligned with domestic users

To verify the second hypothesis, we consider different countries and compare the behavior of domestic users with that of foreign visitors inside the same country. To have a meaningful comparison to the extent possible, we focus on the top-5 countries with the *highest number of foreign users*: United States (US), United Kingdom (GB), France (FR), Germany (DE) and Netherlands (NL). We look for the differences with respect to category and time of the check-ins, with a separation between check-ins generated on weekdays and on weekends. More precisely, using check-ins generated during weekends, we construct the domestic and foreign check-in distribution matrices (see definitions in 4.2) $\mathbf{P}_c^d, \mathbf{P}_c^f$ for each selected country. We also do the same thing using check-ins generated during weekdays. We show in Figure 11 the results for five selected countries.

We can see a few differences between domestic and foreign users in the same country. For example, we see that during weekdays in France and United Kingdom foreign users have more check-ins between 11pm (23h) and 5am as compared to domestic users. During weekdays, foreign users check in more in Art category than domestic users. Another example is that in Netherlands foreign users check in Outdoor venues much less than local users in both weekdays and weekends; outdoor activities might hence, be deemed to be part of the Dutch culture. On the other hand, we also observe that, for example, the distributions of check-ins in Food category are quite similar for domestic and foreign users in the US.

In order to quantify the similarity/difference between domestic and foreign users in country c during weekdays or

	F1	F2	F3	F4	F5	F6	F7
Art	33.07	5.55	6.53	8.18	7.57	2.93	4.05
College	0.68	0.91	1.63	1.53	1.24	53.39	3.69
Food	12.89	13.65	20.55	14.54	36.85	8.71	12.60
Professional	12.85	11.48	7.09	28.43	10.76	2.03	9.86
Nightlife	12.59	4.63	2.66	4.16	7.02	3.01	3.06
Outdoor	6.05	4.24	6.75	11.06	6.79	2.81	4.59
Shop	6.41	7.44	33.90	8.82	9.75	10.18	10.07
Transport	14.69	51.69	19.49	22.36	18.52	13.97	15.62
Residence	0.76	0.41	1.40	0.91	1.50	2.98	36.15

13.84	1.75	17.86	9.47	14.05	8.40	16.43	16.41	1.80
7.04	2.95	29.35	16.11	3.89	8.79	17.59	10.76	3.52
4.24	2.22	13.49	11.55	3.02	4.86	8.91	50.04	1.65
3.95	2.68	12.81	15.71	2.92	4.39	10.89	15.80	31.15
6.45	2.21	16.25	39.04	3.70	5.99	7.48	15.93	3.25
5.40	1.78	51.11	11.06	6.96	3.43	8.65	10.34	1.27
2.54	40.61	11.10	10.04	3.49	2.22	10.99	10.14	8.88

Cluster	F1	F2	F3	F4	F5	F6	F7	
D1	16	46	15	47	64	6	6	(200)
D2	13	60	35	84	116	5	8	(321)
D3	6	65	13	28	27	2	9	(150)
D4	6	46	14	36	25	3	13	(143)
D5	11	52	12	52	37	2	6	(172)
D6	12	24	18	28	102	0	6	(190)
D7	0	10	6	8	9	3	6	(42)
	(64)	(303)	(113)	(283)	(380)	(21)	(54)	

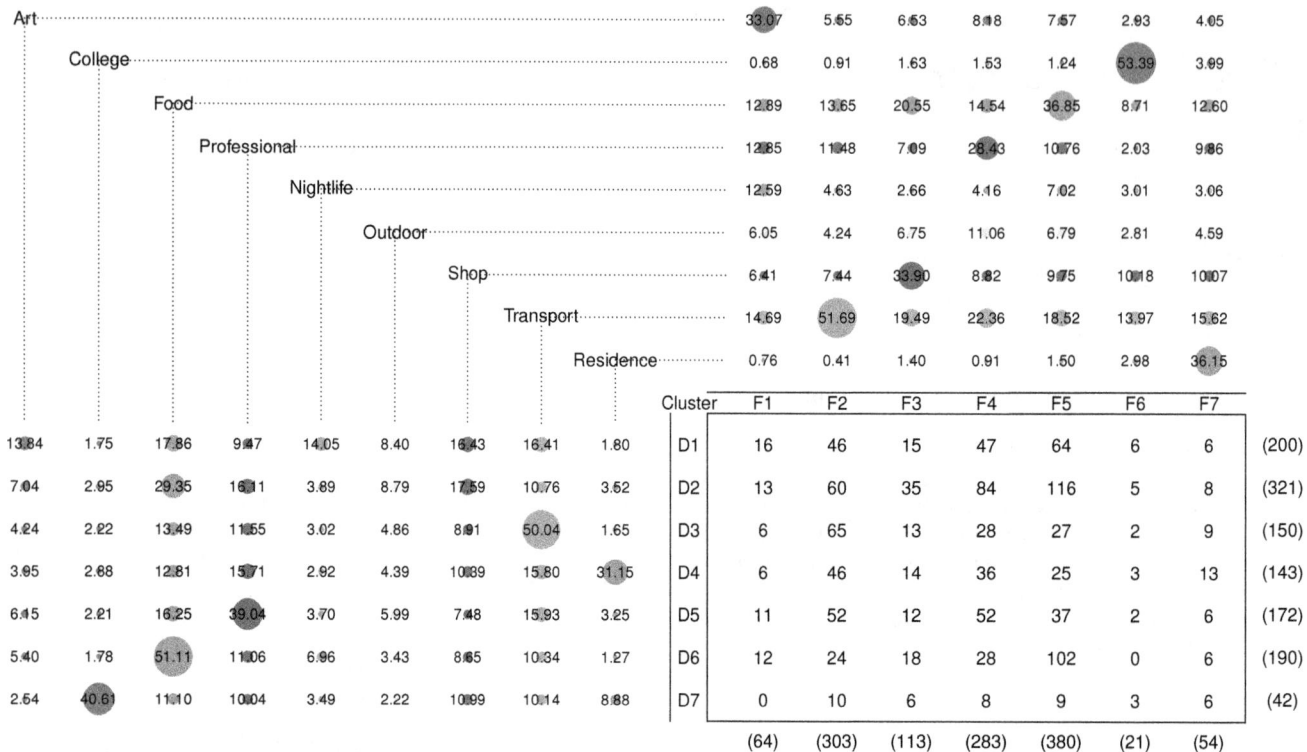

Figure 10: Clustering users by domestic and foreign check-ins in four main categories. Transport category attracts more foreign check-ins (F2 vs. D3). There is also a group of users (F3) showing interest in Shoping venues in foreign countries.

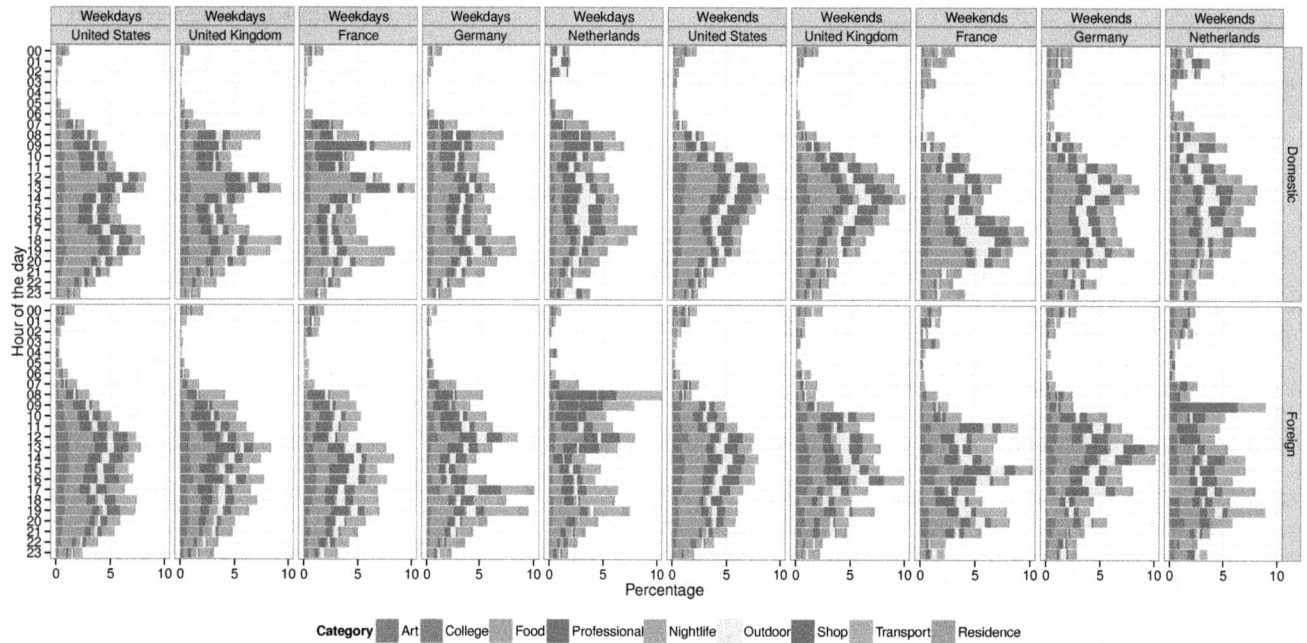

Figure 11: Distribution of domestic and foreign check-ins over 24 hours and 9 categories in five countries with the highest number of foreign visitors. We can spot a few differences between domestic users and foreign visitors. For example, foreign users in France have more proportion of check-ins in Art category during weekdays, or domestic users in Neitherlands are more interested in Outdoor category than foreign visitors in both weekdays and weekends.

weekends we construct the vector of difference $\mathbf{g}_c$ where its i-th component is the Canberra distance[5] between two corresponding i-th column vectors from the two check-in distribution matrices: $\mathbf{g}_c[i] = distance(\mathbf{P}_c^d[i], \mathbf{P}_c^f[i])$. Canberra distance, which has been successfully used in image retrieval and other fields [14, 8], is chosen here because it is more sensitive to small values. In the case of small values (caused by small percentage of check-ins) a metric like Euclidean distance could cause false similarity. Here the Canberra distance serves as a metric to quantify how domestic and foreign users generate check-ins differently in a specific category through the 24 hours of the day. A small distance for a category indicates that domestic and foreign users behave similarly in that category.

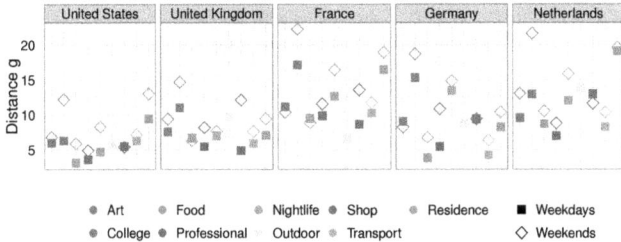

Figure 12: Distance between foreign and domestic check-in patterns in the nine categories in selected countries. The distances in Food and Professional categories are among the smallest for all countries. The other categories having small distances differ for different countries. For example, on weekdays, foreign and domestic users in France have similar check-in patterns in Outdoor category.

Figure 12 plots the values of $\mathbf{g}_c$. We observe that, in general, the distance is slightly higher for weekends. This could possibly be explained as follows: during weekdays people use their time in similar ways since activities are shaped by schedules. On the contrary, during weekends, people have the freedom to use their time differently. The US appears to be the country where the distances are the smallest in all categories, while France is the country where distances are the largest. We can further see that the distances in Food and Professional are among the smallest ones for *all* five countries. Nevertheless, there are other categories that have a small distance and they differ for different countries. For instance, in the US we see Shop and Nightlife as categories with a small distance. Our dataset shows that shopping in malls and going to bars appear to be common activities in the US, so foreign visitors may also follow that trend. Inspecting the dataset confirms that locations with highest number of foreign check-ins in Shop are big malls and in Nightlife are bars. For each of the five selected countries, Table 4 shows categories (in addition to Food and Professional) that foreign visitors and domestic users have similar check-in patterns and some example locations where both foreign and domestic users make a high number of check-ins. These country-specific places might allow for activities in which foreign visitors tend to follow the habits of local people.

---

[5]Canberra distance between two vectors x and y of length n is defined as $\sum_{i=1}^{n} \frac{|x_i - y_i|}{|x_i| + |y_i|}$.

Table 4: Categories with small domestic-foreign distances. Besides Food and Professional, in each country there are categories where foreign visitors and domestic users have similar check-in patterns.

Country	Categories	Example locations
US	Shop, Nightlife	Malls and bars
UK	Transport, Shop	Heathrow airport, chain stores
FR	Outdoor	Elysee Palace, Pont Neuf
DE	Transport	Frankfurt airport, train stations
NL	Art, Transport	Galleries, Amsterdam Arena, Rotterdam Central station

4.5 Summary

By analyzing check-ins of users from two major LBSNs (Gowalla and Foursquare), we verify two hypotheses: (1) users change their check-in patterns when they travel abroad; and (2) foreign visitors have their own check-in patterns but can also be aligned with domestic users. The first hypothesis is supported by a variety of results at different aggregate levels. Considering all users as a whole, we find that the distribution of check-ins in home and foreign countries are different with regards to the time of check-ins, the time between check-ins, the revisiting frequency and the category of repeated check-ins. Specifically, in foreign countries, the time of check-ins do not show the "three peaks" patterns during weekdays, while the time between consecutive check-ins tend to be shorter. Furthermore, the chance of returning to the same location is higher for time intervals less than one day and there are more chances to repeatedly check-in at Transport locations and less so at Professional venues. By grouping users based on their home country, we see that users from different countries can exhibit different changes in the check-in categories. By looking at individual users, we see that in foreign countries, average inter-check-in time is shorter for 70% of users; some users keep their main interest (e.g., high Food check-ins), while a larger part exhibit different interests. The second hypothesis is supported by our analysis of the similarity in the check-in patterns between foreign visitors and domestic users in the same country. We observe that there is a dependence on the country and there are categories where foreign visitors have check-in patterns similar to that of domestic users. This closeness might be attributed to the local cultural specifics (e.g., shopping in the US or visiting galleries in Netherlands).

5. DISCUSSION AND CONCLUSIONS

Our objective is to explore the spatial behavioral dynamics of people as a function of their location and as captured through the content they generate on LBSNs. While location can be defined at different granularities, the focus on the country-level provides significant physical separation. With different granularity of aggregation, we are able to highlight differences in the way users generate check-ins. Our observations confirm that behavior of LBSN users changes not only over time, but also over space. The LBSN service designers can take this into account when design their system to improve users' experience. For example, if the data show that users from country X visiting country Y will be more interested in category Z, then an LBSN may select the better recommendations of places to visit to visitors.

Of course, we are aware that there are potential biases to our results as we explain in the following.

Technology Bias: Throughout our analysis, we have implicitly assumed that all users are able to check-in to locations outside their home country. However, data roaming is still expensive and it might be the case that many users do not perform foreign check-ins due to their inability to do so. Even users that do have foreign check-ins, might be able to check-in only at locations with open Internet connectivity (e.g., a public WiFi hotspot). We expect such biases to be reduced in the future and especially with the very recent significant reduction in roaming costs that big telecommunication providers have announced (e.g., T-mobile USA). Future studies may reveal if the bias is significant. In addition, the Foursquare dataset has bias itself because only check-ins that were pushed to the Twitter public stream could be collected.

Quality of Data: Traditional sociology studies that rely on interviews for obtaining the required data are known to exhibit biases such as the difference between the declared and actual social behavior of the subjects. The emerging field of computational sociology relies upon digital trails of people's activity. However, this approach can also exhibit quality of data problems. For example, before filtering the data, we observed that in the Foursquare dataset Indonesia forms the foreign country with largest number of user check-ins in the US. It turns out that there are many Indonesian users making fake check-ins in the US to collect badges [10]. Although we applied simple sanity check filter, other kinds of fake check-ins may still remain.

Demographic Bias: Another possible source of bias for the conclusions drawn from the results, is that of demographic biases. By integrating the two different datasets we are able to possibly account for different user bases that use the two different systems (Gowalla and Foursquare), but the final dataset still includes demographic biases. In particular, it captures the behavior only of "tech savvy" people that use LBSNs and even more their early adopters (since the datasets span the early adoption period of LBSNs).

Despite the possible biases, we believe that our analysis still provides some insights that can be useful to a number of disciplines. By studying the behavioral changes across people and between their behavior in the home country and when traveling abroad, we may reveal and highlight hidden cultural differences. Furthermore, tourist services may benefit from similar studies. Now they can not only track where visitors come from (after all, this information is available from other sources as well), but they can also examine the behavioral changes of users and hence, develop relevant infrastructure to support tourism.

6. REFERENCES

[1] L. Backstrom, E. Sun, and C. Marlow. Find me if you can: improving geographical prediction with social and spatial proximity. In *Proceedings of the 19th WWW*, 2010.

[2] Z. Cheng, J. Caverlee, K. Lee, and D. Sui. Exploring millions of footprints in location sharing services. In *Proceedings of AAAI ICWSM*, 2011.

[3] E. Cho, S. A. Myers, and J. Leskovec. Friendship and mobility: Friendship and mobility: User movement in location-based social networks. In *Proceedings of ACM KDD*, 2011.

[4] H. Cramer, M. Rost, and L. E. Holmquist. Performing a check-in: Emerging practices, norms and conflicts in location-sharing using foursquare. In *Proceedings of the 13th International Conference on Human Computer Interaction with Mobile Devices and Services*, MobileHCI, pages 57–66, New York, NY, USA, 2011. ACM.

[5] D. Crandall, L. Backstrom, D. Cosley, S. Suri, D. Huttenlocher, and J. Kleinberg. Inferring social ties from geographic coincidences. *Proceedings of the National Academy of Sciences*, 107(52):22436–22441, 2010.

[6] J. Cranshaw, E. Toch, J. Hong, A. Kittur, and N. Sadeh. Bridging the gap between physical location and online social networks. In *Proceedings of UbiComp*, pages 119–128. ACM, 2010.

[7] Efele. Timezones. http://efele.net/maps/tz/world/, 2012.

[8] S. M. Emran and N. Ye. Robustness of canberra metric in computer intrusion detection. In *Proc. IEEE Workshop on Information Assurance and Security, West Point, NY, USA*, 2001.

[9] A. Field. The college student market segment: A comparative study of travel behaviors of international and domestic students at a southeastern university. *Journal of Travel Research*, 37(4):375–381, 1999.

[10] Foursquare-About. Foursquare's Indonesia problem. http://aboutfoursquare.com/ foursquare-indonesia/, 2009.

[11] B. J. Frey and D. Dueck. Clustering by passing messages between data points. *Science*, 315(5814):972–976, 2007.

[12] R. Garcia-Gavilanes, D. Quercia, and A. Jaimes. Cultural dimensions in twitter: Time, individualism and power. In *Proceedings of AAAI ICWSM*, 2013.

[13] A. Kaltenbrunner, S. Scellato, Y. Volkovich, D. Laniado, D. Currie, E. Jutemar, and C. Mascolo. Far from the eyes, close on the web: impact of geographic distance on online social interactions. In *Proceedings of ACM WOSN*, 2012.

[14] M. Kokare, B. N. Chatterji, and P. Biswas. Comparison of similarity metrics for texture image retrieval. In *Proceedings of TENCON*, 2003.

[15] R. Lambiotte, V. Blondel, C. De Kerchove, E. Huens, C. Prieur, Z. Smoreda, and P. Van Dooren. Geographical dispersal of mobile communication networks. *Physica A: Statistical Mechanics and its Applications*, 387(21):5317, 2008.

[16] J. Lindqvist, J. Cranshaw, J. Wiese, J. Hong, and J. Zimmerman. I'm the mayor of my house: examining why people use foursquare - a social-driven location sharing application. In *Proceedings of the SIGCHI Conference on Human Factors in Computing Systems*, CHI, pages 2409–2418, New York, NY, USA, 2011. ACM.

[17] D. Mok, B. Wellman, and J. Carrasco. Does distance matter in the age of the internet? *Urban Studies*, 47(13):2747, 2010.

[18] A. Noulas, S. Scellato, C. Mascolo, and M. Pontil. An empirical study of geographic user activity patterns in foursquare. In *Proceedings of AAAI ICWSM*, 2011.

[19] D. Preotiuc-Pietro and T. Cohn. Mining user behaviours: A study of check-in patterns in location-based social networks. In *Proceedings of ACM WebSci*, 2013.

[20] S. Scellato, C. Mascolo, M. Musolesi, and V. Latora. Distance matters: Geo-social metrics for online social networks. In *Proceedings of WOSN*, 2010.

[21] S. Scellato, A. Noulas, R. Lambiotte, and C. Mascolo. Socio-spatial properties of online location-based social networks. In *Proceedings of AAAI ICWSM*, 2011.

[22] L. Sproull and S. Kiesler. Reducing social context cues: Electronic mail in organizational communication. In *Management Science, Volume 31, Issue 11, November*, 1986.

[23] P. Sullivan. It's easier to be yourself when you are invisible: Female college students discuss their online classroom experiences. *Innovative Higher Education*, 27(2):129–144, 2002.

[24] Thematicmapping. Worldmap. http://thematicmapping. org/downloads/world_borders.php, 2012.

[25] C. L. Toma, J. T. Hancock, and N. B. Ellison. Separating fact from fiction: An examination of deceptive self-presentation in online dating profiles. *Personality and Social Psychology Bulletin*, 34(8):1023–1036, 2008.

Evolution of Online User Behavior During a Social Upheaval

Onur Varol, Emilio Ferrara[*], Christine L. Ogan, Filippo Menczer, Alessandro Flammini

Center for Complex Networks and Systems Research
School of Informatics and Computing, Indiana University, Bloomington, USA

ABSTRACT

Social media represent powerful tools of mass communication and information diffusion. They played a pivotal role during recent social uprisings and political mobilizations across the world. Here we present a study of the Gezi Park movement in Turkey through the lens of Twitter. We analyze over 2.3 million tweets produced during the 25 days of protest occurred between May and June 2013. We first characterize the spatio-temporal nature of the conversation about the Gezi Park demonstrations, showing that similarity in trends of discussion mirrors geographic cues. We then describe the characteristics of the users involved in this conversation and what roles they played. We study how roles and individual influence evolved during the period of the upheaval. This analysis reveals that the conversation becomes more democratic as events unfold, with a redistribution of influence over time in the user population. We conclude by observing how the online and offline worlds are tightly intertwined, showing that exogenous events, such as political speeches or police actions, affect social media conversations and trigger changes in individual behavior.

Categories and Subject Descriptors

[Human-centered computing]: Collaborative and social computing—*Social media*; [Information systems]: World Wide Web—*Social networks*; [Networks]: Network types—*Social media networks*

Keywords

Social media analysis, social protest, political mobilization, online user behavior

1. INTRODUCTION

Technologically mediated communication systems, like social media platforms and online social networks, support in-

[*]Corresponding author: `ferrarae@indiana.edu`

formation sharing and foster the connectivity of hundreds of millions of users across the world every day [12, 38]. The adoption of these platforms has been associated with profound changes in 21st-century society: they affect how we produce and consume information [2, 10], shifting the paradigm from a broadcasting model (one-to-many, like radio and TV) to a peer-to-peer (many-to-many) distribution system. They have also altered the ways we seek information to understand societal events surrounding us [31, 32], and how we interact with our peers [14, 15].

The use of online social media to discuss politics and policy has recently been associated with political uprisings and social protests around the world. Prominent examples include the revolution in Egypt [17], the American anti-capitalist Occupy Wall Street movement [13, 16, 19, 20], and the Spanish May 15th protests [11, 25]. Social media have played a pivotal role in the development and increasing frequency of these social movements [8, 22, 33]. Using survey methodology, Tufekci and Wilson [34] found that the use of social media in the Egyptian protests allowed people to make informed decisions about participation in the movement, provided new sources of information outside of the regime's control, and increased the odds that people participated in the protests on the first day. Another survey found Facebook use for news and socializing in Chile's youth movement to be positively associated with participation in the protests [36]. Chief among social platforms used for protests is Twitter that, with more than a half billion users, provides a high-visibility window on real-world events and an active forum for discussion of political and social issues. The mostly ungoverned nature of this platform ensures a democratic, peer-to-peer discussion, aiming at both creating a framing language to set goals for the protest, and as a vehicle for mobilizing resources and social capital to sustain it [1, 26, 29, 19]. Individuals and organizations can discuss and share information on Twitter about the movement's political and social objectives [6, 7]. They can also coordinate to marshal the resources needed to carry out on-the-ground activities like encampments or marches [27, 30].

In this work we focus on the Gezi Park protest, a social uprising whose events unfolded during May and June 2013 in Turkey. Political and policy issues related to this movement have been recently discussed in the social science literature [23, 28]. Here instead we present an empirical analysis of the conversation about Gezi Park that occurred on Twitter. Our goal is to gain insight to the protest discussion dynamics. In particular, we aim at exploring three different aspects of this conversation: *(i)* its spatio-temporal dimen-

Table 1: List of relevant events during the protest divided in three categories.

	Code	Event date	Event description
Government	A1	2013-05-29	Prime minister Erdogan's statement: "No matter what you do, we took our final decision about Gezi Park."
	A2	2013-06-02	Erdogan refers to protesters as marauders (*çapulcu*).
	A3	2013-06-03	Erdogan says "There is 50 percent, and we can barely keep them at home. But we have called on them to calm down" before his trip to Morocco.
Police	B1	2013-05-30	Police forces raids Gezi Park by using tear gas and destroys tents of protesters without any notice.
	B2	2013-06-03	Official statements about the first death and many injuries all around Turkey.
	B3	2013-06-11	Riot police enters Taksim square with water cannons and uses tear gas against the protesters.
	B4	2013-06-15	Police clears Gezi Park and takes out the protesters. Police starts to stake out Gezi Park.
Protests	C1	2013-06-04	A library is built by the protesters in Gezi Park.
	C2	2013-06-13	Mothers join protests after Huseyin Mutlu's (Governor of Istanbul) calls to mothers to bring their children home.
	C3	2013-06-17	Silent protest in Taksim square held by a standing man. Many others gather after his protest.

sion, to determine whether it was concentrated only in the country of inception, or if it acquired significant attention worldwide, and to assess how it started and what trends it generated; *(ii)* what roles individuals played in this conversation and what influence they had on others, and whether such roles changed over time as information was diffused and the protests unfolded; *(iii)* and how the online behavior of individuals changed over time in response to real-world events. To the best of our knowledge, this is the first study to explore the temporal evolution of online user roles and behaviors as a reflection of on-the-ground events during a social upheaval. We do so by means of computational tools and data-driven analyses.

Contribution and outline

- We present methods to extract topically focused conversations about the social uprising surrounding Gezi Park and related trending topics of conversation on Twitter. (See § 3.)

- We explore the spatio-temporal characteristics of the conversation; that is, where tweets about Gezi Park originated and what locations shared the most similar topics and trends. This analysis yields clusters of cities that are mostly consistent with the country's geopolitics. (See § 4.1.)

- We analyze the emerging characteristics of users involved in the conversation about Gezi Park protests on Twitter, the roles they played in this context, and how these roles evolved as the protest unfolded. We find that influence was redistributed in the user population over time, making the conversation more democratic. (See § 4.2.)

- We show that online user behavior was affected by external factors, such as speeches by political leaders or police action to hinder or suffocate the protests. (See § 4.3.)

2. BACKGROUND ABOUT THE PROTEST

In this section we provide some background information about the Gezi Park movement, explaining the context of the protests, the triggers for the mobilization, the timeline of events, and the ways which those events unfolded.

The protests began quietly in an already politically divided Turkey on May 28, 2013 with about 50–100 environmental activists who gathered for a sit-in at Gezi Park in Taksim Square, Istambul. They were there to demonstrate against the destruction of one of the last public green spaces in central Istanbul. The government had slated the space for the construction of a replica of an Ottoman-era barracks that would be the site of luxury residences and a shopping mall. The peaceful encampment successfully resisted the demolition of the park by bulldozers when demonstrators refused to leave. At dawn on the morning of May 30, and then again the next morning, the protesters were attacked by the police using tear gas and water cannons, triggering clashes between authorities and the demonstrators that lasted until the end of the park occupation on June 15. During that time period, the size of the groups of demonstrators escalated to about 10,000 on both the European and Asian sides of the Bosphorus and many thousands more in major cities across the country. The focus of the protests grew from upset over Gezi Park's potential destruction to widespread criticism of the government's increasingly authoritarian practices and intrusions into the private lives of its citizens. As the New York Times reported,

> In full public view, a long struggle over urban spaces is erupting as a broader fight over Turkish identity, where difficult issues of religion, social class and politics intersect. [3]

Throughout the struggle, the protesters, who mostly consisted of middle-class secular Turks but also included some members of left-wing groups and nationalists, used social media to alert others to their plans, urge others to join them, warn participants of police attacks and potential danger spots, provide information about makeshift medical assistance locations, and announce their goals. A poll of about 3,000 activists found that the motivation of the demonstrators was their anger with Prime Minister Erdogan and not

Table 2: Set of hashtags commonly used by protesters and government supporters.

Commonly used hashtags		Local protest hashtags	Government supporters' hashtags
#direngeziparki	#bizeheryertaksim	#direnankara	#dunyaliderierdogan
#occupygezi	#gezideyim	#direnbesiktas	#seviyoruzsenierdogan
#eylemvakti	#7den77yedireniyoruz	#direnizmir	#seninleyizerdogan
#occupyturkey	#heryertaksimheryerdirenis	#direntaksim	#seninleyiztayyiperdogan
#direngezi	#korkakmedya	#direnadana	#youcantstopturkishsuccess
#tayyipistifa	#hukumetistifa	#direndersim	#weareerdogan
#bubirsivildirenis	#dictatorerdogan	#direnistanbul	#yedirmeyiz
#wearegezi	#siddetidurdurun	#direnrize	#turkiyebasbakanininyaninda

Table 3: Trends in Turkey (country level) and in 12 Turkish cities during the observation period.

Trend Location	Top 5 trending hashtags/phrases
Turkey	Turkey, Necati Şaşmaz, #DirenGeziSeninleyiz, #OyunaGelmiyoruzTakipleşiyoruz, #ProvokatörlereUYMA
Istanbul	Turkey, Necati Şaşmaz, #DirenGeziSeninleyiz, Bruno Alves, #OyunaGelmiyoruzTakipleşiyoruz
Ankara	Turkey, Necati Şaşmaz, Bruno Alves, #DirenGeziSeninleyiz, #ProvokatörlereUYMA
Izmir	Turkey, Necati Şaşmaz, #DirenGeziSeninleyiz, #TatilöncesiTakipleşelim, #ProvokatörlereUYMA
Bursa	Turkey, #TatilöncesiTakipleşelim, Necati Şaşmaz, #KızlarTakipleşiyor, #çapulcularTakipleşirse
Adana	Turkey, #çapulcularTakipleşirse, #TatilöncesiTakipleşelim, Necati Şaşmaz, #DirenGeziSeninleyiz
Gaziantep	Turkey, Necati Şaşmaz, #SesVerTürkiyeBuÜlkeSahipsizDeğil, #DirenGeziSeninleyiz, #OyunaGelmiyoruzTakipleşiyoruz
Konya	#TatilöncesiTakipleşelim, Turkey, #BizimDelilerTakipleşiyor, Necati Şaşmaz, #SesVerTürkiyeBuÜlkeSahipsizDeğil
Antalya	Turkey, #KızlarTakipleşiyor, #CapulchularTakipleşiyor, #TürkiyeBaşbakanınınYanında, Necati Şaşmaz
Diyarbakir	Turkey, Necati Şaşmaz, #DirenGeziSeninleyiz, #OyunaGelmiyoruzTakipleşiyoruz, #ProvokatörlereUYMA
Mersin	#HayranGruplarıTakipleşiyor, Turkey, #TatilöncesiTakipleşelim, #TürkiyemDireniyor, #direnankara
Kayseri	Turkey, Necati Şaşmaz, #DirenGeziSeninleyiz, #Seni_Görünce, #ProvokatörlereUYMA
Eskisehir	Turkey, Necati Şaşmaz, #DirenGeziSeninleyiz, #OyunaGelmiyoruzTakipleşiyoruz, #ProvokatörlereUYMA

his political party or his aides. More than 90% of the respondents said they took to the streets because of Erdogan's authoritarian attitude [35].

A detailed timeline of the Gezi Park protests' major events during this period is provided in Table 1.

3. DATA COLLECTION

Our analysis is based on data collected from Twitter. Twitter users can post *tweets* up to 140 characters in length, which might contain URLs and media alongside text. Users can also interact with each other through various means, including the creation of directed social links (follower/followee relations), *retweeting* content (*i.e.*, rebroadcasting messages to their followers), and *mentioning* other users in their posts. Tweets may also contain *hashtags*, that are keywords used to give a topical connotation to the tweets (like #direngeziparki and #occupygezi). Multiple hashtags might co-occur in the same tweet.

The dataset collected for our study comes from a 10% random sample of all tweets streamed in real time, which was stored, post-processed and analyzed in-house. The observation period covers 27 days, from May 25th to June 20th, 2013: this time window started four days prior to the beginning of the Gezi Park events, and fully covered the three weeks during which the main protests unfolded. The short period prior to the protest inception is used as baseline to define user activity and interests.

Our sample not only contains information about the tweets, but also meta-data about the users, including their *screen names*, follower/followee counts, self-reported locations, and more. Additionally, for content posted with a GPS-enabled smartphone, we have access to the geographic location from which the tweets were generated.

To isolate a representative sample of topical discussion about Gezi Park events, we adopted a hashtag seed-expansion procedure [18]: first, we hand-picked the most popular Gezi Park related hashtag (#diregeziparki) and we extracted all tweets containing this hashtag during our 27-day long period of interest. We then built the hashtag co-occurrence list, and we selected the top 100 hashtags co-occurring with our seed (#diregeziparki). We generated our final list of hashtags of interest to include the set of commonly co-occurring hashtags and expanded our dataset collecting all tweets containing any of these hashtags. These hashtags were manu-

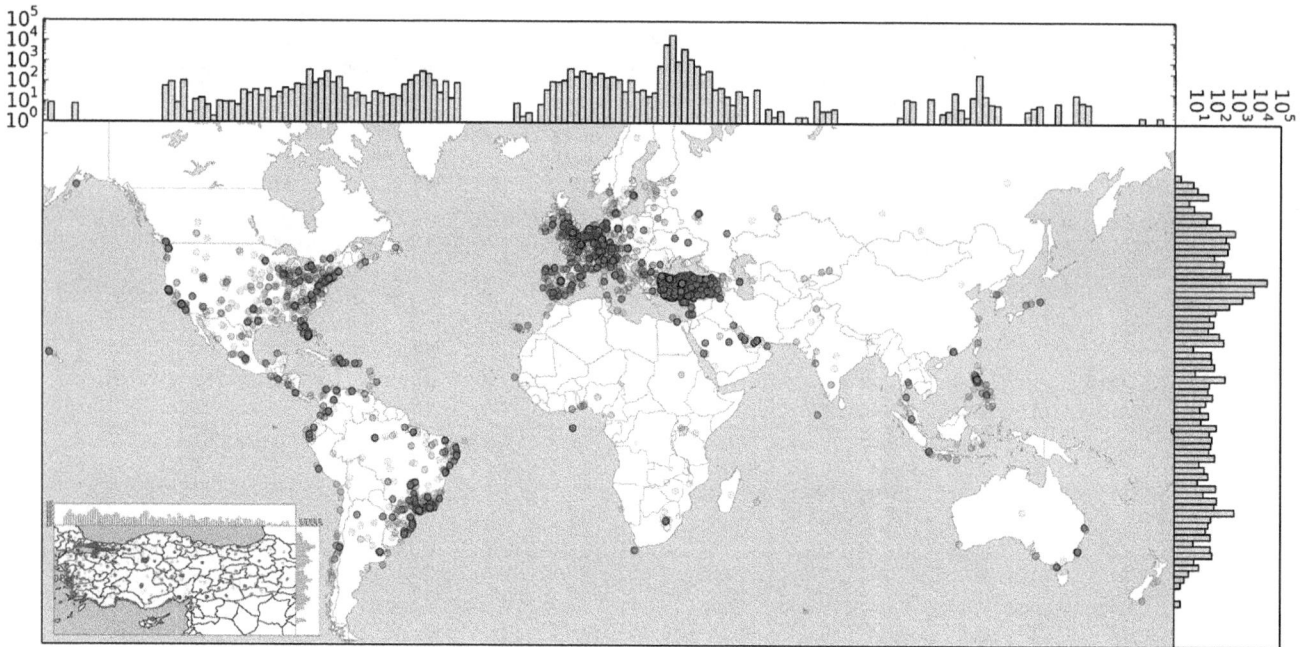

Figure 1: Geographic distribution of tweets in our sample related to the discussion of Gezi Park events. The histograms represent the total volume by latitude and longitude. Content production crossed the Turkish national boundaries and spread in Europe, North and South America.

ally divided in three categories: general-interest hashtags, local protest related ones, and finally those used by government supporters. A detailed list containing the top general-purpose, local-protest, and government-support hashtags are listed in Table 2.

Overall, we collected 2,361,335 tweets associated with the Gezi Park movement, generated by 855,616 distinct users and containing a total of 64,668 unique hashtags. Among these 2.3 million tweets, 1,475,494 are retweets and 47,163 are replies from one users to another. Also, 43,646 tweets have latitude/longitude coordinates. We adopt this subset of geolocated tweets to study the spatio-temporal nature of the protest (see § 4.1).

During the same 27-day long observation period, we monitored the Twitter trends occurring at the country level in Turkey, and at the metropolitan area level in 12 major cities as provided by Twitter, namely: Adana, Bursa, Istanbul, Izmir, Kayseri, Gaziantep, Diyarbakir, Eskisehir, Antalya, Konya and Mersin. The list of top 10 hashtags and phrases trending both at the country level and at the city level were pulled from the platform at regular intervals of 10 minutes. This method [21] is used in our analysis to define the similarity of topical interests and the patterns of collective attention towards Gezi Park conversation in the country. During this period we also monitored worldwide trends to determine whether and when the discussion about the protest achieved global visibility. A detailed list of the top popular trending hashtags and phrases for each location and at the country level is provided in Table 3.

4. RESULTS

In this section we present the results of our analyses on spatio-temporal characteristics of the Gezi Park conversa-

tion on Twitter, evolving roles of the users involved, and effects of real-world events on online behaviors.

4.1 Spatio-temporal cues of the conversation

Our first analysis aims at determining the extent to which the discussion about Gezi Park attracted individual attention inside the national boundaries of Turkey, where the movement began, and how much of this conversation spread worldwide.

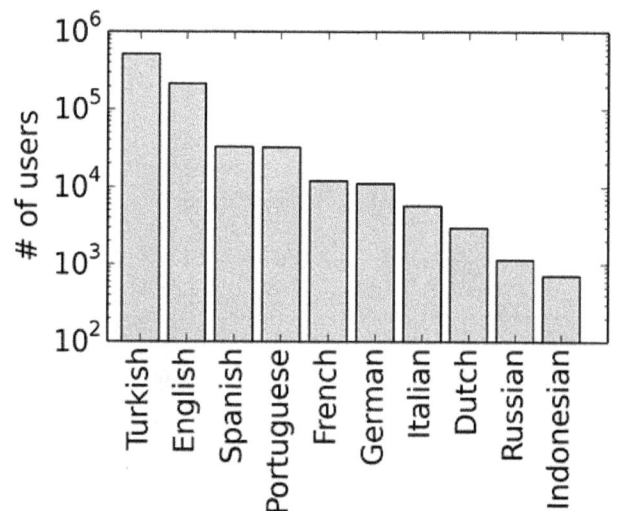

Figure 2: Distribution of top 10 languages in tweets about the protest. Language information was extracted from the tweet meta-data.

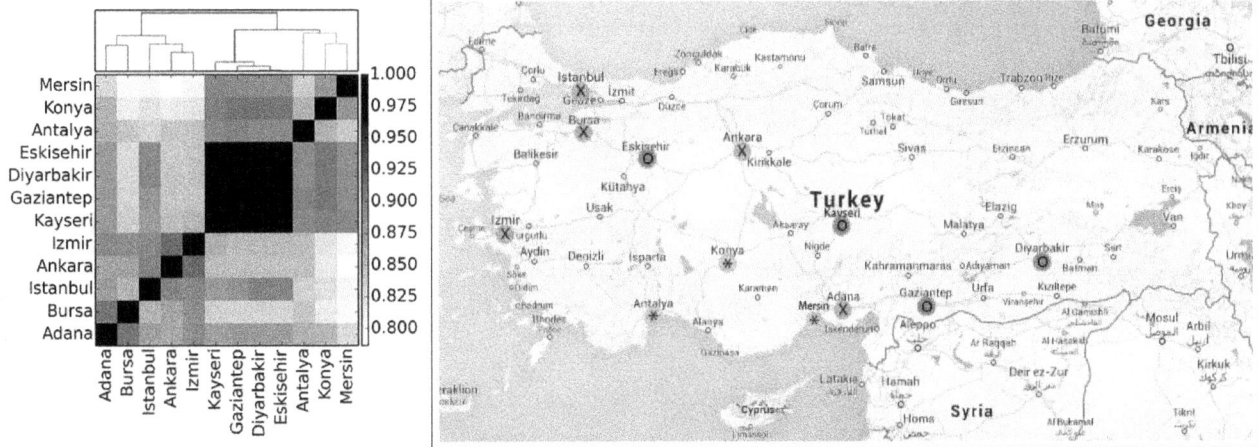

Figure 3: Left: Trend similarity matrix for 12 cities in Turkey. From the dendrogram on top we can isolate three distinct clusters. Right: Location of the cities with trend information, labeled by the three clusters induced by trend similarity.

We focus on the subset of tweets in our dataset that have geo-coordinates attached (in the form of latitude/longitude). Such tweets are likely to be posted by GPS-enabled devices (like smartphones) and represent only a small fraction of total tweets ($\approx 1.84\%$ of our sample), which is consistent with similar studies [19]. Yet they provide a very precise picture of the geospatial dynamics of content production. Figure 1 maps the sources of these tweets. The figure also shows histograms on the horizontal and vertical axes, that illustrate the distribution of tweets occurring in the corresponding locations, binned by latitude and longitude. From this figure the global nature of the discussion about Gezi Park events clearly emerges. Although a large fraction of tweets originated in Turkey, a significant amount was produced in Europe, North and South America (especially the United States and Brazil). Other noteworthy countries involved in the discussion are the Philippines, Bahrain, Qatar and the United Arab Emirates.

Attention abroad was signaled by the presence of trending hashtags and phrases in the worldwide Twitter trends. Among these, the main protest hashtag, #direngeziparki, trended several times between May 31st and June 2nd, 2013; #TayipIstifa, invoking Erdogan's resignation, appeared on June 6th, 2013. Worldwide attention is also evident in the variety of languages exhibiting hashtags related to the Gezi Park events, as displayed in Figure 2. After Turkish, the most popular languages were English, Spanish, and Portuguese.

We also explored the local dimension of the conversation, focusing on the discussion inside the Turkish borders. Our goal was to determine whether any patterns of discussion of similar topics of conversation emerged. In Figure 3 we show the trend similarity matrix computed among the sets of trending hashtags and phrases occurring in each of the 12 cities where Twitter trends are monitored. Each location is described by a frequency vector of occurrences of the observed trends. The similarity between pairs of cities is calculated as the cosine similarity of their trends frequency vectors. Above the matrix we show the dendrogram produced by hierarchical clustering, where it is possible to appreciate the separation in three clusters. Such clusters neatly corre-

spond to three different geographic areas of Turkey. Physical proximity seems to play a crucial role in determining the similarity of topical interests of individuals, consistent with other recent results [21].

The clusters found with our trend similarity analysis also seem to match the Turkish geopolitical profiles. Eskisehir, Kayseri and Gaziantep (in the red cluster) are all central Anatolian cities where the president's party (AKP) has a stronghold (though the CHP opposition party edged out the AKP in the March 2014 mayoral race); they are more culturally conservative and homogeneous. Izmir, Istanbul, Bursa, Ankara, and Adana (green cluster) are the largest cities in Turkey with diverse populations. Finally, Antalya and Mersin (blue cluster) are seacoast cities that are known for supporting the one of the main opposition parties (CHP or MHP). Further work is needed to understand why Konya is assigned to this cluster, as it is considered a major religiously conservative center (where the AKP mayoral candidate secured more than 64% of the vote in the 2014 mayoral elections) that has little in common with the Mediterranean cities.

Let us explore the temporal dimension of the Gezi Park discussion. We wanted to determine whether the activity on social media mirrored on-the-ground events, and whether bursts of online attention coincided with real-world protest actions. We analyzed the time series of the volume of tweets, retweets and replies occurring during the 27-day-long observation window, as reported in Figure 4 (top panel). The discussion was driven by bursts of attention that largely corresponded to major on-the-ground events (cf. Table 1), similar to what has been observed during other social protests [20]. It is also worth noting that the numbers of tweets and retweets are comparable throughout the entire duration of the conversation, suggesting a balance between content production (i.e., writing novel posts) and consumption (i.e., reading and rebroadcasting posts via retweets). In the middle panel of Figure 4 we report the number of users involved in the conversation at a given time, and the cumulative number of distinct users over time (dashed red line); similarly, in the bottom panel of the figure, we show the total number of hashtags related to Gezi Park observed at a given

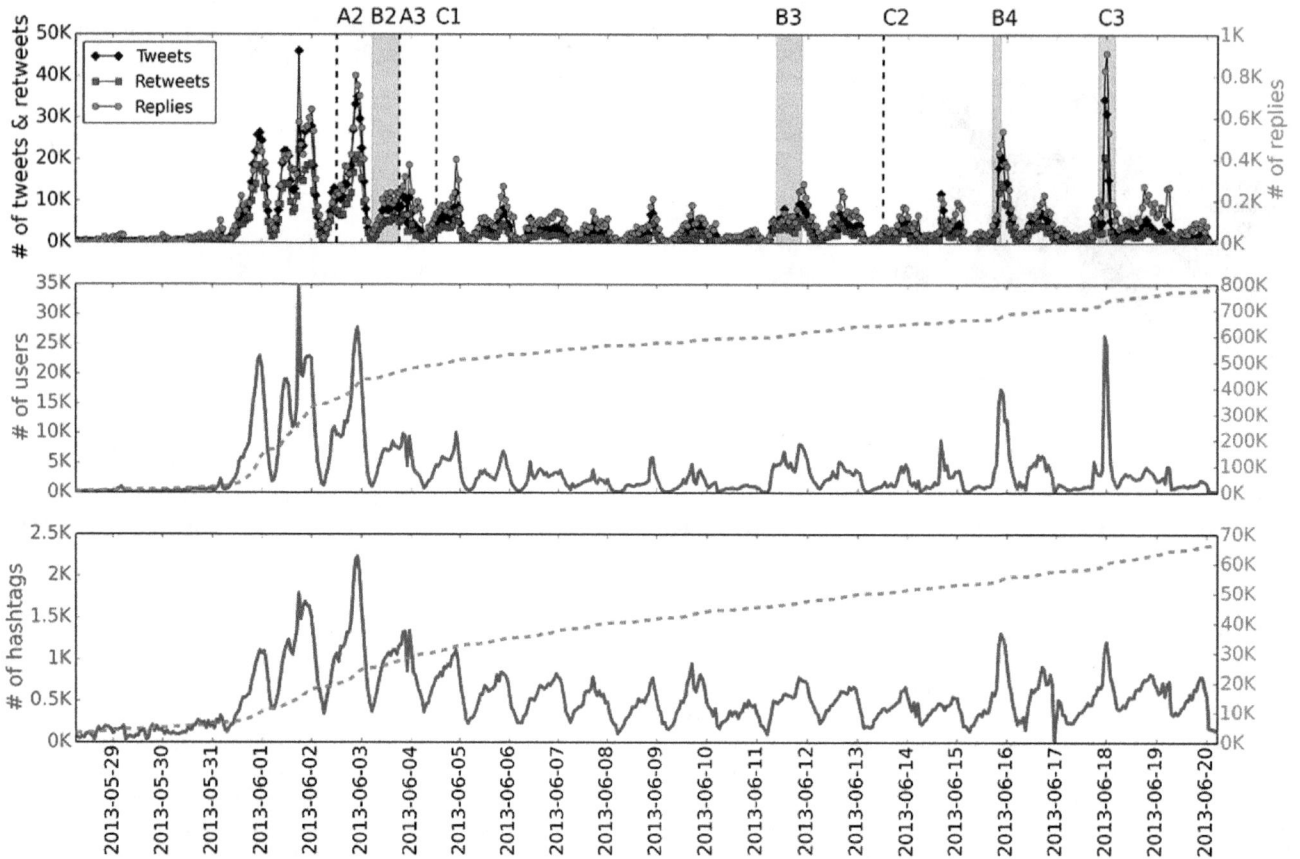

Figure 4: Hourly volume of tweets, retweets and replies between May 30th and June 20th, 2013 (top). The timeline is annotated with events from Table 1. User (center) and hashtag (bottom) hourly and cumulative volume of tweets over time.

time, and the cumulative number of distinct hashtags over time. We note that approximately 60% of all users observed during the entire discussion joined in the very first few days, whereas additional hashtags emerged at a more regular pace throughout a longer period. This suggests that the conversation acquired traction immediately, and exploded when the first on-the-ground events and police action occurred.

4.2 User roles and their evolution

Our second experiment aims at investigating what roles users played in the Gezi Park conversation and how they exercised their influence on others. We also seek to understand whether such roles changed over time, and, if so, to what extent such transformation reshaped the conversation.

Figure 5 shows the distribution of social ties reporting the two modalities of user connectivity, namely followers (incoming) and followees (outgoing) relations. The dark cells along the diagonal indicate that most users have a balanced ratio of ingoing and outgoing ties. Users below the diagonal follow more than they are followed. Note that most users are allowed to follow at most 1000 people. Finally, above the diagonal, we observe users with many followers. Note the presence of extremely popular users with hundreds of thousands or even millions of followers. The number of followers has a broad distributions and seems largely independent of the number of followees.

The presence of highly followed users in this conversation raises the question of whether their content is highly influential. Following a methodology inspired by González-Bailón et al. [24], we determined user roles as a function of their social connectivity and interactions. Figure 6 gives an aggregated picture of the distribution of user roles during the Gezi Park conversation. The y-axis shows the ratio between number of followees and followers of a given user; the x-axis shows the ratio between the number of retweets produced by a user and the number of times other users retweet that user. In other words, the vertical dimension represents social connectivity, whereas the horizontal dimension accounts for information diffusion. We can draw a vertical line to separate influential users on the left (*i.e.,* those whose content is most often retweeted by others) and information consumers on the right (those who mostly retweet other people's content). Influential users can be further divided in two classes: those with more followers than followees (bottom-left) and those with fewer followers (top-left), which we call *hidden influentials*. Similarly, information consumers can be divided in two groups–rebroadcasters with a large audience (bottom-right), and common users (top-right).

Figure 6 shows a static picture of aggregated data over the 27-day observation period. To study how roles evolve as events unfold, we carried out a longitudinal analysis whose results are provided in Figure 7. This figure shows the av-

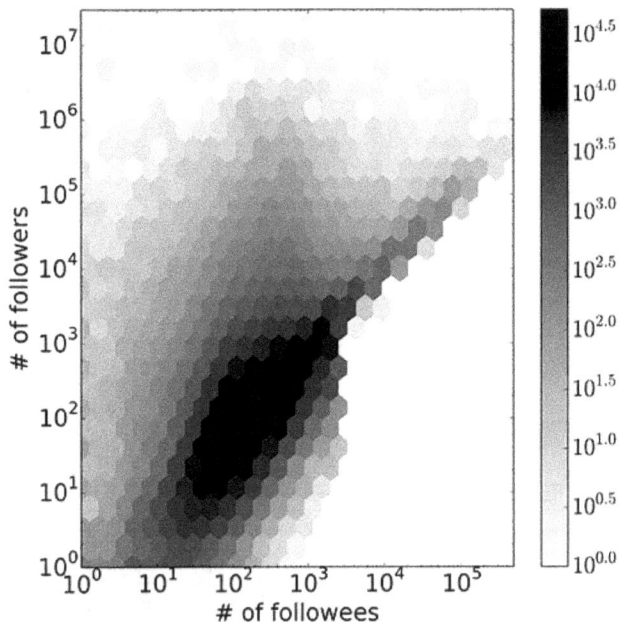

Figure 5: Distribution of friends and followers of users involved in the Gezi Park conversation.

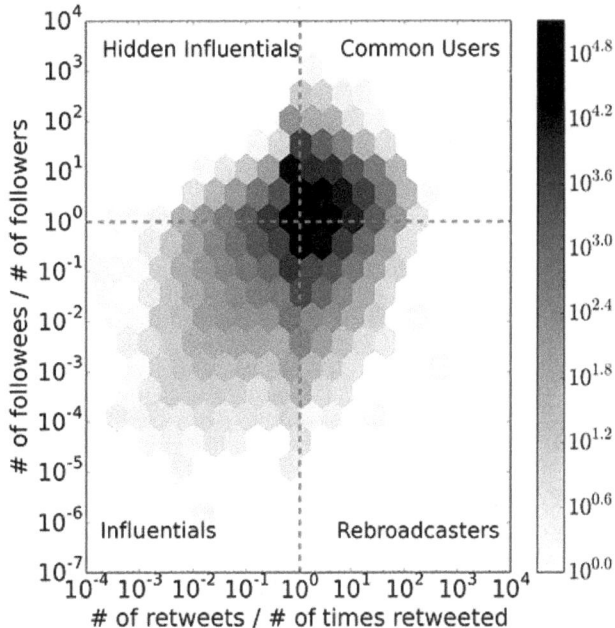

Figure 6: Distribution of user roles as function of social ties and interactions.

erage displacement of each role class, and the number of individuals in each class (circles), for each day. The displacement is computed in the role space (that is, the space defined by the two dimensions of Figure 6). Larger displacements suggest that individuals in a class, on average, are moving toward other roles.

Various insights emerge from Figure 7: first, we observed that the classes of information producers (influentials and hidden influentials) are relatively stable over time; together they include more than 50% of users every day, suggesting that many individuals in the conversation had large audiences, and the content they produced was heavily rebroadcasted by others (information consumers as well as other influentials). On the other hand, information consumers show strong fluctuation: starting from an initial configuration with stable roles (May 29–31), common users and rebroadcasters subsequently exhibit large aggregate displacements in the role space (June 1–4). We also note a redistribution of the users in each role: at the beginning of the protest a large fraction represents common users and rebroadcasters, while, as time passed and events unfolded, these two classes shrank. This suggests that common users and rebroadcasters acquired visibility and influence over time: some fraction of these users moved from the role of information consumers to that of influentials, such that their content wass consumed and rebroadcasted by others. In other words, the discussion became more *democratic* over time, in that the control of information production was redistributed to a larger population, and individuals acquired influence as the protests unfolded.

4.3 Online behavior and exogenous factors

Our concluding analysis focused on the way on-the-ground events affected online user behavior. While analyzing our dataset we noticed an abnormal number of screen name changes, as reported in Figure 8 (the screen name, not to be

confused with the user name, is the name displayed in one's Twitter account). Many users changed their screen names five or more times. This was an unusual observation that attracted our attention.

Further investigation revealed a collective synchronization process, as displayed in Figure 9. The changes in screen names represent reactions of users involved in the Gezi Park conversation to external events: these users changed their Twitter screen names to reflect sobriquets attributed to them by their political leaders. One example is the adoption of "TC" (standing for *Turkiye Cumhuriyeti* — Turkish Republic). As a reaction to identity issues, several users started using TC in front of their screen names. Another relevant example is Erdogan's speech of June 2, during which he referred to protesters as marauders (*çapulcu*), marginals (*marjinal* or drunks (*ayyas*). Individuals responded by changing their screen names to include such nicknames as a sign of protest against the government's attempt to discredit the protest participants and minimize the relevance of their actions. This phenomenon illustrates how online and offline worlds are tightly interconnected, deeply affecting each other.

5. RELATED WORK

The role of communication technologies used during social upheavals has been studied in the context of different events, including Arab Spring movements, Occupy Wall Street, and the Spanish 'Indignados' uprisings [11, 17, 19, 20, 25]. The benefits resulting from the adoption of social media include lowered barriers to participation, increased ease with which small-scale acts can be aggregated, the rapid propagation of logistic information and narrative frames, and a heightened sense of community and collective identity [8, 9, 33, 37, 39].

González-Bailón *et al.* [25] collected a large corpus of tweets related to the Spanish social and economic 'Indig-

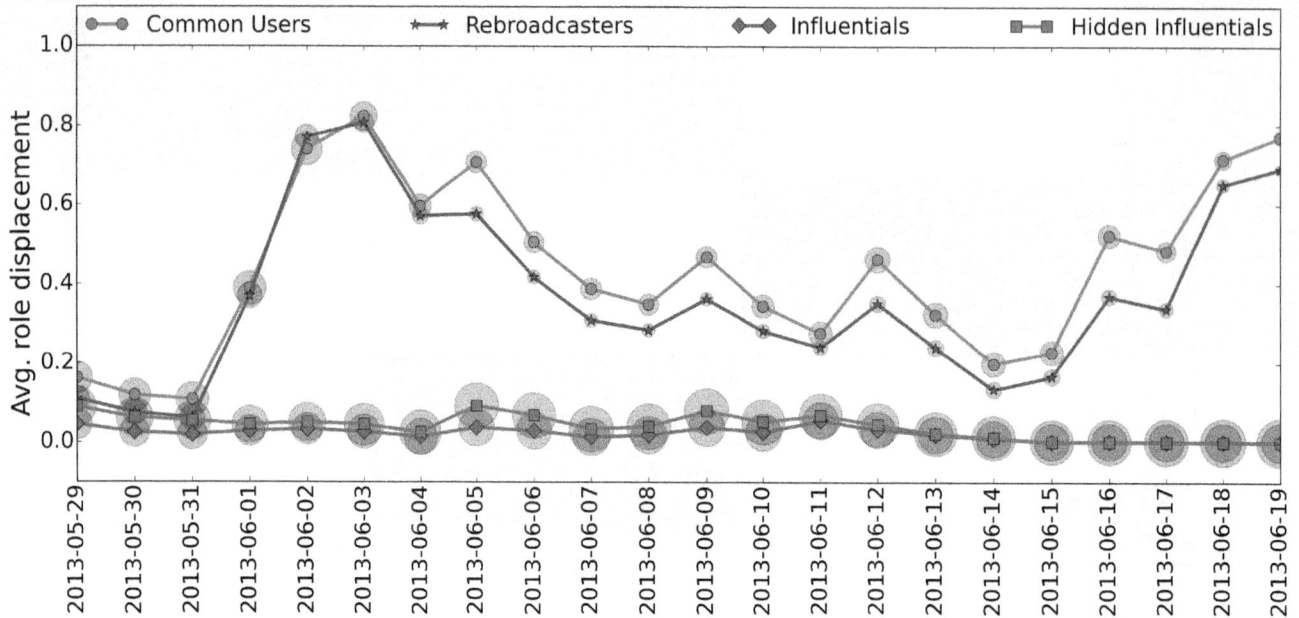

Figure 7: Average displacement of roles over time for the four different classes of roles. The size of the circles represents the number of individuals in each role.

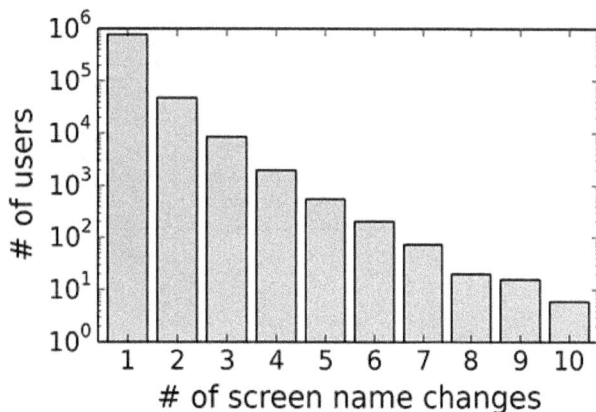

Figure 8: Distribution of the number of screen name changes among users during the Gezi Park events.

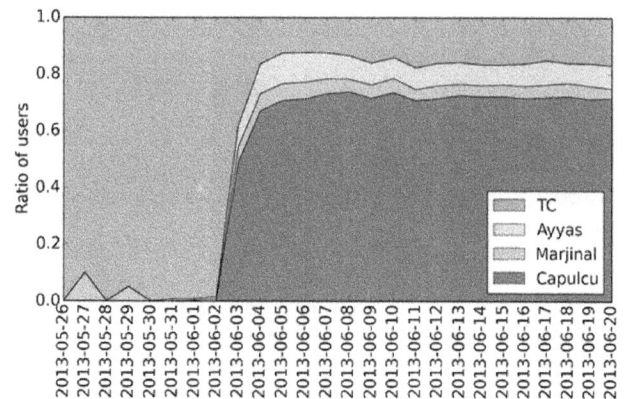

Figure 9: Among the many users who changed screen names, this chart plots the fractions who adopted different nicknames over time in respons to external events.

nados' protest that unfolded during May 2011. Their work provides evidence that Twitter played a role in the recruitment of new individuals to the protest movement as well as in the dissemination of information related to mass mobilization activities.

Choudhary *et al.* [17] analyzed the aggregate tweet sentiment during the 2011 Egyptian revolution, observing that fluctuations in positive and negative sentiment were closely correlated with the sentiment expressed by influential users worldwide. The authors also observed that users tweeting about the Egyptian revolution were distributed both inside and outside Egypt. Our work supports the global dimension of social protest discussion on social media: here we showed how Twitter brought worldwide visibility to the discussion of the Gezi Park protest, crossing the boundaries of its country of origin.

Recently, Baños *et al.* [4, 5] highlighted the role of social media users in the diffusion of information related to mass political mobilizations, unveiling the presence of hidden influentials who foster large cascades. The authors also observed how the topology of the communication network during such events reflects underlying dynamics like information diffusion and group emergence. Our analysis builds on this work and shows that user roles are not static, but rather evolve dynamically as the protest unfolds.

In our recent work we studied the Occupy Wall Street uprising. First, we focused on the geospatial characteristic of the protest [19]. We observed that highly-localized discussions mirrored individuals' attempts to organize and coordinate mobilization on the ground. Interstate discussion channels driving long-distance communications fostered the collective framing process that imbues social movements with a shared language, purpose and identity. A longitudinal analysis [20] revealed that users did not change their connectivity, interests and attention patterns with respect to baseline activity prior to the beginning of the protest. These findings left open the question whether Occupy had any long-lasting effect on its online community of participants.

6. CONCLUSIONS

In this paper we focused on the analysis of the conversation about the Gezi Park protest that took place on Twitter. We collected a large dataset spanning the time from May 25th to June 20th, 2013, during which the main events of the protests unfolded.

Our analysis of the spatial dynamics of the communication brought two different interesting findings. First, we observed that the discussion about Gezi Park events spread worldwide, and a sustained number of tweets was produced over time outside of Turkey — in Europe, North and South America. International attention was underscored by trending hashtags related to Gezi Park at the worldwide level. Second, we observed that local trends followed geographic and political patterns. Among the 12 cities whose trends we monitored, three clear geographic clusters emerge. This result is consistent with our recent analysis of geospatial spreading patterns of Twitter trends [21]. The discussion was driven by bursts of attention that largely correlated with on-the-ground events.

Focusing on users, we identified four types of roles (common users, rebroadcasters, influentials and hidden influentials). We tracked their evolution over time as events unfolded. As time passed, the discussion about Gezi Park became more democratic, with an increased number of influential users.

Our analysis concluded by studying an effect of real-world events, such as political speeches, on online user behavior. We found that individuals responded to such external provocations by exhibiting collective actions, namely the change of their Twitter screen names to reflect sobriquets attributed to them by their political leaders.

Our analysis uncovered various interesting dynamics, yet much remains to be done. It would be interesting to investigate whether universal patterns of communication emerge from different classes of conversation, including those about social and political issues, if contrasted with other types like sports, news, or entertainment. This would allow us to separate intrinsic characteristics of human communication dynamics from topic specific patterns.

Acknowledgments

This work was partially supported by NSF (grant CCF-1101743), DARPA (grant W911NF-12-1-0037), and the McDonnell Foundation. The funders had no role in study design, data collection and analysis, decision to publish, or preparation of the manuscript.

7. REFERENCES

[1] S. Aday, H. Farrel, M. Lynch, J. Sides, J. Kelly, and E. Zuckerman. Blogs and bullets: New media in contentious politics. Technical report, U.S. Institute of Peace, 2010.

[2] S. Aral and D. Walker. Identifying influential and susceptible members of social networks. *Science*, 337(6092):337–341, 2012.

[3] T. Arango. Protests in turkey reveal a larger fight over identity. *NY Times*, June 2, 2013.

[4] R. A. Baños, J. Borge-Holthoefer, and Y. Moreno. The role of hidden influentials in the diffusion of online information cascades. *EPJ Data Science*, 2(1):1–16, 2013.

[5] R. A. Baños, J. Borge-Holthoefer, N. Wang, Y. Moreno, and S. González-Bailón. Diffusion dynamics with changing network composition. *Entropy*, 15(11):4553–4568, 2013.

[6] R. Benford. An insider's critique of the social movement framing perspective. *Sociological Inquiry*, 67(4):409–430, 1997.

[7] R. Benford and D. Snow. Framing processes and social movements: An overview and assessment. *Annual Review of Sociology*, 26(1):611–639, 2000.

[8] W. Bennett. Communicating global activism: Strength and vulnerabilities of networked politics. *Information, Communication & Society*, 6(2):143–168, 2003.

[9] W. Bennett. Changing citizenship in the digital age. *The John D. and Catherine T. MacArthur Foundation Series on Digital Media and Learning*, pages 1–24, 2007.

[10] R. M. Bond, C. J. Fariss, J. J. Jones, A. D. Kramer, C. Marlow, J. E. Settle, and J. H. Fowler. A 61-million-person experiment in social influence and political mobilization. *Nature*, 489(7415):295–298, 2012.

[11] J. Borge-Holthoefer, A. Rivero, I. García, E. Cauhé, A. Ferrer, D. Ferrer, D. Francos, D. Iñiguez, M. P. Pérez, G. Ruiz, et al. Structural and dynamical patterns on online social networks: the spanish may 15th movement as a case study. *PLoS One*, 6(8):e23883, 2011.

[12] d. boyd and N. B. Ellison. Social network sites: Definition, history, and scholarship. 2007. *Journal of Computer-Mediated Communication*, 13(1), 2010.

[13] J. Byrne. Occupy the media: Journalism for (and by) the 99 percent. In J. Bryne, editor, *The Occupy Handbook*, pages 256–264. Little, Brown, 2012.

[14] D. Centola. The spread of behavior in an online social network experiment. *Science*, 329(5996):1194–1197, 2010.

[15] D. Centola. An experimental study of homophily in the adoption of health behavior. *Science*, 334(6060):1269–1272, 2011.

[16] N. Chomsky. *Occupy*. Zuccotti Park Press, 2012.

[17] A. Choudhary, W. Hendrix, K. Lee, D. Palsetia, and W. Liao. Social media evolution of the egyptian revolution. *Communications of the ACM*, 55(5):74–80, 2012.

[18] M. Conover, J. Ratkiewicz, M. Francisco, B. Gonçalves, A. Flammini, and F. Menczer. Political polarization on Twitter. *Proceedings of the 5th International AAAI Conference on Weblogs and Social Media*, 2011.

[19] M. D. Conover, C. Davis, E. Ferrara, K. McKelvey, F. Menczer, and A. Flammini. The geospatial

characteristics of a social movement communication network. *PloS One*, 8(3):e55957, 2013.

[20] M. D. Conover, E. Ferrara, F. Menczer, and A. Flammini. The digital evolution of occupy wall street. *PloS One*, 8(5):e64679, 2013.

[21] E. Ferrara, O. Varol, F. Menczer, and A. Flammini. Traveling trends: social butterflies or frequent fliers? In *Proceedings of the 1st ACM Conference on Online Social Networks*, pages 213–222. ACM, 2013.

[22] R. Garrett. Protest in an information society: A review of literature on social movements and new ICTs. *Information, Communication & Society*, 9(02):202–224, 2006.

[23] N. Göle. Gezi–anatomy of a public square movement. *Insight Turkey*, 15(3), 2013.

[24] S. González-Bailón, J. Borge-Holthoefer, and Y. Moreno. Broadcasters and hidden influentials in online protest diffusion. *American Behavioral Scientist*, 57(7):943–965, 2013.

[25] S. González-Bailón, J. Borge-Holthoefer, A. Rivero, and Y. Moreno. The dynamics of protest recruitment through an online network. *Scientific Reports*, 1, 2011.

[26] P. Howard, A. Duffy, D. Freelon, M. Hussain, W. Mari, and M. Mazaid. Opening closed regimes: What was the role of social media during the arab spring. Technical Report 2011.1, Project on Information Technology and Political Islam, 2011.

[27] J. Jenkins. Resource mobilization theory and the study of social movements. *Annual Review of Sociology*, 9:527–553, 1983.

[28] M. B. Kuymulu. Reclaiming the right to the city: Reflections on the urban uprisings in turkey. *City*, 17(3):274–278, 2013.

[29] G. Lotan, E. Graeff, M. Ananny, D. Gaffney, I. Pearce, and danah boyd. The revolutions were tweeted: Information flows during the 2011 Tunisian and Egyptian revolutions. *International Journal of Communication*, 5:1375–1405, 2011.

[30] J. McCarthy and M. Zald. Resource mobilization and social movements: A partial theory. *American Journal of Sociology*, 82(6):1212–1241, 1977.

[31] P. Metaxas and E. Mustafaraj. The rise and the fall of a citizen reporter. In *Proceedings of the 5th Annual ACM Web Science Conference*, pages 248–257. ACM, 2013.

[32] P. T. Metaxas and E. Mustafaraj. Social media and the elections. *Science*, 338(6106):472–473, 2012.

[33] D. Myers. Communication technology and social movements: Contributions of computer networks to activism. *Social Science Computer Review*, 12(2):250–260, 1994.

[34] Z. Tufekci and C. Wilson. Social Media and the Decision to Participate in Political Protest: Observation from Tahrir Square. *Journal of Communication*, 62:363–379, 2012.

[35] U. Uras. What inspires turkey's protest movement. *Al Jazeera*, June 5, 2013.

[36] S. Valenzuela, A. Arrigada, and A. Scherman. The Social Media Basis of Youth Protest Behavior: The Case of Chile. *Journal of Communication*, 62(2):299–314, 2012.

[37] J. Van Laer and P. Van Aelst. Cyber-protest and civil society: the internet and action repertoires in social movements. *Handbook on Internet Crime*, pages 230–254, 2009.

[38] A. Vespignani. Predicting the behavior of techno-social systems. *Science*, 325(5939):425, 2009.

[39] S. Wray. On electronic civil disobedience. *Peace Review*, 11(1):107–111, 1999.

"I Always Feel It Must Be Great to Be a Hacker!"
The Role of Interdisciplinary Work in Social Media Research

Katharina Kinder-Kurlanda
GESIS Leibniz Institute for the Social Sciences
Data Archive for the Social Sciences
Phone: 0049 (0) 221 47694 449

katharina.kinder-kurlanda@gesis.org

Katrin Weller
GESIS Leibniz Institute for the Social Sciences
Data Archive for the Social Sciences
Phone: 0049 (0) 221 47694 472

katrin.weller@gesis.org

ABSTRACT

This paper presents first results from a series of qualitative interviews with social media researchers concerning their methods, objectives and challenges in dealing with social media data for their research. Twenty face-to-face, semi-structured interviews were conducted with researchers who have a social science background and work in different disciplines. The interviews were transcribed and coded. While many dimensions were identified concerning the whole research process of social media studies, this paper focuses on the dimension of interdisciplinarity in social media research. It looks at how social scientists describe the need for (interdisciplinary) collaboration and what experiences they have made in working with computer scientists in particular.

Categories and Subject Descriptors
J.4 SOCIAL AND BEHAVIORAL SCIENCES

General Terms
Management, Human Factors.

Keywords
Interdisciplinarity, research methods, collaboration, social science, computational social science, social media, qualitative research, interviews.

1. INTRODUCTION

In this paper we explore interdisciplinary collaboration of social scientists and computer scientists for the purpose of social media research as a growing field within the broader context of web research. We provide insights from a qualitative inquiry into

social scientists' viewpoints with the aim to inform computer scientists interested in working interdisciplinarily in this field.

Right from its beginnings, web science has been envisioned as an interdisciplinary field of research [1], [2], [3] and efforts continue to bring people from different backgrounds together e.g. during events such as the ACM Web Science conference series – with some noteworthy success in including, e.g., sociology [4]. While web science has its origins in computer science and related fields, other communities have also started to explore interdisciplinary approaches for studying web users and web-related phenomena. For example, from the social science and humanities perspectives, terms like "internet studies" or "internet research" (as in the Association of Internet Researchers, AoIR), "web social science" [5] and "digital methods" [6] are used to refer to efforts of studying web usage "independent from traditional disciplines and existing across academic borders" [7]. However, so far there is still relatively little overlap between more social science-based communities and more computer science-based communities. While we focus on these two broad communities in this paper we acknowledge that other fields such as the natural sciences, economics, educational science, linguistics, law, medical science, etc. may also be relevant for interdisciplinary approaches to studying the web.

New methods based on "computational social science" aim to address the gap between social and computer sciences by providing social scientists with the "capacity to collect and analyze massive amounts of data" [8], with commercial internet companies like Yahoo being quick to apply such methods before social scientists in academia have done so. This might be due to the fact that "as for infrastructure, the leap from social science to a computational social science is larger than from biology to a computational biology, largely due to the requirements of distributed monitoring, permission seeking, and encryption" [8].

Just like studies of the web in general, studies of the social web or social media applications can benefit from innovative combinations of methods grounded in different disciplines and could become a broad application area for computational social science. Studying social media is a still growing research field – the number of papers featuring either "Twitter" or "Facebook" in their title has been four times as large in 2012 as four years earlier in 2008 (based on Scopus data, 508 publications in 2008 and 2,171 publications in 2012, while the overall number of publications on Scopus has grown by a factor of roughly 1.2 in the same time period). The possibility to access data via platforms' APIs may have contributed to this rapid growth. Furthermore, the availability of data may have helped to inspire different research communities that can now access the respective data. Regarding research based on social media data, [9] point out that "while in many research fields related to online social activities, ethnographic approaches have predated statistical and, especially, computational approaches in the 'Twitter field' computational approaches appeared first, as can be observed by the venues or by the authors of the very first academic research on the topic." Twitter research, as one main area of social media research, is still dominated by computer science approaches, although there is also a growing number of social science based publications.

There are some indications that social scientists' appropriation of social media research may be connected to successful adoption of technical skills and interdisciplinary approaches, as "collecting, storing and analyzing these data often requires technical skills beyond the traditional curricula of social scientists. These projects require, in fact, collaboration with computer scientists. Nevertheless developing a common interdisciplinary project is often challenging because of the different backgrounds of researchers" [10].

Addressing the issues of interdisciplinary collaboration and the role of technical skills in social media research this paper contributes to:

- a more detailed understanding of the challenges that researchers from the social sciences and humanities face when they work with data gathered from social media platforms,

- a furthering of computer scientists' understanding of social scientists' motivations for using social media data by revealing reasons for their interest in social media,

- and an exploration of social media researchers' experiences in interdisciplinary collaboration involving computer scientists.

We make available our insights into when and how interdisciplinary efforts between social scientists and computer scientists joining up to conduct social media research succeed. Our aim in doing so is to facilitate the crossing of traditional disciplinary boundaries, which is necessary in the pursuit of understanding the web [3]. This paper therefore answers the call of furthering the richness of disciplines and methods in the field of web research by providing a basis for more discussion about how collaboration can be accomplished:

"The future of Web Science depends on maintaining our cohesive, balances community in which no single discipline dominates. To this end, we would like more discussion about how disciplines collaborate: What are the stumbling blocks? Where do misunderstandings arise?" [11].

We have chosen to answer this call for exploring 'stumbling blocks' by focusing on concerns connected to the various steps of data analysis as the actual points of collaboration between social scientists and computer scientists in social media projects. Our paper is part of a broader project called "The Hidden Data of Social Media Research", in which we investigate the meta-level of social media research by focusing on the multiple phases of research: the research data cycle. Project topics include theory building and epistemology as well as technical dimensions of data collection, processing, management and sharing. Practical implications for everyday work, for example, in terms of research

ethics and collaboration workflow are addressed as well. The initial motivation for the project was the assumption that social media is currently being studied by a variety of different groups and individuals, many of them creating their own ad-hoc approaches and methods while broadly accepted theories and shared standards are still to come. We wanted to capture this exciting state of the (potential) formation of a new research field while it is developing.

During the initial project phase we have so far conducted twenty interviews with researchers from social science backgrounds. This paper presents our first results from these interviews. Some related work has been conducted by [12], who asked academics on their approaches to work with "big data". To our knowledge, our project is the first to investigate data management practices of researchers specifically working with social media data.

2. METHOD

The exploration of the issues social media researchers currently face in dealing with social media data and an understanding of their motivations entails asking these researchers for detailed explanations and to explore meanings and contexts. We therefore decided on the qualitative approach of conducting face-to-face, semi-structured interviews, which, while unstructured enough to allow interviewees to introduce topics, employed "a thematic guide with probes and invitations to expand on issues raised" [13] in order to enable some comparison between interviewees [14]. Qualitative methods are especially useful when the aim is to discover meaning, rather than to make generalized hypothesis statements [15]. Relatively small, distinct groups are analyzed with the aim to achieve a point at which no new themes emerge from the data [16].

Following this approach we conducted twenty interviews with social media researchers from the social sciences in the first phase of this project. Interviews were conducted during a major international internet studies conference in the United States in 2013. Interviewing scientists at a conference is a convenient and approved way of gathering insights from these experts in an environment conducive to discussion and reflection [e.g. 17]. Potential candidates (i.e. researchers who had experience in working with data gathered from social media platforms) were identified from the online conference program and sent an email invitation. We were able to recruit twenty social media researchers, most of them with a background in media, communication or internet studies for interviews about their experiences with social media data (out of the 30 candidates we invited, 7 did not respond and 3 were willing to participate but were unable to arrange for a meeting during the selected conference). Eight interviewees were working in Europe, seven in the United States, and five in Australia. In terms of professional levels nine participants were PhD students, five were postdocs or assistant professors, and six were senior lecturers, associate professors or full professors. Most interviewees had experiences in research based on social media data from several platforms. In addition to having conducted various research projects on social media, thirteen researchers had specifically based research on data gathered from Twitter data before, ten on blog data, five on data from Facebook, and many had also gathered or analyzed other data from platforms such as Foursquare, Tumblr, 4chan or reddit.

We were interested in what interviewees viewed as the potential of the research with social media data and what they saw as the challenges and opportunities of interdisciplinary collaboration. In order to explore this we asked questions on how researchers' everyday work with social media data looked like in actual projects and practice. Topics discussed in the interviews hence ranged from methods for data collection, data analysis and management as well as ethical and epistemological concerns. Most of the interviews were conducted jointly by both authors of this paper. We used an interview guide which covered the main topics to be addressed (like practical workflow or research ethics) rather than specific questions – besides some initial questions about interviewees' background and a concluding question. In addition to allowing explanation, correction, thinking-aloud and discussion, the face-to-face interview situations also prove to be beneficial in providing an atmosphere of trust and non-judgment when addressing sensitive topics such as ethical concerns or the lack of best practice standards in data management. A follow-up questionnaire was also sent to participants to cover more detailed questions concerning data collection and analysis and to allow interviewees to submit additional information at their leisure. The topic of interdisciplinarity was mainly covered in the interviews, however, so results from the questionnaire have only been used to fill in details of participants' experiences with various types of social media data in this paper.

The collected interview data were transcribed into text, and interpreted using the atlas.ti software and a 'lean coding' approach in which themes were built through reducing and combining categories found in the data [18]. Codes were discussed and iteratively defined by both authors.

3. RESULTS AND DISCUSSION

Our first results show researchers' high awareness of the unregulated and developing character of social media research methods. The highly interdisciplinary research initiatives were shaped both by the necessity to acquire technical skills and by researchers having to develop novel epistemological foundations. Participants discussed the establishment of shared methods (on concerning comparability, validity, ethics) as important for the emerging field and recognized common shortcomings of current approaches. The following results are based on the first twenty interviews within the project only and therefore focus on social media researchers from the social sciences. Further research is planned to include additional interviews, especially with social media researchers from other disciplines.

3.1 Interdisciplinarity in social media research

3.1.1 Social media researchers are already interdisciplinary

When asking social media researchers about which discipline they were located in (one of the few predefined questions in our interview guide which otherwise contained no concrete questions but rather topics to be covered) it became apparent that for most of them this constituted a very difficult question answered usually with statements such as "This is really a huge question for me right now". One researcher even dismissed disciplinarity, saying: "I'm trying not to be in a specific discipline, on the contrary. (…) Actually I'm objecting to the idea of putting me in a specific discipline." While most of the researchers had training in media

and communication studies, their interests and methods were inherently interdisciplinary. Typical answers were statements such as "I think it's weird. (…) I'm hooked into projects rather than any particular field" or "definitely I am per se interdisciplinary because (…) I really have three totally different areas of perspective, of method, of theory, that I feel I am trying to combine", or even stating that their disciplinary background was "a bit of a mess". One participant even assumed not to have a proper method ("and also I don't really have a method (…) it comes with not having a core discipline, it's a mixed method"), which was seen as detrimental with regards to competing on the academic job market where disciplines are often tightly coupled to methods. Interdisciplinarity was also apparent in biographies and researchers would "arrive from many different fields". We heard statements such as:

> "My undergraduate background is in English and radio-television-film production (…). And then I was a professional librarian."

> "I did my PhD in architectural theory. I worked in an Australian studies research institute for a while. I taught in cultural studies. Now I'm back researching in media and communications."

> "…the research team is kind of a human interaction group. But my background is media studies and cultural studies. So, I've kind of come to there from a different area. But, that area is kind of interdisciplinary anyway, so…"

Descriptions of what they thought of as their 'home' discipline therefore became complicated, an example was: "I guess that I am some kind of sociologist with a network analysis methodology applied to online social data."

Most researchers worked in institutions such as interdisciplinary grad schools, which were interdisciplinary or experimental. But some of these institutions were also new and still "trying to find [their] own feet in some way". The sense of disciplinary boundaries being challenged emerged as very prevalent in social media research, shaping research, biographies and affiliations.

3.1.2 Social media research needs to be interdisciplinary

Often, social media research teams were comprised of people with experiences in various sub-disciplines in the social sciences and also those with other disciplinary backgrounds:

> "I think this research has brought us into contact with people from computer sciences and other disciplines like that more."

Even more, all interviewees agreed that social media research was inherently interdisciplinary:

> "Everyone is more or less on the margin of their home fields, because the core disciplines usually don't deal with those subjects like mobile media (…). I think that most people don't have a home discipline called internet research."

One reason given for the inherent interdisciplinarity in social media research was the field being so new, that there were only few people who were trained as social media researchers, and that there was no typical researcher 'profile' yet. One researcher said, for example, that social media research was still in a "pioneering phase" and would at some point "settle down somehow."

However, while it is possibly due to the novelty of the area that those drawn into it embrace the richness of contrasting perspectives, researchers agreed with the statement that "as the field grows it is worth remembering that this mutual respect is powerful, precious and worth actively preserving" [11]. Researchers deemed interdisciplinarity as important in order to be able to accomplish social media research. Most even thought that it was a requirement in order to further the understanding of and the exchange on social media:

"The whole media studies sphere is a (...) mélange of different fields and I think this is very positive because it enhances the options to tackle the material, find material, methods, perspectives, theory."

When talking about interdisciplinarity, participants discussed both working with people from other social science disciplines and working with computer scientists. They perceived some challenges of the inherent interdisciplinarity in the field (challenges for collaborating with computer scientists follow in section 3.2), often relating to different methodologies underlying the sub-disciplines. One assumption was that interdisciplinary efforts often struggled because little common understanding of what constitutes validity can be established: "The disadvantage is that it is not so easy to have a common language."

Some addressed the distinction of qualitative and quantitative methods that still seem to divide the social sciences into different camps – although participants mostly claimed that different methods "complemented each other". However, interviewees pointed out the disciplinary rift between those who work with (quantitative) data and those who do not. And some observed that "those people who don't have data sometimes feel beneath those who have data – but that's totally wrong."

3.1.3 Social media researchers from the social sciences challenge 'traditional' academic structures
Besides methodological challenges there are also challenges in the logistics of research. As has been mentioned above, this can play out as difficulties – but also as a rather productive variation – in individual researchers' biographies and careers. Practical challenges are also to be found in the process of publishing research results:

"It's difficult to publish, right. Because you don't belong anywhere. So now we have a little bit of venues like JCMC, New media & Society, Information Society (...). But it's the tip of the iceberg. I mean (...) we don't belong anywhere. You go to the American Political Science Review, they were like, what is this, that is not really political science tradition. Breaking those silos, it's like you are really fighting."

Social media based studies may not fit into mainstream social science publications, especially if the journals are focused on traditional methodological practices. One participant reported problems with reviewers who were demanding quotes from social media data as a proof for originality ("You don't have any quotes! How do I know that you did in this study?") while the researcher deliberately decided not to include verbatim quotes from tweets due to privacy issues. Another researcher related how the entire section on data collection in a paper on Twitter had to be removed on reviewers' requests – which meant that the paper was published without the part originally written by the co-authoring computer scientist. From the interviews we also gathered that in many projects computer scientists faced similar problems with regards to computer science work packages in interdisciplinary projects.

3.2 The role of computer science and computer scientists

3.2.1 Social media researchers are aware of the necessity to collaborate
Interviewees believed strongly in the necessity of collaboration in general and that researchers with different competencies are required to achieve the best possible results in social media research: "It seems very hard, or nearly impossible, to do this kind of stuff in the future as a single or individual researcher."

One reason given for the need to work interdisciplinarily was the fact that data collection was both time-intensive and difficult: "It's just too much for one person to do individually" which resulted in having to 'outsource' different parts of a project which previously may have been possible to deal with on one's own.

The second reason for the need to work interdisciplinarily was seen in the newness of the field, as new fields require an open mind: "Anybody who is very closely tied to a discipline won't find the same things that other people find."

Academics from the social sciences were therefore expected to "have to learn to work – even more than before – in teams", with the social media researchers being in good positions to accomplish this due to usually already having interdisciplinary outlooks. However, interviewees did not always find that others agreed with their viewpoint: "... my approach to things has always been very much interdisciplinary in how I view things. And I'm constantly amazed at how people don't share that view. And that there are still these disciplinary and methodological silos – that just drives me nuts." Interdisciplinarity was therefore seen as a challenge for researchers less inclined or experienced in it. However, because interdisciplinary collaboration was seen as necessary for accomplishing social media research, researchers were required to "either (...) work per se, you know, forced, with people from other disciplines, or, and that's what I would really think is the better way, you keep open yourself."

Even though the need to connect people with different skills is recognized, bringing those people together is not always easy and depends on good networking skills and the availability of research infrastructure: "It's just, I guess, luck and the size of our institution that we had enough students and professors, that some had the skills needed."

3.2.2 Role for computer scientists
The value of computer scientists and their skills for social media research projects was often acknowledged in the interviews. Approaches in projects seem to vary with regards to how much members of an interdisciplinary undertaking are involved in each other's specific methods and activities. Some groups take a lot of effort to let everybody understand the whole workflow: "That is one of the pedagogical goals of the group (...), which is really trying to make it so everybody understands every part of the process." Another interviewee told us he does not want to collaborate if not everybody also engages with the others' methods and in the past had even refused to collaborate in a setting where each member of a team just worked with his/her own methods and 'puts the pieces together afterwards'. There was

generally a longing for the "productive tension" of negotiating methods.

In other cases, especially when working with bigger datasets, there often is a delegation of roles in the teams. It is seen as useful and easier to collaborate with others who take care of data collection "because I don't have to think about all the technical issues. (...) We are working really closely together and try to find solutions for the technical problems. But (...) they are the programmers and they are the ones that put it into the software. We are just those analyzing and finding new methods they can put into software again." The fact that reducing the roles of computer scientists to those of 'mere' data collectors could be problematic was also mentioned and will be explored in the next section.

Social media researchers were also hoping that computer scientists might be able to shed light on previously unsolvable problems connected to big data. For example, traditional social science methods do not seem sufficient for capturing phenomena such as memes, because "questions of spread are really hard to get to from a qualitative point of view and even from a quantitative standpoint I think that it would take some really big systematic work". A participant wished for "a really systematic way to be able to trace spread and then creation" in order to study social media memes.

3.2.3 Computer scientists have different approaches, questions and methodology

Social media researchers noticed both the overlap in interest with computer scientists as well as the differences regarding research foci and methods. Overlaps mostly occurred through working on the same data. Differences pertained to standards, research questions and expectations and could, for example, concern topics such as how to make sense of user experience. Differences would often become critical at points when it came to decisions about data collection and data analysis. While social scientists in a research team would look for "single examples and they're going to do close textual analysis and build a whole story around those", computer scientists would, for example, ask for "more noise in their data, because they want to make an algorithm that can clean out the noise or something like that". Very different requirements concerning the data would therefore have to be accommodated. Different approaches needed to be allowed to co-exist, even though they might seem "fascinating and mysterious". Otherwise collaboration could become impossible, especially when ideas about the method differed considerably as is the case for those branches of the social sciences in which data collection is seen as part of the research or even coding process. On researcher put it as follows:

"So that process of gathering, of collecting is not just something to be done automated and then a bunch of different questions applied to it. The collection process is part of the coding process, the understanding process. And it is a really foreign idea to me that you're just like, well, I've got these questions that maybe are related to gender and I have these questions that maybe are related to intensity of tweets, Hey, let's both look at the same billion tweets set. It's a different way of thinking. Not that it's invalid, but it's, I don't think I would…"

One researcher told us of the difficulties he had initially experienced when trying to interest computer scientists in social media. Computer scientists had to be convinced that social media

research was worthwhile. To other researchers it seemed that computer scientists were not interested in producing negative results, which can however be beneficial for social media researchers in order to learn about which approaches are successful and which are not. Interviewees realized that computer scientists had their own research agenda and that often the tasks that social scientists required were not interesting to them:

"They can't publish results on the things we need from them. Like collecting data or creating something to collect data. We collaborated with (...) experts in databases. And it was very difficult to find something that was useful also for them under the academic point of view."

Some social scientists were not sure about what computer scientists expected from a collaboration and even doubted that they had any incentives to participate in an interdisciplinary project. Conversely, other social scientists thought that the issue of computer scientists' role as 'mere' data collectors originated in the fact that computer scientists themselves perceived social scientists "as an end user that they need to provide a technological solution for", rather than as a collaborator in challenging traditional paradigms and methods.

In other cases, collaboration worked well, for example, because the computer scientist in a project "was really interested in doing this, because he wanted to learn". But even if there is a shared interest, or if everybody is motivated to work together, problems may occur. Some participants reported difficulties in communicating effectively:

"I always think about, I don't know, whether he can do this. So I just suggest it, right, and then he comes and tells me a week after, 'You know, I can also give you *this*'. And I, 'Why didn't you tell me?'"

The establishment of a common language to facilitate communication about issues of method, validity and research foci appeared to be a prerequisite for facilitating interdisciplinary collaboration in social media research projects.

3.2.4 Social media researchers are aware of the need for computer science competencies

Social media researchers were especially concerned about computer scientists' motivations and interests because they often struggled with technical aspects in social media research themselves and hoped to acquire technical skills through collaboration. Working with social media data requires different skills and different tools than social scientists are used to working with: "…it's totally different than surveys and interviews and stuff." Many researchers felt the need to acquire new technical skills:

"Yeah, I always feel it must be great to be a hacker because you can get hold of all these great datasets."

Social media researchers believed that a lack of technical skills affected their work: "My questions are limited to what I can do." In some cases, they even perceived their own lack of programming skills as a deficiency:

"It is kind of ironic that I'm studying, you know, new media, but unlike a lot of other researchers I know I don't have any of that kind of hands-on practical skills in that area. I'd love to be able to do that."

In the cases where researchers did possess technical skills, they were aware that others, who had the same disciplinary training but no skills or interest in programming, would not be able to work with social media data: "I'm lucky because I was always interested in these things, so I'm able to write simple programs and I understand more or less the architecture of the APIs, but most of the people in my field of course need someone to collaborate with to explain this kind of data." Some interviewees had even started to learn new methods and skills by visiting training courses. The opportunity that computer science skills offered with regards to analytical potential were valued as very high:

"I keep running up against this issue of how much of a computer scientist you have to be to competently work with large volumes of data. If you work with smaller samples or if you do something that's sort of more the typical approach of a humanist or social scientist, then it feels a bit like you're not exploiting the advantages of specifically social media data."

However, learning skills such as programming could be a drawn-out process and might not lead to sufficient results in time. Learning may also consume time needed for other tasks, such as reviewing literature or studying the material. One researcher said:

"I think you would be able also as a social science researcher to learn that [Python programming] stuff, but then you don't have time to theorize."

So while acquiring some new technical skills was seen as worthwhile researchers realized that they needed to compromise: "It's also about putting in time and money (…). And you know: I'm not a renaissance man – I can't do everything."

Learning technical skills was also connected to a longing for gaining back 'control' over the research process. Researchers wanted to be independent: "I would like to do as much as I can by myself." Many of them did not enjoy having to rely on others and their judgment "I try to have a really good understanding of the system, so I can explain what we actually did, so I don't like the idea that it's just like a black box, that you don't understand anything about it and it's just outsourced". Consequently, social media researchers sometimes wished for a tool that would allow them to collect data without requiring computer science skills or colleagues to depend upon. It appears that social media research has placed them into a new situation, where their research is not yet supported by a substantial research infrastructure and data access possibilities, which they are used to in other fields of study:

"I would like to be able to not need advanced computer science knowledge in order to just get my dataset. (…) If I do a content analysis from just traditional media I just buy my papers, or I go to an archive, I can do it. I'd like to be able to do the same with Twitter."

Some participants felt that they had been left alone with the task of acquiring necessary skills ("basically I'm doing most of it on my own") and were calling for programming to become a standard part of the curriculum in media and communication studies, especially as more and more communication in all areas of society I being mediated by computers.

Acquiring technical skills eventually seemed to come down to two options: "You can collaborate with someone with technical skills, someone from computer sciences or sometimes even statistics. (…) And otherwise you have to develop your own skills." Advanced researchers would usually 'outsource' data gathering to PhD students or hire student assistants to do the job, probably also due to the lack of time that would be needed to learn – while again struggling with the disadvantages of having to depend on others:

"My PhD students are collecting the data for me. So if I had to go and collect data I wouldn't know how to do that. (…) So I'm not anymore independent – as I used to be."

3.3 Value of social media research

We saw that conducting social media research as a social scientist could be challenging and even risky for social scientists. We therefore also asked what unique value social media could offer to researchers and social science disciplines in order to better understand why they chose to address this novel field rather than sticking with traditional methods. Most of all, the social media researchers in our study were very curious and excited about the new developments in and through social media.

3.3.1 Social media researchers value the 'newness' and excitement in the field

Researchers expressed their positive experiences in being part of an emerging field and were driven by their own interest ("Everything is interesting in social media"). They enjoyed the novelty of the topic, highlighting that "it's fascinating because it's totally different" and that "there's a feeling of being able to explore, of being able to do new things." They felt that others were also inspired by the new possibilities of social media research and described it as "good to be in a field where there is a lot of excitement"

By exploring the chances and challenges of social media as an object of study they also hoped to contribute to new research directions that would become even more important in the future: "I think that there are researchers and attempts to create some kind of common social media related knowledge. That's going to be (…) useful for something else in the future." And they also saw that they could help to pave the road for other researchers to follow them into this new field: "I see ourselves as pioneers, we have to do that. It's, we are starting, we are working with the flame for the whole. You know the young generation who would come after." There sometimes even was a feeling of responsibility to move forwards into such new topics and new (interdisciplinary) methods: "It's our obligation as researchers, really to open the road and not to close our eyes and not to allow ourselves to be stagnated in one of the disciplines."

3.3.2 Social media researchers value the availability of data

Despite the technical challenges in data access, social media researchers were impressed by the possibilities of new data collection approaches ("And we had all this data and we were like: Oh my gosh, we have this amazing data!"). Even though they often cannot perform the computational tasks themselves, they get the impression that collecting data has become much easier ("Because it's so easy to gather data, because anyone can do it now, because we have established tools.") and that you can collect data for a variety of topics: "You can gather data from any context you want. So you can... you could be a researcher in Australia and look at the Arab spring and you could be a researcher in Germany and look at protests in Brazil." For them, social media data is "very available compared to ethnographic research. (…) If you do ethnographic research you have to go into the field. You have to go to the gatekeepers. And inform those people about your research (…) and build up a relationship to the ones that you're doing research about."

Sometimes there even seems to be so much data that one does not know where to start: "I have death by opportunities." And some researchers had collected more data than they could use for their studies: "I thought it would be interesting, and it *would* be interesting, just, I haven't had time to look at everything".

This richness of available data also comes with a lot of critique, such as that researchers use this type of data just for "convenience", not because it necessarily helps with their research question ("So: I wanna do research on language. And Twitter happens to be a really good way to get a whole bunch of data about language"). In some cases this critique seemed not too far-fetched as single researchers were indeed inspired by this particular availability of data and turned to it simply "because it's there": "It doesn't make intuitive sense to keep trying to think about the representative sample when you have these huge amounts of digital traces of activities on a particular topic. It doesn't seem to make sense not to do it, I suppose. Why not, because it's there." The critical reflection of social media as a source of research data – and the challenges posed to epistemology and methodology – were major elements in the interviews and we intend to publish them as a separate study in the future.

3.3.3 Social media researchers value the potential of immediacy

It is not only the availability of data that drives social media research. Researchers also see a particular value in the specific type of communication one can observe in social media. Because especially Twitter is easy to use and characterised by both the brevity and the instantaneousness of posts (spread happens immediately) it becomes possible for users to share information unidirectionally with many others. This allows researchers to observe previously hidden or at least not easily accessible aspects of human activities, such as protests or discussions about TV shows and sports events, where "you can map the audience conversation."

While it takes a long time to prepare a survey to inquire people's opinions about a topic, social media conversations happen while a topic or event unfolds: "It's publically available interactions (…) on large scale." Social media promises immediate access to reactions and opinions, i.e. one does not need to ask people a long time after an event but can capture immediate reactions. It might thus be less influenced by memory lapses. And it also profits from the absence of the researcher: Compared to survey data or interview data "another great advantage of Twitter data is that I think this is something that I'd label as naturally occurring data. So this data is not motivated by means of researchers." For social scientists this can be an interesting addition to other methods, as it can help to discover the "discrepancies" between "what people say they do" and "what they actually do".

3.3.4 Social media researchers value the opportunity to observe society

Ultimately, researchers are exploring the possibilities of observing society through social media. They recognize its value as a communication channel that is "being used by a very large population for a variety of functions" and "where we can see people's activities over long periods of time." Within internet environments, communication structure that used to be "ephemeral" becomes "manifest", "visible", "crawlable" and "analyzable" and researchers in our interviews were concerned with analyzing the "relationship between the structure we see on the internet and the structure of society".

Yet, the interviewees did not expect social media to be a mirror of society per se. Rather they demonstrated a critical reflection of the reciprocal relationship between society and the internet, recognizing that one can influence the other. Not only researchers look at society through social media but also society can observe itself through this channel "for the first time (…) in a new way." There is a chance that society is again affected by this observation, and researchers were also interested in studying the effects this can have on society. Some effects had already been described, for example that the "internet has and social media has created an interesting kind of shift of the structure of power between institutions, between the traditional elites, between users." To study such developments it might not always be feasible to exclusively work with data collected from social media. The adaptation of new social media can further tell us a lot about culture in general:

"So I think how people handle Twitter, how it kind of sparks extremes, dystopian, utopian notions, it says a lot about culture. So Twitter in itself is interesting, not just the debates on it as a window into elite voices in society, but in itself it is interesting to see what people do with something new in terms of media."

It is recognized that social media data can yield quite different advantages and insights for scholars from different disciplines, for example linguists or economists and researchers were curious to see other disciplines involved in discussions ("I would love to have more psychology in some of these panels because it is extremely interesting from their perspective"). Again there were also very critical discussions about the use of social media to study society and about the respective methodologies, but these topics are beyond the scope of this paper and will be presented in more detail in the future.

4. CONCLUSION AND OUTLOOK

In this paper we have investigated experiences of social scientists who study social media, focusing on different dimensions of interdisciplinarity in social media research. We could therefore present results illustrating a) the general need for interdiscplinarity for this particular research field, b) the more specific need to work with computer scientists, and c) the specific value social media adds to social scientists research. All results were drawn from semi-structured interviews with twenty social science researchers. Our approach enabled us to capture a detailed and fine-grained image of the facets of interdisciplinarity from social media researchers' point of view and thus allowed us to present first insights in the challenges and chances perceived.

Studying social media brings with it both chances and challenges for social scientists. In addition to technical difficulties with the scale and size of data – which can be addressed by making data and skills available for social media researchers as proposed, for example, in computational social science approaches – we found that there are also other challenges. First, the interdisciplinary work presents challenges due to differing ideas about validity, best practice and research interests. Such difficulties have already been described as common obstacles in interdisciplinarity [19]. Second, there is in particular a lack of clarity about the derivation, validity and explanatory power of the new 'type' of data being made available through APIs and other crawlable sources. On the other hand there is obviously a lot of potential to try and accomplish new things and to learn by doing. And, last but not least, there are differing ideas about what data needs to look like in order to be understandable and interesting to the different disciplines.

While much work is understandably 'result driven' – in the sense that interdisciplinary collaboration is made to work regardless of difficulties in order to produce scientific output, there is still more research needed to define, test and learn how social scientists and computer scientists can work together productively. As is the case for most interdisciplinary work it seems that in order to allow for successful collaboration the way in which validity in research is achieved needs to match or at least a way needs to be found for different disciplines to fulfill the respective validity requirements.

This paper presents first results from a larger project on studying the evolving field of social media research. Not all insights from the first round of interviewing social media researchers could be presented here and thus we will in the future present more detailed results concerning in particular the epistemological shift in social media research, the issues around personal data, trust and privacy and general social media research ethics. We are aware that these dimensions especially demand interdisciplinary perspectives and will therefore conduct more interviews with researchers from additional disciplines. We especially expect further insights into interdisciplinary collaboration by gathering perspectives from computer scientists and by comparing these to the results presented here. Furthermore, researchers from communities such as digital humanities or network studies should be included in future interviews.

5. ACKNOWLEDGMENTS

Many thanks to the researchers who participated in our interviews – we really appreciate the valuable insights they shared with us! We would also like to thank our student assistants who helped to transcribe the audio recordings.

6. REFERENCES

[1] Hendler, J., Shadbolt, N., Hall, W., Berners-Lee, T., and Weitzner, D. 2008. Web science: An interdisciplinary approach to understanding the web. Communications of the ACM 7(51), 60-69.

[2] Shneiderman, B. 2007. Web science. A provocative invitation to computer science. Communications of the ACM 50 (6), 25–27.

[3] Berners-Lee, T., Hall, W., Hendler, J., Shadbolt, N. and Weitzner, D.J. 2006. Creating a Science of the Web. Science 313 (5788), 769-771.

[4] Hooper, C.J., Bordea, and G., Buitelaar, P. 2013. Web science and the two (hundred) cultures. Representation of disciplines publishing in web science. In: Proceedings of the 5th Annual ACM Web Science Conference. Paris, France. New York: ACM, 162–171.

[5] Ackland, R. 2013. Web Social Science: Concepts, data and tools for social scientists in the digital age. Los Angeles: SAGE.

[6] Rogers, R. 2013. Digital Methods. Cambridge, MA, London: The MIT Press.

[7] AoIR 2013. Association of Internet Research - About. Retrieved from http://aoir.org/about/

[8] Lazer, D., Pentland, A., Adamic, L., Aral, S., Barabasi, A.L.m Brewer, D./ Christakis, N., Contractor, N., Fowler, J., Gutmann, M., Jebara, T., King, G., Macy, M., Roy, D. and Van Alstyne, M. 2009. Life in the network: The coming age of computational social science. Science 323(5915), 721-723.

[9] Giglietto, F., Rossi, L., and Bennato, D. 2012. The open laboratory: Limits and possibilities of using Facebook, Twitter, and YouTube as a research data source. Journal of Technology in Human Services 30(3-4), 145-159.

[10] Giglietto, F., and Rossi, L. 2012. Ethics and interdisciplinarity in computational social science. Methodological Innovations Online 7(1), 25-36.

[11] Hooper, C., and Dix, A. 2012. Web science and human-computer interaction: when disciplines collide. In Proceedings of the 3rd Annual ACM Web Science Conference (WebSci '12). ACM, New York, NY, USA, 128-136.

[12] Taylor, L., Meyer, E.T., and Schroeder, R. (in press). Bigger and better, or more of the same? Emerging practices and perspectives on big data analysis in economics. Big Data and Society.

[13] Fielding, N. 1988. Joining forces: Police training, Socialization and Occupational Competence. London: Routledge.

[14] May, T. 2011. Social research: Issues, methods and process. Maidenhead, New York: Open University Press.

[15] Crouch, M., and McKenzie, H. 2006. The logic of small samples in interview based qualitative research. Social Science Information, 45(4), 483-499.

[16] Strauss, A., and Corbin, J. 1998. Basics of qualitative research: Techniques and procedures for developing grounded theory. Thousand Oaks, CA: Sage.

[17] Sim, S.E., and Alspaugh, T.A. 2011. Getting the Whole Story: An Experience Report on Analyzing Data Elicited Using the War Stories Procedure. Empirical Software Engineering: An International Journal 16(4), 460-486.

[18] Creswell, J. 2013. Qualitative Inquiry & Research Design: Choosing Among Five Approaches. Los Angeles, London, New Delhi et al., Sage.

[19] Brewer, G.D. 1999. The challenges of interdisciplinarity. Policy Sciences 32: 327-337.

Multilinguals and Wikipedia Editing

Scott A. Hale
Oxford Internet Institute, University of Oxford
1 St Giles, Oxford, UK OX1 3JS
scott.hale@oii.ox.ac.uk

ABSTRACT

This article analyzes one month of edits to Wikipedia in order to examine the role of users editing multiple language editions (referred to as multilingual users). Such multilingual users may serve an important function in diffusing information across different language editions of the encyclopedia, and prior work has suggested this could reduce the level of self-focus bias in each edition. This study finds multilingual users are much more active than their single-edition (monolingual) counterparts. They are found in all language editions, but smaller-sized editions with fewer users have a higher percentage of multilingual users than larger-sized editions. About a quarter of multilingual users always edit the same articles in multiple languages, while just over 40% of multilingual users edit different articles in different languages. When non-English users do edit a second language edition, that edition is most frequently English. Nonetheless, several regional and linguistic cross-editing patterns are also present.

Categories and Subject Descriptors

H.5.4 [**Information Interfaces and Presentation (e.g. HCI)**]: Hypertext/Hypermedia; H.5.3 [**Information Interfaces and Presentation (e.g. HCI)**]: Group and Organization Interfaces

General Terms

Human Factors; Design

Keywords

Social Media; Information Discovery; Social Network Analysis; Information Diffusion; Cross-language; Wikipedia; Multilingual

1. INTRODUCTION

Wikipedia, the free, peer-produced online encyclopedia, contains a large collection of human knowledge. The foundation behind Wikipedia has characterized the encyclopedia as trying to provide access to "the sum of all human knowledge."[1] If any one language edition of Wikipedia were to achieve the goal of "all human knowledge," then that language should contain (at a minimum) all the information found in other language editions of the encyclopedia. Studies comparing content across language editions, however, have found a "surprisingly small amount of content overlap between languages of Wikipedia" [11, p. 295]. No one edition contains all the information found in other language editions, and the largest language edition, English, contains only 51% of the articles in the second-largest edition, German [11, p. 295]. Nonetheless, there clearly is some overlap in content between languages, and a greater sharing of information between the language editions would enable monolingual readers of the encyclopedia to access a larger variety of content.

This paper examines one month of all edits to the top 46 language editions of Wikipedia. This comprises all editions with at least 100,000 articles at the time of data collection in July 2013.[2] It identifies users who contribute to multiple language editions (these users are referred to as multilingual users in this paper) and compares their contributions to that of users who edit only one language edition of the encyclopedia (monolingual users). It asks if multilingual editors play a unique bridging role diffusing information between different language editions.

2. RELATED WORK

Language is a large factor in the network structure of communication patterns on many platforms including telephone communications [1], Twitter messaging [3, 9], and blog linking [8, 12]. Consistent with this previous work on other platforms, Hecht and Gergle [11] found there was low overlap in articles between different language editions of Wikipedia. In a separate study, they also found that most language editions exhibited a self-focus bias where articles about places, people, and events where the language of the edition was spoken were more prominent than those in other regions [10]. While past work has not specifically looked at what percentage of users contribute to multiple language editions of the

[1] http://www.theatlantic.com/technology/archive/2011/05/is-wikipedia-a-world-cultural-repository/239274/

[2] http://meta.wikimedia.org/wiki/List_of_Wikipedias

encyclopedia, studies of other platforms and the low overlap in content between different language editions of Wikipedia suggest that *most editors will edit only one language edition* (H1).

Previous research about Wikipedia has tended to focus on the English-language edition. These studies have found that the scientific articles in the English edition compared favorably with Encyclopedia Britannica [5]. However, studies have also suggested the edition suffers from issues of coverage and bias [6, 10, 13].

Among these biases, multilingual studies of Wikipedia have revealed each language edition has a self-focus bias [10]. This bias manifests itself in both the articles users choose to write (and not write) and also in the content of the articles. Hecht and Gergle [11] give an example where the article on psychology in the Spanish-language edition has a section about contributions to the field from Latin America while other language editions do not.

Even so, a 2011 survey of Wikipedia editors found that just over "half of Wikipedia editors contribute to more than one language Wikipedia, and an overwhelming majority (72%) read Wikipedia in more than one language" (N=4,930).[3] In addition, Yasseri et al. [20] found registered users from many different timezones contribute to many language editions of Wikipedia. For example, 25% of edits to the Arabic and Persian editions likely came from users in North America. This suggests diaspora, language learners, or other speakers of these languages play an important role in editing the encyclopedia. Furthermore, the location of these users in North America suggests many of them might speak another language in addition to Arabic or Persian. If so, these users could introduce new information from other language sources and reduce the amount of self-focus in the edition.

Self-focus results were not reported for Arabic or Persian by Hecht and Gergle [10], but the Dutch and Swedish editions were found to exhibit less self-focus. The authors speculated that high bilingualism with English in Dutch and Swedish societies could explain why the Swedish and Dutch editions exhibited less self-focus in their study. They write that users contributing to the Dutch and Swedish editions, "may have gained significantly more guidance from the English Wikipedia, muting their spatial self-focus effect" [10, p. 17]. This idea, however, is not specifically tested in their paper.

The literature therefore suggests that multilingual users who edit multiple language editions of Wikipedia could play a unique role in diffusing content between different language editions. From seemingly small changes like updated population numbers or new website addresses to large, fast-breaking news developments (e.g. the Japanese tsunami and earthquake discussed by Hale [7]), multilingual users may help keep content in sync and reduce self-focus bias by introducing new content, updating old content, and correcting errors across multiple language editions.

This paper examines this idea in two ways. First, the articles edited by multilingual users are compared to the articles edited by monolingual users. It is expected that *multilingual users will edit different articles than monolingual users* (H2). Second, this paper compares the articles edited across language editions by the same user to the network of interlanguage links that link articles on the same concept across language editions. If multilingual Wikipedia users serve as information bridges contributing similar information across multiple editions, then it is expected that *when a user edits an article in another language that same user will usually also edit the corresponding article in his native language* (H3).

The idea of network effects from network studies or positive externalities from economics may explain in part the reason editors of Wikipedia would contribute to a foreign language edition of the encyclopedia. Network effects suggest that larger-sized platforms or networks have more communicative value than similar, smaller networks. This is obvious in the trivial observation that if only one person in the world had a telephone it would be utterly useless to that person as he would have no one to call. More generally, a social media platform, like a telephone, is only valuable if one's social contacts also use the platform. For without this, a user would have no one with whom to communicate. With each additional social media user, the value of the network grows for the existing users because each person now has a wider array of individuals who they may contact through the network. Crystal [2] relates this network effect to languages arguing that the more individuals who use a common language, the more valuable it is for additional individuals to also learn that language. He speculates this effect might account in part for the growth and staying power of English as a global language. This idea is also suggested by Zuckerman [23]. Similarly, editions of Wikipedia written in more widely spoken languages have the possibility of reaching larger audiences, and past research has suggested an important factor motivating content production is the extent to which authors believe there is an audience to engage with the content [22].

These ideas of network effects related to language size suggest two related hypotheses. The users who cross-language boundaries will *come from* smaller, less-represented languages and will *cross to* larger, more-represented languages. More specifically, *users writing primarily in smaller-sized language editions will be more likely to cross-language boundaries than users writing primarily in larger-sized language editions* (H4). When these users cross languages, they will most likely cross to a larger-sized language edition (e.g. English, German, French). As a consequence of this, *larger-sized language editions, English chief among them, will be more likely to have contributions from editors of different languages than smaller-sized language editions* (H5).

3. DATA

Edits to Wikipedia are broadcast in near real-time over Internet Relay Chat (IRC).[4] Each edit to any Wikipedia edition is broadcast on the irc.wikimedia.org server on an IRC channel with a name in the format of #lang.wikipedia (e.g. #en.wikipedia for the English edition of Wikipedia, #de.wikipedia for the German edition, etc.). Each entry contains the username (or IP address for anonymous users), the title of the article edited, comments written by the user about the edit, the size of the edit (how many bytes larger or smaller the result of the edit is compared to the previous version), and a link to the differences from the previous version. The date and time of the edit is not included, but

---

[3] https://meta.wikimedia.org/w/index.php?title=Editor_Survey_2011/Location_%26_Language&oldid=8409990

[4] http://meta.wikimedia.org/wiki/IRC/Channels#Raw_feeds

this information was added by consulting the system clock. Similarly, the IRC channel of the message was recorded to know which language edition the user edited.[5]

All edits for the 46 language editions with 100,000 or more articles[6] were recorded through IRC from July 8, 2013, to August 9, 2013. Edits to the Simple English edition are excluded for most of the analysis and the role of the Simple English edition is addressed separately in Section 4.4. In addition to the main, article namespace, Wikipedia has separate namespaces for other content including user pages, portals, and administrative activity. This paper focuses on the main namespace to which the majority of the edits (63%) were directed. Consistent with prior research, many of these edits (15% of non-minor edits) were created by bots—automated scripts editing the encyclopedia for consistency, fixing common mistakes, and detecting and reverting vandalism (malicious edits). A number of edits were also from anonymous users without an account (28% of non-minor edits). Since IP addresses change over time and multiple users may edit from the same IP address, these edits were removed from the dataset. In order to focus on the activity of human editors, only non-minor edits from registered users, who were not listed as bots were considered for further analysis.

Initial analysis of the data suggested that there were many bots operating on the encyclopedia without being officially declared as bots. These suspected bots had very high edit counts across a large number of languages, and human examination of their contributions and user pages suggested most were indeed bots. A number of ideas drawn from the literature were examined and ad hoc subsets of users were manually inspected to arrive at a method to filter these unregistered bots. The most successful approach found was to examine the maximum amount of time between two successive edits from the same user. In accordance with past research, edits for most users (registered bots excluded) were bursty: that is, the edits were clustered such that many edits occurred in small amounts of time separated by comparatively longer absences of edits [4, 21]. Looking at the length of the longest break between bursts of edits revealed that many users without the bot flag set never had a rest of more than a couple of hours over the entire 32-day data collection window. As most human editors would need to break longer than this for sleep—and editing activity has previously been shown to follow circadian cycles [20]—these users are likely undeclared bots.

Through manual examination of different thresholds, six hours was chosen. Overall, 114,376 accounts did not have any break in editing of more than six hours over the course of the 32 days in the sample. These users were assumed to be bots (or humans with only one editing burst) and excluded from further analysis.

One edit is insufficient to determine whether a user edits in multiple languages, while with two edits in two different languages it is unclear which language is the user's primary language. To be certain multilingual users were identified as such and to be able to identify users' primary languages, all users with less than four edits overall (21%) or less than two edits in their most-edited language (0.6%) were excluded. As

a result, this study focuses on the most active users. This is not, however, a major limitation, as past work has shown the most active users produce a disproportionate majority of the content in the encyclopedia [16].

3.1 Cross-language alignment

Previous cross-language studies on Wikipedia relied on the interlanguage links found in each edition of the encyclopedia. These links were maintained by a mixture of humans and machines (bots), but nonetheless contained a number of errors [10]. The issues were often compounded by having dumps of each language from slightly different dates.

This study uses a new source of inter-language information, WikiData.[7] This new initiative centralizes all interwiki references and category information (and, in the future, statistics and other structured data) in one location. This avoids some previous issues with out-of-date or conflicting interlanguage links. Further study of the impact of the WikiData project on Wikipedia and its editors is not within the scope of this paper, but would be a fruitful area for future research.

When Wikipedia began, each language edition was run independently. User accounts were created separately on each language edition, and thus the same username on different editions may refer to two different persons. As Wikipedia matured, a central authorization system was built to provide for unified login. Unified login allows users to unite their accounts across multiple language editions (and other projects: Wiktionary, Wikiquote, Wikibooks, etc.) and be able to login to all projects and editions at one time. Users who have unified their accounts have "global accounts" and information about the user is available from the *Global account manager*.[8]

There was an announcement in April 2013 that any remaining conflicts where different persons had accounts with the same usernames on different editions would be resolved and the accounts renamed.[9] This was to take place in May 2013, but was delayed first to August 2013 and then to an unspecified future date. Once this step is taken it will be trivially easy to determine if one user edits multiple language editions. At the point of data collection, however, it still remained technically possible for one person to have two differently named accounts on different editions, or for two persons to have accounts of the same name on different editions.

The publicly-available data makes it difficult to identify one person with multiple accounts (false-negative monolingual). It is possible, however, to check whether a given account is a global account. If it is a global account, it is possible to get a list of all the language editions on which the user is active. This makes it possible to avoid any false-positive multilingual user classifications.

For this study, all usernames were first assumed to be unique across the editions. The usernames editing multiple language editions were identified and classified as possible multilingual users. Each of these usernames was checked against the *Global account manager* to ensure that the user was a global user registered with all the language editions the

---

[5]The code used to record the IRC streams (Java), construct the network (Java/Hadoop), and perform the analysis (Python/R) are available at http://www.scotthale.net/pubs/?websci2014.

[6]http://meta.wikimedia.org/wiki/List_of_Wikipedias

[7]http://www.wikidata.org/

[8]http://meta.wikimedia.org/w/index.php?title=Special:CentralAuth

[9]http://meta.wikimedia.org/wiki/Single_User_Login_finalisation_announcement

Language	Edits	Articles	Users	NP users	NP edits
English	1,389,647	518,405	27,476	18%	3%
German	256,495	125,647	5,967	18%	2%
French	250,828	106,027	4,549	25%	3%
Spanish	191,934	66,848	4,338	24%	3%
Russian	239,267	92,326	3,961	16%	1%
Japanese	106,848	56,406	3,551	11%	2%
Italian	160,191	69,534	2,919	25%	2%
Chinese	112,888	42,937	2,309	14%	1%
Portuguese	67,505	32,753	1,730	29%	4%
Dutch	80,535	39,463	1,500	33%	3%
Polish	67,038	37,393	1,454	30%	3%
Swedish	42,390	25,269	904	43%	4%
Ukrainian	54,241	22,537	898	36%	3%
Hebrew	37,889	13,224	832	16%	2%
Arabic	43,924	15,993	729	20%	3%

Table 1: Statistics for the top 15 language editions in the sample. The *Users* column includes all users who edited the edition during the data collection period. A percentage of these users (*NP users*) are non-primary users who edited a different language edition more frequently. *Edits* and and *NP Edits* are defined similarly.

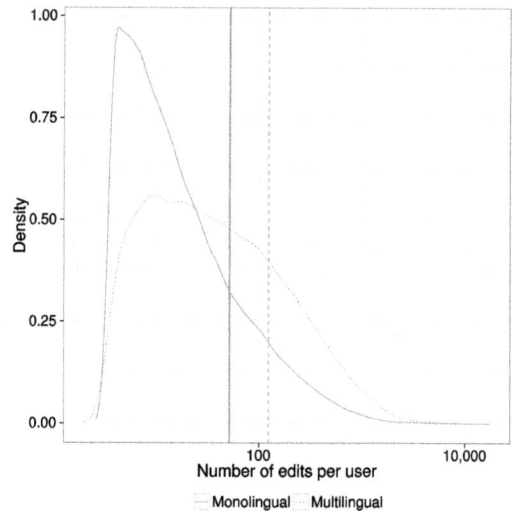

Figure 1: Density plot comparing the number of edits made by monolingual and multilingual Wikipedia users.

user was recorded as having edited during the data collection period. Users who were not registered as global users or whose global username was not associated with all the editions the user was recorded as having edited were treated as separate users.

There were very few false-positive matches found. Only 572 usernames found to be editing multiple editions were not global accounts. In a further 50 cases, a global username existed but was not associated with all language editions where the username was used. These local, non-global users were treated as separate users. The small number of these matches means that this correction has minimal effect on the results.

The available data does not easily allow the discovery of false-negatives—one user with different usernames on different editions. In addition, it is not possible to know if a user reads multiple language editions, while editing only one edition. Therefore, the number of multilingual users presented in this paper is a lower bound on the actual amount of multilingual activity happening on Wikipedia.

4. ANALYSIS

Excluding the Simple English edition, 55,568 registered, human users edited at least one edition of Wikipedia two times or more and had at least four edits across all editions during the 32-day data collection period. This resulted in a total of 3,518,955 edits. Most of these edits (39%) were to the English language edition. Similarly, most users (40%) edited the English-language edition of the encyclopedia more than any other edition (Table 1).

Consistent with H1 a relatively small number of users (8,544 or 15.4%) edited multiple editions of the encyclopedia. These users were categorized as *multilingual* while all remaining users were classified as *monolingual*. Multilin-

gual users were significantly more active than their monolingual counterparts. Multilingual users made a mean 124 (median 32, sd 299) edits overall, while monolingual users made only a mean 52 (median 13, sd 192) edits overall (Figure 1). These additional edits by multilinguals are not only in other language editions but also in each user's primary language edition that the user edited most frequently. Multilinguals made a mean 113 (median 26, sd 285) edits to their primary language editions of the encyclopedia. Indeed, while only 15.4% of all users, multilingual users were responsible for 30.1% of all edits captured during the month.

Multilingual users were not just editing the same articles more, but also edited a wider number of articles. Multilingual users edited a mean 69 (median 16, sd 191) articles while monolinguals edited a mean 27 (median 5, sd 133) articles. Logically following from the fact that multilingual users were more active in their primary languages than monolingual users, it is clear multilinguals were not more active simply because they had more articles across more languages they could have edited. As discussed in the next subsection, multilinguals only directed a small percentage of their edits to their non-primary languages. Multilingual users were still more active than their monolingual counterparts after collapsing together articles in different languages on the same concept as determined by interlanguage article links. In this way, for example, editing United States (English) and Estados Unidos (Spanish) only counted as editing one "concept" since the two articles are linked together by interlanguage article links. Monolingual users edited the same number of concepts as articles since they only edited one language, while multilingual users edited a mean 65 (median 15, sd 185) concepts. All of these differences are significant as established with two-tailed t-tests ($p < 2.2 \times 10^{-16}$).

In contrast, the size of the edits made by multilinguals and monolinguals do not differ significantly. Edits by multilinguals had a mean size of 331 bytes (median 143, sd 912),

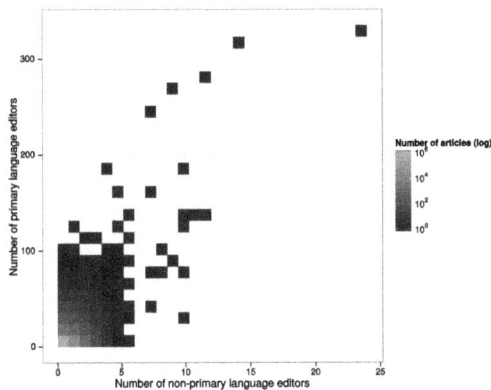

Figure 2: 2D density plot of the number of multilingual users editing articles in a non-primary language against the number of monolingual users editing the articles.

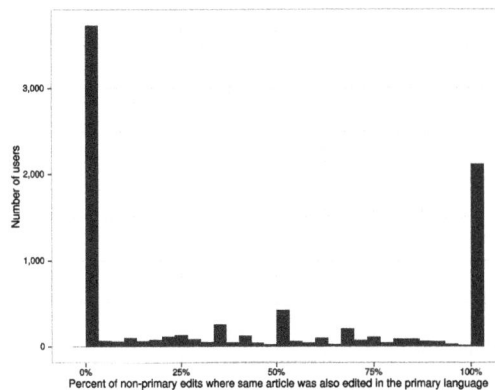

Figure 3: Histogram showing the distribution with which multilingual users edited articles in other languages that they also edited in their primary languages. The distribution is bimodal. A large number of users did not edit any of the same articles in their primary languages, but a large number of users always edited the same articles in their primary languages.

while edits by monolinguals had a mean size of 339 bytes (median 125, sd 1327).

4.1 What do multilinguals edit?

Given the low overlap in content between language editions of Wikipedia, multilingual users may offer unique contributions to the editions they edit. This section examines the edits of multilingual users to their non-primary language editions (that is, to editions other than the editions they edited most frequently).

Edits from multilingual users writing in their non-primary language are an extremely small fraction of all edits to Wikipedia. Only 2.6% of edits are from users writing in their non-primary languages. To some extent, multilingual users edit similar articles in their non-primary languages as do monolingual users. The 2D density plot in Figure 2 shows that the articles with the largest number of non-primary users also have a large number of primary users. There's a positive correlation of 0.25 between the number of multilingual users editing an article in a second language and the number of monolingual users editing the article. The most dense region is near the origin where most articles are edited by a small number of users. Within this region, however, multilingual users are often editing articles not edited by other users: 44% of the articles edited by multilingual users in their non-primary languages were not edited by any monolingual user during the data collection period.

Using the WikiData information for interlanguage article links, it is possible to connect articles across languages (e.g. the English-language *United Nations* article is on the same concept as the Spanish-language *Organización de las Naciones Unidas* article). This makes it possible to check when a multilingual user edited an article in a non-primary language, if that user also had edited the equivalent article in his or her primary language. Overall, 44.5% of the edits to non-primary languages by multilingual users were to articles where the user had edited the same article in his or her primary language. The underlying distribution per user, however, is bimodal at the two extremes (Figure 3). 43% of multilingual users did not edit the equivalent articles in their primary languages at all. On the other hand, 25% of mul-

tilingual users always edited the equivalent articles in their primary languages.

Part of this behavior is explained by the fact that some of the articles edited by multilingual users in their non-primary languages did not exist in their primary languages. Overall, 73% of the articles edited by multilingual users in a non-primary language existed in the primary languages of those users. Ignoring the instances where an equivalent article did not exist in the users' primary languages, 59.8% of edits to non-primary languages by multilingual users were to articles the user had edited in his or her primary language. The distribution remains bimodal with 34% of users not editing the equivalent articles in their primary languages, and 37% of users always editing the equivalent articles in their primary languages.

While the size of edits made by multilingual and monolingual users did not differ significantly, the size of edits multilingual users made in their non-primary languages were significantly smaller than the edits they made in their primary languages. Considering only edits with a positive size (i.e. not edits that removed more text than was added) multilingual users made edits with a mean size of 569 bytes (median 260, sd 1327) in their primary languages and a mean size of 468 bytes (median 83, sd 2156) in their non-primary languages. Nonetheless, 25% of multilingual users actually made larger positive-sized edits in their non-primary languages as compared to positive-sized edits in their primary languages.

Comparisons of edit sizes across languages is difficult for two reasons: first, different characters require a different number of bytes to store, and second, the information content contained in one character differs across languages. One standard English character is usually one byte, while a special or accented character (e.g. á) is usually two bytes, and a character from a more complex language like Japanese, Chinese, or Korean is generally three bytes. In contrast, however, one English character usually contains less information content than one Japanese or Chinese character, which could represent a full word. An information-theoretic approach, using entropy, has previously been employed to compare the information content per character across different languages on Twitter [15], and a similar approach could be employed to compare Wikipedia edit sizes across languages. Such an approach, however, would require the content of the edits rather than the meta-data about edits used here.

Overall, these findings support H2 that multilingual users would make unique contributions to the encyclopedia by editing articles less edited by monolingual users. The data is mixed for H3 which suggested multilingual users would often edit the same article in their primary and non-primary languages. For a quarter of users this was always true. However, just over two-fifths of multilingual users did not edit the equivalent articles in their primary languages. Data on the articles users view is not available to know whether these users viewed the equivalent articles in their primary languages before editing in another language.

4.2 Variations by language

The percentage of users classified as multilingual varied across the language editions studied. Previous research suggested this variation would correlate with the total number of users and/or the number of articles in each edition. Figure 4 shows the percentage of users primarily editing each language edition that also edited a second language edition compared with the total number of users primarily editing the language edition. Consistent with the suggestions of prior research, there is a strong correlation between the two variables. Looking only at languages with at least 10 users in the sample to avoid small number issues, the log of the number of users primarily editing each edition and the percentage of users editing multiple editions are correlated with a coefficient of -0.69. Similar results hold for comparing the percentage of users who are multilingual to the number of articles in each language edition, where the correlation coefficient is -0.46. (These two measures are interdependent as the total number of articles per edition and the number of users in the sample per edition have a correlation coefficient of 0.90.)

Among the smallest-sized editions, Esperanto (eo) and Malay (ms) stand out as two languages with high levels of multilingualism among their primary editors. It is surprising that Esperanto was not higher given that it is a constructed language and thus has no native speakers. Nonetheless, nearly 46% of the editors of the Esperanto edition edited that edition more than any other. Italian (it), Slovenian (sl), and Slovak (sk) are similarly sized but with far lower levels of multilingualism.

Among larger-sized languages, Catalan (ca), Swedish (sv), Ukrainian (uk), and Dutch (nl) all had relatively high levels of multilingualism. In contrast, the lowest level of multilingualism is found among users primarily editing the Japanese (ja) language edition, where only 6% of the users edited another edition.

While some exceptions emerge, the findings support H4: in general a larger percentage of the users primarily editing smaller-sized editions are multilingual.

4.3 Language crossings

Hypothesis H5 predicted that when users did edit a second edition, that edition would almost always be English

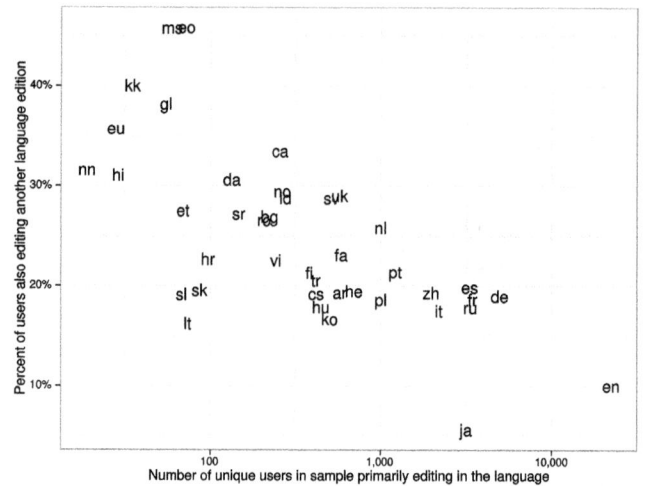

Figure 4: Scatter plot of language size (number of unique users) and percentage of users who are multilingual (edit more than one language edition). The three editions with less than 10 users in the sample are omitted (Uzbek, Cebuano, and Waray-Waray).

or, to a lesser degree, another large edition. In order by the number of users active in the last 30 days, the largest editions of Wikipedia are English (129,900 active users), German (20,300), Spanish (15,800), French (15,500), Japanese (11,400), Russian (10,800).[10]

The bipartite network of users and articles was collapsed to a network of language relationships. Each article was assigned to the node corresponding to the language edition to which it belonged. Similarly, users were grouped with the node representing the language they edited most frequently. Each directed, weighted edge e_{ij} records the log of the number of editors primarily editing language edition i that also edited language edition j. This network is shown in Figure 5a.

The number of users represented by each edge ranged from 1 to 775 with a mean value of 15.3 and a standard deviation of 50.7. Only edges with a log value at least 1.96 standard deviations above the mean of all log values are shown on the graph. This corresponds to edges with 60 or more users. Isolates (languages unconnected to any other language) are removed from the network diagram. Note that in contrast to the previous section, the network graph shows the logarithm of the number of users editing multiple editions and not the percentages of users editing each edition that also edit another edition.

The network reveals the English edition (en) does receive a large amount of attention from multilingual users in other languages. Every node in the graph is connected to English. Most of these edges are reciprocal, but in three-quarters of the cases more users from another language edited English than users from English edited the other language. Despite the very large size of English, this also holds globally as 4,659 users from other languages edited English while only a total

---

[10]The latest information on the number of users and articles for all editions of Wikipedia is online at http://meta.wikimedia.org/wiki/List_of_Wikipedias

of 3,673 primary users of English edited another language. When users primarily editing the English edition did edit another language edition, the largest number of users edited the Spanish (es), German (de), and French (fr) editions.

There are only four languages that have a directed edge from English that is not reciprocated. These languages are Romanian (ro), Danish (da), Bulgarian (bg), and Catalan (ca). Each of these four languages is quite small, and while a sizable percentage of the users primarily editing these language editions also edited English[11] they simply did not constitute sufficient volume to rise above the edge weight threshold and appear on the graph.

There are are some strongly connected language pairs not involving English. German users edit the French edition, and Russian and Ukrainian users edit each others' editions with some frequency. Figure 5b shows the same network, but with English removed. The edge weight distribution is recalculated and edges with 33 or more users are shown (corresponding to 1.96 standard deviations above the mean of the log values with English removed).

Even with the English edition removed, editions with a larger number of active users continue to structure the network. The second-largest edition, German, is connected to every node except Ukrainian (uk), Japanese (ja), and Chinese (zh).

The infomap community detection algorithm [17, 18] finds the same community structure with and without English as shown with node color in Figure 5. The largest community is centered around the largest language, English or German. A strong relationship is present between Ukrainian and Russian (ru) where Ukrainian users edit Russian and English but rarely another language edition. Similarly, Chinese users edit Japanese and English but rarely any other edition. Unlike the Russian/Ukrainian relationship, the edge from Chinese to Japanese is one way. Indeed, apart from editing English, Japanese users rarely edit any other language.

With English removed, it is also worth noting that all the romance languages (Spanish [es], Italian [it], French [fr], and Portuguese [pt]) have mutual edges between them. The only exception is Catalan (ca), which is only connected to Spanish and German. Nonetheless, the many links to German from other language editions overshadow these connections in the community detection algorithm.

These findings support hypothesis H5 that multilingual users from smaller languages would mostly cross language boundaries to edit larger-sized languages. English receives edits from users in almost every other edition. Even with English removed, the second-largest edition, German, receives edits from users in a large number of other editions. Nonetheless, regional and linguistic patterns are also evident in the co-editing network.

4.4 The role of Simple English

The Simple English edition of Wikipedia (hereafter Simple) is written in English, but aims to use simpler grammar and shorter sentences. While intended to be primarily read by children, adults with learning difficulties, and second-

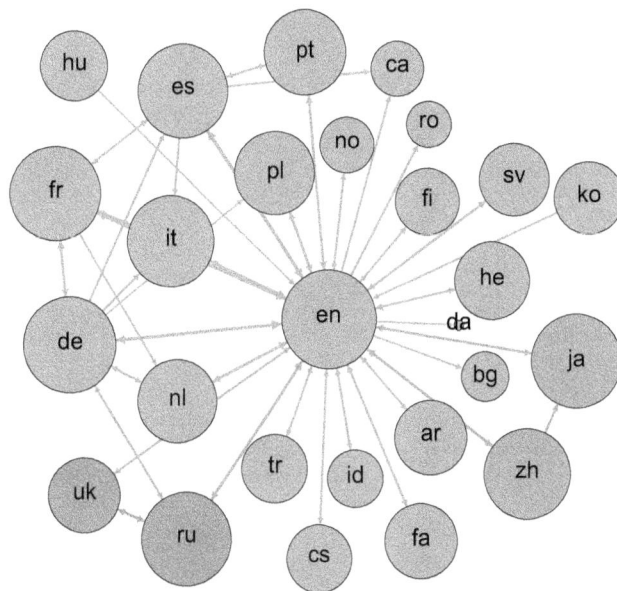

(a) Network graph with English

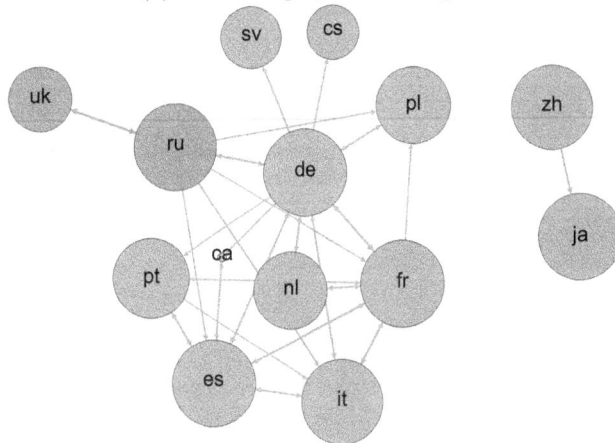

(b) Network graph with English removed

Figure 5: Network graphs of co-editing patterns. Nodes represent language editions of the encyclopedia and the directed, weighted edges show the log of the number of users primarily editing one language edition who edited another edition as well. Both graphs show only edges with weights over 1.96 standard deviations above the mean. The top graph shows all language editions. In the bottom graph, the English edition is removed and the distribution of edges recalculated. Colors indicate communities found by the infomap community detection algorithm.

---

[11]27–33% of the users in each of these four languages edited multiple editions. Most of these multilingual users edited English in the case of Romanian (95%), Danish (88%), and Bulgarian (88%). Of the multilingual users that primarily edited Catalan, 50% also edited English.

language learners of English, past research has indicated it may also be edited by many speakers of other languages [20].

The findings presented so far in this paper have excluded all edits to Simple. Its inclusion, however, makes little difference to the findings. There is a strong link between Simple and the English edition. Of the 221 users in the data sample who edited Simple, over half (124 users) primarily edited English. Users editing Simple and primarily editing a non-English edition were spread thinly over 26 other languages. The four largest of these languages were German (13 users), French (10), Dutch (9), and Russian (8). Two-thirds of the users editing Simple were multilingual users, who already edited at least two other language editions. Of the 76 users editing Simple who were previously classified as editing only one edition, 66 were primarily editors of the English edition. Simple makes little difference to the structure of the co-editing networks in Figure 5. Enough English users edit Simple to have a small directed edge from English to Simple, but no other edges are added.

Like the Esperanto edition, there appears to be a cohort of users dedicated more to Simple than to their native languages. There are 21 users in the dataset who edited Simple more than any other edition (14 of these users edited the English edition second-most). In addition, there are a further 44 users not in the dataset, who edited Simple more than two times but did not have at least four edits across all editions when their edits to Simple were excluded. Just under half (45%) of all the users who edited Simple most often did not edit any other edition at all. Of those users that did edit a second edition less frequently than Simple, that edition was English for all but 9 users.

There have been two proposals in the past to close Simple, both of which have failed. Whatever the utility of the edition to readers, it does have a dedicated community of editors. In this respect, it is very similar to the Esperanto edition, where 54% of the users that primarily edited Esperanto edited no other language edition.

5. DISCUSSION

By far, most Wikipedia users edited only one language edition, confirming H1. However, just over 15% of users also edited multiple language editions. These multilingual users were found to be more active than their monolingual counterparts making more than 2.3 times as many edits per user on average. Most of this additional activity occurred in the users' primary languages, with only 2.6% of all edits being made by users in their non-primary languages. It is important to note that this is a correlation between multilingualism and activity and not causation. It may be that the most dedicated and active users of Wikipedia contribute to multiple language editions regardless of how great their foreign-language skills really are. Survey work, for instance, has shown many Internet users in Uzbekistan engaged with foreign-language content even while simultaneously reporting low comfort with foreign languages [19]. Regardless of the direction of this relationship, it will be important to keep these multilingual users in mind when considering design changes to Wikipedia.

The percentage of users editing multiple languages on Wikipedia is similar to the 11% of users found to tweet in multiple languages on Twitter [9]. On the other hand, the percentage of users editing multiple language editions is far less than the 50% of users that self-reported editing mul-

tiple language editions in the 2011 Wikipedia editors survey.[12] This could perhaps follow from the idea that the most dedicated users are multilingual and thus more likely to take the time to respond to a survey about Wikipedia when given the opportunity. Alternatively, given that multilinguals only made a small fraction of their edits to their non-primary language editions, it is possible that more users would be observed editing multiple language editions if they were observed for a longer period of time.

Multilingual users editing more than one edition of Wikipedia can bring information, sources, and perspectives from the primary edition they edit to other editions. A large portion (44%) of the articles edited by multilinguals in their non-primary languages were to articles that no monolingual users in that language edited during the month of study. A similar percentage of all edits by multilinguals in their non-primary languages were to articles that the same multilingual user had edited in his or her primary language. This suggests that multilingual users are making unique contributions not duplicated by monolingual users and that in many cases multilingual users are working on the same article in multiple languages.

Hecht and Gergle [10] have previously suggested that users crossing between different languages like this might reduce the amount of self-focus bias in Wikipedia. They found the Dutch and Swedish editions to be less self-focused than other editions. The research presented in this paper supports their conjecture that this is likely due to higher levels of multilingualism among speakers of these languages. This research shows that a relatively higher percentage of users primarily editing the Dutch or Swedish editions also edit another language edition. Hecht and Gergle [10] also found the Portuguese edition to be less self-focused. The rate of multilingualism among users primarily editing the Portuguese edition in this study is slightly above the mean, but is mostly explained by the size of the Portuguese edition. Overall self-focus bias among the 15 editions studied by Hecht and Gergle [10] is negatively correlated with the level of multilingualism found in this study. That is higher levels of multilingualism are generally associated with less self-focus bias. The correlation coefficient between the measures is -0.67, although this drops to -0.33 if English and Japanese are excluded. Multilingualism is one of perhaps several factors affecting the level of self-focus bias in different editions of Wikipedia, and this study has only been able to observe cross-language editing and not cross-language reading. Further study should identify additional factors affecting self-focus bias and their relative roles.

Multilingual users are found in all language editions. Generally, however, a higher percentage of users primarily editing smaller-sized language editions are multilingual compared to users primarily editing larger-sized editions, supporting H4. This is also consistent with prior qualitative and survey work. Of the outliers found, Esperanto and Malay had higher percentages of multilingual users than their sizes would predict, while Japanese had a much lower percentage than its size would predict. Malay users have previously been found to be among the most multilingual user groups on Twitter, while Japanese users were similarly found to be the least multilingual group on Twitter [9]. This points to

---

[12]https://meta.wikimedia.org/w/index.php?title=
Editor_Survey_2011/Location_%26_Language&oldid=
8409990

the importance of language-specific factors, which are also shown in the rather simple case of Esperanto being a constructed language with no native speakers.

Differences between the results on Twitter [9] and those found here on Wikipedia also suggest platform-specific characteristics affect the levels of multilingualism users exhibit. For example, in the Twitter study Italian users were more multilingual on Twitter than their size suggested, while the opposite was found here. In addition, the correlation in the Twitter study between language size and levels of multilingualism was very weak whereas the correlation on Wikipedia was much stronger. Further research will be needed to untangle the role of design and platform-specific characteristics affecting the levels of multilingualism on different platforms.

When users did edit a second language edition, that edition was most often English, supporting H5. English users did edit many other language editions, but these users were a much small percentage of the English user total than the percentage of users primarily editing other languages that also edited English. Even with English removed, the network of language crossings was centered around German, the second-largest edition. Some regional and linguistic groups were also apparent, pointing towards the importance of geo-linguistic factors [14] in the cross-language activity of Wikipedia users.

Including or excluding the Simple English edition of Wikipedia had little impact on the findings of this paper. Many users editing Simple already edited two other editions and were classified as multilingual. Past research analyzing the location of users through the circadian rhythms of their edits found more editors of Simple were in Europe and the Far East/Australia compared to the English edition [20]. This raised speculation that English as a second language (ESL) speakers might edit Simple more than the English edition. This research finds, however, that the English edition is edited much more by users of other languages than is Simple. Thus, the difference in geographic spread between the two editions is more likely one of awareness and commitment to editing among English speakers rather than a native/ESL divide. Indeed, this research has shown that like Esperanto, there is a dedicated editing community for Simple. Many users edit Simple (or Esperanto) more than any other edition despite no one being a native speaker of Simple (or Esperanto).

Overall, this study shows multilingual users play a unique role on Wikipedia editing articles different to those edited by monolingual users. Multilingual users may further transfer information between language editions and thereby reduce the levels of self-focus bias in the encyclopedia. The correlation between self-focus bias and multilingualism is present, but noisy, and further research is needed to identify other factors that also affect self-focus bias. Finally, differences between the levels of multilingualism by language previously found on Twitter with the levels found in this research on Wikipedia indicate design and platform-specific factors that future research should explore.

6. ACKNOWLEDGMENTS

I would like to thank Taha Yasseri, Eric T. Meyer, Jonathan Bright, and Mike Thelwall, as well as the anonymous reviewers who provided helpful comments on previous versions of this paper.

7. REFERENCES

[1] G. A. Barnett and Y. Choi. Physical distance and language as determinants of the international telecommunications network. *International Political Science Review*, 16(3):249–265, 1995.

[2] D. Crystal. *English as a Global Language*. Cambridge University Press, Cambridge, 2nd edition, 2003.

[3] I. Eleta and J. Golbeck. Bridging languages in social networks: How multilingual users of Twitter connect language communities. *Proceedings of the American Society for Information Science and Technology*, 49(1):1–4, 2012.

[4] R. S. Geiger and A. Halfaker. Using edit sessions to measure participation in Wikipedia. In *Proceedings of the 2013 Conference on Computer Supported Cooperative Work*, CSCW '13, pages 861–870, New York, NY, USA, 2013. ACM.

[5] J. Giles. Internet encyclopaedias go head to head. *Nature*, 438(7070):900–1, Dec. 2005.

[6] A. Halavais and D. Lackaff. An analysis of topical coverage of Wikipedia. *Journal of Computer-Mediated Communication*, 13(2):429–440, 2008.

[7] S. A. Hale. Impact of platform design on cross-language information exchange. In *Proceedings of the 2012 ACM Annual Conference on Human Factors in Computing Systems Extended Abstracts*, CHI EA '12, pages 1363–1368, New York, NY, USA, 2012. ACM.

[8] S. A. Hale. Net increase? Cross-lingual linking in the blogosphere. *Journal of Computer-Mediated Communication*, 17(2):135–151, 2012.

[9] S. A. Hale. Global connectivity and multilinguals in the Twitter network. In *Proceedings of the SIGCHI Conference on Human Factors in Computing Systems*, CHI '14, pages 833–842, New York, NY, USA, 2014. ACM.

[10] B. Hecht and D. Gergle. Measuring self-focus bias in community-maintained knowledge repositories. In *Proceedings of the Fourth International Conference on Communities and Technologies*, C&T '09, pages 11–20, New York, NY, USA, 2009. ACM.

[11] B. Hecht and D. Gergle. The Tower of Babel meets Web 2.0: User-generated content and its applications in a multilingual context. In *Proceedings of the 28th International Conference on Human Factors in Computing Systems*, CHI '10, pages 291–300, New York, NY, USA, 2010. ACM.

[12] S. C. Herring, J. C. Paolillo, I. Ramos-Vielba, I. Kouper, E. Wright, S. Stoerger, L. A. Scheidt, and B. Clark. Language networks on LiveJournal. In *Proceedings of the 40th Annual Hawaii International Conference on System Sciences*, HICSS '07, Washington, DC, USA, 2007. IEEE Computer Society.

[13] T. Holloway, M. Bozicevic, and K. Börner. Analyzing and visualizing the semantic coverage of Wikipedia and its authors. *Complexity*, 12(3):30–40, 2007.

[14] H.-T. Liao and T. Petzold. Analysing geo-linguistic dynamics of the World Wide Web: The use of cartograms and network analysis to understand linguistic development in Wikipedia. *Cultural Science*, 3(2), 2010.

[15] G. Neubig and K. Duh. How much is said in a tweet? A multilingual, information-theoretic perspective. In *AAAI Spring Symposium Series*, 2013.

[16] F. Ortega, J. M. Gonzalez-Barahona, and G. Robles. On the inequality of contributions to Wikipedia. In *Hawaii International Conference on System Sciences, Proceedings of the 41st Annual*, HICSS '08, page 304, 2008.

[17] M. Rosvall, D. Axelsson, and C. T. Bergstrom. The map equation. *The European Physical Journal Special Topics*, 178(1):13–23, 2009.

[18] M. Rosvall and C. T. Bergstrom. Maps of random walks on complex networks reveal community structure. *Proceedings of the National Academy of Sciences*, 105(4):1118–1123, 2008.

[19] C. Y. Wei and B. E. Kolko. Resistance to globalization: Language and Internet diffusion patterns in Uzbekistan. *New Review of Hypermedia and Multimedia*, 11(2):205–220, 2005.

[20] T. Yasseri, R. Sumi, and J. Kertész. Circadian patterns of Wikipedia editorial activity: A demographic analysis. *PLoS ONE*, 7(1):e30091, 2012.

[21] T. Yasseri, R. Sumi, A. Rung, A. Kornai, and J. Kertész. Dynamics of conflicts in Wikipedia. *PLoS ONE*, 7(6):e38869, 2012.

[22] E. Zuckerman. Meet the bridgebloggers. *Public Choice*, 134(1):47–65, 2008.

[23] E. Zuckerman. *Rewire: Digital Cosmopolitans in the Age of Connection*. W. W. Norton & Company, London, 2013.

Motivating Online Engagement and Debates on Energy Consumption

Lara S. G. Piccolo

Institute of Computing (IC) - UNICAMP
Knowledge Media Institute (KMi)
The Open University
piccolo@ic.unicamp.br

Harith Alani, Anna De Liddo

Knowledge Media Institute (KMi)
The Open University, United Kingdom
{h.alani, anna.deliddo}
@open.ac.uk

Cecilia Baranauskas

Institute of Computing (IC)
The State University of Campinas –
UNICAMP, Brazil
cecilia@ic.unicamp.br

ABSTRACT

Several studies and official reports argue that changing people's behavior towards energy consumption is a vital part of our fight against climate change. Engaging people into this issue is the first step towards a social change. However, it has been shown that information campaigns and technology alone are insufficient to achieve such engagement. Understanding what motivate people, in which contexts and combinations, and for which individuals, is therefore key to engaging the public more successfully in such crucial debates. This work investigates the role and impact of motivational strategies on promoting engagement in online energy debates. We report our results from running an experiment in the workplace, in which 33 people contributed to an online discussion on reducing energy consumption. A public and tangible feedback of contributions to the online debate, as well as social comparison and competition were analyzed as motivational strategies. Our results point out that engagement goes beyond intrinsic motivation, and that a set of interplaying factors influenced by the social context was found to be the stronger motivational force of engagement.

Categories and Subject Descriptors

H.5.3 [Group and Organization Interfaces]: Computer-supported cooperative work, Web-based interaction.

Keywords

Engagement, motivation, energy awareness, online debate.

1. INTRODUCTION

The acknowledged power of social media of gathering people around common societal problems is unarguable. However, not all online initiatives are well succeeded, often due to issues of user's engagement and motivation. Engaging participants is a concern that challenges online community managers, designers and sponsors, especially those who aim to exploit the full potential of online tools to promote social change, such as governments, NGOs, and policy makers.

The term engagement can be understood from different but complementary perspectives. Yates and Lalmas [1] define *user engagement* as "the phenomena associated with wanting to use that application longer and frequently", as a result of "the quality of the user experience that emphasizes the positive aspects of the interaction with a web application". Malliaros and Vazirgiannis [2] adopted the definition of "the extent that an individual is encouraged to participate in the activities of a community". When social change is the target, engagement might be also related to the *civic engagement* defined by [3] as "individual and collective actions designed to identify and address issues of public concern.".

From the Web Science perspective, investigating engagement with online tools requires understanding the forces that drive human behavior towards technology, be they individual, social or influenced by the environment. Motivation determines the force and direction of behavior [5], therefore, a crucial aspect towards engagement.

Motivation theories from Social Psychology have the purpose of explaining why people show great effort and persistence on doing things, which may comprehend interacting with a system or being active in a community [5]. This paper is grounded on concepts of the Self-Determination Theory (SDT) [6], which considers that motivation emerges intrinsically for satisfying needs, due to emotion or cognition, and extrinsically, i.e. by means of prizes or rewards. Still, individuals and the environment influence each other supporting or undermining motivation. From the individual side, i.e. psychological needs, interests and values can stimulate engagement with activities and with social groups. The environment, on the other hand, plays a role offering challenges and interesting things to do, providing feedback, imposing goals, and offering opportunities to potentiate the individuals' development [5][7].

This work focuses on understanding the role and impact of motivational strategies on promoting engagement in online energy debates. We build on SDT main elements to evaluate the impact of some motivational strategies not only to promote engagement in terms of online participation but also to connect people to a common issue. Namely, we present a user study in which an online argumentation tool has been used for raising energy awareness and fostering social change towards energy conservation in the workplace. By means of the debate tool, users from a computer science lab discussed about current consumption issues and possibilities to change behavior, building the knowledge collectively and collaboratively.

As expected, the voluntary adoption of this tool by employees required a certain level of motivation, since it was competing in terms of time allocation with other daily obligations. Moreover' the "intangible" aspect of the debated issue can also be seen as an additional challenge to attract people for debating online. This is due to the fact that energy consumption is perceived influenced by habits and environment more than by individual decisions [8][10] and, therefore, people may fail to understand how this issue can relate to individual behavior.

Finding ways to engage people with energy consumption towards conservation has been a concern also for governments and police makers, requiring from them the understanding of the behavior change dynamics and motivational strategies to promote it [9][11][12]. Individually, we see engagement as a precursor of behavior change. Collectively, it is the first necessary component leading to a social change.

We hypothesize that engagement with "intangible" issues, such as energy consumption, may benefit from "tangible" feedback to improve users understanding and appropriation of the problem. To test this hypothesis we built the Energy Tree, a public tangible artifact with visual feedback of contributions to the online tool. We added to this analysis the influence of social dynamics of collaborative work and competition on engagement with the online debate.

Composing this exploratory study we:

- Assessed to what extent the presence of the Energy Tree promoted engagement with the energy debate by comparing online engagement during two identical workshops, the first without the tree and the second with it;
- Associated the tangible feedback with social comparison (and the consequent competition) to promote online participation after the workshops, and evaluated qualitatively how they impacted engagement.
- With the lenses of the SDT, analyzed the interplay of intrinsic and extrinsic motivational forces that have led to the engagement in this research scenario.

In the next session we present related works with regard to motivation, online participation and energy awareness/savings. The following session describes the overall methodology, which includes the description of the debate tool and the Energy Tree in terms of features to support the experiment. Then, we describe the experimental setting, which is followed by the results related to online participation and self-assessments. Combining the collected data, we analyze our findings, and subsequently discuss the limitations of the study. We then conclude the paper.

2. RELATED WORK

From the Human-Computer Interaction perspective, Shneiderman [13] sheds light to the current need of better understanding people's behavior, collaborative strategies, engagement, and cooperation to improve social media potential. He illustrates this challenge by underlining the subjectivity and ephemeral aspect of related concepts, such as motivation, an ancient notion that was brought to technology design only recently, according to him.

In [14], Lee et al. evaluated individual achievements, social achievements and gamification strategies in the design of an application that aggregates the Tweets of the employees in a company. Their analysis pointed out that over using motivational strategies (including gamification) may lead the user to lose their intrinsic motivation.

According to Vassileva [15], theories from psychology have been applied in literature to motivate specific behaviors or behaviors change, but not explicitly to motivate a person to contribute to a community. The author analyzed different approaches to motivate participation and found out that money or status rewards may jeopardize the quality of contributions, since people may act for results and not inline with their intrinsic motivations. She also

highlights the importance of visualizations and states the need to consider both the user (micro level) and the community model (macro level) for providing incentives. Involving users' real communities beyond the online one is also an important motivational strategy for her.

2.1 Acting socially to promote energy awareness

Working socially to foster energy savings has been a recent approach. According to Pierce and Paulos' literature review in 2012 [16], the vast majority of studies related to energy conservation had been focused on the individual behavior disregarding social changes dynamics. Most of the studies had been evaluated in terms of consumption reduction as a consequence of information provision, either as consumption feedback or by providing hints for saving. A number of initiatives launched by governments and NGO's are found in the literature since the 70's leading to marginal effects on savings [18][19].

Instead of connecting individual's actions to their consequences, as the usual approach, Dourish [20] suggests the need to "connect people through their actions and their consequences", persuading people by the empowerment of collective actions. According to the Climate Change Communication advisory group [21], "there are few influences more powerful than an individual's social network" to promote pro-environmental behavior. People tend to act in a certain way to be in line with others in similar context, following social norms [22]. But just adopting social norms to avoid guilty, or the fear of not 'fitting in' usually produces low level of motivation. When combined with intrinsic motivations, the social norms can be more effective and persistent [21].

Then, studies that associate motivational strategies (social comparison, competition) to engage people via online social networks started to emerge leading to a higher level of savings, such as [23] and [24]. However, factors that contribute to their success are most of the times unclear [25]. Petkov [24] affirmed that users prefer to compare their data against users they know (even if the households present significant differences), suggesting that in the context of real community, such as a working place, this strategy may be even more effective. Welectricity [26] and Opower [27] are examples of online tools that allow users to compare their energy consumption with similar houses.

Competition is a controversial motivational strategy, with some positive results, but yet not so positive effects [19][28] especially when targeting behavior change. In fact, it is found that competition might even encourage the development of unsustainable energy consumption practices [4]. Competition can be associated to rewards, e.g. money or prizes, such as the San Diego Energy Challenge [29]. Although, some authors argue that extrinsic rewards may even undermine intrinsic motivation in some situations [30].

Competition and collaboration can be applied together in different levels, such as teams collaborating internally and competing against each other. A collaborative approach was found in [31], relying on collective savings to reduce the need of energy generation. Projecting consumption data in the street for engaging neighbors to work together is a design alternative evaluated by the authors. Watt-Lite [32] publicly represented statistical data of energy consumption projected on the floor of a factory. It was successful to engage people in the topic when they were close to the installation but not enough visiting the project website afterwards.

Differently from the above-mentioned, evaluating savings or assessing behavior change is out of the scope of this study. We consider engagement as the fundamental step leading to behavior change, and then analyze how engagement in the debate of energy saving issues can be promoted by comparison, competition and public feedback in the context of a working place.

3. METHODOLOGY

In line with [21] and [33], this work relies on the potential of peer-to-peer learning, dialogue and argumentation of different viewpoints to build contextualized knowledge about energy usage. Engaging participants in this collaborative knowledge building process is the first step towards fostering longer-term changes.

For promoting engagement, we designed the Energy Tree, a public tangible artifact with visual feedback of contributions to the online tool. We combined face-to-face group activities with online participation to explore the impact of the Energy Tree on participants' engagement with the online debate on energy conservation. The methodology comprehended qualitative analysis applied to:

1) **The assessment of the impact of tangible and public feedback on engagement.** Two identical workshops promoting the online debate, one with and the other without the Energy Tree were conducted. Resulting contributions to the online debate associated to self-assessment questionnaires provided data for the analysis of the role of the tangible feedback on engagement.

2) **Evaluation of the tangible feedback associated to social comparison dynamics.** After the workshop, the Energy Tree was placed in a public area providing feedback of new contributions for both workshop groups, alternately, for 10 days. The impact of comparing group performances by means of the tree was evaluated supported by a sample interview with the top contributors and people who completely stopped contributing after the workshop.

3) **Analysis of motivational forces considering intrinsic and extrinsic sources.** Participants of the first workshop, the one without the tree, were told about a prize (no money related) that would be offered to the top contributor, adding an extrinsic motivation element to the study. The analysis of the motivational forces, intrinsic and extrinsic, on engagement took into account the main elements of the Self-Determination Theory. Qualitative study of contributions to the online debate, self-assessments responses and outcomes of interviews subsidized the analysis.

How this methodology was applied to this experimental setting is further detailed. The experiment relied on the adequacy of the technical artifacts, both the debate tool and the Energy Tree, in providing features that motivate engagement. In the next sessions we describe how these artifacts were conceived and configured to support this study.

3.1 The debate tool

Energy saving and behavioral change are complex domains to be discussed, in which there are no right answers, or unique world views. Then, a debate tool must be featured to provide the expected contrast and connections of opinions. The Evidence Hub is a kind of Contested Collective Intelligence Platforms [34] applied to this study, suitable to support the complexity of discussion domain.

As an argumentative knowledge construction tool [35], instead of leading to find the best and quickest answer to a question, the Evidence Hub promotes the development of critical thinking and

collective assessment of several solutions in order to support a higher-level reflection on the different aspects of a debate.

Users can create **issues**, and **ideas** that overcome issues. Both issues and ideas can be supported or challenged by **arguments,** promoted by **votes for** and demoted by **votes against.** Users can also add **Facts** or Web **resources** to enrich the debate. Figure 1 illustrates a Knowledge Tree connecting an Issue to Ideas, Arguments and Facts.

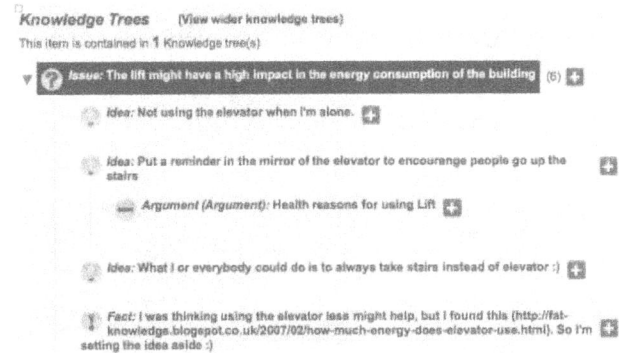

Figure 1 – Screenshot of a knowledge tree in the Evidence Hub

Based on the nature of the content expected to be generated by participants, the Evidence Hub was set up with six main themes to debate on: 1) Behavior Change; 2) Consuming Energy, mostly issues about how energy has been used and eventually wasted; 3) Environmental Impact; 4) Good Practices, a theme that emerged for need of sharing the good behaviors that people already had; 5) Institutional Actions, identifying constraints associated to the building or to the institution, therefore out of individual control; and 6) The Tree – a space for ideas of how to apply the tangible device for the experiment.

Besides navigating content by tags, key challenges or type of contribution, users can also explore the map of connected people and ideas. Figure 2 illustrates the dynamic social network visualization. By means of this polarized semantic map, users can identify those who they mostly agreed, disagreed or expressed neutral comments within the conversation. The colors green, red and grey represent these levels of connections.

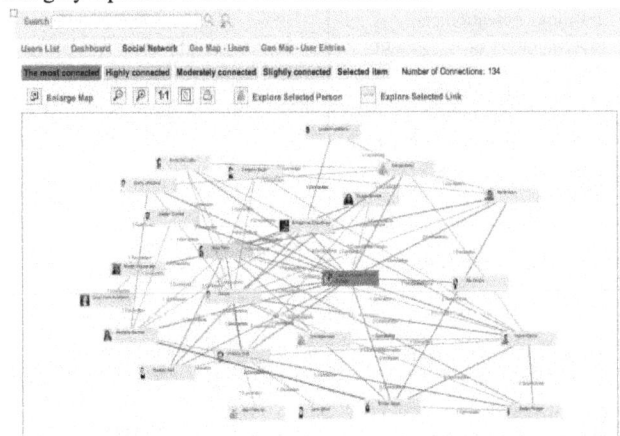

Figure 2 – Screenshot of the users connection map

The Energy Tree was connected to the Evidence Hub database to provide a visual feedback of the number of contributions to the online debate. In the next section we describe the Energy tree functioning and its expected role to promote engagement.

3.2 The expected role of the Tree

Technically, the Energy Tree is a led-lights tree (Figure 3) designed to be solar powered, with seven branches that illuminate independently. It was developed upon the Microsoft Gadgteer Fez Spider Kit and connected to the Evidence Hub in such way that every 60 new user-contributions to the tool lighted on a new branch of the tree.

Conceptually, it is a Socially-inspired Energy-Eco-Feedback Technology [36] [37], conceived to promote new patterns of behavior

Figure 3 - The Energy Tree

(social affordances) within a social group [38] by promoting the connection between energy consumption and natural environment impact.

The Energy Tree was conceived to be a motivational artifact. In Table 1, we describe how the tree and the debate tool together are featured to promote motivation according to a set of ten design principles for *motivational affordances* [39]. These motivational affordances, which are also based on the SDT main concepts, refer to properties of objects that determine whether and how they can support one's motivation, considering psychological needs, cognition, social needs, and emotion as possible sources of motivation [39].

Table 1 – The Energy Tree and Evidence Hub features related to motivational design principles [39]

Design principles	Features
Psychological needs	- Users of the debate tool have their profile with pictures.
1. Support autonomy	
2. Promote creation and representation of self-identity	- The Energy Tree represents results of a pre-established group of users.
Cognition	- The target established to light on the tree was previously calculated to be feasible, but not too easy to achieve.
3. Design for optimal challenge	
4. Provide timely and positive feedback	- The tree provides instant feedback of new contributions.
Social and Psychological needs	- Being publicly displayed, the tree aims at promoting collaboration among participants towards lightening it on completely.
5. Facilitate human-human interaction	- It has also the intended role to trigger online and real discussions about energy consumption.
6. Represent human social bond	
7. Facilitate one's desire to influence others	- The debate tool provides visualizations of people connected by their content (Figure 2).
8. Facilitate one's desire to be influenced by others	- By voting and arguing, users can explicit support or oppose others' idea.

Emotion	- The tree was designed intending to be visually attractive, calling people's attention and reminding them about the current energy awareness initiative.
9. Induce intended emotions via initial exposure to ICT	
10. Induce intended emotions via intensive interaction with ICT	- The novelty aspect of a tangible feedback can be considered as a motivation.

The Energy Tree was originally conceived as a tangible feedback of group energy savings [36][37], but the need to first promote engagement has lead to a change in the design. How the tree was applied in the experimental setting is described below.

4. EXPERIMENTAL SETTING

The study took place in a research university department in the UK during October-November of 2013. Four phases shaped the experiment that together implemented the methodology. The phases are:

1) Online survey. Aimed at collecting initial perceptions about how energy has been consumed in the lab and preliminary ideas for behavior change. The participation was opened to everyone in the department by means of an online form with three simple questions. The results of the online survey were then used to pre-seed the Evidence Hub with meaningful content, thus providing a useful starting point for the online debate.

2) Two workshops (WS1 and WS2) were organized to promote the online debate by gathering volunteers to use the Evidence Hub. The two workshops had the same dynamic, except by the presence of the Energy Tree in WS2, making it possible to compare results and infer about effects of the Energy Tree on engagement. The Energy Tree was centrally located as a feedback mechanism during WS2 by reflecting the number of new submitted contributions. Each workshop lasted 2 hours and was run in a meeting room. Participants were asked to create, promote or demote Facts, Arguments, Issues, and Ideas online. Some face-to-face discussions enriched the online debate, but most of the time participants interacted individually with the online tool. The content generated in the WS1 was not visible for the participants of the WS2 to avoid influence. For assessing possible effects of extrinsic motivation on engagement, participants of WS1 only were told about a non-monetary prize (indeterminate) that would be offered to the top contributor in the end of the study.

After interacting, the attendees completed usability and motivational assessments.

3) 10 days of online debate. For evaluating motivation and, complementary to the workshop dynamic, "spontaneous" engagement with the debate, Group1 from WS1 and Group 2 from WS2 were asked to continue contributing to the online debate for 10 days, each group contributing to a different website. During that time, participants could optionally make use of energy monitoring devices for learning and sharing knowledge about individual consumption. The Energy Tree was placed in a social area as a feedback of engagement. Every 60 new contributions to the tool (new issues, ideas, arguments, facts, resources or votes) turned on a new branch of the tree. Results of each group were identified by a sign and kept alternating from time to time. The competition between groups was not clearly promoted.

4) Sample interview. To understand what motivated participation, perceptions, as well as their overall experience towards this study, a sample of participants that included the top and bottom contributors was interviewed.

4.1 Motivational assessments

We applied two self-assessments artifacts to workshop attendees aiming at finding qualitative evidences of potential motivational forces related to engagement:

- The Self-Assessment Manikin – SAM [40] was applied to evaluate the affective quality of the interaction with the debate tool, potentially under influence of the Energy Tree for Group 2. It consists on a pictographic questionnaire that assesses three dimensions of emotions: valence, the positive or negative feeling caused by the experience; arousal that means the level or excitement or boredom; and dominance, in this case, it means the perception of control interacting with the Evidence Hub.

- Intrinsic Motivation Inventory (IMI) [41]. This questionnaire is part of the SDT framework. We applied the shortest version with 9 items consisting of three subscales: *Interest/enjoyment* that measures the intrinsic motivation directly; *Perceived competence*, a positive predictor of motivation related to how adequate the interaction was to participants' skill; and *Pressure/tension*, a negative predictor of intrinsic motivation related to external factors. Lower values are preferable for this subscale. Usually the IMI is applied to larger samples making it possible to explore correlations statistically. In this limited research scenario, the IMI was applied to point directions of the eventual impact and influence on intrinsic motivation.

4.2 Calculating contributions

Voting clearly requires less effort from the Evidence Hub user when comparing to the action of creating a new idea or issue, for example. For this reason, a system of points was established to calculate participation and identify the top contributors. Any new Idea, Issue, Fact or Web Resource value 3 points; Arguments value 2 points and votes 1 point each.

5. RESULTS

Numbers related to participation and self-assessments are presented here, supporting the qualitative analysis and discussion in the next session.

5.1 Participation

The four phases of the study involved a total of 33 participants, most of them researchers and some PhD students of the computer science lab. The workshops gathered 24 voluntary participants (12 people per workshop), including 10 of the 19 respondents of the online survey.

The total of contributions generated in the debate tool is synthetized in the chart in Figure 4. Group 1 generated less contributions in the workshop (348) compared to Group 2 (542), which had the tree. The score inverted when the tree was installed in the public area as a feedback of contributions for both groups alternately (phase 3). Group 1 created 247 new contributions and Group 2 only 78. These numbers suggest that the Energy Tree had a potential impact on participation when seen as a novelty. This result though must be associated to other assessments and variables to be conclusive.

In terms of type of contributions among votes, ideas, issues, arguments, facts and resources, both groups had comparable distribution as represented by the chart in Figure 5. These distributions can be considered adequate for the debate balance, such as the higher number of ideas than issues, as well as the expected high number of votes, which reflects that users accessed other people's contribution and expressed their opinion.

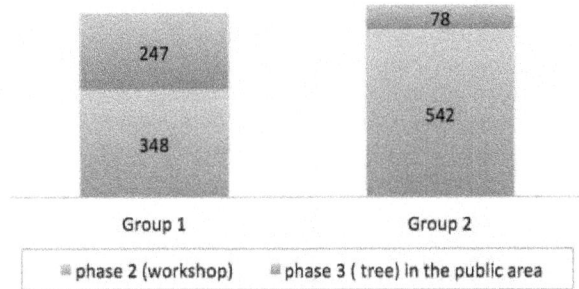

Figure 4 - Contributions to the debate tool per group

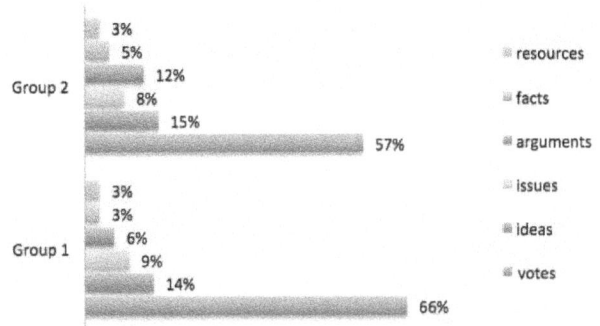

Figure 5 - Distribution of types of content in the debate

The most significant distinction between the groups is the number of arguments created by Group 2, twice as many posted by Group 1, possibly reflecting a characteristic of the group.

The main challenge of promoting engagement was keeping people motivated to access the debate tool during the phase 3, after the workshop. The chart in Figure 6 illustrates the number of contributions day by day during this phase. The number remained stable between D3 (Friday) and D7 (Tuesday), when an external intervention occurred: an email ranking results of both groups was launched. Just after that, the number of Group 1 contributions increased 37% (59 new posts) and 201% (31 new posts) for Group 2. The score was published again on D8 and D10 also reminding participants about the last day of the study. The last increased the participation once again in 9% for Group 1 and 70% for Group 2.

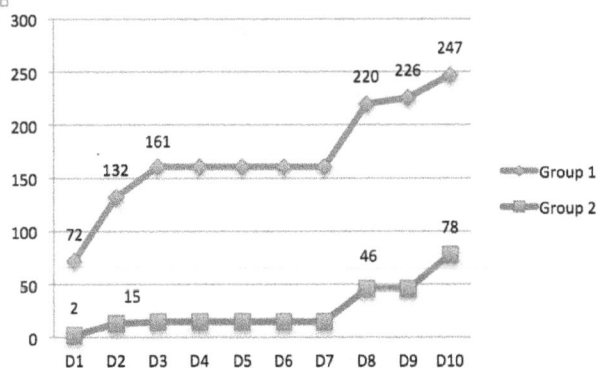

Figure 6 - Contributions generated per day

5.2 Assessments and sample interview

Figure 7 presents comparative results of the affective quality assessment [40] regarding to valence, motivation, and dominance. These aspects were scored from 1 to 5, in which 5 is the most

113

positive answer. Participants of WS1 demonstrated slightly more positive perception (valence). The average was 4.26 for Group 1 and 3.83 for Group 2. Despite of being differently distributed, the mean of motivation was identical, 4 for both groups. Dominance was the aspect worst scored with 2.6 of average for Group 1 and 3.0 for Group 2, suggesting that people from both workshops felt a bit too challenged when interacting to the debate tool.

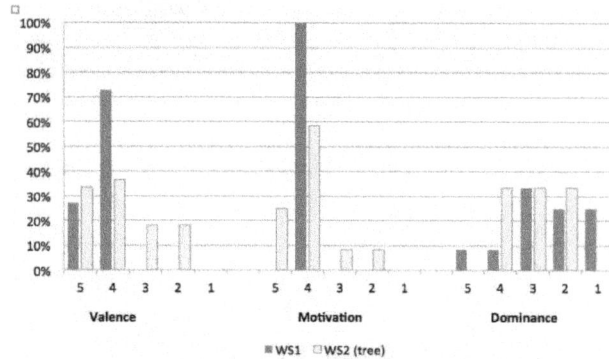

Figure 7 - Results of the SAM

The concepts related to motivation were scored from 1 to 7 in the IMI [41]. The results presented in Table 2 are statistically limited (high standard deviation) due to the small sample of this study, but it suggests higher motivation by participants of WS1 than WS2, which had the tree. The competence subscale results are proportionally comparable to the dominance assessment by the SAM [40]. Both groups expressed having an autonomous behavior at a certain degree by the low score of Pressure/Tension.

Table 2 – Results of the IMI

		Mean	Median	Mode	SD
Interest/ Enjoyment	G1	**5.22**	5.00	6.00	1.20
	G2	4.60	5.00	5.00	1.42
Perceived competence	G1	**4.67**	5.00	6.00	1.78
	G2	4.13	4.00	4.00	1.62
Pressure/ Tension	G1	2.25	2.00	1.00	1.72
	G2	2.25	2.00	1.00	1.36

Details of the usability evaluation of the Evidence Hub are out of the scope of this paper. However, how participants perceived the online tool might influence engagement and motivation. The Table 3, thus, summarizes the average score (from 1-5) of positive and negative usability aspects by both groups, pointing out that Group 1 had a better perception in terms of the ease of leaning and use, complexity, etc. The complexity was the main issue pointed out by participants.

Table 3 - Summary of usability evaluation

Usability aspects	Group 1	Group 2
Positive	3.40	2.96
Negative	2.15	2.42

As part of the usability assessment, when asked about the effectiveness of the Evidence Hub to raise energy awareness, workshop participants highlighted mostly aspects related to debate, as enumerated in Table 4.

Table 4 – Mentioned aspects of the debate tool that contribute to energy awareness and % of answers that refers to it

The informative aspect, new ideas, knowledge sharing	44%
The debate elements (contrast opinion, arguments)	31%
It made me think	6%
Potential to organize a community around a problem	6%
Connecting ideas	3%
Funny	3%
The tree as motivational aspect	3%
Goes from discussing issues until finding solutions	3%

Nevertheless, one participant pointed out his/her dissatisfaction by saying: "*I would prefer to search Google/newspaper for facts and reports rather than view other people's claim / notes*". This particular participant also reported the lowest level of intrinsic motivation (2.8) for using the debate tool.

The interview with a sample of participants revealed aspects related to their overall experience towards the study. Regarding reasons to participate, respondents were asked to choose up to tree reasons to be engaged in this study. The results are quantified in the chart (Figure 8), evidencing that the tree was the second main reason for participating, more than all other technical artifacts or the social aspect of the activities.

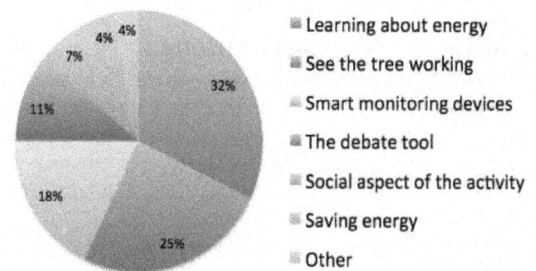

Figure 8 - Reasons to be part of the study (chosen among a set)

Interviewees also scored (1 to 5) the level of attention they spent to the tree during the WS2 and during the time it was installed in the public area. The average score of attention in the workshop by Group 2 was 3.5, while in the public space was higher, 3.9. Figure 9 represents the score distribution.

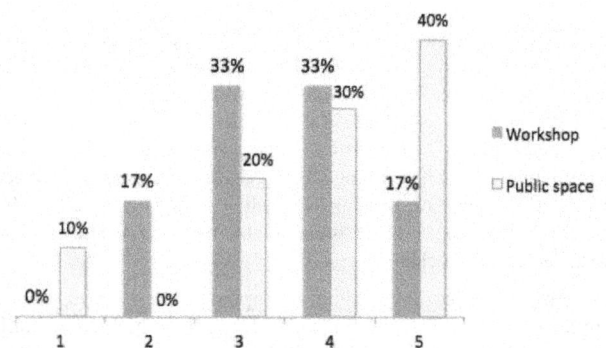

Figure 9 - Score of the level of attention to the tree

Table 5 relates a sample participants' data, including the top 2 contributors of each group, plus one person of each that did not contribute at all after the workshop. Data from different sources were associated: the user's participation in points, as described in the section 4.2, the Interest/enjoyment subscale of IMI score, the stated main reason for being part of the activity, and the meaning of the tree for them when they used to see it in the public space.

Table 5 - Cross data of a sample of participants

		Points	Interest / enjoyment	Main reason for contributing	The tree meaning
Top 1	G1	244	6.20	Learning	The progress, competition
	G2	99	5.40	Environmental	Competition
Top 2	G1	99	4.60	Learning	Competition
	G2	58	4.80	Learning	Guilty
No participation	G1	34	5.20	Social aspect of the activity	Someone is doing
	G2	12	4.80	Learning	Guilty

From this group of interviewees, only the G1 participant that did not contribute admitted to not have changed any behavior as a consequence of the study. All the others mentioned examples of changes both at the workplace and at home, suggesting the positive effect of the study in raising awareness, i.e., referring to longer-term changes in behaviour: *"I am more attentive to energy consumption in general and whenever I have the chance in the future, energy consumption of devices I purchase will play a more important role"*. And *"I recently got a table lamp and use it instead of the main lights when I am alone in the open space)"*, referring to changes in the workspace.

6. ANALISYS

By connecting results from the Evidence Hub, self-assessments and the sample interview, we analyze and discuss the impact of the tangible device, as well as the effect of social comparison and competition on engagement. Then, we analyze results taking into account the main SDT concepts.

6.1 The tangible device effect

Results of self-assessment pointed out higher level of motivation (Table 2) and a better perception of the tool by participants of Group 1 (Table 3). However, Group 2 produced 56% more during the workshop, as illustrated by the chart in Figure 4, evidencing the impact of the tangible device on participation. The Energy Tree was also declared as the second reason for people to be engaged in the study, more than the smart monitoring device and the debate tool (Figure 8).

However, the presence of the tree in the public area was not enough to keep Group 2 participants engaged. A possible explanation is that the novelty aspect of the technology, which may increase motivation, was not present anymore for this group that had already lighted on the Energy Tree completely beforehand, during the WS2.

In the workshop, the effect of the tree could be even stronger if there was no pre-established goal to light it on, which was perceived as a limit by workshop attendees. When the tree was completed, and the last branch was lightened, typical reactions from the participants were: *"and now?"*, and *"we don't need to contribute more"*. Similar effect of loosing motivation was

observed in on-line communities where users had to achieve a goal to have access to new features [42]. Design alternatives to go beyond the goal - more levels of contributions represented by unexpected lightening effects, for instance, should have overcome this constraint.

Placed in the public area, the visual feedback of the tree was more effective in attracting participants' attention (Figure 9). Differently from the workshop, in which people spent most of the time working online, in the public space the tree was considered mainly a reminder that the study was going on, as suggested by our previous analysis with regard to energy awareness.

The expected effect of the artifact leading to new patterns of behavior was identified as a post to the debate tool: *"It looks like thanks to the tree we started switching off the lights during the day"*, however, this effect could not be identified by the sample interview, in which the tree was said to be perceived mostly as signal of competition or guilty for those who were not collaborating, as further described.

6.2 Social comparison and competition

Learning about energy was stated by participants as the main reason to engage with the study (Figure 8). We see comparison as central aspect in a collective learning process, for this reason social comparison has not been evaluated in terms of effectiveness in this study.

The debate potentiates the comparison not only in terms of number of posts created, but also by the possibility to contrast opinions. Participants highlighted these aspects positively when discussing about the effectiveness of the tool to raise awareness in Table 4, as well as they made evident the value of arguments and the possibility to see connected people and ideas.

The public feedback by the Energy Tree was also a tangible way to provide social comparison both within the groups and especially between them. A participant from Group 1 declared to think that *"some people are saving energy"* when seeing the tree in a public place, meaning that him/herself was not contributing, although the group result was evident.

Making public results of both groups changed the perceived meaning of the tree for them: the group with better result mostly associated the tree with a feedback of their performance (including competition), while for the Group 2, the tree was a signal of guilty: - *" it's like I am not fulfilling my responsibilities"*, declared a Group 2 interviewee.

Social comparison is actually a predictor of competition, which was reported as an important trigger for the most engaged people in Table 5. The Group 1 second contributor said about his/her thoughts when seeing the tree in the public space: *"Shamelessly competitive: Is my group doing best?"*. Another important aspect to be highlighted is that the both top contributors claimed for a public reward.

Comments during the WS2, such as *"Does the tree refer to everyone?"*, expressing disappointment, and *"We should compete against each other!"* illustrate the preference for the competition approach instead of working collaboratively.

In terms of number of contributions, the curve associated to daily contributions in (Figure 6) made clear that the first intervention of publishing the ranking of both groups' contributions on D7 impacted participation. The importance of competition stated by the top contributors suggests that the ranking had a motivational meaning. The same effect of the intervention was not observed in the following day though, suggesting that the frequency of interventions must be carefully planned to be effective.

In terms of quality of contributions, the controversial effects of competition found in the literature, such as cheating and loosing the quality [28], were not confirmed in this research scenario. Group 1 had a higher number of votes. For being the simplest way to interact to the system, it can be considered as a consequence of the individual prize offered for the Group 1. However, voting is also a relevant way to promote the debate, so, in this context, it cannot be seen as cheating or quality loss.

Despite of presenting the highest level of intrinsic motivation towards the debate tool during the workshop, the top contributor also declared the interest by the competition, prize and reward, suggesting that the intrinsic motivation was not the only responsible for the engagement.

6.3 Motivation and engagement

Satisfying a need leads to well being, for this reason Autonomy, Competence, and Relatedness are considered the most important needs that lead to intrinsic motivation according to SDT [5][7].

More **Autonomy** means stronger motivation. The behavior is said to be autonomous (or self-determined) when in line with one's interests, preferences and wants; otherwise, external forces, like pressure, guide it. **Competence** reflects the interest in applying and developing our skill performing a task; to enhance intrinsic motivation, competence must be accompanied by autonomy. **Relatedness** refers to the need to establish close emotional bonds with other people. Relatedness may also be a reason to internalize extrinsically motivated behaviors, since people are willing to have the behaviors valued as significant by others to whom they want to be connected, whether a family, a peer group, or a society [6].

Autonomy

As voluntary participation, contributing to the online debate relies on autonomous behavior, which in turn is related to intrinsic motivation, interest, and enjoyment. Individually, intrinsic motivation measurements could not be directly associated as an indicator of engagement in this research scenario. People who did not keep contributing after the workshop had similar or even higher level of intrinsic motivation than people among the top contributors (Table 5).

However, the novelty aspect of the Energy Tree seemed to promote initial engagement, leading to a higher number of contributions to the debate tool in the first contact of users with the tangible technology.

Competence

In this study context, competence was mainly related to the perception of usability aspects of the tool, declared to be complex by users. The Group 1 participants' higher intrinsic motivation (and perceived competence) seems to be associated to the experienced affective quality (Figure 7), also higher in average. They better evaluated the tool in terms of usability than participants of WS2, with the tree.

Low levels of competence may prevent users to adopt a tool after the first contact. Although usability aspects are out of the scope of this paper, the adequacy of the online solution to the user skills and expectation must be ensured to motivate engagement. Results pointed out that the group with higher competence continued contributing, but it is not possible to affirm that it happened due to this correlation, since the presence of the tree, as describe below, had others more evident influence.

Relatedness

By far, relatedness is the strongest motivational aspect in this experimental setting that relies on a collective platform. Elements associated to the debate such as argumentation, contrast of opinions, support or opposition to others' contribution, were mentioned as strengths for promoting energy awareness, as describe in Table 4.

Competition and public reward played an important role on engagement of those who most contributed to the online debate, demonstrating the importance of human bonds and social influence. Differently from reported by [37], a study that also evaluated the Energy Tree in the context of an elementary school, competition did not affect the quality of contributions. A possible explanation refers to the social context; in a working environment, people tend be more careful about preserving their image.

The consequent changes in behavior declared by most of the interviewees suggest the effectiveness of this experimental setting to raise energy awareness. Associated, intrinsic and extrinsic reasons together strengthened motivation and promoted engagement.

7. Discussion

Vassileva [15] states that relating motivation and online community engagement requires dealing with the influence of external factors that may lead to unpredictable behavior by the participants. We argue that the methodology and the experiment design must consider alternatives to overcome possible influences created by the environment. In the context of a workplace, for example, hierarchical pressure for participation or the lack of institutional support could bias results of engagement. In this research scenario, we did not detect unpredicted behavior, possibly due to the controlled and familiar environment where the experiment took place, its short-term run, and the relatively small number of participants.

These characteristics made it difficult to statistically analyze the impact of our motivational strategies on online engagement. Despite all that, qualitative results pointed out some interesting directions with regards to:

- **The tangible feedback of contributions**: the presence of the Energy Tree promoted engagement in a situated interaction (the workshop), possibly due to the novelty aspect of it. When placed in a public space, the artifact was mostly perceived as a reminder of the study.
- **Social comparison and competition**: even though competition was not strongly promoted, the top contributors in the study declared it as an important motivational force behind their engagement. No negative aspects were reported or found to be associated with competition in this research scenario.
- **Intrinsic and extrinsic motivations**: engagement could not be explained by intrinsic motivation alone. The top contributors requested public rewards as well as declared their interest in the prize, suggesting that intrinsic and extrinsic motivations must be combined to promote engagement.
- **Characteristics of the online debate**: participants evaluated the debate as effective to raise energy awareness due to the possibility of comparing and contrasting their opinions and ideas.

As an exploratory study, we mixed some motivational strategies, such as the presence of the Energy Tree and social comparison/competition, thus making it more difficult to evaluate the potential impact of isolated strategies. However, studying the impact of multiple interplaying strategies is the focus of this work, which is also supported by the literature on behavior change which argues for using a combination of motivational strategies to engage people more effectivly [11].

Vassileva [15] argues that results associated with successful incentives in one community cannot be easily generalized to other communities. The users in our study were all computer science researchers, wich limits our ability to generalise our findings to other user groups. Nevertheless, our results can act as pointers to further research directions, and to experiments involving a wider variety of users.

8. CONCLUSION

This exploratory study analyzed motivational strategies related to the engagement of users with online debate on energy saving. A public tangible feedback of online participation was proposed as a motivational strategy. The impact of this device on engagement and how the social dynamic of competition and collaboration influenced participation were analyzed qualitatively.

In the context of this research scenario, external factors were found as positively impacting engagement. While scores of intrinsic motivation alone could not suggest engagement, competition and public reward were mentioned as crucial for those participants who most contributed.

Possibly due to the novelty aspect associated to the device, which attracted participants' curiosity, the Energy Tree was effective on promoting situated engagement. However, placed in a public area, the presence of the tree promoted competition between groups of users, and worked as a symbol, a reminder of the ongoing energy awareness study.

For promoting Relatedness, one of the most important needs that lead to motivation, participants judged the Evidence Hub as effective to raise awareness and highlighted debate elements (arguments, contrasting opinion) as the strengths. These elements of collective knowledge building are important to promote engagement not only in terms of online participation, but also to establish and promote new social norms, leading to a desired social change.

In the Web Science perspective, our results contributed to the understanding of the relationship between motivation, a force that drives behavior, and engagement with an online tool. Even though situated, the findings point directions to further investigations in different research scenarios.

9. ACKNOWLEDGMENTS

The authors thank CAPES (PDSE program) – process 3355/13-6, Green Energy Options (GEO), the UNICAMP, Microsoft Research, DecarboNet (FP7 program – grant agreement 265454), and Catalyst (FP7 program - grant agreement #6111188).

10. REFERENCES

[1] Yates, R. B., Lalmas, M. 2012. User engagement: the network effect matters!. In *Proc.of the 21st ACM Intl. conference on Information and knowledge management (CIKM '12)*. ACM, New York, NY, USA, 1-2.

[2] Malliaros. D. F., Vazirgiannis, M. 2013. To stay or not to stay: modeling engagement dynamics in social graphs. In *Proc. of the 22nd ACM international conference on Conference on information & knowledge management (CIKM '13)*. ACM, New York, NY, USA, 469-478.

[3] American Psychological Association. Civic Engagement. http://www.apa.org/education/undergrad/civic-engagement.aspx

[4] Brewer, R.S, Lee, G. E., Johnson, P. M. 2011. The Kukui Cup: a dorm energy competition focused on sustainable behavior change and energy literacy. In *Proceedings of the 44th Hawaii Intl. Conf. on System Sciences*, January 2011.

[5] Reeve, J. 2009. *Understanding Motivation and Emotion*, 5th ed. Hoboken, NJ: Wiley.

[6] Deci, E. L., Ryan, R. M. 1985. Intrinsic Motivation and Self-Determination in Human Behavior. NY: Plenum.

[7] Piccolo, L.S.G., Baranauskas, M.C.C. 2012. Basis and prospects of motivation informing design: requirements for situated eco-feedback technology. Proc. of the 11th Brazilian Symposium on Human Factors in Computing Systems (IHC '12). SBC, Brazil, 137-146.

[8] Pierce, J., Schiano, D.J., Paulos, E. 2010. Home, habits, and energy: examining domestic interactions and energy consumption. *Proc. of CHI '10*. ACM, 1985-1994.

[9] EEA (European Environment Agency). 2013. Achieving energy efficiency through behaviour change: what does it that? Technical Report N5/2013.

[10] Jelsma, J. 2006. Designing 'Moralized' products: theory and practice. *User Behaviour and Technology Development*, Verbeek, P-P. and Slob, A. (eds) Springer, 221–231.

[11] Houses of Parliament. 2012. *Energy Use Behaviour Change*. N 417. http://www.parliament.uk/briefing-papers/POST-PN-417.pdf

[12] Darnton A. 2008. GSR Behaviour Change Knowledge Review. *Reference Report: An overview of behaviour change models and their uses*, HMT Publishing Unit, London. http://www.civilservice.gov.uk/Assets/Behaviour_change_re ference_report_tcm6-9697.pdf

[13] Shneiderman, B. 2011. Technology-mediated social participation: the next 25 years of HCI challenges. *In Proceedings of HCII'11*. Vol. Part I. Springer, 3-14.

[14] Lee et al. 2013. Experiments on Motivational Feedback for Crowdsourced Workers. *In Proc. of the 7th International AAAI Conference on Weblogs and Social Media*. http://www.aaai.org/ocs/index.php/ICWSM/ICWSM13/pape r/view/6118

[15] Vassileva, J. 2012. Motivating participation in social computing applications: a user modeling perspective. User Modeling and User-Adapted Interaction, April 2012, V 22, Issue 1-2, 177-201

[16] Pierce, J., Paulos, E. 2012. Beyond energy monitors: interaction, energy, and emerging energy systems. In *Proceedings of CHI '12*. ACM, 665-674.

[17] Froehlich, J., Findlater, L., Landay, J. 2010. The design of eco-feedback technology. *Proc. of CHI '10*. ACM, 1999-2008

[18] Abrahamse, W. et al. 2005. A Review of Intervention Studies Aimed at Household Energy Conservation, *Journal of Environmental Psychology*, 25(3), 273-291.

[19] Froehlich, J. et al. 2012. The design and evaluation of prototype eco-feedback displays for fixture-level water usage data. *Proceedings of CHI'2012*, 2367-2376.

[20] Dourish, P. 2010. HCI and environmental sustainability: the politics of design and the design of politics. In *Proceedings of the DIS '10*. ACM, 1-10.

[21] Climate Change Communication Advisory Group. 2010. *Communicating climate change to mass public audiences.* Public Interest Research Centre. http://psych.cf.ac.uk/understandingrisk/docs/cccag.pdf

[22] Goldstein, J. N., Cialdini, R. B., Griskevicius, V. 2008. A Room with a Viewpoint: Using Social Norms to Motivate Environ. Conservation in Hotels, *Journal of Consumer Research*, Oct, 2008.

[23] Foster, D. et al. 2010. Wattsup?: motivating reductions in domestic energy consumption using social networks. In *Proc. of the NordiCHI '10*. ACM, New York, 178-187

[24] Petkov, P. et al. 2011. Motivating domestic energy conservation through comparative, community-based feedback in mobile and social media. In Proc. of the 5th Intl. Conf. on Communities and Technologies. ACM. 21-30

[25] Dillahunt, T., Mankoff, J. 2014. Understanding factors of successful engagement around energy consumption between and among households. Proc. of the 17th Intl. conf. of the Computer Supported Cooperative Work and Social Computing Conference (CSCW'14), 1246-1257.

[26] Welectricity. http://welectricity.com/

[27] Opower. https://social.opower.com

[28] Johnson, P.M. et al. 2012. Beyond kWh: Myths and Fixes for Energy Competition Game Design. *Meaningful Play Conference*. East Lansing, USA.

[29] San Diego Energy Challenge. https://www.sdenergychallenge.com

[30] Kersten, G., Wu, S., Oertel, C. 2011. Extrinsic or Intrinsic Motivation of E-Negotiation Experiments' Participants. In *Proc. HICSS' 2011*, IEEE (2011), 1-10.

[31] Boucher, A., Cameron, D., Jarvis, N. 2012. Power to the people: dynamic energy management through communal cooperation. In *Proc. of the Designing Interactive Systems Conference (DIS '12)*. ACM, 612-620

[32] Jönsson, L., Broms, L., Katzeff, C. 2010. Watt-Lite: energy statistics made tangible. *Proc. of the 8th ACM Conference on Designing Interactive Systems DIS '10*, 240-243

[33] Concannon S., Healey P.G.T. 2013. Social Media for Social Change? *CHI 2013 Workshop Designing Social Media for Change*, Paris, France. http://socialmedia4change.org/concannon/

[34] De Liddo, A., Sándor, Á., Buckingham Shum, S. 2012. Contested Collective Intelligence: Rationale, Technologies, and a Human-Machine Annotation Study. *Computer Supported Cooperative Work*, 21, 4-5, 417-448. http://oro.open.ac.uk/31052

[35] De Liddo, A., Buckingham Shum, S. 2013. The Evidence Hub: harnessing the collective intelligence of communities to build evidence-based knowledge. Large Scale Ideation and Deliberation Workshop, 6th *Intl. Conference on Communities and Technologies (C&T2013)*, Munich, Germany.

[36] Piccolo, L.S.G., et al. 2013. Designing to Promote a New Social Affordance for Energy Consumption. In *Proc. of 12th IFIP Conf.on e-Business, e-Services, e-Society.* (I3E' 2013). 213-225.

[37] Piccolo, L.S.G., Baranauskas, C. Azevedo, R.J. 2014. Evaluating an Energy Feedback Technology in a Social Developing Scenario. *Paper submitted.*

[38] Stamper, R.K. 1973. Information in Business and Administrative Systems, John Wiley and Sons, New York

[39] Zhang, P. 2008. Motivational affordances: Reasons for ICT design and use, In Communications, ACM, vol 51, n°11.

[40] Bradley, M., Lang, P. 2000. Measuring emotion: Behavior, feeling, and physiology. *Cognitive neuroscience of emotion*. NY: Oxford University Press, 242–276.

[41] Intrinsic Motivation Inventory, http://www.selfdeterminationtheory.org/questionnaires/10-questionnaires/50

[42] Mamykina, L. et al. 2011. Design lessons from the fastest Q&A site in the west. In *Proc. of CHI '11*. ACM, New York, NY, USA, 2857-2866.

Graph Structure in the Web – Aggregated by Pay-Level Domain

Oliver Lehmberg
Data and Web Science Group
University of Mannheim
Germany
oli@informatik.uni-mannheim.de

Robert Meusel
Data and Web Science Group
University of Mannheim
Germany
robert@informatik.uni-mannheim.de

Christian Bizer
Data and Web Science Group
University of Mannheim
Germany
chris@informatik.uni-mannheim.de

ABSTRACT

Previous research on the overall graph structure of the World Wide Web mostly focused on the page level, meaning that the graph that directly results from hyperlinks between individual web pages was analyzed. This paper aims to provide additional insights about the macroscopic structure of the World Web Web by analyzing an aggregated version of a recent web graph. The graph covers over 3.5 billion web pages and 128 billion hyperlinks between pages. It was crawled in the first half of 2012. We aggregate this graph by pay-level domain (PLD), meaning that all pages that belong to the same pay-level domain are represented by a single node and that an arc exists between two nodes if there is at least one hyperlink between pages of the corresponding pay-level domains. The resulting PLD graph covers 43 million PLDs and contains 623 million arcs between PLDs. Analyzing this aggregated graph allows us to present findings about linkage patterns between complete websites and not only individual HTML pages. In this paper, we present basic statistics about the PLD graph, such as degree distributions, top-ranked PLDs, distances and diameter. We analyze whether the bow-tie structure introduced by Broder et al. can also be identified in our PLD graph and reveal a backbone of highly interlinked websites within the graph. We group the websites by top-level domain and report findings about the overall linkage within and between different top-level domains. In a last experiment, we use data from the Open Directory Project (DMOZ) to categorize websites by topic and report findings about linkage patterns between websites belonging to different topical categories.

Categories and Subject Descriptors

H.3.4 [**INFORMATION STORAGE AND RETRIEVAL**]: System and Software - World Wide Web

Keywords

World Wide Web, Web Graph, Network Analysis, Graph Analysis, Web Mining, Web Science

WebSci'14, June 23–26, 2014, Bloomington, IN, USA.
Copyright is held by the owner/author(s). Publication rights licensed to ACM.
ACM 978-1-4503-2622-3/14/06 ...$15.00.
http://dx.doi.org/10.1145/2615569.2615674.

1. INTRODUCTION

With the growth of the World Wide Web, the corresponding web graph has evolved in size and complexity. Knowledge about the macroscopic structure of this graph is useful within various application domains. It forms the basis for designing the ranking methods of web search engines. In turn, search engine optimization (SEO) efforts exploit the link structure of the Web in order to fool search engines and increase the ranking of target websites. An extreme appearance of such manipulations are spam networks, which consist of large numbers of websites that are created for the sole purpose of influencing rankings. Knowledge about the graph structure of the Web is also important for the seed selection of general web crawlers. Knowledge about linkage patterns within specific topical domains can help focused crawlers to adapt their crawling strategy. In addition, such patterns might also revile interesting findings about the social mechanisms that govern a specific domain.

We have extracted a large web graph from the 2012 version of the Common Crawl.[1] The graph covers over 3.5 billion web pages which are connected by over 128 billion hyperlinks. It is the largest web graph that is currently (May 2014) available to the public. In [13], we analyze the structure of this graph on page level. The paper updates the findings of Broder *et al.* [6], who did a similar page-level analysis over a decade ago, concerning in- and outdegree distributions, the distributions of the sizes of weakly and strongly connected components, distances within the graph, as well as the size of the components of the bow tie. In contrast to earlier studies and using the power law fitting methodology proposed Clauset *et al.* in [7], we find that the in- and outdegree distributions on page-level do not follow power laws.

In this paper, we analyze an aggregated version of the same graph. This aggregation is based on the pay-level domain of each HTML page. In addition to the analysis on page level, the PLD aggregation gives us the possibility to draw conclusions about the connectivity amongst complete websites[2] and not only individual pages. The paper makes the following contributions: (1) We report the results of a structural analysis of the PLD graph including degree distributions, distances, and diameter (Section 3). We present several rankings of pay-level domains which are particularly interesting for search engine optimization and spam detection. We analyze whether the bow-tie structure introduced by Broder *et al.* can also be identified in our PLD graph and report the sizes of the components of this bow tie (Section 3.4). Additional experiments (2) reveal a backbone of highly interlinked websites (Section 3.6) and enable us to (3) infer a two-layer model explaining the largest

---

[1] http://commoncrawl.org
[2] We will use the term website synonymously to the term pay-level domain.

strongly connected component and the low average shortest path length within the graph (Section 3.7). (4) We group the websites by top-level domain and report findings about the linkage within and between different top-level domains[3] (Section 4). In addition, (5) we use data from the Open Directory Project[4] to categorize the websites by topic and describe the structural properties of the websites assigned to different topical categories (Section 5). (6) The page- and PLD graph as well as the code used for the analysis are made publicly available via the *WebDataCommons.org* website[5] as we want to encourage other researchers to validate our findings and to be able to further analyze the graphs.

2. CRAWLING STRATEGY AND PLD COVERAGE

The web crawl from which we extracted our web graphs was collected in the first half of 2012 by the Common Crawl Foundation. Their crawler used a breath-first crawling strategy and was seeded with over 71 million different URLs from previous crawls and from Wikipedia pages. Unfortunately, the Common Crawl Foundation does not provide detailed information about banned pages, crawling limitations, as well as the stopping conditions of the crawler. Additional statistics about the crawl are provided in [18]. We aggregate the web graph by merging all pages from the same pay-level domain into a single node and remove internal and duplicate arcs. This results in a PLD graph containing 43 million nodes and 623 million arcs. We used the WebGraph library [4] to shrink the page graph into the PLD graph.

While we do not know the overall number of HTML pages on the Web, we know how many PLDs were registered at the time of crawling. This allows us to estimate the percentage of all registered PLDs that are covered by our graph. The number of registered domains is frequently reported by Verisign. In their report from October 2012[6] about the second quarter of the same year, they state a total of 240 million registered domain names. With our graph covering 43 million domains, this means we have (at least partial[7]) data about 18% of all domains that were registered at that time. The report further states that only 66% of all ".com" and ".net" domains contain real websites, meaning that one third of all registered domains forward to other domains or do not contain any web pages. We hence assume that our graph effectively covers more than the 18% that we can state with certainty: Assuming that the 66% hold for all domains, only 158 million domains have to be considered, resulting in a coverage of 27%.

3. ANALYSIS OF THE PLD GRAPH

In the following, we first have a closer look at the distribution of indegree, outdegree (Section 3.1), and PageRank (Section 3.2), and identify the top ranked PLDs according to several ranking methods (Section 3.3). Next, we present our findings about the connectivity of the PLD graph and examine whether the bow-tie structure introduced by Broder *et al.* [6] can also be found in our graph. In Section 3.5, we examine paths and reachability of websites in the

bow-tie components. Afterwards, we investigate the robustness of the PLD graph and have a closer look at groups of strongly linked websites which connect a large part of the PLD graph (Section 3.6). Finally, we combine these findings into a two-layer model which explains the largest strongly connected component and the low average shortest path length within the graph (Section 3.7).

3.1 In- and Outdegree Distributions

Figure 1 displays the in- and outdegree distributions of the PLD graph, showing the number of PLDs (y-axis) for a certain degree (x-axis) using a log-log scale. The grey dots show the actual distribution of the degree values. We also include the *Fibonacci Binning* [19] of the degree values into the figure to give a better impression of the distribution. In order to test the hypothesis that the distribution follows a power law, we employ the methodology proposed by Clauset *et al.* [7]. As concrete implementation, we use the plfit[8] tool to estimate the power law that fits our data with the maximum-likelihood. We also perform a goodness-of-fit test. The test produces a p-value, which tells us to reject the hypothesis that the distribution follows a power law if the value is smaller than 0.1. In the diagrams, the black line represents the best-fitting power law for the given distribution.

For the indegree distribution, the best-fitting pow law has an exponent of 2.40 and starts at a degree of 3 062. The p-value of the best fit for the indegree distribution is $0.43 \pm (0.01)$, meaning that the distribution follows a power law. The best-fitting power law for the outdegree distribution starts at 496 and has an exponent of 2.39. The p-value of this fit is $0 \pm (0.01)$. It is thus very likely that the outdegree distribution does not follow a power law. In [13], we found the largest outdegree value within the page graph to be three orders of magnitude smaller than the largest indegree value. Within the PLD graph the largest outdegree and indegree values are quite similar.

Both the indegree and the outdegree distribution (Figure 1) show several outliers above the rest of the distribution. In addition, both degree distributions display spikes at an indegree of roughly 3 000 and an outdegree of roughly 8 500. Examining a sample of those data points, we find that the corresponding websites can be classified as spam sites or domain seller sites. This has also been observed by Fetterly *et al.* [10] for the degree distributions on page level. Beside obvious spam sites, some companies register a separate PLD for every city that matters to their business. An example is a group of job-search websites following the pattern "*-jobs.co.uk", while each website links to all the other websites.

3.2 PageRank Distribution

In addition to the in- and outdegree, we also examined the distribution of PageRank values. PageRank is a popular measure for the prestige of a website, as it cannot be tricked by spammers as easily as indegree [14]. The PageRank distribution has been shown by Pandurangan *et al.* [15] to have approximately the same power-law exponent as the indegree distribution.

The right-most diagram in Figure 1 shows the PageRank distribution for the PLD graph. We can report a best-fit power law exponent of 2.27, which differs by 0.13 from the exponent of the indegree distribution. Generally, we can say that the PageRank distribution is much cleaner than the distribution of the indegree and does not contain any extreme outliers (like spikes within the distribution).

---

[3]More precisely *public suffixes* which are domain endings under which a domain name can be registered. Examples are ".com" or ".co.uk".

[4]http://dmoz.org

[5]http://webdatacommons.org/hyperlinkgraph/

[6]http://www.verisigninc.com/assets/domain-name-brief-oct2012.pdf

[7]We can say for sure that we have at least one page from each of these domains. Again, it is not possible to determine whether our data contains all pages from a specific domain.

[8]https://github.com/ntamas/plfit

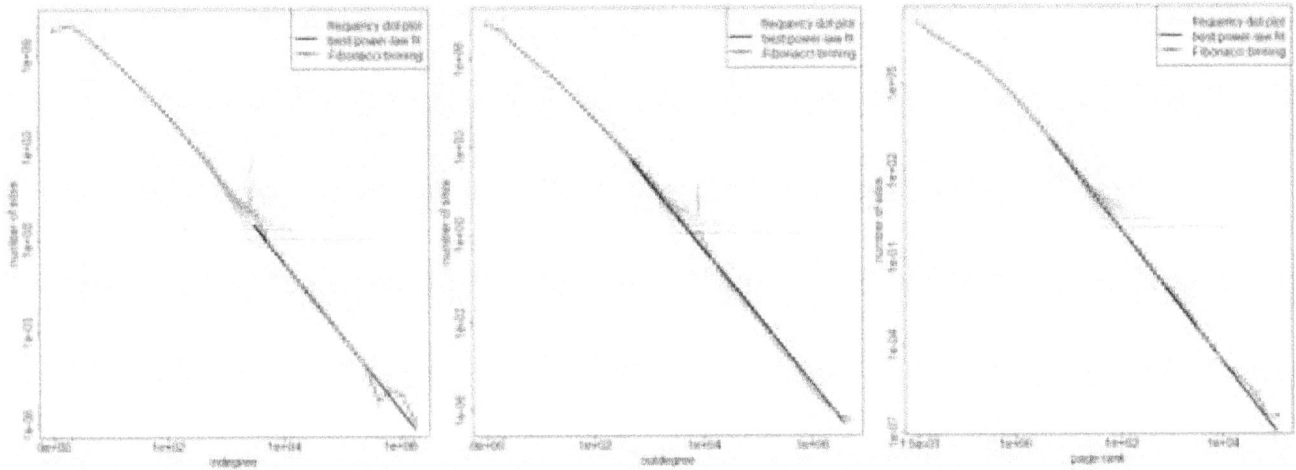

Figure 1: Distributions of indegree, outdegree and PageRank of the PLD graph

3.3 Top Ranked PLDs

We now have a look at the top ranked websites with respect to the in- and outdegree as well as the PageRank. This gives us an impression about the most important websites in our graph. Table 1 lists the top 20 websites in our PLD graph, ordered by their out- respectively indegree.

Regarding the outdegree, the highest ranked website is *blogspot.com*. We assume the reason for this high rank to be our aggregation. On this website, every user can create a personal blog and is provided with a sub domain under *blogspot.com*. Hence, this high outdegree can be assumed to be the sum of the outdegrees of all personal blogs hosted by *blogspot*.

Ordered by indegree, the most prominent website is *wordpress.org*. We assume that this is due to a large number of blogs that use *wordpress*' blog software and hence all of them also set links to the central *wordpress.org* website. The second ranked website is *youtube.com* followed by the online encyclopedia *wikipedia.org*.

Table 2 shows the top 20 websites according to their PageRank values. In this table, we find many websites that are also in the top list for the indegree. The highest ranked websites are *wordpress.com*, *gmpg.org* and *youtube.com*. The website *gmpg.org* provides a vocabulary for describing relationships. From the high PageRank we can assume this vocabulary is used frequently by rather popular websites.

3.4 Bow-Tie Structure

Broder *et al.* [6] have set up the hypothesis that the macroscopic structure of the Web has the form of a bow tie. The bow-tie structure has a large strongly connected component (LSCC) as its core. The sets containing the remaining nodes that can reach the LSCC or that can be reached from there are called IN and OUT respectively. The nodes that do not belong to any of these three sets are either TENDRILS, if they can either be reached from IN or can reach OUT, TUBES if they are located on a connected path from IN to OUT without passing the LSCC, or DISCONNECTED otherwise.

In this section we test whether we also find a bow-tie structure in our PLD graph and determine the sizes of the components. Before determining this structure, we examine the overall connectedness of the PLD graph, using a weakly connected component (WCC) analysis. We discover a giant WCC, covering 39 374 588 (91.8%) websites. The largest strongly connected component (SCC) in the PLD graph contains 22 274 865 (51.9%) PLDs. The next largest

	Website	Outdegree	Website	Indegree
1	blogspot.com	3 898 561	wordpress.org	1 822 440
2	wordpress.com	2 249 553	youtube.com	1 319 548
3	youtube.com	1 078 938	wikipedia.org	1 243 291
4	wikipedia.org	862 705	gmpg.org	1 156 727
5	serebella.com	699 609	blogspot.com	1 034 450
6	refertus.info	668 271	google.com	782 660
7	top20directory.com	650 884	wordpress.com	710 590
8	typepad.com	551 360	twitter.com	646 239
9	botw.org	496 645	yahoo.com	554 251
10	tumblr.com	496 045	flickr.com	339 231
11	dmoz.org	476 890	facebook.com	314 051
12	vindhetviahier.nl	424 646	apple.com	312 396
13	jcsearch.com	423 918	miibeian.gov.cn	289 605
14	startpagina.nl	392 543	vimeo.com	269 003
15	yahoo.com	371 087	tumblr.com	226 596
16	tatu.us	370 918	joomla.org	201 863
17	freeseek.org	362 310	amazon.com	196 690
18	lap.hu	352 668	w3.org	196 507
19	blau-webkatalog.com	312 924	nytimes.com	193 907
20	allepaginas.nl	276 578	sourceforge.net	189 663

Table 1: Top 20 websites ordered by in- and outdegree

components are much smaller with maximum sizes of around 1 000 PLDs for SCCs and less than 100 PLDs for WCCs.

Having identified the largest WCC and SCC, we now examine the bow-tie structure of our PLD graph. The results are shown in Figure 2. We find that the LSCC is referenced by a small IN component, consisting of 7.65% of all websites. The OUT component contains 30.98% of all nodes. TUBES and TENDRILS together amount to 1.24%.

Table 3 shows the sizes of the different bow-tie components of our PLD graph in comparison to the sizes in the page graph from which we constructed the PLD graph. The LSCC has a similar relative size. In contrast, the relative sizes of the IN and OUT component are exchanged. While the page graph has a large IN component (cf. [13]), we can only find a rather small one in the PLD graph. For the OUT component, the opposite effect appears. In order to understand this effect, one has to keep the applied aggregation in mind. Pages from the IN component are now counted to the LSCC whenever at least one page of the same PLD receives one link from a page in the LSSC component. The same holds for

	Website	PR		Website	PR
1	wordpress.org	113 388	11	apple.com	23 929
2	gmpg.org	111 173	12	phpbb.com	22 329
3	youtube.com	88 206	13	miibeian.gov.cn	22 165
4	twitter.com	54 644	14	hugedomains.com	20 793
5	wikipedia.org	54 081	15	facebook.com	20 254
6	blogspot.com	40 901	16	joomla.org	18 146
7	google.com	40 799	17	flickr.com	17 966
8	wordpress.com	28 018	18	adobe.com	17 903
9	yahoo.com	27 594	19	linkedin.com	16 083
10	networkadvertising.org	27 395	20	w3.org	15 539

Table 2: Top 20 websites ordered by PageRank (PR)

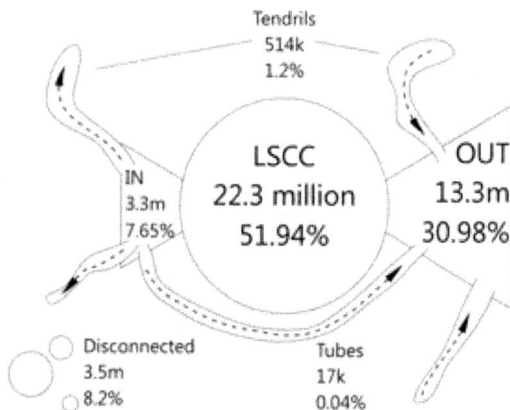

Figure 2: Bow-tie structure of the PLD graph

the OUT component, for PLDs including at least one page pointing back to the LSCC. In addition, we have to keep in mind that the crawl is biased towards some PLDs. For example *youtube.com* contains more than one million pages where other PLDs contain less than ten crawled pages. This skewed distribution in the number of pages per PLD can substantially change the picture, as we measure the sizes of the components relative to the total number of nodes in the respective graph. Beside these general factors, we find that a very large number of pages from the IN component belong to the LSCC after aggregating the page graph to the PLD graph. This means that pages from the IN component often belong to a website that has at least one page in the LSCC. Most pages from the OUT component, however, do not change the component after the aggregation. Hence, these pages belong to websites that are located completely in the OUT component.

	LSCC	IN	OUT	TENDR. TUBES	DISC
PLD graph	51.94	7.65	30.98	1.24	8.20
page graph [13]	51.28	31.96	6.05	4.87	5.84

Table 3: Comparison of the sizes of the different bow-tie components between PLD and page graph in percentages.

3.5 Distances and Diameter

As we now have an impression about the macroscopic structure of the graph and have determined which sets of websites could potentially reach others, we are interested in the distances between pairs of websites. We use the Hyperball method by [5] to calculate

an approximation of the distance distribution for our graph (technically, we computed five runs, which give us an approximation with the relative standard deviation 7.66%).

In the PLD graph, $42.42 \pm 3.59\%$ of the pairs of nodes are connected by a directed path between them. Moreover the length of the average shortest path is 4.27 ± 0.085. This means that from large proportion of the websites it is possible to reach almost all other websites by crossing only three others. Figure 3 shows the distance distribution, concentrated around the average. Using Hyperball, we can further estimate the diameter, i.e. the longest shortest path, to be at least 48.

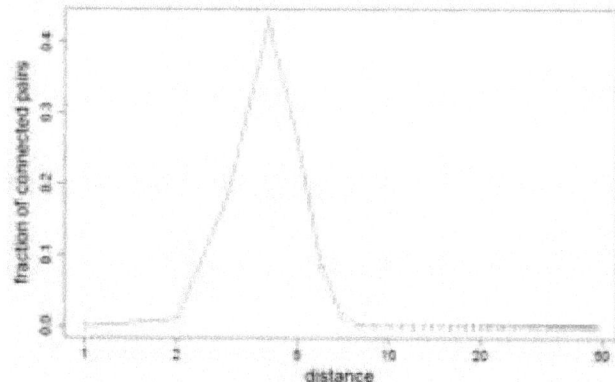

Figure 3: Distance distribution

Having calculated the basic distance measures within the whole graph, we are interested in the diameters of the different bow-tie components. Donato *et al.* [9] showed that both the IN and OUT component are very shallow. Our experiments, running breath-first search from the different components (we used a sample of 500 randomly chosen websites) in both directions lead to the following results: (a) the IN and OUT components are shallow as we found a diameter of two within both components and (b) the overall diameter of the graph is embedded in the LSCC, as the maximal diameter from the IN component is shorter than the one starting in the LSCC. This leads to the assumption that the LSCC contains chains of websites, which are very sparsely connected to other websites. We manually pick such chains from our results and have a look at the pay-level domains. As an example, one chain of length 43 has only domain names containing the keywords "sports" and "bet"/"betting". Another chain of length 26 has a comparably suspicious naming scheme. These domain names contain the keyword "ringtones" in combination with a singer's or a band's name. This indicates that very long paths are likely to be spam and arise due to the artificial or automated generation of websites.

3.6 Backbone of Highly Interlinked Websites

We further want to determine, if there are some particular websites which are responsible for the wide connectivity of the graph and the short average distances. In particular we want to find out if there exists a *hub and spoke* system, or if there is a finely woven structure which connects all websites. For this reason, we attempt to remove links from the PLD graph and measure to which degree the connectedness changes, as proposed by Broder *et al.* [6].

3.6.1 Removing Strongly Connected Websites

To determine the role of hubs, i.e. sites with very large indegree, in connecting the PLD graph, we start with removing all links to websites with an indegree of at least k. We then measure the sizes of the largest remaining weakly and strongly connected components.

Table 4 shows the experimental results for different values of k. We observe that for a k equal to or smaller than ten large strongly connected components are practically absent. This means that, if there were no hubs, i. e. websites with high indegree, most websites could never be reached by following hyperlinks from other websites. In the case of weakly connected components, for a k of five, only half of all nodes in the graph are still weakly connected. This shows that the graph is not composed of many completely isolated components that are connected by hubs. There are rather resilient connections between the low indegree websites, but for wide navigability, hubs are needed.

	all	10 000	1 000	100	10	5	4
WCC	91.8	90.3	89.4	87.6	73.7	56.8	48.0
SCC	51.9	45.1	39.7	27.8	0.1	< 0.1	< 0.1

Table 4: Percentage of nodes in the largest components for websites with indegree smaller than k

3.6.2 Removing Weakly Connected Websites

We now remove all links to nodes with indegree less than k. Table 5 shows the sizes of the largest remaining weakly and strongly connected components. From the indegree distribution we know that the majority of nodes has low values. As we remove the links to these nodes they can no longer be part of an SCC. For a k of ten, for example, we remove all links to a total of 33 957 836 nodes, which is about 79% of our whole PLD graph. These numbers are reported in the third row of Table 5 for every k.

	10	100	1 000	10 000	100 000
WCC	62.6	48.7	38.6	28.4	18.1
SCC	16.1	1.7	0.1	< 0.1	< 0.1
% removed	79.2	97.9	99.9	> 99.9	> 99.9

Table 5: Percentage of nodes in the largest components for websites with indegree at least k

For a k of ten, we see that the size of the largest WCC decreases from 91% to 62%. This means that links to nodes with low indegree are very important for the overall connectivity of the graph. The remaining 62% of the nodes are still connected, are nodes that link to other nodes with an indegree of ten or higher. As we increase k, we see how the size of the largest WCC decreases. Concerning the largest SCC, the picture now becomes clearer. From the previous experiment we know that the nodes with indegree smaller than ten do not form a large SCC. We now see that the nodes with indegree at least ten form an SCC spanning 16% of the whole graph. Recall that we removed incoming links to 79% of all nodes, which cannot participate in an SCC any more. So this SCC contains 76% of the remaining nodes. For a k of 100, the SCC contains 1.7% of all nodes and 97.9% of all nodes cannot participate in any SCC. This means, almost 81% of the remaining nodes are included in the largest SCC. Summing up, we can say that for our PLD graph the nodes with indegree at least ten form the core of the largest strongly connected component. The nodes with indegree less than ten do not form a large strongly connected component, but a large fraction is weakly connected.

3.6.3 Using a Weighted Graph

In order to find websites that are massively interlinked, we remove all arcs from the PLD graph that represent less than k links in the page graph. This means we practically assign weights to the arcs of the PLD graph. Table 6 shows the results for k values of 500 000, 100 000, 1 000 and 100. As the resulting numbers decrease rapidly, we report absolute numbers instead of percentages. For comparison, the largest weakly connected component for a k of 100 contains 3.9 million websites, which is around 9% of the PLD graph.

	500 000	100 000	10 000	1 000	100
WCC	106	2 331	45 396	642 276	3 908 604
SCC	10	65	1 900	33 300	381 000

Table 6: Number of nodes in the largest components for websites with at least k links between them

We now focus our attention to $k = 500\,000$. In this case, the largest remaining weakly connected component contains 106 websites. These are the pay-level domains that are most frequently being linked to in our PLD graph, as each of them receives at least half a million incoming links. Figure 4 shows this sub graph, where we visualize the topical areas of the included websites, using the best fitting category from the Open Directory Project.

Looking at this sub graph, we can make some detailed observations. The WCC can be split into two parts that are only connected via *imdb.com*. The smaller part, around the domain *amazon.com*, belongs mostly to the shopping category. The other part contains various other well-known PLDs like *google.com*, *facebook.com* and *blogspot.com*. In the centre of this second part, we find an SCC of size seven containing *youtube.com*, *google.com*, *sapo.pt*, *wordpress.com*, *typepad.com*, *blogspot.com* and *blogalaxia.com*. From this centre, several links to groups of other PLDs can be observed. *youtube.com* links to several PLDs that belong to various categories. *blogspot.com* links to many blogs, blog-hosting sites and news sites. Further analysis shows that the 106 PLDs from this WCC are connected, either by inlinks or by outlinks, to a total of 10 456 257 PLDs, which is almost a quarter of all PLDs in our PLD graph.

The largest strongly connected component comprises ten websites with adult content. Further inspection of the next largest SCCs for a k of 500 000 reveals the previously mentioned one SCC with seven PLDs. The domain *universehotels*, represented with five different top-level domains, forms another strongly connected component. Another eight SCCs with a total of 48 PLDs contain adult content.

3.7 Two-Layer Model of the PDL Graph

Combining all our observations, we hypothesize that the structure of the PLD graph can be explained using a *Two-Layer Model*, as depicted in Figure 5. The *Low Degree Layer* (LDL) contains the majority of websites that are sparsely connected, forming the giant weakly connected component. Within the *High Degree Layer* (HDL) we find websites with high indegree and large amounts of links between the websites.

From Table 4, we know that a large strongly connected component does not exist for nodes with indegree ten or lower. In case we include nodes with indegree up to 100, we find such a component.[9] Thus, we infer that the LDL consists of nodes with a maximum

---

[9]From our experiments, this is the smallest value of k that resulted in a large SCC. A more exact definition of this border is left for future research.

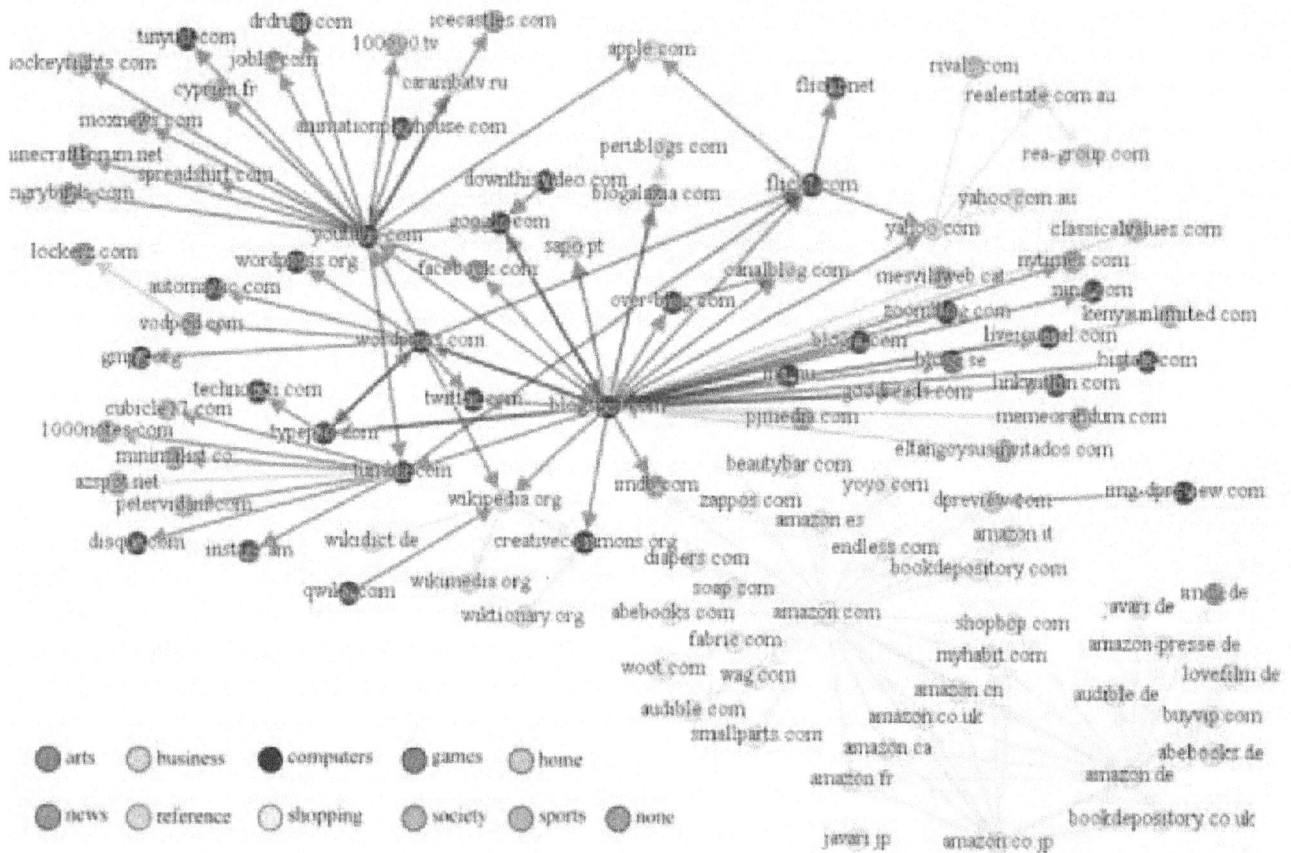

Figure 4: Largest WCC with more than $500\,000$ **links**

indegree ranging between ten and 100. As we know from the distribution of the indegree, this is the majority of all nodes. There are 34.6 million nodes with an indegree up to ten and additional 7.3 million nodes with indegree between 11 and 100. This leaves 881 thousand nodes with an indegree higher than 100. Hence, the LDL contains between 80% and 97% of all nodes of our PLD graph. Assuming the LDL includes all nodes with indegree up to 100, we find that 30 million nodes of this layer (71% of the PLD graph) being directly connected to the HDL formed by the remaining nodes.

We now compare the *Two-Layer Model* to the bow-tie structure and outline how the bow tie can, partially, be explained by our hypothesis. A large part of the giant WCC, containing 91.8% of all nodes, is explained by the LDL, which has a WCC containing between 73.7% to 87.6% of all nodes. The LSCC of the bow-tie structure comprises 51.9% of all nodes and can only be formed by the HDL. We find that 781 722 (89%) nodes from the HDL belong to the LSCC. The links between these nodes and the LDL create the LSCC with 22.3 million nodes. Hence, the nodes from the HDL are also likely to have a rather high outdegree. The remaining nodes from the HDL mostly belong to the OUT component. Only a few can also be found in the other components of the largest WCC.

We further suppose that the HDL provides short-cuts through the graph. The nodes with indegree higher than 100, which are definitely located in the HDL, are source or target of 421 million links, which is 68% of all links in the graph. 124 million of these links have both their source and target inside the HDL, leaving 297 million inter-layer links. This linkage pattern can be used to explain the small distances between a large proportion of pairs of nodes, as shown in Section 3.5.

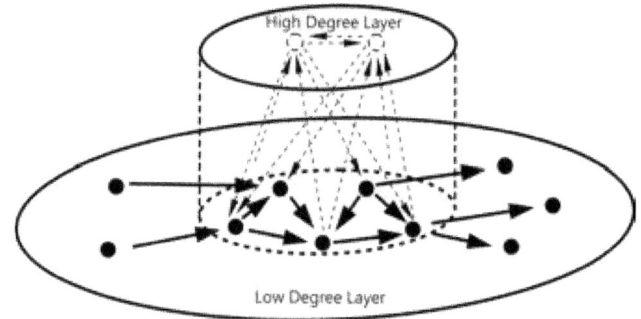

Figure 5: Two-Layer Model of the PLD Graph

An interesting question that we did not investigate and which is left for future research is how our hypothesized *Two-Layer Model* is in agreement with the Core-Periphery Structure as described by Rombach *et al.* [16].

4. LINKAGE BETWEEN TOP-LEVEL DO-MAINS

Besides the general connectivity and linkage on PLD level, we are also interested in linkage patterns that exist between websites that belong to different public suffixes. For this analysis we select the top ten public suffixes (PS) based on the number of websites included in our PLD graph. In addition, we introduce a group "others" that covers the remaining websites. Altogether, websites from the top ten PS amount for a total of 78.98% of all nodes of the PLD graph. Nodes belonging to the group of the ".com" websites cover almost half of all nodes of our graph. The distribution of the different PS in our dataset generally agrees with the Verisign Domain Industry Brief from October 2012.

Figure 6 shows the links between these 11 groups. In this diagram, the outermost circle labelled with percentages represents the total number of links for each group. Directly adjacent to this circle are two smaller bars for each group. The outer bar represents the number of inlinks while the inner bar represents the number of outlinks. Further to the centre there is another circle labelled with absolute numbers. This circle, again, represents the total number of links. From this circle ribbons spanning through the middle represent interconnections between the different groups. Incoming links have a white gap between the ribbon spanning in the middle and the circle part labelled with absolute numbers. Also, the ribbon has the same colour as the group that it originates from.

The two largest public suffixes, ".com" and ".de", exhibit an outstandingly high number of intra-group links. On the opposite, a rather low number of such links exists within the ".org", ".info" and ".net" suffixes. Besides, we can observe a general trend. Public suffixes with country code top-level domains (TLDs) tend to have a larger fraction of intra-group links than those with general TLDs, such as ".org" or ".net". The ".com" TLD does not follow this trend. An explanation for this exception is that the ".com" TLD is used accross all countries. This also manifests in the fact that the largest fraction of inter-group links for every public suffix is from and to the ".com" TLD.

Further inspection of the ".de" TLD links reveals an interesting fact. A total of 11 171 PLDs are either linking to *verleihcenter.de* or *verleihcenter.eu*. All those websites are hosted on nine different IP-addresses, meaning they mainly share the same servers. The summed outdegree of all PLDs hosted on these nine IP-addresses amounts to 21 801 852 which is almost half of all intra-".de"-links. Also, these spam PLDs are responsible for the spikes in the in- and outdegree distributions of the PLD graph (see section 3.1).

5. LINKAGE OF CATEGORIZED WEBSITES

Adding category information using data obtained from DMOZ to our websites, we add a content-based perspective to our analysis. Combined with our large amount of linkage information, we can analyse the websites of each topical category for their structural properties. Besides a visualization of the linkage between the topical categories, we detail statistics about incoming and outgoing links as well as the average clustering coefficient for each category.

5.1 Category Statistics

We matched the websites for all 15 relevant DMOZ top-level categories,[10] excluding the categories "regional" and "world" as they provide a geographical and not a content based categorisation. Within DMOZ categories can be maintained for different granularities, meaning that a large number of categorizations are done on page level. As we apply the categorisation to our PLD graph, we obtain multiple categories for some pay-level domains. For example, the video portal *youtube.com* is found in almost all categories. In order to obtain a distinct categorisation we only use those websites that are assigned only a single category. This results in 743 686 distinctly categorised PLDs out of the 796 251 PLDs

---

[10]The data set is available as public RDF data: http://www.dmoz.org/docs/en/rdf.html

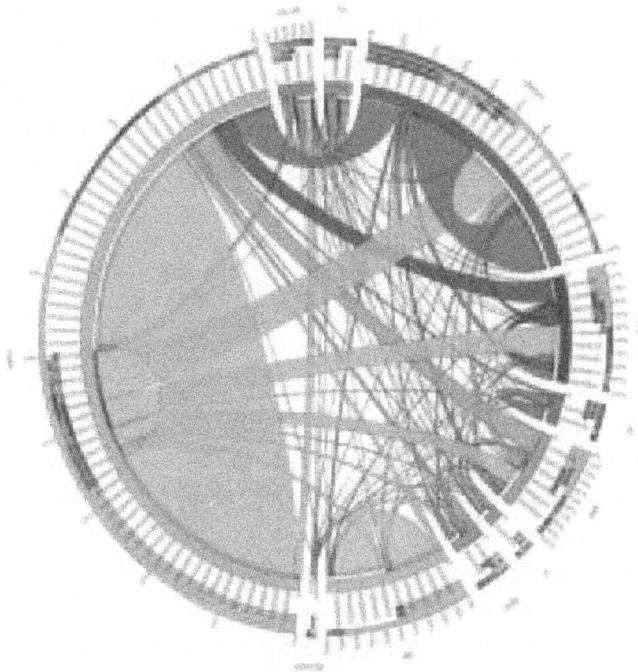

Figure 6: Linkage of websites grouped by TLDs

we obtained from the matching of our PLD graph with the DMOZ data.

Table 7 shows the number of matched websites for each category. The numbers reported refer to pay-level domains that were categorised distinctly. The second column gives the absolute number and the third column contains the percentage of this number relative to the total number of categorized websites.

The largest categories we obtain are "business" and "society". The categories with the least number of websites are "home" and "news".

Category	Number of PLDs	Percentage
business	176 890	26
society	99 801	14
arts	75 978	11
shopping	67 477	10
recreation	54 721	8
computers	52 995	8
sports	43 334	6
science	28 717	4
health	28 571	4
adult	12 475	2
reference	14 329	2
kids and teens	11 742	2
games	10 885	2
home	7 577	1
news	4 118	1

Table 7: Websites distinctly categorized by DMOZ

5.2 Linkage between Categories

Combining the DMOZ data with our PLD graph gives us the opportunity to analyse the linkage between the categories. For the visualisation of our results, we use the same diagram layout as in Section 4. In Figure 7, the outer circle represents the categories, sized by their respective number of links. In the centre of the circle, the interconnections of the categories are displayed by ribbons spanning in between. Although we hoped to find groups of categories that show a clearly distinguishable linkage pattern, our results show that there are no clear preferences concerning which categories link to each other.

Looking at the figure, we see that the "computers" category plays a dominant role. It has the largest number of links, although it is only the sixth largest category by the number of websites. We observe that for connections with other categories, it has more outgoing than incoming links. The opposite applies for the "business" category, which receives more incoming links than outgoing links.

Overall, we can say that most categories have a large fraction of internal links. However, this does not endure for some categories. For example, the "shopping" and "reference" categories only have few internal links. In the case of the "shopping" category, this may be explained by the fact that different shopping websites are competitors and hence do not link to each other. This was also hypothesized by Broder *et al.* [6], assuming that those are mainly located in the OUT component.

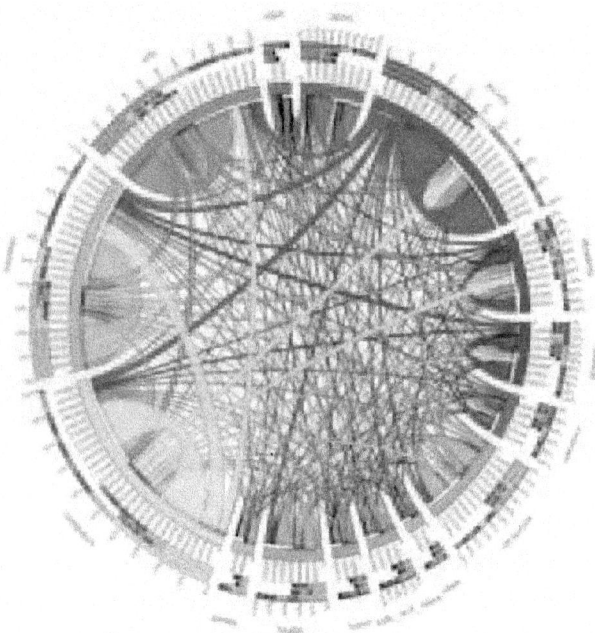

Figure 7: Linkage of websites grouped by categories

5.3 In- and Outdegree

In a next step, we have a closer look at the distribution of links among the categories. To this end, we determine the total number of links as well as the average in- and outdegree. Note that, contrary to the previous section, we now take all links, including those to and from uncategorised websites, into account.

Table 8 lists the average in- and outdegree as well as the total number of outgoing links for each category. We observe the highest average indegree for the categories "computers", "kids and teens" and "news". The categories with the highest average outdegree are the same, but in a different order: "kids and teens", "news" and "computers". As mentioned before, the "business" and "shopping" categories have a low average outdegree. These sites most likely refrain from placing links to their competitors. For most categories, the average indegree is higher than the average outdegree, except for the categories "adult" and "games".

Category	Avg. indegree	Avg. outdegree	total in-links	total out-links
adult	103	116	1 297 359	1 451 297
arts	91	69	6 918 096	5 282 143
business	70	29	12 455 999	5 142 553
computers	279	133	14 807 829	7 091 805
games	101	102	1 101 279	1 113 447
health	109	48	3 129 440	1 381 696
home	177	117	1 348 016	890 686
kids and teens	257	169	3 024 563	1 988 132
news	233	155	962 152	641 919
recreation	83	52	4 559 801	2 882 297
reference	173	98	2 491 173	1 408 763
science	107	62	3 091 737	1 805 970
shopping	79	24	5 365 656	1 622 528
society	81	57	8 134 803	5 763 999
sports	65	41	2 832 955	1 813 262

Table 8: Degree statistics of websites distinctly categorized by DMOZ ordered by category

5.4 Clustering Coefficient

We now also take the vicinity of the categorised websites into account and compute the clustering coefficient. By this, we can get an impression about the structural environment the categorised websites are embedded in. Due to the computation time required to determine the clustering coefficient, we cannot use all PLDs, but used a sample of 1 000 pay-level domains per category.

Figure 8 plots the clustering coefficients for all categories. The dark blue line represents the average clustering coefficient as obtained from our sample. The light blue area around this line visualizes the positive and negative standard deviation.

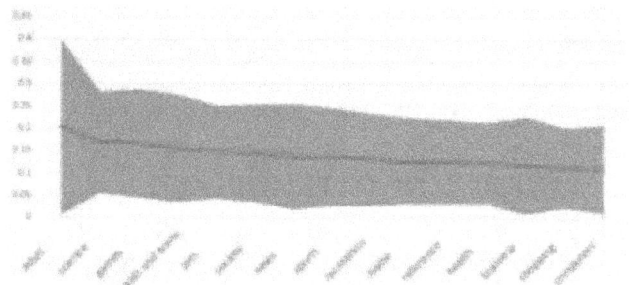

Figure 8: Average clustering coefficient by category

All values obtained for our sample fall in a range between 0.11 and 0.19 with standard deviations from 0.09 to 0.19. The highest clustering coefficients are observed for the categories "adult", "science" and "games". These categories also show the largest standard deviation. The lowest values are again observed for the "business" and "shopping" categories, which are now unexpectedly joined by the "computers" category.

5.5 Summary

Figure 9 shows a diagram summarizing our findings about the topical categories. To fit all this data into one chart, we computed several ratios to reduce the number of dimensions. The x-axis charts the ratio of in- and outdegree, which we know from Section 5.3. A value of one means both are the same, while a value higher than one means the indegree is higher than the outdegree. The y-axis represents the average number of links per website, incorporating data from Section 5.1. Finally, the size of each bubble is relative to the clustering coefficient as reported in Section 5.4.

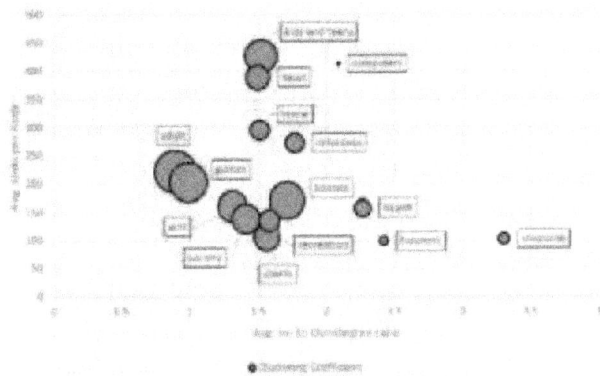

Figure 9: Structural description of the DMOZ categories

6. RELATED WORK

This section gives an overview of related research in the area of web graph analysis. First, we discuss research that analyzes the Web graph on page level. Afterwards, we describe related work analyzing web graphs on a higher aggregation level.

6.1 Page-Level Graphs

Most existing studies analyze the structure of web graphs on page level. Among these studies, one of the most influential and often cited is the work of Broder *et al.* [6] from the year 2000. Their study is based on two crawls from AltaVista with over 200 million pages and 1.5 billion links each. They introduce the bow-tie structure which gives an overview of the macroscopic structure of the Web. Further, they find that the average distance in their graph is about 16, if there is a directed path between two pages. According to them, such a path exists in only 25% of all cases. In addition, Broder *et al.* claim that in- and outdegree distributions exhibit a power law. Kumar *et al.* [12] and Barabási and Albert [2] reported similar results.

The inner structure of the bow-tie components was analyzed by Donato *et al.* [9] in their work from 2005 using four different crawls. They found weakly connected components in IN and OUT to be rather small and that most webpages are isolated, meaning that the paths to and from the LSCC are rather short. Concluding, they propose a *"daisy"* structure to replace the bow-tie structure of the Web. In this *"daisy"* structure, the IN and OUT components are represented by many small WCCs around the LSCC. Within our PLD graph, we could identify similar characteristics, where we observe a maximum length of paths inside the IN and OUT component of two.

Using different data sets, various numbers for the proportions of the bow-tie components have been reported in the past. Examples include the works of Serrano *et al.* [17], Boldi and Codenotti [3], Baeza-Yates and Poblete [1] and Zhu *et al.* [20]. As the reported numbers show strong variations, it can be assumed that the crawling strategy has a non-negligible impact on the size of the components. But, as in our case, details about the exact crawling strategy and parameters are not always known.

We have already published a page level analysis [13] of the same graph that was used to create the aggregated graph presented in this paper. For the in- and outdegree distributions, we report an estimate of the power law using maximum-likelihood fitting and perform a goodness-of-fit test [7]. The test shows that both distributions do not follow a power law. Further, we report that approximately 48% of all nodes are connected by a directed path and the average

distance is around 12.84. The graph exhibits a bow-tie structure with large LSCC (51.28%) and IN (31.96%) components and a small OUT component (6.05%).

6.2 Aggregated Graphs

Only a few studies have been published that analyze the web graph on a higher aggregation level.

Hirate *et al.* [11] gathered a large crawl between 2004 and 2005, which they analysed using a host level reduction. Although their reduction method is the same as ours, they did not use the same aggregation level. As the host may contain sub domains, the resulting graph has several nodes per pay-level domain. They found that the bow tie shows a rather small IN component (10%) and quite large LSCC and OUT components with (41%) of all nodes each.

Zhu *et al.* [20] analysed the structure of the Chinese Web. They compared their results on three different aggregation levels: the page level, the host level and the domain level. On the page level, they found a large IN component, which disappears on the host and the domain level. Analogously, the LSCC and OUT components of the host and domain level are larger than on the page level.

Dill *et al.* [8] compared several sub graphs, one of which is the "hostgraph". The indegree power law exponent for their graph is 2.34 and hence close to the value we reported. Concerning the bow-tie structure, they found an LSCC of 82%. This result led them to the conclusion that almost every website has a page belonging to the LSCC.

Interestingly, the trend that can be seen in the results of Hirate *et al.* [11] and Zhu *et al.* [20] can also be found in our results: On the page level, the IN component is larger than the OUT component, but on an aggregated level, the opposite is true. Obviously, the aggregation from the page level to a higher level shrinks the IN component of the bow tie and simultaneously inflates the OUT component. The results of Dill *et al.* [8] do not really fit to these observations. As we do not have further information about the methodology Dill *et al.* applied to gather their data, we cannot say whether this is as phenomenon that has changed since 2002 or whether the results of Dill *et al.* are an artefact of their crawling strategy.

7. CONCLUSION

In this paper, we have analysed the aggregated version of the largest publicly available web graph, extracted from a web crawl from 2012. This PLD graph includes at least one page of between 18% and 27% of all registered domains from the time of the crawl. We have shown that using a PLD aggregation level, we can overcome the effect of website-internal links on graph measures, and hence give insights about the graph structure on website level.

First, we analysed basic graph statistics of our graph and showed that the outdegree distribution does not follow a power law. Further, we found a diameter of at least 48 in our graph and an average distance of 4.27. When examining the overall graph structure, we calculated the bow-tie structure and detected a similar shift in IN and OUT components in comparison to the page graph as previously observed by Zhu *et al.* [20].

Further, we hypothesize a two-layer model explaining the LSCC and the short distances in the graph. This model describes a large group of finely woven, weakly connected websites with a relatively low degree – the Low Degree Layer. This layer is responsible for the overall connectedness of the graph. In addition, we identify a second layer of websites with high degrees – the High Degree Layer – which we assume is responsible for the short average distance within the whole graph.

Looking at the linkage between PLDs belonging to different top-level domains, we found two patterns: generic top-level domains, for example ".org", have more external links than links pointing to websites within the same top-level domain. Public suffixes based on country-specific top-level domains have a larger proportion of internal links. The ".com" domains do not follow these patterns, which we presume to be due to its usage across all languages and countries.

As we grouped pay-level domains by the topical category obtained from DMOZ, we measured more detailed properties of the different categories. By combining these properties, we find indications for how categories can be distinguished on an aggregate level.

8. REFERENCES

[1] R. Baeza-Yates and B. Poblete. Evolution of the chilean web structure composition. In *Web Congress, 2003. Proceedings. First Latin American*, pages 11–13, 2003.

[2] A.-L. Barabási and R. Albert. Emergence of scaling in random networks. *Science*, 286:209–512, October 1999.

[3] P. Boldi, B. Codenotti, M. Santini, and S. Vigna. Structural properties of the african web. In *WWW '02*, volume 66, 2002.

[4] P. Boldi and S. Vigna. The webgraph framework I: compression techniques. In *WWW '04*, pages 595–602. ACM, 2004.

[5] P. Boldi and S. Vigna. In-core computation of geometric centralities with HyperBall: A hundred billion nodes and beyond. In *ICDMW 2013*. IEEE, 2013.

[6] A. Broder, R. Kumar, F. Maghoul, P. Raghavan, S. Rajagopalan, R. Stata, A. Tomkins, and J. Wiener. Graph structure in the web. *Computer networks*, 33(1):309–320, 2000.

[7] A. Clauset, C. R. Shalizi, and M. E. Newman. Power-law distributions in empirical data. *SIAM review*, 51(4):661–703, 2009.

[8] S. Dill, R. Kumar, K. S. Mccurley, S. Rajagopalan, D. Sivakumar, and A. Tomkins. Self-similarity in the web. *ACM Trans. Internet Technol.*, 2(3):205–223, Aug. 2002.

[9] D. Donato, S. Leonardi, S. Millozzi, and P. Tsaparas. Mining the inner structure of the web graph. In *WebDB*, pages 145–150, 2005.

[10] D. Fetterly, M. Manasse, and M. Najork. Spam, damn spam, and statistics: Using statistical analysis to locate spam web pages. *International Workshop on the Web*, pages 1–6, 2004.

[11] Y. Hirate, S. Kato, and H. Yamana. Web structure in 2005. In *Algorithms and models for the web-graph*, pages 36–46. Springer, 2008.

[12] R. Kumar, P. Raghavan, S. Rajagopalan, and A. Tomkins. Trawling the web for emerging cyber-communities. *Computer Networks*, 31(11 - 16):1481 – 1493, 1999.

[13] R. Meusel, S. Vigna, O. Lehmberg, and C. Bizer. Graph structure in the web — revisited: A trick of the heavy tail. In *Proc. of WWW Companion '14*, pages 427–432, 2014.

[14] L. Page, S. Brin, R. Motwani, and T. Winograd. The PageRank citation ranking: bringing order to the web. pages 1–17, 1999.

[15] G. Pandurangan, P. Raghavan, and E. Upfal. Using Pagerank to characterize web structure. *Computing and Combinatorics*, pages 330–339, 2002.

[16] M. P. Rombach, M. A. Porter, J. H. Fowler, and P. J. Mucha. Core-periphery structure in networks. *arXiv preprint arXiv:1202.2684*, 2012.

[17] M. Serrano, A. Maguitman, M. Boguñá, S. Fortunato, and A. Vespignani. Decoding the structure of the www: A comparative analysis of web crawls. *ACM Transactions on the Web (TWEB)*, 1(2):10, 2007.

[18] S. Spiegler. Statistcs of the common crawl corpus 2012. Technical report, SwiftKey, June 2013. Document viewed on September 16th 2013 from https docs.google.comfiled1_9698uglerxB9nAglvaHkEgU-iZNm1TvVGuCW7245-WGvZq47teNpb_uL5N9.

[19] S. Vigna. Fibonacci binning. *CoRR*, abs/1312.3749, 2013.

[20] J. J. H. Zhu, T. Meng, Z. Xie, G. Li, and X. Li. A teapot graph and its hierarchical structure of the chinese web. *WWW '08*, pages 1133–1134, 2008.

"Supertagger" Behavior in Building Folksonomies

Jared Lorince[*†]
jlorince@indiana.edu

Sam Zorowitz[§]
szorowi1@jhu.edu

Jaimie Murdock[*‡]
jammurdo@indiana.edu

Peter M. Todd[*†‡]
pmtodd@indiana.edu

Indiana University:
[*]Cognitive Science,[†]Psychological & Brain Sciences,[‡]Informatics
John Hopkins University:
[§]Psychological & Brain Sciences

ABSTRACT

A folksonomy is ostensibly an information structure built up by the "wisdom of the crowds", but is the "crowd" really doing the work? Tagging is in fact a sharply skewed process in which a small minority of users generate an overwhelming majority of the annotations. Using data from the social music site Last.fm as a case study, this paper explores the implications of this tagging imbalance. Partitioning the folksonomy into two halves — one created by the prolific minority and the other by the non-prolific majority of taggers — we examine the large-scale differences in these two sub-folksonomies and the users generating them, and then explore several possible accounts of what might be driving these differences. We find that prolific taggers preferentially annotate content in the long-tail of less popular items, use tags with higher information content, and show greater tagging expertise. These results indicate that "supertaggers" not only tag *more* than their counterparts, but in quantifiably *different* ways.

Categories and Subject Descriptors

H.1.2 [**User/Machine Systems**]: Human information processing; H.5.3 [**Information Interfaces and Presentation**]: Group and Organization Interfaces—Collaborative computing, Web-based interaction

Keywords

Collaborative tagging, Folksonomy, Supertaggers

1. INTRODUCTION

Participation rates in a social tagging system vary widely. The semantic structure of a folksonomy — the collaboratively-generated classification scheme that emerges from many individual, assignments of free-form textual labels to content

— is available and potentially useful to all users of a system with tagging features. But most users are precisely that: users. They may use tags to search for or gain information about resources, but only a minority of users actively contribute to the knowledge-generation process by assigning metadata to content. Even among those who do tag, only a small percentage do most of the work, with a small number of taggers contributing most of the annotations (i.e. tag assignments), and a comparatively large number only tagging a few times. The implications of these participation rates have deep consequences for the information architect wishing to implement a tagging system. Does the folksonomy represent the aggregated knowledge of its users, or only the few "supertaggers" among them? Would the behavior of prolific and non-prolific taggers actually create two distinct folksonomies?

We can partly attribute this lack of participation to the fact that tagging is most often a secondary feature of a given system. To tag is to make a deliberate choice with costs of time and effort outside the primary use of a service. Users may, for instance, use Flickr to find and share photos or Last.fm to listen to and learn about music, without making any substantive contribution to the folksonomies embedded in these systems. This fact is more pronounced in the latter case, where the principal activity on the site — listening to music — is a passive activity, while tagging requires active effort.

Underlying questions about folksonomy creation is the fundamental issue of motivation — why do users contribute to social tagging systems? A substantial literature has explored this topic in terms of why users tag in one manner rather than another [16, 1, 19], but there is little work addressing the question of why users choose to participate in the tagging process to begin with. By comparing the tagging patterns of the minority of prolific taggers to the majority of non-prolific taggers, here we contribute to an understanding of what differentiates the heavy contributors from their low-tagging counterparts in social tagging, what motivational factors distinguish these two groups, and whether their tags reflect different underlying folksonomies.

In summary, there are two high-level questions that interest us: First, how do the tagging patterns of the minority of prolific taggers differ from the majority of non-prolific taggers, and what does this suggest about motivations for tagging? Second, does the disproportionate contribution to the folksonomy by a small number of users compromise the presumed crowdsourced nature of tagging? In other words, does the folksonomy truly represent the collective knowledge of its users, or just a subset who may or may not be representative of the general user base? Though we cannot offer complete answers to these questions, we present methods and results that help shed light on these relatively unexplored issues.

In this paper, we address these questions using a dataset of approximately 1.9 million users, with over 50 million annotations across 4.5 million items[1] crawled from the social music site Last.fm (Section 3.1). After presenting related work (Section 2) and an overview of the dataset (Section 3), we illustrate and formalize the the prolific- vs. non-prolific tagger dichotomy in Section 4. In Section 5 we present our main descriptive analyses showing differences in the tagging patterns and attributes of users in each of the two groups. Next, in Section 6, we explore possible causal accounts for the observed differences, focusing on expertise effects and differences in motivation. We conclude in Section 7 by synthesizing our results and considering their implications.

2. RELATED WORK

2.1 Folksonomies

A *folksonomy* is a collaborative organization scheme which uses tags (words or short phrases) to annotate objects for later retrieval. Thomas Vander Wal coined the word "folksonomy" in a 2004 listserv posting[20]. Folksonomies are most often social endeavors, with multiple users annotating the same objects with user-generated vocabulary.

Whereas many classification schemes are "top-down" hierarchies, a folksonomy is "bottom-up". In a taxonomy, a discrete set of pre-existing, often expert-generated, categories are assigned to resources. In a folksonomy, the vocabulary is unconstrained and comes from the users themselves, who may or may not be domain experts, bringing "power to the people" [17]. Many efforts have been made to infer taxonomies from folksonomies, synthesizing the advantages of controlled vocabulary and crowdsourced curation [10, 14].

The information retrieval advantages of folksonomies, combined with low economic cost of implementation and essentially free creation, provide a strong motivation for their use. Many folksonomies have been studied in diverse domains, including Flickr (photos, [15]), Delicious (web bookmarks, [3]), Last.fm (music, [11]), and BibSonomy (academic papers, [5]). A review of many early social tagging systems can be found in [12].

2.2 Tagging Motivation

One possible distinction between prolific and non-prolific taggers is tagging motivations. Though motivation in tagging behaviors has been operationalized in numerous ways, one prominent approach [9] characterizes users as either categorizers or describers. When tagging, categorizers use a limited vocabulary to construct a personal taxonomy conducive to later personal search. In contrast, describers do not constrain their vocabulary; instead they freely choose a variety of informative keywords to describe items. Strohmaier et al. [19] and Körner et al. [9] present several metrics with which to categorize users according to this dichotomy, discussed in Section 6.2.

Content produced by describers and categorizers has been shown to be useful for disparate tasks. Tags produced by describers, for example, are more useful in information retrieval [4] and knowledge acquisition [8]. Conversely, tags produced by categorizers are more useful for social classification tasks [25]. As such, it is important to determine whether prolific and non-prolific taggers differ in their tagging motivations along the lines of describers versus categorizers, to help understand how the folksonomy created by the top taggers may differ from that created by the rest.

2.3 Expertise in tagging

Another possible distinction between tagger types is level of expertise. In other words, do prolific taggers demonstrate greater or lesser expertise than non-prolific taggers when annotating items? Detecting expert users in a folksonomy is motivated by an increasing need to distinguish users providing informative contributions from those producing unhelpful contributions (especially spammers) in large folksonomies [6, 22].

One noteworthy approach to expert detection is Spamming-Resistant Expertise Analysis and Ranking (SPEAR) [22, 23], a variant of the HITS Web page ranking algorithm [7], that identifies experts according to two principles: First, there should be mutual reinforcement between user expertise and the quality of the annotated items. In other words, an expert user is not only more adept at identifying high quality items, but is also defined by the quality of the items annotated. Second, expert users are more likely to "discover" quality items than less expert users.

Here, we utilize the SPEAR algorithm to quantify expertise among prolific and non-prolific taggers. The use of a spam-robust expertise measure is important, as Wetzker et al. [21] found an overwhelming majority of the most prolific taggers in a large taxonomy were spammers. SPEAR is particularly appropriate for detecting expertise in our dataset as users on Last.fm are provided tag recommendations when annotating items, and SPEAR reasonably assigns greater expertise to users who first annotate an item with a given tag than to users who tag later.

3. DATASET

To address our questions, we utilize a dataset crawled from the social music site Last.fm with data spanning July 2005 through December 2012. The data was first presented in [11], but has since been expanded to not only include tagging data, but friends, group memberships, items listened to, and loved/banned tracks[2] for an increased number of users.

3.1 Crawling Methodology

We crawled data with a combination of API queries and HTML scraping of users' publicly available profile pages. We did so on a user-by-user basis, such that we have the

---

[1] An "item" is a generic term referring to an atomic target of tagging activity on Last.fm, and can be an artist, album, or song. Although there is a hierarchical structure inherent to these item types (an artist has a set of albums, each made up of a set of songs), tag distributions exist on Last.fm at the item level, and we therefore perform our analyses at that level, as well.

[2] "Loving" a track is roughly equivalent to favoriting a tweet, or other similarly-defined activities, while "banning" allows a user to indicate disliked items and exclude them from any recommendations by Last.fm.

complete tagging history for every user in our data, but not necessarily the complete tagging history for any particular item. All temporal annotation data is at a monthly granularity, as users' profiles only list the month and year in which an item was tagged (no such data is available from the API).

Because users were crawled by traversing the site's social network, we necessarily only include those users with at least one friendship on the site, but we do not believe this is problematic for our analyses. See [11] for further discussion of our crawling methods and its limitations.

3.2 Data Summary

We crawled a total of nearly 1.9 million users, extracting the behavioral measures mentioned above, as well as self-reported demographic data. An "annotation" refers to a given instance of a user assigning a particular tag to a particular item at a particular time. It is best thought of as a four-element tuple in the form user-item-tag-time. For a subset of our users, we also have collected full scrobble histories[3]. Table 1 summarizes the data collected. All tagging analyses presented here reflect only those users with ≥ 1 annotation.

Total users	1,884,597
Friendship relations	24,320,919
Total annotations	50,372,895
Users with ≥ 1 annotation	521,780
Total unique tags	1,029,091
Unique items tagged	4,477,593
Total Scrobbles	1,181,674,857
Users with scrobbles recorded	73,251
Unique items scrobbled	32,864,795
Total loved tracks	162,788,213
Users with ≥ 1 loved track	1,355,859
Total banned tracks	23,321,347
Users with ≥ 1 banned track	502,758
Unique Groups	117,663
Users with ≥ 1 group membership	827,232

Table 1: Dataset summary.

The data show a long-tailed distribution for per-use annotation counts, with similar distributions[4] for other tagging (total uses of each tag, total annotations per item) and behavioral (number of groups, loved tracks, and banned tracks per user) measures of interest, as well as the total number of scrobbles per track. Figure 1 summarizes this data. The distribution of scrobbles differs from the others in lacking a long tail, showing that most users listen to a large number of items. While these scrobble counts come from a relatively small subsample of our users, the pattern is consistent with the distinction between passive listening and active tagging mentioned earlier.

---

[3]A "scrobble" is Last.fm's term for an instance of a user listening to a particular song at a particular time. The service tracks users' listening habits (either through the site directly, or via a plugin installed in a media player) providing recommendations and aggregated listening statistics, and each listen logged is a "scrobble".

[4]Though clearly long-tailed, we remain agnostic as to the precise mathematical form (e.g. power-law, lognormal) of these distributions, as it does not meaningfully affect our analyses.

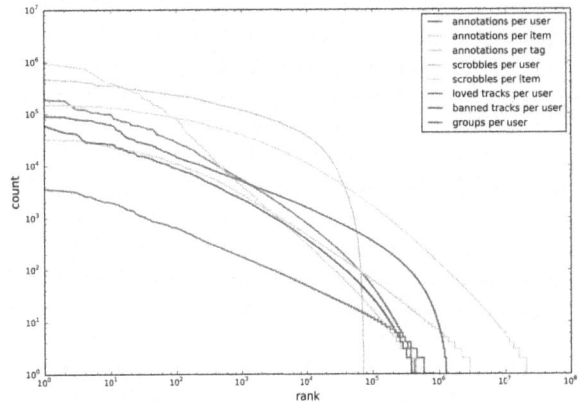

Figure 1: Rank-frequency plots for main measures from the dataset, on a log-log scale.

4. PROBLEM FORMALIZATION

The long-tail distribution of annotation counts in our data suggest the existence of two populations: a prolific-tagging minority and a non-prolific-tagging majority. To attempt to distinguish these two populations, we calculated the relative contributions of annotations across divisions between prolific and non-prolific taggers. We compared the proportion of taggers included in the prolific-tagger group to the proportion of annotations generated by that group (Figure 2). The top 20% of users generate over 90% of all tagging activity in our data, more skewed than the 20%/80% pattern commonly described by the Pareto Principle [13].

With this distribution in mind, we explored a variety of methods to seek a "natural" split between the prolific and non-prolific tagger populations, settling upon a 50-50 split in the number of annotations. This split at a threshold of 1,457 total annotations per user placed 5,086 users (0.97%) in the prolific-tagger group, and the remaining 516,694 users (99.03%) in the non-prolific group.

While this partitioning is arbitrary, it yields two large folksonomic structures of equal size (in terms of total annotations) amenable to analysis, and also highlights the extreme

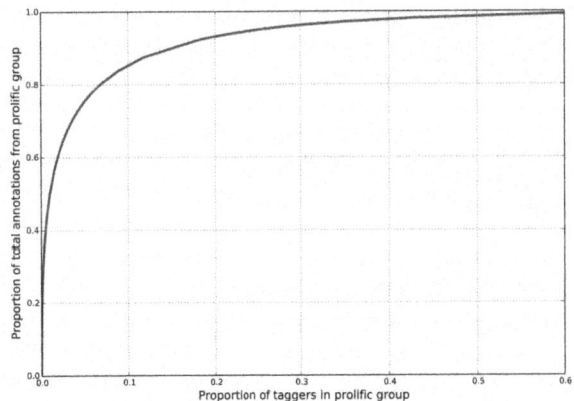

Figure 2: Proportion of total annotations created by the prolific taggers as a function of the proportion of top users included the prolific-tagging group.

skew in the behaviors of users on the site. Although other measures, such as the number of actual unique tags, users, and items vary between the two folkosnomies, this partitioning ensures that the total amount of tagging performed is equal in both.

5. DESCRIPTIVE ANALYSES & RESULTS

In this section we examine, at a descriptive level, how the *users* in each group defined by our partition differ, and how the two *folksonomies* generated by those groups differ.

5.1 User Attributes

Are the groups similar in terms of demographics and other attributes? There were few interesting demographic differences of note, but three points do warrant mention. First, prolific taggers are older on average than non-prolific taggers ($m = 31.1$ vs. $m = 26.4$). Second, they are more likely to be subscribers (users who pay a monthly fee for premium features): 7.3% of prolific taggers versus 1.2% of non-prolific taggers are subscribers. Finally, they are slightly more likely to report optional demographic data such as age (73.9 % versus 71.7%) and country (90.7% versus 84.5%)

Are the groups similar with respect to other behavioral measures? The behavioral measures we collected tend to show weak, but positive cross-correlations (with some exceptions, see Table 2), but our main interest is in how these measures covary with annotation volume. Following analyses in [18], we plot these measures for all users as a function of annotation count, binned logarithmically, in Figure 3. Users in the non-prolific tagging group appear on the left of the dashed line, and prolific taggers on the right.

Though the data is much noisier for the prolific taggers, the general trend is that of prolific taggers being more active than non-prolific taggers across all behavioral measures. This suggests that being a prolific tagger may, in part, be an artifact of being a heavy user of the site more generally (though not for all users; there are clear outliers in Figure 3).

	N_f	N_a	N_l	N_s	N_b	N_g
N_f		0.075	0.155	0.146	0.015	0.225
N_a	0.075		0.209	0.204	0.062	0.139
N_l	0.155	0.209		0.226	0.113	0.191
N_s	0.146	0.204	0.226		0.056	0.211
N_b	0.015	0.062	0.113	0.056		0.012
N_g	0.225	0.139	0.191	0.211	0.012	

Table 2: Cross-correlations (Pearson's r) between per-user counts of friends (N_f), annotations (N_a), loved tracks (N_l), scrobbles (N_s), banned tracks (N_b), and groups (N_g). In all cases $P \ll 0.0001$

5.2 Folksonomy Attributes

Table 3 presents several high-level measures of the two folksonomies. P denotes the prolific-tagger folksonomy, and NP denotes the non-prolific tagger folksonomy. With these global measures as our starting point, we can ask several concrete questions about the attributes of P and NP.

Do both groups use a similar global vocabulary? The non-prolific taggers clearly have a larger vocabulary overall, but note that both groups' vocabularies are largely shared:

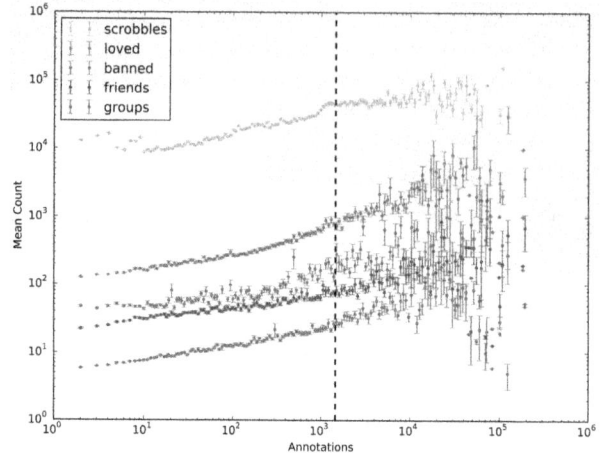

Figure 3: Users' mean number of scrobbles, loved tracks, banned tracks, friends and groups as a function of logarithmically binned annotation count. Error bars show +/- 1 SE, and the vertical line shows the prolific/non-prolific tagger threshold.

Though NP contains almost two times the tags of P, more than 90% of all annotations by both groups use one of the 168,245 tags the groups share (i.e. tags that occurred at least once in both folksonomies). This suggests the existence of many "singletons" — tags used only once, or a small number of times. This is verified in Figure 4A, which shows the distribution of annotation counts by tag for both groups.

The solid points in Figure 4A show, for a given number of annotations N, the proportion of unique tags in each folksonomy that are used N total times (i.e. having that many annotations). Clearly, more tags are used once overall than any other frequency for both P and NP. P does show, however, proportionally more tags with larger annotation counts (it follows that NP, which contains more unique tags than P, has a greater raw number of true singletons and other tags used a small number of times). This is an unsurprising result, given the very different number of users in each group. The crosses on the plot show the proportion of total annotations corresponding to a given N; that is, for a given N, the corresponding dot shows what proportion of tags were used N times, while the cross shows the combined propotion of annotations from all tags with N annotations. The most popular tags (far right of plot) represent the greatest overall contribution to the folksonomies, while the combined annotations of the many rarely used tags outweigh the contribution of the tags in between, creating a U-shaped relationship. P does have, however, more tags in this middle range (i.e. tags used 100 − 10000 times).

In Figure 4B we show how this same data is distributed over users: For a given N, what proportion of tags (within each folksonomy) are used by N users? Consistent with the first plot, more tags are used by a single user than by any other number of users for both folksonomies. We again plot the corresponding annotation proptions, which show a similar U-shaped pattern. This indicates that annotations are concentrated among the few most popular tags (in this case defined in terms of number of users instead of total annotations) and the many tags used by the fewest users.

	P	NP
Total Users	5,086	516,694
Total Tags	399,552	797,784
Unique Tags	231,307	629,539
Shared Tags	168,245	
Total Items	2,992,046	2,515,070
Unique Items	1,962,523	1,485,547
Shared Items	1,029,523	

Table 3: Summary measures of prolific- and non-prolific tagger folksonomies.

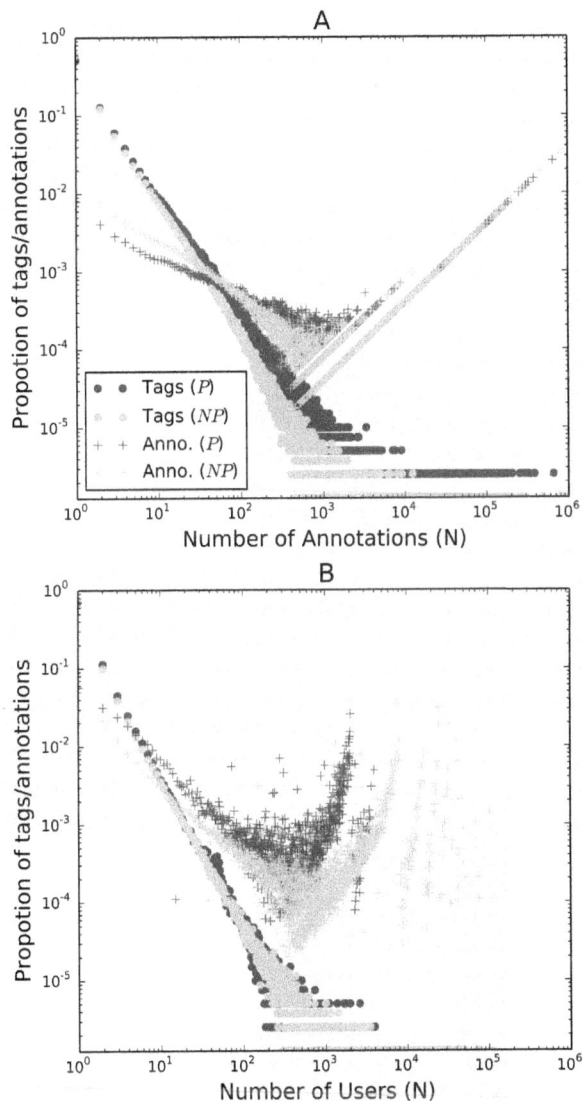

Figure 4: Log-log probability distributions of number of unique *tags* with N total annotations (A) and N total users (B), marked with dots. Crosses indicate the corresponding proportions of total *annotations* from tags with the corresponding annotation/user count.

Two simple summary measures of the similarity between P and NP are the rank correlation, Spearman's ρ, of tags for each folksonomy (i.e. is the rank order of overall tag popularity the same in both distributions) and the cosine similarity between the two global tag vocabularies (i.e. calculated across vectors of the frequency of each tag in each of the two folksonomies). Considering all tags, we find a rank correlation $\rho = -0.219$ and a cosine similarity of 0.8719 between P and NP. These give rather opposing impressions of the distribution similarities, so it is informative to consider these measures for smaller subsets of the data. We calculated both measures for the top N tags in both folksonomies, and in Figure 5 plot the results as a function of increasing N[5]. We find that the rank correlation coefficient is maximized by only considering the top 225 tags from each folksonomy, yielding $R = 0.836$. Considering more tags leads to monotonic decreases in ρ. The cosine similarity does increase as we consider more tags, but only marginally (for the top 225 tags the cosine similarity is .8713). These results indicate that there are substantial differences in the use of the many, rare tags in the tail of the distribution (hence the decreasing ρ past the top 225 tags), but that these do little to affect the overall similarity of the two vocabularies. The lower ρ and decreasing cosine similarity when considering fewer than the top 225 tags shows, however, that there are non-negligible differences in the most popular tags used by the two groups.

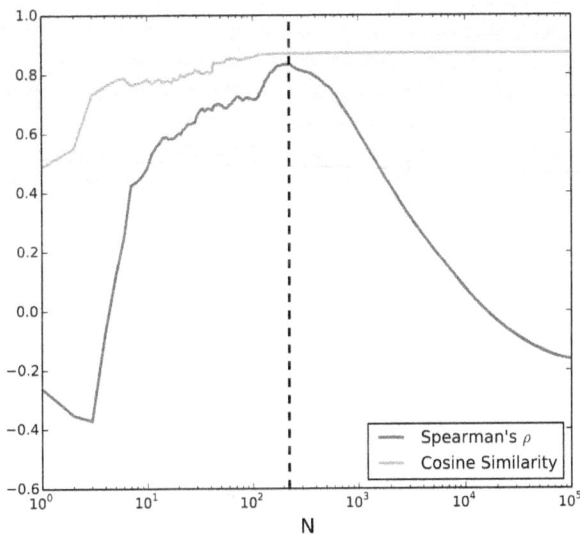

Figure 5: Spearman's ρ and cosine similarity between P and NP as a function of N, considering only the top N most popular tags overall from each folksonomy. The dashed line shows $N = 225$.

Do both groups tag the same content? P clearly covers a larger number of items than does NP, but the overlap is substantial, with 72.6 and 83.7 percent, respectively, of the annotations in P and NP allocated to items tagged by both groups. The higher percentage for NP suggests that they are concentrating their tagging on popular items more so than P. To better understand these patterns, we repli-

[5] As an example for clarification, if $N = 100$, we consider the top 100 most frequent tags in each folksonomy. Tags that appear in P but not NP (and vice versa) are assumed to have rank $N + 1$ for the purposes of calculating the rank correlation. This was repeated for N from 1 to 100000.

cate the analyses shown in in Figures 4 and 5 for items as opposed to tags.

In Figure 6A and B we see that, just as many *tags* are only used once, many *items* are tagged only once. Unlike the tags, however, we do not find highly-annotated items with combined totals of annotations rivaling those of the singleton items. In other words, for neither P nor NP is the item distribution as skewed as the overall tag distribution.

The notable differences between the folksonomies is that annotations in P are skewed towards items with proportionally fewer total items and taggers, suggesting that prolific taggers not only tag more items, but preferentially tag less popular, more obscure music. We confirm this in Figure 6C, plotting the mean number of annotations for items with a given *global* number of scrobbles (i.e. across all users). Though there is a general trend of items with more scrobbles attracting more annotations, there is clear pattern of users in P allocating more annotations to items with low scrobble counts.

We also repeat the cosine similarity and rank correlation measurements at the item level. That is, we calculate the rank correlation and cosine similarity over the distributions of items tagged (as opposed to tag vocabularies) for both folksonomies. Calculated over the entireties of P and NP, we find a rank correlation of $R = 0.216$, and a cosine similarity of 0.768, but considering smaller subsets of the data is again informative. Figure 7 shows cosine similarities and rank correlations between the folksonomies when only considering the top N most tagged items overall. There is clearly greater disagreement between P and NP when it comes to which items are tagged than which tags are used. The rank correlation peaks at 0.540 when considering the top 944 items, while the corresponding cosine similarity is 0.760. These results indicate that the overall differences between P and NP with respect to items tagged are more extreme than differences with respect to the tags used. Furthermore, there is relatively greater deviance in the top tagged items within each group as compared to the top used tags. In other words, prolific and non-prolific taggers agree more regarding what the most popular tags are than regarding what the most popular (or, at least, tag-deserving) items are.

5.3 Information Theoretic Measures

In addition to traditional statistical methods, we examined several information theoretic differences between P and NP. These metrics enable us to express differences not just in *what* is being tagged, but in *how* they are being tagged. Combined with a time-dependent analysis of cumulative tagging behaviors, we can also see if the prolific and non-prolific populations diverge as the folksonomies grow.

Are tags generated by prolific taggers more informative than those generated by non-prolific taggers? To answer this question, we calculated naive Shannon entropy for items and tags, as defined below:

$$H(T) = - \sum_i p(i) \log p(i)$$

where $p(i)$ is the ratio of appearances of that entity to the total number of annotations. The results are shown in Table 4. We see that the tags provided by the prolific and non-prolific taggers have roughly equivalent uncertainty with slightly higher uncertainty for the prolific taggers. Given

that there are 399,552 tags used by the prolific taggers and 797,784 tags used by the non-prolific taggers (see Table 3), the roughly equivalent entropy shows that each tag contains roughly equivalent information, no matter how often it is used. Similarly, the item entropy is higher for the prolific taggers (with 2,992,046 items tagged by the prolific group and 2,515,070 items tagged by the non-prolific group), consistent with the greater diversity of items observed in Section 5.2.

	P	NP
tag	11.7548	11.2922
item	19.2823	17.8425

Table 4: Entropy of each annotation component for the prolific and non-prolific folksonomies.

Does the behavior of each population change over time? To answer this question, we calculated the monthly Kullback-Leibler (KL) divergence for the cumulative folksonomies for both the items tagged and the tags used. KL divergence is also known as the "relative entropy" and can be interpreted as the amount of information gained by using the distribution A instead of B. It is formally defined as:

$$D_{KL}(A||B) = \sum_i \ln \left(\frac{A(i)}{B(i)} \right) A(i)$$

KL divergence is asymmetric, which allows us to tell if one distribution is mimicking the other. If a distribution has a low divergence relative to another, it requires little information to transcode into the other distribution. A higher divergence indicated that more bits are required to store the same amount of information in the second distribution. If these divergence scores differ widely between distributions, the direction with a lower divergence indicates that the other set has a better fit to the underlying information. KL divergence is often used in a modeling context, in which the second distribution is a model, and the first distribution is the observed data. As opposed to a correlative measure, it is able to show changes in *how* items are tagged as opposed to *what* items are tagged.

Thus, we calculated KL in both directions ($P \rightarrow NP$ and $NP \rightarrow P$) and only over elements (items or tags) contained in both populations at that point in time. For tagging divergence, we calculated the cumulative divergence at each time step by creating a new folksonomy P_m and NP_m which consisted of all annotations containing tags present in both folksonomies up to that point of time. Thus, annotations which were previously excluded may be included once a given time step is reached. Figure 8 shows the results. Similarly, monthly folksonomies were generated based on the intersection of item annotations. Item folksonomies may have non-intersecting tags, and tag folksonomies may have non-intersecting items.

We found that for tags (solid lines) the KL divergence grew over time, indicating that the ability of each population to fully capture the other's annotations decreased. Furthermore, as the $P \rightarrow NP$ non-prolific divergence was larger than the $NP \rightarrow P$ divergence, highlighting that the prolific taggers were generating a schema that more closely matched the communal tag usage than the non-prolific taggers. This emphasizes some of the expertise effects noted

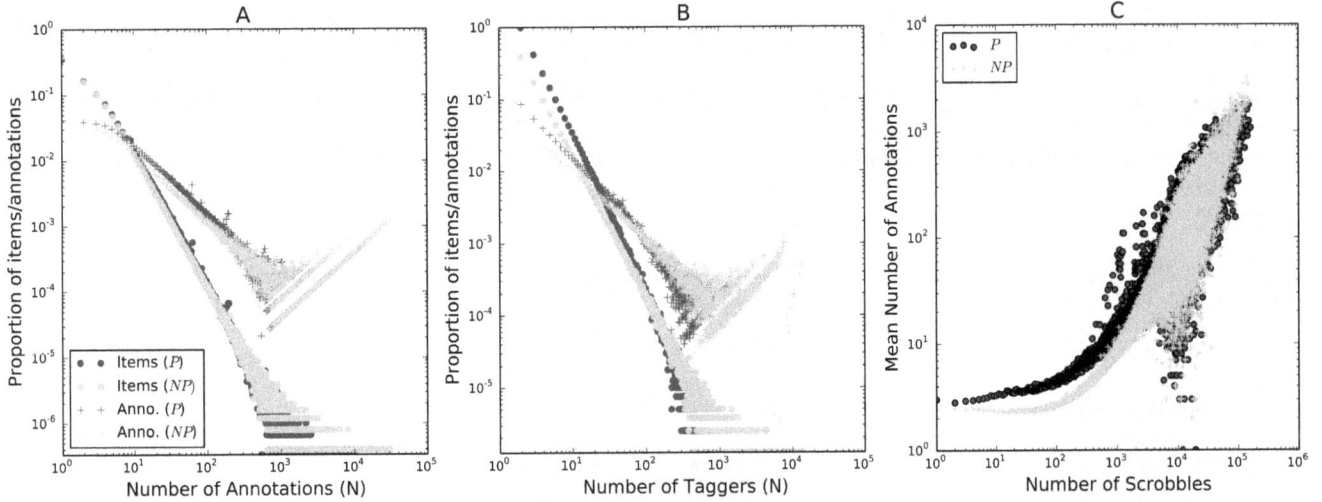

Figure 6: Log-log probability distributions of number of *items* with N total annotations (A) and N total taggers (B), marked with dots. Crosses indicate the corresponding proportions of total *annotations* assigned to items with the corresponding annotation/user count. C shows the mean number of annotations for items with a given global scrobble count.

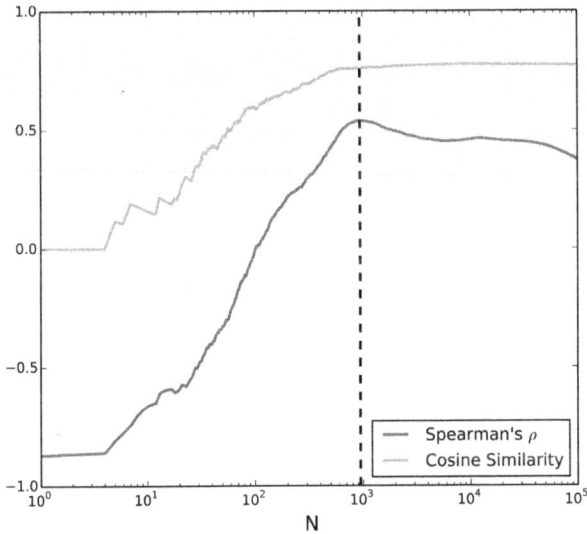

Figure 7: Spearman's ρ and cosine similarity between P and NP as a function of N, considering only the top N items from each folksonomy. The dashed line shows $N = 943$.

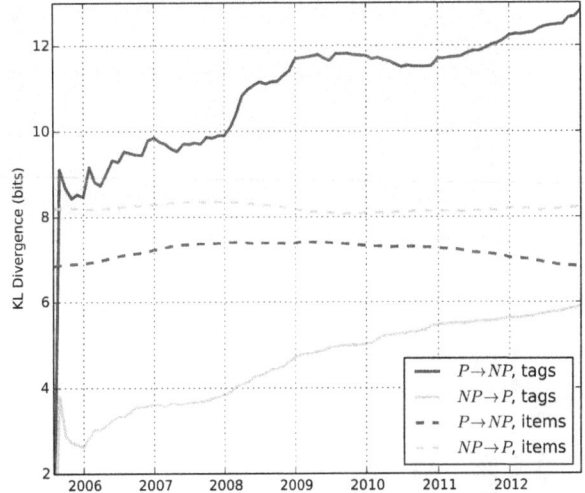

Figure 8: Kullback-Leibler (KL) divergence between P and NP, calculated over tags (solid lines) and items (dashed lines).

below in Section 6.1. However, for items (dashed lines), the KL divergence stayed fairly consistent, indicating that the types of objects annotated were equally accessible to either population.

6. POSSIBLE CAUSAL FACTORS

6.1 Expertise Effects

To measure expertise, we implemented the SPEAR algorithm using its associated package in Python. Briefly, SPEAR works as follows. For every tag t, there are two corresponding vectors: E, a vector of expertise scores of users annotating with t, i.e. $E = (e1; e2; \ldots; e_M)$, and Q, a vector of quality scores for items annotated with tag t, i.e. $Q = (q1; q2; \ldots; q_N)$, where M and N are the total number of users and items associated with t, respectively. From this, an adjacency matrix A of size $M \times N$ is constructed, where $A_{m,n} = 1 + k$ if user m had assigned a tag to item n, and k users had assigned tags to item n after user m, and $A_{m,n} = 0$ otherwise. Thus, if user m was the first to tag item n, $A_{m,n}$ would be set to the total number of users who tag resource n; but if user m was the last one, then $A_{m,n}$ would be set to 1. Following recommendations by [22, 23], the value of $A_{m,n}$ was adjusted by the square root function, such that $A_{m,n} = \sqrt{A_{m,n}}$. Then, user expertise scores per tag are derived by $E = Q \times A^T$.

135

In computing user expertise scores, we included the first 5,000 most popular tags of the entire folksonomy. In doing so, we obtain a set of 908,494 total across 5,086 users in P, and a set of 5,060,983 expertise scores across 516,694 users in NP. A majority of these expertise scores exhibit an apparent floor effect, with nearly all values less than 0.1. In fact, only 4317 (0.475%) and 587 (0.011%) expertise scores from 1358 users in P and 561 users in NP, respectively, are above 0.1. Thus, a much larger proportion of users from P (27%) have non-negliglbile expertise scores as compared to users in NP (0.1%). In order to get a clearer picture of the distribution of expertise across the two folksonomies of users, we only show scores above this threshold. In addition, we do not compute average expertise scores by user, reflecting the intuition that being an expert in one or several tags does not necessitate being an expert in most or all tags.

Figure 9 presents the distribution of expertise values across P and NP. The differences are most striking in the extremes of expertise scores. A greater proportion of expertise scores in NP are clustered towards the lower end of the range of expertise scores. In contrast, a greater proportion of expertise scores in P are clustered towards the higher end of the range of expertise scores. To reiterate, the SPEAR algorithm assigns higher expertise scores per tag to users annotating quality items (i.e. items more associated with a given tag) more often and earlier than other users. Therefore, the results suggest that users in P are more adept than users in NP at identifying and annotating quality items associated with the 5000 most popular tags.

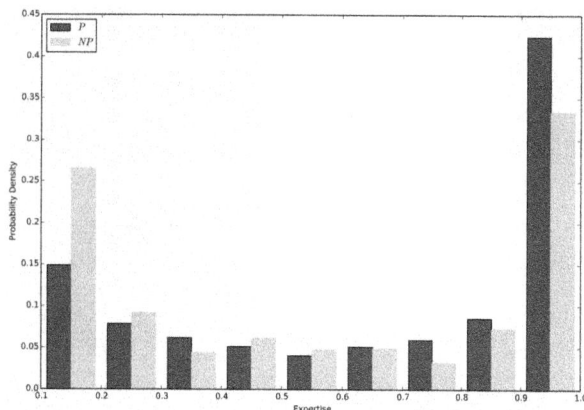

Figure 9: Histogram of all expertise scores exceeding 0.1 for P and NP

6.2 Motivational Effects

To quantify user motivations along the describer-categorizer spectrum, we employed three common metrics: tags per post (TPP), tag/resource ratio (TRR), and the orphan ratio (OR). TPP measures a user's number of total annotations to the total number of annotated items. We expect describers to, on average, annotate items with a greater number of tags and thus score higher on this measure. TRR compares the size of a user's tag vocabulary to the total number of annotated items. We expect categorizers to maintain a constricted vocabulary, and thus score lower on this measure. OR compares a user's number of seldom used tags to the tag vocabulary. We expect describers to be minimally motivated to reuse tags, and thus score higher on this measure.

Though there exist other measures, we limit our analyses to these three in light of previous research reporting high correlations between TPP, TRR, OR, and other measures [25]. For full details on the calculations of each measure, see [9].

Figure 10 present, as function of total annotations N, the TPP, TRR, and OR scores for P and NP. As is evident in Figure 10A, user TPP scores increase as total annotations increase. This suggests that P are not simply annotating more items than NP; rather, P are, on average, annotating any given item with more tags than are NP. Similarly, Figure 10C presents a trend of increasing OR scores as total annotations increase. As such, P appear to have far more orphaned tags in their vocabulary than do NP. These two results indicate that P is populated with a far greater number of describers than is NP.

Figure 10B presents an anomaly then to the above interpretation. Indeed, it presents an unclear, if not negative, relationship between total user annotations and TRR. If greater TRR scores are representative of describers, then the TRR scores are contrary to the TPP and OR scores described above. We believe the discrepancy can be resolved, however, by looking at the relation between total items annotated and the size of user tag vocabularies. For NP, there is a strong correlation of 0.522 between these two values across users; this correlation decreases dramatically to 0.143 for P. This is in line with the results of Cattuto and Baldassarri [2] who report sub-linear growth of user tag vocabularies as compared to total annotated items, perhaps reflecting a saturation point in user tag vocabularies. In sum then, the results suggest that P and NP differ in tagging motivations, where P is populated with more describers than NP.

7. DISCUSSION AND CONCLUSIONS

The principal contributions of this work are the following:

- A formalization of the disproportionate contribution by "supertaggers" to a folksonomy;

- an analysis of the differences between these prolific taggers and their non-prolific counterparts, at the levels of the users themselves and the folksonomic structures they generate; and

- analysis of how these two groups of taggers differ in terms of established measures of expertise and tagging motivation.

Our results demonstrate that, while it is the case that they are more active across a variety of behavioral measures, the most prolific taggers are not simply generating a greater volume of annotations in a manner consistent with "the crowd". Instead, their tagging patterns quantifiably different from the non-prolific taggers. With respect to tag vocabulary, we find that both groups use many of the same most popular tags, but disagree on the long-tail of less common tags, with prolific taggers using fewer true singletons and more moderate popularity (100-10000 total annotations). With respect to items tagged, prolific taggers allocate proportionally more annotations to less popular items, while non-prolific taggers are more likely to tag more popular items. This suggests that the tagging of users in P is more exploratory, favoring items further down the long-tail of popularity instead of tagging the most popular items.

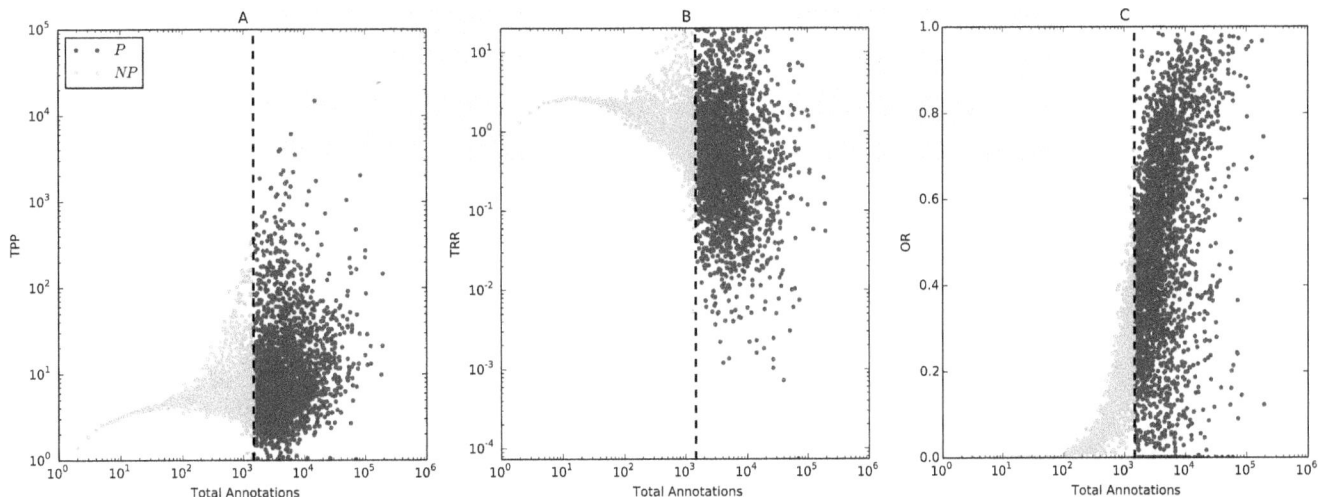

Figure 10: Scatterplots of principal categorizer/describer measures from [25], averaged over users with a given number of annotations. Shown are Tags Per Post (TPP, A), Tag-Resource Ratio (TRR, B), and Orphan Ratio (OR, C).

Though in the aggregate expertise scores from the SPEAR algorithm are low, the "supertaggers" make up a disproportionate number of those users with higher expertise scores. Furthermore, the divergence metrics presented in Section 5.3 are consistent with the SPEAR algorithm, which favors "discoverers" who tag content earlier. Finally, with respect to tagging motivation as formalized in [25], we find the prolific taggers show tagging habits more consistent with describers than categorizers.

The implications of these findings are significant. They reveal that the most prolific taggers on Last.fm exhibit behavior systematically distinct from that of the majority of the tagging population. Our results suggest that the minority of prolific taggers annotate more obscure items using more describer-like vocabularies, and the non-prolific taggers annotate more popular content with categorizer-like vocabularies. This, combined with our information theoretic analyses, challenges the notion that collaborative tagging truly captures the "wisdom of the crowd" in the traditional sense of the term. Whether or not this is "good" for the folksonomy is an entirely different question, however. It may be the case that such a "division of labor" between prolific and non-prolific taggers serves to generate a more usable semantic structure than would be created by users with more homogenized tagging strategies. Addressing this question (e.g. via multi-agent modeling) is a promising direction for future research that is beyond the scope of this paper.

There are, of course, unaddressed complexities at play here. It could be the case, for instance, that the measured differences in motivation of "supertaggers" are partly a function of their tagging more obscure items. This might occur if more obscure items do not fit canonical musical categories and demand multiple classifications such that users tagging them appear more like describers than categorizers, even when this does not reflect a fundamental motivational difference. Relatedly, the motivations of "supertaggers" may not reflect internal, stable user traits but may instead result from interacting with the folksonomy over time. By virtue of discovering more obscure items through increasing use,

users' motivations may transition from resembling categorizer to describer behavior for the reasons described above. There also is the question of spam tagging, which we did not address here, other than to use the SPEAR expertise assessment methods to avoid spam tagging problems. Effective identification and elimination of prolific spam taggers might shift the dominance in annotation counts away from the most prolific taggers. A final issue is that the two folksonomies we analyzed here are not independent; a user we have classified as "prolific" could certainly see and be influenced by tags assigned by a non-prolific user, and vice versa. A possible approach to address this would be to only consider items uniquely tagged by users in one folksonomy or the other (i.e. for P, limit analysis to those items tagged *only* by users in P, and vice versa), but more work is needed to determine if and how this might alter our conclusions.

Other future work will need to examine a number of issues, including methods for for identifying more formally what constitutes a "supertagger" and determining other relevant metrics along which these users may differ from the general tagging population. It will also be important to replicate these analyses on more datasets from different tagging systems, to help determine if the patterns observed are idiosyncratic aspects of Last.fm or common across tagging systems in general. At a minimum, we would expect different dynamics in tagging systems with differing (or non-existent) tag recommendation functionality [24], a feature prominent on Last.fm

Nevertheless, our work presents compelling evidence that the bulk of tagging activity comes from a minority of users. Moreover, the tagging patterns of this unique minority are quantifiably distinct from other users. Thus, it is important for both researchers and designers of collaborative tagging systems to identify and differentially interpret the metadata generated by these "supertaggers".

8. REFERENCES

[1] M. Ames and M. Naaman. Why we tag: motivations for annotation in mobile and online media. In *SIGCHI conference on Human factors in computing systems*, pages 971–980. ACM, 2007.

[2] C. Cattuto, A. Baldassarri, V. D. P. Servedio, and V. Loreto. Vocabulary growth in collaborative tagging systems. *ArXiv e-prints*, Apr. 2007.

[3] S. A. Golder and B. A. Huberman. Usage patterns of collaborative tagging systems. *Journal of Information Science*, 32(2):198–208, Apr. 2006.

[4] P. Heymann, G. Koutrika, and H. Garcia-Molina. Can social bookmarking improve web search? In *Proceedings of the international conference on Web search and web data mining - WSDM '08*, pages 195–206, New York, New York, USA, 2008. ACM Press.

[5] A. Hotho, R. Jäschke, C. Schmitz, and G. Stumme. BibSonomy: A social bookmark and publication sharing system. In *Proceedings of the Conceptual Structures Tool Interoperability Workshop at the 14th International Conference on Conceptual Structures*, pages 87–102, 2006.

[6] I. Ivanov, P. Vajda, and T. Ebrahimi. In tags we trust: Trust modeling in social tagging of multimedia content. *Signal Processing Magazine, IEEE*, 29(2):98–107, 2012.

[7] J. M. Kleinberg. Authoritative sources in a hyperlinked environment. *Journal of the ACM*, 46(5):604–632, Sept. 1999.

[8] C. Körner, D. Benz, A. Hotho, and M. Strohmaier. Stop Thinking , Start Tagging : Tag Semantics Emerge from Collaborative Verbosity. In *In Proceedings of the 19th international conference on World wide web*, pages 521–530, 2010.

[9] C. Körner, R. Kern, H.-P. Grahsl, and M. Strohmaier. Of categorizers and describers: An evaluation of quantitative measures for tagging motivation. In *Proceedings of the 21st ACM conference on Hypertext and hypermedia*, pages 157–166. ACM, 2010.

[10] M. Kubek, J. Nützel, and F. Zimmerman. Automatic Taxonomy Extraction through Mining Social Networks. In *Proc. of the 8th International Workshop for Technical, Economic and Legal Aspects of Business Models for Virtual Goods*, pages 109–114, Namur, Belgium, 2010.

[11] J. Lorince and P. M. Todd. Can simple social copying heuristics explain tag popularity in a collaborative tagging system? In *Proceedings of the 5th Annual ACM Web Science Conference*, pages 215–224, Paris, France, 2013. ACM.

[12] C. Marlow, M. Naaman, D. Boyd, and M. Davis. HT06, tagging paper, taxonomy, Flickr, academic article, to read.

[13] M. E. Newman. Power laws, pareto distributions and zipf's law. *Contemporary physics*, 46(5):323–351, 2005.

[14] M. Niepert, C. Buckner, and C. Allen. A dynamic ontology for a dynamic reference work. In *Proceedings of the 7th ACM/IEEE Joint Conference on Digital Libraries (JCDL)*, pages 288–297, Vancouver, British Columbia, 2007. ACM Press.

[15] O. Nov, M. Naaman, and C. Ye. What drives content tagging: the case of photos on Flickr. In *Proceedings of the SIGCHI conference on Human factors in computing systems*, pages 1097–1100. ACM, 2008.

[16] O. Nov and C. Ye. Why do people tag? *Communications of the ACM*, 53(7):128–131, July 2010.

[17] E. Quintarelli. Folksonomies: Power to the People. In *Proceedings of the 1st International Society for Knowledge Organization (Italy) (ISKOI), UniMIB Meeting*, Milan, Italy, June 2005.

[18] R. Schifanella, A. Barrat, C. Cattuto, B. Markines, and F. Menczer. Folks in folksonomies: social link prediction from shared metadata. In *Proceedings of the third ACM international conference on Web search and data mining*, pages 271–280. ACM, 2010.

[19] M. Strohmaier, C. Körner, and R. Kern. Why do users tag? detecting users' motivation for tagging in social tagging systems. In *ICWSM*, 2010.

[20] T. Vander Wal. Folksonomy: Coinage and Definition, 2007.

[21] R. Wetzker, C. Zimmermann, and C. Bauckhage. Analyzing Social Bookmarking Systems : A del.icio.us Cookbook. In *Proceedings of the ECAI 2008 Mining Social Data Workshop.*, pages 3–7, 2008.

[22] C.-m. A. Yeung, M. G. Noll, N. Gibbins, C. Meinel, and N. Shadbolt. SPEAR: Spamming-Resistant Expertise Analysis amd Ranking in Collaborative Tagging Systems. *Computational Intelligence*, 27(3):458–488, 2009.

[23] C.-m. A. Yeung, M. G. Noll, C. Meinel, N. Gibbins, and N. Shadbolt. Measuring Expertise in Online Communities. *IEEE Intelligent Systems*, 26(1):26–32, Jan. 2011.

[24] A. Zubiaga, V. Fresno, R. Martinez, and A. P. Garcia-Plaza. Harnessing Folksonomies to Produce a Social Classification of Resources. *IEEE transactions on knowledge and data engineering*, 25(8):1801–1813, 2013.

[25] A. Zubiaga, C. Körner, and M. Strohmaier. Tags vs shelves: from social tagging to social classification. In *Proceedings of the 22nd ACM conference on Hypertext and hypermedia*, pages 93–102. ACM, 2011.

Reading the Source Code of Social Ties

Luca Maria Aiello
Yahoo Labs
Barcelona, Spain
alucca@yahoo-inc.com

Rossano Schifanella
University of Torino
Torino, Italy
schifane@di.unito.it

Bogdan State[*]
Stanford University
Palo Alto, CA, USA
bstate@stanford.edu

ABSTRACT

Though online social network research has exploded during the past years, not much thought has been given to the exploration of the nature of social links. Online interactions have been interpreted as indicative of one social process or another (e.g., status exchange or trust), often with little systematic justification regarding the relation between observed data and theoretical concept. Our research aims to breach this gap in computational social science by proposing an unsupervised, parameter-free method to discover, with high accuracy, the fundamental domains of interaction occurring in social networks. By applying this method on two online datasets different by scope and type of interaction (aNobii and Flickr) we observe the spontaneous emergence of three domains of interaction representing the exchange of status, knowledge and social support. By finding significant relations between the domains of interaction and classic social network analysis issues (e.g., tie strength, dyadic interaction over time) we show how the network of interactions induced by the extracted domains can be used as a starting point for more nuanced analysis of online social data that may one day incorporate the normative grammar of social interaction. Our methods finds applications in online social media services ranging from recommendation to visual link summarization.

Categories and Subject Descriptors

H.1.2 [**User/Machine Systems**]: Human Factors

Keywords

Computational sociology; social exchange; domains of interaction; aNobii; Flickr

1. INTRODUCTION

The explosion of data from online social media has encouraged the often uncritical adoption of the notion of *social tie* as the atomic interaction quantum of any social network structure. Social ties

[*]All authors contributed equally to this work, that was done when R. Schifanella and B. State were visiting Yahoo Labs Barcelona.

are usually treated as *a priori* entities, immediately available to the researcher from the graph of online-mediated interactions such as emailing, following on Twitter, or friending on Facebook. The social tie is indeed a powerful abstraction that has allowed researchers to build rigorous models to describe the evolution of social networks and the dynamics of information exchange [23].

Even though previous research on social networks has explored the *intensity* of social links, as well as their *polarity* [22, 34], there is still much to investigate about the *nature* of the social interactions implied by social ties. One way to overcome this limitation is to look into the *content* of social links, the *messages* exchanged between actors.

For these reasons, online *conversations* – the object of our study – have emerged as an important domain of research for social link characterization [14, 4]. Although the tools to mine the *syntactics* and *semantics* of online conversations are available and have been used extensively [39], to date there is no way to automatically capture the *pragmatics* of communication. From the angle of pragmatics, messages are not just defined by their intensity, structure or topic but can be instead interpreted as *communicative acts* that contribute to the incremental definition of the nature of the social relationship between pairs of individuals. We understand this process of construction of social ties through the lens of Social Exchange Theory [6], conceiving every dyad as a repeated set of exchanges of different types of non-material *resources* transacted in an interpersonal situation, such as knowledge, social support or manifestation of approval [18]. Being able to describe a conversation in terms of these resources would overcome[*] the limitations of the current representations of social links.

This work gives a contribution in this direction by defining a method to *discover* the types of resources exchanged in a social network and to cluster messages by the type of resource they convey, rather than by their topical aspect. Our algorithm is unsupervised and parameter-free, as the number of clusters is detected automatically and it can be applied to different languages. The algorithm is based on the intuition that in a dyad, social interactions conveying a resource tend to be reciprocated with the same resource type. As an illustration, if two individuals exchange knowledge now, their next exchange will be most likely to also involve knowledge, rather than affection. This intuition has been validated for a wide range of social interactions in both the offline [24, 2] and online world. In this work we make the following main contributions:

- We propose a novel method to cluster messages based on the type of resource they convey (§3). Using the bibliophile community aNobii and the photo sharing service Flickr as case study (§4), our algorithm yields edifying results in detecting meaningful and coherent domains of interaction when compared to a ground truth generated by human coders (§6).

- We apply our methodology to two datasets of different nature and we observe the spontaneous emergence of three main domains that are identified by as many social exchange processes, namely *status exchange*, *social support*, and *knowledge exchange* (§5).

- We provide a framework that enables a direct validation of social theories about well-known interaction types (e.g., status giving) that are difficult to test in practice with a conventional tie representation. We take on the issues of tie strength, dyadic interaction over time, and inequality of resource exchange in relation to the different domains of interaction, finding striking regularities across the two datasets (§7).

2. RELATED WORK

Online conversations. A branch of the research studying online conversations has focused on the characterization of the users based on the *conventions* they use, especially in Twitter [29, 7]. Correa *et al.* [12] conducted interviews to investigate the correlation between psychological indicators, such as emotional stability and openness to new experiences, with propensity to engage online conversations. On a similar note, Celli and Rossi [10] studied Twitter conversational data, estimated the user emotional stability from the text and correlated it with the tendency to engage conversations.

Conversations around items have been studied also in relation with the *engagement* of users in online communities. De Choundhry *et al.* [14] studied discussions around YouTube videos and estimate the thread interestingness using a random walk model. Backstrom *et al.* [4] used a machine learning model to predict the number of entries and the probability for a user to submit a new post in Twitter discussion threads. Harper *et al.* [28] interpret participation in conversations as a proxy for engagement and, to limit user churn, they proposed to send personalized and familiar invitations to join threads. Budak and Agrawal [9] studied factors that affect continued user participation in Twitter chats and identify through surveys the distinct dimensions of informational and emotional exchange in messages. Similarly, the application of our method to online datasets finds the emergence of a social support dimension.

A line of work more similar to ours was devoted to the investigation of the properties of conversations. Kumar *et al.* [33] built a model able to reproduce the size and depth of multi-user conversations in Twitter and Yahoo Groups. Java *et al.* [31] studied the *intent* behind Twitter conversations and based on that they identify different behaviours and types of users. Although informed by hub-authority computation and inspection of communities on the mention graph, their classification is ultimately performed manually. The aspect of emotions conveyed in conversations has been recently studied by Kim *et al.* [32]. They extracted LDA topics in Twitter conversations, used a framework based on the Plutchik's wheel to assign emotions to them, and analyzed the transitions between emotions in conversations. Similarly to what we find for resource exchange, they verified that a conversation that conveys a certain sentiment tends do it consistently in the following exchanges ("nice words for nice words"). Very recently, more nuanced studies have been done around online conversations, touching upon the concepts of social cohesion and social identity and their implications on group discussion divergence [38], and discussing the social power dynamics they contribute to create [44].

Link characterization. Research on characterization of social links has focused primarily on the concept of *tie strength* on *interaction* networks [45, 48]. Gilbert and Karahalios [22] used a supervised method to predict the tie strength in Facebook using textual, profile and graph structural features. We use apply their framework to characterize the average tie intensity for different social exchange processes (§7.2). Xiang *et al.* [49] addressed the same problem with an unsupervised model instead, using a latent variable model based on some profile features, assuming that the higher the profile similarity the higher the strength of the link. Grabowicz *et al.* [26] studied the strength of ties in relation with the communities in the Twitter interaction graphs and identified weak ties as the ones towards community intermediaries. Besides link strength, research has been done on the sign of edges in network with positive and negative links (e.g., Slashdot) mostly in the direction of link sign prediction [34]. So far, little attention has been devoted to characterize the type of social links according to sociological dimensions, and recent work on the accommodation of linguistic styles according to power differentials provides an example of the intellectual opportunities now available at the intersection of social theory and conversational data [13]. A step to fill that gap has been recently done by Bramsen *et al.* [8], who have introduced a supervised approach to identify social power relationships in social dyads using ad-hoc texual features. Our method provides a means for the discovery of multiple kinds of social exchange in an unsupervised way, rather than limiting the interaction to status exchange.

3. METHODOLOGY

3.1 Problem Definition

The general problem we address is defined as follows.
Input: a population of users U and a set of messages M where each message $m_{u,v}^t \in M$ is a textual communication between source $u \in U$ and destination $v \in U$ at time t.
Output: a probabilistic clustering of messages in M with probability of a message m to be assigned to cluster D being $p(m, D) \geq 0$.

The novel aspect of the method is the nature of the clusters in output, that do not group together messages based on their topical aspects, but instead according to the type of social exchange those messages convey. The algorithm is composed by four phases: 1) preprocessing and distillation of the raw text messages, 2) clustering of messages in buckets according to their textual similarity, 3) creation of a conversation graph that models the transitions between buckets during social interactions, and 4) extraction of dense portions of the conversation graph through a community detection algorithm. We will describe in details each step in the following sections.

3.2 Preprocessing

We apply to the raw text a series of filters commonly used in information retrieval. The filters include the removal of non-alphanumeric strings, stopwords, and very frequent and infrequent terms, namely those who appear in more than 60% and less than 1% of the corpus. To reduce inflected forms to their root we apply a stemming algorithm. After a tokenization phase, a message representation is expanded with the insertion of bi-grams and tri-grams to take into account the discriminative power of sequences over single terms (e.g., the bigram *"great shot"* is more informative than the individual terms *great* and *shot*).

The adoption of n-grams can lead to an explosion of the dimensionality of the feature space and, in a practical scenario, an upper bound based on term frequency is needed. We consider only the most frequent 10,000 n-grams with $n \in [1...3]$ and we filter out messages that do not contain elements in that vocabulary (less of 1.5% for both corpora).

The vector of stemmed terms representing the messages are stacked in a *term-document matrix* $\Gamma_{m \times n} : w_{ij}$ where m is the number of terms in the vocabulary and n is the number of messages in the corpus. A generic element w_{ij} reflects the importance of the corresponding term i with respect to the semantics of message j and it is calculated with a standard TF-IDF weighting scheme with sublinear TF scaling. This matrix is the only input to the next stages of the pipeline.

3.3 Message Bucketing

Modern social media convey a huge volume of information through the interactions between users. Modeling these dynamics as message-to-message communication process can raise practical issues due to the dimensionality of the data flow. Moreover, conversations are often characterized by variations of recurrent patterns that use similar sentences and words for conveying the object of the conversation. For instance, greetings in an online community could be coded in different variations (e.g., *"Hi, how are you?"* or *"Hello, how do you do?"*). These observations suggest the possibility to model conversations not as transitions between single messages but instead as transitions between classes of homogeneous messages.

To this extent, we leverage a probabilistic generative model based on a low rank *Non-negative Matrix Factorization (NMF)* method to cluster messages in coherent groups according to their textual content. We name these homogeneous clusters *message buckets*. NMF has been successfully used in document clustering [50] and topic detection tasks [3] and it allows a part-based representation where a document is modeled as an additive combinations of topics vectors due to the non-negativity constraint. In a text mining framework, this property differentiates NMF from other existing matrix decomposition approaches like *Singular Value Decomposition (SVD)* or *Principal Component Analysis (PCA)* that force a document to belong to a single topic or are able to recover only the span of the topic vectors instead of the topic vectors themselves [3].

The NMF model is able to factor the previously defined non-negative *term-document matrix* $\Gamma_{m \times n} : w_{ij}$ into two matrices $W_{m \times k}$ and $H_{k \times n}$ such that $\Gamma = WH + e$, where e is a $m \times n$ matrix of approximation errors, and where $k \ll m$. In short, entries of the matrix W represent the probability of each of the m terms to belong to each of the k buckets, whereas the matrix H embeds the probability of each bucket to include each of the n messages. This approach fits well into the assumption that a message can convey multiple informational units and then belong to different buckets. The matrix decomposition enables the definition of two functions:

1. $\mathscr{B}(H, m_i)$, maps a message m_i into the set of most representative buckets,

2. $\mathscr{T}(W, b_i, n)$, maps a bucket b_i into the set of n most characterizing terms.

The choice of the number of buckets k is generally application-dependent. Many different methods for evaluating the optimal number of underlying components k have been developed in this context [19]. In particular, we use an iterative approach that selects the k that minimizes the *Frobenius norm* of the error matrix e.

3.4 Building The Conversation Graph

To shape the conversational aspect of between-user interactions, we introduce the concept of *Conversation Graph* – a weighted directed graph where nodes are buckets and edges represent transitions between buckets determined by the conversational flow. Intuitively, an edge (i, j) captures the following notion: given a message from ego to alter classified in bucket i, what is the likelihood that alter will reply back to ego with a message in bucket j?

Consider a dyad involving users u and v and the time-ordered sequence of messages between them, that is part of the algorithm's

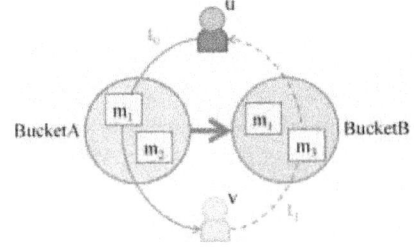

Figure 1: Example of construction of the Conversation Graph from conversation data.

input. We define a *transition* $t_{uv} = (m_{uv}^{t_0}, m_{vu}^{t_1}), t_0 < t_1$ to be a pair of two consecutive mutual messages sent between user u and v. Similarly to web browsing session analysis, a threshold on the the elapsed time between messages could be used to avoid considering transitions between messages sent with a big temporal gap between each other, and therefore likely to be part of two separate conversations. However, such threshold could vary significantly depending on the medium (e.g., longer time could elapse in email conversations than in instant messaging) and even on the specific user pair, so to keep our approach as general as possible we do not introduce this filtering step.

With this definition in mind, we create the Conversation Graph following these steps:

- For each pair of users u and v we extract the set of transitions T_{uv} between them.

- For each transition $t \in T_{uv}$, with $t = (m_x, m_y)$, we derive the sets of most representative buckets using the function defined in §3.3. We obtain $\mathscr{B}(H, m_x) = B_i$ and $\mathscr{B}(H, m_y) = B_j$.

- $\forall b_i \in B_i$ and $\forall b_j \in B_j$ with $b_i \neq b_j$ we add a directed edge $b_i \rightarrow b_j$ with weight $w_{ij} \in [0, 1]$ that is proportional to the probability of the messages m_x and m_y to belong to the corresponding buckets. Such weights are extracted from the matrix H computed in §3.3.

The process of construction of the Conversation Graph is illustrated in Figure 1. In the example, a user u writes a message m_1, belonging to bucket A, to user v and gets as reply a message m_3, belonging to bucket B. This interaction implies that there is a conversational transition from messages in A to messages in B, and a directed arc between them is created accordingly.

3.5 Extracting Domains of Interaction

The Conversation Graph shapes the transition between classes of coherent messages during social interactions. We conceive these interactions as the realizations of underlying processes of social resources exchange and we assume that a message that conveys a certain type of resource will most likely get a reply that conveys the same resource type.

In offline social networks the propensity to reciprocal interactions has been derived as a theoretical necessity in the exchange of status [24] and has been shown to exist empirically in the case of social support [2]. Moreover, in the online world reciprocity has been found to exist for a wide range of social interactions [32].

Our work does not make the assumption that reciprocity is ubiquitous in human interactions. Rather, we follow previous work in assuming that if reciprocation is observed, then the reciprocal interaction will be likely in the same social domain (e.g., of status exchange, or of social support, etc.) as the initial interaction. For instance, we would expect a person who receives social support for the loss of a grieving relative ("I'm sorry for your loss") to reply in kind (if at all) with another social support interaction ("Thank you for being a good friend") rather than a status-exchange interaction ("You're such a great photographer!"). Indeed, we verify this assumption in our experimental setting, which yields coherent domains of interaction for two independent datasets (see §6).

Under this interpretation, highly-clustered parts of the Conversation Graph aggregate buckets that carry homogeneous patterns of social exchange and will have fewer edges connecting them to the rest of the graph. This scenario is consistent with the most common definition of graph *community* [20], therefore network community detection algorithms could be applied to the Conversation Graph to discover these dense areas. In our experiments we use the the Spinglass algorithm [40] available in the igraph library.

We name *Domains of Interaction* (DoIs) the communities given as output by the community detection algorithm, as in our conception they contain messages that belong to a domain in which the resources exchanged during interactions tend to be homogeneous. The final output of the community detection step is a fuzzy assignment of messages to a set of DoIs: every message is assigned to every DoI that includes at least one bucket containing that message, with a probability equal to the maximum probability of the message belonging to one of those buckets.

The algorithm is fully unsupervised, but it does not allow us to assign labels to the extracted domains. The interpretation of the nature of the domain is admittedly a task that is hard to accomplish automatically and social-scientific input is necessary to provide *qualitative* insights into the algorithm's findings, combining the emerging clustering with social theory. Next (§4) we present the details of the two datasets we used to test our method and after that (§5) we describe the application of our method to them and the process of interpretation of the domains we obtained.

4. DATASETS

We test our framework on datasets extracted from two social media: aNobii, a website for book lovers, and Flickr, the popular image sharing website. Both have similar mechanisms for the creation of social connections: social ties are directed and, similarly to the "following" relation available in other mainstream social media, they allow users to receive all the updates of the profiles they are linked with. Social links can be created towards any other user, without the need of any authorization. Peculiar aspects of the two networks are discussed next.

aNobii. User profiles in aNobii are centered around a personal digital library containing the titles the users have read. The main channel of interaction is the public messaging activity: every profile page contains a public *shoutbox* where any user can leave a message and see the messages written by others. It is common practice for pairs of users to engage conversations by writing on each other's shoutbox. We use a public aNobii dataset recently released to the public [1] and we model conversations through a *communication graph* where nodes are users and directed arcs represent the messages exchanged between them. Users write in different languages, but the biggest community is the Italian one, accounting for around 35% of the user base and for 76% of the message traffic. A cross-language analysis is outside the scope of this work, so we focus on the Italian community only. We consider all the messages (around $1M$) exchanged over the $\sim 545k$ unique pairs of Italian users between year 2006 and end of year 2011.

Flickr. Differently from aNobii, Flickr does not provide any tool for sending direct public messages between users, therefore communication is mainly mediated by the activity of photo comment-

	Users	Conversations	$conv_{len}$	msg_{len}
aNobii	62,235	545,656	1.75 (1)	18.75 (13)
Flickr	95,397	100,000	10.84 (3)	6.90 (5)

Table 1: Size of the two datasets, average value and median (in paranthesis) of message length (number of tokens) and conversation length (number of messages).

ing: a pair of users can either initiate a communication thread by commenting under a user's photo or by writing comments on each other's photos. Although both are possible, we consider the second option only. This choice appears reasonable first because, even if the direct target of the comment is the photo, its main recipient is always the photo owner, who is the only one being explicitly notified of the new comment. Additionally, since a Flickr persona is defined mainly by its photos, writing on a photo is a quite common practice to convey a message directly to the owner, as observed in previous studies on item-mediated communication [35]. On the other hand, the first option is not practical because identifying the communication flow (who is writing to whom) in a thread with potentially many commenters is an arduous task [42], and the assumption of a message being always delivered in broadcast to all the thread participants would be an unacceptable oversimplification.

Similarly to aNobii, we model the interactions with a communication graph, arcs of which go from the commenters to the owners of the commented photos. To get a sample of conversations, we randomly selected 100k anonymized user pairs who commented on each other's photos at least once. For each of these pairs we collect the full history of their comment exchange, getting around 2M messages in total.

A summary of some basic quantities of the two dataset is provided in Table 1. Although they share commonalities, Flickr and aNobii are quite different domains for scope and norms of interaction, beginning with the different ways of exchanging messages (direct vs. item-mediated). This difference is already surfaced by basic statistics such as the average message length, that is way lower in Flickr. Given the short length of Flickr messages, we assume the likelihood of a message conveying multiple resources will be low. For this reason, in the case of Flickr we don't consider a probabilistic assignment of message to buckets, but instead we assign each message to the most likely bucket.

5. EXTRACTION OF DOMAINS OF INTERACTION

We apply the methodology described in §3 to both datasets, thus obtaining a mapping of each message to DoIs. The Conversation Graph of message buckets is depicted in Figure 2. The optimal number of buckets k we found for aNobii and Flickr (as determined by the error computed on the output of the NFM algorithm described in §3.3) are 350 and 250 respectively, but we also verified the DoIs boundaries to be resilient to significant changes of k. The Spinglass community detection algorithm yields three distinct communities in aNobii and two in Flickr.

For illustration we show in Table 2 the most representative terms for the five domains, selected by summing the weights of the terms in each bucket. To get a first interpretation of their nature, we have shown the most frequent terms and a sample of messages from each cluster to a sociologist. This inspection suggests that the three domains in aNobii correspond to as many fundamental processes of social exchange: *Knowledge exchange*, *Status exchange*, and *Social Support*. Accordingly, in Flickr analogous domains emerge, with the exception of the one related to knowledge exchange.

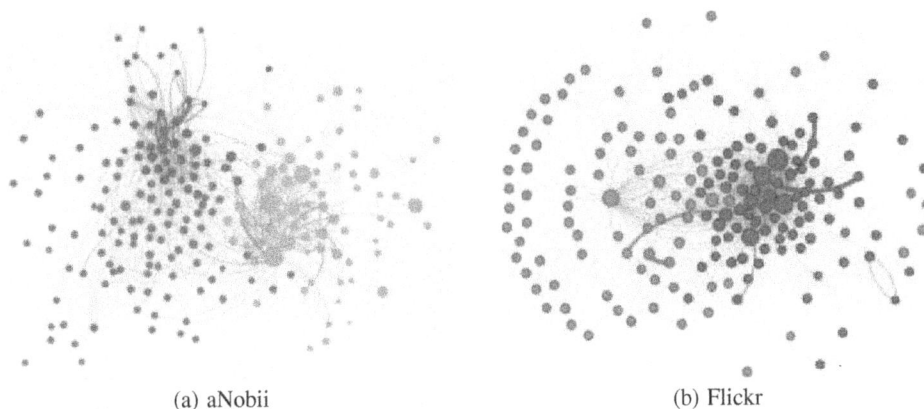

	(a) aNobii	(b) Flickr

Figure 2: Conversation Graphs. Nodes represent message buckets and edges the transitions between them. Colors encode the Domains of Interaction of *Social Support* (red), *Status Exchange* (green), and *Knowledge Exchange* (blue). Edge thickness is proportional to the weighted number of transitions between buckets and the size of nodes is proportional to the number of messages in the bucket. Graph layout is arranged according to the Yifan-Hu algorithm, edges with low weight are not displayed. Graph drawing powered by gephi.org.

	DoI	Most representative tokens
aNobii	Status	neighbor · library · like · congratulations · visit
	Support	wish · dear · good day · greeting · friend · soon
	Knowledge	book · read · know · think · advice
Flickr	Status	beautiful · wonderful · photo · capture · great shot
	Support	guy · haha · year · happy · lol · day

Table 2: Selection of the most representative words (and *n*-grams) in the DoIs, according to the NMF weighting. For the sake of presentation, stems used in NMF are inflected and then translated from Italian in the case of aNobii.

Albeit we do not consider this classification to be exhaustive of all the possible types of interaction, and many other kinds of resources could spawn other forms of social exchange [18, 16], we see social exchange processes occurring in these domains as essential for the development of most social ties, especially in the wide context of online, task-oriented communities.

Next we report an interpretation of the three domains found, along with some representative messages.

5.1 Status exchange

In most social contexts the possession of resources is often non-uniformly distributed across the actors. In a task-oriented online social network, for example, some people can own more items (photos, books, social contacts) than others, and the distribution of item possession is usually heavy-tailed. According to the Power-Dependence Theory [11], this heterogeneity of resource endowments in a dyadic relationship leads to *power imbalances* and a situation of power inequality induces a behavior that may bring the relationship closer to a more balanced state. Among the power-balancing mechanisms, *status giving* is a way in which a low-power actor may attempt to lessen their dependence on a more powerful partner [43]. In practical terms, status giving is often instantiated in messages displaying appreciation, esteem, or admiration sent to social partners with higher power. Expressions of status giving in aNobii and Flickr are often related to the display of admiration for other people's books or photo collections, such as "very interesting library" or "excellent shot". In both cases, besides the appreciation for the showcased items in the user profile (e.g., "Beautiful

scene and well captured by you"), the explicit declaration of the act of creating a new social link is also a communicative act that implies status giving (e.g., "Hi, interesting profile, I added you as my neighbor"). This is coherent with the notion of *prestige* in social network analysis being related to the centrality of an actor in the social graph [46]. Symmetrically, acknowledging the attention received (e.g., "Thank you very much for your visit") is also a way to express gratitude that is part of the status exchange ritual.

5.2 Social Support

Many everyday interactions have comparatively little to do with the previously described process of status giving. Indeed, many interactions seem inconsequential: greetings, chit-chat with a coworker, gossiping with a friend, wishing a person well, or discussing everyday problems with a sibling. These usually-minute exchanges between individuals form the essential structure of social interactions, that of social support, a basic process of friendship through which one partner provides emotional valuation to another.

A first attempt of generalization of the concept comes from House et al. ([30]), who define social support as "the positive [...] aspects of relationships, such as instrumental aid, emotional caring or concern, and information." This wider notion of support has been studied in web-mediated interaction [41] and in the context of urban areas [47], in which companionship and minor emotional aid are part of the daily interpersonal interactions.

In the datasets we consider, expressions of social support are varied, ranging from sending good wishes ("Bye, I wish you a merry Christmas and a happy 2012") to colloquial chat ("My dear, I found you also here! How are you doing?", "sooo soo cute! you looked good as a baby"), jokes and laughter ("lol, thanks! Right back at ya!"). In Flickr especially this seems to reflect quite well the type of interaction happening in social groups (as opposed to the topical ones) that has been detected in previous work [25].

5.3 Knowledge exchange

Often the main resource being exchanged on a social media platform is knowledge related to the platform's orientation: technical knowledge on stackoverflow.com, knowledge about music on last.fm, or book-related knowledge on aNobii. Even though we have no direct way of gauging the nature and quality of the infor-

Message	DoI
Have a good weekend my dear.	*Sup*
Hi! very interesting library! I added you as my neighbor.	*Sta*
No, haven't read it, but I read some good reviews.	*Kno*
Of course I remember you, how are you? You've a very good library!	*Sup* *Sta*
Merry Christmas to you! Yes, I've really enjoyed the last one from Pennac.	*Sup* *Kno*
It's a pleasure to add you back. I see you like Sci-fi!	*Sta* *Kno*
Hi, hope you're doing well. Your latest reviews are good! I just started Harry Potter and I'm loving it.	*Sup* *Sta* *Kno*
Yes, but today is Monday	*?*

Table 3: Examples of aNobii messages (tr. from Italian) along with the domain of interaction they belong to, according to the editorial labeling process (§6.1).

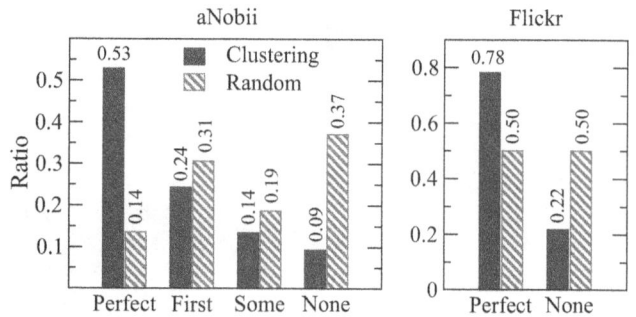

Figure 3: Match of clustering algorithm against the ground truth. Ratio of instances with different level of matching, together with the same values computed for a random clustering.

mation particular individuals possess, we can observe the act of sharing one's knowledge or opinions with others (e.g., "To have a general overview on this, my advice is to read the introductory books by Todorov and Baudot", "I appreciate the author, he is still young but very good and it reminds me the Baricco's writing style"). Given that knowledge about books represents the main resource available to aNobii users, they are expected to provide ample evidence of what books they know about in their messages sent to others. We therefore identify as displaying (or asking for) knowledge the language where works of literature figure prominently.

Even if some traces of knowledge exchange can be found in Flickr comments (e.g., exchanging opinions on camera models), these kind of conversations appear to be very rare if compared to the other social interaction types and our algorithm does not detect them as a separate domain. Intuitively, this is due to the focus of the platform: while the core purpose of aNobii is to foster discussions about books, Flickr facilitates more the users to focus on the aspect of multimedia exploration and discovery rather than on discussions driven by specific topics.

6. EVALUATION

A first inspection of the algorithm output made by an expert of the domain allowed us to label each community according to the most likely DoIs informed by the literature. We hypothesize that the clusters found coincide with the domains described in §5. To verify that, we resort to human evaluation: we produce labeled corpus of messages as ground truth (§6.1) and we match it with the automatically extracted DoIs to check their quality (§6.2).

6.1 Ground truth extraction

To gauge the quality of the output of our method, we produce an editorial ground truth to assess whether a message is assigned to the proper DoI. Two editors read a sample of 1,000 randomly selected messages from each website and label them according to the DoI they belong to. To help the editors with their decision, we provided a description of the DoIs, similar to what is presented in §5, and a set of guidelines to perform the assignment. We summarize the guidelines as follows:

- A message belongs to the *status exchange* DoI when: it contains explicit appreciation for the profile or activity of another user (e.g., his reviews, his tastes, the size of the library or the quality of photos); it announces the creation of a social tie; it points out commonalities between users and taste compatibility; it acknowledges the attention received from others.

- A message belongs to the *social support* DoI when: its main purpose is to greet or welcome someone to the website; it explicitly expresses affection or attachment; it contains wishes, jokes, or laughter.

- A message belongs to the *knowledge exchange* DoI when: its purpose is to share information and personal experience about books, reading, or related events such as book lovers' meetups; it asks for opinions or suggestions; it displays knowledge of the literary field; it asks for recommendations or suggestions.

If the message appears to be a concatenation of two or more messages that could be standalone messages belonging to different DoIs, then they should be marked with multiple labels. The three DoIs we analyze are *not* supposed to cover all the possible communication patterns in the social network, so no label is given when the message does not seem to belong to any of those reported above. We find that the portion of unlabeled message is quite small ($< 10\%$), supporting the intuition that the three DoIs under examination include the vast majority of social interaction types in the social network. The inter-label agreement between the two labelers, measured as Fleiss' Kappa, is 0.70, indicating substantial agreement. Examples of aNobii messages with different labels are displayed in Table 3.

6.2 Validation

The soft clustering method assigns every message to at least one of the detected DoIs. When a multiple assignment occurs, the DoIs are sorted by the probability of membership. For every message in the ground truth corpus, we compare the sorted list of automatically extracted DoIs ($\mathscr{L}_{algo}^{DoI}$) with the set of DoIs assigned by the editors ($\mathscr{S}_{edit}^{DoI}$). We compute the match between them as follows. We consider a *perfect match* when $set(\mathscr{L}_{algo}^{DoI}) \equiv \mathscr{S}_{edit}^{DoI}$; a *first match* occurs instead when $\mathscr{L}_{algo}^{DoI}[0] \in \mathscr{S}_{edit}^{DoI}$; a *partial match* occurs when there is no first match but $set(\mathscr{L}_{algo}^{DoI}) \cap \mathscr{S}_{edit}^{DoI} \neq \varnothing$; there is *no match* when the two sets are disjoint. To compare the obtained results with a baseline, we also compare the ground against random lists of labels ($\mathscr{L}_{rand}^{DoI}$) assigned to every message.

As described in §4, we run a soft clustering on aNobii and a hard clustering on Flickr, therefore in Flickr only the perfect match and no match categories apply. The results are shown in Figure 3. In aNobii the proportion of perfect matches is close to 53%, and the sum of perfect matches and first matches reaches around 77%, which is an extremely good results for an unsupervised method

144

		Nodes	Edges	Messages	Reciprocity
aNobii	Status	0.877	0.753	0.552	0.861
	Support	0.726	0.400	0.409	0.783
	Knowledge	0.861	0.594	0.648	0.798
Flickr	Status	0.821	0.660	0.368	0.757
	Support	0.910	0.639	0.501	0.737

Table 4: Statistics about the subgraphs of the communication network induced by the DoIs. Number of nodes, edges, and messages are divided by the same quantities in the full datasets.

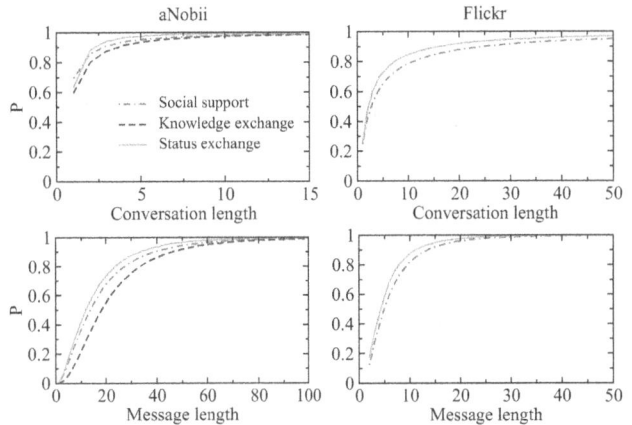

Figure 4: Cumulative probability distributions of length of conversations (number of messages exchanges) and length of messages (number of tokens).

dealing with multiple labelled message instances. The second series of bars shows the ratios for the random model, in which the number of perfect matches drops to 14% and the number of wrong matches rises up to almost 40%. A similar performance is obtained in the case of Flickr, with an accuracy of 78%. In aNobii, the average clustering precision (i.e, ratio between the number of correctly assigned DoIs and the number of automatically detected DoIs, per message) is around 0.76 for the clustering algorithm, 78% higher than the random case, whose accuracy is around 0.45.

7. ANALYSIS

The possibility of automated extraction of Domains of Interaction opens opportunities in the field of computational social science, as it allows the social analyst to quantitatively check theories specific to defined sociological categories (e.g., status giving) directly against the detected domain. To illustrate this opportunity we study the structural and evolutionary properties of the communication graphs denoted by each DoI we extracted, namely the subgraphs of the communication networks induced by the edges over which the messages belonging to that specific DoI are delivered.

7.1 Coverage and reciprocation

The first question that comes naturally is about how much the different DoIs spread over the communication network. Statistics on the size and link reciprocity of each DoI graph are reported in Table 4. In the case of aNobii, the difference in the number of edges involved is quite significant, although not very unbalanced in terms of nodes, with the status exchange domain spanning over 75% of the links and social support covering only 40% of them. Consistently with the main purpose of the service, the overall number of messages is instead imbalanced towards the knowledge exchange domain (60% of ties have a component of domain-related information transmission). In Flickr, instead, the proportion of edges in each domain in more balanced (about 66% for status and 64% for support). The overall reciprocity in the actors' behavior over the span of a conversation, computed as the ratio of reciprocated messages between two endpoints (disregarding their temporal order) is reported as well. In aNobii, most conversations involve a relatively balanced exchange of messages, on average there being 0.834 messages sent one way in a conversation for every one message sent in the other direction. The same measure is the highest (0.861) for status exchange, likely a reflection of social norms imposing the ritualized reciprocation of status exchange [24]. A similar pattern is found for Flickr. Conversely, both social support and knowledge exchange are less balanced, suggesting slightly more lopsided relationships in these domains of interaction.

7.2 Tie composition and strength

Our approach allows us to decompose a social link in the DoIs that constitute the communication between its endpoints. We study the proportion of different resources exchanged over a communication tie. The portions of messages per dyad belonging to each DoI, averaged over all the dyads, is reported in the "tie share" column in Table 5. In aNobii, status giving is the most frequent interaction. This finding is rather intuitive: status giving is predominant in very short messages – the archetypal message in this context being "nice library!" – and many messages are relatively short. In Flickr the proportion is very balanced instead, with no domain being predominant on average. This finding is consistent with recent studies on group interactions in Flickr that identify a dichotomy between *social* and *topical* interactions in the network [25].

In Figure 4 we show the distributions of message length (in number of tokens) and conversation length for the three domains. This difference is not only helpful in characterizing the interactions but it also means that the DoI can potentially serve as an additional feature in the task of conversation length prediction [4].

Another important aspect that connects our work with previous studies in social link characterization is the measurement of the average strength of the link in the different DoI graphs. To understand whether differences in the strength of the ties hold between different domains, we adopt the framework presented by Gilbert and Karahalios [22] based on Granovetter's definition of tie strength [27]. Unlike in Gilbert's experiment, we do not have a crowdsourced ground truth about tie strength in our datasets. However, our aim here is not to determine which metrics are better proxies for tie strength, but to compare individual strength indicators across DoIs, to spot differences between them. We measure the strength based on three main families of metrics [22]: *structural similarity* (extent to which the tied individuals share common acquaintances and features), *intensity* (duration of their interaction), and *sentiment* (amount of words expressing intimacy and emotions). To quantify the sentiment dimension, we process the text of conversations using the English and Italian versions of the "Linguistic Inquiry Word Count" (LIWC) dictionary [37]. LIWC is a dictionary that maps words into 72 categories, such as positive and negative emotional words, words implying cognitive processes, psychological constructs, and so on. To capture the notion of intimacy and emotion, we use the LIWC intimacy categories previously identified in [22]. In addition, Flickr data allows us to investigate also the *kinship* dimension, namely whether a social partners declared to be friends or member of the same family.

Results are presented in Table 5. In aNobii, ties in the Status Exchange network exhibit the lowest strength in terms of all indica-

	DoI	Tie Share	Structural sim			Intensity		Sentiment		Kinship
			σ_n	σ_g	σ_i	$\langle conv_{len} \rangle$	$\langle msg_{len} \rangle$	Intim.	Emo.	
aNobii	*Status*	0.48	0.045	0.062	0.041	2.13	16.32	0.026	0.033	n/a
	Support	0.33	0.064	0.077	0.054	3.03	18.81	0.040	0.040	n/a
	Knowledge	0.19	0.068	0.075	0.059	2.48	23.27	0.038	0.036	n/a
Flickr	*Status*	0.51	0.028	0.024	0.0011	8.83	6.26	0.370	0.393	0.049
	Support	0.49	0.040	0.024	0.0013	12.70	7.35	0.410	0.440	0.057

Table 5: Strength of ties connecting pairs of users, in terms of: i) Jaccard similarity σ between their neighbors (n), the groups they are subscribed (g) and their items (i), books for aNobii and favorited photos for Flickr; ii) lenght of the conversation in terms of number of messages exchanged; iii) ratio of words belonging to the intimacy and emotions categories in the LIWC categories; iv) ratio of dyads reciprocally declaring a "family" or "friend" relation (available for Flickr only). The portions of messages per dyad belonging to each DoI, averaged over all the dyads, is also reported as *tie share*.

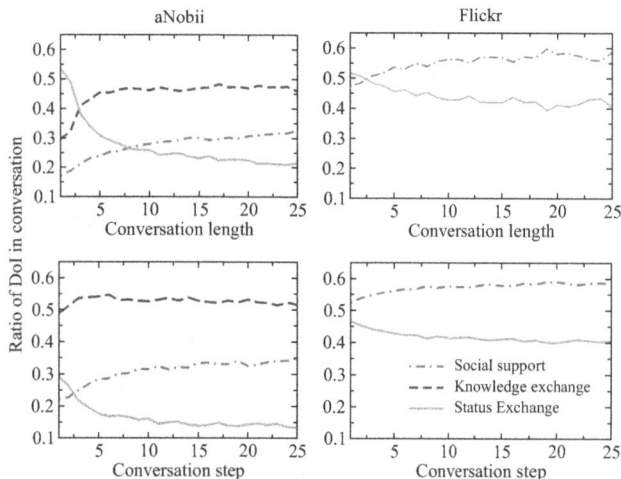

Figure 5: Average proportion of messages belonging to each DoI for pairs of users with fixed conversation length (top) and after n conversation steps (bottom).

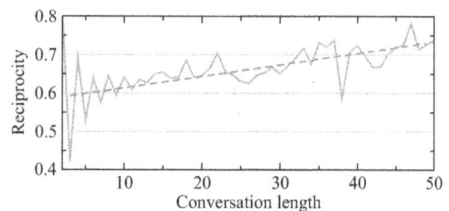

Figure 6: Average reciprocity of interactions at fixed conversation length. Linear fitting is reported.

tors. Support and Knowledge networks have more similar features, with the Knowledge Exchange ties having slightly higher similarity in terms of books shared between the endpoints and the Social Support ties having longer conversations, on average. Flickr has consistent results for all the feature categories even if the signal is weaker for some structural indicators, as the structural similarity is substantially different only when considering the similarity of common friends. Also, the probability of people exchanging support being real life friends or kins is 16% higher than for status.

In summary, in both networks weaker ties tend to convey status giving and stronger ties either social support or knowledge.

7.3 Tie evolution

Intuitively, the role and importance of each domain in a dyadic relation could potentially change as the relationship evolves in time. To study the evolution of social processes along a tie after its creation, we compute across all the users the average ratio of messages belonging to each DoI in i) conversations with different lengths and ii) in messages belonging to the nth conversation step. Figure 5 shows the dynamic of this evolution. Status exchange is particularly present in short conversations or, more in general, in the first stages of a conversation, after which the average tie moves to a mix of knowledge exchange and social support. It thus appears that status exchange serves to set the foundation for the future relationship, fading to the interactional background after the tie-formation stage. Interestingly, the same pattern (even if smoother) is found

for Flickr, where status giving is predominant at the beginning and then slowly loses its importance. Even more surprisingly, in both datasets the status giving curve starts losing its predominance exactly after 3 messages exchanged.

Even though highly-reciprocal status decreases as a conversation grows in length, reciprocity nonetheless tends to *increase* in a relationship over time (Figure 6). This is a likely example of survival bias among social ties. Power-imbalanced relations, where only one individual provides resources and the other cannot reciprocate, are assumed to be more vulnerable to dissolution through the dependent actor's withdrawal from the relationship [17]. Thus, we are more likely to observe long conversations stemming from reciprocal relationships than from non-reciprocal ones.

7.4 Inequality and assortativity

In our conception, inspired by the Social Exchange Theory, knowledge, status, and support can be considered as *goods* generated by the social actors and exchanged between them. We investigate the way in which the exchange of such goods is distributed in the network. A common way to measure the *social inequality*, i.e., the tendency of small circles of people to accumulate the vast majority of the global wealth, is to draw the Lorenz curve of any wealth indicator. The curve plots the proportion of the global wealth retained by the poorest x% of the population: the farther the curve is from the diagonal, the greater the inequality between individuals. In Figure 7 we plot the Lorenz curve by using the indegree (similar results are obtained with the in-strength) of each DoI graph as a proxy of wealth (e.g., number of alters giving status to ego) and we compute the Gini coefficient $G \in [0,1]$ as a quantitative measure of the inequality [21]. In general, the distribution of resources is very unequal in all the domains but in particular for the status giving, which has the highest Gini coefficient: in aNobii $G_{sta} = 0.72$, $G_{sup} = 0.69$, and $G_{kno} = 0.68$ and in Flickr $G_{sta} = 0.53$, $G_{sup} = 0.43$). This supports the intuition that the status, more than other goods, tends to flow unidirectionally from low- to high-status individuals.

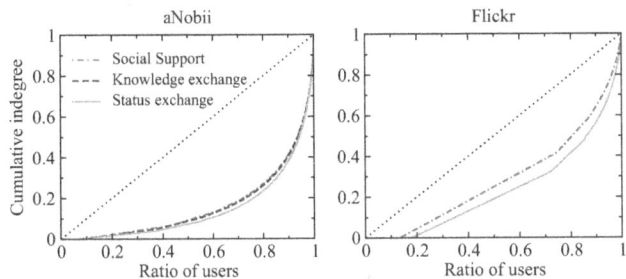

Figure 7: Lorenz curve for the indegree (unweighted on the left and weighted on the right) in the three DoI graphs.

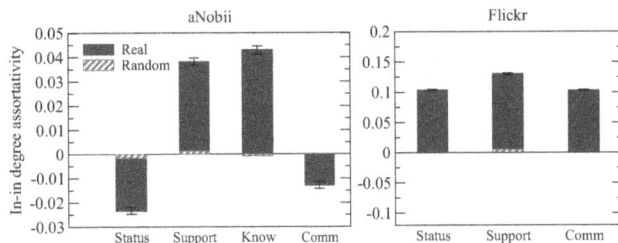

Figure 8: In-in assortativity in the DoI graphs and in the full graphs. Errors estimated with jackknife resampling are always $< 10^{-3}$ and are showed as error bars. Values computed on randomly rewired networks are shown with striped bars.

We investigate the social stratification also by measuring the in-in assortativity of the graphs, namely the tendency of individuals to connect with people with similar indegree [36]. In Figure 8 we report the assortativity values for the three subgraphs and the full communication graph. To check the statistical significance of results, i) we compute the same values on randomly rewired versions of the graphs and ii) we compute the error on the assortativity estimation through jackknife resampling [36]. Surprisingly, in aNobii all the assortativity absolute values tend to zero, meaning that the connectivity patterns in all the networks are very mixed. Status is the only DoI that tends to disassortativity, thus confirming the tendency of unidirectional status flow (i.e., people with higher status receiving status from people with lower status). The full communication network is disassortative as well because dominated by the signal of the Status DoI, which covers the highest number of edges (see Table 4). In Flickr, assortative patterns are more evident but, consistently with aNobii, status assortativity is lower than for social support, with a statistically significant difference.

8. DISCUSSION AND CONCLUSIONS

The methodology we propose has two immediate outcomes. First it provides an unsupervised way to discover the type of social exchange (e.g., status giving) that happens with dyadic passing of messages, in contrast with other methods that are able to capture the message's topic or sentiment. The accuracy of our approach in assigning messages to different domains is high, as assessed by human evaluators and consistently good in networks with direct user-to-user messaging (aNobii) as well as with item-mediated communication (Flickr). Last, it allows us to study the structure of the different interaction networks and to check our quantitative findings against well-established sociological theories. Among other findings, we verify that strong links in the communication network tend to convey either social support or knowledge, while weaker links convey more status giving. We also gain insights into the way ties evolve over time with status exchange gradually giving way to exchanges of knowledge or social support. Interestingly, the predominance of status exchange fades after 3 message exchanges on average in both the datasets we tested.

The characterization of messages in terms of their type of social exchange opens a plethora of unexplored opportunities for applications, not limited to analytics. First is *user profiling*: users engaged in conversations that are predominantly characterized by different DoIs would be presumably interested in different types of activities (e.g., socialization vs. item consumption). Second is *link profiling*: dyads exchanging different social resources might react differently to signals. For example, when considering a process of information diffusion (e.g., diffusion of product ads via viral marketing), considering the knowledge, status or social support networks may yield

very different results. Last, we see opportunities for the *summarization* of social relationships. For example, Facebook's friendship page[1] displays a relationship between two connected users with a timeline of their shared experiences. Our tie decomposition in domains would allow a different way of summarizing a social link, e.g., "based on their conversations, Alice and Bob's relationship has been made 30% by knowledge exchange, 20% by status giving and 50% by social support."

Our method has also some limitations that we plan to address in the future and that we summarize as follows.

Supervised vs. unsupervised. Our approach is fully unsupervised. This choice is motivated by the purpose of *discovery* of the framework: detecting the domains of interaction in *any* communication network. Supervised alternatives are possible. If a ground truth is available, a training set could be built from any set of features (textual, social, and so on). However, such approach would need i) an initial labeling effort, ii) to build different ground truth corpora for different domains, and iii) to know in advance the number and type of resources that are exchanged in the network. Our approach is free from these constraints and therefore more general. We plan to explore combinations of supervised and unsupervised approaches for a classification of messages on the fly.

Clustering alternatives. We used NMF in the message bucketing stage (§3.3) and Spinglass as community detection algorithm in the phase of DoI extraction (§3.5), but a plethora of alternatives for clustering and community detection are available. We also conducted experiments using Latent Dirichlet Allocation (LDA) and Fuzzy K-Means in alternative to NMF and we found analogous results. We plan as a future work to experiment more community detection algorithms in alternative to Spinglass.

Message bucketing. The bucketing phase groups messages by the similarity of their bags of words but other types of aggregation to better capture the semantics of messages would be possible. We partially address this point by giving in input to the clustering also bi-grams and tri-grams, that are needed to account for associations of words with slightly more complex meaning. Also clustering messages by their sentiment would be an interesting extension.

Concluding remarks. The representation of a social tie as a sequence of individual exchanges naturally leads one to the idea of understanding social ties as strings of interactions. With this understanding, we can use insights from theoretical Computer Science to establish the computational properties of social rituals. Indeed, this idea has already been leveraged by DeDeo [15], who gives evidence of the insufficiency of finite-state machines for the description of social interactions. The ultimate goal of such analysis is the unpacking of "culture" as a formal, computational concept. If

---

[1] newsroom.fb.com/News/531/A-New-Look-for-Friendship-Pages

we see social ties as interactional sequences, then we may understand the Domains of Interaction we discover as the "grammar of society" [5] – in other words, the bits of "source-code" that prescribe how individuals are to act in a certain situation. We hope our work provides yet another step towards a truly computational understanding of human societies.

Acknowledgments

This research is supported by EU Community's Seventh Framework Programme FP7/2007-2013 under the ARCOMEM and Social Sensor projects, by the Spanish Centre for the Development of Industrial Technology under the CENIT program, project CEN-20101037 "Social Media", and by Grant TIN2009-14560-C03-01 of the Ministry of Science and Innovation of Spain. R. Schifanella was partially supported by the Yahoo FREP grant.

9. REFERENCES

[1] L. M. Aiello, M. Deplano, R. Schifanella, and G. Ruffo. People are Strange when you're a Stranger: Impact and Influence of Bots on Social Networks. In *ICWSM*, 2012.

[2] T. Antonucci, R. Fuhrer, and J. Jackson. Social Support and Reciprocity: A Cross-Ethnic and Cross-National Perspective. *Journal of Social and Personal Relationships*, 7(4), 1990.

[3] S. Arora, R. Ge, and A. Moitra. Learning Topic Models – Going Beyond SVD. In *FOCS*, 2012.

[4] L. Backstrom, J. Kleinberg, L. Lee, and C. Danescu-Niculescu-Mizil. Characterizing and Curating Conversation Threads: Expansion, Focus, Volume, Re-entry. In *WSDM*, 2013.

[5] C. Bicchieri. *The Grammar of Society: The Nature and Dynamics of Social Norms*. Cambridge University Press, 2006.

[6] P. Blau. *Exchange and Power in Social Life*. Transaction Publishers, 1964.

[7] d. boyd, S. Golder, and G. Lotan. Tweet, Tweet, Retweet: Conversational Aspects of Retweeting on Twitter. In *HICSS*, 2010.

[8] P. Bramsen, M. Escobar-Molano, A. Patel, and R. Alonso. Extracting Social Power Relationships from Natural Language. In *Human Language Technologies - Volume 1*. Association for Computational Linguistics, 2011.

[9] C. Budak and R. Agrawal. On Participation in Group Chats on Twitter. In *WWW*, 2013.

[10] F. Celli and L. Rossi. The Role of Emotional Stability in Twitter Conversations. In *Workshop on Semantic Analysis in Social Media*, 2012.

[11] K. S. Cook and R. M. Emerson. Power, Equity and Commitment in Exchange Networks. *American Sociological Review*, 43(5), 1978.

[12] T. Correa, A. W. Hinsley, and H. G. de Zúñiga. Who Interacts on the Web? The Intersection of Users' Personality and Social Media Use. *Computers in Human Behaviour*, 26(2), 2010.

[13] C. Danescu-Niculescu-Mizil, L. Lee, B. Pang, and J. Kleinberg. Echoes of Power: Language Effects and Power Differences in Social Interaction. In *WWW*, 2012.

[14] M. De Choudhury, H. Sundaram, A. John, and D. D. Seligmann. What Makes Conversations Interesting? Themes, Participants and Consequences of Conversations in Online Social Media. In *WWW*, 2009.

[15] S. DeDeo. Collective Phenomena and Non-Finite State Computation in a Human Social System. *PLoS ONE*, 8(10), 10 2013.

[16] D. Derks, A. E. Bos, and J. v. Grumbkow. Emoticons and Social Interaction on the Internet: the Importance of Social Context. *Computers in Human Behavior*, 23(1), 2007.

[17] R. Emerson. Power-dependence Relations. *American Sociological Review*, 1962.

[18] E. Foa and U. Foa. Resource Theory: Interpersonal Behavior as Exchange. In *Social exchange: Advances in theory and research*. Plenum Press, 1980.

[19] P. Fogel, S. S. Young, D. M. Hawkins, and N. Ledirac. Inferential, Robust Non-negative Matrix Factorization Analysis of Microarray Data. *Bioinformatics*, 23(1), 2007.

[20] S. Fortunato. Community Detection in Graphs. *Physics Reports*, 486(3-5), 2010.

[21] J. L. Gastwirth. The estimation of the Lorenz curve and Gini index. *The Review of Economics and Statistics*, 54(3), 1972.

[22] E. Gilbert and K. Karahalios. Predicting Tie Strength with Social Media. In *CHI*, 2009.

[23] M. Gomez-Rodriguez, J. Leskovec, and B. Schölkopf. Structure and Dynamics of Information Pathways in Online Media. In *WSDM*, 2013.

[24] R. V. Gould. The Origins of Status Hierarchies: A Formal Theory and Empirical Test. *American Journal of Sociology*, 107(5), 2002.

[25] P. A. Grabowicz, L. M. Aiello, V. M. Eguiluz, and A. Jaimes. Distinguishing Topical and Social Groups Based on Common Identity and Bond theory. In *WSDM*, 2013.

[26] P. A. Grabowicz, J. J. Ramasco, E. Moro, J. M. Pujol, and V. M. Eguiluz. Social Features of Online Networks: The Strength of Intermediary Ties in Online Social Media. *PLoS ONE*, 7(1), 2012.

[27] M. S. Granovetter. The Strength of Weak Ties. *American Journal of Sociology*, 1973.

[28] F. M. Harper, D. Frankowski, S. Drenner, Y. Ren, S. Kiesler, L. Terveen, R. Kraut, and J. Riedl. Talk Amongst Yourselves: Inviting Users to Participate in Online Conversations. In *IUI*, 2007.

[29] C. Honeycutt and S. Herring. Beyond Microblogging: Conversation and Collaboration via Twitter. In *HICSS*, 2009.

[30] J. House, D. Umberson, and K. Landis. Structures and Processes of Social Support. *Annual Review of Sociology*, 1988.

[31] A. Java, X. Song, T. Finin, and B. Tseng. Why We Twitter: Understanding Microblogging Usage and Communities. In *WebKDD/SNA-KDD*, 2007.

[32] S. Kim, J. Bak, and A. Oh. Do You Feel what I Feel? Social Aspects of Emotions in Twitter Conversations. In *ICWSM*, 2012.

[33] R. Kumar, M. Mahdian, and M. McGlohon. Dynamics of Conversations. In *KDD*, 2010.

[34] J. Leskovec, D. Huttenlocher, and J. Kleinberg. Predicting Positive and Negative Links in Online Social Networks. In *WWW*, 2010.

[35] M. Mitrovic and B. Tadic. Dynamics of Bloggers' Communities: Bipartite Networks from Empirical Data and Agent-based Modeling. *Physica A*, 391(21), 2012.

[36] M. E. J. Newman. Assortative Mixing in Networks. *Phys. Rev. Lett.*, 89, 2002.

[37] J. Pennebaker. *The Secret Life of Pronouns: What Our Words Say About Us*. Bloomsbury, 2013.

[38] H. Purohit, Y. Ruan, D. Fuhry, S. Parthasarathy, and A. Sheth. On Understanding Divergence of Online Social Group Discussion. In *ICWSM*, 2014.

[39] D. Ramage, S. Dumais, and D. Liebling. Characterizing Microblogs with Topic Models. In *ICWSM*, 2010.

[40] J. Reichardt and S. Bornholdt. Statistical Mechanics of Community Detection. *Phys. Rev. E*, 74(1), 2006.

[41] H. Rheingold. *The virtual community: Finding commection in a computerized world*. Addison-Wesley Longman, 1993.

[42] A. Ritter, C. Cherry, and B. Dolan. Unsupervised Modeling of Twitter Conversations. In *HLT*, 2010.

[43] B. State, B. Abrahao, and K. Cook. From Power to Status in Online Exchange. In *WebSci*, 2012.

[44] S. Tchokni, D. Ó Séaghdha, and D. Quercia. Emoticons and Phrases: Status Symbols in Social Media. In *ICWSM*, 2014.

[45] B. Viswanath, A. Mislove, M. Cha, and K. P. Gummadi. On the Evolution of User Interaction in Facebook. In *WOSN*, 2009.

[46] S. Wasserman and K. Faust. *Social Network Analysis: Methods and Applications*. Cambridge University Press, 1994.

[47] B. Wellman and S. Wortley. Different Strokes from Different Folks: Community Ties and Social Support. *American Journal of Sociology*, 96(3), 1990.

[48] C. Wilson, B. Boe, A. Sala, K. P. Puttaswamy, and B. Y. Zhao. User Interactions in Social Networks and their Implications. In *EuroSys*, 2009.

[49] R. Xiang, J. Neville, and M. Rogati. Modeling Relationship Strength in Online Social Networks. In *WWW*, 2010.

[50] W. Xu, X. Liu, and Y. Gong. Document Clustering Based on Non-negative Matrix Factorization. In *SIGIR*, 2003.

Centrality Rankings in Multiplex Networks

Albert Solé-Ribalta
Departament d'Enginyeria
Informàtica i
Matemàtiques,Universitat
Rovira i Virgili
43007, Tarragona, Spain
albert.sole@urv.cat

Manlio De Domenico
Departament d'Enginyeria
Informàtica i
Matemàtiques,Universitat
Rovira i Virgili
43007, Tarragona, Spain
manlio.dedomenico@urv.cat

Sergio Gómez
Departament d'Enginyeria
Informàtica i
Matemàtiques,Universitat
Rovira i Virgili
43007, Tarragona, Spain
sergio.gomez@urv.cat

Alex Arenas
Departament d'Enginyeria
Informàtica i
Matemàtiques,Universitat
Rovira i Virgili
43007, Tarragona, Spain
alex.arenas@urv.cat

ABSTRACT

The vertiginous increase of e-platforms for social communication has boosted the ways people use to interact each other. Micro-blogging and decentralized posts are used indistinctly for social interaction, usually by the same individuals acting simultaneously in the different platforms. Multiplex networks are the natural abstraction representation of such "layered" relationships and others, like co-authorship. Here, we re-define the betweenness centrality measure to account for the inherent structure of multiplex networks and propose an algorithm to compute it in an efficient way. To show the necessity and the advantage of the proposed definition, we analyze the obtained centralities for two real multiplex networks, a social multiplex of two layers obtained from Twitter and Instagram and a co-authorship network of four layers obtained from arXiv. Results show that the proposed definition provides more accurate results than the current approach of evaluating the classical betweenness centrality on the aggregated network, in particular for the middle ranked nodes. We also analyze the computational cost of the presented algorithm.

Categories and Subject Descriptors

H.4 [**Information Systems Applications**]: Miscellaneous;
J.4 [**Social and Behavioral Sciences**]: Web Science

Keywords

Betweenness centrality; Multiplex networks; Multilayer networks

WebSci'14, June 23–26, 2014, Bloomington, IN, USA.
Copyright 2014 ACM 978-1-4503-2622-3/14/06 ...$15.00.
http://dx.doi.org/10.1145/2615569.2615687.

1. INTRODUCTION

Complex networks have become a natural abstraction of the interactions between elements in complex systems [20]. When the type of interaction is essentially identical between any two elements, the theory of complex networks provides with a wide set of tools and diagnostics that turn out to be very useful to gain insight of the system under study. However, there exist particular cases where this classical approach may lead to misleading results. Specifically, when the entities under study are related with each other using different types of relations. Representative examples are provided by temporal networks [19, 11], where edge connectivity may vary on time, transportation networks [6], where two geographic places may be connected by different transport modes, or social networks [18] where users are connected using several platforms or different categorical layers (for example, in co-authorship networks the categories of the field of study).

Here, we focus our study on a particular type of interconnected multilayer network [7] called "multiplex", where each object, if it exists, is univocally represented in each independent layer and so the interconnectivity pattern among layers becomes one-to-one. Figure 1b, 1c shows some representative examples of multiplex networks where it is possible to see the characteristics of the related topology. The examples show a multiplex with two layers where entities s, b, t exist in both layers. The interconnectivity between them is different in both layers.

Note that the existence of several topological structures similar to the one used in this work requires special care in their differentiation. Several works [16, 23, 3, 2, 25] have used a structure similar to multiplex networks. The main difference being that the topology adopted here relies on the connectivity between nodes representing the same entity in the different layers. In some of these studies, each layer is treated independently and metrics are evaluated on each of them to aggregate later the results in different ways. In the others, the different layers are projected into a single layer network by aggregating the edges of the individual layers and the metrics are computed over this aggregated network. Another approach that has been considered is the aggregation of all layers into a single layer with some differentiation between the connectivity of the different layers, like edge-colored graphs. Other structures similar to multiplex networks are interdependent networks [10]. The main difference between those type of networks and the one used here is more conceptual than structural. In the case of interconnected networks elements of layers have no counterparts on the other layers and consequently the one-to-one structural relation between elements of the different layers does not exist. For further details about the classification of such multilayer networks we refer to [12] and references therein. In the proposed approach, we do not perform any type of prior aggregation and keep the inherent structure of the interconnected layers in the multiplex to define the desired diagnostic, in our case the computation of shortest-path betweenness centrality.

The paper is structured as follows. Section 2 reviews centrality measures on multiplex networks and particularly focus on the problem of defining the shortest-path betweenness centrality for these type of networks. Section 2.1 describes our new proposed definition. Section 2.2 presents a computationally efficient algorithm to compute the proposed betweenness. Next, Section 3 presents results on real data, compares this results to the ones obtained by the aggregated network and experimentally evaluates the computational complexity of the algorithm. Eventually, Section 4 summarizes the main findings.

2. CENTRALITY MEASURES ON MULTIPLEX NETWORKS

In network theory, centrality diagnostics are aimed to measure the relative importance of a node, an edge, or some other subgraph [26, 20]. This diagnostic measure is specially interesting in social sciences since it is a proxy to determine influential nodes. However, centrality measures are also extremely important to address the problem of blind search and efficient navigation, e.g. PageRank [24] or HITS [13]. The generalization of these particular measures to multiplex is proposed in [22, 27, 15, 14, 17, 8].

Here, we focus on the definition of shortest path (or geodesic) betweenness centrality [9] for multiplex networks. As motivated in the previous section, social networks are usually composed by several types of relations, or ties, between individuals. Consider, for example, the ego network of an individual. Family, work, and hobbies are likely to be among his relationships as well as some others are likely to be maintained with on-line social platforms. In this scenario, the classical procedure of studying such networks is to project all this information into a single network by collapsing all the relations. However, using this aggregation procedure, as we will show, the resulting network may not accurately reflect the real topology.

Consider the scenario described in Figure 1. Figure 1a shows a network of three individuals $\{s, b, t\}$, edges between individuals indicate a relation between them. However, since the aggregation procedure is not injective several scenarios can lead to the same aggregated network, as shown in Figure 1b and 1c. In Figure 1b, individuals s and t can communicate through individual b in layer 1. This reduces to the classical approach where all the relations are within a single layer. Consider now the scenario of Figure 1c, this time

individuals s and t are disconnected in both layers and individual b acts as a bridge allowing information to flow from layer 1 to layer 2. Note that without individual b connecting the two layers, individuals s and t will be disconnected. Undoubtedly, individual b in the scenario described by Figure 1c has more importance than individual b in the scenario of Figure 1b and centrality measures should reflect this fact. Thus, to obtain reliable centrality measures that accurately reflect the real structure it is mandatory to analyze the relations between individuals considering the full multiplex architecture when performing the respective analysis.

2.1 Shortest path betweenness centrality on multiplex networks

First of all, we define a path, $p_{s_\alpha \to t_\beta} \in \mathcal{P}_{s_\alpha \to t_\beta}$, on a multiplex network consisting of L layers and N nodes per layer, as an ordered sequence of nodes which starts from node s in layer α and finish in node t in layer β, with the restriction that an edge exists between every pair of consecutive nodes in p. $\mathcal{P}_{s_\alpha \to t_\beta}$ indicates the set of all possible paths between node s in layer α and node t in layer β. For every path $p_{s_\alpha \to t_\beta}$ it is possible to define a distance function $d\left(p_{s_\alpha \to t_\beta}\right)$, usually depending on the weight of the edges the path traverses to account for the "length" of the path. Without loss of generality, we define this distance function as the number of traversed edges in the path. Hence, the set of shortest-paths $P^*_{s \to t}$, from node s to node t, in the multiplex is defined as the set of paths which minimize the distance function between the two nodes,

$$P^*_{s \to t} = \underset{\substack{p_{s_\alpha \to t_\beta} \in \mathcal{P}_{[s_\alpha \to t_\beta]} \\ \alpha, \beta \in \{1, \dots, L\}}}{\arg \min} \, d(p_{s_\alpha \to t_\beta}) \qquad (1)$$

That is, a shortest-path between two individuals, in a multiplex network, is a minimum path that starts from the source node in any layer, and reaches the destination node in any layer. See that this definition is coherent with the definition of a multiplex network since the same node in the different layers represent the same physical entity.

Considering (1), the shortest-path betweenness of node v on layer l, $g(v_l)$ is defined as the sum, for every possible origin-destination pair (s, t), of the fraction of times that node v on layer l, belongs to a path in $P^*_{[s \to t]}$. Specifically, the shortest-path betweenness centrality on a multiplex network is obtained by:

$$g(v_l) = \sum_{\substack{s, t = 1 \\ s \neq t \neq v}}^N \frac{\sigma_{s,t}(v_l)}{\sigma_{s,t}}, \qquad (2)$$

where $\sigma_{s,t} = |P^*_{[s \to t]}|$ is the number of shortest-paths from s to t and $\sigma_{s,t}(v_l)$ is the number of times node v_l is in a shortest-path from s to t.

Note that with the given definition the shortest path degeneration increases. $P^*_{[s \to t]}$ may contain several shortest paths between s and t in same layer (classical shortest path degeneration) together with shortest paths that start and end in the same node but in different layers (multiplex shortest path degeneration).

Eventually, the shortest-path betweenness of a node, in a multiplex network, can be obtained by:

$$g(v) = \sum_{l=1}^L g(v_l). \qquad (3)$$

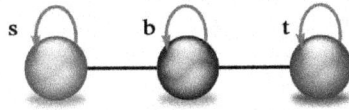

(a) Aggregated Network.

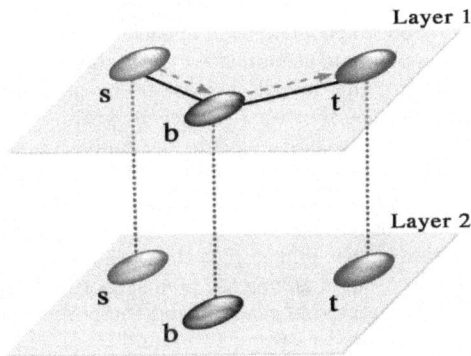

(b) Individuals are only connected in one layer.

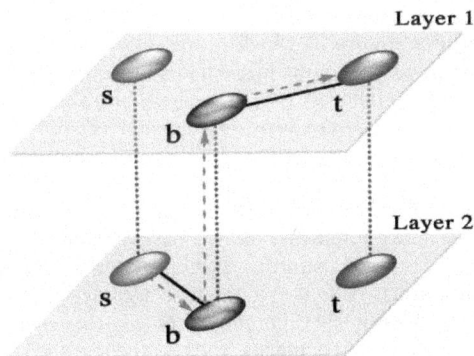

(c) Individual *b* acts as a bridge between the layers.

Figure 1: Example of possible multiplex configurations for the same aggregated network

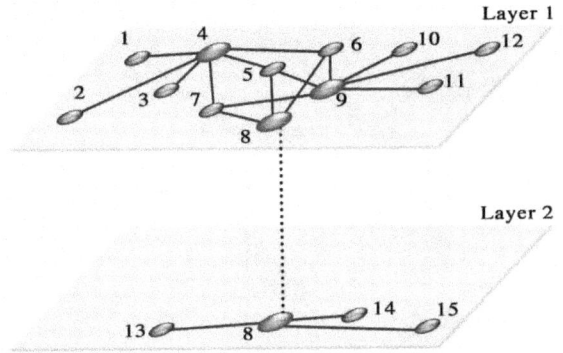

(a) Example of a multiplex with three hubs, one acting as a bridge between layers.

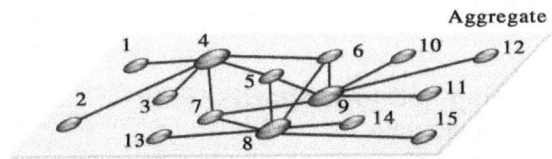

(b) Aggregated network of Figure 2a. Still contains three hubs, but all have the same centrality.

Figure 2: Example of how the multiplex obtains different centrality rankings than the aggregated network.

Usually, not only the numerical value of the betweenness centrality is of interest [1] about a particular network but also the ranking of the nodes it provides [4]. In the scenarios described in Figure 1, although the betweenness given by the aggregated network is different from the betweenness given by the multiplex network, the rankings are equivalent. In both cases, node *b* becomes the most central node in the network while *s* and *t* are ranked as second. However, this situation is not common. Usually, rankings are substantially different. To illustrate the situation, consider the scenario given in Figure 2. Figure 2a represents a multiplex network with two hubs in layer 1 and a third hub linked to some nodes on layer 1 and some nodes on layer 2. Figure 2b shows the aggregated version of the multiplex in Figure 2a. It is easy to see that the shortest-path betweenness on the aggregate network of hubs numbered 4, 8 and 9 is the highest and the same. These nodes are ranked the first on the aggregated network. However, in the multiplex network node 8 is ranked the first and nodes 4 and 9 are ranked second exhibiting equal betweenness. It is worth noting how the multiplex representation disambiguates the betweenness of the aggregated network providing more centrality to the hub which acts as a bridge between nodes connected in the different layers. This change in the centrality allows that a node, which is not central in any single layer, to be ranked the first in the multiplex network.

151

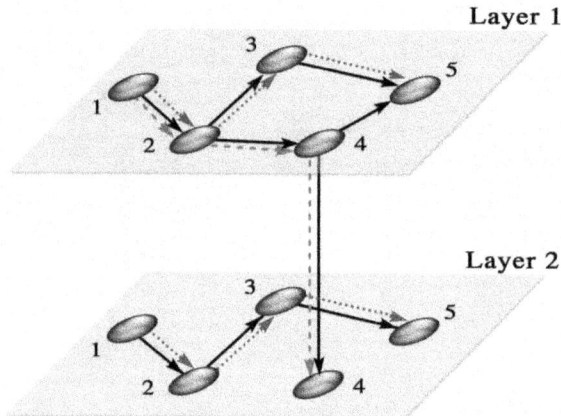

Figure 3: Shortest-paths acyclic graph with multiple paths reaching the same node in different layers.

2.2 Computation of Shortest Path betweenness

It is a common approach to compute the betweenness centrality in two steps. In the first, the shortest-paths, in form of a predecessor list, are computed using well known algorithms such as Breadth First Search (with a computational cost of $\mathcal{O}(NE)$ per source node), Dijkstra (with a computational cost of $\mathcal{O}(NE + N^2 \log N)$ per source node, when implemented using a Fibonacci Heap) or Floyd-Warshall (with a computational cost of $\mathcal{O}(N^3)$), where N and E are the number of nodes and edges, respectively. Once the shortest-paths information is obtained, each shortest-path is reconstructed and the corresponding betweenness is accumulated for the traversed nodes. It is easy to see that the betweenness computation yields to $\mathcal{O}(N^3)$ algorithm. Note that, except for the Floyd-Warshall algorithm, the computational complexity of the full algorithm is dominated by the calculus of the betweenness not by the shortest-path. To reduce the complexity, as Brandes [5] and Newman [21] show, it is possible to perform a recursive computation of the betweenness using a backtracking procedure over the shortest-paths acyclic graph.

Our procedure is inspired in that proposed in [5], and is outlined in Algorithm 1 for the simple unweighted case[1].The algorithm is divided in two steps. In the first step (line 11 to 27), for a single source node s all the shortest path to all other nodes are computed. The shortest-path acyclic graph is stored in variable P as well as the the number of shortest path that pass thought each node σ. The initialization of the Breadth First Search differs from the classical one to consider the source node s can be localized in any layer. Thus, the neighbors of source node s are the union of the neighbors of s in all layers (line 17). Besides, note that the short-

---

[1]The adaptation to the weighted case is straightforward, it is only required to replace the shortest-paths acyclic graph generation for the Dijkstra algorithm instead of the current Breadth First Search procedure.

est paths are computed considering the destination nodes in the different layers correspond to different entities. The equivalence of entities in the different layers is performed in the computation of the betweenness (second step). To correctly account for these equivalences, we keep track of the first accessed node (independently of the layer) though variable $vOrder$ and of shortest path distance in the multiplex though variable d_M. The necessity of variable d_M should not be confused with d which stores the distance to every node in every layer. d_M is used to keep track of the first time a node is accessed independently of the layer as well as to account for multiplex path degeneracy. However, d is still necessary since the shortest path search procedure must travel through the different layers. Once the all shortest path are found, to correctly account for the multiplex path degeneracy the number of shortest paths that pass though each node independently of the layer is computed (lines 28 to 31). In the second step, the contribution of each shortest path in P to the betweenness is accumulated in the betweenness vector C_B. To account for all shortest path contributions in an efficient way the shortest path acyclic graph is traversed starting from the farthest nodes to the source. That is, the shortest-path acyclic graph is traversed in a backtracking fashion. In a single layer graph, where only classical path degeneracy needs to be accounted, at each traversed node w, the paths that go thought w plus the path that starts at w are correct distributed among the predecessors v considering the number of paths that reach w and the number of paths that reach each predecessor v ($\sigma[w]$ and $\sigma[v]$). Each fraction of paths is accumulated in each $\delta[v]$. Eventually, when all nodes farther than w to the source are explored, $\delta[w]$ can be safely accumulated in the betweenness of w. However, in a multiplex network this procedure is substantially more complex since we need to account not only for the first node it is accessed independently of the layer but also for multiplex path degeneracy. To illustrate these particularities, consider Figure 3, which represents a possible acyclic graph (in black solid arrows) that generates all shortest-path from node labelled 1, independently on the layer, to all other nodes. There are two possible shortest-paths (shown in dashed red arrows) from individual 1 to individual 4 in the acyclic graph, $\{1_{L1}, 2_{L1}, 4_{L1}\}$ and $\{1_{L1}, 2_{L1}, 4_{L1}, 4_{L2}\}$. However, the shortest-path reaching node 4 in layer 2 is not a valid one, since it exists a shorter path that reaches node 4 in layer 1. To avoid counting these paths, we only consider a new path starts at w if w is the first accessed node considering its replicas in the different layers (see this check in line 35). The second particularity that we need to account for is multiplex path degeneracy, the case of node 5 (in layers 1 and 2) in Figure 3. There are two shortest-paths (shown in dotted blue) that reach node 5, one reaches node 5 in layer 1 and the other reaches node 5 in layer 2. Thus, for walks that end at node 5, the betweenness contribution to its predecessors, such as node 3 in layer 1, corresponds to the number of times we reach 5 considering the layer where it was reached divided by the times we reach 5 independently of the layer where it was reached. See in the Algorithm (line 36) how the contribution to predecessor v of w of the path that ends at w is given by $\frac{\sigma[w]}{\sigma_M[w]}$.

3. EXPERIMENTAL RESULTS

To analyze the computational cost of the algorithm and provide empirical evidences that the ranking of nodes is affected by the mutiplex structure, we performed numerical experiments on two real-multiplex networks. The first multiplex corresponds to a co-authorship network obtained from the arXiv repository (http://arxiv.org/). It is composed by 4 layers and 310 nodes per layer. Each layer corresponds to a category specially selected to have a certain fraction of authors in common in the layers. We selected: Physics and Society (physics.soc-ph), Condensed Matter (cond-mat.soft), Adaptation and Self-Organizing Systems (nlin.ao) and Social and Information Networks (cs.si). Within each layer, we only consider authors with at least six co-authors, and two authors have a tie if they co-authored at least two papers. With the largest connected component of each layer, we created the multiplex network by connecting the same author in the different layers with an edge. We did not consider any disambiguation mechanism since, in the selected subset, we detected less than 1% author names with a normalized Levenshtein distance greater than 0.95. The second multiplex corresponds to a directed ego multiplex of two layers, built gathering data from two on-line social networks: Twitter (https://twitter.com) and Instagram (http://instagram.com). From a list of 13297 users, obtained using an on-line ranking platform, we obtained their Twitter and Instagram Id. Neither disambiguation of names nor matching between them in both platforms was needed since users provide their user Id on both platforms. To construct the network, we selected users which have more than 21 friends on Twitter (obtaining 2000 individuals) and 10 friends in Instagram (obtaining 2756 individuals). The topology of each on-line social network was derived from the user's friend list. Thus, a user has a tie with another one if he/she is in his/her friend list. Equivalently to the co-authorship, to create the multiplex network, we inter-connected the users in both layers when possible.

Figure 4a and 4b show two plots with the difference of the rankings obtained with the aggregated network and with the multiplex network for the co-authorship and social networks, respectively. The values of the ranking have been computed using the Dense Ranking approach, and then normalized to be on the same scale. We see that the amount of entities that obtain different ranking on the two networks is notable in both cases. In the Arxiv co-authorship network 54% of the entities obtain different ranking and in the Twitter+Instagram network 87%. With respect to the relationship of the rankings obtained in the multiplex and in the aggregated network, we observe that there is a correlation of both measures. The amount of entities that obtained the same ranking can be seen in the central plateau of the figures. This plateau is greater in the co-authorship network where the lower differences are observed in the first ranked and last ranked entities. This tendency is justifiable since the centrality of the first ranked nodes is notably higher than middle ranked ones and the changes on the rankings is of few positions. In order to see this, we provide in Table 1 the first twelve ranked authors for the co-authorship network. Last ranked nodes have zero centrality in both rankings. On the Twitter+Instagram network, we also observe the lower differences for first ranked and last ranked entities. However, these differences are smaller, giving a narrower plateau and wider tails. The maximum difference on the rankings provided by the multiplex network and aggregated network is an increase 21% in the ranking for the co-authorship network and a decrease of 25% in the ranking for the on-line

---

Algorithm 1: Shortest path betweenness for multiplex networks. N corresponds to the number of nodes per layer, and L to the number of layers in the multiplex.

Data: G
Result: C_B

1   $C_B[1..N] \leftarrow 0$;
2   **for** $s \in 1 \ldots N$ **do**
3    $S \leftarrow$ empty stack;
4    $P[1..NL] \leftarrow$ empty list;
5    $\sigma[1..NL] \leftarrow 0, \sigma[w] \leftarrow 1, s \equiv w \mod N$;
6    $d[1..NL] \leftarrow -1, d[w] \leftarrow 0, s \equiv w \mod N$;
7    $d_M[1..NL] \leftarrow -1, d_M[w] \leftarrow 0, s \equiv w \mod N$;
8    $vOrder[1..N] \leftarrow$ empty list;
9    $Q \leftarrow$ empty queue;
10   Q enqueue s;
11   **while** Q *not empty* **do**
12     $v \leftarrow \text{first}(Q)$;
13   S push v;
14   **if** $v \neq s$ **then**
15      $W =$ neighbor of v in G
16   **else**
17      $W = \bigcup\limits_{\substack{v' \in \{1..NL\} \\ v' \equiv s \mod N}}$ neighbor of v' in G
18   **for** $w \in W$ **do**
19   **if** $d[w] < 0$ **then**
20   Q enqueue w;
21       $d[w] = d[v] + 1$;
22   **if** $d_M[w \mod N] < 0 \vee d_M[w \mod N] == d[w]$ **then**
23        $d_M[w \mod N] = d[w]$;
24        $vOrder[w \mod N]$ add w;
25   **if** $d[w] = d[v] + 1$ **then**
26       $\sigma[w] \leftarrow \sigma[w] + \sigma[v]$;
27       $P[w]$ add v
28   **for** $w \in \{1..N\}$ **do**
29     $\sigma_M[w] \leftarrow 0$;
30   **for** $v \in vOrder[w]$ **do**
31      $\sigma_M[w] \leftarrow \sigma_M[w] + \sigma[v]$
32   **while** S *not empty* **do**
33     $w \leftarrow pop(S)$;
34   **for** $v \in P[w]$ **do**
35   **if** $w \in vOrder[w \mod N]$ **then**
36       $\delta[v] \leftarrow \delta[v] + \frac{\sigma[v]}{\sigma[w]}\left(\frac{\sigma[w]}{\sigma_M[w]} + \delta[w]\right)$
37   **else**
38       $\delta[v] \leftarrow \delta[v] + \frac{\sigma[v]}{\sigma[w]}\delta[w]$
39   **if** $w \neq s$ **then**
40      $C_B[w \mod M] \leftarrow C_B[w \mod N] + \delta[w]$

social network. As a result, we can conclude that the centrality computed on the aggregated network is usually different than the centrality on the multiplex network. Thus, to obtain accurate betweenness centrality rankings it is crucial to compute these centralities directly on the multiplex structure.

A crucial point to consider on the definition of measures for networks is the computational cost of the algorithm required to compute them. Since most of real networks contain large number of nodes and also large number of edges, only algorithms with low computational cost are able to run over those networks. The theoretical computational complexity of the algorithm developed here is $\mathcal{O}(NLE)$ for unweighted mutiplex networks and $\mathcal{O}(NLE+N^2L^2\log NL)$ for weighted multiplex networks. N corresponds to the number of nodes per layer, L to the number of layers and E to the number of edges in the mutiplex structure.

Ranking	Multiplex	Aggregated
1	s.havlin	s.havlin
2	m.barthelemy	z.di
3	z.di	m.barthelemy
4	j.wu	h.e.stanley
5	h.e.stanley	j.wu
6	p.holme	h.jeong
7	a.l.barabasi	v.latora
8	r.lambiotte	r.lambiotte
9	m.barahona	s.sreenivasan
10	h.jeong	m.barahona
11	a.vespignani	p.holme
12	v.latora	a.l.barabasi

Table 1: First twelve ranked authors of the arXiv co-authorship dataset.

4. SUMMARY

Multiplex networks are state-of-the-art structures to represent social interaction, allowing to accurately represent different types of relation between individuals such as family relations, friendship relations or on-line social platforms communication. However, classical measures developed for single layer networks cannot be trivially extended (e.g. degree of the node, clustering coefficient or centrality) to this type of networks. This situation requires a careful re-definition of the classical measures and a brand new set of measures specific for multiplex networks. Among those measures, in this paper, we focus on shortest-path betweenness centrality. In the first part of the paper, we extended the classical definition and provide an appropriate interpretation of its meaning. We showed, my means of representative examples that shortest-path betweenness on multiplex networks tend to favor individuals which act as a bridge between layers allowing to connect individuals which are disconnected inside layers. In the second part of the paper, we provide an algorithm to compute the shortest-path betweenness with a computational cost of $\mathcal{O}(NLE)$ for unweighted multiplex networks and $\mathcal{O}(NLE + N^2L^2\log NL)$ for weighted multiplex networks.

To validate the convenience and the accuracy of the given centrality measure we conducted experiments on two real data multiplex networks, a co-authorship multiplex of 4 layers and an on-line social multiplex of 2 layers. Results show

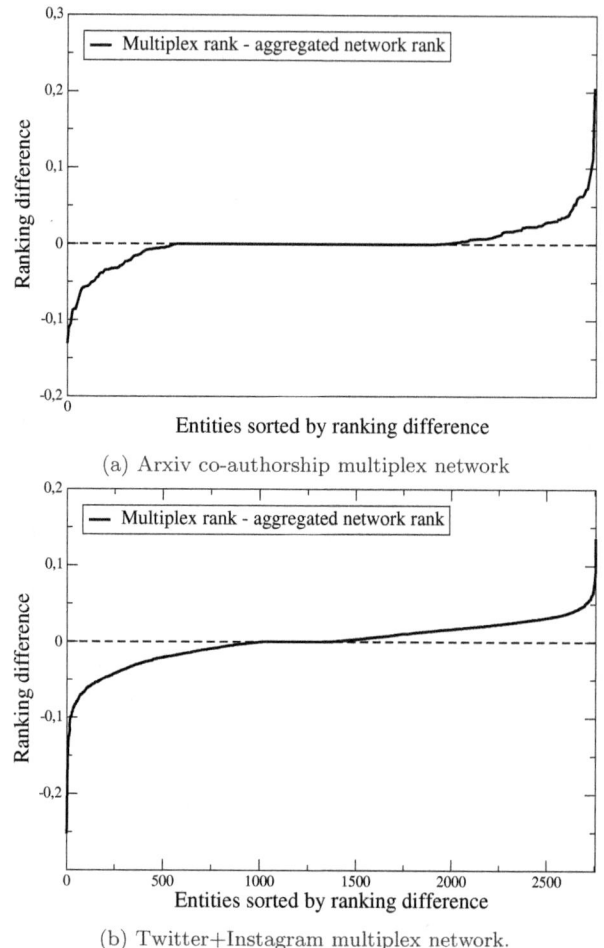

(a) Arxiv co-authorship multiplex network

(b) Twitter+Instagram multiplex network.

Figure 4: Plot showing the difference of the rankings obtained with the multiplex and with the aggregated network.

a clear difference between the rankings computed on the multiplex structure and the ones computed with the classical shortest-path betweenness on the aggregated network. From the results, we can conclude that the rankings computed on the aggregated network are a proxy of the multiplex rankings but to obtain accurate results these need to be computed directly on the multiplex structure.

5. ACKNOWLEDGMENTS

Manlio de Domenico, and Albert Solé-Ribalta are supported by the European Commission FET-Proactive project PLEXMATH (Grant No. 317614), Alex Arenas and Sergio Gómez acknowledge support from the project MULTIPLEX (grant 317532) and the Generalitat de Catalunya 2009-SGR-838. Alex Arenas also acknowledges financial support from the ICREA Academia and the James S. McDonnell Foundation, and Sergio Gómez and Alex Arenas are also supported by FIS2012-38266.

6. REFERENCES

[1] A. Arenas, L. Danon, A. Díaz-Guilera, and R. Guimerà. Local search with congestion in complex communication networks. In *International Conference on Computational Science*, volume 3038 of *Lecture*

Notes in Computer Science, pages 1078–1085. Springer, 2004.

[2] F. Battiston, V. Nicosia, and V. Latora. Metrics for the analysis of multiplex networks. *arXiv:1308.3182*, 2013.

[3] G. Bianconi. Statistical mechanics of multiplex networks: Entropy and overlap. *Phys. Rev. E*, 87:062806, 2013.

[4] S. P. Borgatti. Centrality and network flow. *Social Networks*, 27(1):55–71, Jan. 2005.

[5] U. Brandes. A faster algorithm for betweenness centrality. *Journal of Mathematical Sociology*, 25:163–177, 2001.

[6] A. Cardillo, M. Zanin, J. Gómez-Gardeñes, M. Romance, A. García-del Amo, and S. Boccaletti. Modeling the multi-layer nature of the european air transport network: Resilience and passengers re-scheduling under random failures. *The European Physical Journal Special Topics*, 215(1):23–33, 2013.

[7] M. De Domenico, A. Solé-Ribalta, E. Cozzo, M. Kivelä, Y. Moreno, M. A. Porter, S. Gómez, and A. Arenas. Mathematical formulation of multi-layer networks. *Phys. Rev. X*, 3:041022, 2013.

[8] M. De Domenico, A. Solé-Ribalta, E. Omodei, S. Gómez, and A. Arenas. Centrality in interconnected multilayer networks. *arXiv:1311.2906*, 2013.

[9] L. C. Freeman. Centrality in social networks conceptual clarification. *Social networks*, 1(3):215–239, 1979.

[10] J. Gao, S. V. Buldyrev, H. E. Stanley, and S. Havlin. Networks formed from interdependent networks. *Nature Phys.*, 8(1):40–48, 2011.

[11] P. Holme and J. Saramäki. Temporal networks. *Physics Reports*, 519:97–125, 2012.

[12] M. Kivelä, A. Arenas, M. Barthelemy, J. P. Gleeson, Y. Moreno, and M. A. Porter. Multilayer networks. *arXiv:1309.7233*, 2013.

[13] J. Kleinberg. Authoritative sources in a hyperlinked environment. *Journal of the ACM 46*, pages 604–632, 1999.

[14] T. G. Kolda and B. W. Bader. The TOPHITS model for higher-order web link analysis. In *Workshop on link analysis, counterterrorism and security*, volume 7, pages 26–29, 2006.

[15] T. G. Kolda, B. W. Bader, and J. P. Kenny. Higher-order web link analysis using multilinear algebra. In *IEEE INTERNATIONAL CONFERENCE ON DATA MINING*, pages 242–249. IEEE Computer Society, 2005.

[16] K.-M. Lee, J. Y. Kim, W.-K. Cho, K.-I. Goh, and I.-M. Kim. Correlated multiplexity and connectivity of multiplex random networks. *New J. Phys.*, 14:033027, 2012.

[17] X. Li, M. K. Ng, and Y. Ye. Har: Hub, authority and relevance scores in multi-relational data for query search. In *SDM*, pages 141–152. SIAM / Omnipress, 2012.

[18] M. Magnani and L. Rossi. The ml-model for multi-layer social networks. In *Proceedings of the 2011 International Conference on Advances in Social Networks Analysis and Mining*, ASONAM '11, pages 5–12, Washington, DC, USA, 2011. IEEE Computer Society.

[19] P. Mucha, T. Richardson, K. Macon, M. Porter, and J. Onnela. Community Structure in Time-Dependent, Multiscale, and Multiplex Networks. *Science*, 328(5980):876–878, May 2010.

[20] M. Newman. *Networks: An Introduction*. Oxford University Press, Inc., New York, NY, USA, 2010.

[21] M. E. J. Newman. Scientific collaboration networks. ii. shortest paths, weighted networks, and centrality. *Phys. Rev. E*, 64:016132, Jun 2001.

[22] M. K.-P. Ng, X. Li, and Y. Ye. Multirank: co-ranking for objects and relations in multi-relational data. In C. Apte, J. Ghosh, and P. Smyth, editors, *KDD*, pages 1217–1225. ACM, 2011.

[23] V. Nicosia, G. Bianconi, V. Latora, and M. Barthelemy. Growing multiplex networks. *Phys. Rev. Lett.*, 111:058701, 2013.

[24] L. Page, S. Brin, R. Motwani, and T. Winograd. The pagerank citation ranking: Bringing order to the web, 1999.

[25] L. Sola, M. Romance, R. Criado, J. Flores, A. G. del Amo, and S. Boccaletti. Eigenvector centrality of nodes in multiplex networks. *Chaos*, 3:033131, 2013.

[26] S. Wasserman and K. Faust. *Social Network Analysis: Methods and Applications*. Cambridge University Press, 1994.

[27] D. Zhou, S. A. Orshanskiy, H. Zha, and C. L. Giles. Co-ranking authors and documents in a heterogeneous network. In *INTERNATIONAL CONFERENCE ON DATA MINING*, pages 739–744. IEEE Computer Society, 2007.

Noticing the Other Gender on Google+

Diego Las Casas[1], Gabriel Magno[1], Evandro Cunha[1,2],
Marcos André Gonçalves[1], César Cambraia[2] and Virgilio Almeida[1]
[1]Dept. of Computer Science, [2]College of Letters – Federal University of Minas Gerais
Belo Horizonte, Minas Gerais, Brazil
{diegolascasas, magno, evandrocunha, mgoncalv, virgilio}@dcc.ufmg.br, nardelli@ufmg.br

ABSTRACT

Google+ provides a feature that has been overlooked in social media studies: the possibility of users setting their gender information not only as *female* or *male*, but as *other*
instead. In this paper, we discuss this particularity and,
more broadly, the issue of non-binary gender roles in the
Web. By analyzing a large dataset, we characterize some
aspects of self presentation, word use, network information
and country of residence among users who choose different
alternatives in the field *Gender*. On the whole, our main
contributions are to present preliminary results and to shed
light into the topic considered here – namely, the implications of having a third gender option to present oneself in
an online social networking service.

Categories and Subject Descriptors

K.4 [**Computers and Society**]: Social Issues

Keywords

Online social networks; Gender issues; Google+

1. INTRODUCTION

Google+ is a major online social networking service
launched by Google Inc. in June 2011. According to a recent
report [14], Google+ grew in terms of active usage by 33%
from June 2012 to May 2013 and was, in mid-2013, the second largest social platform in number of users, with about
360 million active profiles. As a comparison, at that time,
Facebook, the most popular online social network (OSN),
had almost 700 million active users; YouTube and Twitter,
respectively the third and the fourth most popular ones, had
slightly less than 300 million active users.

An interesting aspect of Google+ is that, during registration or any subsequent profile update, its users are given
the option of setting their gender information not only as
female or *male*, but also as *other*. This is an especially useful feature for profiles of members who do not associate with

a particular gender – like, from one side, profiles of couples,
groups and organizations; and from another side, profiles of
users who identify themselves as, for instance, non-gender,
transgender or intersex.

The main goals of this study are (a) to characterize the usage of an online social networking service by members who,
for any reason, declare themselves as neither female nor male
individuals, but as *other*; and (b) to raise awareness to the issue of non-binary gendered Web users. By investigating how
users who declare themselves as other-gendered in Google+
behave in this network, we also provide contrastive information on the behavior of declaredly female and male members
– and of Google+ users in general.

2. BACKGROUND

In gender studies, the term *gender* is often used to refer
to the social constructions of femininities and masculinities.
It does not refer to biological differences – which are usually
assigned to *sex* – but rather to cultural differences. In this
section, we briefly review how gender is framed in OSNs, as
well as how it has been studied by scholars.

2.1 Profile field "Gender" across networks

Until recently, Google+ was, among the most popular online social networking systems, the only one that provided
to its users the option *other* as an alternative to *female*
and *male* in the profile field *Gender*. Table 1 shows that,
among the ten most popular OSNs and social curating websites in the beginning of 2014 [4], three did not provide a
profile field *Gender* and only four provided an alternative
to *female* and *male*. It is worth noticing that Pinterest and
MySpace offered the *unspecified* alternative, which seems to
give an idea of indefiniteness not given by *other*.

Table 1: Answer options for the field *Gender* during
registration in the most popular OSNs

Online social network	Answer options for the field *Gender*	Is the answer compulsory?
Facebook	*Female / Male / Custom*	Yes
Twitter	Does not provide a field *Gender*	
LinkedIn	Does not provide a field *Gender*	
Google+	*Female / Male / Other*	Yes
Pinterest	*Female / Male / Unspecified*	Yes
Tumblr	Does not provide a field *Gender*	
Flickr	*Female / Male*	Yes
VK	*Female / Male*	Yes
Instagram	*Female / Male*	No
MySpace	*Female / Male / Unspecified*	Yes

There is a variety of reasons for a user choosing *other* as gender in an OSN. In the following lines, we will describe the three that we find most relevant for this study.

2.1.1 Not a person

As uses of social media are widely varied, many profiles can actually represent groups (e.g. bands), aggregations (e.g. couples), personas (e.g. fictional characters) or institutions (e.g. brands). All these kinds of profiles may eventually set *other* as gender.

In November 2011, Google+ added the possibility of creating special profile pages for institutions and organizations [5], which meant that these groups would not need to create new other-gendered profiles for this purpose. However, since a fraction of old business profiles did not enable this functionality, there are still organizations with profiles very similar to the ones of individual users.

2.1.2 Privacy worries

The option of setting gender information as private was enabled by Google+ in July 2011 [10] and those English-speaking users who set this information as private are identified by the pronoun *they* (as in *Alex updated **their** profile*), just like users who set their gender information as *other*[1].

Privacy-concerned users may declare their gender as *other* due to lack of knowledge of the feature of setting it as private, lack of interest in updating this field (if the profile was created before the pro-privacy feature was available) or because they do not want even Google and its commercial partners to have access to their gender identities.

2.1.3 Non-binarism

The *gender binary system* is a model of gender construction that classifies people into either *feminine* or *masculine*, *female* or *male*, *man* or *woman*, always as categorically distinct and mutually exclusive roles. It has been strongly criticized in the past decades as it is seen as a false dichotomy, since there are many more expressions of gender identities that cannot be collapsed into two discrete categories. Even the concept of *sex*, generally related to a biological basis, has its binarism called to question as it was shown to consist of numerous parts (e.g. chromossomal sex, anatomical sex, reproductive sex) and shades of gray (e.g. genital ambiguity and intersex conditions) [9]. Those who reject this binarism acknowledge *non-binary* or *transgender* identities. By allowing users to state that they are neither *female* nor *male*, Google+ opens up for non-binary gender identities to be expressed.

In February 2014, this subject made headlines due to the announcement that Facebook would allow users to pick a *custom gender* and it raised the discussion on the tailoring of online social media to transgender people [6].

2.2 On gender issues in social media

Two main approaches were identified by Van Doorn and Van Zoonen [13] as being taken by studies that address gender issues in digital environments: a) studies on *gender as identity* analyze the individual behavior of users of different genders either by enumerating gender differences in Internet usage or highlighting the importance of practices of ex-

perimentation of different gender roles in online situations; b) studies on *gender as social structure* describe gender inequalities, oppression or empowerment in technological settings. The authors noticed that both approaches frequently consider online and offline environments as separated entities, with one influencing the other but not the other way round. They suggest that gender roles should be approached as something that is both "shaping and shaped" by technology.

They also conclude that most studies show that the Internet reproduces inequalities and existing differences, but also enables new forms of transgressions of stereotypical gendered practices. This view is further explored by Van Doorn [12], who investigates micro-networks formed by close acquaintances in MySpace and concludes that these networks allow users to challenge standard norms of sexuality and gender roles through a cheerful interplay of stylistic forms.

Another work in this line is presented by De Ridder and Van Bauwel [3], who demonstrate how young users act their gender identities through commentaries in photos posted by other young users. They describe a rich symbolic environment in which gender roles are continually displaced and reaffirmed, showing tensions and contradictions that young users live in online interaction.

As boyd and Heer [1] frame it, social communication can be understood as performance, which is inherently embodied and contextually dependent. In this sense, *profiles* are digital bodies that interact to create social context within the network, which orients this performance. One of our goals is to explore empirically whether Google+ third gender option has had its effect in how users digital bodies interact in the online social environment.

3. DATA COLLECTION

To conduct this research, we collected Google+ public profiles of millions of users. Google+ members are able to choose the degree of visibility of the information available in their own profiles: social information, friends lists and posts published may be visible to friends, friends of friends, the general public or to customized lists of users, known as *circles*. For ethical and legal reasons, we only collected information set as public and did not attempt to access private information. Since our dataset was crawled from public Web pages, we can make it available upon request.

The data collection ran from March 23rd to June 1st, 2012. In order to retrieve the list of profiles to collect, we inspected the `robots.txt` file provided by Google+ and followed the corresponding sitemap to compile the lists of URLs of profiles. Because we collected the complete list of profiles provided by Google+, we believe that we collected information from all users with public profiles at the time of the data collection, gathering information from 160,304,954 profiles. By requesting the corresponding public friends list in the users' profiles, we also collected network information.

4. ANALYSES AND RESULTS

According to Magno et al. [7], *Gender* is the most shared profile field among those that can be set as private by Google+ users[2]: in our dataset, 126,531,842 (78.93%) of the more than 160 million users with profiles collected set their

---

[1] It is important to notice that the pronoun *they* is a common *preferred gender pronoun (PGP)* among transgenders and gender nonconforming people.

[2] *Name* is the most shared profile field, but users do not have the option of setting it as private.

gender information as public. Considering users who publicly shared their gender information, 80,683,714 (63.77%) declared themselves as *male*, 43,506,597 (34.38%) as *female* and 2,341,531 (1.85%) as *other*. In this section, we present the gender-related investigations performed in our dataset and the results obtained, as well as discuss findings.

4.1 Self presentation

Profile information is the first impression that users give to other network members. Here, we contrast profile information provided by Google+ users who report themselves as *female*, *male* and *other*, which should give insights into how they build their digital personas.

4.1.1 Looking for and Relationship status

Besides the field *Gender*, two Google+ profile fields have closed answer alternatives: *Looking for*, which suggests four alternatives, and *Relationship status*, which offers nine alternatives. In *Looking for*, network members can answer *friends*, *dating*, *relationship* and *networking*. Response to this field is not exclusive, meaning that users can choose from zero to all four alternatives. In our dataset, only 2,971,031 (1.9%) profiles filled this field in and set this information as public. In *Relationship status*, nine alternatives are available, going from traditional marital status (like *single* and *married*) to a joke option (*it's complicated*). This information is provided and set as public by 4,057,966 users (2.5% of the dataset).

Table 2 depicts information on the answers to these fields, showing the percentage of users who selected each option among those who made them available. Since members can select multiple options in the field *Looking for*, the sum of the percentages for each gender exceeds the value of 100.

Other-gendered users are less interested in *friends* (62.2% of other-gendered against 83.3% of females and 78.5% of males) and more interested in *networking* (62.5% of other-gendered against 40.2% of females and 55.7% of males) than the remaining users. This fact suggests that many of them are companies or organizations instead of individuals. For the remaining items, however, other-gendered users show interests in between of females and males.

Regarding relationship status, the large ratio of other-gendered users who reported their status as a non conventional or a non traditional one is meaningful: these users are the main selectors of the alternatives *it's complicated*, *in an open relationship*, *in a domestic partnership* and *in a civil union* – which together correspond to 33.0% of their responses, against only 8.0% of the responses of females and 7.6% of the responses of males.

4.1.2 Self-descriptive fields

Google+ profiles have three self-descriptive fields: *Tagline*, that invites users to shortly introduce themselves; *Introduction*, in which network members provide extended self-presentations; and *Bragging rights*, where they are encouraged to talk about their own reasons for pride.

Table 3 depicts the most frequent nouns in each of these fields by gender in order to exhibit common elements of self-presentation. The high prevalence of words related to business among other-gendered users (like *service*, *business* and *company*) reinforces our hypothesis that most users in this category are actually companies and commercial ventures. For this reason, we also provide the same information

Table 2: Information available in the fields *Looking for* and *Relationship status* by gender

Looking for	Total	Female	Male	Other
Friends	79.7%	83.2%	78.5%	62.2%
Networking	50.0%	40.2%	55.7%	62.5%
Relationship	25.3%	13.7%	32.3%	19.9%
Dating	22.3%	11.8%	28.7%	18.4%

Relationship status	Total	Female	Male	Other
Single	42.4%	35.4%	47.7%	24.0%
Married	27.2%	28.0%	26.7%	20.1%
In a relationship	17.3%	22.3%	13.8%	13.7%
Engaged	4.3%	5.4%	3.5%	4.5%
It's complicated	4.3%	4.7%	3.7%	16.3%
In an open relationship	2.0%	1.4%	2.3%	8.6%
In a domestic partnership	1.3%	1.4%	1.1%	3.7%
Widowed	0.7%	0.8%	0.6%	4.0%
In a civil union	0.5%	0.5%	0.5%	4.4%

for users who not only report themselves as other-gendered, but publicly inform their relationship status – institutions and organizations will hardly fill this profile field in. We named this category as *other (V.R.)* (as in *visible relationship*) and Table 3 suggests that this filtering may be effective to help identifying individual users, as the most frequent words among them are similar to the ones of declared female and male members. This gives us a useful preliminary way of distinguishing between two kinds of other-gendered users, which we will use frequently along the paper.

Table 3: Most frequent nouns in each self-descriptive field by gender

Tagline				
Rank	Female	Male	Other	Other (V.R.)
1st	love	life	love	love
2nd	life	love	life	life
3rd	girl	man	music	fun
4th	fun	music	world	people
5th	world	guy	service	world

Introduction				
Rank	Female	Male	Other	Other (V.R.)
1st	love	love	service	love
2nd	life	life	business	life
3rd	years	years	people	people
4th	people	music	world	name
5th	name	time	company	time

Bragging rights				
Rank	Female	Male	Other	Other (V.R.)
1st	school	school	years	school
2nd	kids	kids	school	kids
3rd	children	years	world	years
4th	love	college	service	love
5th	years	life	business	life

4.2 Word use

Users communicate with others in Google+ through posts and comments. Since communication is gendered, users express their gender identities in their choice of words, as seen in a number of studies [8, 2]. We wished to understand how other-gendered users express themselves in relation to those with different gender identities: if they are conforming to a binary identity, they will tend to have an expression that is similar to one gender or another; otherwise, their expression will be in between the binaries.

For each gender, we calculated the frequency of usage of each word in the posts shared by its members and selected the 1% most common words. Then, we found the percentage of male users who employed each word present in the *male + female* frequency count and calculated the z-score of the percentages. This gave us a rough empirical measure representing how "masculine" a given word is in relation to an arbitrary "binary-only" basis: negative values mean words predominantly used by women (i.e., very feminine), while positive values indicate words employed mostly by men (i.e., very masculine). *User scores* were then obtained by averaging the score of all words employed by each user. This analysis was also focused in users filtered by the visibility of their relationship status, as described above.

Figure 1 shows the distribution of *user scores* by gender. There is a significant overlap between the distributions and, by construction, male users are shifted to the right, whereas female users are shifted to the left. This shows that our measure does differentiate between these two genders, which, however, are not completely separated – since they, as expected, do not have entirely different vocabularies. Other-gendered users are more spread than the other two genders and their distribution is centered between females and males. This hints to our hypothesis that their expression is less bounded by binary gender roles, as they seem to be able to transit between identities more associated with "masculine" and "feminine" performances.

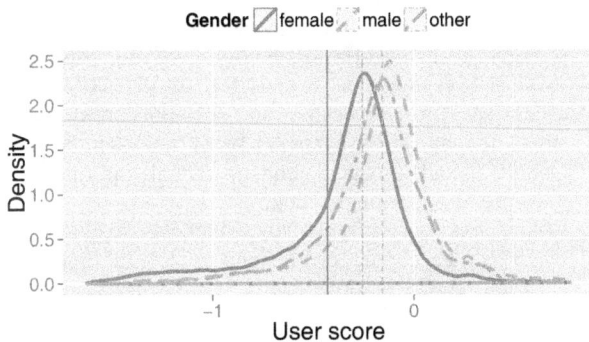

Figure 1: Density distribution of *user scores* by gender. Vertical Lines represent the averages.

4.3 Network structure

To undestand how other-gendered users are situated inside the network, we examined fundamental whole network and ego-network[3] metrics. Here, again, we also consider the visibility of the field *Relationship status*, since we observed that users who share more social information are likely to be more active(*e.g.* Users who share this field have higher average out-degree (46) than those who do not (19).

4.3.1 Clustering coefficient

The local clustering coefficient (CC) of an user is the probability of any two of its neighbors being neighbors themselves. Figure 2 depicts the mean value of CC for each gender. It shows that, independently of the visibility of the relationship status, other-gendered users have higher CC values than female and male users, which indicates that their ego-networks tend to be more densely connected.

---

[3]The ego-network of an user is formed by the user herself, her 1-hop neighbors and the respective connections among them.

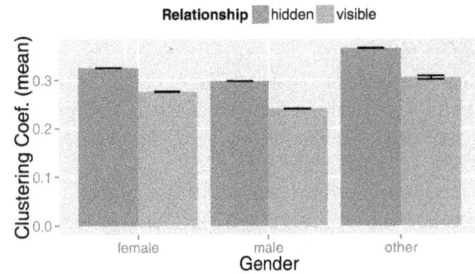

Figure 2: Mean clustering coefficient by gender ± standard errors

4.3.2 Homophily

In this analysis, we investigate the rate of homophily among gender groups in the network – that is, if users of a particular gender are more prone to connect to users of that same gender. For a given user, we calculated the fractions of neighbors of each gender, considering only neighbors with public gender information, so that the sum of the three fractions for a particular user is equal to 1.0. Although we present only the results for the outgoing edges, the incoming edges produce qualitatively equivalent results. Figure 3 shows the cumulative distribution functions of the three fractions for users with visible relationship information. We observe that users of a particular gender have higher fractions of neighbors of that same gender, indicating that there is, indeed, homophily in the network. Interestingly, values for all fractions of other-gendered members are in between those of female and male users, except for the fraction of neighbors of their own group.

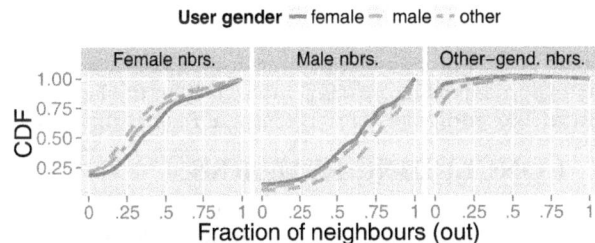

Figure 3: Cumulative distribution functions of fractions of neighbors by gender

Taken together, these results suggest that other-gendered users tend to be connected by a rich network with more other-gendered users, perhaps in a community fashion.

4.4 Country of residence as social context

Google+ has an international penetration, and thus its users are exposed to widely different social realities. Although describing the relationship that users from different societies have with gender identities is beyond our scope, we can investigate how expressive are other-gendered profiles across countries.

Users are able to supply a list of names of places where they have lived in the field *Places lived*. They can be as specific as they want and can describe a particular location in distinct ways (e.g. "Rio de Janeiro", "Rio", "RJ") and levels of precision (e.g. "Paris", "Île-de-France", "France"). We extracted the geographic coordinates of the most recent information on the list – which is expected to indicate a user's current location – and translated them into valid location identifiers, which allowed us to identify the country of 22,578,898 (14.08%) users.

For each country in our dataset, we calculated the fraction of other-gendered users relative to the total amount of users. We call this measure *Other-Gendered Proportion* (OGP). To avoid biases and "mock locations"[4], we excluded from this analysis countries with less than 10,000 users in the dataset, which left us with a total of 21,563,667 users in 96 countries.

Figure 4 shows countries with highest and smallest OGPs. Some of them have extremely inexpressive OGPs, and it is worth noticing that some of the countries in the bottom 10 list are also countries with poor indicators of gender equality. In fact, a country's OGP seems to be related to gender equality indicators: the Spearman correlation between OGP and the Gender Inequality Index from 2012's Human Development Report [11] is -0.53, or -0.57 if we consider only users with visible relationship status (both values are statistically significant under $p < 0.0001$). Note that the correlations are negative because the indexes measure *inequality*.

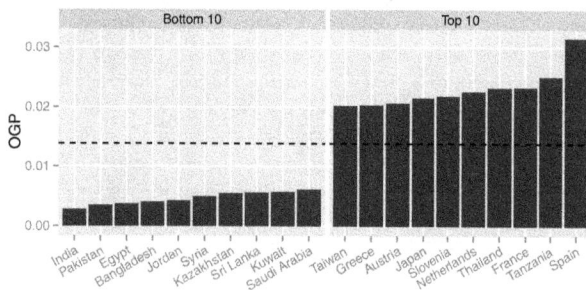

Figure 4: Country-wise proportion of users who declare themselves as *other-gendered*. The dashed horizontal bar indicates the average across countries

5. CONCLUDING REMARKS

In this paper, we analyzed users who chose *other* as their gender identity in Google+. We started by describing the profile information that they make public to show how they present themselves to the online world. We also related their word choices to those from binary-gendered users and showed that they are able to situate themselves in between the binary. By looking at their network features, we suggested that they link to additional other-gendered users and have, in general, dense ego-networks. We also observed that users from distinct countries have different dispositions towards expressing themselves as other-gendered, and we correlated this disposition to a social measure associated to gender equality. It should be noted that our results might be biased by the fact that the percentage of users from each gender who declare their own gender information can be asymmetric. Also, gender swapping is a known behavior in several online situations. These factors could not be controlled here and shall be addressed in future studies.

---

[4]Many users seem to state fake locations as a humorous tweak in their profiles.

Although *other* as a gender option impacts users' digital identities, its vagueness foreshadows the importance of OSNs allowing users to express their personal struggles through the network. The lack of a proper word for transgender identities hinders the clarity and profundity of this impact, as it unables users to distinguish among institutions, privacy-worried individuals and transgender users. Given the possibility, users will shape their profiles to better match their identities, and this will spread within the network.

Users tell stories by interacting with others in a (semi-) public environment. These stories are bounded by different media logics – such as an OSN user interface –, which in turn shape the representations that users build for themselves. The possibility of declaring oneself as *other* instead of collapsing to standard binarism allows network members to reshape their digital bodies, impacting gender identities and social contexts around them.

6. REFERENCES

[1] d. boyd and J. Heer. Profiles as conversation: Networked identity performance on Friendster. In *Proc. of Hawaii Int'l Conf. on System Sciences*, 2006.

[2] E. Cunha, G. Magno, M. A. Gonçalves, C. Cambraia, and V. Almeida. He votes or she votes? Female and male discursive strategies in Twitter political hashtags. *PLOS ONE*, 9(1):e87041, 2014.

[3] S. De Ridder and S. Van Bauwel. Commenting on pictures: teens negotiating gender and sexualities on social networking sites. *Sexualities*, 16(5-6), 2013.

[4] eBizMBA. Top 15 most popular social networking sites | January 2014. http://bit.ly/1d2L2hr, 2014.

[5] Google. Google+ pages: connect with all the things you care about. Google Blog, http://bit.ly/1czGpxI, November 2011.

[6] B. Griggs. Facebook goes beyond 'male' and 'female' with new gender options. CNN, http://cnn.it/1l3zn9o, February 2014.

[7] G. Magno, G. Comarela, D. Saez-Trumper, M. Cha, and V. Almeida. New kid on the block: exploring the Google+ social graph. In *Proceedings of the ACM Internet Measurement Conference (IMC'12)*, 2012.

[8] H. A. Schwartz, J. C. Eichstaedt, M. Kern, et al. Personality, gender, and age in the language of social media: The open-vocabulary approach. *PLOS ONE*, 8(9):e73791, 2013.

[9] S. Stryker and S. Whittle, editors. *The Transgender Studies Reader*. Routledge/Taylor & Francis, 2006.

[10] H. Tsukayama. Google Plus makes gender a private matter. The Washington Post, http://wapo.st/1fMfmj9, July 2011.

[11] United Nations Development Programme. Human development report. http://hdr.undp.org, 2012.

[12] N. Van Doorn. The ties that bind: the networked performance of gender, sexuality and friendship on MySpace. *New Media & Society*, 12(4), Nov. 2009.

[13] N. Van Doorn and L. Van Zoonen. Theorizing gender and the Internet: Past, present, and future. *The Routledge Handbook of Internet Politics*, 2008.

[14] T. Watkins. Suddenly, Google Plus is outpacing Twitter to become the world's second largest social network. http://read.bi/1khuhED, May 2013.

Latent Dirichlet Allocation: Stability and Applications to Studies of User-Generated Content

Sergei Koltcov
National Research University
Higher School of Economics
ul. Soyuza Pechatnikov, 27
St. Petersburg, Russia
skoltsov@hse.ru

Olessia Koltsova
National Research University
Higher School of Economics
ul. Soyuza Pechatnikov, 27
St. Petersburg, Russia
ekoltsova@hse.ru

Sergey Nikolenko
National Research University
Higher School of Economics
ul. Soyuza Pechatnikov, 27
St. Petersburg, Russia
sergey@logic.pdmi.ras.ru

ABSTRACT

Topic modeling, in particular the Latent Dirichlet Allocation (LDA) model, has recently emerged as an important tool for understanding large datasets, in particular, user-generated datasets in social studies of the Web. In this work, we investigate the instability of LDA inference, propose a new metric of similarity between topics and a criterion of vocabulary reduction. We show the limitations of the LDA approach for the purposes of qualitative analysis in social science and sketch some ways for improvement.

Categories and Subject Descriptors

G.3 [**Mathematics of Computing**]: Probability and Statistics – Probabilistic algorithms (including Monte Carlo); G.1.0 [**Mathematics of Computing**]: Numerical Analysis – stability (and instability); I.1.2 [**Computing Methodologies**]: Algorithms – analysis of algorithms; I.2.7 [**Artificial Intelligence**]: Natural Language Processing – text analysis

Keywords

Latent Dirichlet Allocation, topic modeling, social analysis

1. INTRODUCTION

With huge growth of online text data, it is becoming vitally important for social scientists to have reliable methods for fast automated analysis of such data. Researchers are, in particular, interested in methods able to track agendas, topics, opinions, and sentiments in user-generated content that can later be used for the purposes of political science, sociology, marketing, and other disciplines. One of the methods aimed at detecting topical structure in large text collections is a class of probabilistic models called Latent Dirichlet Allocation (LDA); these models have become the *de facto* standard in the field of topic modeling. However, comprehensive investigations of the quality of these models for qualitative studies are very scarce, and some indicators of quality, such

as reproducibility of results, have hardly been researched at all. Instead, complex extensions of the algorithm are rapidly proliferating [2,4,9,18], as well as applications of topic modeling to specific datasets and applied goals, e.g., qualitative studies, without comprehensive prior testing [7].

Informally speaking, quality for social scientists means that the algorithm is able to show the topics "that are really there". In particular, a social scientist would expect that a topic modeling algorithm detects all "existing" topics, does not show any "non-existing" topics, and shows their "true" proportion. Then the researcher would conclude, say, whether the online public is currently talking more about elections than about popstars (in sociological context), or more about one brand than another (in marketing context). While it is unclear how to judge this notion of quality, stability is obviously an important sanity check: if a model gives different results each time it is run on the same data, it certainly does not draw the "true" picture of social reality.

In LDA, each document expresses multiple topics at once, each with a certain affinity. Likewise, each topic is a distribution on words. Thus, from the mathematical point of view each document is a mixture of distributions. To find the word-topic and topic-document matrices (probabilities of words appearing in topics and topics appearing in documents), one has to approximate the initial set of documents by these distributions. Two most popular approaches are based on variational approximations [1,3] and Gibbs sampling [5] respectively. These algorithms find a local maximum of the joint likelihood function of the dataset; this is accepted as a solution for the topic modeling problem. Moreover, the LDA approach has been further developed by offering more complex model extensions with additional parameters and additional information [2,4,9,18]. However, from the end user's point of view a local maximum does not necessarily represent a satisfactory solution for the topic modeling problem. In the case of LDA, there are plenty of local maxima [5], which may lead to instability in the output. Therefore, before using LDA social scientists have to understand how stable the output will be; this, in turn, calls for an instrument of comparison between different solutions that would be able to capture similarity between topics as sets of words with probabilities. One important problem is the huge "long tail" of words with low probabilities that are mostly irrelevant for qualitative analysis but may contribute to the level of similarity between topics. Therefore, we may need additional criteria for reducing these sets of words.

WebSci'14, June 23–26, 2014, Bloomington, IN, USA.
Copyright 2014 ACM 978-1-4503-2622-3/14/06 ...$15.00.
http://dx.doi.org/10.1145/2615569.2615680.

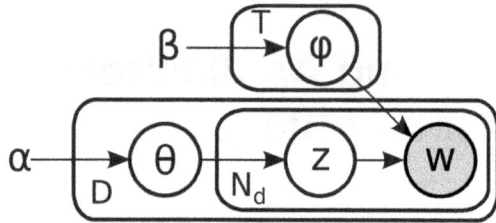

Figure 1: LDA graphical model.

In this work, we investigate the instability of the LDA algorithm, proposing a new metric of similarity between topics and a method for vocabulary reduction. We show the limitations of LDA for the purposes of qualitative analysis in social sciences and sketch some ways to improvement. Section 2 shows related work and our contributions. In Section 3, we introduce the new similarity metric, in Section 4 we use it to evaluate LDA stability, and Section 5 concludes the paper.

2. LDA AND OUR CONTRIBUTIONS

2.1 LDA

The basic latent Dirichlet allocation (LDA) model [3,5] is depicted on Fig. 1. In this model, a collection of D documents is assumed to contain T topics expressed with W different words. Each document $d \in D$ is modeled as a discrete distribution $\theta^{(d)}$ over the set of topics: $p(z_w = j) = \theta_j^{(d)}$, where z is a discrete variable that defines the topic for each word $w \in d$. Each topic, in turn, corresponds to a multinomial distribution over the words, $p(w \mid z_w = j) = \phi_w^{(j)}$. The model also introduces Dirichlet priors α for the distribution over documents (topic vectors) $\theta \sim \mathrm{Dir}(\alpha)$, and β for topical word distributions, $\phi \sim \mathrm{Dir}(\beta)$. The inference problem in LDA is to find hidden topic variables $\boldsymbol{z}$, a vector spanning all instances of all words in the dataset. There are two approaches to LDA inference: variational approximations and MCMC sampling which in this case is convenient to frame as Gibbs sampling. After easy transformations [5], Gibbs sampling reduces to the so-called *collapsed Gibbs sampling*, where z_w are iteratively resampled with distributions

$$p(z_w = t \mid \boldsymbol{z}_{-w}, \boldsymbol{w}, \alpha, \beta) \propto p(z_w, t, \boldsymbol{z}_{-w}, \boldsymbol{w}, \alpha, \beta) =$$
$$= \frac{n_{-w,t}^{(d)} + \alpha}{\sum_{t' \in T} \left(n_{-w,t'}^{(d)} + \alpha \right)} \frac{n_{-w,t}^{(w)} + \beta}{\sum_{w' \in W} \left(n_{-w,t}^{(w')} + \beta \right)},$$

where $n_{-w,t}^{(d)}$ is the number of times topic t occurs in document d and $n_{-w,t}^{(w)}$ is the number of times word w is generated by topic t, not counting the current value z_w.

2.2 Evaluating LDA quality with perplexity

One well established method for numerical evaluation of topic modeling results is to measure *perplexity*. Perplexity shows how well the model predicts new test samples; for a set of held-out documents D_{test} one computes $p(d \mid D) = \int p(d \mid \phi, \theta) p(\phi, \theta \mid D) \mathrm{d}\theta \mathrm{d}\phi$ for each held-out document d and then normalizes the result as $\mathrm{perplexity}(D_{\text{test}}) = \exp\left(-\frac{\sum_{d \in D_{\text{test}}} \log p(d)}{\sum_{d \in D_{\text{test}}} N_d}\right)$. To compute $p(d \mid D)$, various algorithms have been proposed, the current standard being the so-called left-to-right algorithm [16,17].

The smaller the perplexity, the better (less uniform) is the LDA model and the more it differs from the starting distribution. However, an important drawback of evaluating the quality of a parametric LDA model with perplexity is the fact that the value of perplexity drops as the number of topics grows, so perplexity does not really yield a way to find the optimal number of topics either numerically or qualitatively. In general, topic modeling can be thought of as clustering, and it inherits certain problems of clustering, including the problem of finding the optimal number of clusters (model selection). Moreover, perplexity depends on the dictionary size which further complicates the comparison of different results. De Waal and Barnard [15] studied perplexity as a function of dictionary size (for a fixed number of topics and documents) and showed that when the dictionary was reduced by 70%, perplexity dropped by a factor of three. Unfortunately, the authors do not analyze how these changes affect the final result of topic modeling, i.e., how well the topics represent the actual contents of the dataset.

In general, perplexity is a good measure to estimate convergence of the iterative process but it is unclear how to use it to evaluate the quality of topic modeling, especially from the point of view of human interpretation.

2.3 Evaluating LDA quality with Kullback–Leibler divergence and topic correlation

Steyvers and Griffiths [6] propose to evaluate LDA quality with a symmetric Kullback–Leibler divergence. This approach is based on pairwise comparisons of two solutions to the topic modeling problem. The pairwise comparison is computed as

$$\mathrm{KL} = \frac{1}{2} \sum_w \phi_w^1 \log \frac{\phi_w^1}{\phi_w^2} + \frac{1}{2} \sum_w \phi_w^2 \log \frac{\phi_w^2}{\phi_w^1},$$

where ϕ_w^1 is the word distribution for the first topic; ϕ_w^2, for the second topic. This metric shows similarity between two topics, but further analysis that would analyze the stability of topic reproduction in multiple topic modeling experiments on the same dataset has not been performed. Besides, the Kullback–Leibler divergence only gives an estimate of the similarity of two topics while detailed analysis would have to take into account some evaluation of the *dis*similarity between two topics.

A different approach to pairwise comparisons between topics was proposed by de Waal and Barnard [15]. Instead of Kullback–Leibler divergence, they propose a method to compute correlation between documents from two topic modeling experiments. The method consists of the following steps: (1) construct a bipartite graph based on two topical solutions; (2) compute the minimal distance between topics in this bipartite graph; (3) compare topics between two cluster solutions based on the minimal distance. This means that two topics are similar if they have the smallest distance between them as compared to the distance from these two topics to other topics. To compute minimal distances in the bipartite graph, the authors use the so-called Hungarian method, also known as Kuhn's method [8]. The authors show that correlation between documents does not depend on dictionary size as much as perplexity.

2.4 Our contributions

In this work, we propose several new metrics for evaluating different aspects of topic modeling. Namely, we introduce the notions of document and word ratios that show the fraction of words and documents that are actually relevant to specific topics. This lets us drastically cut the vocabulary in our novel topic similarity metric based on Kullback–Leibler divergence; we show that this metric matches qualitative expectations of the notion of similar topics quite well. Armed with this metric, we study the stability of Gibbs sampling for LDA inference and discover that modeling results are unstable, and sociological analysis based on topic modeling should proceed with extra care. We conclude with recommendations for further studies.

In numerical experiments, we used a popular LDA inference implementation based on Gibbs sampling, GibbsLDA++ [10]. The dataset for experiments consists of Russian language LiveJournal posts for October 2013 that we have collected for the purposes of qualitative sociological and media studies. There are 298,967 posts in the dataset with 35,049,514 instances of 153,536 unique words.

3. EVALUATING SPARSITY

3.1 Word and document ratios

LDA inference algorithms based on Gibbs sampling rely upon random sampling used to generate topic variables z for document instances on each iteration. Thus, topic modeling by itself is influenced by random noise: topic variables for both documents and topics fluctuate randomly during modeling. However, the LDA inference algorithm guarantees that the iterative process converges to a certain value of perplexity with some noise, which means that the number of words and documents used in modeling also converge to a certain value.

To estimate the number of high probability words and documents, we introduce the notion of *ratio*. Ratio is closely related to the notion of perplexity. The initial distribution for words and documents is uniform, so the probability of each topic in each document starts from $1/K$, where K is the number of topics, and the probability of each word in each topic starts from $1/V$, where V is the dictionary size. During inference, probabilities of words and topics in documents change, but they still, obviously, sum up to one; some words and topics rise above the average values of $1/K$ and $1/V$, and the others sink below it.

We introduce *document ratio* as the parameter that characterizes the ratio of the total number of topics with probability greater than $1/K$ over all documents:

$$\mathrm{DR} = \frac{1}{K|D|} \sum_{d \in D} \sum_k \left[\theta_k^{(d)} > \frac{1}{2} \right].$$

At the beginning of the first iteration, $\mathrm{DR} = 1$; over Gibbs sampling iterations, DR begins to drop and then, at some point, it stabilizes and converges to some value; we can stop the Gibbs sampling as fluctuations of DR attenuate. Similarly, we formulate the notion of *words ratio* which is the ratio of the number of words in all topics with probability higher than $1/V$ to the total number of words in all topics:

$$\mathrm{WR} = \frac{1}{KW} \sum_w \sum_k \left[\phi_w^k > \frac{1}{2} \right].$$

Note that the same document (resp., word) may participate in the computation of document ratio (resp., word ratio) several times.

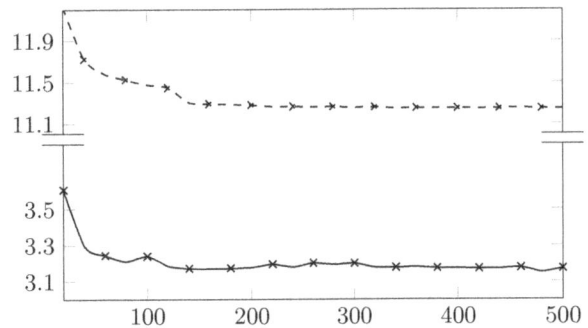

Figure 2: Sample document ratio (dashed line, %) and word ratio (solid line, %) as a function of iteration index.

Figure 2 shows the behaviour of word and document ratios for a sample run of LDA inference with 120 topics. In this case, the word ratio stabilized after 150–200 iterations around 3.2%; document ratio, around 11.5%. One can also introduce the average word ratio over a set of samples as $\mathrm{AWR} = \frac{1}{n} \sum_{i=1}^n \mathrm{WR}_i$, where WR_i is the word ratio measured at the ith sample; similarly, the average document ratio is introduced as $\mathrm{ADR} = \frac{1}{n} \sum_{i=1}^n \mathrm{DR}_i$. Our experiments with different number of topics (from 50 to 280) have shown that the word ratio stabilizes around 3.5% and document ratio stabilizes around 11.5% in all experiments, with standard deviation of the results being about 0.5-1%.

3.2 KL-based similarity metric

The Kullback–Leibler divergence is a widely accepted distance measure between two probability distributions. However, directly computing KL divergence to measure similarity between two topics in a topic modeling result does not lead to a good result since the KL value is dominated by the long tail of low probability words that do not define the topic in any qualitative way and are mostly random. Therefore, in this section we devise a modification for the KL metric to measure similarity between topics.

As we have shown above, the number of words with above average probabilities in our experiments was about 3.5% of the total number of unique words in all topics. We left only words top probabilities in at least one topic reducing the dictionary from 153,536 tokens (words) to 8000 (about 5.2%). This also lets us compute KL divergence faster since it has complexity $O(K^2W)$, where K is the number of topics and W is the dictionary size.

Another deficiency of the "vanilla" Kullback–Leibler divergence is that it significantly depends on the dictionary size [15]. This means that while the KL divergence is always zero (or very close to zero) when two distributions coincide almost exactly, it may have values all over the $[0, 1]$ for two very distinct topics if we consider different dictionaries and different pairs of topics, so it is hard to find a good general threshold for KL divergence. To get such a threshold, we propose to normalize KL divergence by making the distance between two least similar topics artificially equal to 1. Thus, we introduce the normalized KL similarity measure as

$$\mathrm{NKLS}(t_1, t_2) = \left(1 - \frac{\mathrm{KL}(t_1, t_2)}{\max_{t_1', t_2'} \mathrm{KL}(t_1', t_2')} \right),$$

where KL denotes the regular KL divergence. In the NLKS measure, 1 corresponds to a perfect match and 0 corresponds to the furthest possible distributions among given sets of topics.

3.3 Topic similarity thresholds

Kullback–Leibler divergence takes into account the long tail of topic-word distributions, and it may happen (and often does) that large deviations in KL-based metrics do not really correspond to significant differences in top words, i.e., the words that a qualitative researcher would use to define and understand a topic. To estimate this effect, we need to study how similarity between top words relates to the NLKS similarity measure.

Our studies have shown that in topics with similarity $0.93 - 0.95$ and higher, the 30-50 most probable words coincide almost exactly, and the sequences in which they appear in the list sorted by probability are also very similar; thus, similarity levels of 0.93 and higher indicate that a qualitative researcher would almost certainly treat these topics as the same. Similarity level about 0.9 usually corresponds to the situation when the first 30-50 words in the ranked list do match, but they have different probabilities and go in a different order; Table 1 shows a sample pair of such topics. The similarity level of 0.85 usually corresponds to a situation when two topics have a completely different set of top words.

Therefore, our experiments indicate that the proposed NLKS metric does correspond well to a qualitative estimation of topic similarity, and the similarity threshold for "truly similar" topics appears to be around 0.9. In the next section, we apply this metric to study the stability of Gibbs sampling.

4. TOPIC STABILITY

4.1 Experimental setting

In topic modeling, the posterior distribution which is maximized during inference may have a very complex and certainly nonconvex shape. This leads to multiple local maxima; in practical terms, it means that different runs of the same software may lead to different results, in particular, different word-topic distributions. Therefore, it becomes of primary importance to test the stability of topic reproduction. We propose the following method to estimate the stability of reconstructing topical solutions for given (unchanged) α and β parameters and a fixed number of topics. We perform several runs of the LDA inference software GibbsLDA++ [10] with the same parameters, getting several word-topic and topic-document distributions. Since these distributions result from the same dataset with the same vocabulary and model parameters, any differences between them are entirely due to the randomness in Gibbs sampling. This randomness affects perplexity variations, word and document ratios, and the reproducibility of the qualitative topical solution. Words may change their probabilities in topics, and it makes sense to use a KL-based measure to compare topical solutions. We use the normalized measure NLKS introduced above.

In our experiments, we performed six runs with $K = 120$ topics with model parameters $\alpha = 0.5$, $\beta = 0.1$ on our dataset with 298,967 documents and a vocabulary of 153,536 unique words. Then we performed pairwise comparisons of the results with the NLKS metric, computing how similar

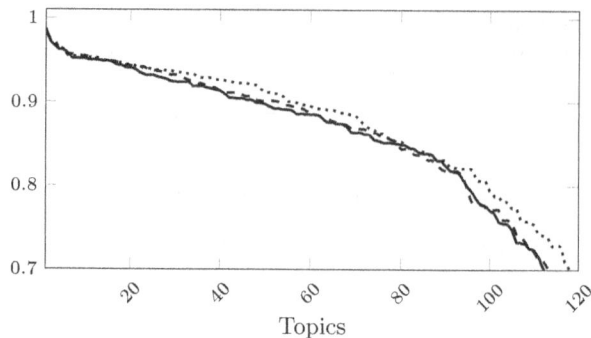

Figure 3: Topic similarity sorted in decreasing order; lines correspond to different test run comparisons.

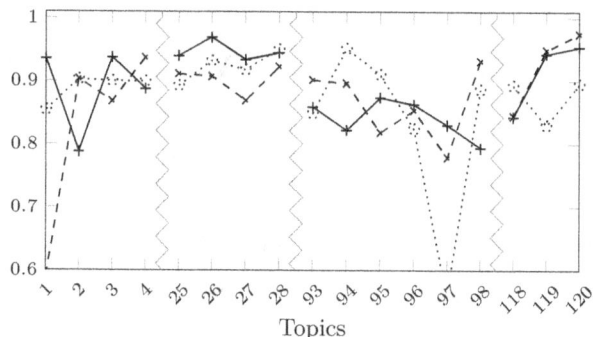

Figure 4: Sample topic similarities across test runs.

the topics are across different runs, for each pair of models getting a $K \times K$ matrix whose elements represent the similarity metric between topics. Then, for each topic of one model (i.e., a row of the similarity matrix) we find the most similar topic in the second model (i.e., a column).

4.2 Results

Fig. 3 shows topics sorted according to similarity in three comparisons between different runs of LDA inference. It shows that less than half of the topics are reproduced with reliable stability (similarity > 0.9); this share would be even smaller if we required more than two matches. Fig. 4 shows several sample similarities between specific topics (showing the top similarity value among topics from another test). Some topics, (e.g., topics 25–28) fluctuate very little across the runs, with NLKS similarity of 0.95-1.0, while others (e.g., 1 and 97) have large deviation, with fluctuations around 40%; in practice this means that in some runs, these topics are simply not found at all. On average, fluctuations amount to 0.2065 per topic.

One might expect that the topics that do not reproduce well are "trash" topics based on common words or that would not be of interest for social studies anyway. Unfortunately, this is not the case; for instance, an interesting and readily interpretable topic on the war in Syria (first pair of topics in Table 1) reproduced only three times out of six runs in our experiments. Hence, a qualitative study might conclude that war in Syria either is very interesting for Russian bloggers or goes completely unnoticed, depending on the random number generator in Gibbs sampling.

Similarity 0.935				Similarity 0.9				Similarity 0.854			
USA	0.04734	USA	0.03567	tree	0.03195	tree	0.03321	USA	0.04734	water	0.01758
American	0.02406	American	0.01804	forest	0.021	forest	0.01918	American	0.02406	help	0.01296
Syria	0.02082	Syria	0.01758	garden	0.01527	green	0.01631	Syria	0.02082	city	0.01262
Obama	0.01374	country	0.01495	mushroom	0.015	mushroom	0.01563	Obama	0.01374	far	0.01199
weapon	0.01343	war	0.01361	leaf	0.01389	garden	0.01478	weapon	0.01343	house	0.01064
war	0.01309	military	0.01246	plant	0.01291	leaf	0.01453	war	0.01309	east	0.0104
president	0.01169	weapon	0.01084	grow	0.01146	plant	0.0135	president	0.01169	region	0.00945
UN	0.01018	Russia	0.01004	green	0.00873	grow	0.01277	UN	0.01018	dam	0.0091
military	0.01014	Obama	0.00996	collect	0.00779	color	0.01045	military	0.01014	flood	0.00904
country	0.01005	president	0.0096	rose	0.00764	flower	0.00809	country	0.01005	resident	0.00839
chemical	0.00944	UN	0.00869	flower	0.00744	rose	0.00809	chemical	0.00944	injured	0.00714
Syrian	0.00851	international	0.00769	color	0.00701	collect	0.00766	Syrian	0.00851	FRS	0.00698

Table 1: Three pairs of topics with NLKS measures. The first pair of topics did not reproduce in other runs.

5. CONCLUSION

In automated analysis of user-generated content on the Web, topic modeling provides unparalleled possibilities for sociological analysis by allowing the researcher to quickly evaluate the topical map of a corpus of texts, draw conclusions on what topics are discussed there and how intensively. However, in this work we show that classical implementations of inference in LDA models should be applied with care, since the algorithms contain inherent uncertainty in regard to which local maximum they arrive to, and unlike some other nonconvex optimization problems, in the case of LDA this does in fact matter. We show that even topics that can be easily interpreted qualitatively and appear to be full of meaning for a sociologist may be in fact unstable, showing up only in a fraction of LDA inference runs.

Therefore, to be able to draw specific sociological conclusions we recommend researchers to run topic modeling multiple times (even with the same parameters), then distinguish stable topics that reappear across multiple runs and analyze only those. We have proposed a new topic similarity measure based on Kullback–Leibler divergence.

LDA has already been critiqued for lack of stability and similar faults [11]. Our results show that further work is required to solve the underlying problem, namely to improve stability of topic modeling. One recently initiated direction of studies that we believe to be promising in this regard deals with regularized topic models. It appears that instead of Bayesian regularization it may be better to use more general Tikhonov regularizers; however, Tychonoff regularization in application to topic modeling is a research direction still in its infancy [13,14], and further work is required.

6. REFERENCES

[1] D. M. Blei. Introduction to probabilistic topic models. *Communications of the ACM*, 2011.

[2] D. M. Blei and J. D. Lafferty. Correlated topic models. *Advances in Neural Information Processing Systems*, 18, 2006.

[3] D. M. Blei, A. Y. Ng, and M. I. Jordan. Latent Dirichlet allocation. *Journal of Machine Learning Research*, 3(4–5):993–1022, 2003.

[4] A. Daud, J. Li, L. Zhou, and F. Muhammad. Knowledge discovery through directed probabilistic topic models: a survey. *Frontiers of Computer Science in China*, 4(2):280–301, 2010.

[5] T. Griffiths and M. Steyvers. Finding scientific topics. *Proceedings of the National Academy of Sciences*, 101 (Suppl. 1):5228–5335, 2004.

[6] T. Griffiths and M. Steyvers. Probabilistic topic models. In T. Landauer, D. Mcnamara, S. Dennis, and W. Kintsch, editors, *Latent Semantic Analysis: A Road to Meaning*. Laurence Erlbaum, 2006.

[7] O. Koltsova and S. Koltcov. Mapping the public agenda with topic modeling: The case of the Russian livejournal. *Policy & Internet*, 5(2):207–227, 2013.

[8] H. W. Kuhn. The Hungarian method for the assignment problem. *Naval Research Logistics Quarterly*, 2:83–97, 1955.

[9] S. Z. Li. *Markov Random Field Modeling in Image Analysis*. Advances in Pattern Recognition. Springer, Berlin Heidelberg, 2009.

[10] X.-H. Phan and C.-T. Nguyen. GibbsLDA++: A C/C++ implementation of latent Dirichlet allocation (LDA), 2007.

[11] A. Potapenko and K. Vorontsov. Robust PLSA performs better than LDA. In P. Serdyukov, P. Braslavski, S. O. Kuznetsov, J. Kamps, S. M. Rüger, E. Agichtein, I. Segalovich, and E. Yilmaz, editors, *Advances in Information Retrieval - 35th European Conference on IR Research, ECIR 2013, Moscow, Russia, March 24-27, 2013. Proceedings*, volume 7814 of *Lecture Notes in Computer Science*, pages 784–787. Springer, 2013.

[12] A. N. Tikhonov and V. Y. Arsenin. *Solution of Ill-posed Problems*. Washington: Winston & Sons, 1977.

[13] K. V. Vorontsov. Additive regularization of topic models. In *Proc. 16th Russian Conf. on Mathematical Methods for Image Recognition*, page 88. MAKS Press, 2013.

[14] K. V. Vorontsov and A. A. Potapenko. Modifications of EM algorithm for probabilistic topic modeling. *Machine Learning and Data Mining*, 1(6), 2013.

[15] A. D. Waal and E. Barnard. Evaluating topic models with stability, 2008.

[16] H. M. Wallach. *Structured topic models for language*. PhD thesis, University of Cambridge, 2008.

[17] H. M. Wallach, I. Murray, R. Salakhutdinov, and D. Mimno. Evaluation methods for topic models. In *Proceedings of the 26th International Conference on Machine Learning*, pages 1105–1112, New York, NY, USA, 2009. ACM.

[18] X. Wang and A. McCallum. Topics over time: a non-Markov continuous-time model of topical trends. In *Proceedings of the 12th ACM SIGKDD International Conference on Knowledge Discovery and Data Mining*, pages 424–433, New York, NY, USA, 2006. ACM.

Do Ordinary Bloggers Really Differ From Blog Celebrities?

Olessia Koltsova[*]
National Research University
Higher School of Economics
16 ul. Soyuza Pechatnikov
St. Petersburg, Russia
ekoltsova@hse.ru

Sergei Koltcov
National Research University
Higher School of Economics
16 ul. Soyuza Pechatnikov
St. Petersburg, Russia
skoltsov@hse.ru

Svetlana Alexeeva
National Research University
Higher School of Economics
16 ul. Soyuza Pechatnikov
St. Petersburg, Russia
salexeeva@hse.ru

ABSTRACT

In this paper we describe structural and topical properties of "ordinary" blogs versus "popular" blogs. Using the complete directory of the Russian language LiveJournal, we sample both groups and show that the main difference between them is in the volume of posting activity and of commenting feedback and in the skewedness of respective distributions. No substantial differences in topical structure obtained with the LDA algorithm are found, which suggests that ordinary bloggers do not hold specific vision of topic salience and do not set their own "grassroots" agendas.

Categories and Subject Descriptors

G.3. [**Mathematics of Computing**]: Probability and Statistics – *Probabilistic algorithms (including Monte Carlo)*; I.2.7 [**Artificial Intelligence**]: Natural Language Processing - *text analysis*; J.4 [**Computer Applications**]: Social and Behavioral Sciences – *sociology*.

Keywords: Live Journal, blogger, public opinion, topic modeling.

1. INTRODUCTION

User-generated content in blogs and social media may be a valuable source (and a new form of existence) of public opinion and of public agendas [8; 15; 17] of internet-active fraction of the population. Blogs as long-form user media provide a possibility to develop arguments at length and thus present a richer material for opinion and agenda analysis than social networking sites. Bloggers do not represent the entire population of a country or of a language community, but since they are those who choose to explicitly articulate their views and have a chance to influence the society through public dissemination of those, they are of interest per se. However, making samples of blogs and bloggers so that they are representative of a country's blogosphere, is also problematic. Complete directories of blogs are extremely rare, while lists of most popular bloggers are not. Therefore, A-list bloggers are the most available and the most studied [16]; however, this approach might have certain limitations. Top bloggers are often regarded "regular" media than as vox populi

---

[*] Corresponding author.

WebSci'14, June 23–26, 2014, Bloomington, IN, USA.
Copyright 2014 ACM 978-1-4503-2622-3/14/06 ...$15.00.
http://dx.doi.org/10.1145/2615569.2615675

since they are publicity oriented and often pursue commercial interests. Agendas, visions of topic salience and opinions of "ordinary" bloggers situated in the long-tail of the blogosphere might differ from those on the top. In this paper, we seek to check this assumption (in relation to agendas) and to reveal other basic features of "ordinary" bloggers as compared to "popular" authors which may help building more accurate and better justified samples.

2. RELATED WORK

Massive sampling of blogs and blog texts has been rare, therefore, we know little about the basic structural properties of the blogosphere as a collection of texts (this is true for social networking sites as well, although this is beyond the scope of this paper). Attempts to model the blogosphere have usually centered around its hyperlinking structure [10; 18]. On the contrary, works on text classification (clustering, topic modeling) of blogs have used conventional text collections that were cut out of the body of the blogosphere with little concern about their representativeness since the main goal of such works has always been methodological [11; 13]. Berkman center has made a series of blogosphere maps based on hyperlink analysis and subsequent, relatively sketchy hand coding of selected blogs in clusters produced by links between the most active blogs [1; 2; 5]. This means that it maps well the most vibrant part of the blogosphere only. A study on the Russian language blogosphere topical structure with a topic modeling algorithm that includes massive sampling has however been based on top 2000 most popular bloggers [8]. A few other studies of ordinary bloggers by social scientists have all been done by hand coding of small samples of texts [4; 14; 17]. The lion share of the works have been devoted to English-language blogs, with only some attention to other languages, Chinese above all [2; 5; 6; 12].

3. GOALS AND HYPOTHESES

The goal of this work is to compare the agendas, that is the topical structures of the "popular" and the "ordinary" bloggers in the Russian language blogosphere, as well as some other features of these two groups of bloggers. Given the assumption about top bloggers as media professionals versus ordinary bloggers as lay agenda generators, we have formulated the following hypotheses:

H1: since top bloggers are publicity and influence oriented, they devote their blogs to public affairs more than ordinary bloggers who seek for interpersonal communication with friends and thus tend to write about private and recreational issues.

H2: activity of ordinary bloggers is significantly lower and shifted towards weekends, in contrast to professional top bloggers.

H3: as devoted to trivial private issues, texts of ordinary bloggers are significantly shorter and less commented.

4. DATA, SAMPLE AND METHOD

The research is based on the data retrieved from the Russian language LiveJournal as the leading blogging platform in Russia – both in terms of the number of accounts and activity [1]. The list of the LJ "Cyrillic" accounts is publicly available, which gives a rare possibility to dig into the structural properties of the entire blogging service. The bloggers in the list are rated according to their popularity based on the number of their friends who have recently visited their blog. The precise methodology is the LJ commercial secret. Before the main sampling, a series of tests was run retrieving monthly collections of all texts of 5,000 blogs cut out of different parts of the rating list, with step 50,000, down to place 505,000. Spam accounts were filtered out manually. It has shown a fast decrease of the number of posts per blogger and the number of comments per post as we move down the rating list. At the range of places 150,000 – 200,000 that was studied in more detail the number of posts drops especially dramatically and stabilizes at the level of a few hundred per 5,000 bloggers per month, and a few dozens of comments. This means that the rest part of LJ is virtually inactive and does not worth sampling.

Table 1. Basic properties of blogs

	Popular bloggers	Ordinary bloggers	Ordinary bloggers without e_kopylov
Bloggers, total	2000	20004	20003
Bloggers with posts (active bloggers), abs.	1907	9683	9682
Active bloggers, %	95,3	48,4	48,4
Comments, total	2501821	298333	298333
Posts, total	135083	163884	121584
Posts per blogger	67,5	8,2	6,1
Posts per active blogger	70,8	16,9	12,6
Comments per post	18,5	1,8	2,5
Comments per blogger	1250,9	14,9	14,9
Comments per active blogger	1311, 9	30,8	30,8
Commented bloggers, abs.	1895	5631	5631
Commented bloggers %	94,8	28,2	28,2
Active non-commented bloggers, abs.	12	4052	4051
Active non-commented bloggers, %	0,6	41,8	41,8
Commented posts, abs.	95067	32338	32338
Commented posts, %	70,4	3,4	26,6
Mean post length, words	269		255

The sample of popular bloggers has comprised all posts written by top 2000 bloggers, the threshold being taken from the previous research [8]. "Ordinary" bloggers were sampled randomly from the range 2,001-150,000 so that the total number of posts be equal to that of the top bloggers, which resulted in the sample of 20,000 "ordinary" bloggers. The period of study has been selected so as to contain no major political events or large-scale disasters, and it spans from September 14 to October 14, 2013. Altogether, 298967 posts and 2800154 comments were retrieved. Basic descriptive statistics is represented in Table 1. While plotting basic distributions it was found out that 42,300 messages (25% of all ordinary posts) were "written" by e_kopylov around October 12; all of them contained the same spam (students' works for sale); this was acknowledged in further calculations.

As in previous studies, we have used topic modeling approach to discover the topical structure in the selected blogs. A Latent Dirichlet Allocation (LDA) algorithm with Gibbs sampling [3] was run over the joint collection of pre-processed posts yielding the probabilities of each topic in each text, as well as the probabilities of each unique word in each topic (topic-document matrix and word-topic matrix, respectively). The number of topics was set = 120 based on earlier experiments [8]. The probabilities of each topic in texts were then summed up separately for each group of bloggers ("top" vs "long tail"), which gave us the "weights" of each topic in the two groups. As we show elsewhere [7], LDA does not give stable solutions when run multiple times on the same data. Therefore, five runs of the algorithm were performed, the latter four being compared to the initial one. Topics from the initial solution were hand-labeled by two independent coders who later agreed on their coding, after which the topics were grouped into four broader categories: public affairs, recreational, private, and noise (topics that human coders can not interpret and label).

5. RESULTS

5.1. Structural properties of top and long-tail blogs

As shown in Table 1, posts of ordinary bloggers are not much shorter if e_kopylov's texts 46-52 words each are disregarded. The distributions are also identical and power-law. However, the number of posts per blogger is actually one order of magnitude less, and the distribution is different. Only half of ordinary bloggers have authored at least one post during the period of study against 95% of popular bloggers. Posts of active ordinary bloggers are distributed by power-law with 10% of authors having written only one text (Figure 1b), while the distribution of posts among popular bloggers is, albeit highly skewed, still of a bell shape and peaks at the range of 4-10 posts per blogger (Figure 1a). At the same time, 20 most active bloggers in both groups generate around a thousand of posts each, which means that activity among ordinary authors is present, but is very uneven and hard to find if the sample size is small.

A more striking difference can be observed in the level of commenting (Figures 1c, 1d). Around 40% of ordinary bloggers among those who have authored at least one post get no comments at all, against less than 1% of popular bloggers. Posts that generate comment threads of more than ten entries amount to about fifty thousand among popular bloggers and to less than 3,000 among ordinary bloggers. It means that the long tail is an unlikely place to find elaborated discussions where opinions, conflicts and solidarities may emerge, and that the communication in the long tail is mostly monologic.

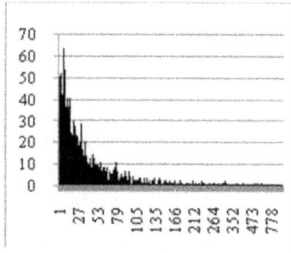

Figure 1a. Posts per blogger, top

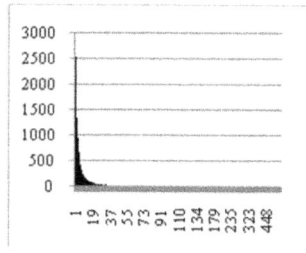

Figure 1b. Posts per blogger, long tail

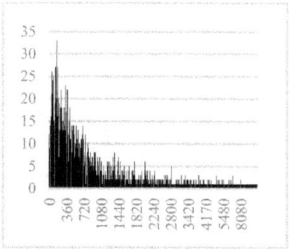

Figure 1c. Comments per blogger, top

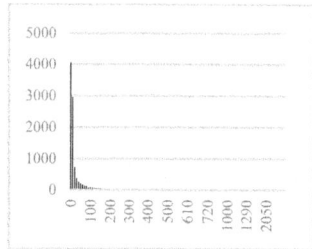

Figure 1d. Comments per blogger, long tail

One might argue that getting a few replies from your close friends might be not less meaningful than a hundred comments from unknown fans. However, many features indicate dominance or at least abundance of non-lay activity in "ordinary" blogs. One of such indicators is post to comment ratio of a blogger. Its distribution among ordinary authors looks artificial and gives strange peaks at integers and other "nice" values: 2 (the largest peak), 2.5 (a little lower), 2.25, 2.75 (still a little lower) etc. (Figures 2a, 2b). This can happen if comments are automatically generated in pre-set numbers, which points at substantial presence of spambots in the long tail. This is not seen among the popular bloggers and, in general, nothing resembling automatic commercial content has been observed during our three-year study of this group.

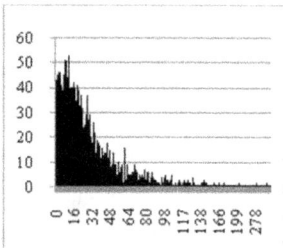

Figure 2a. Comment to post ratio of popular bloggers

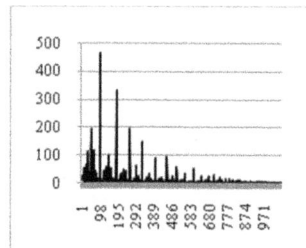

Figure 2b. Comment to post ratio of ordinary bloggers

Lay character of long-tail bloggers' activity is not confirmed by its distribution over the days of the week. Both popular and ordinary bloggers write less on the week-ends, and the difference between week-ends and working days is statistically significant in both cases (with dependent variable "number of posts", Eta coefficients are 0.976 for top bloggers and 0.723 for ordinary bloggers).

5.2. Topical composition of the top and the long-tail blogs

Topical composition of the joint collection has been found to be not much different from our earlier research [8] which indicates that the selected period of study is not an outlier. The differences in totaled weights of each topic between the sample of popular bloggers' posts and that of the ordinary bloggers are shown in Figure 3. The positive part of Y axis shows topics prevailing in the long tail; the negative part – topics prevailing in the top of LJ. Since the absolute number of posts of popular bloggers is slightly larger, first, the totaled weights of each topic were normalized to the range 0-100. Then the difference between the weights of each topic in the top vs the long tail was expressed in % of the sum of its two normalized weights (e.g. if the weight of topic X comprises 1,5% of the top and 1% of the long tail, these weights relate as 60 to 40 and thus differ by 20%).

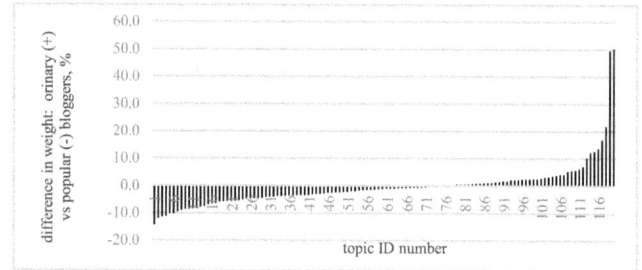

Figure 3. Prevalence of topics among popular and ordinary bloggers

Tables 2 and 3 show 15 topics most prevailing in top and in the long tail respectively, with corresponding difference scores.

Table 2. Topics prevailing in the top

Topics prevailing in the top	diff., %	stab.
Livejournal	-14,3	5
World's most beautiful places	-12,0	5
Unusual animals	-11,3	5
LJ competitions	-11,0	3
Architecture	-10,2	4
Movies	-10,2	2
Photo	-9,5	2
Visual art	-8,9	4
Top USA issues	-8,5	2
Middle East was	-8,4	5
Russia and USA in the Syrian conflict	-8,3	3
Ancient history	-8,2	4
Tourism and leisure	-7,7	4
European history	-7,4	4
Alcohol drinks	-6,8	3

No meaningful reason can be seen for some topics to prevail over others in the two groups. Indeed, no statistically significant difference was revealed between weights of merged topic categories: political affairs, private, recreational and noise.

Table 3. Topics prevailing in the long tail

Topics prevailing in the long tail	diff., %	stab.
Classical scholars	50,2	3
Student papers to download	49,4	3
Uninterpretable (noise)	21,7	4
Uninterpretable (noise)	16,8	3
Automobile industry news	13,6	5
Schedule of the day	12,6	3
DotA computer game	12,3	5
Uninterpretable (noise)	10,3	2
Russian and Ukrainian economics	7,1	4
Discussions on family law	6,2	2
Esoteric practices	5,7	4
Uninterpretable (noise)	5,6	5
legislation	5,3	4
Uninterpretable (noise)	4,1	2
transcendent domain	4,1	5

The same result was received when recreational and private topics were united (see Table 4). Thus the differences look like random fluctuations.

Table 4. Topic clusters and ordinary/popular bloggers

Blogger groups		Topic groups		
		public affairs	recreatioanl & private	Noise
all topics	popular bloggers	35.6%	42.9%	21.5%
	ordinary bloggers	34.9%	43.4%	21.6%
stable topics	popular bloggers	17.2%	16.5%	3.8%
	ordinary bloggers	16.4%	15.9%	4.1%

6. CONCLUSIONS AND FURTHER RESEARCH

It may be concluded that ordinary bloggers do not significantly differ from popular bloggers in the agendas they set, in the length of their posts and in the time cycles of posting. Their main difference is in the amount of posting activity and in the volume of feedback they get. Since posting activity is distributed among ordinary bloggers even more unevenly than among popular authors, it may be concluded that those ordinary bloggers who generate content (and who are not bots) do not differ in it from top users at all, however, they are diluted with inactive and spam accounts. This suggests that there is no hidden public holding a vision of topic salience different from that of the most popular media-like and publicity oriented bloggers.

However, firstly, it is a question whether this is a feature of the Russian LiveJournal or of any blogging service and any blogosphere in general. Secondly, it is not yet known if ordinary bloggers have the same attitudes to same agendas: LDA usually unites "PRO" and "CONTRA" utterances into the same topic if the utterances are devoted to the same issue (and share the same vocabulary). Thus, earlier it was shown that political messages of popular LJ bloggers are predominantly oppositional [9], but this does not mean that the LJ long-tail is as full of oppositional moods as its top.

Secondly, it is not yet clear whether LDA, as well as other automatic methods of text analysis, is able to detect private topics. Trivial everyday conversations usually lack specific vocabularies, their difference from each other and from the more vocabulary-specific talk thus being quite low. Therefore, when private messages are united with vocabulary-specific texts such as reposted media news, the differences between the former may be overshadowed with larger differences between the latter. It thus may happen that, when reliably detected, private topics may show up in the long tail to a much greater extent than in the top. Therefore, more experiments are needed that among other things might include tests with training collections of posts using everyday speech.

Another direction for further research is improving LDA stability that will allow more precise judgments on salience of individual topics in the long tail rather than of broad categories. Finally, ordinary bloggers might also differ not in their vision of topic salience, but in their attitudes to the same agendas. This demands further development of opinion mining and sentiment analysis approaches. Meanwhile, top bloggers can be viewed as a fair and a reasonably easy-to-reach proxy of the blogosphere, or of the Russian language LiveJournal at the very least.

7. ACKNOWLEDGEMENTS

This research was carried out at the Laboratory for Internet Studies at the National Research University Higher School of Economics (HSE), Russia with the funding from the Basic Research Program of HSE in 2013.

8. REFERENCES

[1] Etling B., Alexanyan, K., Kelly, J., Faris, R., Palfrey, J. and Gasser, U. (2010). "Public Discourse in the Russian Blogosphere: Mapping RuNet Politics and Mobilization". Berkman Center Research Publication. October 19, 2010. http://cyber.law.harvard.edu/publications/2010/Public_Disco urse_Russian_Blogosphere

[2] Etling D., Kelly J., Faris R., Palfrey J. (2009) Mapping the Arabic Blogosphere: Politics, Culture and Dissent. *Berkman Center for Internet and Society Research Publication* No. 2009-06.

http://cyber.law.harvard.edu/sites/cyber.law.harvard.edu/files /Mapping_the_Arabic_Blogosphere_0.pdf

[3] Griffiths T.L., Steyvers M. (2004) Finding scientific topics. *Proceedings of the National Academy of Sciences*, 101. P. 5228–5235.

[4] Herring, S. C., Scheidt, L. A., Bonus, S., and Wright, E. (2005). Weblogs as a bridging genre. Information, Technology & People, 18 (2), 142-171.

[5] Kelly J., Etling B.(2008) Mapping Iran's Online Public: Politics and Culture in the Persian Blogosphere. *Berkman Center for Internet and Society Research Publication* No. 2008-01. http://cyber.law.harvard.edu/sites/cyber.law.harvard.edu/files/Kelly&Etling_Mapping_Irans_Online_Public_2008.pdf

[6] King, G., Pan J., and Roberts. M.E. (2013). How Censorship in China Allows Government Criticism but Silences Collective Expression. *American Political Science Review* 107(2 (May): 1-18

[7] Koltcov S., Koltsova O., Nikolenko S. Latent Dirichlet Allocation: Stability and Applications to Studies of Usergenerated Content. Preprint. http://www.hse.ru/data/2014/02/21/1331648934/websci_01.pdf

[8] Koltsova O., Koltcov S. Mapping the public agenda with topic modeling: The case of the Russian Livejournal. Policy & Internet. – UK: Wiley-Blackwell, 2013. Vol. 5. № 2. P. 207–227

[9] Koltsova, O., Shcherbak, A. (2014) 'LiveJournal Libra!': The political blogosphere and voting preferences in Russia in 2011–2012. *New Media and Society*, April 2014.

[10] Lescovec J., McGlohon M., Faloutsos C., Glance N., Hurst M. (2007)Patterns of Cascading Behavior in Large Blog Graphs. Proceedings of the 2007 SIAM International Conference on Data Mining.

DOI:http://dx.doi.org/10.1137/1.9781611972771.60

[11] Li, B.; Xu, S. and Zhang, J. (2007). "Enhancing Clustering Blog Documents by Utilizing Author/Reader Comments". In *Proceedings of the 45th ACM Southeast Conference*

(ACMSE 2007), pages 94-99, Winston-Sale, North Carolina http://portal.acm.org/citation.cfm?id=1233359 (accessed 16 February 2011).

[12] Mandl. Th. (2009). Comparing Chinese and German blogs. HT '09 Proceedings of the 20th ACM conference on Hypertext and hypermedia. Pages 299-308. ACM New York, NY, USA.

[13] Nallapati R. and Cohen W.W. (2008). "Link-PLSA-LDA: A New Unsupervised Model for Topics and Influence of Blogs". *Proceedings of ICWSM 2008*.

[14] Papacharissi, Z. (2007). "Audiences as Media Producers: Content Analysis of 260 blogs". In Tremayne, Mark (ed). *Blogging, Citizenship and the Future of Media.* NY&London: Routledge.

[15] Sayre B., Bode, L., Shan, D., Wilcox, D. and Shah, C. (2010). "Agenda Setting in a Digital Age: Tracking Attention 8 in Social Media, Online News, and Conventional News". *Policy and Internet*, Vol.2, Iss. 2, article 2.

[16] Trammell K. D., Keshelashvili A. (2005) Examining the New Influencers: A Self-Presentation Study of A-List Blogs. Journalism & Mass Communication Quarterly December 2005 vol. 82 no. 4968-982.

[17] Wallsten K. (2007). Agenda Setting and the Blogosphere: An Analysis of the Relationship between Mainstream Media and Political Blogs. *Review of Policy Research*, Vol. 24, N.6, pages 567-587.

[18] Zakharov P. (2007) Structure of LiveJournal social network. *Proc. SPI 6601, Noise and Stochastics in Complex Systems and Finance*, 660109.

Multimodal Communication on Tumblr: "I Have So Many Feels!"

Elli Bourlai
Indiana University
ebourlai@indiana.edu

Susan C. Herring
Indiana University
herring@indiana.edu

ABSTRACT

We manually analyzed a corpus of Tumblr posts for sentiment, looking at images, text, and their combination. A dataset was constructed of posts with both text and images, as well as a dataset of posts containing only text, along with a codebook for classifying and counting the content in each. This paper reports on the construction of the overall corpus and the codebook, and presents the results of a preliminary analysis that focuses on emotion. Posts containing images expressed more emotion, more intense emotion, and were more positive in valence than posts containing only text. The study contributes a micro-level analysis of multimodal communication in a social media platform, as well as a gold standard corpus that can be used to train learning algorithms to identify sentiment in multimodal Tumblr data.

Categories and Subject Descriptors

K.4.m [Computing Milieu]: Computers and Society – *miscellaneous*.

General Terms

Measurement, Human Factors.

Keywords

Communication, GIF, image analysis, meme, multimodality, sarcasm, sentiment, social media.

1. INTRODUCTION

Increasingly, meanings are expressed through images in social media. The use of animated GIFs to express opinions and reactions, for example, is popular on sites such as 4chan and Tumblr, as well as in the comment sections of forums and blogs. On some sites, users continuously create new GIFs to express a range of attitudes and emotions, some of which become memes [11] and spread to other internet contexts [2]. What research methods should be used to analyze these new meaning units?

One possibility is to employ sentiment analysis and machine learning to analyze attitudes expressed through images. However, although sentiment analysis (SA) has been an active area of research in recent years [12], most SA research focuses on text; fewer studies have analyzed images, let alone animated GIFs. This is because automating image SA is challenging; thus far, it has tended to rely on textual tags/metadata provided by users and low-level visual features [22]. Manual annotation of the expressive meanings conveyed in images would provide richer information and could raise the quality of sentiment studies that make use of machine learning, but it is a time-consuming process.

Moreover, it is not enough to analyze images alone. Images and text work together to create meaning on multimodal social media sites: The text often provides context for the images,

indicating, for example, that the image's apparent message is intended sarcastically. Sarcasm is especially difficult to detect using automated methods [7]. Furthermore, text is sometimes embedded directly into images [13], making it part of the image's meaning. Thus text and image need to be analyzed in relation to one another. Few studies have done this in a systematic way.

In the study reported in this paper, we manually analyzed a corpus of Tumblr posts for sentiment, looking at images, text, and their combination. Two datasets were constructed – one of posts with both text and images, and the other of posts containing only text – along with a codebook for classifying and counting the content in each. Here we report on the construction of the two datasets and the codebook, and present the results of a preliminary study of a subset of the corpus that focused on emotion. The results indicate that posts with images express more emotion, more intense emotion, and are more positive in valence than posts containing only text. The study thus makes two contributions: It advances knowledge of multimodal (especially image) communication in social media, and it provides a manually-tagged gold standard corpus [20] that could be used to train learning algorithms to identify sentiment in multimodal Tumblr data.

2. BACKGROUND

2.1 Tumblr

Tumblr is a microblogging service that was founded in February 2007 by David Karp. As of 2014, it had 172.2 million blogs and 77.2 billion posts [19]. Tumblr users have their own individual blog(s), on which they can post new content or "reblog" content posted by other Tumblr users. Users can choose among seven rebloggable types of posts: text, photo, link, audio, video, chat, and quote. Tumblr also has a Private Messaging (PM) feature that lets users reply to messages received either privately or publicly. Most Tumblr users are female and under 34 years old [15].

Tumblr is especially known for its use of reaction GIFs: short clips of movies and television shows that communicate emotions ("feels"), reactions, and everyday events [4]. These images typically originate in Tumblr and spread to other electronic environments [6]; some of them become associated with specific meanings and functions, and acquire the status of internet memes. Despite Tumblr's popularity and reputation as a source of reaction GIFs, however, we are not aware of any studies that have been conducted of such images.

2.2 Relevant Literature

Several studies have applied machine learning techniques to predict the sentiment of images in social media. For example, [17] analyzed a corpus of Flickr photographs using user-generated text tags and low-level visual features such as color to train a classifier. [21] leveraged mid-level attributes of Twitter images to predict their sentiment, including material (e.g., metal), function (e.g., playing), surface property (e.g., glossy), spatial envelope (e.g., man-made), and facial expression in images of people.

Multimodal online content has also been analyzed using discourse and content analysis methods, although few such studies have considered images. An exception is McDonald [13], who qualitatively analyzed interactive image-based communication on a community image blog. He identified four styles of visual 'conversation' in interactive image exchanges: positional play, image quote, text-in-picture, and animation. An image quote, in which a participant takes a picture posted by another participant, modifies it, and reposts the picture, is similar to a meme.

Internet memes have attracted research attention independent of their function in conversational exchanges. [11] used discourse analysis methods to identify key characteristics of successful internet memes reported in mainstream media venues between 2001 and 2005. The successful memes contained humor, wry intertextual cross-references to everyday and popular culture events, and/or anomalous juxtapositions. The study proposed a typology of meme purposes that includes social commentary, absurdist humor, and hoaxes. [2] investigated the spread of 150 famous Internet memes using time series data from Google Insights, Delicious, Digg, and StumbleUpon, and discovered that the temporal distributions that characterize meme popularity are mostly heavily skewed and long-tailed.

With the exception of [13], none of these studies analyzed image use in interactive online communication. Although some consider animated images, including YouTube videos, none include GIFs, whose popularity is a recent phenomenon. Moreover, we found no studies of Tumblr images. The present study contributes to filling these gaps.

2.3 Research Questions
This study addresses the following research questions:

- Do Tumblr users communicate differently in text vs. images?
- If so, how do textual and image communication differ?

Specifically, we focus in this paper on the expression of emotion in text versus images.

3. METHODOLOGY
3.1 Corpus Construction
In order to examine the use of the two modes on Tumblr, a systematic corpus with two datasets was constructed. The first (TXT dataset) comprises posts containing only text, and the second (IMG dataset) comprises posts with images and/or images and text. In order to collect user-generated data representing both text and image use efficiently, we sampled from popular user-generated tags. We first examined the 10 most popular user-generated tags [1] to identify tags that referenced posts with images (at least 10 of the 50 most recent posts). Four of the tags met these criteria, and a fifth tag that was very popular at the time of our data collection (December 2012) but was not mentioned in [1] was added. The first five tags are mostly used by fan communities ("fandoms"), the majority users of Tumblr. A sixth more generic tag (#feels) was added to diversify the sample.

The IMG dataset was collected first on five different days (three weekdays and two weekend days) during peak posting times on Tumblr (6:00pm-12:00am EST), then the TXT dataset was collected using the same systematic procedure. We manually examined the 100 most recent posts for the five fandom-based tags and the 200 most recent posts for the generic tag on each of the five days, selecting posts according to the following criteria:

a) The language used is English.
b) For the image dataset, each post includes at least one image used for discourse purposes (as opposed to simple reblogging of images). For the text dataset, posts contain only text.
c) Each post appears only once in the dataset (we excluded identical reblogged posts).

Table 1 shows the frequencies of the posts collected for each tag in each dataset.

Table 1. Post frequencies by tag and dataset

Tag	IMG Dataset	TXT Dataset	Total
#onedirection	56	103	159
#tomhiddleston	178	94	272
#legendofkorra	62	153	215
#loki	144	101	245
#supernatural	191	241	432
#feels	436	393	829
Total	1,067	1,085	2,152

The posts were imported as text into two Microsoft Excel spreadsheets (one for each dataset), preserving as much of their formatting as possible (e.g., italics and bold font for emphasis), where each row represents a functional move. Because Excel does not allow the insertion of pictures into cells, images were inserted as links in the location they would appear in the post. Posts on Tumblr can be ephemeral, either because users delete posts or change their usernames (which are part of their blogs' URL). This meant that some links saved in the spreadsheet would not work when we tried to access them to code the images. To address this problem, screenshots were taken of image posts during data collection and were saved in a separate folder for reference.

3.2 Content Analysis Codebook
The methodology employed for analyzing the posts is content analysis using a grounded theory approach, which allows coding categories to emerge from the data. The first step was to identify the coding unit. While some categories of interest can be applied to posts as a whole, the content of a Tumblr post is often heterogeneous across its different sections (title, body, tags) and/or within a section (e.g., a section may contain different modes and/or different emotion polarities). In addition, the images should be analyzed as part of the posts rather than as separate entities, because they play an integral role in the overall meaning of the post. We addressed these issues by subdividing posts into *functional moves*, a concept from linguistic text analysis that breaks down larger entities into a "schematic organization" or "conventional sequence of 'chunks'" [8]. Dividing a post into smaller, internally consistent parts allowed the same coding categories to be used for both modes (text and image).

For the corpus as a whole, since this is an exploratory study, the codebook includes multiple variables in three categories: demographics (gender and age of poster), structure, and function. The first is coded at the post level; the last two are coded at the post or functional move level, depending on whether the variable refers to the whole post or part of it, as described further below.

3.2.1 Demographics
Demographic information about the posters was coded during data collection. All posts were coded for gender and age of the users. Gender and age information was extracted from usernames, bio descriptions, and post content on the users' Tumblr blogs.

The users for 1,698 posts out of the total 2,152 were clearly identifiable as male or female. Females are equally distributed between the two datasets, while 60% of males use image communication and 40% use textual communication.[1]

3.2.2 Structure
Structural variables are identified from the format of the post itself. The variables and their code values are shown in Table 2.

---

[1] The overall posting patterns of the genders across the two datasets are significantly different, $\chi^2(1, N=1{,}698)=7.605, p=.006$.

Table 2. Codebook for structure variables

Unit of Analysis	Variable	Values
Post	Post Type	Text, Photo, Link, Audio, Video, Chat, Quote, Reply, N/A
Post	Interaction Type	PM + PR (rebloggable), PM + PR (non-rebloggable), PP + Reply/Comment, N/A
Post	Text in Post	Yes, No, N/A
Functional Move	Location of Text	Title, Body, Tag (+ Text-in-Image and N/A for IMG Dataset)

The variables coded at post level describe technically-specified characteristics of the posts' format. Post Type includes the seven types of posts offered by Tumblr and what users call a "reply" post, a private message (PM) with a public reply (PR). At the time of our data collection, replies could not be reblogged by other users. To overcome this limitation, Tumblr users took screenshots of private messages they received and embedded them into one of the seven rebloggable types of posts, adding their reply below the screenshot.[2] The Interaction Type of each post is thus coded according to whether it is a non-rebloggable Reply (PM + PR), a rebloggable Reply (PM + PR), or any other type of public post (PP) that was reblogged and contained a comment added by another user. The value N/A for Post Type and Interaction Type is used in cases where either is unclear or information is missing.

At the functional move level, the location of the text is coded for both datasets for the title, body, and tag sections. Two values were added for the IMG dataset: Text-in-Image for images that contain text and N/A for images that do not contain text.

3.2.3 Function

The codebook for function variables is shown in Table 3. Function is expressed mostly on the semantic and pragmatic levels of discourse and requires human interpretation. Because functions can be ambiguous, content analysis employs multiple coders to increase the reliability of functional codes. In the study described in section 4, the authors discussed all ambiguous cases in order to reach agreement for coding.

Table 3. Codebook for function variables

Unit of Analysis	Variable	Values
Post	Role-play	Yes, No
Post	Purpose	GIF Challenge, Personal Situation, Fandom-related Situation, Mixed, Other
Functional Move	Expression	Self-expression, Expression other than self, Mixed, N/A
Functional Move	Reaction	Yes, No, N/A
Functional Move	Presence of Emotion	Yes, No, Unclear
Functional Move	Polarity of Emotion	Positive, Negative, Mixed, N/A
Functional Move	Type of Emotion	Anger, Anticipation, Disgust, Fear, Joy, Sadness, Surprise, Trust, N/A
Functional Move	Intensity of Emotion	Extreme, Non-Extreme, N/A
Functional Move	Bona Fide	Yes, No, N/A

Functional Move	Person in Image Saying the Same as Text	Yes + Text-in-Image, Yes + Text-Outside-Image, No, N/A
Functional Move	Image Function	Mention, Use, Unclear, N/A
Functional Move	Image Format	Static, Dynamic, N/A

At the post level, the data are coded for role-playing, i.e., whether the user was posing as a fictional character from a fandom universe. The posts are also coded for purpose based on whether their content describes a personal situation, a fandom-related situation, a mixture of the two, or a GIF Challenge game, where users have to pick the nth GIF from their personal GIF folder on their computer, which then represents their reaction to a situation described in the directions for the game.

Most of the function variables require separate analysis of each section of the post and are coded at the functional move level. Each functional move is coded for whether the text or image expresses the perspective of the user, another individual, or both (identified, e.g., by use of 1st vs. 3rd person pronouns); whether it is a reaction to something (as indicated by expressions such as "and then I was like", "I freaked out"); presence, polarity, and type of emotion[3] (as determined by words expressing emotion in text or facial expressions in images); intensity of emotion (as determined by capitalization of words, repetition of letters and punctuation, bold or italic fonts in text; intense movements and facial expressions in images); and sarcasm (whether the communication is bona fide/genuine or not).

The image dataset is additionally coded for three variables. Animated images featuring a person (or a personified object or animal) are coded for whether the person appears to say the same thing as the text in the image, the text around the image, or something different. The N/A code is used for images not featuring talking. Images are also coded for their function: as part of discourse ('use') or as a picture that was simply reblogged and commented upon ('mention'). Finally, images are coded as static (usually in JPG or PNG format) or dynamic (GIF format). Most of the images in the IMG dataset are dynamic GIFs.

4. PRELIMINARY ANALYSIS
4.1 Data

For the preliminary analysis, we coded a subset of the data in the corpus from the #tomhiddleston and #feels tags. The first 50 posts in each tag were coded from each of the datasets (100 posts from each dataset, for a total of 200 posts). Table 4 displays the frequencies of the posts and the functional moves contained in the subset. The IMG Dataset has more functional moves than the TXT Dataset, because its posts were considerably longer, and each image was coded as a separate functional move.

Table 4. Subset post and functional move (FM) frequencies

Tag	IMG Dataset	TXT Dataset	Total
Posts	100	100	200
Functional Moves	609	323	932

Analysis of the data subset using chi-square tests was conducted on variables relating to the expression of emotion. The variable tested at the post level was posting Purpose, and the variables tested at the functional move level were Emotion

---

[2] Tumblr recently modified public reply posts to make them rebloggable.

[3] The typology used for the types of emotions was taken from the NRC Word-Emotion Association Lexicon [14].

Presence, Emotion Intensity, Emotion Polarity, and Sarcasm (the Bona Fide variable). Most of the variables tested showed significantly different mode patterns across the two datasets.

4.2 Results

4.2.1 Purpose

The subset analyzed did not contain any GIF Challenge posts; therefore only the posting purposes personal situation, fandom-related situation, and mixed were tested. Because of the small number of posts (N=200), the results of the tests for significance were inconclusive. However, the proportions show a preference for image use when describing a fandom-related situation and for text use when describing a personal or mixed situation.

4.2.2 Emotion

Three variables related to emotion were tested for overall pattern differences and for pattern differences within each dataset. Excluding cases where emotion was not clearly present, the two datasets show differences overall in emotion presence, $\chi^2(1, N=899)=48.481$, $p<.001$. For cases where emotion is present, intensity of emotion is also significantly different overall, $\chi^2(1, N=660)=8.652$, $p=.003$. Finally, excluding cases where emotion polarity is mixed or unclear, there are significantly different distributions overall of negative and positive emotion in the two datasets, $\chi^2(1, N=532)=26.751$, $p<.001$. Binomial tests were conducted to examine differences within each dataset; the results are presented in Tables 5-7.

Table 5. Binomial test results for emotion presence

Dataset	Observed Prop. (Yes)	Observed Prop. (No)	Significance
IMG	.81	.19	<.001
TXT	.59	.41	.002

Although both datasets are emotional, posts containing images are much more emotional than plain text posts.

Table 6. Binomial test results for emotion intensity

Dataset	Observed Prop. (Extreme)	Observed Prop. (Non-Extreme)	Significance
IMG	.41	.59	<.001
TXT	.28	.72	<.001

Neither textual nor image posts usually convey extreme emotion. However, there is more extreme emotion in the image dataset.

Table 7. Binomial test results for emotion polarity

Dataset	Observed Prop. (Positive)	Observed Prop. (Negative)	Significance
IMG	.57	.43	<.001
TXT	.32	.68	<.001

Table 7 shows a reversal of proportions in the two datasets. Posts containing images are mostly positive, while posts with plain text are mostly negative in emotion polarity.

4.2.3 Sarcasm

Each functional move was coded for whether it showed genuine communication (bona fide) or sarcasm (non-bona fide). The patterns are overall significantly different between the two datasets, $\chi^2(1, N=803)=5.643$, $p=.018$, as well as within each dataset, as Table 8 shows.

Table 8. Binomial test results for sarcasm

Dataset	Observed Prop. (Bona Fide)	Observed Prop. (Non-Bona Fide)	Significance
IMG	.69	.31	<.001
TXT	.61	.39	<.001

Most functional moves in both datasets convey genuine messages. However, there is more sarcasm in purely textual communication than in communication using images.

4.3 Discussion

It appears that mode choice on Tumblr is not arbitrary. The results of our preliminary study suggest that Tumblr users communicate differently in text and image posts. Image communication is used more for describing fandom-related situations; it conveys more emotion than textual communication, greater intensity of emotion, and the emotion expressed in images is mostly positive. Text, in contrast, is used more to describe personal situations and express sarcasm, and it conveys more negative emotion compared to images. The greater negativity of text is consistent with what Herring and Demarest [9] found for text vs. audio and video posts on the multimodal commenting site Voicethread.com.

Communication in both Tumblr modes is mostly bona fide (although there is a considerable amount of sarcasm), and it is quite emotional overall. A possible explanation for the latter finding is that the #feels tag analyzed in the data subset conveys emotion by definition; it might be biasing the results. We checked for this possibility by analyzing the #tomhiddleston tag separately; the results were similar to those for both tags combined. Another possible explanation is that a majority of Tumblr users (as well as in our dataset) are female; previous research has found that females tend to express more emotion online, especially positive emotion, than males do [8][18]. Moreover, the tags used for data collection are mostly fandom-related and attract a younger audience, and young women in western cultures are socialized to be emotional [5]. These findings underscore the importance of taking user demographics and topic of communication into consideration when analyzing emotion in social media.

The differences between the two datasets can be explained in terms of the nature of the two modes. Image is a socially richer mode than text [16]: It can express facial expressions[4] and other iconic representations of emotion (e.g., a wave breaking over a person to show overwhelming emotion[5]). Moreover, images are more efficient at depicting humorous situations (e.g., boxes falling on top of a person[6]), which might explain the positive orientation of the image dataset. Image memes also tend to be rich in intertextuality [11], which may be why they are preferred when users post about fandom-related subjects. Previous studies [e.g., 11] have claimed that text is more distancing; this could help explain why the textual dataset has more negative polarity. Additionally, many of the textual posts that have negative emotion include the hashtags "#vent" and "#rant," suggesting that the users wanted to "let out" their feelings quickly, rather than following the more time-consuming process of selecting and inserting an image in a post. Finally, a possible reason that textual communication is more sarcastic than image communication is

---

[4] See, e.g., http://media.tumblr.com/d5c26c47423209fa62a47391843972 b6/tumblr_inline_mhtdvjq4Lq1qz4rgp.gif
[5] See, e.g., http://media.tumblr.com/1c63b3ba7349f2a9f2572ed3120e209 a/tumblr_inline_mhtdtzBQew1qz4rgp.gif
[6] See, e.g., http://media.tumblr.com/f2a7bf22bc7228381063228a65a18b 4a/ tumblr_inline_mhthw2aoTi1qz4rgp.gif

that sarcasm relies on ambiguity. Text, being less rich in social cues [16], may lend itself better to ambiguity.

5. CONCLUSIONS

This paper described the construction of two datasets to analyze Tumblr text and image content, as well as the creation of a content analysis codebook for analyzing the corpus manually. It further presented the results of a preliminary analysis of a subset of the corpus using code variables focused on emotion expression.

This research has several implications, especially for sentiment analysis. Image memes, both static and dynamic, are becoming more common and are spreading across the social web, for example, in the comment sections of blogs and forums. Our findings indicate that images convey more emotion than plain text. It follows that analyzing images along with text in multimodal environments should improve the performance and result in greater accuracy of sentiment analysis. Our hand-coded image dataset can also be used further as a training dataset for sentiment analysis using machine learning. As a research study, the paper contributes a micro-level analysis of multimodal communication in a social media platform, especially of image communication, which has been understudied. Finally, it sheds light on the production of Tumblr memes.

Our future work will follow the agenda set out in this paper. We are currently analyzing the whole corpus using the full codebook. We plan to separate dynamic from static images in future analyses; dynamic images should be socially richer than static images, in that they add movement [16], and therefore they can be expected to express meaning differently. Finally, we plan to collect additional Tumblr corpora from randomly-selected tags to evaluate the extent to which our preliminary findings, which are oriented towards fandom, can be generalized across the Tumblr platform.

6. REFERENCES

[1] Alfonso, F. 2012, June. The 10 most popular tags on Tumblr. *The Daily Dot.* Retrieved from http://www.dailydot.com/entertainment/10-most-popular-tags-tumblr/

[2] Bauckhage, C. 2011. Insights into internet memes. *Proceedings of the Fifth International AAAI Conference on Weblogs and Social Media* (Barcelona, Spain, July 17-21). The AAAI Press, Menlo Park, CA, 42-49.

[3] Borth, D., J. Rongrong, Chen, T., Breuel, T., and Chang, S-F. 2013. Large-scale visual sentiment ontology and detectors using adjective noun pairs. *Proceedings of the 21st ACM International Conference on Multimedia* (Barcelona, Spain, October 21-25). ACM, New York, 223-232.

[4] Casserly, M. 2012, March. #WhatShouldWeCallMe revealed: the 24-year old law students behind the new Tumblr darling. *Forbes.* Retrieved from http://www.forbes.com/sites/meghancasserly/2012/03/29/whatshouldwecallme-revealed-24-year-old-law-students-tumblr-darling/

[5] Currie, D. H., Kelly, D. M., and Pomerantz, S. 2006. The geeks shall inherit the earth. *Journal of Youth Studies*, 9, 4 (Sep. 2006), 419-436.

[6] Faircloth, K. 2012, October. Tumblr is down, so how're we supposed to get our GIFs now? *BETABEAT.* Retrieved from http://betabeat.com/2012/10/tumblr-is-down/

[7] González-Ibáñez, R., Muresan, S., and Wacholder, N. 2011. Identifying sarcasm in Twitter: A closer look. *Proceedings of the 49th Annual Meeting of the Association for Computational Linguistics: Human Language Technologies* (Portland, OR, June 19-24). *Scopus®*, 581–586.

[8] Herring, S. C. 1996. Two variants of an electronic message schema. In *Computer-Mediated Communication: Linguistic, Social and Cross-Cultural Perspectives,* S. C. Herring, Ed. John Benjamins, Amsterdam, 81-101.

[9] Herring, S. C., and Demarest, B. 2011. Mode choice in multimodal comment threads: Effects on participation and language use. Unpublished ms.

[10] Kiesler, S., Siegel, J., and McGuire, T. W. 1984. Social psychological aspects of computer-mediated communication. *American Psychologist*, 39 (Oct. 1984), 1123-1134.

[11] Knobel, M., and C. Lankshear 2006. Online memes, affinities, and cultural production. *A New Literacies Sampler*, M. Knobel and C. Lankshear, Eds. Peter Lang, 199-227.

[12] Liu, B., and Zhang, L. 2012. A survey of opinion mining and sentiment analysis. *Mining Text Data*, C. C. Aggarwal and C. Zhai, Eds. Springer US, 415-463.

[13] McDonald, D. 2007. Visual conversation styles in web communities. *Proceedings of the 40th Hawaii International Conference on System Sciences.* IEEE Computer Society Washington, DC, 76.

[14] Mohammad, S., and Turney, P. 2010. Emotions evoked by common words and phrases: Using mechanical turk to create an emotion lexicon. *Proceedings of Workshop on Computational Approaches to Analysis and Generation of Emotion in Text* (Los Angeles, CA, June 5). ACL, Stroudsburg, PA, 26-34.

[15] Pingdom, 2012. Social network demographics in 2012. *Royal Pingdom.* Retrieved from http://royal.pingdom.com/2012/08/21/report-social-network-demographics-in-2012/

[16] Short, J., Williams, E., & Christie, B. 1976. *The social psychology of telecommunications.* London: Wiley.

[17] Siersdorfer, S., and Hare, M. 2010. Analyzing and predicting sentiment of images on the social web. *Proceedings of the 18th ACM International Conference on Multimedia* (Firenze, Italy, October 25-29). ACM, New York, 715-718.

[18] Thelwall, M., Wilkinson, D., and Uppal, S. 2010. Data mining emotion in social network communication: Gender differences in MySpace. *Journal of the American Society for Information Science and Technology*, 61(1), 190–199.

[19] Tumblr. (2014). *About* page. Retrieved February 19, 2014 from http://www.tumblr.com/about

[20] Wiebe, J., Bruce, R., and O'Hara, T. 1999. Development and use of a gold-standard data set for subjectivity classifications. *Proceedings of the 37th annual meeting of the Association for Computational Linguistics* (College Park, MD, June 20-26). ACL, Stroudsburg, PA, 246-253.

[21] Yuan, J., Mcdonough, S., You, Q., and Luo, J. 2013. Sentribute: Image sentiment analysis from a mid-level perspective. *Proceedings of the Second International Workshop on Issues of Sentiment Discovery and Opinion Mining* (Chicago, IL, August 11-14). ACM, New York.

[22] Zha, Z-J., Wang, M., Shen, J., and Chua, T-S. 2010. Text mining in multimedia. *Mining Text Data*, C. C. Aggarwal and C. Zhai, Eds. Springer US, 361-384.

Friends You Haven't Met Yet:
A Documentary Short Film

Jesse Vigil
Writer and Director
Psychic Bunny, Inc.
jesse@psychicbunny.com

Asa Shumskas Tait
Executive Producer
Psychic Bunny, Inc.
asa@psychicbunny.com

Christopher Wienberg
University of Southern
California
cwienberg@ict.usc.edu

Andrew S. Gordon
University of Southern
California
gordon@ict.usc.edu

Categories and Subject Descriptors

K.7.4 [**THE COMPUTING PROFESSION**]: Professional Ethics – *Ethical dilemmas.*

1. SUMMARY

"Friends You Haven't Met Yet" is a documentary short film that chronicles encounters between extremely prolific bloggers and a computer scientist who uses their personal narratives for research. It explores issues related to public sharing of personal stories, the ethical obligations of researchers who use web data, and the changing nature of online privacy.

The film was conceived by Andrew Gordon and Christopher Wienberg at the University of Southern California, whose research involves the collection of millions of personal stories posted to internet weblogs. In analyzing their data, these researchers discovered an unusual population of extremely prolific bloggers, people who post personal stories about their daily lives everyday over the course of many years. They posed three questions about this population:

1. What motivates these people to post so frequently and publicly about their personal life?

2. To what degree do these people embellish their stories to make them more interesting than reality?

3. What expectations do these authors have about their readers, and what are the ethical implications for researchers like us who analyze their posts?

To answer these questions, PhD Student Christopher Wienberg contacted many of these bloggers directly and set up face-to-face interviews at their homes. Accompanied by a documentary film crew, Christopher traveled to locations around California, in both urban and rural settings, to better understand the people whose contributions on the web serve as data in social media research.

WebSci '14, Jun 23-26 2014, Bloomington, IN, USA
ACM 978-1-4503-2622-3/14/06.
http://dx.doi.org/10.1145/2615569.2617797

Challenging Social Media Analytics:
Web Science Perspectives

Ramine Tinati, Olivier Philippe, Catherine Pope, Leslie Carr, Susan Halford
Web Science Institute, University of Southampton
Southampton, Hampshire
United Kingdom

{R.Tinati, op1e10, C.J.Pope, lac, Susan.Halford }@soton.ac.uk

ABSTRACT

In this paper we outline some of the challenges for social media analytics and – at the same time - challenge existing approaches to social media analysis. Specifically, we suggest that there is an unhelpful gulf between social scientific approaches, which offer rich theoretical and methodological understandings of the social; and computational approaches which offer sophisticated methods for data harvesting, interrogation and modelling. Brought together these approaches might meet the challenges facing social media analytics and produce a different order of understanding. We offer two preliminary examples of this synthesis in practice: first, we show how established computational tools might be harnessed to address theoretically grounded empirical questions about the social; and second we consider social theories might inspire the development of new methodological tools for social media analytics. In doing so, we aim to contribute to the development of interdisciplinary social media analytics with in a broader framework of Web Science.

Categories and Subject Descriptors

H.1.1 Systems and Information Theory

Keywords

Social Theory, Social Media, Twitter, Methodology, Interdisciplinarity

1. INTRODUCTION

The phenomenal growth of Web-based social media data over recent years is currently provoking enormous interest and activity from researchers across a range of disciplines. For most, if not all, the lure of these data is that they offer important insights into *the social*: that is, into the nature of interactions between individuals; the formation of, and distinction between, groups; and the shared meanings and practices – as well as the divisions and inequalities – that characterise our everyday lives. In this respect, social media data offer information at a scale hitherto unimagined in social research [38]. Furthermore, the proportionality of social media offers information (in principle at least) on 'whole' populations, rather than sub-sets; the information is dynamic – captured in real time and over time; and

social media provide data on what people say and do 'in the wild', rather than what they say they do in response to researchers' questionnaires and interviews. Furthermore, the digital nature of the data offers unparalleled opportunities for data mining and linking [5,18]. In short, the promise is that social media data will mark a step-change in our understanding of the social world.

However, there are some considerable challenges to be faced before this promise might be realised. Specifically, these relate to the development of data sources and methodologies that will allow us to interrogate and interpret social media data in ways that address complex questions about the social. In part this is a question of data construction (harvesting and archiving). As Geoffrey Bowker now famously observed, '... raw data is an oxymoron' (p.g. 184) [4]. Choices are always made about how to simplify and structure data and these choices bear implications for the kinds of questions that can be asked, and answered. However, in this paper we concentrate on the related question of methodology: that is, the overall design of research from the conceptualisation of questions, to methods and tools, to data analysis and interpretation. Specifically, we will suggest that there is currently a methodological impasse in social media research that must be overcome if we are to realise the contribution that social media data might make to understanding the social. To put it bluntly, whilst the social sciences bring the expertise to construct and interrogate social research questions, underpinned by rich theoretical and methodological traditions, they lack the repertoire of methods necessary to engage with the inherent qualities of social media data. Meanwhile, the computer sciences bring critical expertise for the interrogation of social media data, underpinned by rich computational techniques of large scale data management and modelling, but they lack the theoretical and methodological repertoire necessary to make the most of the methods in addressing complex questions about the social.

This may seem provocative but it is not intended to be so. The historical evolution of academic disciplines has produced divisions of labour that enable the growth of in-depth expertise but – as is increasingly recognised by governments, funding councils and researchers alike – this has siloed knowledge and expertise and, in doing so, limited our understanding of the world. Rather than falling into familiar routines linked to one disciplinary approach over another, our aim here is to evaluate how the combined strengths of the social and computational sciences set an agenda for social media analytics that transcends both the historical divisions and the hierarchical politics of the academy. In what follows, we begin with an outline of the conceptual and methodological framings that drive social science interest in social media, taking Twitter as one example. Next, we consider the methods developed for analysis of Twitter data in computational research. To illustrate the potential for synthesis across these two streams of Twitter research, we present vignettes of two new studies: one that develops a new form of Social Network Analysis to study political protest; and another that draws on social theory to develop a new computational tool for social media analysis. Finally in our conclusion we suggest some key concerns for the future development of social media analytics.

2. TWITTER AND THE SOCIAL

Social media platforms like Twitter provide a digital trace of human expression, action and interaction of interest to social scientists across the spectrum from psychology to political science, geography and sociology. These digital traces provide us with data at a scale rarely encountered in the social sciences and of a nature that is tremendously time consuming and often difficult to come by: as Latour [28] suggests '… it is as if the inner workings of private worlds have been pried open' (p.2).Broadly speaking, we can identify two distinct types of social science interest in Twitter.

First, social media offer social scientists new data on the subjects that are already well established topics of research. For example, Geographers can use geo-tagging to learn more about the spatialities of social ties [41]; Political Scientists can follow unfolding political protests online [40,43] and the exchange of information between communities of different languages [7], and Sociologists have new data with which to explore identity [19,30,31]. *Second, social media are sometimes seen as part of a paradigmatic shift in the nature of society itself* linked to the emergence of the 'information age' [2],'network society' [8,9,10] and the 'mobilities' turn [46,47] in social theory. This turns the process of social research on its head. Instead of starting with categories or concepts assumed to define the social and seeking to trace their iteration in the empirical world, the point becomes to trace the *emergence of the social in the dynamic flows of people, objects, images and information* (p.g. 190) [46].

In both cases, social scientists' experience in researching these areas raises challenges for social media analytics. Contrary to first appearances, it is no simple matter to link social scientific understandings of the social to social media data. Not least, there are sophisticated and competing approaches to *theorising core concepts* - friendship, influence and identity, for instance – that have rich histories in the social sciences and cannot be taken as self-evident. Think of identity for example. This subject evokes enormous contention both between and within disciplines: is identity innate, contextual or discursive? Is it static or dynamic? Are identities coherent or fragmented? The answers to these questions are linked to wider epistemological positions with enormous consequences for the way that research questions are framed, the methods chosen and interpret findings. Linked to this, social scientists have developed an *extensive repertoire of research methods* with which to pursue these complex concepts. Whilst quantitative modelling of large data sets might allow us to answer some questions; others will require in-depth interviews, visual methods of data collection, focus groups or oral histories. We know that different methods will produce different types of data, and different insights. Ticking a box in a questionnaire is not the same as articulating complex emotions in an interview; or recording a visual diary over a longer period of time. Similarly, methods of analysis will – of course – shape the findings. The point is that *theory, methods and interpretation are interwoven* and we must attend to the implications of this for social media research.

However, whilst this substantive and methodological expertise is key to analysing social media data we suggest that, to date, the scope for social scientific research using social media data has been limited by their methodological repertoire. Specifically, that social scientists have approached Big Data with methods that cannot explore many of the particular qualities that make it so appealing to use *viz.* the scale, proportionality, dynamism and relationality described above. Rather, Big Data has commonly been approached with *small scale* content analysis – looking at small numbers of users – or larger scale *random or purposive samples* of tweets. Rendering Twitter data manageable in this way overrides its nature as 'big' data, by-passing the scale of the data for its availability or imposing an external structure by sampling users or tweets according to a priori criteria, external to the data themselves. Furthermore, most previous social science studies are snapshots, categorising content and user-types rather than following the data as it emerges dynamically or exploring the nature of online social networks.

3. COMPUTATIONAL APPROACHES TO TWITTER

Meanwhile, the computer sciences' interest in Twitter begins from quite a different starting point. In particular, there is interest in understanding Twitter at the macro level. These studies aim to explore *the network as a whole*, using computational social network analysis (SNA); well-documented techniques for analysing network graphs which have often been applied to other – similar – large-scale network sources (e.g. the Web graph). These studies use SNA to describe aspects of the Twitter network (friends, followers, retweets, mentions) reveal characteristics including size [42], connectivity [50] and its small-world features [24]. These techniques allow comparison with other Web phenomenon [16] and indeed, other network structures (cancer cells or neural networks [14]). In short, these methods have been driven by questions about the mathematical structure of nodes and edges and by data modelling rather than analyses of the specifically social nature of Twitter.

Beyond this, we see two broad strands of Twitter research in the computational sciences. First, there is growing interest in the *textual data 'inside' the Twitter network*. Named Entity Recognition (NER), is used in order to detect and extract vocabulary within tweets. This research is driven largely by the technical challenges involved: for example, how to apply NER to large streaming data sources [29]; or improve the reliability of data extraction from large volumes of unstructured textual data [36]. Way beyond anything achievable though manual processes of analysis [33,37] machine learning techniques can be used to identify events [48], to measure topic frequency and 'popularity', and model local and global trends [13]. These findings can be extended with sentiment analysis using Natural Language Processing (NLP) [3,20,32] (usually) to produce a quantifiable value representing positive or negative sentiment e.g. regarding political opinion and mobilization [25,40], health issues [17], and well-being [12]. These techniques have also been applied to more technical challenges such as the detection and filtering of 'spam' from large streams of text information [6,21,51]. Meanwhile a second strand of research pays attention to *community and user identification* [15,34] detecting user latent attributes [23,35] and user influence [1,11] *and community formation* around specific topics or events. Here complex algorithms and taxonomic models are used to identify and classify individual behavior behave within a network, and to model and predict future behaviour patterns [22].

This brief review of computational research on Twitter demonstrates the successful application of computer science techniques in the fields of data mining and NLP to social media analytics. This facilitates increasingly fast and reliable data extraction and interrogation at a scale unachievable with social science methods. Not least, these techniques allow us to engage with the particular qualities that make social media data so appealing to social scientists, particularly those concerned with networks, mobilities and flow viz. the proportionality, temporality and dynamism of social practice 'in the wild'. However whilst this computational expertise is key to developing social media analytics, we suggest that the scope for computational research has been limited by its a-theoretical and largely technical and/or mathematical orientation. Analysing Twitter data in this way overrides its nature as 'social' data, by-passing the theoretical and methodological complexity of the data for its scale. In and of itself this may be unproblematic, depending on the questions being asked. So long as these are technical or mathematical this is entirely appropriate. However if our intention is to explore the 'social' in social media it is more troublesome.

4. WEB SCIENCE TWITTER METHODS

From the brief review above, we are only too aware of the challenges facing interdisciplinary social media analytics. At the same time, there are clearly many ways forward. In what follows we explore two examples, in this case drawing together social theory and computational techniques to achieve a richer and more insightful analysis of Twitter data.

4.1 Using SNA to Trace Information Flows and Emergent Network Roles

Flow 140 (described in detail in [44,45]) is a new network analytics platform built on the well-established techniques and metrics developed in social network analysis (SNA) studies, adjusted to explore the emergence of information flows and network roles over time. Following the sociology of networks, mobilities and flows *Flow 140* is distinguished from conventional SNA in three key ways. First, rather than providing a snapshot of the final network structure, *Flow 140* provides a dynamic mapping of the conversations and flows of information to demonstrate process: that is, how the social emerges over time. Second, and linked to the previous point, unlike traditional approaches to SNA which search for a set of *a priori* characteristics related to the structure and connectively of a network, *Flow140* attends to the roles that emerge as the network grows over time interactions and activities of the individuals involved [27]. As such it provides a method to follow the digital traces of the social as it evolves [26]. Third, and finally, Flow 140 transcends the distinction between macro and micro analysis, enabling both large scale data capture of the network as a whole, and associated analysis of network metrics; and in-depth qualitative analysis of the content of individual tweets. We can see not only how information flows, but what information flows; which users are connected in what ways and the roles that emerge in the process of this information flow and network formation.

Using Flow 140 for a case study of the use of Twitter in political protest [45] revealed which users were key to the generation and flow of information and the different types of roles that were involved. These stretch beyond quantitative measures of re-tweets to include 'amplifiers' and 'aggregators' who – whilst not necessarily highly retweeted themselves play an important role in the diffusion of information and in building connections between discrete networks. We can also see how quickly particular pieces of information flowed, through which parts of the network and that some limited pieces of information came to dominate the network over time. .

In theoretical terms, Flow 140 traces the emergence of the social in Twitter activities. Furthermore, by allowing in-depth analysis of the tweet contents Flow 140 drew attention to the importance of a wider eco-system of interactions with other socio-technical systems such as YouTube, Blogs, and photo sharing sites (and here there are promising connections to computational research making the same point more generally.

Following these links offered a richer understanding of the emerging activities and – critically – how these were connected to activities off-line. In this sense then Flow 140 extends 'network analysis' beyond the mathematical structure of nodes and edges within Twitter platform – although these are helpful metrics. Instead, this network analysis demands attention to the connections and disconnections online and offline, across diverse fields of action. In this sense, the term 'network' refers not just to a social media network in and of itself but to the wider network in which this might play a part.

4.2 Using Social Theory to Develop New Methods for Twitter Analytics

Our second example takes social theory as its starting point – specifically, theories of social action that emphasise the emergent nature of social outcomes in the flow of everyday action [27,49] - and considers what kinds of methods would be necessary to explore questions of the social from this starting point. From a sociological perspective, the point is not to study individual, discrete actions in and of themselves but rather to understand the contexts and processes that shape these and – in turn – how these actions (re)produce the social world. Considering Twitter, we might ask: why do people tweet, why do people follow particular individuals, or what is the relationship between tweets and followers? However, by asking these questions we must confront methods - both for collecting and for analysing data.

Whilst the dominant paradigm in computational methodologies for social media generates quantitative descriptions of large data for *modelling* and *prediction* [26,39] this does not help us to explore these interactive relationships on Twitter or how they evolve over time. Rather, from this perspective, the tweet is simply a unit of data. It is only *after* collection, during the analysis, that meaning is imputed: the tweets, filtered intentionally or not, (e.g. by technical limitations or sampling techniques), are conceived as raw data, meaningless until clustering or network analysis is applied to make sense of them. This reduces interaction on Twitter to the tweet alone, rather than to the broader range of contexts and relationships in play. In comparison with off-line methods, this is analogous to reducing our understanding of complex social relationships to tick boxes in a survey asking about very particular and actions, rather than asking more in-depth questions about underlying processes and meanings or the wider contexts of action.

Developing an approach where a tweet is meaningful in its context of production rather than during the analysis forces us to rethink the method of collection [27]. This led us to the following principles for our study: (1) Define the population of interest theoretically, rather than solely by reference to technical capacities e.g. hashtag or location; (2) position the individual as the producer of action; (3) place the individual in relevant social context. Consequently, the tweet is understood as a temporal intersection of the individual, situated in context, responding to and (potentially) producing a range of other interactions and subject to multiple meaning making. *The tweet is a link in the process of interaction and not the sole product of this interaction.* Data produced from these principles not only provides an account of the communications, but also the emerging and re-shifting of the social basis on these interactions.

The practical consequences of this are that we must collect information about the users' profile, including their network of followers and friends as well as their interactions with other users and information contained within the tweet by the use of mention or retweet. This allows us to trace the context of the tweet from its production environment and later, its consequence on the user's profile, adjusting the sampling to the field as the processes evolve over time. The interaction between users becomes the rule – with users included/excluded from the dataset following the flow of action, creating a dynamic sampling based on the activity and the context where it is produced. Social action becomes an essential part of the *data collection* rather than only a product of analysis.

In short, this approach brings together sociological and computational approaches in the processes of collection and analysis, not only at the very end, such as it occurs now with network analysis, or at the very beginning with visualization; but within the entire collection-curation-analysis process. From a computational perspective, the scalability and the issues raised by a dataset is partially driven by a theoretical approach to sampling. From a sociological perspective, the reshaping of the data collection techniques provide a richer and contextualized data resource, which is embedded with a theoretically-driven framing to understanding the data.

5. CONCLUSION

In this paper we have argued that there lies a gap between the social and computer sciences. Our argument considers both perspectives: on the one hand, computer science have sophisticated methods and techniques to analyse this new forms of 'social' data, the discipline provides fewer theoretical and methodological tools with which to address the social. On the other hand, social scientists have well-developed theories and great experience with asking questions and understanding the social, yet lack the tools and computations skills (in general) to be able to engage with this data.

We would be the first to acknowledge that this is a very broad brush account. There may be many in both the computational and social sciences who can point to exceptions, where the characterisation that we have presented here becomes fuzzier in practice. If so, we applaud these. Our point is not to cast criticism but to recognise the historical legacies in the divisions of academic labour and to seek synthesis that will take us beyond the painful 'science wars' of earlier times. We aim to generate dialogue in doing so to enable social medial analytics that can rise to the challenge of the extraordinary social data being generated around us day by day.

6. ACKNOWLEDGEMENTS

This work is supported by the RCUK Doctoral Training Centre in Web Science and SOCIAM: The Theory and Practice of Social Machines. The SOCIAM Project is funded by the UK Engineering and Physical Sciences Research Council (EPSRC) under grant number EP/J017728/1 and comprises the Universities of Southampton, Oxford and Edinburgh.

REFERENCES

[1] Anger, I. and Kittl, C. Measuring Influence on Twitter. *Proceedings of the 11th International Conference on Knowledge Management and Knowledge Technologies*, (2011).

[2] Bell. D. *The Coming Of Post Industrial Society*. Basic Books, New York, NY, USA, 1974.

[3] Bertrand, K.Z., Bialik, M., Virdee, K., Gros, A., and Bar-yam, Y. Sentiment in New York City: A High Resolution Spatial and Temporal View. *NECSI Report*, (2013), 1–12.

[4] Bowker, G.C. "Raw Data" Is An Oxymoron. In L. Gitelman, ed., *"raw data" is an oxymoron*. The MIT Press, 2005, 184.

[5] Boyd, D., Golder, S., and Lotan, G. Tweet, Tweet, Retweet: Conversational Aspects of Retweeting on Twitter. *HICSS-43*, IEEE Comput. Soc (2010).

[6] Brody, S. and Diakopoulos, N. Cooooooooooooooooolllllllllllllll!!!!!!!!!!!!!!!: using word lengthening to detect sentiment in microblogs. *EMNLP '11 Proceedings of the Conference on Empirical Methods in Natural Language Processing*, (2011), 562–570.

[7] Bruns, A., Highfield, T., and Burgess, J. The Arab Spring and Social Media Audiences English and Arabic Twitter Users and Their Networks. *American Behavioral Scientist 57*, (2013), 871–898.

[8] Castells, M. *The Rise of the Network Society, The Information Age: Economy, Society and Culture Vol. I.* Blackwell Publishing Inc, Cambridge, MA, 1996.

[9] Castells, M. *The Power of Identity, The Information Age: Economy, Society and Culture Vol. II.* Blackwell Publishing Inc, Cambridge, MA, 1997.

[10] Castells, M. *End of Millennium, The Information Age: Economy, Society and Culture Vol. III.* Blackwell Publishing Inc, Cambridge, MA, 1998.

[11] Cha, M. and Gummadi, K.P. Measuring User Influence in Twitter: The Million Follower Fallacy. *ICWSM '10: Proceedings of international AAAI Conference on Weblogs and Social*, (2010).

[12] De Choudhury, M., Counts, S., and Horvitz, E. Social media as a measurement tool of depression in populations. *Proceedings of the 5th Annual ACM Web Science Conference on - WebSci '13*, (2013), 47–56.

[13] Dave, K., Bhatt, R., and Varma, V. Modelling Action Cascades in Social Networks. *Proceedings of the Fifth International AAAI Conference on Weblogs and Social Media*, (2011), 121–128.

[14] Dorogovtsev, S.N., Mendes, J.F., and Samukhin, a N. Structure of growing networks with preferential linking. *Physical review letters 85*, 21 (2000), 4633–6.

[15] Enoki, M., Ikawa, Y., and Rudy, R. User community reconstruction using sampled microblogging data. *Proceedings of the 21st international conference companion on World Wide Web - WWW '12 Companion*, (2012), 657.

[16] Gao, Q., Abel, F., Houben, G., and Yu, Y. A Comparative Study of Users ' Microblogging Behavior on Sina Weibo and Twitter. (2012), 88–101.

[17] Ginsberg, J., Mohebbi, M.H., Patel, R.S., Brammer, L., Smolinski, M.S., and Brilliant, L. Detecting influenza epidemics using search engine query data. *Nature 457*, 7232 (2009), 1012–4.

[18] Halford, S., Pope, C., and Weal, M. Digital Futures? Sociological Challenges and Opportunities in the Emergent Semantic Web. *Sociology 47*, 1 (2012), 173–189.

[19] Hargittai, E. and Litt, E. The tweet smell of celebrity success: Explaining variation in Twitter adoption among a diverse group of young adults. *New Media & Society 13*, 2011, 824–842.

[20] Hu, X., Tang, L., Tang, J., and Liu, H. Exploiting social relations for sentiment analysis in microblogging. *Proceedings of the sixth ACM international conference on Web search and data mining - WSDM '13*, (2013), 537.

[21] Hurlock, J. and Wilson, M.L. Searching Twitter: Separating the Tweet from the Chaff. *Proceedings of the Fifth International AAAI Conference on Weblogs and Social Media*, AAAI (2011), 161–168.

[22] Kairam, S., Wang, D., and Leskovec, J. The life and death of online groups: Predicting group growth and longevity. *WSDM'12*, (2012).

[23] Kim, D., Jo, Y., Moon, I.-C., and Oh, A. Analysis of Twitter Lists as a Potential Source for Discovering Latent Characteristics of Users. *CHI 2010 Workshop on Microblogging: What and How Can We Learn From It?*, (2010).

[24] Kwak, H., Lee, C., Park, H., and Moon, S. What is Twitter, a social network or a news media? *19th international conference on the World Wide Web*, (2010), 591–600.

[25] Larsson, a. O. and Moe, H. Studying political microblogging: Twitter users in the 2010 Swedish election campaign. *New Media & Society 14*, 5 (2011), 729–747.

[26] Latour, B., Jensen, P., Venturini, T., Grauwin, S., and Boullier, D. The Whole is Always Smaller Than Its Parts - A Digital Test of Gabriel Tarde's Monads. *British Journal of Sociology*, (2011), 1–21.

[27] Latour, B. *Reassembling the Social: An Introduction to Actor-Network-Theory by Bruno Latour*. Oxford University Press, 2005.

[28] Latour, B. Beware, your imagination leaves digital traces. *Times Higher Literary Supplement*, April (2007).

[29] Li, C., Weng, J., He, Q., Yao, Y., and Datta, A. TwiNER: named entity recognition in targeted twitter stream. *SIGIR '12 Proceedings of the 35th international ACM SIGIR conference on Research and development in information retrieval*, (2012), 721–730.

[30] Marwick, A. and boyd, danah. To See and Be Seen: Celebrity Practice on Twitter. *Convergence: The International Journal of Research into New Media Technologies 17*, 2 (2011), 139.

[31] Murthy, D. Towards a Sociological Understanding of Social Media: Theorizing Twitter. *Sociology 46*, 6 (2012), 1059–1073.

[32] Park, J. and Lee, W. Revolution 2.0 in Tunisia and Egypt: Reactions and sentiments in the online world. *Proceedings of the Fifth International AAAI Conference on Weblogs and Social Media*, AAAI (2011).

[33] Paul, M.J. and Dredze, M. You Are What You Tweet: Analyzing Twitter for Public Health. *Artificial Intelligence*, (2011), 265–272.

[34] Pennacchiotti, M. and Popescu, A. A Machine Learning Approach to Twitter User Classification. *Proceedings of the Fifth International AAAI Conference on Weblogs and Social Media*, (2011), 281–288.

[35] Rao, D., Yarowsky, D., Shreevats, A., and Gupta, M. Classifying Latent User Attributes in Twitter. *Proceedings of the 2nd international workshop on Search and mining user-generated*, ACM Press (2010).

[36] Ritter, A., Clark, S., and Etzioni, O. Named entity recognition in tweets: an experimental study. *Conference on Empirical Methods*, (2011), 1524–1534.

[37] Sadilek, A. and Kautz, H. Modeling spread of disease from social interactions. *Proceedings of the Sixth International AAAI Conference on Weblogs and Social Media*, (2012), 322–329.

[38] Savage, M. and Burrows, R. The Coming Crisis of Empirical Sociology. *Sociology The Journal Of The British Sociological Association 41*, 5 (2007), 885–899.

[39] Savage, M. and Burrows, R. Some Further Reflections on the Coming Crisis of Empirical Sociology. *Sociology The Journal Of The British Sociological Association 43*, 4 (2009), 762–772.

[40] Segerberg, A. and Bennett, W.L. Social Media and the Organization of Collective Action: Using Twitter to Explore the Ecologies of Two Climate Change Protests. *The Communication Review 14*, 3 (2011), 197–215.

[41] Takhteyev, Y., Gruzd, A., and Wellman, B. Geography of Twitter networks. *Social Networks 34*, 1 (2011), 1–25.

[42] Teutle, A.R.M. Twitter: Network properties analysis. *2010 20th International Conference on Electronics Communications and Computers (CONIELECOMP)*, (2010), 180–186.

[43] Theocharis, Y. Young people, political participation and online postmaterialism in Greece. *New Media & Society 13*, 2 (2011), 203–223.

[44] Tinati, R., Carr, L., and Hall, W. Identifying communicator roles in twitter. *Proceedings of the 21st international conference companion on World Wide Web*, (2012), 1161–1168.

[45] Tinati, R., Halford, S., Carr, L., and Pope, C. Big Data: Methodological Challenges and Approaches for Sociological Analysis. *Sociology*, (2014).

[46] Urry, J. Mobile sociology. *British Journal of Sociology 51*, 1 (2000), 185–203.

[47] Urry, J. *Mobilities*. Wiley, 2007.

[48] Weng, J. and Lee, B. Event Detection in Twitter. *Proceedings of the Fifth International AAAI Conference on Weblogs and Social Media*, AAAI (2011).

[49] Wittel, A. Toward a Network Sociality. *Theory, Culture & Society 18*, 2001, 51–76.

[50] Wu, S., Hofman, J.M., Watts, D.J., and Mason, W.A. Who Says What to Whom on Twitter. *Proceedings of the World Wide Web 2011*, (2011).

[51] Yardi, S., Romero, D., Schoenebeck, G., and Boyd, D. Detecting spam in a twitter network. *First Monday 15*, 1 (2010).

How "Big Vs" dominate Chinese Microblog

A comparison of verified and unverified users on Sina Weibo

Ning Wang
Oxford Internet Institute
University of Oxford
1 St Giles', Oxford, UK
ning.wang@oii.ox.ac.uk

James She
HKUST-NIE Social Media Lab
Hong Kong University of
Science and Technology
eejames@ust.hk

Junting Chen
HKUST-NIE Social Media Lab
Hong Kong University of
Science and Technology
eejtchen@ust.hk

ABSTRACT

Sina Weibo has become the most popular microblogging platform in the Chinese-speaking community. Verification scheme is a distinctive element of Weibo with an aim to help the public to identify genuine accounts and select trustworthy information sources. Verified users are also known as "Big Vs", who are identified by a verification badge, a capitalised letter "V" added alongside account name. By comparing statistical characteristics of both verified and unverified users, this paper presents that a minority of verified users are largely consider as influentials, who tend to be more central in the networks and play vital roles in keeping connectivity as well as network robustness. Although verification scheme is likely to draw more users to become influentials, user behaviours are still considerably more influenced by user roles rather than by verification scheme.

Keywords

Sina Weibo; Microblog; Verification; Online Social Network.

1. INTRODUCTION

Sina Weibo[1], an equivalent of Twitter in China, has become the most popular microblogging platform in the Chinese-speaking community. First launched in 2009, Weibo had attracted over half billion registered users and the number of daily average users had soared to 61 million in December 2013 [1]. Every day there are over 100 million statuses (equivalent to the tweets in Twitter) posted on Weibo [2]. Being the most influential microblog platform in China, Weibo is operated as a public medium to facilitate social activities in different levels: not only can celebrities and media use Weibo to share their statuses and engage with their followers, but the general public also uses this platform to spread their public opinions; more and more companies and organisations open their official channels on Weibo to

---

[1]For simplicity we use Weibo refers to Sina Weibo throughout this paper.

promote new products and services as well as to collect feedbacks from customers; Chinese government also commences on using Weibo to publish information and communicate with the public for emergencies and public affairs.

Verified users on Weibo are comparable to the well-known people or organisations on Twitter. Weibo imposed verification scheme in 2009 with an aim to help the public to identify the genuineness of user accounts. Verified users are also known as "Big Vs", who are identified by a verification badge, a capitalised letter "V" added alongside account name. The verification procedure is quite complicated and requires users to fulfil specific requirements, e.g., providing mobile phone number and real profile image, and proving to have more than 30 followings, 100 followers, and 2 mutually followed verified users. The verification also requires to meet different criteria for individual and organisation: the individuals must submit their identification, proof of employment or professional certification; the organisations are required to provide more documents depending on different categories, i.e., government, media, enterprise, etc.

Some research has been done on analysing user behaviour, influence and topology on Weibo and Twitter [3], [4], [5]. However, it is still not sufficient to understand the different roles played by verified and unverified users on Weibo, as it generally needs a large amount of data from closely monitored user activities. A few recent works have attempted to address this problem. Our preliminary study on the statistical characteristics of verified and unverified users is carried out in [2], which, however, only limits to user activities and network growth. This paper employs new analysis techniques, such as user categorisation and structural holes, to analyse the influence of verification scheme on user behaviours by comparing the characteristics of both verified and unverified users. The results not only strengthen the conclusions in [2], but also present an in-depth study on classifying user attributes into different user roles and comparing them inside each groups.

The rest of the paper is organised as follows: Section 2 introduces the process of data collection. Section 3 presents the empirical comparison of verified and unverified users. Finally, in section 4, the conclusion of the work is presented.

2. DATA COLLECTION

We collected data using public Application Programming Interfaces (APIs) provided by Weibo for the period between July 2012 and August 2012. The rate of data collection in the Weibo's APIs is limited to 150 queries/hour in every testing account[2]. Our collected data includes user's profile and their interactions from 14th August 2009 (The first date Weibo started to provide the services) to 3rd August 2012, which contains user ID, nickname, registration time and number of followings, followers and statuses. We also collected specific information from user's profile, such as information ID, number of comments and number of reposts.

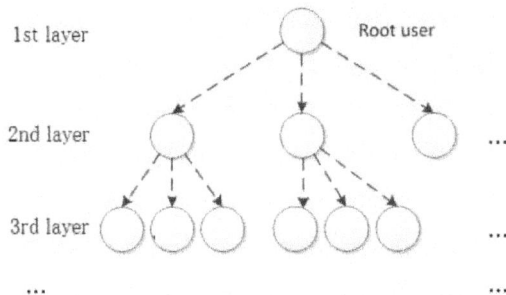

Figure 1: Data collection process

The procedure of data collection is illustrated in Fig.1. Snowball sampling was applied in data collection: starting from a random root user, identical data collection process was recursively operated on the user's followers and followings. The followers or followings of a root user are regarded as second-layer users. The data collection continues from the root user to each member in the second-layer. In order to avoid deadlocks in data collection, the users in upper layer will not appear in the next layer. As a result, a significant amount of user information including followers and followings can be collected and stored in our database for further data preparation and analysis. In the end, our dataset contained 493,470 user profiles in total, including 52,467 verified users and 441,003 unverified users. Table 1 summarises the descriptive statistics of our dataset.

	Verified users	Unverified users
Number of users	52,467	441,003
Total number of statuses	122,748,308	340,237,633
Maximum number of statuses	100,081	197,852
Average number of statuses	2,340	772

Table 1: Data summary

3. DATA ANALYSIS

In this section, the data collected from Weibo is prepared to analyse how different roles played by verified and unverified influence user behaviours on Weibo. It proceeds by giving an in-depth study on describing user properties inside each role and comparing them between verified and unverified users.

3.1 Categorisation of user roles

The direction of links determines the information flows on online social networks. Users with different out-degree play different roles in affecting information flows in a network, whereas users with large in-degree can effectively spread information to a large number of users [6]. As suggested in

[2]See http://open.weibo.com/wiki/api, accessed in January 2014.

[7], we use γ to categories user roles. The γ is defined in the equation(1), where the out-degree is the number of followings of a user and the in-degree is the number of followers of a user. In this paper we consider all users with zero in-degree as spams which are filtered out in further analysis.

$$\gamma = \frac{out - degree}{in - degree} \qquad (1)$$

In Fig.2, the x axis is represented by γ which symbolises the potential influence of a user, while the y axis exhibits the number of statuses of a user which implies the level of active engagement. The colour in Fig.2 presents the number of users, i.e., darker colour means more users in the area. Furthermore, it can be observed that Fig.2 is divided into 4 quadrants, which present 4 distinctive categories of users [8]: the upper left corner highlights influentials; the bottom left corner represents hidden influentials; the top right corner presents broadcasters; the bottom right corner implies listeners; and users fall at the intersection of dashed lines represents ordinary users.

Fig.2 (a) uncovers that most verified users are very unevenly distributed in the top left quadrant, which implies that a minority of verified users generally play a role as influentials, who concentrate a substantial amount of audiences and are actively involved in stimulating participation. In contrast, unverified users differ largely: most unverified users fall at the intersection of dashed lines and some even fall into the area of right bottom corner as listeners, indicating that they perform averagely in both influence and participation and have a tendency to receive more information rather than to spread out information. It is also interesting to note that verification scheme helps verified users to attract more listeners which in return stimulate their level of active engagement.

In order to further elaborate users roles, we analyse the CDF (Cumulative Probability Function) of γ for both verified and unverified users, and further categorise the user roles into following 3 categories:

- $\gamma > 10$: Users who typically seek knowledge or collect information. This kind of user is defined as a listener.

- $0.1 < \gamma \leq 10$: This represents a typical community. Users can interact with each other fully. This kind of user is defined as a typical user.

- $\gamma \leq 0.1$: General media or famous people who mainly spread their ideas or opinions on the network. This kind of user is defined as an influential user.

Fig.3 displays the CDF of γ for verified and unverified users. It is exhibited that γ normally ranges from 0.1 to 10^4. As shown in Fig.3, roughly 50% of verified users have a γ less than 0.1, and consequently they are described as influentials; in contrast, only 3.3% of unverified users play a role as influentials. Moreover, 20% of unverified users act as listeners with γ greater than 10; in comparison, there are merely no listeners in verified users. As a result, verified users mostly have a smaller γ than unverified users, suggesting that verified users are the dominant user group to spread information more widely and effectively.

Note that the curve of unverified users does not reach 1 because the users with zero in-degrees are ignored when we calculate γ. Although both verified users and unverified

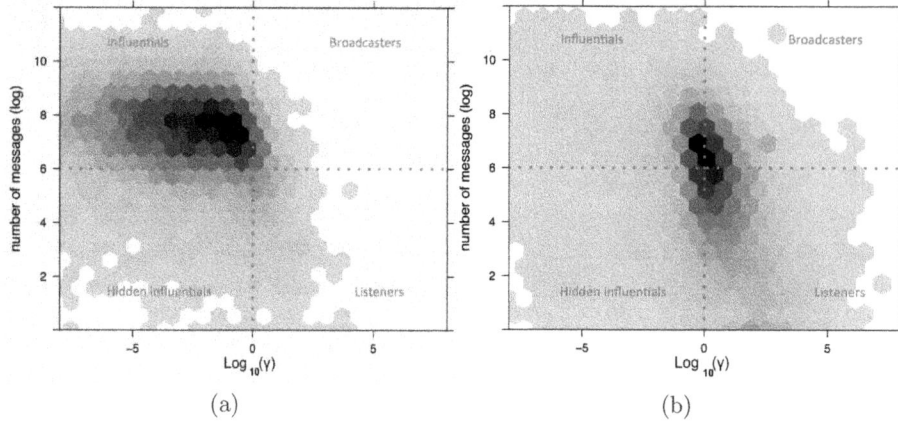

Figure 2: Categorisation of user roles for (a) verified and (b) unverified users

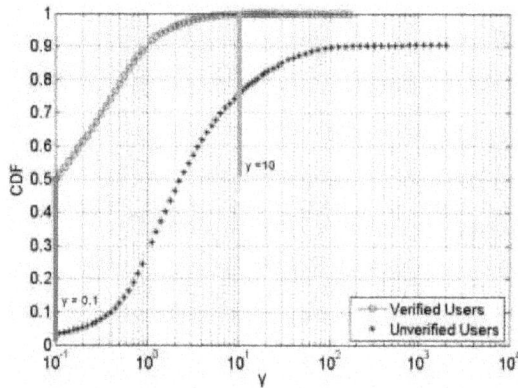

Figure 3: CDF (Cumulative Probability Function) of γ for verified and unverified users

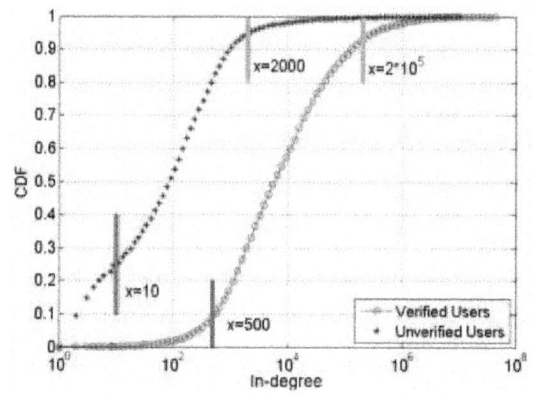

Figure 4: CDF (Cumulative Probability Function) of in-degree for verified and unverified users

users have zero in-degree users, there are roughly 13 verified spam users versus 41,946 unverified spam users (the ratio is 0.025% versus 9.5%). This explains the fact that there are more spams in unverified users who may affect the distribution of unverified user group.

3.2 User groups comparison

In addition to the comparisons among different user roles, verified and unverified users can be subsequently separated into three groups according to the CDF of in-degrees in Fig.4. Although the common property of degree distributions follows long tails, it is worthwhile to note that there are some points in Fig.3 where the curves slope suddenly upward or downward. These points are selected as the boundaries of different user groups. The boundary is between 500 and 2×10^5 for verified users and between 10 and 2,000 for unverified users. By using these boundaries, we can classify users into following three groups: the first group is of users who are among the least-connected in the networks; the second group is of users who are well-connected; the last group is of users who are among the most-connected.

Verified and unverified users are classified into three groups in Table 2. It can be discovered that the composition of unverified users tends to be categorised into all three user roles with a reasonable probability distribution. However, verified

users are more unevenly distributed than verified users: the well-connected and the most-connected groups are generally classified as influentials for verified users. Not surprisingly, all three groups of influentials look similar in terms of number of statuses and followers, and listeners possess the least number of statuses and followers. It is interesting to observe that the influentials in unverified users follow and post relatively more than that the influentials in verified users. One possible explanation is that unverified users who want to be influentials require to be more active than verified users in order to achieve the same influence (i.e., keeping the similar number of followers).

Considering that both verified and unverified users contains influentials and typical users, the next questions are these: 1) Does the influentials in verified users behave similarly as the influentials in unverified users? 2) What is the difference between the typical users in verified and unverified users? Fig.5 employs PDF (Probability Distribution Function) to demonstrate the distributions of number of statuses and followings for verified and unverified users within a specific categorised group. In general, the PDF distributions for both verified and unverified users present a similar tendency. Fig.5 (a) demonstrates that when the number of statuses related to influentials is around 1000, the PDF value of verified users is higher than unverified users; when the num-

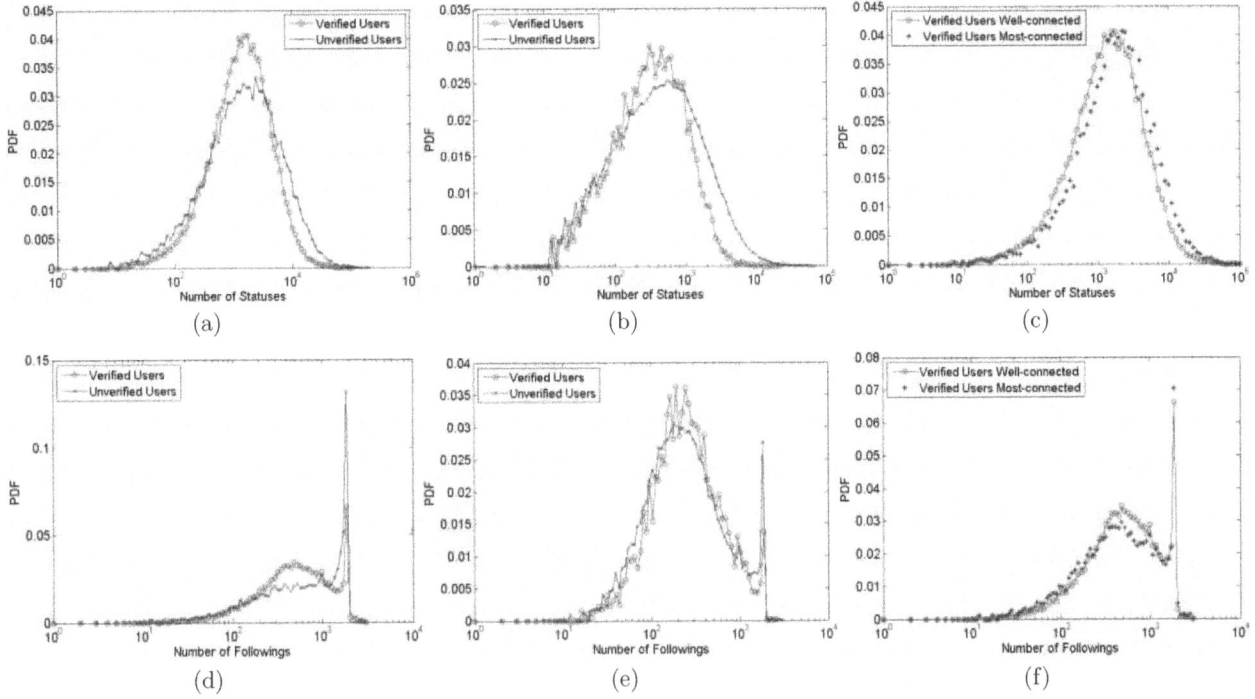

Figure 5: Comparison of the number of statuses and followings between influentials users (a) and (d); typical users (b) and (e); well-connected and most-connected verified users (c) and (f)

Table 2: Categorisation of user roles and user groups

	Verified Users			Unverified Users		
Average γ	1.413	0.033	0.005	34.236	1.343	0.014
Average statuses	493.76	2.47×10^3	2.88×10^3	9.11	885.76	3.61×10^3
Average followers	249.43	2.05×10^4	1.35×10^5	2.15	275.54	6.22×10^4
Average followings	352.45	680.18	691.12	73.46	369.78	885.13
User Groups	Least-connected	Well-connected	Most-connected	Least-connected	Well-connected	Most-connected
User Roles	Typical Users	Influentials	Influentials	Listeners	Typical Users	Influentials

ber of statuses is larger than 5,000, unverified users maintain a higher probability. Influentials present a similar pattern on the PDF of the number of followings in Fig.5 (d): when the number of followings is approximately 500, the probability of verified users is greater than that of unverified users. When the number is higher than 1,000, unverified users end up with a higher probability. Identical trends appear for typical users in Fig.5 (b) and (d). Furthermore, it can be observed that there exists an impulse when the number of followings is about 2,000, and the probability curve of verified users is higher than that of unverified users at the peak of the impulses. The reason behind the impulses may be due to the limitation of following number applied by Weibo, which is restricted to 2,000 for normal users and 3,000 for members (users who pay membership fees which is different from the verification).

Fig.5 (c) and (f) present the comparison of the well-connected and the most-connected users who are influentials in verified users. It is seen that when users become influentials, the distributions of the number of statuses and the number of followings are nearly indistinguishable, indicating that the user behaviours are more stable when users become influentials in verified users.

In summary, the results in this section demonstrate that unverified users have to be more active (i.e. posting more statuses) in order to become influentials; however, the verification may not be the substantial factor alone to affect user influences within the same role, as user behaviours are still considerably more affected by user roles rather than their verified identities.

3.3 Structural holes analysis

In order to understand how verified users dominate most of connections in the network, a simulation of structural holes [9] is performed in this section. Since verified users are the minority in our datasets, we intend to see how network structure reacts by removing specific number of verified users from reconstructed social networks. In comparison, the same quantity of unverified users are also randomly chosen and removed accordingly. The intuition is that if verified users tend to be more crucial in building connections in the network, the network actually will break into more segmented components by removing them. Therefore those users serve as more important structural holes in the network.

Fig.6 presents the results of structural holes analysis, where the the number of components (y axis) is recorded as a re-

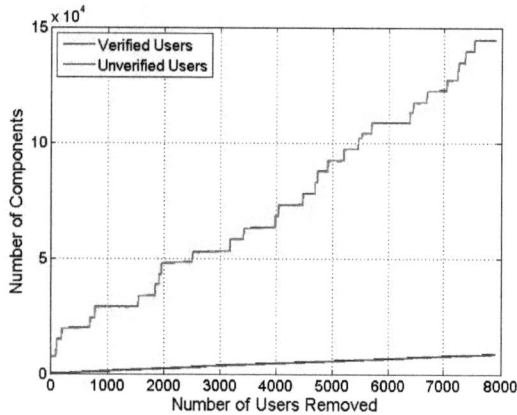

Figure 6: Structural holes simulation

sult of the number of users removed (x axis). Here verified users are removed one by one in a sequence arranged by the registration time, while unverified users are randomly chosen and removed with the same quantity of verified users. As shown in Fig.6, the red line corresponds to the removal of verified users and the blue line represents average value of 100 random runs of the removal of unverified users. It can be noticed that, as expected, the number of components increases as the number of users removed. However, although the same number of users is removed each time, the network breaks into segmented components much faster by removing verified users than by removing unverified users. There are also some sudden increases in the red line, which shows the importance of certain user in connecting other users in the network together.

4. CONCLUSIONS

This paper has investigated the influence of verification scheme on user behaviours by comparing different user roles played by both verified and unverified users on Sina Weibo. Based on the statistical characteristics of dataset collected from Weibo, different user roles of both verified and unverified users have been analysed within specific categorised groups. The results have demonstrated that the social network resources are unevenly distributed on Weibo: a minority of verified users are largely considered as influentials, while unverified users adhere to regular distribution with a standard user community, including listeners, typical users, and influentials. Despite the fact that the verification scheme is likely to bring more users to become influentials, user behaviours are still considerably more influenced by user roles rather than by their verified identities alone, i.e., the verification may not be the substantial factor alone to affect user influences within the same role. In the end, verified users play vital roles in dominating connectivities and robustness of a social network based on the results of structural holes analysis.

The results confirm the fact that a small number of verified users who play active roles like influentials, dominate the connectivities in a social structure on Weibo. From the network point of view, this kind of hierarchal structure is efficient for the information diffusion. This is in principle more resilient to random failure, but could be vulnerable and fragile for purposive attacks. However, verified users provide

a convenient approach for Weibo censorship, because it is much easier to censor a small number of key users rather than a large number of majority. In worst situation, it is easy to break down the whole network just by taking down a few nodes which are important to structure holes. One evidence is the that the activities have fallen by as much as 70% as "Big Vs" abandon Weibo [10]. Sometimes it is difficult to fix this situation because it might take even long time for a certain user to become an influential user by acquiring enough social networking resources like followers.

5. ACKNOWLEDGMENTS

We are grateful to the three anonymous reviewers for their insightful comments. This work is supported by HKUST-NIE Social Media Lab. (http://smedia.ust.hk) with contributions by Mr Suiliang Wang for data collections. Ning Wang thanks Google for funding support.

6. REFERENCES

[1] S. Mishkin, "Weibo user growth slows to record low.," *Financial Times Chinese. From* *http://www.ftchinese.com/story/001054966*, 2014.

[2] J. Chen and J. She, "An analysis of verifications in microblogging social networks–sina weibo," in *2012 32nd International Conference on Distributed Computing Systems Workshops (ICDCS Workshops)*, pp. 147–154, IEEE, 2012.

[3] G. Song, Z. Li, and H. Tu, "Forward or ignore: User behavior analysis and prediction on microblogging," in *2012 IEEE 16th International Conference on Computer Supported Cooperative Work in Design (CSCWD)*, pp. 678–684, 2012.

[4] M. Cha, H. Haddadi, F. Benevenuto, and P. K. Gummadi, "Measuring user influence in twitter: The million follower fallacy.," *4th International AAAI Conference on Weblogs and Social Media (ICWSM)*, vol. 10, pp. 10–17, 2010.

[5] Z. Guo, Z. Li, and H. Tu, "Sina microblog: an information-driven online social network," in *2011 International Conference on Cyberworlds (CW)*, pp. 160–167, IEEE, 2011.

[6] M. Cha, F. Benevenuto, H. Haddadi, and K. Gummadi, "The world of connections and information flow in twitter," *IEEE Transactions on Systems, Man and Cybernetics, Part A: Systems and Humans*, vol. 42, no. 4, pp. 991–998, 2012.

[7] A. R. M. Teutle, "Twitter: Network properties analysis," in *20th International Conference on Electronics, Communications and Computer (CONIELECOMP)*, pp. 180–186, IEEE, 2010.

[8] S. González-Bailón, J. Borge-Holthoefer, and Y. Moreno, "Broadcasters and Hidden Influentials in Online Protest Diffusion," *American Behavioral*, 2013.

[9] R. S. Burt, "Structural holes and good ideas," *American journal of sociology*, vol. 110, no. 2, pp. 349–399, 2004.

[10] M. O. Malcolm Moore, "China kills off discussion on weibo after internet crackdown.," *Telegraph. From* *http://www.telegraph.co.uk/news/worldnews*, 2014.

An Activity-Based Information-Theoretic Annotation of Social Graphs

Arun V. Sathanur
Department of Electrical Engineering
University of Washington
Seattle, WA – 98195
1-206-616-5606
arunsv@uw.edu

Vikram Jandhyala
Department of Electrical Engineering
University of Washington
Seattle, WA - 98195
1- 206-543-6515
vj@uw.edu

ABSTRACT

The explosion in social media adoption has opened up new opportunities to understand human interaction and information flow at an unprecedented scale. Influence between people represented as nodes of a social graph is best characterized in terms of the direction, the volume and the delay associated with the information flow. In this work we investigate the relatively new information-theoretic measure called *transfer entropy* as a measure of directed causal influence in online social interactions. The classical definition of transfer entropy is extended to a form applicable to activity on social graphs characterized by causal influence through delayed responses. For fixed but arbitrary interaction delays, we show that the swept delayed transfer entropy (DTE) profile peaks at the true delay. By extending the results to discrete and continuous distributions of interaction delays, the efficacy of DTE in recovering the interaction delay distributions between two causally related signals is demonstrated. An information theoretic annotation of social graphs that captures the volume and velocity of information transfer is presented based on the swept DTE.

Categories and Subject Descriptors

H.1.1 [**Systems and Information Theory**]: Information Theory; J.4 [**Social and Behavioral Sciences**]: Sociology

General Terms

Measurement, Performance, Reliability, Human Factors

Keywords

Time Series, Transfer Entropy, Information Theory, Social Networks, Causality, Directed Influence, Delay Distribution

1. INTRODUCTION & RELATED WORK

With a significant fraction of the human population partaking in one or more online social networks (OSNs), the volume and velocity of big-social data is leading to information transfer at an extraordinary scale. Data from social media can best be visualized as a collection of a large number of time series with causal interdependence. Treating every node on an OSN as a source of time series data that is causally influenced by that of friends and followees allows mature information-theoretic and signal

processing concepts [1, 2] to be applied in the rigorous influence analysis of big social data. Tie-strengths or connectedness measures on social graphs can represent the extent of similarity between the pair of nodes that constitute an edge, over a set of attributes [3]. However in the case of OSN graphs, such measures usually denoted as edge-weights are in general asymmetric and are a reflection of the directed influence of one node on the other in terms of activity [4]. Another distinguishing feature of OSNs is the causality-based influence that is implicit in the mechanism of activity generation. Hence an influence measure that can capture the volume and velocity (causal delay) of the interaction between nodes will be extremely beneficial as a directed influence measure in OSNs that can then be leveraged by a variety of graph-analytics applications. In this paper we investigate transfer entropy [5] as such a measure of directed influence based on causal responses in OSNs.

Related work in the area of influence detection in OSNs comprises of a number of topology and activity-based approaches. Widely used topology-based approaches include metrics such as the number of followers the user has accumulated, PageRank and its variants [6-9]. Recently, activity-based approaches that make use of weighted digraphs have been proposed to identify influential users on OSNs [10, 11]. The above approaches are rooted in the magnitude of the edge weights that characterizes the local influence model between the nodes constituting the edge while neglecting the delay aspect of the influence. Very recently researchers have started applying information-theoretic [12] and in particular transfer entropy concepts [13-15] to study activity and influence in OSNs. Transfer entropy is well studied in neurobiology where its potential in accurately identifying causal connections between individual neurons and between groups of neurons has been demonstrated [16-18].

In the context of OSNs, transfer entropy is particularly useful when only the activity traces are available and a causal relationship is sought. Thus in its native form, transfer entropy is particularly attractive to analyze networks such as Wikipedia and YouTube. Even in the case of additional headers such as retweets or sharing information being available, transfer entropy analysis can assist in uncovering patterns not captured by simple weight-based approaches. For example, a person not responding when a particular connection posts a message, or posting similar content without acknowledging as retweets or shares. Transfer entropy-based analysis can also point to causal influence between two nodes due to factors outside the network. Such an analysis can help uncover covert groups on OSNs that are not connected at the network level. Similar arguments expand the utility of transfer entropy to human networks beyond OSNs where individual activity traces can be observed and a causal link is sought including in a number of practical online applications.

In this work we investigate some modifications to the original transfer entropy definition that enable deeper insights into the nature of causal influence between nodes on an OSN. Section 2 defines transfer entropy and discusses the treatment of delay models in social networks within the transfer entropy framework. In section 3, the original transfer entropy definition is extended to include arbitrary but fixed delays. Tradeoffs involving the choice of bin size are examined. Section 4 examines parameterized distributions of interaction delay and demonstrates the recovery of delay distributions from the delayed transfer entropy profiles while introducing an associated information-theoretic annotation of social graphs. Section 5 concludes the paper and outlines ongoing and future work.

2. TRANSFER ENTROPY DEFINITIONS

One distinguishing feature of OSNs is the directed causality-based influence that is implicit in the mechanism of activity generation. Thus correlation-based measures struggle to capture the directed causal influence, as do symmetric information-theoretic measures such as mutual information [5]. Transfer entropy, first proposed by Schreiber [5], overcomes these limitations by specifically incorporating directedness and causality in the definition that is based on the Kullback relative entropy.

Consider two discrete-valued, discrete-time stochastic processes X and Y over a common alphabet Ψ. It is assumed that $\Psi = [0,1]$ where a 0 denotes absence of activity and a 1 denotes presence of activity such as posting a message, uploading a photo or a video, commenting, sharing and re-tweeting. The transfer entropy from X to Y is given by

$$TE_{X \to Y} = H\left(Y_{n+1}\big|Y_n^k\right) - H\left(Y_{n+1}\big|Y_n^k, X_n^l\right) \quad (1)$$

Here Y_n^k is the vector $[Y_n \, Y_{n-1} Y_{n-2} \ldots Y_{n-k+1}]$ that denotes the k-length history of Y at the time snapshot n upon which Y_{n+1} might depend. Similarly X_n^l is the l-length history of X at n. The difference of the two conditional entropies as in eq. (1) is non-negative and is a measure of the causal influence from X to Y.

The quantity defined in eq. (1) is called the delay-1 transfer entropy since it relates the past values of X and Y at time n to the value of Y at time $(n + 1)$. The definition in eq. (1) however cannot be generally applied to time series from social data since it requires extension to the wide range of delays encountered in responses on human networks including OSNs [19, 20]. Ver Steeg and Galystyan [14] address this issue by increasing the length of the history of X and by using non-uniform bin sizes. Bauer et al. [13] also increase the length of the history of X but the approach is an empirical one based on testing different values of l. It is known that increasing the order, which amounts to conditioning on multiple variables, results in increased computational complexity and leads to accuracy issues when dealing with sparse data because of the exponentially larger alphabet size [5, 17].

3. DELAYED TRANSFER ENTROPY

Consider two binary processes $X(t)$ and $Y(t)$ with $Y(t)$ causally dependent on $X(t)$ with a delay of t_d. By using an appropriate choice of the bin size, $X(t)$ and $Y(t)$ can be converted to discrete-time processes such that the original delay-1 transfer entropy is still applicable. However, the loss of resolution by using a large bin size can be a serious handicap. To circumvent this the delay-1 transfer entropy can be extended to delay-d transfer entropy by replacing X_n^l with X_{n-d}^l where d is the discrete time equivalent of the delay t_d [17, 21]. Thus

$$TE_{X \to Y}^d = H\left(Y_{n+1}\big|Y_n^k\right) - H\left(Y_{n+1}\big|Y_n^k, X_{n-d}^l\right) \quad (2)$$

To further clarify the definition of delayed transfer entropy, it can be noted that under stationarity, $TE_{X \to Y}^d = H\left(Y_{n+d+1}\big|Y_{n+d}^k\right) - H\left(Y_{n+d+1}\big|Y_{n+d}^k, X_n^l\right)$ whereas $TE_{X \to Y}^d \neq H\left(Y_{n+d+1}\big|Y_n^k\right) - H\left(Y_{n+d+1}\big|Y_n^k, X_n^l\right)$ [21]. The dependence of Y_{n+1} on the history of X is delayed while the dependence on the history of Y is still retained at the previous time-step. $TE_{X \to Y}^d$ is called the delayed transfer entropy (DTE). The efficacy of DTE in recovering the interaction delay distribution is investigated via the following steps.

1. A receiver point process $Y(t)$ that is causally dependent on a source point process $X(t)$ according to a known forward delay model is generated. In this section, in order to emphasize the delay aspects, all the spikes in the activity of X appear in the activity of Y according to the various delay models discussed.

2. Working with only the two time series, binning them and sweeping the delay in eq. (2) a profile of the DTE is built to relate to the original model-based delay. The simplicity and efficiency of computation can be retained by choosing $k = l = 1$ while the effect of increasing history length is addressed through the delay parameter. Further independent computations mean that parallel implementations are very straightforward.

Consider a message source X on an OSN generating activity in the form of a Poisson process. Let Y be a follower of X that engages in influenced activity (for example retweeting on Twitter) after a fixed delay of t_d. The choice of Poisson process is representative and the analysis can be easily applied to other types of stationary point processes. For further discussion on the stationarity aspects involved in transfer entropy estimation the reader is referred to the work by Kaiser and Schreiber [22]. Figure 1 shows the profile of the swept DTE for the process rate $\lambda = 1 \, hr^{-1}$ and $t_d = 6 \, hr$ at three different bin widths of $0.05 \, hr$, $0.2 \, hr$ and $0.5 \, hr$. The computation of $TE_{X \to Y}^d$ can be considerably simplified by adopting the formula based on joint Shannon entropies [22] namely

$$TE_{X \to Y}^d = H\left(Y_n^k \otimes X_{n-d}^l\right) - H\left(Y_{n+1} \otimes Y_n^k \otimes X_{n-d}^l\right) + H\left(Y_{n+1} \otimes Y_n^k\right) - H\left(Y_n^k\right) \quad (3)$$

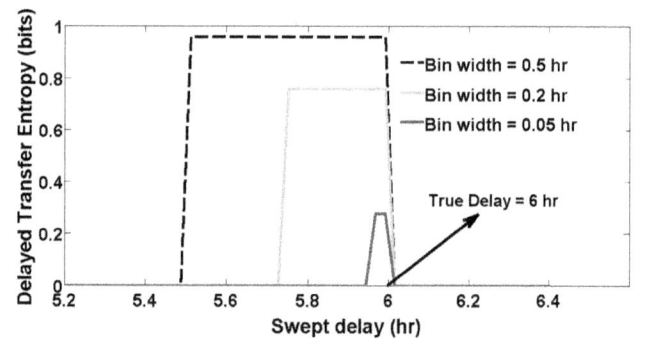

FIG. 1. For a forward model with a single delay, the swept delayed transfer entropy profile has a maximum at the true delay. The resolution and the profile peak are dependent on the bin width used in the discretization.

The following points are noteworthy in the above figure.

a. Transfer entropy is maximized at the true delay. Wibral et al. [21] provide a theoretical justification of this result based on the data processing inequality.

b. Bin size has an effect on the maximum value of transfer entropy.

c. A larger bin size, while reducing the computational burden, introduces ambiguity in the delay estimation.

While point (c) is apparent, the rest can be understood by the following analysis. Let $h(\lambda, b_W)$ denote the Shannon entropy of a binned Poisson point process X. Let t_{d_1} be the swept delay used in the transfer entropy computation and let d_1 and d be the discrete time versions t_{d_1} and t_d respectively. In the above scenario $Y_{n+1} = X_{n-d_1}$ for $d_1 = d$. Otherwise Y_{n+1} is independent of X_{n-d_1}. From eq. (3), it is apparent that

$$TE_{X \to Y}^{d_1} = TE_{X \to Y}^{max} = h(\lambda, b_W) \, ; d_1 = d \quad (4a)$$

$$TE_{X \to Y}^{d_1} = 0 \, ; d_1 \neq d \quad (4b)$$

For a Poisson point process with rate λ characterized by an exponential inter-arrival density function of $\lambda e^{-\lambda t}$, the probability that there is at-least one spike in the time interval corresponding to b_W is $\int_0^{b_W} \lambda e^{-\lambda t} = \left(1 - e^{-\lambda b_W}\right)$ leading to

$$TE_{X \to Y}^{d} = h(\lambda, b_W) = \left(\left(1 - e^{-\lambda b_W}\right) log_2\left(1 - e^{-\lambda b_W}\right) + e^{-\lambda b_W} log_2\left(e^{-\lambda b_W}\right)\right) \quad (5)$$

$TE_{X \to Y}^{d}$ is maximized at $b_W = \left(\frac{\ln 2}{\lambda}\right)$. Assuming that the rate can be estimated from the data, the choice of optimum bin size for sampling boils down to the tradeoff between acceptable delay uncertainty, the computational complexity and the height of the DTE profile especially in the presence of noise. The optimum delay step itself is the same as the bin width and a bin width of about a third of the optimum works well in practice given the various considerations.

Figure 2 shows the tradeoff by sweeping the bin sizes for various η where η is the parameter of the Bernoulli noise process added to the receiver signal $Y(t)$. The rate of the source Poisson process is $2.3 hr^{-1}$. It must be noted that when the unknown delay is not an integral multiple of the bin width, during the process of digitizing the signals, there can be leaks into the adjacent bins due to rounding off errors. In such cases the transfer entropy peak may not be sharp as predicted by eqs. (4a) and (4b). This can be remedied by searching in the local space around a given bin width for the maximum transfer entropy.

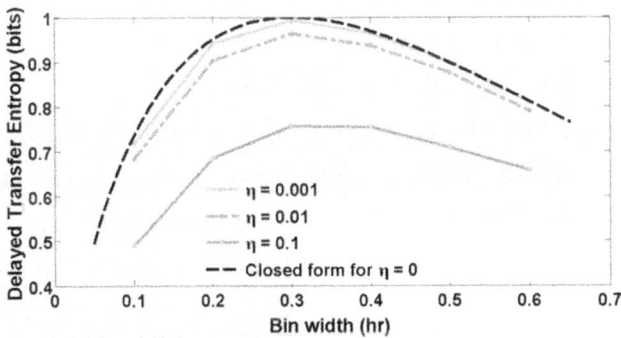

FIG. 2. The peak of the swept delayed transfer entropy (Fig. 1) depends on the bin width and has an optimum with respect to it. The peak transfer entropy also reduces in the presence of noise.

4. SWEPT DELAYED TRANSFER ENTROPY FOR DISTRIBUTIONS OF DELAY

We now introduce a multiple-delay model before moving to distribution of delays. First, three different delays $t_{d_1}, t_{d_2}, t_{d_3}$ are introduced with the delays being selected in the forward model with probabilities w_1, w_2, w_3 respectively and $w_1 + w_2 + w_3 = 1$. The swept DTE profiles are shown in figure 3 where it can be seen that the strongest delay components are easily recovered. The DTE peaks corresponding to the true delays depend in a non-linear fashion on the delay selection probabilities w_1, w_2, w_3. This can be understood by the following analysis.

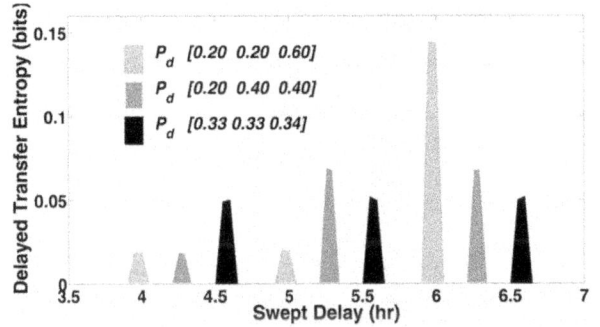

FIG. 3. The delayed transfer entropy response for the three-delay model for different probability distributions of the delays. The delays are purposely misaligned for the three different cases to improve visualization. P_d refers to the vector of probabilities [w_1 w_2 w_3]. The nonlinear dependence of the DTE peak values on the probability of the delay occurring is evident.

Consider a Poisson process X with rate λ and a process Y that is influenced by X such that a portion w (< 1) of the spikes in X appear in Y with a delay t_d. By treating a binned Poisson process (with bin size b_W) as a Bernoulli process with $p(1) = p(\lambda, b_W) = (1 - e^{-\lambda b_W})$, using eq. (3), after some algebra the peak DTE value corresponding to a delay of t_d becomes

$$TE_{X \to Y}^{d} = \xi(w, p) = 2g(wp) + g((1-w)p) + g(1 - wp) - g(w^2 p) - 2g((1-w)wp) - g((1-w)^2 p) \quad (6)$$

Here $g(x) = -x log_2(x)$ and $p = p(\lambda, b_W) = (1 - e^{-\lambda b_W})$. It can be seen that $\xi(w, p)$ is approximately linear in w for small $p(\lambda, b_W)$. However in the presence of multiple delays as in the case of figure 3, when computing the DTE, at any given physical delay (t_{d_1} or t_{d_2} or t_{d_3} in the above example), the interference due to other spikes that suffer a different delay but still appear within the bin corresponding to the delay under consideration reduces the height of the transfer entropy peak. It can be shown that under these circumstances with the total delay probabilities summing to 1, the DTE for the delay under consideration can be approximated by $\xi(w^2, p(\lambda, b_W))$ which by prior considerations is close to quadratic in w. The same is verified in figure 4. Here, a Bernoulli process with probability of the symbol '1' given by $p = 0.2$ undergoes four different delays with probabilities given by $\left[w \quad \frac{2(1-w)}{3} \quad \frac{(1-w)}{6} \quad \frac{(1-w)}{6}\right]$ respectively. The figure shows the analytical and simulated DTE profiles for delay 1 and delay 2 as w

is varied. The simulated curves were obtained from averaging over a 25 Monte Carlo run.

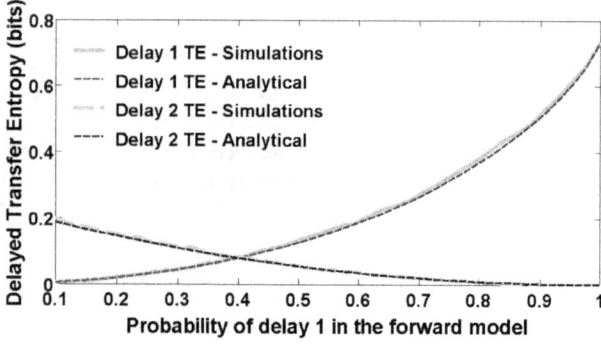

FIG. 4. A Bernoulli process undergoes four different delays according to a probability mass function characterized by one parameter namely the probability of the first delay. The simulated and analytical results for the delayed transfer entropy at two different delays show excellent agreement enabling generalization to arbitrary delay distributions.

In the most general case of the interaction delays following a probability distribution, the possibility of estimating the underlying distribution of the delay from DTE is examined next. Let the delay distribution density be given by $f_{t_d}(T_D)$ where T_D is the random variable representing the delay t_d. When the delay is scanned as a parameter in the swept DTE computation, for a given Δt_d denoting the spacing between the adjacent delays scanned and an index k for the delay under consideration, the probability of the forward model delay being in the interval $[k\Delta t_d \ (k+1)\Delta t_d]$ is given by

$$w(k) = \int_{k\Delta t_d}^{(k+1)\Delta t_d} f_{t_d}(T_D)dt_d \approx f\left(\left(k+\tfrac{1}{2}\right)\Delta t_d\right)\Delta t_d \qquad (7)$$

This amounts to discretizing the density function $f()$ to a sum of impulses as $\sum_k w(k)\delta\left(t_d - \left(k+\tfrac{1}{2}\right)\Delta t_d\right)$. From the earlier discussion on the multiple delay case, the profile of the DTE (at delay d_k) is therefore a discretized, nonlinear version of the underlying forward delay profile is approximately given by

$$TE_{X \to Y}^{d_k} \approx \xi\left(\left(f\left(\left(k+\tfrac{1}{2}\right)\Delta t_d\right)\Delta t_d\right)^2, p(\lambda, b_W)\right) \qquad (8)$$

This is best illustrated for the pathological case of a triangular delay distribution as in figure 5 where simulated and analytical results are shown for a Poisson process with $\lambda = 2.3 \ hr^{-1}$, $b_W = 0.1 \ hr$ and the delay follows a triangular distribution with minimum and maximum values of $2.4 \ hr$ and $5.6 \ hr$ respectively. The simulations involved averaging over a 25 run Monte Carlo. To emphasize the nonlinear transformation, the underlying triangular distribution of the delay is also shown. To facilitate the comparison, the DTE curves are normalized such that the area under the respective curves is unity.

Figures 6a and 6b show the recovered delay distribution for a delay with uniform distribution and a Gaussian distribution. In both the cases, two different standard deviations are shown to illustrate the efficacy of the method. The underlying process was a binned Poisson process with $\lambda = 2.3 \ hr^{-1}$, $b_W = 0.1 \ hr$. The $w(k)^2$ dependence of the DTE magnitude can be perceived from the fact that the standard deviation inferred from the DTE profile is $\frac{\sigma}{\sqrt{2}}$ where σ is the standard deviation of the underlying delay distribution in the forward model. Thus the swept DTE profile is a *signature* of the underlying delay distribution in the forward

model. The inference of the delay distribution can therefore be accomplished by in numerous ways including inverting eq. (8) by leveraging the square root of the DTE profile, lookup tables and formal machine learning methods.

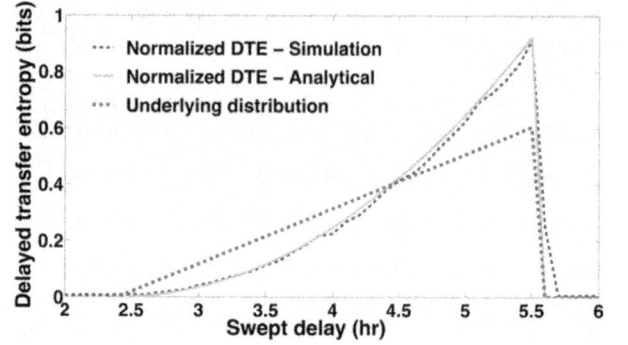

FIG. 5. A triangular delay distribution in the forward model is considered in order to illustrate the non-linear map from the probability density function of the delay to that of the swept profile of the delayed transfer entropy. To facilitate comparison the delayed transfer entropy curves are normalized so that the corresponding areas under the curves are each unity.

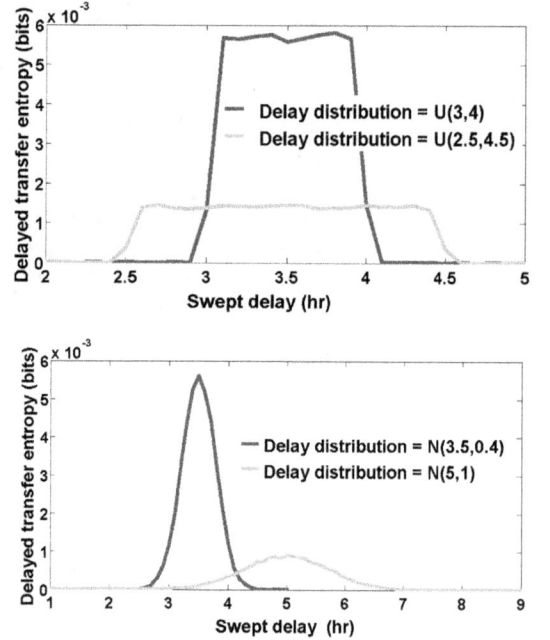

FIG. 6. The swept delayed transfer entropy profiles for two different uniform (a) and Gaussian (b) delay distributions are illustrated. The swept delayed transfer entropy profiles enable the recovery of causal interaction delay distributions between two time series denoting activity.

The swept DTE profile also allows for an *information-theoretic annotation* of an edge in a social graph that takes into account both the magnitude and delay involved in the causal influence. One such annotation is illustrated in figure 7. Here TE^μ refers to the average height of the DTE profile and $[t_d^{min} \ t_d^{max}]$ refers to the interval corresponding to the DTE above a given threshold. Annotations based on other statistical measures around the DTE profile are conceivable. Such an annotation allows for complex optimizations to be performed on social graphs to achieve specific outcomes in diverse application areas such as social marketing campaigns, project management in organizations and mobilization for collective action where time-sensitive information transfer plays a major role.

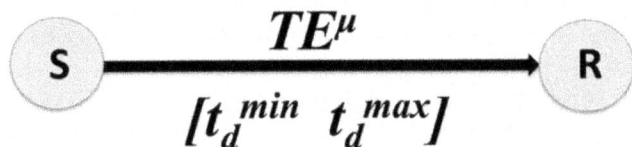

FIG. 7. The swept DTE profile leads to an information theoretic annotation of an edge in a social graph. The annotation captures the magnitude of the causal influence in addition to the delay bounds

5. CONCLUSIONS AND FUTURE WORK

In this work the effectiveness of swept DTE in recovering arbitrary distributions of delays in causal interactions characteristic of social networks was demonstrated. The swept DTE profile also allows an information-theoretic annotation on social graphs that capture the volume and velocity of causal influence and hence can be used in a variety of applications involving time-sensitive information transfer. Current and future work involve extending the swept DTE concepts to facilitate discovery of more complex activity mechanisms, application to real-world social data and exploring the effect of sampling.

6. REFERENCES

[1]   T. M. Cover and J. A. Thomas, *Elements of information theory*: John Wiley & Sons, 2012.

[2]   J. D. Hamilton, *Time series analysis* vol. 2: Princeton university press Princeton, 1994.

[3]   M. Gupte and T. Eliassi-Rad, "Measuring tie strength in implicit social networks," in *Proceedings of the 3rd Annual ACM Web Science Conference*, 2012, pp. 109-118.

[4]   S. Hangal, D. MacLean, M. S. Lam, and J. Heer, "All friends are not equal: Using weights in social graphs to improve search," *Workshop on Social Networking Mining and Analysis, ACM KDD*, 2010

[5]   T. Schreiber, "Measuring information transfer," *Physical review letters,* vol. 85, p. 461, 2000.

[6]   B. Bahmani, A. Chowdhury, and A. Goel, "Fast incremental and personalized PageRank," *Proceedings of the VLDB Endowment,* vol. 4, pp. 173-184, 2010.

[7]   S. Brin and L. Page, "The anatomy of a large-scale hypertextual Web search engine," *Computer networks and ISDN systems,* vol. 30, pp. 107-117, 1998.

[8]   B. Hajian and T. White, "Modelling influence in a social network: Metrics and evaluation," in *Privacy, security, risk and trust (PASSAT), Third IEEE international*

conference on social computing (socialcom), 2011, pp. 497-500.

[9]   Y. Yamaguchi, T. Takahashi, T. Amagasa, and H. Kitagawa, "Turank: Twitter user ranking based on user-tweet graph analysis," in *Web Information Systems Engineering–WISE 2010*, ed: Springer, 2010, pp. 240-253.

[10]   A. V. Sathanur, V. Jandhyala, and C. Xing, "PHYSENSE: Scalable sociological interaction models for influence estimation on online social networks," in *Intelligence and Security Informatics (ISI), 2013 IEEE International Conference on*, 2013, pp. 358-363.

[11]   J. Weng, E.-P. Lim, J. Jiang, and Q. He, "Twitterrank: finding topic-sensitive influential twitterers," in *Proceedings of the third ACM international conference on Web search and data mining*, 2010, pp. 261-270.

[12]   C. Wang and B. A. Huberman, "How random are online social interactions?," *Scientific reports,* vol. 2, 2012.

[13]   T. L. Bauer, R. Colbaugh, K. Glass, and D. Schnizlein, "Use of transfer entropy to infer relationships from behavior," in *Proceedings of the Eighth Annual Cyber Security and Information Intelligence Research Workshop*, 2013, p. 35.

[14]   G. Ver Steeg and A. Galstyan, "Information transfer in social media," in *Proceedings of the 21st international conference on World Wide Web*, 2012, pp. 509-518.

[15]   G. Ver Steeg and A. Galstyan, "Information-theoretic measures of influence based on content dynamics," in *Proceedings of the sixth ACM international conference on Web search and data mining*, 2013, pp. 3-12.

[16]   B. Gourévitch and J. J. Eggermont, "Evaluating information transfer between auditory cortical neurons," *Journal of Neurophysiology,* vol. 97, pp. 2533-2543, 2007.

[17]   S. Ito, M. E. Hansen, R. Heiland, A. Lumsdaine, A. M. Litke, and J. M. Beggs, "Extending transfer entropy improves identification of effective connectivity in a spiking cortical network model," *PloS one,* vol. 6, p. e27431, 2011.

[18]   R. Vicente, M. Wibral, M. Lindner, and G. Pipa, "Transfer entropy—a model-free measure of effective connectivity for the neurosciences," *Journal of computational neuroscience,* vol. 30, pp. 45-67, 2011.

[19]   A. Vázquez, J. G. Oliveira, Z. Dezsö, K.-I. Goh, I. Kondor, and A.-L. Barabási, "Modeling bursts and heavy tails in human dynamics," *Physical Review E,* vol. 73, p. 036127, 2006.

[20]   Z. Yang, J. Guo, K. Cai, J. Tang, J. Li, L. Zhang, *et al.* (2010, Understanding retweeting behaviors in social networks. *Proceedings of the 19th ACM international conference on Information and knowledge management,* 1633-1636.

[21]   M. Wibral, N. Pampu, V. Priesemann, F. Siebenhühner, H. Seiwert, M. Lindner, *et al.*, "Measuring information-transfer delays," *PloS one,* vol. 8, p. e55809, 2013.

[22]   A. Kaiser and T. Schreiber, "Information transfer in continuous processes," *Physica D: Nonlinear Phenomena,* vol. 166, pp. 43-62, 2002.

Detecting and Forecasting Domestic Political Crises: A Graph-based Approach

Yaser Keneshloo
Department of Computer
Science
Virginia Tech
Blacksburg, VA
yaserkl@cs.vt.edu

Jose Cadena
Virginia Bioinformatics
Institute
Virginia Tech
Blacksburg, VA
jcadena@vbi.vt.edu

Gizem Korkmaz
Virginia Bioinformatics
Institute
Virginia Tech
Blacksburg, VA
gkorkmaz@vbi.vt.edu

Naren Ramakrishnan
Department of Computer
Science
Virginia Tech
Blacksburg, VA
naren@cs.vt.edu

ABSTRACT

Forecasting a domestic political crisis (DPC) in a country of interest is a very useful tool for social scientists and policy makers. A wealth of event data is now available for historical as well as prospective analysis. Using the publicly available GDELT dataset, we illustrate the use of frequent subgraph mining to identify signatures preceding DPCs, and the predictive utility of these signatures through both qualitative and quantitative results.

Categories and Subject Descriptors

H.2.8 [**Database Management**]: Database Applications–Data Mining

Keywords

GDELT, event forecasting, graph mining, domestic political crises.

1. INTRODUCTION

Predicting and monitoring political events is known to be an important and challenging task in social science research [2]. Of particular interest is forecasting domestic political crises (DPCs), which refer to significant opposition against the government usually triggered by an election or legalizing an unfavorable law [22, 15]. As discussed in [1], forecasting a DPC is an arduous tasks compared to prediction of other types of events such as rebellion and international crises.

Recent times have significantly increased the wealth of resources available to the computational social scientist. Resources such as ICEWS [9] and GDELT [12] span most of the

countries of the world and have been used to develop prediction models for a range of events such as international and domestic crises, insurgency, rebellion, and ethic and religion violence [3, 4]. Methods used include discriminant analysis [17], HMMs [16], Bayesian time series forecasting [14, 5, 19, 11], and vector auto regression (VAR) methods [10, 6]. For a survey on these predictive models, we point the readers to [18].

We take a *contrast data mining* approach wherein we seek patterns in interaction graphs that are frequent in situations with DPCs but infrequent in situations without DPCs, and thus discriminative. To the best of our knowledge, our work is the first graph mining analysis of intra-country events from GDELT. Using the features (interaction patterns) extracted, we demonstrate how they are both explanatory for the underlying crises and predictive of future DPCs.

2. PRELIMINARIES

2.1 The GDELT Dataset

The Global Database of Events, Language, and Tone (GDELT) is a new CAMEO-coded dataset containing geolocated events with global coverage from 1979 to the present [12]. The data are collected from news reports throughout the world. Currently, this dataset provides daily coverage on the events found in news coverage published on that day. The event types in CAMEO taxonomy are divided into four primary classifications: verbal cooperation and material cooperation, which are represented by numbers 1 to 10, and verbal conflict and material conflict, which are represented by numbers 11 to 20. Moreover, there are 32 different roles for the actors in each event, e.g., Police Forces, Government, and Military.

In GDELT, each record captures information pertaining to a specific event. To generate our models, we use the following attributes from an event: MonthYear, Actor1Type, Actor2Type, RootEventCode, AvgTone, and GoldsteinScale, where Actor1Type and Actor2Type store the role of the actors participating in the event, RootEventCode $\in \{1, \ldots, 20\}$ identifies whether this event is cooperative or conflicting, AvgTone is a subtle measure of the importance of an event and plays as a proxy for the impact of that event, and the

Primary Role Codes	Description
COP	Police forces, officers
GOV	Government: the executive, governing parties, coalitions partners
JUD	Judiciary: judges, courts
MIL	Military: troops, soldiers, all state-military personnel
OPP	Political opposition: opposition parties, individuals, activists
REB	Rebels: armed and violent (non-state) groups, individuals
SPY	State intelligence, secret service
Secondary Role Codes	**Description**
BUS	Business: businessmen, companies, etc.
CVL	Civilian individual or group
EDU	Education: educators, schools, students
ELI	Elites: former government officials or celebrities
LAB	Labor: workers, unions
LEG	Legislature: parliaments, assemblies, "lawmakers"
MED	Media: journalists, newspapers, television stations,etc.
REF	Refugees
Tertiary Role Codes	**Description**
MOD	Moderate: "moderate," "mainstream," etc.
RAD	Radical: "radical," "extremist," "fundamentalist," etc.
UAF	Armed forces that cannot be identified as MIL, COP, or REB

Figure 1: Actors defined in the CAMEO codebook.

GoldsteinScale captures the impact of this event on stability of a country.

2.2 Modeling Domestic Interactions

We define an *interaction graph* of CAMEO event-types involving CAMEO actors. Let $G = (V, E, l, w)$ denote an undirected, labeled multigraph. The set of nodes V represent CAMEO actors; each node is given a distinct actor code (label) by the *node label function l*. The set of edges E represent the CAMEO interactions (events) between actors. The *edge label function w* assigns a label to an edge e corresponding to the type of an interaction.

We construct the interaction graph from a collection of entries in the GDELT dataset. For example, a record indicating a "Demand" interaction (type 10) between government (GOV) and refugees (REF) is represented in the interaction graph as an edge $e = (u, v)$ between the nodes with labels $l(u) = $ GOV and $l(v) = $ REF; the label of this edge is $w(e) = 10$. In this paper, we use *monthly* interactions graphs; for a given country, we compile the entries in GDELT for one month and construct the graph as described above.

We now present several definitions that will be used in the detection and forecasting tasks of Section 3:

Support. Let G_s and G be two graphs, $D = \{G_1, \ldots, G_N\}$ be a collection of graphs, and let $G_s \sqsubseteq G$ denote that G_s is a subgraph of G. We define the support of G_s in dataset D, denoted as $supp(G_s, D)$, as the number of graphs $G \in D$ for which $G_s \sqsubseteq G$. In other words, $supp(G_s, D) = |\{G \in D \mid G_s \sqsubseteq G\}|$

Frequent Subgraph. Given a collection of graphs $D = \{G_1, \ldots, G_N\}$ and a threshold value $\theta \in (0, 1]$, a graph G_s is *frequent* if it is a subgraph of at least $\theta \times N$ graphs in D, or, equivalently, $supp(G_s, D) >= \theta N$.

Subgraph Matching. If a graph S is isomorphic to at least one subgraph G_s of G, then G_s is a *match* of S in G.

3. PROPOSED METHODS

We hypothesize that the interactions between specific actors of a country are important indicators of a DPC in that country. For instance, if there are a high number of conflicts between the government and civilians, the country is likely to experience a DPC imminently or in the near future. Furthermore, interactions between actors during a DPC should be different from interactions in periods of peace. The methods presented below are motivated by this idea.

3.1 Classifying and Detecting DPCs

We pose the problem of detecting DPCs as a classification task. Given the interaction graph G of a country for some period of time t, we use a subset of the subgraphs of G to classify t as *DPC* or *non-DPC*. Formally, let $X = \{x_1, x_2, \ldots, x_n\}$ be a set of multigraphs; the nodes of a graph in X are a subset of the CAMEO actor codes, and its edges represent CAMEO interactions. We refer to X as the *feature set*. Let G^t be an interaction graph corresponding to a period of time t, and let G_X^t be a vector of length n, where the the ith entry in G_X^t is 1 if $x_i \in X$ is a subgraph of G^t, and 0 otherwise. We call G_X^t the *feature vector* of G^t. Our task is to find a *detection function* f that indicates whether a feature vector corresponds to a period of DPC or non-DPC; that is $f : G_X^t \rightarrow \{\text{DPC}, \text{nonDPC}\}$.

A key step in finding a good detection function is to find features, i.e. subgraphs, that appear frequently in interaction graphs and, at the same time, are discerning enough to separate DPC graphs from non-DPC ones. We separate the monthly interaction graphs in our dataset into two groups, D_+ and D_-, representing DPC and non-DPC graphs, respectively. We then find the frequent subgraphs in each dataset, F_+ and F_- using the gSpan algorithm [23]. Since we are interested in finding the most discriminative features for the classification task, we ignore all the subgraphs that are common between F_+ and F_-, thus obtaining a discriminative feature set $DFS = \{F_+ \cup F_-\} - \{F_+ \cap F_-\}$, which we use for classification. As explained in Section 4, at this point in our process, we find that, in most cases, the intersection between F_+ and F_- is very small. This means that actor interactions are very different on months with and without DPC, and the set of frequent subgraphs in the two groups are promising discriminator features for classification.

After obtaining the DFS, we can compute the feature vector of a graph using a subgraph matching algorithm [24, 25, 20]. We use a simplified version of the TreeSpan algorithm [25] to find the exact matching in this paper. Once we have the feature vectors for all graphs in our dataset, we train different classification algorithms to obtain the detection function.

3.2 Forecasting a Domestic Crisis

We now turn to the task of predicting DPCs using the interaction graph. To this end, we develop various regression models that estimate the probability of a DPC occurring in the near future. We employ the LASSO methodology (Least Absolute Shrinkage and Selection Operator) [21]. Like a regular linear regression, LASSO minimizes the sum of squared errors, but with an added constraint on the sum of the absolute values of the coefficients. We use LASSO over a standard linear regression in order to encourage a sparse representation; that is, we are interested in reducing the original feature set, as some of the initial graph properties are expected to be redundant. We develop three types of LASSO-based logistic regression models that use (i) event counts (M_Event), (ii) graph properties (M_Graph), and (iii) features from both M_Event and M_Graph (hybrid model designated as M_Event_Graph).

Event Counts: In this baseline model, we use the monthly counts of each event type in each country as explanatory variables. Moreover, we include the average AvgTone and the average GoldsteinScale associated with these events. Formally, the regression model estimates DPC_t, the probability of a DPC at time t, as

$$DPC_t = \sum_{i=1}^{20} (\alpha_i E_{it-1} + \beta_i T_{it-1} + \gamma_i G_{it-1}) + DPC_{t-1} \quad (1)$$

In the above equation, E_i is the counts of events of type i, T_i is the average AvgTone, G_i is the average GoldsteinScale for the event type i and DPC_t is the dependent variable. We also use the lagged value of DPC in all of the regression models, since DPCs can persist over consecutive months.

Graph Properties: In this regression model, we use graph-based features. We compute structural properties of the interaction graphs: Total Number of Edges ($TotEdge$), Average Weighted Degree ($AvgWDeg$), Diameter ($Diam$), Number of connected components ($Comp$). In addition, we calculate the weighted degree of each actor and their centrality, based on different measures, such as betweenness ($betwCen$), closeness ($closCen$), and degree ($degCen$). The model estimates DPC_t as

$$\begin{aligned} DPC_t = \sum_{i \in V} \alpha_i degCen_{it-1} + \beta_i betwCen_{it-1} + \\ \gamma_i closCen_{it-1} + \omega_1 AvgWDeg_{t-1} + \omega_2 Diam_{t-1} + \\ \omega_2 Comp_{t-1} + \omega_3 TotEdge_{t-1} + DPC_{t-1} \end{aligned} \quad (2)$$

The summation is over all the nodes (actors) of the interaction graph.

Hybrid model: In this model, we combine the features of the event count model and the graph-based model. The performance and predictive power of each model are evaluated in Section 4.

4. EXPERIMENTS

Our experiments are designed to address the following questions:

- Are interactions in a country different during "normal" times and during a DPC? Can we capture this difference and use it to detect DPCs? (Section 4.2)

- How adept are graph-based properties at forecasting DPCs in a country? (Section 4.3)

- Are graph-based models for DPC detection and forecasting better than a history-based approach or a vanilla event count approach? Is there value in combining features from different models? (Sections 4.2 and 4.3)

4.1 Data

We evaluate our methods using GDELT interaction graphs from five countries: Brazil, Colombia, Mexico, Argentina, and Venezuela. The data are collected from January 2003 to the December 2013. Thus, for each country, we have 132 monthly interaction graphs. Table 4.1 shows the number of DPCs in each country for the period mentioned above. GDELT does not include information about DPCs. As ground truth for our experiments, we used the similarly motivated ICEWS dataset, which includes information on whether or not there was a DPC in a country in a given month. We note

Table 1: Number of DPC months in the 132 months of our experiment on different countries

Country	# of Months with DPC (out of 132)
Brazil	6
Argentina	76
Mexico	10
Venezuela	36
Colombia	3

that our proposed methods exhibit quantifiably good detection and predictive power in spite of using features from one dataset and supervisory labels from another.

4.2 Classifying DPC events

We use the gSpan algorithm to find frequent subgraphs in F_+ and F_-. For our experiments, we set the threshold parameter in gSpan to obtain a number of features ranging from 500 to 1,000. Figure 2 represents the top frequent subgraphs associated with DPCs in Brazil, Colombia, Mexico, and Venezuela. The thick edges represent more adversarial interactions (event types 11-20) whereas the thin edges represent cooperative interactions (event types 01-10). The figure shows that, in Colombia, conflicts between Rebellion, Military, and Government are frequent during domestic crises. This graph corresponds to the real-life political tension between the Colombian government and the guerrilla groups in the country. On the other hand, during political crises in Brazil, the actors involved in conflict are Government, Police, Media, and the Opposition. Actors involved in a DPC and the respective interactions vary across different countries. For instance, Goverment and Media seem to engage in more conflict in Brazil than they do in Colombia or Venezuela. Understanding the role of each actor during a DPC requires a thorough analysis of the social and political aspects of each country and is beyond the scope of this paper.

For classification, we use algorithms from the LibSVM [7] and LogitBoost [8] libraries. We compare the performance of the frequent subgraph approach to a baseline model that does not take into account event types (ignoreEventType). In the baseline approach, all graphs are unlabeled which gives us a different set of frequent subgraphs. Our model and the baseline are evaluated using the Area Under Curve (AUC) metric and the Matthews Correlation Coefficient (MCC) measure. MCC is a quality metric for binary classification in unbalanced datasets; its range is $[-1, 1]$, where 1 indicates perfect classification, -1 indicates inverse classification, and 0 represents a random classifier.

Figures 3 and 4 compare our proposed method to the baseline based on the AUC and MCC metrics. We note that, for Brazil and Colombia, the gSpan algorithm could not find the appropriate number of subgraphs for the baseline method, and it runs out of memory; this is the case even if we run a parallel version of the algorithm described in [13]. In every case in the figures, the frequent subgraph approach beats the baseline; the difference is more noticeable when we compare both methods using the MCC metric. For instance, we can see that although we have only three months of DPC for Colombia, the proposed method is able to classify all the graphs in dataset. Moreover, this illustrates the importance

(a) Brazil (b) Colombia

(c) Mexico (d) Venezuela

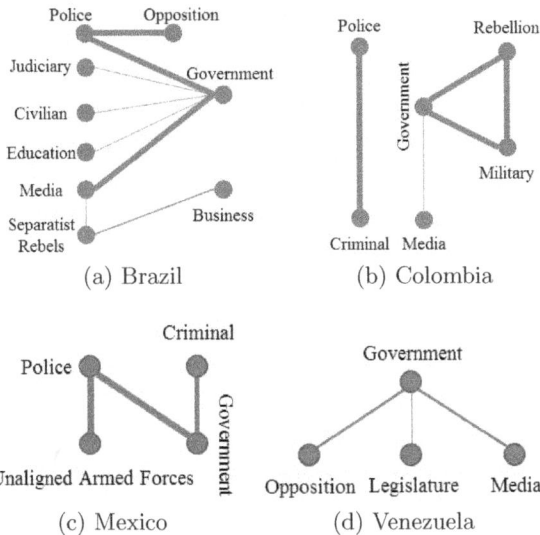

Figure 2: Frequent subgraphs for (a) Brazil, (b) Colombia, (c) Mexico, and (d) Venezuela during DPCs. Thicker edges represent more adversarial interactions.

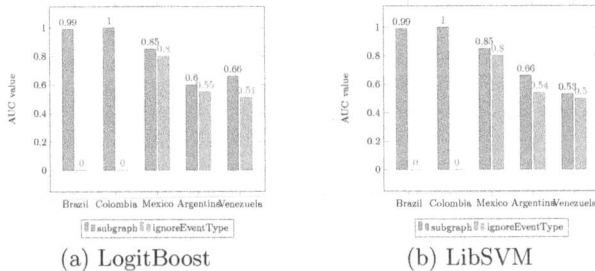

(a) LogitBoost (b) LibSVM

Figure 3: Classifying DPCs (AUC values).

(a) LogitBoost (b) LibSVM

Figure 4: Classification results (MCC measure).

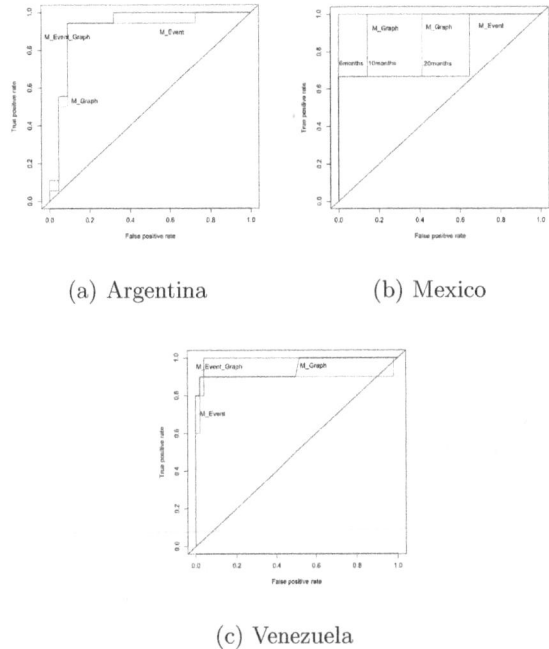

(a) Argentina (b) Mexico

(c) Venezuela

Figure 5: ROC curves for the DPC prediction models. The combination of graph features and event counts outperforms each individual model.

of features that are selected for the classification and solidifies our claim about the effect of actors' interactions on the instability of a country.

4.3 Forecasting DPC events

We evaluate the three regression models described in section 4.2. We focus on Argentina, Mexico, and Venezuela because these countries have a sufficient number of DPCs to train the models. When the distribution of DPC to non-DPC samples is not even, LASSO puts too much weight on the non-DPC months, resulting in a low-performance model. In order to deal with this issue, we focus on the months in which the countries suffered DPC and take the preceding and subsequent months as the training set. (A more systematic approach would be to adopt a classifier specifically meant for imbalanced classes, but our goal here is to explore the utility of graph features using basic machine learning methods.) In the training period (90 months), Argentina experienced 44 months of DPC, compared to 18 in the test period (42 months). For Venezuela, we use a smaller training period —70 months— in order to have a balanced number of DPCs in training and testing data (11 and 10 events, respectively). Finally, Mexico had only 10 months of DPC in 130 months, 3 of which are in the last 3 months of the dataset. Therefore, we only use 45 months to train the model. In

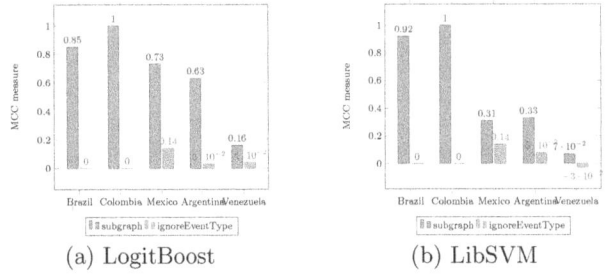

this case, we run experiments with 20 months, 10 months and 6 months as the test set to evaluate the performance of the model over different periods. Figure 4.3 illustrates the performance of the baseline, graph-based and hybrid models for Argentina, Mexico and Venezuela. We observe that the hybrid model outperforms the individual models for all countries. The hybrid model for Argentina and Venezuela result in very high precision (around 0.89 for both), and accuracy reaches 0.92 for Argentina and 0.95 for Venezuela. As we have discussed above, we try different test periods for Mexico and we observe a significant improvement as the number of test days decrease. The precision gets as high as 1, and the accuracy 0.95. When the test period is the last 6 months in our dataset (i.e. July 2013 to December 2013), the model predicts the DPC of the last 3 months and the absence of DPC in the previous months perfectly.

5. DISCUSSION

We have introduced the problem of forecasting DPCs in a given country using graph features. Future work will focus on three aspects. First, we aim to situate our approach

195

in a temporal context so that frequent discriminative subgraphs can be viewed in terms of their evolution over time. Second, we seek to create subgraph features using compositions of basic CAMEO codes, to improve the expressiveness of discovered patterns. Finding such patterns without overwhelming computational complexity is a key issue here. Finally, we aim to develop a maximum entropy modeling of interaction graph evolution so that we can aim to model not just crises but surprising geopolitical developments in general.

Acknowledgements

Supported by the following grants: DTRA Grant HDTRA1-11-1-0016, DTRA CNIMS Contract HDTRA1-11-D-0016-0010, NSF ICES CCF-1216000 and NSF NETSE Grant CNS-1011769. Also supported by the Intelligence Advanced Research Projects Activity (IARPA) via Department of Interior National Business Center (DoI/NBC) contract number D12PC000337, the US Government is authorized to reproduce and distribute reprints for Governmental purposes notwithstanding any copyright annotation thereon. Disclaimer: The views and conclusions contained herein are those of the authors and should not be interpreted as necessarily representing the official policies or endorsements, either expressed or implied, of IARPA, DoI/NBC, or the US Government.

6. REFERENCES

[1] B. Arva, J. Beieler, B. Fisher, G. Lara, P. A. Schrodt, W. Song, M. Sowell, and S. Stehle. Improving forecasts of international events of interest. In *European Political Science Association*, volume 78, 2013.

[2] E. E. Azar. The conflict and peace data bank (COPDAB) project. *Journal of Conflict Resolution*, 24:143–152, 1980.

[3] B. E. Bagozzi. Forecasting civil conflict with zero-inflated count models. *Manuscript, Pennsylvania State University*, 2011.

[4] B. E. Bagozzi. Modeling Two Types of Peace The Zero-inflated Ordered Probit (ZiOP) Model in Conict Research. *Journal of Conflict Resolution*, 58, 2014.

[5] P. T. Brandt and J. R. Freeman. Advances in Bayesian time series modeling and the study of politics: Theory testing, forecasting, and policy analysis. *Political Analysis*, 14(1):1–36, 2006.

[6] P. T. Brandt, J. R. Freeman, and P. A. Schrodt. Real time, time series forecasting of inter-and intra-state political conflict. *Conflict Management and Peace Science*, 28(1):41–64, 2011.

[7] C.-C. Chang and C.-J. Lin. Libsvm: a library for support vector machines. *ACM Transactions on Intelligent Systems and Technology (TIST)*, 2(3):27, 2011.

[8] J. Friedman, T. Hastie, and R. Tibshirani. Additive logistic regression: a statistical view of boosting (with discussion and a rejoinder by the authors). *The Annals of Statistics*, 28(2):337–407, 2000.

[9] D. J. Gerner, P. A. Schrodt, R. A. Francisco, and J. L. Weddle. Machine coding of event data using regional and international sources. *International Studies Quarterly*, pages 91–119, 1994.

[10] J. S. Goldstein. A conflict-cooperation scale for WEIS events data. *Journal of Conflict Resolution*, 36(2):369–385, 1992.

[11] G. R. Harris. Regime switching vector autoregressions: a Bayesian Markov chain Monte Carlo approach. *Conflict Management and Peace Science*, 28(1):41–64, 2011.

[12] K. Leetaru and P. Schrodt. GDELT: Global Data on Events, Language, and Tone, 1979-2012. In *International Studies Association Annual Conference*, 2013.

[13] T. Meinl, I. Fischer, and M. Philippsen. Parallel Mining for Frequent Fragments on a Shared-Memory Multiprocessor-Results and Java-Obstacles. *Lernen, Wissen, Adaption*, 2005.

[14] J. M. Montgomery, F. M. Hollenbach, and M. D. Ward. Improving predictions using ensemble Bayesian model averaging. *Political Analysis*, 20(3):271–291, 2012.

[15] S. P. O'brien. Crisis early warning and decision support: Contemporary approaches and thoughts on future research. *International Studies Review*, 12(1):87–104, 2010.

[16] P. A. Schrodt. Pattern recognition of international crises using hidden markov models. *Political complexity: Nonlinear models of politics*, pages 296–328, 2000.

[17] P. A. Schrodt and D. J. Gerner. Empirical indicators of crisis phase in the Middle East, 1979-1995. *Journal of Conflict Resolution*, 41(4):529–552, 1997.

[18] P. A. Schrodt, J. Yonamine, and B. E. Bagozzi. Data-based computational approaches to forecasting political violence. In *Handbook of Computational Approaches to Counterterrorism*, pages 129–162. Springer, 2013.

[19] S. M. Shellman. Time series intervals and statistical inference: The effects of temporal aggregation on event data analysis. *Political Analysis*, 12(1):97–104, 2004.

[20] Y. Tian, R. C. Mceachin, C. Santos, J. M. Patel, et al. SAGA: a subgraph matching tool for biological graphs. *Bioinformatics*, 23(2):232–239, 2007.

[21] R. Tibshirani. Regression shrinkage and selection via the lasso: a retrospective. *Journal of the Royal Statistical Society: Series B (Statistical Methodology)*, 73(3):273–282, 2011.

[22] M. D. Ward, N. W. Metternich, C. Carrington, C. Dorff, M. Gallop, F. M. Hollenbach, A. Schultz, and S. Weschle. Geographical Models of Crises: Evidence from ICEWS. 2012.

[23] X. Yan and J. Han. gSpan: Graph-based substructure pattern mining. In *Proceedings of IEEE International Conference on Data Mining*, pages 721–724, 2002.

[24] S. Zhang, S. Li, and J. Yang. GADDI: distance index based subgraph matching in biological networks. In *Proceedings of the 12th International Conference on Extending Database Technology: Advances in Database Technology*, pages 192–203. ACM, 2009.

[25] G. Zhu, X. Lin, K. Zhu, W. Zhang, and J. X. Yu. Treespan: efficiently computing similarity all-matching. In *Proceedings of the 2012 ACM SIGMOD International Conference on Management of Data*, pages 529–540. ACM, 2012.

Pelagios and the Emerging Graph of Ancient World Data

Leif Isaksen
University of Southampton
Highfield, Southampton
SO17 1BF United Kingdom
l.isaksen@soton.ac.uk

Rainer Simon
AIT: Austrian Institute of
Technology
1220 Vienna, Austria
Rainer.Simon@ait.ac.at

Elton T. E. Barker
The Open University
Walton Hall, Milton Keynes
MK7 6AA United Kingdom
e.t.e.barker@open.ac.uk

Pau de Soto Cañamares
University of Southampton
Highfield, Southampton
SO17 1BF United Kingdom
p.desotocanamares@soton.ac.uk

ABSTRACT

This paper discusses an emerging cloud of Linked Open Data in the humanities sometimes referred to as the Graph of Ancient World Data (GAWD). It provides historical background to the domain, before gong on to describe the open and decentralised characteristics which have partially characterised its development. This is done principally through the lens of Pelagios, a collaborative initiative led by the authors which connects online historical resources based on common references to places. The benefits and limitations of the approach are evaluated, in particular its low barrier to entry, open architecture and restricted scope. The paper concludes with a number of suggestion for encouraging the adoption of Linked Open Data within other humanities communities and beyond.

Categories and Subject Descriptors

J.2 [**Computer Applications**]: Physical Sciences and Engineering—*Archaeology*; J.5 [**Computer Applications**]: Arts and humanities

Keywords

Linked Open Data; Humanities; Geospatial

1. INTRODUCTION

As recently as 2011, one of the authors of this paper concluded their doctoral thesis with the following claim and query: '*it remains a moot point as to whether Berners-Lee's vision of an open and decentralized Knowledge Representation is possible. The question left for archaeologists to consider is: Could an open and decentralized archaeology be possible?*'[8] This paper argues that since then a quiet revolution has been taking place which suggests that open

and decentralised Linked Data is not only possible in archaeology but in the humanities more widely. This is a different issue from whether the field is willing or able to adopt the *technologies* of the Semantic Web. RDF has been used in a variety of humanities projects since at least the early Noughties[1][7], and conferences and funding organisations continue to deem it an area of significance in the Digital Humanities. Rather, the change has been towards an ecology-driven approach in which a community of independent initiatives has gradually increased mutual connectivity by creating and using Linked Open Data.

Perhaps the most significant area of growth has been in what is sometimes dubbed the Graph of Ancient World Data (GAWD)[13], encompassing both philological and archaeological approaches to the study of antiquity. This trend was unquestionably facilitated by the National Endowment for the Humanities (NEH) funded Linked Ancient World Data Institute summer programme which ran in the summer of 2012 and 2013 and has recently published a series of short articles in a special issue of *ISAW Papers*[6]. Yet these two workshops are in themselves insufficient to explain why more than fifty widely divergent projects and organisations from the public, academic and private sectors have so quickly begun to establish connections through the Semantic Web. This is especially given these fields' historical tendencies to work in comparative isolation, and grant prestige principally to the work of individual scholars rather than collaborative ventures.

This paper attempts to explain: why Linked Open Data approaches have started to gain traction in this area; the current state of play; what it may mean both for the future of academic and public engagement with the ancient world; and subsequently draws wider conclusions for the humanities and Linked Open Data communities.

2. WHY THE ANCIENT WORLD?

Classics and archaeology are not fields which many associate with the bleeding edge of technology, let alone Web Science, but in fact they have formed the domain of several significant initiatives in the history of open digital data, including the Perseus Digital Library[4] and the work of Rahtz, Hall and Allen on hypertext for excavation reports [12]. Are there any particular features of these disciplines, or their union, that either makes them especially well-suited to Linked Open Data or encourages its adoption? We argue that the following factors have all played a role:

A diverse but tractable domain The study of antiquity is divided into a wide array of individual subfields, both in terms of a traditional separation between philological and archeological evidence, but also specialisms which cross this divide, including prosopography (historical individuals and their relationships), numismatics (coins), epigraphy (inscriptions), geography, political, military and social history, and so on. Yet these often starkly differing approaches are united by a reasonably well-defined domain with a limited, if slowly growing, evidence base. A vast proportion of this information is hidden not beneath the soil or on dusty monastery shelves, but within libraries, museums and archives compiled in the nineteenth and twentieth centuries that are increasing available online. Furthermore, as Greece and Rome were literate cultures, at a basic level we are often able to identify and refer to emic concepts, i.e. those which originated in the languages of those periods. These are arguably more stable than the etic conceptual schemes developed by contemporary scholars to describe cultural phenomena for which no linguistic evidence survives.

Controlled vocabularies An extremely important development has been the establishment of services providing stable URIs for shared categorical and instance thesauri. These include place gazetteers,[1] type classifications for coins[2] and canonical citations for classical literature.[3] Without them, earlier attempts at 'interoperability' were seriously hampered by the lack of common reference terms for analogous content despite the availability of ontologies that defined shared or equivalent properties.

Simple ontologies The CIDOC Conceptual Reference Model (CIDOC CRM) remains perhaps the most powerful ontology available for describing the creation, evolution and destruction of cultural heritage[5]. Nonetheless its complexity, in combination with unfamiliar Linked Data technologies such as RDF, has proven off-putting to newcomers. Ontologies such as Open Annotation[4] have offered an easier on-ramp, along with a variety of direct benefits to both contributors and users, without preventing the adoption of additional (and more sophisticated) ontologies later on.

Sufficient open data An enormous amount of information about the ancient world remains inaccessible to the general public and researchers at all but a handful of elite institutions[9]. However, the tightly-knitted nature of the field has meant that much interrelated material, especially ancient text, is increasingly available. The situation for material culture is more varied but pioneering work by organisations such as the German Archaeological Institute, the Alexandria Archive and the UK Archaeological Data Service may be stimulating progress on open archaeological data elsewhere.

The most significant difference between GAWD and earlier 'Semantic Web' developments in the humanities is the increasing interconnection between heterogeneous, independently maintained resources through the common use of URIs. Whereas earlier initiatives were often characterised by intensive collaboration between small numbers of projects, often without persistent URIs or making data openly accessible[8], GAWD is an informal collective of independent participants treating Linked Data as as just one more means of making their data more accessible. So how does this 'ecosystem' work in practice?

3. CASE STUDY: PELAGIOS AND GEOGRAPHIC ANNOTATION IN GAWD

An example of this decentralised structure is the interconnection of resources based on common references to place. The foundations for this were laid by the Pleiades Gazetteer of the Ancient World, developed and hosted by the Institute for the Study of the Ancient World, New York University. Initially conceived of as an online and community-driven continuation of the *Barrington Atlas of the Greek and Roman World*[15], it was soon realised that providing a stable URI would be an essential for each entry in the gazetteer. This would not only allow other projects to derive information such as coordinate locations automatically, but furthermore that they could act as a point of intersection between projects otherwise unknown to one another. The Pelagios project, led by several of this paper's authors and supported by Jisc , a UK funding body, took on the task of formalising this process while seeking to maintain the twin principles of openness and decentralisation[2].

In consultation with a variety of stakeholders it proposed the use of the Open Annotation ontology which describes an annotation comprising a *target* URI representing a document (or fragment thereof) and a *body* representing its content[14]. While the general specification allows the latter to have any value, Pelagios compliance requires it to point to a URI representing a place defined in a digital gazetteer such as Pleiades or Geonames.[5] While such annotations are themselves extremely simple (essentially tripartite links), collectively they form a two-mode graph of associations between document[6] resources and places. This allows not only for the first-order querying of places associated with a document and vice versa, but questions of greater interest to humanists - which places are commonly referred to together? Which documents appear to cover similar geographic territory? Additionally they are language neutral, an important consideration for a field that operates across many modern European languages as well as Latin and Ancient Greek. The addition of further metadata to the annotations, such as the specific toponym used, as well as the date, time and author of the annotation, can collectively provide valuable information for understanding variation in the way geographic concepts are referred to, and help address issues of provenance and trust.

A fundamental premise of the Pelagios initiative was that it should avoid social and technical bottlenecks wherever possible. This was achieved by encouraging individual re-

---

[1]http://pleiades.stoa.org
[2]http://numismatics.org/ocre
[3]http://cts3.sourceforge.net
[4]http://www.openannotation.org

[5]http://geonames.org
[6]'Document' is here used to denote any kind of human interpretable online resource, whether image or text, static or dynamically generated.

source providers to produce and host their own annotations. RDF proved to be a powerful format in this regard. Simple ontologies such as Open Annotation are reasonably comprehensible to the technically literate, can be templated easily, and expressed in a range of notations and technical solutions suited to any level of Web-based hosting. The capability (in terms of both knowledge and resources) to host Web content remained a prerequisite, but one which - almost by definition - any provider of online ancient world resource is likely to meet. On the other hand, allowing third parties to annotate content and host it in a decentralised fashion remains an open challenge in a field where few day-to-day practitioners have either experience or facilities for Web-hosting. In addition to hosting their annotations, resource providers were also encouraged to release them under the most liberal licensing terms possible, ideally CC0.[7] There remains an important question as to whether such annotations should be deemed to constitute data, and thus be licensed under an Open Data Licence such as PDDL.[8] The Pelagios stance is that such annotations usually constitute an interpretive rather than a factual assertion to the affect that 'reference x refers to place y' as the author's intention is inherently inaccessible to the annotator unless they are one and the same person.

Pelagios annotations thus form an interconnected and open set of RDF triples, dispersed across the Web. While this is an important outcome that meets the objectives of both openness and decentralisation, it is also not terribly easy for information consumers to make use of. The Pelagios project therefore established a demonstrator Webservice which harvests such annotations and makes them available through a human-readable search interface, a machine-readable API,[9] and a series of embeddable widgets.[10] The API provides a number of functions of direct benefit to to those who have annotated their own content, not least of which is the ability to access a growing cloud of related content hosted elsewhere, as well as the increased likelihood of discovery by consumers following the same API in the opposite direction. Indeed, it is precisely the utility of this interface that led to a rapid growth in both partners and content - from five institutions in the first phase of the project to almost forty at the time of writing and some 800,000 annotations.[11] It might be asked whether the claim for decentralisation is merely sleight-of-hand if both contributors and consumers are making use of this API rather than the source data? We share concerns that any system which relies too heavily on a single point of failure will ultimately prove unsustainable, and thus encourage the development of alternative APIs and web services, building upon the project's open source code base where this assists, ignoring it where it does not. The fact that every aspect of the project is open access, from content to code, to a cookbook of best practices, means that no aspect is not reproducible elsewhere should the need or desire arise.

Contextualisation and discovery are not the only benefits that large-scale, distributed, but structurally simple, graphs

can bring. Traditional humanistic questions may also be approached with such data. For instance, the latest cycle of Pelagios, funded by the Andrew W. Mellon Foundation, is creating infrastructure and content for the annotation of Early Geospatial Documents (EGDs) extending up to the end of the Pre-Modern period (c. 1500). The ability to compare the places referred to in maps, itineraries and geographic descriptions across diverse linguistic and ethnic traditions is likely to transform our understanding of historical developments in geographic thought. It is also a clear indicator, were it needed, that Linked Open Data is not exclusively suited to classical resources but has much to offer the study of, and engagement with, other regions and periods as well.

Geography is only one of many dimensions across which Linked Open Data can interconnect online resources. Work on Canonical Text Services is creating Web-based infrastructure for uniquely identifying canonical citations in classical texts[3]. Such citations form the backbone of most scholarly research in this literature, providing a global reference system that transcends arbitrary page numbering divisions. The Standards for Networking Ancient Prosopographies (SNAP)[12] project is similarly defining both URI and annotation conventions for referencing ancient people. This introduces new challenges: while identifying a shared conception of a place can often be achieved 'intuitively' by means of geodetic, administrative or mereological relationships, people can be harder to denote, especially where the evidence is fragmentary. Should Aristotle be defined by his place of birth, his association with Athens (of which he was not a citizen), his contributions to philosophy (which?), his tutoring of Alexander the Great, or a combination of these and other 'facts'? What if such identifications are controversial or turn out to be wrong? Establishing best practices for this process will be an important contribution to GAWD. Finally, classificatory thesauri for fields such as numismatics and ceramics may over time greatly assist our ability to compare distribution networks from archaeological excavations which are currently very difficult to assimilate[10].

4. SIGNIFICANCE FOR WEB SCIENCE

Collectively, these developments suggest a number of lessons for those seeking to introduce Linked Open Data practices to the humanities. Despite longstanding concerns as to the the humanities' tendency towards individualism and technical illiteracy, the case is now clear that decentralised Linked Open Data is not only possible but can flourish in this field. Nonetheless, much work remains to be done. Few if any humanities domains have embraced this model to the same degree as the ancient world, although that need not deter us unduly given how rapidly the situation can change. Furthermore, we are at the tip of the iceberg even in this case as the overwhelming majority of classicists and classical archaeologists have never heard of Linked Open Data, let alone contributed to it. It may be an unrealistic, perhaps even undesirable, goal to believe that they should, but we must certainly aim for a scenario in which they can benefit, and ideally offer their own content, regardless of whether they care for the terminology or grasp all of its underlying principles. How might this be achieved? The following suggestions reflect the authors' experiences contributing to GAWD:

---

[7]https://creativecommons.org/publicdomain/zero/1.0

[8]http://opendatacommons.org/licenses/pddl

[9]https://github.com/pelagios/pelagios-cookbook/wiki/Using-the-Pelagios-API

[10]http://pelagios-project.blogspot.co.uk/p/pelagios-in-use.html

[11]http://pelagios.dme.ait.ac.at/api/datasets

---

[12]http://snapdrgn.net/about

1. Simplicity is essential if we are to attract contributors with little prior investment in Semantic Web technologies. A huge advantage of the Linked Data approach over even relational database technologies is that almost everyone is now familiar with URLs, and the conceptual leap to URIs is neither difficult, nor ultimately essential for day-to-day users. Likewise, much of the apparent complexity faced by those acquainting themselves with Linked Data for the first time lies with the ontologies, rather than RDF *per se*. We should seek to attract broader communities by proposing Linked Data activities with immediate benefit, only introducing greater complexity as required. Complex ontologies remain useful however, and initiatives to facilitate their use, such as SENESCHAL[13] and ARCHES[11] are important.

2. Quickly establishing a critical mass of open and related content is a tremendous motivator, as the benefits of Linked Open Data largely derive from the ability to associate the contributor's content with external content. Without it, there are few technical advantages that RDF encoding provides which cannot be achieved by means with which the contributor is likely to be more familiar. Fortunately, once this critical mass is established, there is often a snowballing effect by which the benefits of connecting to the data cloud continually increase against the (stable) cost of contributing to it. Historically, much production of Linked Data has been happenstance, often producing semantic silos of conceptually unrelated content. As a community we should seek to target groups of related datasets, then continuously build around them, bridging between clusters where we can. Wide-application concepts such as geographic location are especially good for this.

3. Linked Data is sometimes discussed as though it exists as its own parallel Web, unpolluted by the Web of Documents. This is highly detrimental to its adoption. Linked Open Data approaches should be used in a 'mixed economy' of multiple technologies, each used for the task to which it is best suited. For instance, the dimensional aspect of geospatial information is poorly suited to expression and visual representation as Linked Data. Likewise, GIS and web mapping technologies require a geometric primitive to locate every entity and handle conceptual associations between places poorly. Attempting to reduce geographic knowledge solely to either is neither necessary nor helpful. The same holds true of web services, relational data formats, statistical datasets and mathematical functions.

4. Just like the Web, the wider graph of humanities data (and indeed all Linked Open Data) will grow organically, not be built according to a software architect's plan. With this in mind it makes sense for us to concentrate on small, individual steps which offer immediate benefits, whilst remaining aware of their limitations. There has been perhaps been too much emphasis by funders on Virtual Research Environments or domain ontologies which are expected to cater to every conceivable humanities question. This is not only a failure to understand the nature of humanistic inquiry (which seeks to challenge conceptual models, rather than defer to them), but can prevent us from focussing on goals more readily within our grasp. Growth can occur in two dimensions - both through the expression of data according to established URI schemes, or through the addition of new infrastructural components such as controlled vocabularies and ontologies. We should expect the former to be far more frequent than the latter and require a far lower level of technical capability. We should also maintain the principle that contribution can be at any level - that as the possibilities for contribution grow more complex, the requirements for doing so do not. A recent positive development in this area has been the Getty Research Institute's publication of its thesauri as Linked Open Data.[14] These widely used datasets could see yet greater adoption as online resources align content with their URIs without the earlier impediment of licensing fees.

5. Such organic growth in turn requires multiple stakeholders to take responsibility for clearly defined aspects of the wider graph. The nature of this responsibility will vary. Those maintaining controlled vocabularies or ontologies will need to guarantee at least a moderate level of stability and documentation, along with clearly defined contingency plans should the service fail or be discontinued. In contrast, the requirements for those aligning otherwise 'non-semantic' content with such services might be requested simply to provide identifying information for the purpose of provenancing and other such metadata.

6. This last point touches on perhaps the most important challenge of all: trust. GAWD has grown largely due to the establishment of trust at a range of levels among the parties involved. This is partly a matter of sustainability. When investing time producing RDF that aligns content with URIs offered by an external body it is important to believe that they will remain online for the foreseeable future, and have a plan for what happens if they do not. There is an additional social component to this trust network, however. If content is accessible through third parties, it is essential that all parties receive appropriate levels of attribution, regardless of licensing stipulations, and provenance be transparent. Obscuring the source of content will disenchant consumers and contributors alike.

5. CONCLUSIONS

Linked Open Data—conceived of as an ecology of independent online resources interconnected by RDF—has finally taken significant hold in an area of the humanities. The factors leading up to this development are manifold and it is not yet clear how easily repeatable they are. Nonetheless, this provides strong evidence that RDF-based approaches are applicable outside the laboratory and in scenarios that do not require extensive financial resources or support for complex technical solutions. Most importantly, they can also work across wide networks of stakeholders and show

[13]http://www.heritagedata.org/blog/about-heritage-data/seneschal

[14]http://www.getty.edu/research/tools/vocabularies/lod/

potential for growth. By fostering open but collaborative initiatives, with institutions taking responsibility for clearly defined roles, a nascent Semantic Web for the humanities is starting to emerge.

6. ACKNOWLEDGMENTS

The authors would like to thank Jisc, the Andrew W. Mellon Foundation, the organisers of the Linked Ancient World Data Institute, and all contributors to the Graph of Ancient World Data.

7. REFERENCES

[1] M. Addis, M. Boniface, S. Goodall, P. Grimwood, S. Kim, P. Lewis, K. Martinez, and A. Stevenson. SCULPTEUR: Towards a New Paradigm for Multimedia Museum Information Handling. pages 582–596. 2003.

[2] E. Barker. Welcome to PELAGIOS, Feb. 2011.

[3] C. Blackwell and N. Smith. A Brief Guide to the Canonical Text Service. Technical report, Homer Multitext Project, May 2013.

[4] G. Crane. The Perseus Project and Beyond: How Building a Digital Library Challenges the Humanities and Technology. *D-Lib Magazine*, Jan. 1998.

[5] N. Crofts, M. Doerr, T. Gill, S. Stead, and M. Stiff. Definition of the CIDOC Conceptual Reference Model. Version 5. Technical report, ICOM, Jan. 2011.

[6] T. Elliott, S. Heath, and J. Muccigrosso, editors. *Current Practice in Linked Open Data for the Ancient World*, volume 7 of *ISAW Papers*. Institute for the Study of the Ancient World, New York, 2014.

[7] B. Fuchs, L. Isaksen, and A. C. Smith. The Virtual Lightbox for Museums and Archives: A Portlet Solution for Structured Data Reuse Across Distributed Visual Resources. In *Museums and the Web 2005*, Victoria, 2005. Archives & Museum Informatics.

[8] L. Isaksen. *Archaeology and the Semantic Web*. PhD thesis, University of Southampton, 2011.

[9] E. Kansa. Openness and Archaeology's Information Ecosystem. *World Archaeology*, 44(4):498–520, 2012.

[10] A. Meadows and E. Gruber. Coinage and Numismatic Methods. A Case Study of Linking a Discipline. *ISAW Papers*, (7), 2014.

[11] D. Myers, Y. Avramides, and A. Dalgity. Changing the Heritage Inventory Paradigm: The Arches Open Source System. *Conservation Perspectives: the GCI Newsletter*, pages 4–9, 2013.

[12] S. Rahtz, W. Hall, and T. Allen. The Development of Dynamic Archaeological Publications. In S. Rahtz and P. Reilly, editors, *Archaeology in the Information Age*. Routledge, 1992.

[13] R. Robineau. Graph of Ancient World Data, June 2012.

[14] R. Sanderson, P. Ciccarese, and V. d. S. Herbert. Open Annotation Data Model. Technical report, W3C, Feb. 2013.

[15] R. J. A. Talbert. *Barrington Atlas of the Greek and Roman World*. Princeton University Press, Princeton, 2000.

It's all in the Content: State of the art Best Answer Prediction based on Discretisation of Shallow Linguistic Features

George Gkotsis, Karen Stepanyan,
Carlos Pedrinaci, John Domingue
Knowledge Media Institute
The Open University
Milton Keynes, UK
firstname.lastname@open.ac.uk

Maria Liakata
Dept. of Computer Science
University of Warwick
Coventry, UK
m.liakata@warwick.ac.uk

ABSTRACT

This paper addresses the problem of determining the best answer in Community-based Question Answering websites by focussing on the content. Previous research on this topic relies on the exploitation of community feedback on the answers, which involves rating of either users (e.g., reputation) or answers (e.g. scores manually assigned to answers). We propose a new technique that leverages the content/textual features of answers in a novel way. Our approach delivers better results than related linguistics-based solutions and manages to match rating-based approaches. More specifically, the gain in performance is achieved by rendering the values of these features into a discretised form. We also show how our technique manages to deliver equally good results in real-time settings, as opposed to having to rely on information not always readily available, such as user ratings and answer scores. We ran an evaluation on 21 StackExchange websites covering around 4 million questions and more than 8 million answers. We obtain 84% average precision and 70% recall, which shows that our technique is robust, effective, and widely applicable.

Categories and Subject Descriptors

H.3.1 [**Information Storage and Retrieval**]: Content Analysis and Indexing—*linguistic processing*

General Terms

Algorithms, Design, Experimentation

Keywords

Community Question Answering, Social Media

1. INTRODUCTION

The proliferation of Community-based Question Answering (CQA) websites and their corresponding data has drawn the attention of computer science researchers. The solution to the problem of identification of the best answer is expected to bring several benefits. First of all, since several answers are provided for each question, the readers of these websites will be able to process the candidate answers more efficiently and mitigate the "information overload" phenomenon. Secondly, a mechanism that identifies the high quality answers will increase awareness within the community and will help to put more effort into questions that remain poorly answered. For instance, in Stackoverflow[1] alone, as of September 2013, we found that approximately 33% of the questions have yet to be marked as resolved (i.e., out of the 5 million, 1.7 million questions have no answer marked as "accepted"). More generally, the study of the characteristics of answers is expected to improve our understanding of information seeking activities and social media reception in general.

Typically, CQAs adopt a simple model where the discussion is centred around a question posted by a user with answers addressing it submitted by community members. A question remains "unresolved" until the questioner marks exactly one of the answers as the "accepted" one. Research so far has indicated that communities cannot be examined statically. In particular, the dynamic nature of online communication and communities alters the distribution of different roles in a community and may affect its sustainability [15]. In this work we also discuss how the content/linguistic features change over time and the implications this change has for the community's perception of good content quality.

The study of publicly available corpora and the continuously increasing volume of user-generated content through social media is at the focus of web science. Researchers in related fields have used lexical, syntactic, and discourse features to produce a predictive model of readers' judgments [14]. In several cases, the use of shallow features, i.e. features that do not employ semantic or syntactic parsing such as sentence length [8] or word length [13], are proven to be effective in assessing properties such as ease of reading or usefulness. However, with respect to CQA, research efforts towards the exploitation of shallow features report

---

[1]http://stackoverflow.com/

relatively low results (e.g., Burel et al. report 70% precision [5] and Tian et al. report 71% prediction accuracy [17] for a balanced dataset). To improve the efficacy of their models, researchers refer to more contextual information, such as the *score* of each answer, the *comments* received or the *reputation* of the user.

Solutions that are based on *answer* or *user ratings* have been shown to be far more effective compared to linguistic ones. For instance Burel et al. [5] achieve 85% precision largely due to the received score (answer rating), while Anderson et al. [3] find that authors with a high reputation are behind good quality answers (user rating). At the same time, there is growing research interest around sites like StackExchange that employ badges and how this may affect the development of a community and the acceptance of answers. There is particular interest in studying well known behaviours, such as preferential attachment (the "rich get richer" effect), which may be a side-effect of systems that support community-based content assessment [11]. In such cases preferential attachment poses a threat to the development of the community, since the reputation framework reinforces the pre-existing community hierarchy.

In addition to the above concerns around the utilisation of reputation-based platforms, another issue pertains to the usage of answers' ratings, since these cannot be applied in a real-time setting due to an inherent delay between the answerer's submission and the expected community feedback. To provide a solution that is applicable in a real-time setting we address the problem of best-answer identification in CQAs by leveraging purely textual features of the candidate answers. Our decision to ignore further contextual information is based on the fact that when examining a question and its candidate answers we do not always have at our disposal information such as answer ratings or the reputation information for new users.

The main goal of our work is to address the problem of best answer identification and prediction using solely textual features. To do so, we examine 21 of the most active StackExchange websites, including the most popular one, Stackoverflow. We study the evolution of language characteristics over time and across different communities. We investigate the distinct properties of accepted answers and we devise a classification strategy to achieve this prediction efficiently. Our paper makes the following contributions:

- We introduce a novel way of exploiting various shallow textual features with state-of-the-art performance that outperforms previous linguistics-based solutions

- We evaluate and validate the results of the proposed technique on 21 StackExchange (SE) websites. To our knowledge, the scope and diversity of this evaluation is the largest so far.

- We show how our solution is generically applicable without the use of training data from the target SE website.

The remainder of the paper is organised as follows: Section 2 reviews related work. Section 3 presents information around StackExchange and the corresponding dataset that we used. Section 4 introduces the features that we used for addressing our problem, including the proposed, novel methodology for devising discretised linguistic features. We

then proceed to Section 5 where we present the results of our evaluation. Finally, Section 6 discusses how our approach compares to others as well as some ideas for future work.

2. RELATED WORK

The past years have seen the publication of several papers addressing the quality of answers in CQA. We first discuss work on best answer identification for StackExchange (SE) and Yahoo! Answers[2] (YA) and then move on to work on quality assessment of answers.

The most recent work on SE comes from Burel et al. [5]. The authors introduce three different classes of features for predicting the best answers. These classes contain features involving the content, user and thread information of answers. The combination of these features yields a precision of 85% for the case of two StackExchange websites (Server Fault and Cooking). The results show that the model deployed is mostly based on the "Score Ratio" feature (the proportion of scores given to a post from all the scores received in a question thread). According to our approach, this feature constitutes part of "future knowledge", as the score value cannot be collected near the submission time of an answer and is therefore against our initial input assumption. Furthermore, when using purely textual features, the authors report a precision drop for Server Fault[3] down to 65%. We show how the textual features can be leveraged to improve performance.

Tian et al. [17] share similar objectives with this work as they focus solely on the content of posts rather than user background information (e.g., user rating). They identify contextual information as the most important factor for successfully predicting the best answer. More specifically, they develop their model by using the questions together with the corresponding answers. However, some of the attributes used include comments, which are disregarded in our approach as they constitute future knowledge. This requirement for the existence of information such as the comments is the reason why the dataset they used included only around 196k answers from Stackoverflow that were at least a year old. The final prediction accuracy reported in this case was 72%. Our solution overcomes this limitation for the need for long-lived questions and answers and exhibits higher performance.

In general, YA adopts similar operation mechanics but differs in the nature of questions submitted by the users, since questions are more debatable, subjective and are hosted on a single website divided into different thematic categories. Shah and Pomerantz [16] construct a dataset of resolved questions each one containing exactly 5 answers (the ratio of answers is 4:1). The model employed contains a number of shallow textual features, such as the length of the subject and content for each answer, as well as information about a user profile and the score received. The authors start by acknowledging that the baseline of the constructed dataset has an accuracy of 80% (i.e. negative classifier classifying all answers as non-accepted) and manage to improve the classification up to 84.52%. The authors also report a lower performance when employing readability annotations from

---

[2]http://answers.yahoo.com/
[3]http://serverfault.com

Mechanical Turk[4] due to the inherent subjectivity of the assessments. This is an important finding that demonstrates the subjectivity and difficulty inherent in best answer identification. Finally, Adamic et al. [1] also focus on YA and introduce a number of thread and content features. Looking at questions under the "Programming" category, they report a precision of 72.9% using features such as thread length, user number of best answers and user number of replies.

Work more broadly related to ours includes papers that study the activity of questions in StackExchange, such as whether a question will receive any answer (Yang et al. [18]), or whether questions have been answered sufficiently (Anderson et al. [3]). Yang et al. [18] use the question length as a linguistic feature in addition to 6 more features pertaining to the asker's background and they experiment with different classification algorithms. The highest reported F-Measure is 0.325. Anderson et al. [3] use several features to assess the longevity of a question and highlight the importance of the number of answers, the sum of scores on answers to question, as well as the length of the highest-scoring answer. Liu et al. [12] present a framework for estimating question difficulty. The authors follow a competition-based approach which models together the level of question difficulty with the level of user expertise.

Finally, numerous papers have been published that focus on the assessment of user-generated content quality. Agichtein et al. [2] use human editors to train a classifier for high and low quality questions and answers in YA. They use different features including baseline linguistic features such as word n-grams and report 67% precision (0.805 AUC) for an unbalanced dataset comprised of a few thousand answers. Furthermore, their study reports that the length of an answer is a significant indicator of answer quality.

3. STACKEXCHANGE DATASET

StackExchange (SE) is the engine that powers some of the most popular CQAs such as Stackoverflow (SO), Mathematics and Server Fault. Webpages in SE consist of one question and an arbitrary number of answers submitted by users. As of February 2014, 115 SE websites are available, each focussing on one topic. Topics are diverse, ranging from programming, system and network administrating to cooking, scientific skepticism and English language. As indicated in the mission statement, SE "is all about getting answers, it's not a discussion forum, there's no chit-chat". In order to maintain the quality of both questions and answers, posts are curated by the members of the community and if a question or an answer is deemed to be inappropriate or irrelevant, the post is removed from the website. In addition to the above, the reputation system introduced incentivises users to receive accreditation from the community and create high quality content, which is rewarded through badges and extra rights (such as the right of content removal). The high quality of the content has lead SE's premier website, Stackoverflow (SO), to grow vigorously and attract almost 3 million users in approximately 5 years[5]. In total, as of February 2014, SE websites host 4.8 million users, 8.3 million questions and 14.7 million answers.

The full content – except users' personal information – of SE is distributed under a Creative Commons licence. For

our work, we downloaded the dump of September 2013[6]. In addition to SO, our focus is on 20 of the biggest SE websites (in terms of generated content size). The total number of answers in our dataset is over 12 million and the number of questions is almost 7 million. For the purposes of the evaluation study, we excluded content created by users that had their account removed or deleted. Furthermore, for evaluating the performance of our model classifier, we only kept questions with an accepted answer. The resulting dataset contains more than 8 million answers and almost 4 million questions (see Table 1 for an overview).

Table 1: Overview of the StackExchange websites dataset. Columns refer to the number of accepted (A), non-accepted (NA) and total number of answers (Total).

SE Website	A	NA	Total
stackoverflow.com	3,375,817	3,795,276	7,171,093
apple[se.com]	14,471	14,149	28,620
askubuntu.com	37,907	33,746	71,653
drupal[se.com]	14,393	8,558	22,951
electronics[se.com]	11,726	14,942	26,668
english[se.com]	17,369	31,617	48,986
gamedev[se.com]	9,866	11,106	20,972
gaming[se.com]	24,019	20,457	44,476
gis[se.com]	10,015	8,724	18,739
math[se.com]	98,351	78,294	176,645
mathoverflow.net	21,447	23,660	45,107
meta.stackoverflow.com	27,682	26,060	53,742
physics[se.com]	10,851	10,389	21,240
programmers[se.com]	15,998	52,694	68,692
serverfault.com	82,315	89,833	172,148
skeptics[se.com]	2,041	1,421	3,462
stats[se.com]	9,360	7,297	16,657
superuser.com	89,251	91,247	180,498
tex[se.com]	30,642	20,249	50,891
unix[se.com]	16,283	16,155	32,438
wordpress[se.com]	19,420	10,788	30,208
Total	3,939,224	4,366,662	8,305,886

[se.com] .stackexchange.com

4. FEATURES FOR BEST ANSWER PREDICTION

In this section we present the features used for training and evaluating our classifier. We initially present some shallow text features and one simple vocabulary, lexical-based feature. We then proceed by showing how we propose to exploit our features more efficiently. In order to assess the performance of the proposed model more holistically, we have also added a number of features referring to the rating of answers and users.

4.1 Linguistic features

The term "shallow features" refers to those used by traditional *readability* metrics [8] which have been used for several decades. The original purpose of these metrics was to estimate the average number of years of education required for being able to read and understand written text. The measurements use "surface", aggregated values of text properties, such as the average word length, the average number

---

[4]https://www.mturk.com/
[5]http://stackexchange.com/sites

[6]http://www.clearbits.net/torrents/2155-sept-2013. The SE dump is now available from the Internet Archive https://archive.org/details/stackexchange.

of words in sentences or the number of sentences in a paragraph. In addition to being simple to understand, these features are computationally cheap compared to other more language-sensitive and context-sensitive features. More specifically, readability metrics are defined through a formula (based on regression analysis) which returns the expected number of years of education. Our metrics originate from similar yet more recent approaches. More specifically, we adopt as our baseline the features in Pitler and Nenkova [14], employed in the context of modelling readability judgements for the Wall Street Journal corpus, in terms of how well the articles are written. These features are the *average number of characters per word, average number of words per sentence, number of words in the longest sentence and answer length* (number of characters).

In addition to the above, we also considered using simple vocabulary features. Vocabulary features, compared to syntactic or discourse features, are cheap in terms of deployment (language-agnostic) as well as cost (linear time and space) and have been proven useful for content assessment [6, 14]. Other studies have examined how the language of a community evolves and affects the language use of individual members. Danescu et al. [7] assessed the evolution of lexical corpora within an online community and use this change to predict a member's lifecycle. To this effect we used a probability-based vocabulary feature from [14] which is constructed from a unigram language model, where the probability of an answer is defined as:

$$\prod_w P(w|M)^{C(w)}$$

$P(w|M)$ is the probability of word w according to a background corpus M, and $C(w)$ is the number of times w appears in the answer. In our case, the background corpus is built from the content of each SE website separately.

The log likelihood (noted as LL from now on) of an answer is then:

$$\sum_w C(w)log(P(w|M))$$

Finally, in order to avoid any bias in favour of short answers, we normalise LL by dividing it over the number of unique words in the answer. Hence, this feature measures the probability of the answer being close to the vocabulary used by the SE community: the closer this value is to 0, the closer the answer is to the "community vocabulary".

Figure 1 shows the average feature values for the accepted answers together with the non-accepted ones of SO using a one-month window time frame[7]. As seen from the figure, the linguistic features manage to clearly differentiate the accepted from the non-accepted answers. More specifically, accepted answers tend to be longer, use a less common vocabulary, contain longer words, more words per sentence and the longest sentences are lengthier. Even though the above remarks look promising concerning best answer prediction, when training a binary classifier *precision* remains weak (58% on average for all SE websites). Since the results that we obtained for a classification based on shallow features are comparable to similar approaches (e.g. [5, 17])

these results will constitute our baseline for evaluating the proposed solution.

A more thorough investigation towards the explanation of this poor performance leads us to identify two main issues. Firstly, as illustrated in Figure 1, the characteristics of language evolve over time; in most SE websites users follow a more eloquent language (perhaps because of the increasing complexity of questions or because of what is considered good practice and is rewarded accordingly). For example, the SE website on English language shows that around early 2012 the average length of accepted answers is lower than the average length of non-accepted answers one year later. Hence, even though there is a steady gap between the values of accepted and non-accepted answers, the rapid change in the *absolute values* of the adopted shallow features is responsible for the poor classification.

We experimented with using a sliding window and examining the features in a narrow time frame (e.g., one month, as used for Figure 1). However, the large inherent *diversity* of the posts persists together with a large variance in values. Since this is not visible in Figure 1, we discuss one example regarding the length: the average length of answers in SO during September 2008 is 482 characters with a standard deviation of 544. More specifically, for the same time period, the shortest accepted answer is only 2 characters[8] whereas the longest is around 18,000 characters. This deviation is also discussed at a later section where features are presented all together.

Finally, even if a well-performing classifier existed for a single SE website and we used the features proposed above, the same classifier would have very low performance on another SE website. Indeed, as the reader may have anticipated, the characteristics of accepted answers vary significantly across the SE websites. For instance the accepted answers in Superuser have overall average length of 577 characters, whereas the corresponding value for Skeptics SE is 2,154 characters. As already stated, our paper aims at developing a best answer prediction model independent of the community website.

4.2 Feature discretisation

In order to overcome the above weaknesses and effectively make use of the linguistic features introduced, our approach is to treat the collection of answers for *each question* as an *information unit* which can improve the training process. Instead of treating each answer independently of the other answers it is competing with, our approach is to assess the value of the features of each answer *in relation* to each other. We introduce a new set of features that stem from the linguistic features used so far: instead of dealing with continuous values, these new features are the result of *grouping, sorting,* and *discretisation*.

We will present an example for the *Length* feature. Let us consider the example of Table 2 where for one question there are two candidate answers (i.e., question with Id 5 having answers with Id 6 and 7). We have already shown in Section 4.1 that the longer an answer is, the more likely it is to be accepted. In order to represent this preference, we group all answers by their corresponding questions (*grouping*). For each group, we then sort the answers in descending order

---

[7]Similar behaviour is identified for all SE websites and is omitted due to space limitations.

[8]"No" is the best answer to the question "Is there any difference between "string" and 'string' in Python?" http://stackoverflow.com/questions/143714

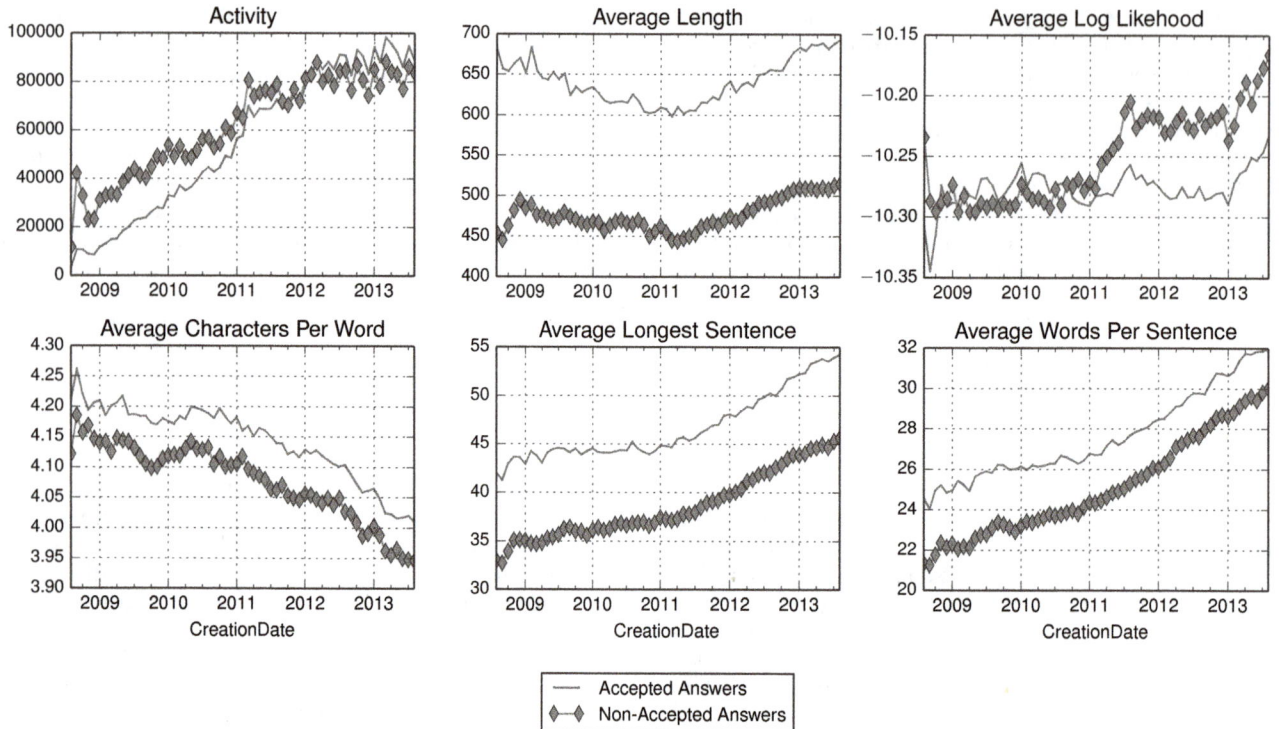

Figure 1: Activity and values of the linguistic features (y-axis) for the Stackoverflow dataset over time (x-axis). Top left sub-plot shows the number of answers posted every month. The remaining sub-plots show the average values for the accepted and non-accepted answers.

Table 2: Example of feature discretisation for the case of *Length*, 5 submitted answers and 2 questions. Column Question Id refers to the question under which the answer is submitted.

Question Id	Answer Id	*Length*	*Length$_D$*
1	2	200	2
	3	150	3
	4	250	1
5	6	250	1
	7	200	2

(*sorting*) and assign a rank for each answer, starting from 1 and incrementing this rank by 1 (*discretisation*). Thus, the answer with the longest *Length* will receive *Length$_D$* of value 1 (answer Id 6 with length 250) while the answer that comes second a value of 2 (answer Id 7 with length 200 - note that we are representing the discretised form of each *feature* as *feature$_D$*). The result of this process is the introduction of an equal number of linguistic features without the usage of any further information (apart from the necessary association of a question and its corresponding answers[9]).

As a result of the discretisation process on all of our shallow features, the information added and used for training purposes improved significantly. This is manifested by the information gain (about 20 times higher) and which we

---
[9]Note that other approaches typically omit this information.

present in the following subsection. Additionally, the benefits of this discretisation are discussed thoroughly in Section 5, where we present the classification results. It may appear that our discretisation process is dependent on "future knowledge", since discretised values may alter as more answers are submitted. Our method is no more time dependent than the notion of a best answer is, as it allows for best answer prediction at any point, in a real-time setting, which is not possible when relying on answer ratings. As more answers are entered, the discretised values change and a new current best answer can be derived.

In the following subsection we will discuss the inclusion in our classifier of two popular non-linguistic features, to allow us a more thorough evaluation.

4.3 User and Answer Rating Features

Until now we have discussed the linguistic features and how the proposed discretisation process is expected to yield better results. In order to have a more complete view of the performance of our classifier we have integrated some non-linguistic features. It is worth noting that these are included for evaluation purposes only; they do not form part of our approach. We group these features into different sets, following the discussion in Section 1. The first set of features (*user*) describes *past* or background knowledge and more specifically the *user profile*, such as the *reputation*, the number of *profile views*, number of *up*- and *down-votes* and the *UserUpDownVotes* feature, which we define as the difference over the sum of *Up* and *Down* votes, as follows:

Table 3: Summary of features used. The last column indicates the improvement on the information gain for the features that have been re-used as discretised. Values are for averages for all SE websites.

Category	Name	Information Gain
Linguistic	$Length$	0.0226
	$LongestSentence$	0.0121
	LL	0.0053
	$WordsPerSentence$	0.0048
	$CharactersPerWord$	0.0052
Linguistic Discretisation	$Length_D$	0.2168
	$LongestSentence_D$	0.1750
	LL_D	0.1180
	$WordsPerSentence_D$	0.1404
	$CharactersPerWord_D$	0.1162
Other	Age	0.0539
	$CreationDate_D$	0.1575
	$AnswerCount$	0.3270
User Rating	$UserReputation$	0.0836
	$UserUpVotes$	0.0535
	$UserDownVotes$	0.0412
	$UserViews$	0.0528
	$UserUpDownVotes$	0.0508
Answer rating	$Score$	0.0792
	$CommentCount$	0.0286
	$ScoreRatio$	0.4539

$$UserUpDownVotes = \frac{|UserUpVotes| - |UserDownVotes|}{|UserUpVotes| + |UserDownVotes|}$$

The second set of features (entitled as *Answer rating*), includes information concerning the community feedback on answers, such as the number of *comments*, the *score* and the *score ratio* ("the proportion of scores given to a post from all the scores received in a question thread", as indicated by Burel et al. as the most informative feature [5]). Finally, another set of features (*Other*) was used, such as the *AnswerCount*, the *Age* (real number representing days) of answers and the corresponding $CreationDate_D$ (answer speed is linked to good answer quality [3]). The total number of features is 21 and are shown in Table 3.

Table 3 shows the values for each feature in addition to their corresponding information gain. Information gain is a measurement based on entropy used for machine learning and has been employed in classification tasks to identify important features. Information gain $InfoGain$ of an attribute A for class C is defined using the entropy H measurement as follows:

$$InfoGain(C, A) = H(C) - H(C|A)$$

We can clearly see that the task of discretisation improves the information gain for all features. In particular, the information gain for *linguistic* features has increased on average 20 times. For the case of *Length*, the improvement is so significant that it manages to outperform well-known features, such as all those based on User Rating, and to rank as the third most important feature. At the same time, both $Length_D$ and $LongestSentence_D$ carry more information gain than $CreationDate_D$ which is also a popular feature shown to yield good performance.

5. EVALUATION: BEST ANSWER PREDICTION

Having experimented with a number of different classifiers, our evaluation shows that we obtain the best results by using *Alternate Decision Trees* (ADT) [9]. Even though we received good results with different classifiers available in Weka [10], we attribute the high performance of ADTs to the fact that they constitute a well-known binary, boosting classifier for numerical data, which suits our goals. Our evaluation was conducted using 10-fold cross-validation. In order to verify the performance of the proposed solution we conducted different experiments, each one aiming at validating the characteristics of the proposed solution.

5.1 Prediction

Table 4 presents the first results concerning the performance of our classifier without the inclusion of features based on answer or user ratings. The table shows that the macro averaged (unweighted) precision using *linguistic* and *other* (namely *Age*, $CreationDate_D$ and *AnswerCount*) features with *discretisation* is *84%*. The remaining evaluation metrics (recall, F-Measure) maintain high values resulting in an average AUC of *0.87*. The website with the lowest precision is Programmers SE with 76%, which can be attributed to the fact that the dataset for this website is heavily imbalanced (only 23% of the dataset's answers are accepted – see Table 1). On the contrary, Skeptics SE has 87% precision with 0.91 AUC value, which can be explained as follows: Firstly 58% of the answers in the dataset are accepted (the third highest ratio from all SE websites). The second reason stems from the website topic and the type of discourse that takes place: questions in Skeptics SE mainly attract scientific reasoning without much technical information, hence prose and linguistic features play a more important role. This performance is also confirmed by the value of information gain for the discretised version of *Length*, which is 0.27 (Skeptics) whereas the average value for $Length_D$ is 0.22 (see Table 3). The English SE dataset is also imbalanced (only 35% of the answers are accepted, close to programmers SE), but language-based features manage to overcome this challenge, most likely due to the nature of the discourse (i.e. similar to skeptics SE). The resulting prediction has 77% precision and 0.83 AUC.

5.2 Improvement due to discretisation

We have already shown the improvement in information gain after discretising the linguistic features (see Table 3). Here we aim to analyse the benefits of this process in the task of best answer prediction. To do so, we compare the performance of our classifier to other classifiers that use more sets of features, including features produced from ratings. Our goal in performing this comparison is to examine the information loss when choosing to disregard information coming from ratings.

Table 5 presents the results when using different sets of features and 10-fold validation. The table contains the average values for all SE websites as the output of different evaluations. Initially, we use the absolute values of textual features (also mentioned in Section 4) with low results 58% (Case 1). The second and third Cases both utilise the discretised features, while the third is additionally using the *other* set of features. Cases 2 and 3 constitute our proposed prediction method (Case 3 was presented in detail in subsection 5.1

Table 4: Results for best answer prediction using *linguistic* and *other* features with discretisation. Columns show macro averaged precision (P), recall (R), F-measure (FM) and Area-Under-Curve (AUC) using 10-fold validation.

SE Website	P	R	FM	AUC
stackoverflow.com	0.82	0.66	0.73	0.85
apple.stackexchange.com	0.84	0.68	0.75	0.86
askubuntu.com	0.84	0.74	0.79	0.88
drupal.stackexchange.com	0.87	0.79	0.83	0.89
electronics.stackexchange.com	0.79	0.65	0.71	0.84
english.stackexchange.com	0.77	0.52	0.62	0.83
gamedev.stackexchange.com	0.82	0.71	0.76	0.87
gaming.stackexchange.com	0.87	0.79	0.83	0.91
gis.stackexchange.com	0.85	0.73	0.78	0.87
math.stackexchange.com	0.85	0.74	0.79	0.87
mathoverflow.net	0.83	0.70	0.76	0.87
meta.stackoverflow.com	0.87	0.69	0.77	0.87
physics.stackexchange.com	0.86	0.71	0.78	0.88
programmers.stackexchange.com	0.76	0.40	0.52	0.84
serverfault.com	0.83	0.66	0.74	0.85
skeptics.stackexchange.com	0.87	0.83	0.85	0.91
stats.stackexchange.com	0.85	0.79	0.82	0.89
superuser.com	0.84	0.65	0.73	0.85
tex.stackexchange.com	0.87	0.77	0.82	0.88
unix.stackexchange.com	0.81	0.68	0.74	0.85
wordpress.stackexchange.com	0.88	0.80	0.84	0.89
Average	0.84	0.70	0.76	0.87

Table 5: Results for best answer prediction using different sets of features (Cases 1 to 6) for all SE websites. Columns show macro average precision (P), recall (R), F-Measure (FM) and Area-Under-Curve (AUC) for all 21 SE websites using 10-fold validation. Case 3 was presented in detail in Table 4.

No.	Features Used	P	R	FM	AUC
1	Linguistic	0.58	0.60	0.56	0.60
2	Linguistic & Discretisation	0.81	0.70	0.74	0.84
3	Linguistic & Discretisation & Other	0.84	0.70	0.76	0.87
4	Linguistic & Other & User Rating (no discretisation)	0.82	0.69	0.75	0.86
5	Linguistic & Other & User Rating (with discretisation)	0.82	0.72	0.77	0.88
6	All features (Answer and User Rating with discretisation)	0.88	0.85	0.86	0.94

and Table 4). Furthermore Case 4 refers to a "traditional" approach that relies in plain linguistics *and* user ratings. We can see that while a whole new set of features is added into the dataset, the performance of classification remains lower than Case 3, which is linguistics-based. Case 5 keeps the user ratings in addition to incorporating all features of Case 3. Hence, classification accuracy is the highest compared to all previous classifications, but almost identical to Case 3 which is strictly based on content and discretisation (lower precision 82% vs. 84%, higher AUC 0.88 vs. 0.87). Finally, Case 6 uses all features presented in Table 3, including the *answer ratings*. This set of features uses all features but most importantly user-entered scores and manages to outperform all of the previous cases. Case 6 shows that the information contained within answer ratings is independent – to a certain extent – of the information found in previous features.

In summary, results in Table 5 show that the discretisation of linguistic features manages to outperform significantly the classifier based on linguistic features only. Moreover, we can also see that user rating features such as reputation do not improve our classification, a sign that discretisation is a process that extracts very useful information and delivers very strong results. Figure 2 shows the AUC curves for Stackoverflow for all 6 cases and confirms the above remarks.

5.3 Generality

The final part of our evaluation aims to examine whether our solution is generic enough to be applied without the need to train our classifier on data from a new website. If the answer to this question is positive, we can assume that our classifier is generic enough to be applied to almost any SE website and to a large extent contains cross-domain intuitions about the mechanics of best answer identification. In order to have a positive answer to our research question,

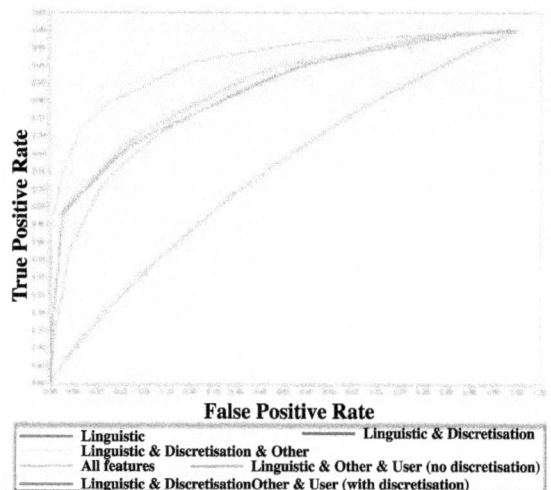

Figure 2: AUC for Stackoverflow. Different curves show the results for 10-fold cross validation using different sets of features (Cases 1 to 6). The 4 overlapping curves in the middle show that the discretisation of features outperforms the linguistic-based approach (bottom curve), matches the classification based on reputation and approaches the classification using all features (top curve) including user and answer ratings.

two requirements must be satisfied. Firstly, our classifier should be able to describe the characteristics of the best answers accurately for each SE website (robustness). Secondly, the features used in this model must neutralise the special characteristics of each SE website (generality). To examine the above hypothesis, we created new datasets following a leave-one-out strategy for each SE website. For instance, for the case of English language SE, we merge the remaining 19 SE websites[10] into one training dataset and use English language as the test dataset. For the evaluation purposes we applied classification using the features of Case 3.

The results of the evaluation shows that the average values for our evaluation metrics remain intact. More specifically, average precision fell by 1%, while recall, F-Measure and AUC remained the same (see Case 3, Table 4 for the values). Hence, we can claim that our classifier manages to remain effective without requiring access to the specific knowledge of the SE website. We believe that this result strengthens the value of discretisation even further. Despite the inherent variance in shallow feature values across answers and – even more – across SE websites, the discretisation process is able to demonstrate both robustness and generality.

6. DISCUSSION

Here we review and discuss our results in relation to previous related work and also discuss some issues raised as a result of the proposed methodology and potential extensions of this work.

6.1 Comparison

As already discussed in Section 2, the paper by Burel et al. [5] predicts accepted answers for Server Fault and Cooking SE. Our work did not include Cooking SE, but we include the larger, more up-to-date dataset of Server Fault (95k vs. 172k answers). Burel et al's classifier based on content delivers a precision of 64.7%, 0.628 F-Measure and 0.679 AUC. Our methodology which employs discretisation of linguistic features outperforms their work by 18-21%, since for Server Fault our precision is 83%, F-Measure is 0.74, AUC is 0.85 (Case 3) and 86% precision, 0.69 F-Measure and 0.83 AUC (Case 2). Moreover, our results when they consider contextual features such as user and answer ratings are similar to ours achieving the same F-Measure 0.84, our precision and AUC being at 89% (5% higher) and 0.93 (0.02 higher) respectively.

Similarly to us Tian et al. [17], look at the content of answers. However, they also exploit features related to what we refer to as answer ratings, since they also consider the number of comments to each answer, a feature which is reported as amongst the most informative ones. The authors report a prediction accuracy of 72.27% on a SO dataset of 196k answers at least one year old. By comparison our SO dataset contains 7.1 million answers and our classier returns 82% precision, 0.73 F-Measure and 77% prediction accuracy, which constitutes a noticeable increase in performance.

While the work concerning YA cannot be compared directly to ours, we highlight some analogies and discuss the results. For instance, Shah and Pomerantz [16] constructed a negative classifier with a dataset comprised of a 1:4 ratio of accepted to non-accepted answers. Adamic et al. [1] consider Programming questions submitted in YA and – similarly to us – disregard the ratings of answers and users. The authors report 72.9% precision, which is similar to our linguistics-based findings. Hence, we can assume that our classifier may be able to increase performance also in the case of YA.

6.2 Future work

To our knowledge, the proposed technique of dealing with continuous and multi-dimensional data found in shallow features constitutes a novel approach for assessing user-generated content. We intend to explore this direction further and apply it on other cases of social media, to fully examine the effectiveness of this technique. For example, one direction would be to analyse the linguistic characteristics of different roles in online communities, such as initiators, conversationalists, etc. (see for example [4]). Another possibility is to follow up on the work conducted by Anderson et al. [3] and explore the assortativity between user reputation and linguistic characteristics of user input.

6.3 Conclusions

Previous research on best answer prediction has shown that linguistics-based features can be helpful to a limited extent. The relevant literature shows that features based on user reputation and answer ratings manage to boost the performance of classifiers and outperform purely content-based approaches. Our approach adopts a novel way of processing linguistic features and manages to bridge the above gap. To do so, instead of processing all answers as one solid training dataset, the proposed discretisation process manages to highlight the distinct characteristics of each answer compared to its candidate, "competing" answers. The information that is produced from this process dramatically improves the performance of our classifier. Our extensive evaluation shows that shallow features, such as length and longest sentence, can be very informative, contradicting the findings of earlier work. Hence, encoding this information into a discretised form allows us to train a classifier that is effective enough to match other classifiers which do use and depend upon non-linguistic contextual information.

Our evaluation shows that the performance of our proposed approach matches the performance of reputation-based classification. Contrary to our intuition, the inclusion of more information such as user background information does not improve the classification, a sign that reputation information is not independent of information found in linguistic features. Finally, our classification methodology is generic and can be applied to the rest of the SE websites, without the need for training data from the target website. Shallow features, such as answer length and longest sentence can be used effectively for assessing user-generated text, following our methodology.

Acknowledgments

This work was supported by the BlogForever (No.269963), COMPOSE (No.317862) and CARRE (No.611140) projects funded by the European Commission Framework Programme 7.

---

[10]We chose to exclude Stackoverflow from training due to its large size which would slow the training process dramatically.

7. REFERENCES

[1] L. A. Adamic, J. Zhang, E. Bakshy, and M. S. Ackerman. Knowledge sharing and yahoo answers: everyone knows something. In *Proceedings of the 17th international conference on World Wide Web*, pages 665–674. ACM, 2008.

[2] E. Agichtein, C. Castillo, D. Donato, A. Gionis, and G. Mishne. Finding high-quality content in social media. In *Proceedings of the 2008 International Conference on Web Search and Data Mining*, pages 183–194. ACM, 2008.

[3] A. Anderson, D. Huttenlocher, J. Kleinberg, and J. Leskovec. Discovering value from community activity on focused question answering sites: a case study of stack overflow. In *Proceedings of the 18th ACM SIGKDD international conference on Knowledge discovery and data mining*, pages 850–858. ACM, 2012.

[4] S. Angeletou, M. Rowe, and H. Alani. Modelling and analysis of user behaviour in online communities. In *The Semantic Web–ISWC 2011*, pages 35–50. Springer, 2011.

[5] G. Burel, Y. He, and H. Alani. Automatic identification of best answers in online enquiry communities. In *The Semantic Web: Research and Applications*, pages 514–529. Springer, 2012.

[6] J. Callan and M. Eskenazi. Combining lexical and grammatical features to improve readability measures for first and second language texts. In *Proceedings of NAACL HLT*, pages 460–467, 2007.

[7] C. Danescu-Niculescu-Mizil, R. West, D. Jurafsky, J. Leskovec, and C. Potts. No country for old members: User lifecycle and linguistic change in online communities. In *Proceedings of the 22nd international conference on World Wide Web*, pages 307–318. International World Wide Web Conferences Steering Committee, 2013.

[8] L. Feng, M. Jansche, M. Huenerfauth, and N. Elhadad. A comparison of features for automatic readability assessment. In *Proceedings of the 23rd International Conference on Computational Linguistics: Posters*, pages 276–284. Association for Computational Linguistics, 2010.

[9] Y. Freund and L. Mason. The alternating decision tree learning algorithm. In *ICML*, volume 99, pages 124–133, 1999.

[10] M. Hall, E. Frank, G. Holmes, B. Pfahringer, P. Reutemann, and I. H. Witten. The weka data mining software: an update. *ACM SIGKDD Explorations Newsletter*, 11(1):10–18, 2009.

[11] J. Jones and N. Altadonna. We don't need no stinkin'badges: examining the social role of badges in the huffington post. In *Proceedings of the ACM 2012 conference on Computer Supported Cooperative Work*, pages 249–252. ACM, 2012.

[12] J. Liu, Q. Wang, C.-Y. Lin, and H.-W. Hon. Question difficulty estimation in community question answering services. In *Proceedings of the 2013 Conference on Empirical Methods in Natural Language Processing*, pages 85–90, 2013.

[13] S. T. Piantadosi, H. Tily, and E. Gibson. Word lengths are optimized for efficient communication. *Proceedings of the National Academy of Sciences*, 108(9):3526–3529, 2011.

[14] E. Pitler and A. Nenkova. Revisiting readability: A unified framework for predicting text quality. In *Proceedings of the Conference on Empirical Methods in Natural Language Processing*, pages 186–195. Association for Computational Linguistics, 2008.

[15] M. Rowe, M. Fernandez, S. Angeletou, and H. Alani. Ontology paper: Community analysis through semantic rules and role composition derivation. *Web Semantics: Science, Services and Agents on the World Wide Web*, 18(1):31–47, 2013.

[16] C. Shah and J. Pomerantz. Evaluating and Predicting Answer Quality in Community QA. In *Proceedings of the 33rd international ACM SIGIR conference on Research and development in information retrieval*, pages 411–418. ACM, 2010.

[17] Q. Tian, P. Zhang, and B. Li. Towards predicting the best answers in community-based question-answering services. In *Seventh International AAAI Conference on Weblogs and Social Media*, 2013.

[18] L. Yang, S. Bao, Q. Lin, X. Wu, D. Han, Z. Su, and Y. Yu. Analyzing and predicting not-answered questions in community-based question answering services. In *AAAI*, 2011.

Skim Reading: An Adaptive Strategy for Reading on the Web

Gemma Fitzsimmons, Mark J Weal, Denis Drieghe
University of Southampton
England, UK
{G.Fitzsimmons, M.Weal, D.Drieghe}@soton.ac.uk

ABSTRACT

It has been suggested that readers spend a great deal of time skim reading on the Web and that if readers skim read they reduce their comprehension of what they have read. There have been a number of studies exploring skim reading, but relatively little exists on the skim reading of hypertext and Webpages.

In the experiment documented here, we utilised eye tracking methodology to explore how readers skim read hypertext and how hyperlinks affect reading behaviour. The results show that the readers read faster when they were skim reading and comprehension was reduced. However, the presence of hyperlinks seemed to assist the readers in picking out important information when skim reading. We suggest that readers engage in an adaptive information foraging strategy where they attempt to minimise comprehension loss while maintaining a high reading speed. Readers use hyperlinks as markers to suggest important information and use them to read through the text in an efficient and effective way. This suggests that skim reading may not be as damaging to comprehension when reading hypertext, but it does mean that the words we choose to hyperlink become very important to comprehension for those skim reading text on the Web.

Categories and Subject Descriptors

H.1.2 [**User/Machine Systems**]: Human Information Processing

Keywords

Hyperlinks; Reading; Skim reading; Web Science; Psychology; Human Computer Interaction; Eye movements

1. INTRODUCTION

We do not always choose to read carefully, sometimes we can skim read for a general impression of the information presented. When there is a large amount of information to read, it is not always efficient or necessary to read everything in great detail. This may equally be true of reading on the Web. There is so much information and text to read that to carefully read and retain everything would not be always possible. Therefore, a strategy of skim reading may be the most effective way to move through the information quickly. However, there is the concern that during skim reading some comprehension may be lost [4, 6, 9, 12]. In this paper, we report an experiment that examined reading

WebSci'14, June 23–26, 2014, Bloomington, IN, USA.
Copyright is held by the owner/author(s). Publication rights licensed to ACM.
ACM 978-1-4503-2622-3/14/06...$15.00.
http://dx.doi.org/10.1145/2615569.2615682

behaviour by recording the eye movements of participants when they read text presented to them. The participants were instructed to read for comprehension or to skim read and they were asked a number of comprehension questions about the texts being read. We will begin by describing the previous research regarding skim reading and reading on the Web, and discuss how the experiment documented here augments what is known regarding how people read and skim read hypertext.

1.1 Eye Movement Methodology

Eye movements during reading are made up of fixations and saccades. When the eye is moving, this movement is called a saccade. In between these saccades our eyes are relatively still, this is called a fixation. We take in visual information during fixations and vision is mostly suppressed during saccades to avoid seeing a blur or smear [13].

Saccades are necessary due to the anatomy of the eye and the retina. The retina contains many photoreceptors called rods and cones. Cones are necessary for high visual acuity. The majority of the cones in the retina are in an area called the fovea which covers about $1°$ degree of visual angle on either side from the fixation point. Moving beyond the fovea, there is a large reduction in the number of cones and therefore a high acuity drop-off. In order to read, we need the words to be positioned on the high acuity fovea to be able to process them. As a result, we need to move our eyes so that the fovea can be utilised to gain the most visual information while reading. It is this fact that makes the eye tracking methodology so useful. Dependent on the size of the object on the retina, individuals need to move their eyes and actually fixate objects in order to see them in detail and process them.

Recording eye movements is an objective way of collecting data about behaviour and a number of studies have shown that eye movements provide an unobtrusive, real-time behavioural index of visual and cognitive processing [10, 19, 20]. The recording of eye movement behaviour enables the researcher to explore the cognitive processes of the online reader in detail.

The experiment we report in the present paper uses eye tracking methodology and building on the existing base of eye movements and reading research (for reviews see [19, 20]) to explore how individuals read hypertext. First, we will discuss the present debate on how hyperlinks may affect reading behaviour.

1.2 Reading Hypertext

There has been a considerable debate as to whether in-text hyperlinks hinder reading. Carr [3] suggested that hyperlinks serve as a distraction and subsequently hinder comprehension of the text. This, he has argued, is because having to evaluate hyperlinks and navigate a path through them is cognitively demanding and draws attention away from the primary task of processing and comprehending the text itself.

Other researchers have suggested that hyperlinks may cause a disruption to reading due to the fact that the salient (typically blue) hyperlinked words attract the attention of the users away from processing and comprehending the text. Related to this, Simola, Kuisma, Oorni, Uusitalo and Hyönä [22] demonstrated that the presence of salient advertisements within a Web page (e.g. those containing motion) can attract disrupt reading of the text and draw the attention of the user. Elsewhere, it has been shown in contrast that learning from electronic texts can be aided by the presence of hyperlinked words, with participants more likely to retain information from hyperlinked words [16].

We previously conducted an experiment [7] exploring how people read text that contained a blue hyperlinked word within a Wikipedia environment. We found that having hyperlinked words in the text did not affect the processing of the text, but when the hyperlinked word was a more difficult or *low frequency* word (such as *skin* vs the low-frequency *pelt* or *plant* vs *shrub*), participants were more likely to re-read the preceding text. These extra fixations did not affect overall reading times suggesting that having salient blue hyperlinks in the passages of text did not hinder overall reading behaviour.

Taken together, these previous studies provide conflicting views in terms of whether hyperlinks are beneficial or are a hindrance to reading. Despite the fact that there has been relatively little research examining how hyperlinks influence reading behaviour on the Web, this is nonetheless an important issue to examine considering how much of our time spent on the Web involves reading and comprehending text. Specifically, if hyperlinks are automatically generated, for example by cross-referencing documents in Wikipedia [14], with no human-authored intentionality, it is important to understand how we read hyperlinked text in order to make sure that the efficiency of reading is not unnecessarily disrupted.

The following section discusses the research on skim reading and whether it is an effective reading strategy when there is a large amount of text to read, or whether there is a comprehension trade-off that makes skim reading faster, but not necessarily more effective when trying to gain comprehension of the text being read.

1.3 Skim Reading

In typical reading studies (for reviews, see [19, 20]), researchers want to ensure that participants are reading for comprehension and fully processing the sentences that are presented. Comprehension questions are often inserted between trials so that researchers can be certain that the participants were fully processing the sentences. However, when reading outside of the laboratory, people may 'skim' through the text and not fully process all aspects of the text that has been presented to them. Current literature suggests that reading on the Web may involve skim reading [11, 15]. Liu [11] suggests that there is a screen-based reading behaviour that is characterised by 'more time spent browsing and scanning, keyword spotting, one-time reading, non-linear reading, and reading more selectively, while less time is spent on in-depth reading, and concentrated reading.' I will now discuss the present literature on skim reading.

One of the first experiments exploring skim reading behaviour used eye movement methodology to investigate the differences in how people read when they are reading normally or reading quickly. Just and Carpenter [9] studied three different types of reading: normal reading; skim reading; and speed reading (using

participants who had graduated from a speed reading course). Just and Carpenter [9] suggested that readers increase their speed by sacrificing the amount they understand from the text, thereby exhibiting a trade-off of greater speed at the cost of reduced comprehension. They found that speed readers were three times faster than normal readers and the skimmers were two and a half times faster than the normal readers in reading through the text presented to them. The eye movement analyses showed that the skimmers and speed readers fixated fewer words than the normal readers and the normal readers had longer fixations when they fixated a word. Speed readers and skimmers were also more likely to skip over multiple words compared to the normal readers.

In terms of which words were fixated, Just and Carpenter [9] found that the normal readers fixated twice as many content words when compared to function words during normal reading. Reasoning that this may have been due to differences in word length between content and function words, they explored their data, but found that readers were more likely to fixate three letter content words than three letter function words, which is consistent with the standard pattern seen in word skipping research [2]. However, a slightly different result was observed for the speed readers and skimmers. They were also more likely to fixate long words compared with short words, but they did not discriminate between short content words and short function words, both were skipped as often as each other suggesting that word length is an important factor for speed readers and skimmers when planning where to move the eyes. Also, because the speed readers and skimmers often skipped more words, the readers are fixating words far into their peripheral vision and therefore cannot gain any useful information other than discriminating word boundaries due to the reduced acuity in the periphery.

Just and Carpenter [9] also examined gaze durations. The gaze durations were shorter for the speed readers and skimmers, who spent on average 100 ms (around one–third) less time on each fixation. However, even with this reduction in fixation times the speed readers and skimmers still showed similar effects of frequency (low frequency words had longer fixation times compared to high frequency words) and word length (longer words had longer fixation times compared to shorter words) as those seen in normal readers, but the sizes of the effects were much smaller. All three groups showed changes in their reading speeds dependent on the sub-section of text they were reading. These changes in speed were roughly parallel across the groups suggesting that they slowed down and speed up their reading rate on the same sub-sections of text. The speed readers and skimmers tended to make more fixations rather than make longer fixations when they spent longer on a section of text. Just and Carpenter [9] suggested that the reading rate varied depending on the section of the text because of "local variables that are idiosyncratic to the text", meaning that some sections of text have denser levels of information, or more difficult information compared to other sections of the same text. They dismissed the suggestion that readers may slow down for sections of text rated independently as more important as they have no suggestion that this could be true from their findings. Instead they suggest that if the reader encountered a difficult to parse phrase they may need to sample more densely in order to understand the text.

Finally, Just and Carpenter [9] found that in terms of comprehension the normal readers had better comprehension than the others two groups. When comparing the speed readers to the skimmers, the speed readers answered more questions correctly (but, it was mostly restricted to general questions rather than those concerning specific details), in spite of reading on average 100 words per minute faster than the skimmers. This is interesting because it would seem that the speed reading training has assisted their speed readers and reduced the speed-accuracy trade off compared to the skimmers.

Other researchers have also shown a reduction in comprehension when reading rate increased. Carver [4] displayed passages of text to participants and gave them varying amounts of time to read the passages. When testing the participants with comprehension questions, those who had the shortest time to read the text performed the worst. This suggests that by increasing reading speed, comprehension is reduced. However, it is difficult to see if comprehension is reduced globally across the text. Other researchers have rated each sentence in the text by independent participants and explored if skim reading is used to skim over the unimportant pieces of text rather than just skim read all of the text. For example, Masson [12] manipulated the time participants had to read passages of text and tested their recognition memory for the text in the passages. The recognition rates decreased when the participants' time to read the text decreased. Also, the faster the text was read, the longer the reaction times were to respond to the recognition questions. However, this was only true for those sentences that were rated as 'unimportant' (as judged by a different set of independent participants). The sentences judged as 'important' did not show the comparitively longer reaction times. Masson [12] suggested that this was due to participants focusing more on relevant and important imformation in the passages to enable faster processing of the text, and paying less attention to the 'unimportant' sentences in order to read more efficiently.

Alternatively, Dyson and Haselgrove [6] found that when participants were asked to either read normally or at a self-paced faster speed (approximately twice as fast) those who read faster had lower scores on the comprehension task. The comprehension task consisted of multiple choice questions and those who read faster recalled more general information and less specific details, but there was no interaction between reading speed and the type of information the participants remembered.

More recently, Reader and Payne [21] examined whether skim readers focus on extracting information from the more important sentences contained within text. Participants were given four texts of different difficulties. Participants spent more time on the higher-level/more difficult texts. Reader and Payne [21] suggested that this was evidence of an 'adaptive allocation of attention' in skim reading tasks, a so-called satisficing strategy.

The concept of a satisficing strategy comes from information foraging research where it is assumed that the readers are sensitive to their 'information gain' (how much useful information they are getting over time) and use this as a basis for what to read and when to stop reading and move on. For example, a reader is monitoring their information gain and they have a threshold of how much information they are happy to get in a certain amount of time. If that information gain drops below that threshold the reader will then stop reading that particular piece of text and move on to a new patch where they might gain more information in the same amount of time.

Pirolli and Card [17] used a metaphor of a bird foraging for berries in patches of bushes as an example of information foraging. The bird must decide how long to spend on one patch before expending time moving onto a new patch to forage for berries. The problem is at what point does the bird decide to move from the one patch to a new one? The most efficient time to leave for a new patch is when the expected future gains from foraging in the current patch decrease to such a level that it is better to expend time moving to a new patch where the future gains may be greater.

Reader and Payne [21] suggested that this information foraging approach of satisficing can be applied to skim reading if we assume that the 'patches' are patches of text or paragraphs, and the reader has a threshold for their information gain that is influenced by the amount of time they have to read the text. If the reader has a short amount of time to read the text, they will want to have a lower threshold for information gain. If they are not receiving enough information from a patch they will want to realize this quickly and move on to a patch that has a higher information gain to make the most efficient use of the limited time. If this is true then the readers will focus on the most important information patches and leave the patches with less important information if their time is limited.

Duggan and Payne [5] conducted several experiments to test if participants focused on the more important information in the text when skim reading. They found that readers who were engaged in skim reading had better memory performance for important details from the text, but not for the unimportant details. Where previous studies that have explored skim reading have shown a decline in comprehension performance, Duggan and Payne [5] found an improvement in comprehension and found higher scores in comprehension questions for sentences rated independently as 'important'. This suggests that skim reading is an adaptive satisficing strategy. By leaving text before it is processed in depth and when information gain begins to drop, readers can efficiently move through the text at an increased speed, while trying to keep comprehension high. Skim reading is a trade-off whereby the reader is trading depth of comprehension for speed, but while trying to minimize the loss of comprehension by using an effective strategy to move through the text quickly without losing comprehension.

The present paper focuses on how hyperlinks impact on skim reading behaviour and how individuals sample the text and extract information from it. With the large amount of information online it can be safely assumed that skim reading is a common behaviour, an efficient way of gaining as much information as possible in the shortest amount of time, while trying not to sacrifice comprehension too much. Hyperlinks may be used to assist in the strategy of determining what parts of the text contain important information and what should be read to gain comprehension.

An experiment was conducted to explore this issue. Participants were either instructed to read normally for comprehension or asked to skim read passages of text that resemble a Wikipedia page. Target words within the passages were manipulated to either be black or blue (resembling a hyperlink) and also their difficulty was manipulated by making the target word either a highly frequent common word (such as *plant*), or a low frequency uncommon word (such as *shrub*). Between each page of text the participant was asked comprehension questions which were either related to important or unimportant sentences in the text (as rated by independent participants not taking part in the main experiment). From previous research we predicted that readers would read faster when asked to skim read, but would have reduced comprehension. It was difficult to suggest whether there

Figure 1. Example stimuli, an edited Wikipedia article.

would be a difference in the comprehension of important and unimportant information because previous research has had conflicting results. However, if skim reading is an efficient strategy to read through text the fastest way possible while minimising comprehension loss then we would expect that the skim readers will perform more poorly on comprehension question about the unimportant information.

2. EXPERIMENT

2.1 Method

Thirty-two native English speakers with normal or corrected-to-normal vision took part in the experiment. Eye movements were measured with an SR-Research Eyelink 1000 system running at 1000Hz (i.e. one sample every millisecond). Viewing was binocular, but eye movements were only recorded from the right eye. The stimuli consisted of forty edited Wikipedia articles (see Figure 1) on a variety of neutral topics. One-hundred and sixty target words were embedded in sentences (one target word per sentence) and four sentences were inserted into each Wikipedia article. In total there were 8 conditions in a 2 (Task Type: Normal, Skimming) x 2 (Word Type: Linked, Unlinked) x 2 (Word Frequency: High, Low) within participants design. The text on the screen was instructed either to be read normally or to be skim read. This was blocked so that the first twenty stimuli were to be read normally and the second twenty to be skim read. We did not counterbalance the Task Type out of worry that the normal reading blocks would be influenced by first having to

skim read. Participants were not told they were going to be skim reading until just before that half of the experiment was due to begin, so as not to effect the first part of the experiment which was to be read normally. At a target word level, the target words within these articles were either displayed in blue or black to denote if the word was a hyperlink or not. There was also a word frequency manipulation where the target word is either high or low frequency. The word frequencies were taken from the Hyperspace Analogue to Language (HAL) corpus, which consists of approximately 131 million words gathered across 3,000 Usenet newsgroups. The frequency norms were used to extract both high and low frequency words to create the experimental stimuli. The high frequency words had an average log transformed HAL frequency of 9.94 and the low frequency words have an average log transformed HAL frequency of 5.81 (according to the norms collected in the HAL corpus [1]. All target words were 4-7 characters in length, the average was 5.60 characters. Word length was matched for each high/low frequency pair).

All characters were lowercase (except when capitals were appropriate) and presented in a monospaced Courier font. The display was 73 cm from the participant's eye and at this distance three characters equal about 1° of visual angle. The participants' head was stabilised in a head/chin rest to reduce head movements that could affect the quality of the calibration of the eye tracker. At the beginning of each trial the participant had to look at a fixation point on the screen. When the eye tracker registered a stable fixation on the fixation point, the sentence was displayed

Table 1. Fixed effect estimates for all eye movement measures in Experiment.

	Skipping Probability Percentage	Single Fixation Duration	Go-Past Times
Intercept	0.09	5.32 ***	5.67 ***
Word Frequency	-0.19 **	0.09 **	0.09 *
Word Type	0.14	0.01	-0.06
Task Type	0.01	-0.04	-0.13 ***
Word Type x Task Type	0.57 ***	0.01	0.01
Word Frequency x Word Type		0.05	0.06
Word Frequency x Task Type		-0.01	-0.08
Word Frequency x Word Type x Task Type		-0.13 *	-0.10

$* p<.05, ** p<.01, *** p<.001$

Table 2. Means of eye movement measures (in ms). Standard deviation in parentheses.

Task Type	Word Type / Word Frequency	Skipping Probability Percentage	Single Fixation Duration (ms)	Go-Past Times (ms)
Normal	Linked/High	52 (20)	221 (44)	378 (223)
	Linked/Low	48 (22)	233 (37)	370 (164)
	Unlinked/High	54 (19)	212 (37)	233 (116)
	Unlinked/Low	51 (20)	246 (45)	375 (140)
Skimming	Linked/High	52 (23)	201 (27)	295 (128)
	Linked/Low	48 (22)	221 (35)	284 (76)
	Unlinked/High	68 (18)	204 (41)	263 (94)
	Unlinked/Low	63 (18)	205 (31)	250 (50)

ensuring that the first fixation fell at the beginning of the text. This is to be certain that the reader is starting at the beginning of the passage and not starting the trial by picking up information from later in the text. When participants finished reading they confirmed they had finished by pressing a button on the response box in front of them. They were then presented with four comprehension questions in a random order. Two questions were related to sentences that were rated as most important by independent participants and two were related to sentences rated as least important. Participants responded to the questions by pressing the appropriate button on a response box. After the questions the next trial would appear. The experiment lasted approximately 90 minutes.

2.2 Results

Eye trackers record a large amount of data (one sample every millisecond) and this data can contain erroneous fixations that are not representative of the dataset. In some cases, these erroneous or outlier fixations will be caused by errors in the eye-tracker (detected by the algorithms used to track the eyes); in other cases, the participant may have had a lapse of concentration, leading to very long fixation durations. Regardless of the cause, and because we were interested only in those instances when the participants were paying attention and reading the text, we cleaned the dataset

before conducting our statistical analyses. In the current experiments we followed the standard procedures for cleaning our data that have been adopted by the reading research community. Trials where there was tracking loss were removed prior to analysis. Fixations shorter than 80 ms that were within one character of the previous or following fixation were merged and all other fixations shorter than 80 ms or longer than 800 ms were removed to eliminate outliers (5.43% of total dataset). When calculating the eye movement measures data that were more than 2.5 standard deviations from the mean for a participant within a specific condition were removed (<1% of dataset). Data loss affected all conditions similarly.

Around each target word an *interest area* was drawn. The interest area is the size of the target word including the space preceding it. The analyses below are conducted using the fixations that landed on the target word, within the interest area drawn around it.

2.2.1 How does Skim Reading affect the Way we Read Hypertext?

Participants were significantly faster to read the passages when they were skim reading ($t(31)=17.38$, $p<.001$). The average time spent reading normally was 39 seconds (SD=8), compared to only 20 seconds (*SD*=6) when asked to skim read. This supports

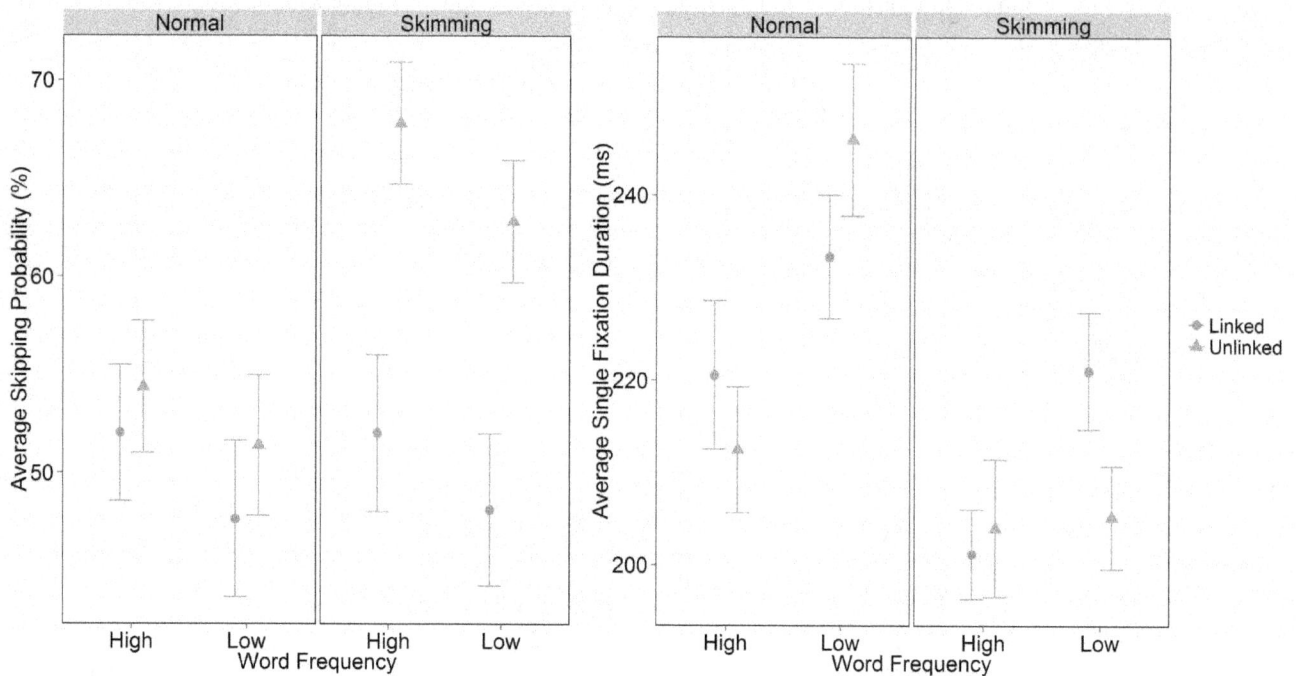

Figure 2. Task Type x Word Type interaction in skipping probability and Task Type x Word Type x Word Frequency interaction in single fixation durations.

previous suggestions that skim reading is around twice as fast as normal reading [6, 9, 12].

We focused out analysis on three key eye movement measures: *Skipping probability, single fixation duration* and *go-past times*. *Skipping probability* is the probability that the target word is skipped in first-pass reading. Skipping rates are used to show the ease of processing a word. If a word is easy to process than is may be fully processed prior to fixating it and skipped completely in first-pass reading. *Single fixation durations* are when the reader makes only one single fixation on the target word in first-pass reading. It is used as a measure to describe how easy a word is to process [19]. Because this measure only includes times where the target word was only fixated once it is one of the cleanest measures to use to represent how difficult a word is to process and can give us a good estimate of how difficult a word is to process. Also, when the target word was fixated, in 93.91% of the cases it received a single fixation. Therefore, we limited the fixation duration analyses to when there was a single fixation on the target word. *Go-past times* are the accumulated time from when a reader fixates the target word until the reader passes to the right after the target word. This measure is often used to explore if a reader has had trouble integrating the target word because it includes the regressive (backward-directed) fixations when a reader has to re-read preceding content.

A series of linear mixed-effects models (lme) using R [18] were used to examine the eye movement measures. Due to the large variation of behaviour often observed between participants and items the models specified participants and items as crossed random effects. The significance values and standard errors reported reflect both participant and item variability. These analyses have the advantage that they result in considerably less loss of statistical power in unbalanced designs due to missing values than traditional ANOVA's. This is especially important for

fixation times when the target word is skipped often, which is the case in this experiment. The *p*-values were estimated using posterior distributions for model parameters obtained by Markov-Chain Monte Carlo (MCMC) sampling.

The three independent variables were included as fixed factors: Task Type (Normal, Skimming), Word Type (Linked, Unlinked) and Word Frequency (High, Low). Model comparisons showed that the three-way interaction between the three fixed factors and the two-way interactions with Word Frequency had to be removed from the skipping probability model because it did not contribute significantly to the fit of the data. All fixed effects estimates are shown in Table 1. The means for all the measures are shown in Table 2.

There was a significant effect of Word Frequency across all eye movement measures. The high frequency words were skipped more often than the low frequency words and if the target was fixated, the fixations times were significantly shorter when the target word was high frequent. This replicates previous experiments that have demonstrated that low frequency words are skipped less often and have longer fixations times because they are more difficult to process than high frequency words [8].

There was no main effect of Word Type on the local analyses, whether the target word was linked had no effect on fixation times (all *p*'s larger than 0.1). This suggests that target words are not more difficult to process when they are linked, replicating our previous findings [7]. However, there was a marginal effect observed in skipping probability. When the target word was linked it was less likely to be skipped. This was qualified by a two-way interaction in skipping probability between Word Type and Task Type (see Figure 2). Subsequent contrasts showed that there was no difference in skipping probability when the target word is linked or unlinked ($z=1.69$, $SE=0.08$, $p=0.09$), but there was a significant difference in the skim reading condition. Linked words are significantly less likely to be skipped compared to unlinked words in the skimming condition ($z=8.26$, $SE=0.08$, $p<001$). This suggests that when the readers are skim reading they are attempting to fixate the linked words. They may be using them as anchor points throughout the passage as the reader may think the linked words may be important words within the passage.

As mentioned previously, there was a significant main effect of Word Frequency in single fixation durations. When the target word was fixated there was significantly shorter fixations time when the target was high frequent. This is qualified by a three-way interaction between Task Type, Word Type and Word Frequency (see Figure 2). Contrasts were conducted to explore this interaction. Fixation times were significantly shorter when the passages were skim read compared to when they were read normally ($t=-4.43$, $SE=0.03$, $p<.001$). This supports previous research that shows shorter fixation times when readers are skim reading [9].

When reading normally there is a significant frequency effect seen in both linked ($t=2.86$, $SE=0.01$, $p<0.01$) and unlinked conditions ($t=4.20$, $SE=0.02$, $p<0.001$). Participants fixated low frequency words for longer than the high frequency words. However, when skim reading a frequency effect is present only when the target word is linked ($t=3.01$, $SE=0.01$, $p<0.01$) and there is no frequency effect when the target word is unlinked ($t=-0.36$, $SE=0.02$, $p=0.75$). This is a very interesting result. Because there is an absence of a frequency effect for the unlinked word in the skim reading condition, this suggests that the readers are not lexically processing the unlinked target words they are landing on. The presence of a frequency effect in the linked words in the skim reading condition suggests they are focusing on the linked words and lexically processing them. If, as previous researchers have suggested, readers skim read when reading on the Web, the words we choose to link become very important if readers are processing them at a deeper level, especially if links are used as anchors to the important information within the text.

In normal reading there was no effect of Word Type. The target word being linked or unlinked had no influence on fixation times when the target word was high or low frequent (high frequency: $t=0.12$, $SE=0.01$, $p=0.89$; low frequency: $t=1.39$, $SE=0.02$, $p=0.16$). There was also no effect of Word Type in the skim reading condition when the target word was high frequent ($t=1.00$, $SE=0.01$, $p=0.32$). However, there were significantly longer fixations on the linked target words in the skim reading condition when the target word was low frequent ($t=-2.53$, $SE=0.01$, $p<0.01$). This is due to the frequency effect being present in the skimming condition for the linked words, but not present for the unlinked words. We see longer fixation times for the low frequent linked words because they are more difficult to process. We do not observe it for the unlinked, low frequency words in the skimming condition because the readers simply were not processing them to the same level, instead focusing on the linked words.

Although the majority of fixations on the target word were single fixations, when the target word was fixated 14.11% of target words had regressions to previous interest areas. Therefore we will also explore go-past times. Go-past times take into account the accumulated time from when the reader first fixated the target word until when they pass to the right, after the target word. All the times where the reader fixated the target word and then made a fixation backward to the preceding text are included in this measure. Again,

there was a significant main effect of Word Frequency with longer fixation times for the low frequency words. There was also a main effect of Task Type, go-past times were shorter in the skimming condition compared to normal reading. This suggests that very little re-reading of preceding content occurs during skim reading, the reader is simply trying to read in the most efficient way possible, and thus limiting their re-reading.

2.2.2 Does Skim Reading affect Comprehension?

Each edited Wikipedia article had every sentence within it rated for its general importance to the meaning of the whole passage by twenty independent participants who did not take part in the main eye tracking study. The two most important and two least important sentences had comprehension questions created about them. This rating study served not only as a useful method to create comprehension questions relating to important or unimportant information, but it also allowed us to observe what participants rated as important and if hyperlinks have any effect on this. The importance rating was created using a 5-point Likert scale, where a response of 1 signified "not important" and 5 signified "very important". Participants could respond anywhere on the scale from 1 to 5 how important they found each sentence for the general meaning of each passage. The sentences rated as most important were of course rated significantly higher than those rated as least important ($t(79)=11.25$, $p<.001$). The average score for the two most important sentences was 4.42 ($SD=0.48$) and the average score for the two least important sentences was 2.24 ($SD=0.44$). What was particularly interesting was the average number of hyperlinks in the most important compared to the least important. The sentences rated as most important had significantly more links than the unimportant sentences ($t(79)=30.38$, $p<.001$). The most important sentences had an average of 2.96 ($SD=1.94$) links per sentences and the least importance sentences had an average of 0.35 ($SD=0.73$) links per sentence. This suggests that readers may use the presence of hyperlinks as a judge of how important a sentence is, or conversely, important sentences may just contain more hyperlinks.

After each stimulus four comprehension questions were presented to the participants, one at a time. Two of the questions were related to sentences within the passage rated as the most important by independent participants and the other two questions were related to the sentences rated as the least important by independent participants. We examined accuracy using a 2 (Importance: High Importance, Low Importance) x 2 (Task Type: Normal, Skimming) within subjects ANOVA (see Table 3 for means). This revealed a main effect of Task Type ($F(1,31)=16.77$, $p<.0001$). The accuracy was significantly lower when the text was being skim read than when it was read normally. This replicates previous research suggesting that comprehension is impaired when skim reading [3, 6, 9, 12]. There was also a marginal main effect of Importance ($F(1,31)=3.58$, $p=0.07$). The accuracy improved when the sentence the questions were related to was a sentence externally rated as important. This effect of Importance may be marginal because of the reasonably high accuracy level overall creating a ceiling effect. This suggests that participants were using a strategy to efficiently and effectively read through the text and pick up the most important information, sacrificing the less important information comprehension for increased reading speed. This adaptive satisficing strategy was also suggested by Duggan and Payne [5] when they found similar results in skim reading.

Table 3. Behavioural results containing accuracy, sensitivity and criterion. Standard deviation in parentheses.

Task Type	Importance	Accuracy Percentage	d'	C
Normal	High Importance	91 (5)	3.03 (0.67)	-0.29 (0.35)
	Low Importance	87 (7)	2.63 (0.74)	-0.32 (0.41)
Skimming	High Importance	90 (5)	2.9 (0.67)	-0.22 (0.35)
	Low Importance	84 (6)	2.4 (0.64)	-0.4 (0.39)

We used the same methodology for analysing the comprehension question results as Duggan and Payne [5]. They used signal detection theory measures to explore participants' comprehension of the text, focusing on sensitivity (d'), which provides an index of overall response accuracy, and response bias (C), which provides an index of the extent to which one response is more probable than another. We used these same measures and examined them using a 2 (Importance: High Importance, Low Importance) x 2 (Task Type: Normal, Skimming) within subjects ANOVA (see Table 3 for means). For d' there was a main effect of Task Type ($F_{(1,31)}$=10.38, p<.0001). The participants' comprehension of the text decreased when they were skim reading. There was also a marginal main effect of Importance($F_{(1,31)}$=3.97, p=0.06), which suggests that the participants were to a degree engaged in an adaptive satisficing strategy because they had improved accuracy for comprehension questions relating to the most important information. When examining the bias (C) there were no significant differences between the measures (all F's smaller than 2.9, all p's larger than .1). This shows that there was no bias when responding to the comprehension questions.

3. CONCLUSION

The present experiment confirms that participants do read faster when skim reading hypertext and also that, when skim reading, comprehension was impaired compared to normal reading. However, the presence of hyperlinks had an impact on skim reading. Participants were less likely to skip linked words when skim reading and when participants did land on linked words the reader processed them fully, as seen by the significant frequency effect observed in linked target words in the skimming condition. Conversely, participants were less likely to fixate the unlinked words when skim reading. If the participants did fixate the unlinked words they did not seem to be processing them to the same degree as they processed the linked words, this is seen by the lack of a frequency effect on the unlinked words during skim reading.

From the comprehension accuracy we observed that comprehension accuracy declined when the participants were skim reading, but we also found that they performed better on the comprehension questions about the sentences which were rated as more important. This suggests that the participants were prioritising the more important information effectively. We found that the sentences rated as more important contained more hyperlinks on average. Participants may have been using the links as anchors throughout the text if the links denote the most important information. Previously it has been shown that hyperlinks can assist in helping learners retain information [16].

If we take both the findings from the eye tracking and the comprehension results together we can suggest that readers could be engaging in an adaptive satisficing strategy, obtaining a speed-comprehension trade-off which is optimal for the task at hand. Participants may have wanted to read quickly while still retaining as much comprehension as possible. From these findings we suggest that participants used the hyperlinks as markers for the presence of important information and used them in a strategy to skim read through the text in the most efficient way possible.

In terms of Web design and the creation of hypertext documents the key lesson here is that if readers are skim reading on the Web as other researchers have suggested [11, 15] then the words that are chosen as hyperlinks have to be taken seriously. These are the words that the reader will be processing and the reader may be using hyperlinks as a marker for the most important information in the page.

The present experiment represents the first steps in understanding how we read hyperlinked text. Even though in the current experiments participants only engaged in reading behaviour and did not have to make decisions and click any hyperlinks, we obtained significant findings regarding skim reading on the Web which can be built upon in future studies. For the current experiments the aim was to tease apart the process of reading or skim reading hyperlinked text. By taking away the decision making required to navigate through different Web pages, we could therefore focus on how hypertext is read. The results presented here serve as the foundation for future experimentation. By basing our future research on the vast amount of research already conducted on eye movements and reading we can build a fuller understanding of how we read hyperlinked text. Future experimentation will expand our experimental task, which is a simplification of live Web behaviour. We aim to further explore reading on the Web and add the additional complexities such as clicking and decision making now we have the basic findings to build upon.

4. ACKNOWLEDGMENTS

This research was funded by the Research Councils UK Digital Economy Programme, Web Science Doctoral Training Centre, University of Southampton. EP/G036926/1.

5. REFERENCES

[1] Burgess, C., & Livesay, K. The effect of corpus size in predicting reaction time in a basic word recognition task: Moving on from Kucera and Francis. Behavior Research Methods, Instruments, & Computers, 30 (1998), 272-277.

[2] Brysbaert, M., Drieghe, D., & Vitu, F. Word skipping: Implications for theories of eye movement control in

reading. In Underwood, G. ed. *Cognitive processes in eye guidance*. Oxford University Press, Oxford, UK, 2005, 53-78.

[3] Carr, N. G. *The Shallows*. W. W. Norton, New York, NY, 2010.

[4] Carver, R. P. Rauding theory predictions of amount comprehended under different purposes and speed reading conditions. *Reading Research Quarterly*, 19, 2 (1984), 205–218.

[5] Duggan, G. B, & Payne, S. J. Text skimming: The process and effectiveness of foraging through text under time pressure. *Journal of Experimental Psychology: Applied*, 15, 3 (2009) 228-252.

[6] Dyson, M. C., & Haselgrove, M. The effects of reading speed and reading patterns on the understanding of text read from screen. *Journal of Research in Reading.* 23, 2 (2000) 210-223.

[7] Fitzsimmons, G., Weal, M. J., & Drieghe, D. On measuring the impact of hyperlinks on reading. In *5th Annual ACM Web Science Conference*, (Paris, France, 2013),

[8] Inhoff, W. A., & Rayner, K. Parafoveal word processing during eye fixations in reading: Effects of word frequency. *Perception psychophysics*, 40, 6 (1986) 431–439.

[9] Just, M. A., & Carpenter, P. A. The psychology of reading and language comprehension. Allyn and Bacon, Newton, MA, 1987.

[10] Liversedge, S., & Findlay, J. Saccadic eye movements and cognition. *Trends in cognitive sciences*, 4, 1 (2000), 6–14.

[11] Lui, Z. Reading behavior in the digital environment: Changes in reading behavior over the past ten years. *Journal of Documentation*, 61, 6 (2005) 700-712.

[12] Masson, M. E. J. Cognitive processes in skimming stories. *Journal of Experimental Psychology: Learning, Memory, and Cognition*, 8, 5 (1982) 400-417.

[13] Matin, E. Saccadic suppression: A review and an analysis. *Psychological bulletin*, 81, 12 (1974), 899–917.

[14] Milne, D., & Witten, I. Learning to link with Wikipedia. *Proc. CIKM '08*, ACM Press, (2008), 509-518.

[15] Morkes, J., & Nielsen, J. Concise, SCANNABLE, and Objective: How to write for the Web. *Nielsen Norman Group*(1997) http://www.nngroup.com/articles/concise-scannable-and-objective-how-to-write-for-the-web/

[16] Nikolova, O. R. Effects of Visible and Invisible Hyperlinks on Vocabulary Acquisition and Reading Comprehension for High- and Average-Foreign. *Apprentissage des langues et systèmes d'information et de communication*, 07 (2004), 29–53.

[17] Pirolli, P., & Card, S. Information foraging. *Psychological Review* 106, 4 (1999) 643-675.

[18] R Development Core Team (2009). R: A language and environment for statistical computing. R Foundation for Statistical Computing, Vienna, Austria: R Foundation for Statistical Computing.

[19] Rayner, K. Eye movements in reading and information processing: 20 years of research. *Psychological bulletin*, 124, 3 (1998), 372–422.

[20] Rayner, K. Eye movements and attention in reading, scene perception, and visual search. *Quarterly journal of experimental psychology*, 62, 8 (2009), 1457–506.

[21] Reader, W. R., & Payne, S. J. Allocating time across multiple texts: Sampling and satisficing. *Human–Computer Interaction* 22, 3 (2007) 263-298.

[22] Simola, J., Kuisma, J., Oörni, A., Uusitalo, L., & Hyönä, J. The impact of salient advertisements on reading and attention on web pages. *Journal of Experimental Psychology: Applied*, 17, 2 (2011), 174–90

Towards Tracking and Analysing Regional Alcohol Consumption Patterns in the UK through the use of Social Media

Daniel Kershaw
Highwire CDT
Lancaster University
d.kershaw1@lancaster.ac.uk

Matthew Rowe
School of Computing and
Communications
Lancaster University
m.rowe@lancaster.ac.uk

Patrick Stacey
Management Science
Lancaster University
p.stacey@lancaster.ac.uk

ABSTRACT

Monitoring rates of alcohol consumption across the UK is a timely problem due to ever-increasing drinking levels [36]. This has led to calls from public services (e.g. police and health services) to assess the effect it is having on people and society. Current research methods that are utilised to assess consumption patterns are costly, time consuming, and do not supply sufficiently detailed results. This is because they look at snapshots of individuals' drinking patterns, which rely on generalised usage patterns, and post consumption recall. In this paper we look into the use of social media such as Twitter (a popular micro blogging site) to monitor the rate of alcohol consumption in regions across the UK by introducing the Social Media Alcohol Index (SMAI). By looking at the variation in term usage, and treating the social network as a spatio-temporal self-reporting sense-network, we aim to discover variation in drinking patterns on both local and national levels within the UK. This study used 31.6 million tweets collected over a 6 week period, and used the Health & Social Care Information Centre (HSCIC) weekly alcohol consumption pattern as a ground truth. High correlations between the ground truth and the computed SMAI (Social Media Alcohol Index) were found on a national and local level, along with the ability to detect variation in consumption on National holidays and celebrations at both local and national levels.

Categories and Subject Descriptors

H.5.m [**Information Systems**]: Information Systems Applications—*Miscellaneous*

Keywords

Twitter, SNS, Keyword Analysis, Alcohol, Trend Detection

1. INTRODUCTION

Alcohol consumption is ingrained in British culture. This is reflected in and reinforced by certain British literature such as Ian Fleming novels, in which James Bond occupies a near alcoholic status [23]. Recently there has been growing concern due to ever-increasing consumption levels. This increase has seen the intake of alcohol rise from 3 litres of pure alcohol per capita in the 1930s to 10 litres per capita in 2006 [35]. The increase in alcohol consumption has been linked to an increase in A&E admittance, anti-social behaviour within town centres [7], and a positive relationship to mortality - the majority of alcohol-related deaths across the world come from injury, liver cirrhosis, poisoning, and malignancy, which contributes to 4% of all fatalities per year [38, 32, 5].

Alcohol-related statistics are compiled from a number of sources in the UK public sector, predominantly from departments within the UK Department of Health (DoH); this includes the NHS (National Health Service). However the collection of data is an expensive and long process, consisting of one-on-one interviews and large-scale surveys. The long lead cycle from data collection to final analysis and release means that the data is only a snapshot of the past and not a current understanding of what is happening. This lack of up-to-date information is at the expense of many services that rely on providing support services in relation to the consumption of alcohol; these include town police forces and A&E departments, which base their staffing levels on historical, out-of-date reports.

The methods currently used to collect the data use quantity-frequency questionnaires (QF), which ask participants to characterise their consumption in averages of drinks over a time period and patterns of beverage-type consumption e.g. how much do you drink in a week, what is the most common drink you consume on a night out? This ignores what different types of beverages may have been consumed at the same time frame, or that all alcohol may have been consumed on one day or a week; these sorts of fine-grained insights can't be determined from QF methods [15]. A more accurate method is the time-line (TL) method - it a gives greater insight into people's consumption patterns by asking for specific drinks consumption over a time-frame e.g. all drinks consumed in the past week. This, has been shown to be a valid method for assessing peoples drinking habits in both problem drinkers and casual drinkers. This is because it allows for a higher quality of data analysis to be applied to the data [37]; though compared to QF it is more expensive to deploy [37].

Comprehensive statistics on alcohol consumption in the UK are compiled by the Health and Social Care Information Centre (HSCIC), who produce the "Statistics on Alcohol" report; this assesses the drinking habits of the adult population (aged 16+) that live in private households in the UK. The questions asked stretch across a week's drinking habits, including the heaviest drinking day [21]. As mentioned before, the lag between gathering the information to publishing it means that it may quickly become obsolete, and the methods used (QF over TL) may not give the necessary insights for stakeholders. Another issue with reports of this nature is that there are tendencies to underestimate the total consumption of alcohol by up to 40% [5]. This can be seen by extrapolating the number of units consumed per capita from the survey data to the total consumed by the population, compared to real sales figures of alcohol in the UK. This under-reporting has been put down to a number of reasons; selective reporting from people unwilling to report how much they actually drink, recall bias from not remembering what has been drunk as a side-effect from excessive consumption, and accidental under-estimation through mis-estimation of measures [5].

1.1 Research Question

Micro-blogging social networking sites such as Twitter allows users to share up to date information in 140 characters. Twitter currently has 200+ million users with the UK accounting for 32.3 million of them [26]. The reasons that bring users to Twitter can be broken down into a number of key concepts under the umbrella of *frequent brief updates about personal life activities* creating *People-based RSS feeds* [39]; these can be understood as interesting things that happen to people in their day-to-day lives. By keeping up-to-date with such information, users can more readily stay in touch with each other and maintain social relationships, as well as raise their visibility, gather information, seek help, and release emotional stress. These are activities that they may not be able to otherwise accomplish on a day-to-day basis. Accessing and using Twitter can be seen as pervasive and unobtrusive - there are many different mediums one can access the system through (e.g. mobile, computer, smartTV), and the limitation of 140 characters requires minimal effort on the part of the user. This induces users to tweet when they are in a variety of situations, such as: consuming or going to consume alcohol, out at a pub/club/bar, and/or are feeling the effects of alcohol [39, 22].

Given the wide spread uptake of Twitter, this poses the question *"is it possible to characterise and model UK alcohol consumption patterns based on social media data such as Twitter, and if so is there a variation across geographical location in drinking patterns and terminology usage?"* This research differs from previous influenza tracking on SNS's (Social Networking System) by analysing Geo-located tweets from the UK to detect variations in alcohol consumption patterns in the UK at a regional, regional postcode and at a postcode level for indication of alcohol consumption. At the same time comparisons between different Geo-locations will be used as a comparative insight into different locations' consumption patterns and language usage.

In this paper we present a method to analyse alcohol-related tweets, how their scores and term frequencies differ across geographical locations and correlate to alcohol consumption patterns. Modelling this data on a ground truth has allowed for the creation of near real-time statistics of alcohol consumption patterns, allowing for the analysis over the long term, as well as on a daily and even hourly basis. This provides a greater insight for services to plan their resource allocation according to new trends.

The contributions of this paper are as follows:

- An approach to model a populations alcohol consumption pattern on Social Media data.

- The discovery of regional variation in relative consumption patterns and term distribution.

- The identification and understanding of how social events effect the overall level of alcohol consumption over an extended period of time.

2. RELATED WORK

There have been many research efforts to utilise social networks and big data to discover real-time information about health-related topics, trends and events. This was first seen in research from Google's Flu Trend[1] and Yahoo;[2] using their search history logs to look for trends in the variation of frequency of terms associated with influenza like illnesses (ILI), over time. This achieved a high coefficient of determination of 0.4250 [30, 20]. This led to similar research that looked for trends in ILI on social media and micro-blogging sites such as Twitter.[3] A number of approaches were taken; for example, during the swine flu outbreak of 2009-2010, outbreaks were assessed and changes in terminology from "Swine Flu" to "H1N1'" were analysed [31, 9]. Their research focused on tweets that expressed concern over H1N1 - they found a strong correlation in conjunction with news stories and reports about the outbreaks. Previously with H5N1 (Bird Flu) there had been the move to detect outbreaks in different regions [11] by modeling trends on Twitter using key term models against health service data on influenza like illness (ILI) outbreaks. This returned a high correlation of above 0.80, and was on the way to predicting outbreak through weighed terminology and semi-dynamic key term sets [24]. This model of monitoring a small number of keywords has also been shown to work for estimating alcohol sales in the USA [12]. It showed that the selection of the keywords can be sometimes be problematic, but a combination of "drunk", "hungover" or "hangover" produced a high estimate of sales of alcohol in the USA, especially when a seven day lag was added to account for drinking the alcohol in the following week.

Analyzing social media content is a growing field of research. One of the main sources of data are sites like Twitter in the West and Weibo[4] in Asia. Initial research looked into topic discovery and which topics were trending [28]. This form of research also performs sentiment analysis of tweets for stock market predictions of certain companies [4], as well as detecting the location of users' tweets concerning earthquakes in Japan, in order to warn other cities of impending shockwaves - tweets are created and communicated at a faster rate than the shock waves can travel [33].

---

[1]Google Flu Trend, http://www.google.org/flutrends/
[2]Yahoo, http://www.yahoo.com/
[3]Twitter, http://www.Twitter.com/
[4]Weibo, http://www.weibo.com/

Geographical locations have been used in the past to model topics and to some extent language on Twitter. Attempts were made to model Twitter users' locations by looking at their tweet history for terms that have a higher Geo-location weight, e.g. 'Purdue' would place the tweet in Indiana. This achieved a 51% accuracy of placing users within 100 miles of their 'home', however this did not take into account diachronic and synchronic differences in users vocabulary [8]. Twitter topics were also modelled by looking for variation between language in topics across locations, but this discovered only moderate differences e.g. the sports teams people were supporting [18]; this is because it was only assessing key terms and not the structure of the tweet itself. This bears similarities to the methods used to measure people's life satisfaction on Twitter by modelling Geo-located tweets with an LDA model in order to compare regions of the USA. Regional correlations were found between tweets about 'disengagement' and lower life expectancy, as well as between 'money' / 'work' and being more "well off" [34]

The combination of time and location has also been used for measuring and monitoring depression among Twitter users [14]. The authors initially formed a ground truth by monitoring known people with depression on Twitter, extracting a number of indicators from their activities online, allowing them to class tweets as "depression inductive". These features were then used to predict which tweets where highly "depression indusive". These models were used over Twitter data sets for different time-frames and granulates, allowing for comparison of states through a measure of Social Media Dispersion Index (SMDI). This showed a high correlation with national data on depression, identifying Detroit as the most depressed and Portland as the least.

3. DATA COLLECTION

For the experiment, that we will describe bellow, we collected six weeks worth of tweets in the time period 27th November 2013 til 9th January 2014. The Twitter public Streaming API[5] was utilised; this allowed for a bounding box to be placed around the UK, only allowing tweets Geotagged to the UK to be mined; in total 31.6 million tweets were collected. During this ten week period there was the Christmas Holiday Period, which also included New Years Eve.

Data from the Health & Social Care Information Centre (HSCIC) was used as the ground truth to test the model on; this came from the 2011 report that showed the last day on which a person binge-drank [21] in the week of the survey. Binge drinking in the UK is defined as drinking twice the recommended units of Alcohol within 24hrs; for a man this would be three strong beers (8 units), and a woman would be 2 large glasses of wine (6 units) [29]. This was chosen as it was the only data available with granularity to a day.

4. METHOD

In this section we will introduce the method which will be used to track mention of alcohol terms in tweets. The complete set of tweets is denoted T with a single tweet defined as t such $t \in T$. However we will need to define the subset of tweets grouped by days, hour in days, and location in hours

[5]Twitter Streaming API, https://dev.Twitter.com/docs/streaming-apis

in days. This will then use the granularity of tweet sets to compare against the ground truth.

To group the tweets by day we created a function $day(t)$ which returns the day the tweet was created on, this is then used to identify the day a tweet was posted:

$$T_k^D = \{t : day(t) = k, t \in T\} \tag{1}$$

$$k \in [1, 2, ..., 42] \tag{2}$$

Where k is the number of days since 27th November 2013.

To group by hour's in a day first we group by the day then by the hour creating a function $hour(t)$ which returns back the hour within the day that the tweet was created on:

$$T_{lk}^H = \left\{t : hour(t) = l, t \in T_k^D\right\} \tag{3}$$

$$l \in [0, 1, ..., 23] \tag{4}$$

Where l is the hour within the day.

To group by location in a given hour we first group to the hour then use the function $location(t)$ which returns the location the tweet was created in.

$$T_{lkp}^P = \left\{t : location(t) = p, t \in T_{lk}^H\right\} \tag{5}$$

$$p \in P \tag{6}$$

Where, P is the set of all the postcodes within the UK.

The function location(t) is used again to find the subset of locations in a subset of tweets in a day.

$$T_{kp}^P = \left\{t : location(t) = p, t \in T_k^D\right\} \tag{7}$$

Key-terms (markers) (Table 1) that denote alcohol consumption are defined as $m \in M$. A tweet t is defined as a bag of words $w \in W$. The list of words defined is returned by a function of a tweet $tokens(t)$; this will return a list of words, including duplicates.

If a key-term m appears in a tweet t then it is marked 1 else it is given 0.

$$c(t, m) = \sum_{w \in tokens(t)} f(w, m) \tag{8}$$

$$f : W \times M \rightarrow \{0, 1\} \tag{9}$$

The sum of all key-terms is taken from $tokens(t)$ and divided by the number of tokens from the key-term list used.

$$s(t, M) = \frac{\sum_{m \in M} c(t, m)}{|tokens(t)|} \tag{10}$$

This would then mean that an SMAI (Social Media Alcohol Score) for a given set of tweets is the average of all the scores.

$$\text{SMAI}(T, M) = \frac{\sum_{t \in T} s(t, M)}{|T|} \tag{11}$$

The model which has been used was based on an influenza-like illness (ILI) detection model for Twitter [24]. It has been modified as the original model placed more relevance on completeness of the keyword set, thus would have a score higher than one. We have modified it so that we can detect a signal which has a score of between 0 and 1, thereby giving the alcohol signal strength of a given day or hour.

drunk	wine	wasted
pissed	hungover	hangover
wine		

Table 1: Keyterms used as markers to indicate alcohol consumption

4.1 Data Processing

The set of tweets (T) are grouped into their respective T^D and T^H groups; then subsets were taken based on the Geo-location of each tweet (t). There are four Geo-location groups; National, Regional, Post Code District and Post Code, e.g. a tweet from Post Code LA1 would appear in the LA1 set, LA set, which is itself part of the North West set, which is in turn part of the national set. The kd-tree data structure in SciPy was used to allow quick nearest-neighbour look-up [27]; this was used to find the shortest distance between a tweet and a central post code.

The whole system was implemented using the map reduce pattern to utilise the parallelisation power of the Hadoop [6] framework. In the map stage the SMAI (Social Media Alcohol Index) was computed for each tweet, which was then mapped onto 8 sets (4 locations sets crossed with 2 time sets) that expands the whole data set from 31.6 million to 252.8 million tweets to be processed. The reduce stage calculated the alcohol score for the set, along with the relative key term probability, and collocations for the corpora of all the tweets in the set which had a score greater than 0.00. Both map and reduce programs were written in Python using the MrJob,[6] this allowed for the NLTK framework [3] to be utilised for text tokenisation, stop word removal and collocation algorithms.

An interactive map[7] of all the Twitter alcohol scores was produced. This shows the Twitter alcohol score output of each Geo-location in the form of a choropleth map, with a time line slider allowing the user to change the data view; giving the ability to see the relative colour changes over time. Zooming to different levels of the map reveal different granularity of the data on a geographical level.

4.2 Quantitative Analysis

A Pearson's coefficient and its significance probability (p-value) was calculated between each of regional daily SMAI (Social Media Alcohol Index) against the ground truth (HSCIC) data (Table 2). This was done on each given week within the six week time frame of the study; thus to see if the model maintained for a given week. The highest correlations were seen in Wales (South) in week one and Yorkshire Humber, East England and Scotland (South Central) in week two with the correlations of 0.97, with low p-values. This showed that the model holds up across the regional and national Twitter sets. However the correlation dropped for each consecutive week; this can be attributed to the period that the Twitter data was collected over as it overlapped on the winter holidays within the UK. This is a period which included Christmas and New Year celebrations, both of which are known for people socialising more than normal leading to a 41% increase in alcohol consumption [1] - this means that the UK is the highest alcohol consuming G7 nation for

[6]MrJob, https://github.com/Yelp/mrjob
[7]Twitter Alcohol Map, http://alcohol-Twitter-map.heroku.com

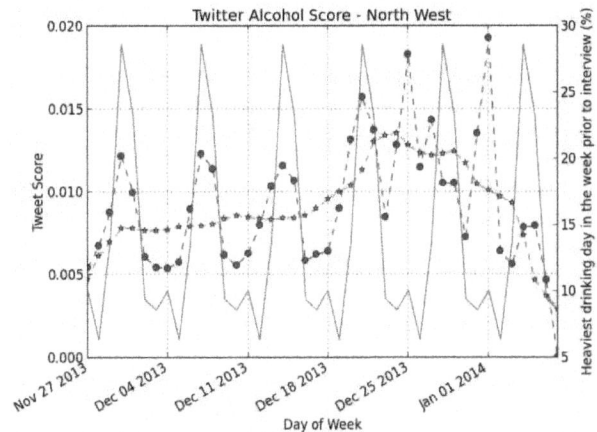

Figure 1: Daily SMAI for whole of UK over 6 week study period. Green line HSCIC Ground Truth data. Blue line daily SMAI. Red Line 7 point moving average.

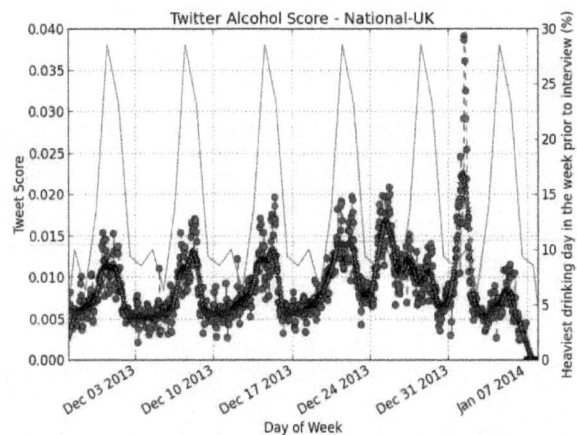

Figure 2: Hourly SMAI for whole of UK over 6 week study period. Green line HSCIC Ground Truth data. Blue line daily SMAI. Red Line 24 point moving average.

that period [2]. This can be seen through the model not maintaining the correlation where the 7 point moving average is increasing on all SMAI graphs at all geographical levels (Figure 1).

As well as computing the SMAI for each set the relative frequency of each term was assessed. This allowed the assessment and comparison of the terms independent of each other. Initially a cross Pearson's correlation (Table 3) was calculated across the term probability for each region; this indicated that each of the regions had a relative similar distribution of relative term usage. Though slight differences can be seen in Northern Ireland and Wales (North) where 10 and 11 correlations where less than 0.9.

Across the board results from the Channel Islands are very low or 0.00 (Table 3). This can be explained by looking at the master Twitter set, which indicated that there were significantly fewer tweets for that region compared to others, this meant that for days key terms may not have

223

	Week 1	Week 2	Week 3	Week 4	Week 5	Week 6
National UK	0.93 ***	0.96 ***	0.86 **	0.74 **	-0.23 *	0.05 *
North West	0.92 ***	0.97 ***	0.84 **	0.76 **	-0.22 *	0.11 *
Yorkshire & Humberside	0.93 ***	0.96 ***	0.79 ***	0.71 **	-0.41 *	0.00 *
Greater London	0.86 **	0.93 ***	0.80 **	0.67 **	-0.27 *	0.06 *
South West	0.94 ***	0.94 ***	0.81 ***	0.66 *	-0.33 *	0.05 *
South East	0.91 ***	0.96 ***	0.87 ***	0.58 **	-0.29	0.06 *
Northern Ireland	0.91 ***	0.89 ***	0.80 **	0.57 **	-0.12 *	0.17 *
West Midlands	0.88 ***	0.96 ***	0.84 **	0.59 *	-0.26 *	0.09 *
Channel Islands	0.00 *	0.00 *	-0.30*	-0.35 *	-0.37 *	-0.22 *
Home Counties	0.91 ***	0.95 ***	0.90 ***	0.78 **	-0.24 *	0.06 *
Scotland (North)	0.93 ***	0.96 ***	0.88 ***	0.95 ***	-0.08 *	-0.06 *
East England	0.94 ***	0.97 ***	0.85 ***	0.72 **	-0.20 *	0.052 *
Scotland (South & Central)	0.89 ***	0.97 ***	0.93 ***	0.88 ***	-0.16 *	-0.08 *
Wales (South)	0.97 ***	0.90 ***	0.89 ***	0.78 **	-0.27 *	-0.04 *
Wales (North)	0.96 ***	0.98 ***	0.93 ***	0.76 **	-0.33 *	0.19 *
East Midlands	0.90 ***	0.90 ***	0.69 **	0.69 **	-0.19 *	0.09 *
North East	0.94 ***	0.91 ***	0.79 **	0.81 **	-0.27 *	0.04 *

Table 2: Pearson Correlation of Regional SMAI with NHS Alcohol Data, $*** = p - value < 0.01, ** = 0.1 < p - value > 0.01, * = p - value > 0.1$

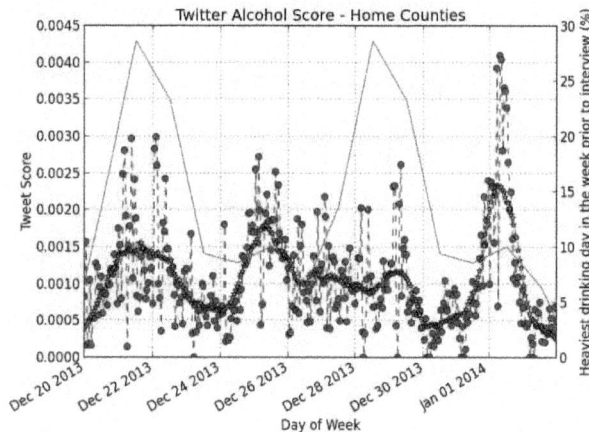

Figure 3: Hourly SMAI for Home Counties over the 2 week Holiday Period. Green line HSCIC Ground Truth data. Blue line hourly SMAI. Red Line 24 point moving average.

been used. This could come from a number of factors; low population density, limited demographics using Twitter, or different culture compared to the rest of the UK, or that the Channel Islands are closer to France than the UK so may not have been included wholly in the bounding box when gathering the tweets.

One final correlation was made against the ranking of regions on if they drank in a week; this was to see if the SMAI indicated variation in tendency to drink over regions and not just variations in patterns in a region over time (Table 4). The rankings of a tendency to drink were based on the HSCIC's Alcohol Statistics report's percentage of a population within each region that drank in a week [21] - this has been used to rank regions across multiple reports. The average SMAI for each region for each week was taken and correlated against the HSCIC data, a Pearson's coefficient of 0.77 was achieved. One of the issues with this measure though is that the data combines the various Wales and

Scotland groups into a combined 'Scotland' and a combined 'Wales', so averages had to be taken to combine the data for the bigger sets.

4.3 Qualitative Analysis

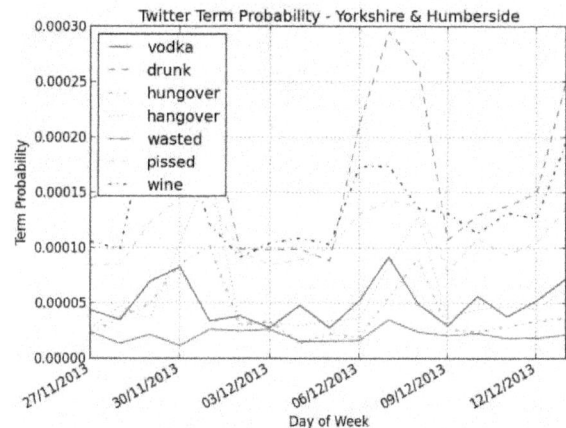

Figure 4: Daily Term Frequency for Yorkshire & Humber 2 weeks starting 27th November

The results indicate that over the winter holidays alcohol consumption increases through the upwards trend of the 7 point moving average on both the hourly and daily charts (Table 1). Although there are lapses in this trend between the two events, this could be due to people going back to work and/or wanting to give their liver a rest.

When looking at a more detailed SMAI graph from the festive holidays there appears to be a trend in increased drinking up to and on Christmas Day (Figure 3), then decreasing afterwards, and spiking upwards again on New Year. There appears to be some interesting increases in SMAI on the weekends either side of Christmas Day - there is a spike in the score; the first one could be an effect of the final day of work and people going out with colleagues to party. Though after Christmas there is a relative plateau (after an initial decrease) which is higher than normal, this could be from people staying off work as Christmas fell mid-week, with reductions only occurring after that weekend before a spike at New Year.

When looking at the hourly graphs from before Christmas a more fine grained understanding can be deduced about potential 'normal habits'. Within the Yorkshire & Humber (Figure 5) on a Saturday from midnight there is a prominent drop in the number of tweets with an increase from Sunday midday, this could be due to people going home and going to sleep, or it may be that they are unable to tweet due to dead barrettes or consuming to much alcohol to tweet.

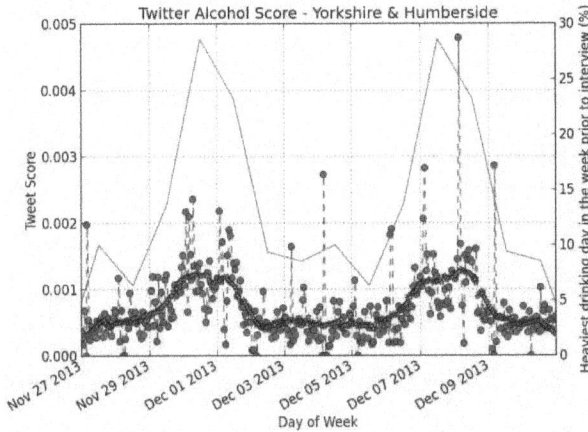

Figure 5: Hourly SMAI for Yorkshire & Humber for initial 2 weeks of study. Green line HSCIC Ground Truth data. Blue line hourly SMAI. Red Line 24 point moving average.

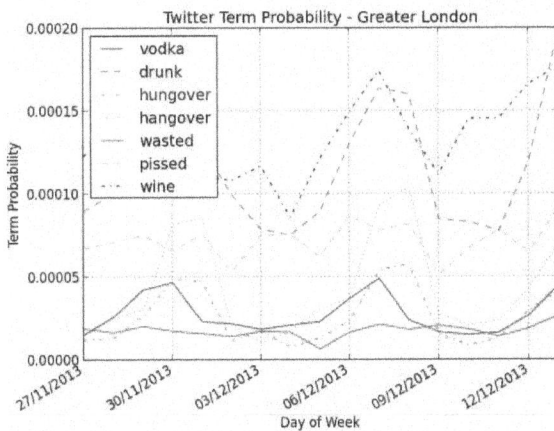

Figure 6: Daily Term Frequency for Greater London 2 weeks starting 27th November.

Though on Sundays a spike in SMAI (Figure 5) can be seen in certain locations, this could come from the change in term distributions as shown in Figure 4 where on the Sunday there is a reduction in the usage of words such as 'vodka', 'wine' and 'drunk', but there is a relative increase in words

such as 'hungover' and 'hangover'. Other variations in term frequency can be seen in Greater London (Figure 6) where there is a more prevalent usage of the word 'pissed' which appears to spike on weekends and midweeks, this could be from 'pissed' being used more by students who traditionally go out more on a Wednesday than many other demographics [19].

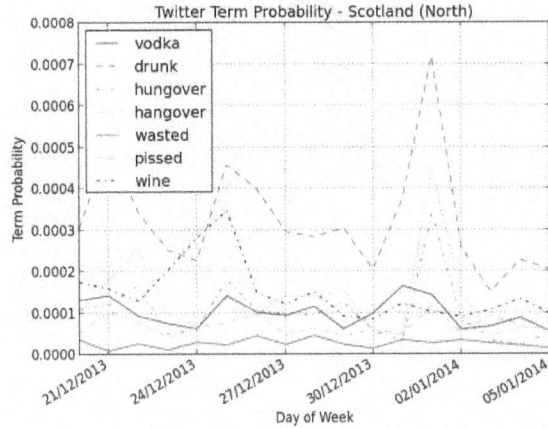

Figure 7: Daily Term Frequency for Scotland (North) 2 weeks starting over Christmas Holiday period.

Around Christmas some terms appear to increase relatively more than others, this can be seen for "wine" which at the time of around Christmas was used more than drunk; this could mean that the drink of choice for around the holidays is Wine and not the other drinks like Vodka (Figure 7). Though generally the terms which were used more are the more prevalent ones in the weeks before.

Some of the characteristics which are seen in the pattern of the probabilities could be down to the concept of the "rich-get-richer phenomenon" where the popularity of already popular items increases faster than less popular items [17]. This was seen in the popularity growth of hash tags on Twitter through a language based study of the spreading of hash tags [13].

(a) Word Cloud for Yorkshire & Humbside for the 6th December 2013 (Friday)

(b) Word Cloud for Yorkshire & Humbside for the 7th December 2013 (Saturday)

Figure 8: Word Cloud for Yorkshire & Humbside

A lot of the collocated words which were coming through were very likely to be talking about the process of getting drunk, such as words "getting" and "drinking" (Figure 9). The aspect of time is also brought in with people reporting that they are going to be drinking in the future by using "tomorrow" or "tonight" (Figure 8). It can also be taken from the data that Red wine appears to be the most Tweeted about wine from Red appearing more than Rose and White across the UK (Figure 10).

Figure 9: Word cloud on all collocation in Home Counties 21st December 2013

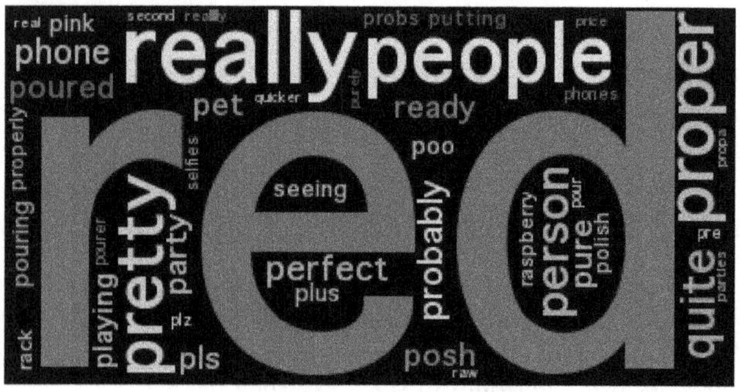

Figure 10: Word cloud on all collocation in North-East

5. CONCLUSIONS AND FUTURE DIRECTIONS

In this paper we presented a method to track variations in drinking throughout regions across the UK by using the social media site Twitter with accuracies as high as 0.97 regionally when compared to the ground truth from HSCIC. The results from this approach could be used in a number of situations from assessing staffing levels in UK A&E departments and policing levels needed in town centres. The method used textual markers as a form of indicator calculating a relative index based on the number of markers in a tweet averaged over a time frame for a Geo-location with data from the HSCIC as ground truth. This shows that there could be many potential benefits of using stream data compares to survey data for time dependent data analysis.

As can be seen through the results above, there is the possibility to model Twitter data against the HSCIC drinking pattern of the nations alcohol consumption. It also shows when nationally and regionally there is a move away from the trend such as national holidays and celebrations. Patterns of lag in terms can be seen across all regions, such as 'hangover' spiking 12 to 24 hours after spikes of 'drunk'. Though there is little word variation between regions in the

UK, with the exceptions such as 'pissed' in Greater London. This work shows that there is also the need for more granular statistics on people's consumption patterns, as this was one of the limitations of the work with the ground truth.

However, one of the limitations is that there is a potential population bias. The data for this in the UK is limited, however in the USA 78% of Adults are on-line, although only 17% are on Twitter, and of these the majority belong to a younger demographic [16]. This means that the population on Twitter which is being analysed may not be an exact representation of the population. This has been highlighted by Lazar et al. [25] which critiqued the use of 'big data' commenting that systems such as this and Google Flu should be in support of existing systems, and not a supplement.

From this initial exploratory work future work will involve research into predicting drinking patterns in regions in the UK, however this will involve filtering the tweets to remove invalid ones which may skew the results e.i. commercial tweets, and an expansion of markers, potentially removing words which would indicate side-effects and increasing words which would indicate drinking (e.g. alcohol types). Other data sources could be included such as check-ins on Foursquare as an indication of an intention to drink.

Further developments of the system will look for words which increase in popularity over time; this could be used to develop the open key term sets, allowing the system to adapt to the ever changing language in on-line social media. As the research suggested there are slight changes in language in regions, and looking more deeply into this language diffusion could reveal cultural changes in the use of language from how people communicate and express themselves; this would potentially mean moving away from specific term subsets to looking at a region's whole corpora. This could be seen as timely as language is believed to be fragmenting more and more through the use of on-line media [10].

6. ACKNOWLEDGEMENTS

This work is funded by the Digital Economy programme (RCUK Grant EP/G037582/1), which supports the High-Wire Centre for Doctoral Training (http://highwire.lancaster.ac.uk).

7. REFERENCES

[1] Christmas statistics - Addaction.
[2] BBC NEWS | World | Europe | UK tops G7 Christmas booze chart, Dec. 2004.
[3] S. Bird. NLTK: The Natural Language Toolkit. *ACL 2006*, 2006.
[4] Bollen, Mao, and Zeng. Twitter mood predicts the stock market. *Journal of Computational Science*, 2(1):8–8, Mar. 2011.
[5] S. Boniface and N. Shelton. How is alcohol consumption affected if we account for under-reporting? A hypothetical scenario. *The European Journal of Public Health*, 23(6):ckt016–1081, Feb. 2013.
[6] D. Borthakur. The hadoop distributed file system: Architecture and design. *Hadoop Project Website*, 11:21, 2007.
[7] R. D. Bromley and A. L. Nelson. Alcohol-related crime and disorder across urban space and time: evidence from a British city. *Geoforum*, 33(2):239–254, 2002.

[8] Z. Cheng, J. Caverlee, and K. Lee. You are where you tweet: a content-based approach to geo-locating twitter users. pages 759–768, 2010.

[9] C. Chew and G. Eysenbach. Pandemics in the Age of Twitter: Content Analysis of Tweets during the 2009 H1N1 Outbreak. *PLoS ONE*, 5(11):e14118, Nov. 2010.

[10] W. Croft. Social factors in the cultural evolution of language. Comment on "Modeling the cultural evolution of language" by Luc Steels. 8(4):359–360, Dec. 2011.

[11] A. Culotta. Detecting influenza outbreaks by analyzing Twitter messages. *arXiv.org*, July 2010.

[12] A. Culotta. Lightweight methods to estimate influenza rates and alcohol sales volume from Twitter messages. *Language Resources and Evaluation*, 2013.

[13] E. Cunha, G. Magno, G. Comarela, V. Almeida, M. A. Gonçalves, and F. Benevenuto. Analyzing the dynamic evolution of hashtags on Twitter: a language-based approach. In *LSM '11: Proceedings of the Workshop on Languages in Social Media*. Association for Computational Linguistics, June 2011.

[14] M. De Choudhury, S. Counts, and E. Horvitz. Social media as a measurement tool of depression in populations. In *WebSci '13: Proceedings of the 5th Annual ACM Web Science Conference*, pages 47–56, New York, New York, USA, May 2013. ACM Request Permissions.

[15] F. K. Del Boca and J. Darkes. The validity of self-reports of alcohol consumption: state of the science and challenges for research. *Addiction*, 98(s2):1–12, 2003.

[16] M. Duggan and A. Smith. Social Media Update 2013. *pewinternet.org*, Dec. 2013.

[17] D. Easley and J. Kleinberg. *Networks, crowds, and markets*, volume 8. Cambridge Univ Press, 2010.

[18] J. Eisenstein, B. O'Connor, N. A. Smith, and E. P. Xing. A latent variable model for geographic lexical variation. pages 1277–1287, 2010.

[19] J. S. Gill. REPORTED LEVELS OF ALCOHOL CONSUMPTION AND BINGE DRINKING WITHIN THE UK UNDERGRADUATE STUDENT POPULATION OVER THE LAST 25 YEARS. *Alcohol and Alcoholism*, 37(2):109–120, Mar. 2002.

[20] J. Ginsberg, M. H. Mohebbi, R. S. Patel, L. Brammer, M. S. Smolinski, and L. Brilliant. Detecting influenza epidemics using search engine query data. *Nature*, 457(7232):1012–1014, 2009.

[21] Health and L. S. Social Care Information Centre. Statistics on Alcohol: England, 2012, May 2012.

[22] C. Honey and S. C. Herring. Beyond Microblogging: Conversation and Collaboration via Twitter. pages 1–10, Jan. 2009.

[23] G. Johnson, I. N. Guha, and P. Davies. Were James Bond's drinks shaken because of alcohol induced tremor? *BMJ : British Medical Journal*, 347(dec12 3):f7255–f7255, Dec. 2013.

[24] V. Lampos and N. Cristianini. Tracking the flu pandemic by monitoring the social web. pages 411–416, 2010.

[25] D. Lazer, R. Kennedy, G. King, and A. Vespignani. The Parable of Google Flu: Traps in Big Data Analysis. *Science*, 343(6):1203–1205, Mar. 2014.

[26] I. Lunden. Analyst: Twitter Passed 500M Users In June 2012, 140M Of Them In US; Jakarta 'Biggest Tweeting' City | TechCrunch, July 2012.

[27] S. Maneewongvatana and D. M. Mount. On the Efficiency of Nearest Neighbor Searching with Data Clustered in Lower Dimensions. In *Computational Science — ICCS 2001*, pages 842–851. Springer Berlin Heidelberg, Berlin, Heidelberg, July 2001.

[28] M. Mathioudakis and N. Koudas. Twittermonitor: trend detection over the twitter stream. pages 1155–1158, 2010.

[29] W. Mistral. Binge Drinking: Consumption, Consequences, Causes and Control. *Emerging Perspectives on Substance Misuse*, 2013.

[30] P. M. Polgreen, Y. Chen, D. M. Pennock, F. D. Nelson, and R. A. Weinstein. Using internet searches for influenza surveillance. *Clinical infectious diseases*, 47(11):1443–1448, 2008.

[31] J. Ritterman, M. Osborne, and E. Klein. Using prediction markets and Twitter to predict a swine flu pandemic. *1st international workshop on . . .*, 2009.

[32] R. Room, T. Babor, and J. Rehm. Alcohol and public health. *The lancet*, 365(9458):519–530, 2005.

[33] T. Sakaki, M. Okazaki, and Y. Matsuo. Earthquake shakes Twitter users: real-time event detection by social sensors. In *WWW '10: Proceedings of the 19th international conference on World wide web*. ACM, Apr. 2010.

[34] H. A. Schwartz, J. C. Eichstaedt, M. L. Kern, and L. Dziurzynski. Characterizing Geographic Variation in Well-Being using Tweets. 2013.

[35] L. Smith and D. R. Foxcroft. Drinking in the UK, 2009.

[36] L. Smith, D. R. Foxcroft, and Joseph Rowntree Foundation. Drinking in the UK, 2009.

[37] L. Strunin. Assessing alcohol consumption: developments from qualitative research methods. *Social science & medicine*, 2001.

[38] World Health Organization. Global Status Report on Alcohol and Health, 2011.

[39] D. Zhao and M. B. Rosson. How and why people Twitter: the role that micro-blogging plays in informal communication at work. pages 243–252, 2009.

	North West	Yorkshire & Humberside	Greater London	South West	South East	Northern Ireland	West Midlands	Channel Islands	Home Counties	Scotland (North)	East England	Scotland (South & Central)	Wales (South)	Wales (North)	East Midlands	North East
North West	1\0	***	***	***	***	***	***	*	***	***	***	***	***	***	***	***
Yorkshire & Humberside	0.96	1\0	***	***	***	***	***	*	***	***	***	***	***	***	***	***
Greater London	0.92	0.94	1\0	***	***	***	***	*	***	***	***	***	***	***	***	***
South West	0.94	0.96	0.94	1\0	***	***	***	*	***	***	***	***	***	***	***	***
South East	0.92	0.95	0.95	0.97	1\0	***	***	*	***	***	***	***	***	***	***	***
Northern Ireland	0.86	0.88	0.83	0.91	0.89	1\0	***	*	***	***	***	***	***	***	***	***
West Midlands	0.96	0.96	0.93	0.96	0.95	0.88	1\0	*	***	***	***	***	***	***	***	***
Channel Islands	0.01	0.02	0.02	0.00	-0.00	0.00	0.01	1\0	*	*	*	*	*	*	*	*
Home Counties	0.93	0.96	0.95	0.97	0.97	0.90	0.96	0.01	1\0	***	***	***	***	***	***	***
Scotland (North)	0.85	0.89	0.86	0.91	0.92	0.90	0.88	0.00	0.91	1\0	***	***	***	***	***	***
East England	0.93	0.96	0.94	0.97	0.98	0.89	0.96	-0.01	0.97	0.91	1\0	***	***	***	***	***
Scotland (South & Central)	0.86	0.90	0.87	0.93	0.93	0.93	0.89	0.01	0.92	0.95	0.91	1\0	***	***	***	***
Wales (South)	0.91	0.92	0.88	0.91	0.91	0.90	0.89	-0.00	0.91	0.90	0.90	0.90	1\0	***	***	***
Wales (North)	0.90	0.89	0.87	0.90	0.88	0.83	0.89	-0.03	0.88	0.84	0.88	0.85	0.89	1\0	***	***
East Midlands	0.94	0.96	0.94	0.97	0.97	0.88	0.97	-0.01	0.96	0.90	0.97	0.90	0.91	0.89	1\0	***
North East	0.93	0.93	0.89	0.93	0.91	0.89	0.91	0.00	0.91	0.90	0.92	0.90	0.94	0.90	0.92	1\0

Table 3: Pearson Cross Correlation or Regional Term Probability Distributions, $*** = p-value < 0.01, ** = 0.1 < p-value > 0.01, * = p-value > 0.1$

Region	Drank Last Week (%)	Average SMAI					
		Week 1	Week 2	Week 3	Week 4	Week 5	Week 6
Yorkshire and the Humber	67	0.00068	0.00066	0.00072	0.00102	0.00111	0.00076
South East	67	0.00063	0.00059	0.00067	0.00087	0.00097	0.00073
South West	66	0.00069	0.00074	0.00076	0.00101	0.00111	0.00079
East of England	66	0.00064	0.00061	0.00070	0.00090	0.00109	0.00075
East Midlands	65	0.00067	0.00072	0.00073	0.00096	0.00108	0.00079
North East	63	0.00072	0.00067	0.00077	0.00103	0.00114	0.00078
North West	63	0.00066	0.00065	0.00069	0.00096	0.00107	0.00075
West Midlands	60	0.00060	0.00059	0.00070	0.00091	0.00101	0.00076
Wales	57	0.00065	0.00069	0.00084	0.00110	0.00114	0.00083
Scotland	56	0.00059	0.00058	0.00066	0.00086	0.00097	0.00079
London	51	0.00048	0.00049	0.00057	0.00065	0.00067	0.00054
Correlation / p-value		0.77 ***	0.60 **	0.36 *	0.52 **	0.67 **	0.47 *

Table 4: Correlations of weekly average SMAI to % people drank in a week, $*** = p-value < 0.01, ** = 0.1 < p-value > 0.01, * = p-value > 0.1$

Mining and Comparing Engagement Dynamics Across Multiple Social Media Platforms

Matthew Rowe
School of Computing and Communications,
Lancaster University,
Lancaster, UK
m.rowe@lancaster.ac.uk

Harith Alani
Knowledge Media Insitutte
Open University,
Milton Keynes, UK
h.alani@open.ac.uk

ABSTRACT

Understanding what attracts users to engage with social media content (i.e. reply-to, share, favourite) is important in domains such as market analytics, advertising, and community management. To date, many pieces of work have examined engagement dynamics in isolated platforms with little consideration or assessment of how these dynamics might vary between disparate social media systems. Additionally, such explorations have often used different features and notions of engagement, thus rendering the cross-platform comparison of engagement dynamics limited. In this paper we define a common framework of engagement analysis and examine and compare engagement dynamics, using *replying* as our chosen engagement modality, across five social media platforms: Facebook, Twitter, Boards.ie, Stack Overflow and the SAP Community Network. We define a variety of common features (social and content) to capture the dynamics that correlate with engagement in multiple social media platforms, and present an evaluation pipeline intended to enable cross-platform comparison. Our comparison results demonstrate the varying factors at play in different platforms, while also exposing several similarities.

Categories and Subject Descriptors

H.4 [**Information Systems Applications**]: Miscellaneous; H.2.8 [**Database Management**]: Database Applications—*Data Mining*

Keywords

Social Media, Engagement, Data Mining

1. INTRODUCTION

The rise of the information age has led to the increased need for users to allocate their attention in a more intelligent and considered fashion. Nowhere better is this manifest than on social media, where the rate at which social data is produced and the scale at which it is available has galvanised

research into understanding attention through the guise of *engagement dynamics*: understanding how and why users engage with (i.e. reply-to, share, favourite) certain pieces of social media content (i.e. status updates) and not others. The free, open and widely-used nature of social media means that several parties have a vested interest in understanding such dynamics for their own needs. For instance, marketing a product or injecting content into a social media platform, with the desire for users to engage with such content, requires understanding what factors are associated with engagement and how these differ between platforms. It could be the case that using familiar language to platform users is important in one context, while not so in another - for instance when advertising a product or event in a dedicated topical web forum.

Despite the emergence of a large-body of literature examining engagement dynamics, such works have thus far focused on different platforms using disparate approaches without considering a unified assessment that spans social media. As a result, findings that have emerged to date have not always been consistent in terms of: (i) examined features; and (ii) the association of such features with engagement in terms of both magnitude and sign - i.e. certain works have concentrated on the role of content features in initiating engagement, whereas other works have only considered social features. Furthermore, the actual action that represents engagement is found to be disparate between such works: for instance, on Twitter this can vary between identifying engagement when an individual *favourites* a status update, *retweets* a message [4, 18, 9, 8], or when a user *replies-to* a message [14, 15, 17], thereby representing differing modalities of engagement.

Social media platforms serve different purposes, offer different capabilities, and cultivate different social norms, therefore one would anticipate the underlying dynamics (communication, interaction, behavioural) on social media to differ from one platform to another. To reach an understanding of the persistent dynamics that emerge on each platform it is therefore necessary to establish a common evaluation framework that can be applied across different social media platforms, and to compare and contrast the results of applying this framework to a range of platforms. This is what we set out to achieve in this paper by presenting a comparative study of the engagement dynamics across five social media platforms: Boards.ie, Twitter, SAP Community Network, Stack Overflow and Facebook; using the action of *replying* as our studied modality of engagement. In performing this study we make the following contributions:

- We define a collection of social and content features that are common across the chosen social platforms, chosen from related work intended to capture factors that influence engagement.

- We present a machine-learning based approach for engagement prediction (defined as a binary classification problem) that includes feature standardisation, dataset balancing via under sampling, and time-ordering to enable inter-social media comparison of engagement dynamics.

- We contrast the role of different features on engagement likelihood across five social media platforms, thereby mining and comparing *engagement dynamics*, and contrast these findings with the engagement dynamics from existing studies on individual social media platforms.

To the best of our knowledge this is the first work that sets out to perform inter-social media analysis of engagement dynamics. By building upon related work for the chosen features to analyse, and comparing our results with prior findings, our work contributes to the domain of Web Science with an understanding of how engagement differs across social media. The findings from our work can be used by, and will have implications for, online product marketers and any content publishers keen to increase the potential for users to engage with their published content.

We have structured the paper as follows: section 2 describes the related work within the field of engagement dynamics, with an emphasis on data mining oriented research towards extracting engagement dynamics. Section 3 describes the datasets that we used for our experiments, the collection methods employed, and information describing the magnitude of the collected datasets. Section 4 explains the features that we engineered for the experiments and how they can be implemented by other researchers. Section 5 details the experiments that were performed to mine engagement dynamics including predicting which posts would be engaged with, the experimental setup that we followed, and the dynamics of engagement that we extracted. Section 6 discusses implications of this work and section 7 finishes the paper with conclusions drawn from the work.

2. RELATED WORK

Recent years have seen a large body of research begining to emerge on measuring and predicting attention generation across social media platforms. Attention has been measured in different forms (e.g. retweets, replies to comments, popularity of posts and answers) in search of a better understanding of its dynamics and the features that influence it. For retweets, it was found that content features were more influential than social features for determining whether a tweet will be retweeted or not [4, 18, 9, 8]. For example, the presence of URLs and hashtags in the tweets were often found to be good indicators of retweetability [12, 18]. Some social features, such as #followers, #followees, and account age were found to have some impact on retweet predictions, although less than content features [18]. Previous tweeting activities of users do not seem to encourage retweets. In fact, it was found that the more users tweet and favourite tweets, the less their tweets get retweeted [18]. Hodas et al [11] stress that the rapid visual decay of tweets on Twitter clients is a significant factor in retweetability. The authors

also found that tweets are less likely to be retweeted by people who follow many users due to the thin spread of their attention to too many users and tweets. The role of topics in attention generation were also investigated. It was found that people are less likely to retweet on topics that they themselves tweet about [9], and that tweets on topics of general interest are more likely to be retweeted [12]. However, in Boards.ie, users with high topic entropy (i.e. tend to post about the same topics) seem to receive more replies [13].

Contradictory to the case with retweets, when predicting replies on Twitter, it was found that social features (e.g., #followers, #lists) play a more important role than content features and tweet topics [14, 15, 17]. Sousa and colleagues showed that Twitter replies by users with smaller social networks are more driven by social aspects than users with larger ego-networks [17]. Nevertheless, as with retweets, combining social and content features produced the best predictions of replies on Twitter [14, 20, 15]. However, when analysing replies on Boards.ie, it was found that content features are better for predictions than social features, thus contradicting the findings obtained from predicting replies on Twitter, and instead agreeing with the predictions of retweets [13]. This highlights the role played by the type and goal of the communities on their engagement dynamics and associated features. For example, the presence of a URL in posts on Boards.ie is only good for generating a reply in general forums, and users with low forum entropy, account age, and #posts, are less likely to get replies in support communities [20]. Other variations in dynamics were observed across topics on Yahoo! Answers [1]. Here it was found that lower entropy of the answerer is good for predicting best answers, but only in technical topics and others where factual information is needed. For Yahoo! Answers, combining content and social features also provided the best predictions of best answers [3], which matches the findings from other social media platforms.

Models for predicting the engagement with comments on various social platform have also been explored in the literature. For example, features such as sentiment, and ratings of new comments were shown to be sufficient for predicting comments' engagement on YouTube [16]. In a study on the comments on Digg, Hsu and colleagues [7] showed that social features were better than content features for predicting comment engagement, which corresponds to the results obtained from predicting Twitter replies. Similar to the studies on Twitter and Boards.ie, combining social and content features also produced best predictions in Digg. Digg comments' engagement dynamics produced a few more patterns that contradict the findings obtained from Twitter. For example, unlike the case with retweets, previous activities of Digg users proved to be important for predicting engagement with comments [7]. On the other hand, account age, which was deemed important for predicting retweets [18], is one of the least influential on Digg predictions. Furthermore, topic entropy, which was found to be good for predicting tweets' retweets [18], is much less useful for predicting Digg comments' engagement [7]. As for predicting the votes of *articles* on Digg, it was found that content feature are most valuable if no *click* data is available yet, whereas social features are more useful for predicting votes when the visibility of a Digg article or a YouTube video is limited to a small number of users [19] . On Slashdot, content features (mainly quality of content) had a significant impact on the number of replies to comments, whereas the influence of the reputation of users was relatively weak [5]. This resembles the case with retweets, and replies on Boards.ie, but not replies on Twitter, or popularity of Digg comments [7]. In Facebook, it was found that social ties between users are good for predicting the length of reply chains [2]; the authors also found that the time it takes for the first reply to arrive is another good indicator of the length of the thread.

The above studies clearly demonstrate the many variations in how the dynamics of engagement differ across the various social platforms. In this paper we concentrate on the process of a user *replying* to content as a modality of engagement and apply a unified collection of features to datasets collected from five social media platforms. In doing so, we aim to reach a better understanding of how general or specific some of these findings are to individual social platforms.

3. SOCIAL MEDIA DATASETS

For our experiments we used data collected from five distinct social media platforms, each platform providing a different type of functionality and set of community forming features. Descriptive statistics for each dataset are shown in Table 1, these datasets were obtained from the following platforms:

3.1 Boards.ie

Boards.ie is the most-popular Irish community message board and provides a large number (>600) of discussion forums where each forum contains posts related to a distinct topic (e.g. Football, Xbox). Users do not build social networks on the platform, and instead the reply graph is used to construct social networks based on implicit edges from which we derive the social features described below. We define a seed post on this platform as a post that is the first in a discussion thread and receives a reply from another user, conversely a non-seed is a post that is not engaged with (has no replies). We use one dataset for our experiments from Boards.ie as described in Table 1.

3.2 Twitter

Twitter is a microblogging platform that allows users to post messages (Tweets) up to 140 characters in length. Users *follow* other users such that they subscribe to their content (Tweets) and receive them in their timeline, users can also *Retweet* other users' messages which then propagates those message through their follower network. We provide three datasets collected for our experiments: a random corpus (Twitter Random), a corpus of Tweets collected during the Haiti earthquake (Twitter Haiti) and a corpus of Tweets collected during president Obama's state of the union address in 2010 (Twitter Union), all of which are described in Table 1. For each dataset we were originally provided with a collection of Tweet IDs that were collected during the event (Haiti earthquake, State of the Union address) or time period (random collection). Some Tweets were replies to others, therefore we had to collect the seed posts that originally started the chain: we iteratively moved up the reply chain - i.e. from reply to parent post - until we reached the seed post in the discussion by querying Twitter's REST API[1] for the original post that was replied-to. Therefore in

the Twitter datasets, collected Tweets that received no reply are non-seeds, and the root post that initiated the discussion chain are seeds.

3.3 SAP Community Network (SAP)

The SAP Community Network is a community question answering system related to SAP technology products and information technologies. Users sign up to the platform and post questions related to technical issues, other users then provide answers to those questions and should any answers satisfy the original query, and therefore solve the issue, the answerer is awarded points. Hence, on SAP, there is prestige attached to the accruing of points over time as a large cumulation indicates expertise within a technical domain. Similar to Boards.ie, SAP provides no explicit means for a user to befriend or follow another user, therefore to construct social networks, and hence derive our social features that we will define below, we use the reply-to graph to form implicit connections between users. We define a seed post on this platform as any post that is the first in a discussion thread, and therefore a post asking for help or a question, that is engaged with by a community member, while conversely, a non-seed post is post that receives no engagement. We use one dataset for our experiments from SAP.

3.4 Server Fault

Similar to SAP, Server Fault is a platform that is part of the Stack Overflow question answering site collection.[2] The platform functions in a similar vein to SAP by providing users with the means to post questions pertaining to a variety of server-related issues, and allowing other community members to reply with potential answers. Answers are then voted by the community as being the best one, and the original question poster can also select his chosen best answer. Similar to SCN, Server Fault also lacks explicit edge-creation features, therefore we use the reply-to graph (i.e. where a user has replied to another user's question) to form an implicit edge between the users. A seed post on Server Fault is any question that is engaged with by community members (i.e. is replied to with answers), while a non-seed post is any post that fails to receive engagement. We use one dataset from Server Fault.

3.5 Facebook

For our final dataset we use data obtained from Facebook groups related to university course discussions. The groups enable users to connect and discuss all kinds of issues with their degree course material and potential avenues for solving any related problems. Although Facebook provides the ability to collect social network data for users, we opted to using the reply-to graph within the groups to build those social networks for individual users. In doing so we would constrain the social dynamics at play to those within the context of the groups. We define a seed post in this context as any post that starts a thread in a discussion group where users engage with the post, while a non-seed is any post that fails to attract engagement from community members.

4. FEATURE ENGINEERING

For our experiments we wanted to see how existing social and content dynamics function across social media. As

---

[1]http://dev.twitter.com

[2]http://stackoverflow.com/

Table 1: Statistics of the collected social media datasets that we used for our experiments. The seeds and non-seeds counts differ for various platforms indicating the extent to which class imbalance is evident.

Platform	Time Span	Post Count	User Count	Seeds	Non-seeds	Replies
Boards.ie	[01-01-2005,13-02-2008]	6,120,008	65,528	398,508	81,273	5,640,227
Twitter Random	[24-03-2007,25-07-2011]	1,468,766	753,722	144,709	930,262	390,795
Twitter Haiti	[28-05-2009,13-10-2010]	65,022	45,238	1,835	60,686	2,501
Twitter Union	[03-08-2009,28-01-2010]	81,458	67,417	11,298	56,135	14,025
SAP	[15-12-2003,20-07-2011]	427,221	32,926	87,542	7,276	332,403
Server Fault	[01-08-2008,31-03-2011]	234,790	33,285	65,515	6,447	162,828
Facebook	[18-08-2007,24-01-2013]	118,432	4,745	15,296	8,123	95,013

we have pointed out in the related work section, there are a variety of works that have examined different features on different platforms. However, in several cases the portability of such features to different platforms is limited (e.g. hashtags on Boards.ie) and therefore considerations must be made when compiling the feature sets to enable cross-platform inspection of engagement dynamics. This section therefore provides descriptions of *intersecting* features that function across all five platforms under inspection. Investigating platform-specific features is out of the scope of this study, where we only focus on common and comparable features. We begin by defining the social features, before going on to explain content features, and at each step highlighting the computational aspects of the features.

4.1 Social Features

Social features capture the social network properties of the author of a post and his activity and time on the platform. These features have been used extensively in previous works when examining the effect that the social network position and audience size has on a user's ability to initiate engagement with platform users. We define five social features as follows:

- *In-degree:* For the author of each post (seed or non-seed), this feature measures the number of incoming connections to the user. On platforms where edges are explicitly defined between users (Twitter) we count the number of followers a user has, on platforms where edges are implicit - i.e. via the reply-to graph where user B replied to a post by user A then we say that a directed edge from user B connects to user A - this is the total number of repliers to a given user (in this instance we use 6-month window prior to when the post was made based on prior work [13]).

- *Out-degree:* This feature measures the number of outgoing connections from the user. In a similar manner to in-degree we use the explicit edges from Twitter and the implicit edges gleaned from the reply-to graph for the other platforms (again a 6-month prior window from the post data is used).

- *Post Count:* Measures the number of posts that the user has made over the previous 6-months.

- *User Age:* Measures the length of time that the user has been a member of the community in days.

- *Post Rate:* Measures the number of posts made by the user per day.

4.2 Content Features

Content features capture the qualities and characteristics of a given post and have also been used throughout the related work. We found that existing attempts to characterise engagement through content dynamics often include features which are not portable to different platforms (e.g. @mentions on Twitter, hashtags, etc.), therefore we have seven common features that can be computed across our five social media platforms. These are defined as follows:

- *Post Length:* Number of word tokens in the post.

- *Complexity:* Measures the cumulative entropy of terms within the post to gauge the concentration of language and its dispersion across different terms. Let $T(p)$ denote a function that returns the unique terms in post p and $tf(t, p)$ denote a function that returns the relative frequency of token $t \in T(p)$ in post p. The complexity of post p is defined as follows:

$$complexity(p) = \frac{1}{|T(p)|} \sum_{t \in T(p)} tf(t,p)(\log |T| - \log tf(t,p))$$

(1)

This measure returns a high entropy if the post contains many terms which are not repeated often, and thus the random variable's entropy is increased, while a low entropy denotes repetition of terms from a limited vocabulary.

- *Readability-Fog:* Gunning fog index using average sentence length (ASL) [6] and the percentage of complex words (PCW): $0.4 * (ASL + PCW)$ This feature gauges how hard the post is to parse by authors.

- *Readability:* LIX Readability metric. As opposed to Gunning Fog, this metric determines complexity of words based on the number of letters rather than on the number of syllables. The Readability of a post is computed as:

$$Readability(p) = \frac{|Words|}{|Sentences|} + \frac{|Words > 6 letters|}{|Words|} * 100$$

(2)

- *Referral Count:* Count of the number of hyperlinks within the post. This measure is sometimes used as a naive spam measure, where posts with many hyperlinks could by for advertising some product or event and might therefore be less likely to lead to engagement.

- *Informativeness:* The novelty of the post's terms with respect to other posts. We derive this measure using the Term Frequency-Inverse Post Frequency (TF-IDF) measure:

$$informativeness(p) = \sum_{t \in T(p)} tf(t,p) \times ipf(t) \quad (3)$$

This measure will return high informativeness if the post contains unique terms with respect to the platform's vocabulary, while if the post contains terms that are familiar to the platform's users it will return a low informativeness value.

- *Polarity:* This measure assesses the average polarity of a post using SentiWordnet.[3] Our inclusion of this feature is to assess whether either positive or negative post polarity is associated with seeds or non-seeds, or whether subjective or objective posts also have an association. Let $T(p)$ denote a function returning the set of unique terms in post p, the function $pos(t)$ returns the positive weight of the term t from the lexicon and $neg(t)$ returns the negative weight of the term. We therefore define the polarity of p as:

$$polarity(p) = \frac{1}{|T(p)|} \sum_{t \in T(p)} pos(t) - neg(t) \quad (4)$$

5. MINING ENGAGEMENT DYNAMICS

Identifying which factors correlate with engagement across different social media platforms requires examining the contribution of individual features to predictive performance and then inspecting the effects of those features. In this section we describe our experiments to predict which posts will be seeds and which will be non-seeds, and compare our results and the findings in relation to existing work from the state of the art.

5.1 Experimental Setup

To uncover engagement dynamics across disparate social media systems we first derived the set of posts that would constitute the instances in each platform's dataset ($D = \{(\mathbf{x}_i, y_i)\}$ - this is to train a machine learning classifier. As shown in Table 1, there are large class imbalances between the seeds and non-seeds in the differing datasets - sometimes where there are more seeds than non-seeds and at other times vice versa. In order to ensure that we have a balanced class distribution in each dataset, we performed random *undersampling* from the dominant class (seed or non-seed) from each respective dataset. This resulted in a 50:50 split between seeds and non-seeds in our datasets - the resultant number of instances within each dataset is shown in Table 2. This method enables the incorporation of several baselines - as we will discuss shortly - that in turn enhance the assessment of model performance and make the process more straightforward.

After balancing the datasets' seeds-to-non-seeds distribution, we then constructed each post's instance features using the previously described features; this resulted in a vector representation of each post ($\mathbf{x} \in \mathbb{R}^{12}$). Within each dataset

[3]http://sentiwordnet.isti.cnr.it/

we then *standardised* each feature by normalising the respective feature value from each instance to have unit variance (i.e. $N(0,1)$) and thus converting it to a *z*-score according to the feature distribution. By performing this conversion we were provided with standardised datasets from which model coefficients can be compared, once induced, without the limitation of outlier values skewing the coefficients. This final process resulted in the construction of each platform's dataset ($D = \{(\mathbf{x}_i, y_i)\}$) as a set of pairs mapping each instance to its class label, where $y_i \in \{0, 1\}$ - with 0 denoting a non-seed and 1 denoting a seed. We maintained time ordering of the datasets such that posts, both seeds and non-seeds, were kept in an ascending publication date order and segmented each dataset into a training and test split using the 80/20% splits respectively.

For our prediction experiment we induced a logistic regression model using the training split and applied it to the test split. We trained the model using different feature sets (e.g. social, content, social+content) to see which feature set performed best and how this differed between the various datasets and platforms. We then inspected the coefficients of the logistic regression model of each platform to see how a change in each feature was associated with the likelihood of engagement. By performing this inspection we could see how engagement dynamics in each of the studied platforms contrasted against the related work - i.e. how a change in the magnitude of a feature would impact the log-odds of the classifier, and hence the likelihood of the post being engaged with.

5.1.1 Evaluation Measures and Baselines

To assess the performance of our models we used the standard classification performance measures of precision, recall and f-measure (F1: with $\beta = 1$ to count precision and recall equally). We also measured the Matthews' Correlation Coefficient (MCC) as a means to contrast our performance against a random guesser baseline. An MCC of +1 indicates perfect performance (i.e. matching predicted labels with observed labels), while a value of -1 indicates complete disagreement between the predictions and observed labels, and a value of 0 indicates that the performance is on a par with a random guesser.[4] Therefore, models should aim to surpass MCC=0, and thus beat a random guessing model.

5.2 Results

We begin by examining the performance of different feature sets on predicting seed posts and how these feature sets differ across the platforms. Table 3 presents the performance that the logistic regression model achieves when trained on isolated feature sets (i.e. social features), and then all features together. We note that for the isolated feature sets **content** achieves the best performance (in terms of F1) for Boards.ie, Twitter Random, Twitter Union and Facebook, while **social** features perform best for Twitter Haiti, Server Fault, and Facebook. When we combine the features together we find that for every platform we exceed the performance of using solitary feature sets. This indicates that different platforms have factors influencing users' engagement with content, however the importance of both

[4]MCC is calculated from classification contingency tables and the χ^2 test statistic divided by the set size and then the square root is taken.

Table 2: Statistics of the social media datasets that we used for our experiments once under sampling has been applied

Platform	Time Span	Seeds	Non-seeds	Instance Count
Boards.ie	[01-01-2005,13-02-2008]	398,508	81,273	162,546
Twitter Random	[24-03-2007,25-07-2011]	144,709	930,262	289,418
Twitter Haiti	[28-05-2009,13-10-2010]	1,835	60,686	3,670
Twitter Union	[03-08-2009,28-01-2010]	11,298	56,135	22,596
SAP	[15-12-2003,20-07-2011]	87,542	7,276	14,552
Server Fault	[01-08-2008,31-03-2011]	65,515	6,447	12,894
Facebook	[18-08-2007,24-01-2013]	15,296	8,123	16,246

social and content dynamics is paramount. We will delve into how such dynamics differ below.

Table 3: Performance of the logistic regression classifier trained over different feature sets and applied to the test set.

(a) Boards.ie

Features	P	R	F1	MCC
Social	0.592	0.591	0.591	0.092
Content	0.664	0.660	0.658	0.162
Social+Content	0.670	0.666	0.665	0.168

(b) Twitter Random

Features	P	R	F1	MCC
Social	0.561	0.561	0.560	0.061
Content	0.612	0.612	0.611	0.112
Social+Content	0.628	0.628	0.628	0.128

(c) Twitter Haiti

Features	P	R	F1	MCC
Social	0.968	0.966	0.966	0.482
Content	0.752	0.747	0.747	0.250
Social+Content	0.974	0.973	0.973	0.493

(d) Twitter Union

Features	P	R	F1	MCC
Social	0.542	0.540	0.539	0.042
Content	0.650	0.642	0.639	0.147
Social+Content	0.656	0.649	0.646	0.153

(e) SAP

Features	P	R	F1	MCC
Social	0.650	0.631	0.628	0.142
Content	0.575	0.541	0.521	0.063
Social+Content	0.652	0.632	0.629	0.144

(f) Server Fault

Features	P	R	F1	MCC
Social	0.528	0.380	0.319	-0.014
Content	0.626	0.380	0.275	0.032
Social+Content	0.568	0.407	0.359	0.012

(g) Facebook

Features	P	R	F1	MCC
Social	0.635	0.632	0.632	0.133
Content	0.641	0.641	0.641	0.140
Social+Content	0.660	0.660	0.660	0.158

5.2.1 Feature Effects

Fig. 1 presents bar plots of the feature coefficients in the logistic regression model. A positive value coefficient for a given feature (i.e. appearing above the x-axis) indicates that an increase in the magnitude of this feature has a positive bearing on the probability of a post initiating engagement.

Conversely, a negative value (i.e. appearing below the x-axis) indicates that the feature has a negative effect on engagement probability, in essence the coefficients are log-odds ratios. Therefore by inspecting the coefficients of the model we can examine how engagement dynamics differ between social media platforms and across the features. The logistic regression model also includes significance probabilities for each calculated coefficient under the null hypothesis a given coefficient is 0 (and thus has no effect on the engagement likelihood). We only report on features whose inclusion in the model is significant at the **5% significance** level - Fig. 2 shows the plot of these significance probabilities for each dataset's features.

Fig. 1 indicates that there are clear differences in the engagement patterns between the examined social media platforms and also within the platforms themselves (i.e. the differing effects for the Twitter datasets between the random corpus, the Haiti-specific corpus and the State of the Union Address corpus). For instance, when we examine the social features we see that for the **in-degree** of users, an increase in the in-degree is associated with an increase in engagement likelihood for all datasets except for Twitter Union, suggesting that the number of followers in this context could have a negative effect on the probability of a user replying to Tweets - i.e. more popular or listened-to individuals were ignored when discussing the political topic of the State of the Union address.

For the **out-degree** of a user a reduced value is associated with an increase in engagement likelihood for all social media datasets except for Twitter Union and Twitter Haiti, suggesting that the propensity of users to follow (Twitter Random) and reply-to (Boards.ie, Server Fault, SAP, Facebook) other users have a negative impact on engagement probability. For the **post count** of users we observe consistent effects for the Twitter datasets: an increase in the number of Tweets that a user publishes is associated with an increase in engagement likelihood. However, for the other datasets we find the opposite to be true: increased posting is associated with a decrease in engagement probability. This suggests that for conversation and discussion-oriented social media (Boards.ie, Server Fault, SAP, Facebook) an increase in a user's activity can have a detrimental effect on the probability of their future posts being engaged with by community members. It could be that in such contexts a user's activity is picked up as an annoyance and therefore leads to more of their posts being ignored.

Assessing the content feature effects we also note marked differences, we now pick out the salient findings. A reduction in the **referral count** (i.e. number of hyperlinks) in a post was found to seed engagement for all platforms, suggesting that URLs have a detrimental effect on yielding replies from other users. One can imagine that a URL posted within a message could denote a website, product, service or event advertisement, thereby not requiring replies (it might instead be retweeted, liked, etc) or leading users to ignoring such content. In terms of **complexity**, an increase in term-entropy was found to be positively associated with engagement for Boards.ie, Twitter Union, SAP and Facebook, while a decrease was found for the remaining datasets. This finding is interesting as it suggests differences in the engagement dynamics between the two question-answering platforms: SAP and ServerFault. For the former, it appears that users respond to posts which have a more varied vocabulary and are longer in describing their issue (shorter **post length** is associated with seeds on SAP), while for the latter a more terse post is preferred on ServerFault (limited vocabulary and longer). Turning now to the **informativeness** of post content we find that unique terminology with respect to the platform, and thus higher **informativeness**, is preferential for engagement on Twitter (Random and Union), however a reduction of unique terminology is preferential on Boards.ie, Server Fault and Facebook. This finding suggests that for discussion-oriented platforms, users are more likely to reply to posts that contain language which they are familiar with, while for microblogging platforms, which restrict the post length, unique terms lead to engagement.

5.2.2 Comparison with Related Work

Analysing the diversity of engagement dynamics both across social media and within the same platform suggests the presence of variance across studies and the disparity between findings from the related work. To ground our findings with that from the related work we compared the engagement dynamics derived from our experiments with findings from the literature. Due to the multidimensional nature of such a comparison, encompassing different feature sets, individual features, and pieces of work, we compiled the table shown in Table 4 to enable a coherent comparison. This table shows how a certain feature performed in our studies versus in other studies that were mostly done on different datasets and platforms. The aim is to highlight general differences and similarities, irrespective of the analysed data and platforms. Inspection of the comparison table reveals some interesting similarities and differences. For example, we found that **in-degree** is consistent across the related work with our findings: higher in-degree is associated with an increase in the likelihood of engagement.

Out-degree, however, differs: we find that a reduction is beneficial for all but Twitter Union, where such a reduction is actually contrary to what is found in the literature (where an increase in the **out-degree** of users is associated with increased engagement). For **post count** we observe that a decrease for all datasets but Twitter Random and Twitter Union is associated with increased engagement: this agrees with work of Suh et al. [18] on Twitter. When inspecting the effect of **age** in the related work we found that an increase in user **age** was found to be beneficial for engagement in the work of Suh et al. [18] on Twitter, whereas a decrease was found to be better by Hsu et al. [7], where the authors rank comments on weblogs. We also see differences too: decrease across Twitter (thus disagreeing with Shuh et al.) and increase on SAP and Facebook. For **referral count** we found a complete disagreement with related works, where

we find an increase in referrals was found to negatively impact engagement likelihood, while the related work found an increase to be better (in Twitter and Weblogs).

6. DISCUSSION AND FUTURE WORK

Our experiments showed that there is a good deal more work to be done in order to reach a greater understanding of how common features influence engagement in different platforms, and even across different datasets from the same platform. In this section we draw attention to a number of related issues that could guide current and future research.

Our selection of features was inspired by the literature, and consisted of features shared by the five platforms we are investigating. This enabled us to compare how these common features correlate with engagement in multiple social platforms. However, we acknowledge the fact that there could be other features, perhaps specific to certain social platforms, that might have a greater influence on engagement. It is also worth noting that the same feature could be used differently in different social platforms, which could explain any variation in their performance for stimulating engagement. These interesting issues are not however within the scope of this study.

For certain features, such as in/out degree, their calculation was done slightly differently across the platform we are investigating. On Twitter, these features were derived from the number of followers and followees (friends), whereas on the other datasets (Boards.ie, Facebook, SAP) they were derived from the user's reply-to network, which was calculated from all the user's reply actions in the past 6 months. It is not possible to mimic this threshold in Twitter, given that the date when a *follow* relationship is created is not supplied by the Twitter API. In future work we intend to harmonise further the calculation of these particular features by collecting timestamped follow relationships on Twitter. We considered *replies* as indicators of engagement. Others exist, such as *Likes* and *Retweets*, that could be considered as indicators of some form of engagement. Although our analysis can be expanded to other indicators, we believe that replies are more likely to indicate a closer or stronger engagement than the other actions - as replying to a person indicates a clear engagement of the replier to the recipient.

Adding more datasets to our analysis, from the same and different platforms, would enrich our experiment and findings. For example, it would be interesting to include additional Twitter and Facebook datasets, to further our study of the impact of topics and non-randomness on engagement dynamics. Adding more datasets could also expand our comparison to the literature, while in this paper the work was intentionally not constrained to like-by-like comparisons (e.g. comparing results across Twitter datasets alone) given that our goal was to study portability of results across multiple platforms. One of the aims of our comparison to the literature is to highlight any inconsistencies. Nevertheless, it is worth acknowledging that results could vary for numerous reasons, such as due to idiosyncrasies of the used datasets or applied analysis. This emphasises the need for reproducing these types of experiment over multiple platforms.

7. CONCLUSIONS

Much research has been carried out in recent years to better understand the dynamics of user engagement in var-

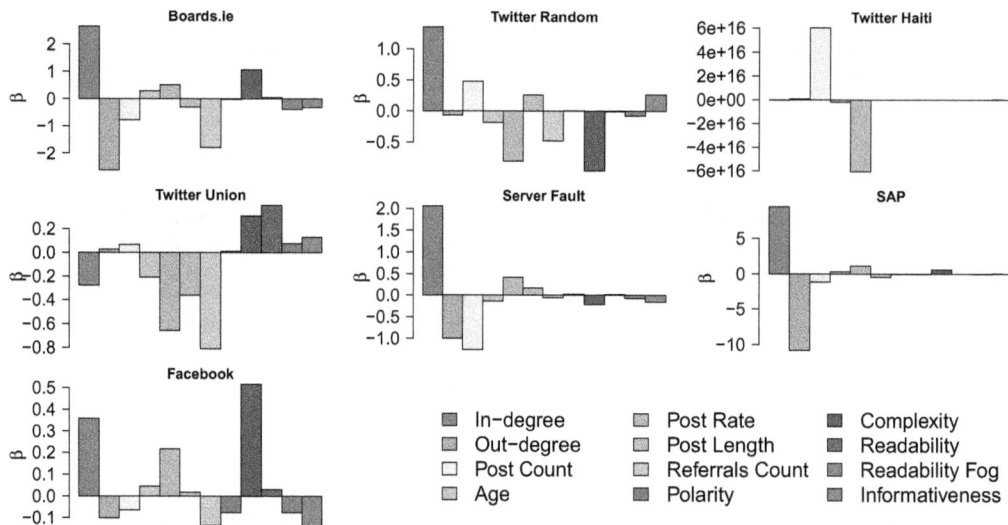

Figure 1: Logistic regression β coefficients for each platform's features. This provides some indication as to the effects of individual features on the response variable (i.e. whether the post seeds engagement or not).

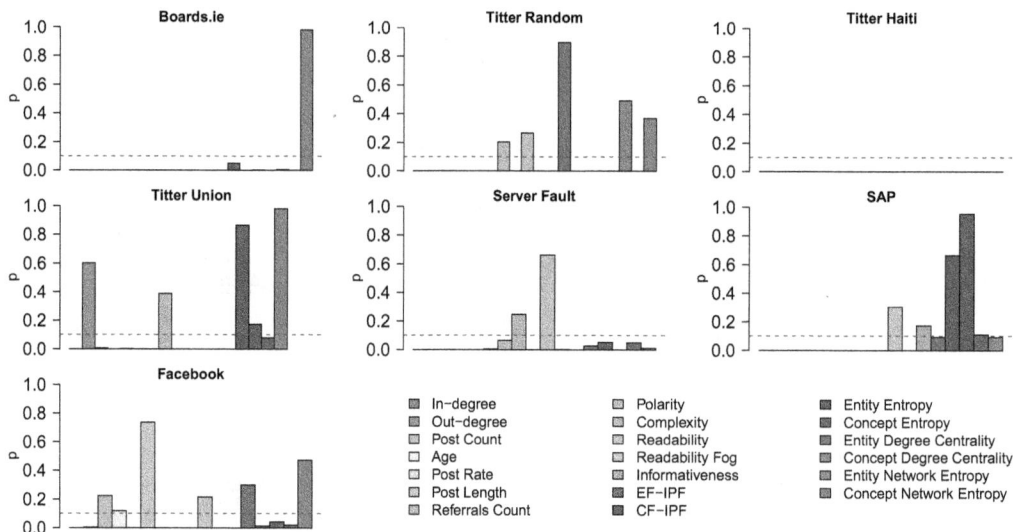

Figure 2: Logistic regression coefficients significance probabilities for each dataset's features. The 5% probability line is marked with the dashed red line.

ious social media platforms. This paper is one of the first to tackle the vital questions of which of those identified patterns are consistent and applicable to multiple platforms. To answer this question, a common set of features and analysis framework are required that apply to several social media platforms.

To this end, we defined a collection of social and content features, chosen from related work, that are common across five social platforms; Twitter, Facebook, Boards.ie, SAP communities, and Server Fault. We then produced and applied a machine-learning based approach for engagement prediction (defined as a binary classification problem) that included standardisation, dataset balancing and time-ordering to enable comparison of engagement dynamics.

We contrasted the role of different features on engagement likelihood across our five social media platforms, thereby comparing engagement dynamics, and contrasting these findings with the engagement dynamics reported in existing studies on individual social media platforms. We went beyond the comparison of results from same platforms (e.g. Twitter vs Twitter) to comparing across multiple and different platforms (e.g. Twitter vs Boards.ie). Our intention was to identify any similarities and differences in the engagement dynamics and feature sets across a variety of platforms.

Our experiments and results demonstrated that different features could have an opposite effect on engagement in different platforms, or across different non-random datasets from the same platform. We hope that the presented evalu-

Table 4: Comparison of the derived engagement dynamics with significant feature findings from the related work. The table is read per-row such that a dot (.) indicates no comparison, ⇑ indicates that the feature is positively associated with engagement while ⇓ being a negative association for a given dataset. The colour coding indicates whether this effect agrees with the finding from the paper in the above column: green for agreement and red for disagreement.

		Naveed et al. [12] (Twitter / RT)	Gomez et al. [5] (Slashdot / Comments)	Rowe et al. [14] (Twitter / Replies)	Adamic et al. [1] (Yahoo! Answers / Replies)	Cha et al. [4] (Twitter / RT)	Hsu et al. [7] (Weblogs / Comments)	Suh et al. [18] (Twitter / RT)	Hodas & Lerman. [11] (Twitter / RT)	Kwak et al. [8] (Twitter / RT)	Mishne et al. [10] (Weblogs / Comments)	Sousa et al. [17] (Twitter / RT)	Wu et al. [21] (Twitter / RT)
Boards.ie	In-Degree	.	⇑	⇑	.	⇑	.	⇑	.	⇑	.	⇑	⇑
	Out-Degree	.	.	⇓	.	.	.	⇓	⇓	.	.	.	.
	Post Count	.	.	.	.	.	.	⇓	.	.	.	.	.
	Age	.	.	.	.	.	⇑	⇑	.	.	.	.	.
	Post Rate	.	.	⇑	.	.	.	.	.	.	.	.	.
	Referral Count	⇓	.	.	.	.	.	⇓	.	.	⇓	.	.
Twitter Rand	In-Degree	.	⇑	⇑	.	⇑	.	⇑	.	⇑	.	⇑	⇑
	Out-Degree	.	.	⇓	.	.	.	⇓	⇓	.	.	.	.
	Post Count	.	.	.	.	.	.	⇑	.	.	.	.	.
	Age	.	.	.	.	.	⇓	⇓	.	.	.	.	.
	Post Rate	.	.	⇓	.	.	.	.	.	.	.	.	.
	Referral Count	⇓	.	.	.	.	.	⇓	.	.	⇓	.	.
Twitter Haiti	In-Degree	.	⇑	⇑	.	⇑	.	⇑	.	⇑	.	⇑	⇑
	Out-Degree	.	.	⇑	.	.	.	⇑	⇑	.	.	.	.
	Post Count	.	.	⇑	.	.	.	⇑	.	.	.	.	.
	Age	.	.	.	.	.	⇓	⇓	.	.	.	.	.
	Post Rate	.	.	⇓	.	.	.	⇓	.	.	.	.	.
	Referral Count	⇓	.	.	.	.	.	⇓	.	.	⇓	.	.
Twitter Union	In-Degree	.	⇓	⇓	.	⇓	.	⇓	.	.	.	⇓	⇓
	Out-Degree	.	.	⇑	.	.	.	⇑	⇑	.	.	.	.
	Post Count	.	.	⇑	.	.	.	.	.	.	.	.	.
	Age	.	.	.	.	.	⇓	⇓	.	.	.	.	.
	Post Rate	.	.	.	.	.	⇓	.	.	.	.	.	.
	Referral Count	⇓	.	.	.	.	.	⇓	.	.	⇓	.	.
	Polarity	⇑	.	.	.	.	.	.	.	.	.	.	.
Server Fault	In-Degree	.	⇑	⇑	.	⇑	.	⇑	.	⇑	.	⇑	⇑
	Out-Degree	.	.	⇓	.	.	.	⇓	⇓	.	.	.	.
	Post Count	.	.	⇓	.	.	.	⇓	.	.	.	.	.
	Age	.	.	.	.	.	⇓	⇓	.	.	.	.	.
	Post Rate	.	.	⇑	.	.	.	⇑	.	.	.	.	.
	Referral Count	⇓	.	.	.	.	.	⇓	.	.	⇓	.	.
	Polarity	⇑	.	.	.	.	.	.	.	.	.	.	.
SAP	In-Degree	.	⇑	⇑	.	⇑	.	⇑	.	⇑	.	⇑	⇑
	Out-Degree	.	.	⇓	.	.	.	⇓	⇓	.	.	.	.
	Post Count	.	.	⇓	.	.	.	⇓	.	.	.	.	.
	Age	.	.	.	.	.	⇑	⇑	.	.	.	.	.
	Post Rate	.	.	⇑	.	.	.	⇑	.	.	.	.	.
	Referral Count	⇓	.	.	.	.	.	⇓	.	.	⇓	.	.
Facebook	In-Degree	.	⇑	⇑	.	⇑	.	⇑	.	⇑	.	⇑	⇑
	Out-Degree	.	.	⇓	.	.	.	⇓	⇓	.	.	.	.
	Post Count	.	.	⇓	.	.	.	⇓	.	.	.	.	.
	Age	.	.	.	.	.	⇑	⇑	.	.	.	.	.
	Post Rate	.	.	.	.	.	⇑	.	.	.	.	.	.
	Referral Count	⇓	.	.	.	.	.	⇓	.	.	⇓	.	.
	Polarity	⇓	.	.	.	.	.	.	.	.	.	.	.

ation framework will serve as a basis for future work within the social web community and enable further research into the cross-platform examination of engagement dynamics.

8. ACKNOWLEDGEMENTS

This work has been part-funded by the DecarboNet project (EU FP7 - grant agreement number: 265454).

9. REFERENCES

[1] L. A. Adamic, J. Zhang, E. Bakshy, and M. S. Ackerman. Knowledge sharing and yahoo answers: Everyone knows something. In *Proc WWW Conf*, 2008.

[2] L. Backstrom, J. Kleinberg, L. Lee, and C. Danescu-Niculescu-Mizil. Characterizing and curating conversation threads: expansion, focus, volume, re-entry. In *Proceedings of the sixth ACM international conference on Web Search and Data Mining (WSDM)*, Rome, Italy, 2013.

[3] J. Bian, Y. Liu, D. Zhou, E. Agichtein, and H. Zha. Learning to Recognize Reliable Users and Content in Social Media with Coupled Mutual Reinforcement. In *18th Int WWW Conf*, April 2009.

[4] M. Cha, H. Haddadi, F. Benevenuto, and K. P. Gummadi. Measuring user influence in twitter: The million follower fallacy. In *Proc. 4th Int. AAAI Conf. on Weblogs and Social Media (ICWSM)*, Washington, DC, 2010.

[5] V. Gómez, A. Kaltenbrunner, and V. López. Statistical analysis of the social network and discussion threads in slashdot. In *WWW '08: Proceeding of the 17th international conference on World Wide Web*, pages 645–654, New York, NY, USA, 2008. ACM.

[6] R. Gunning. *The Technique of Clear Writing*. McGraw-Hill, 1952.

[7] C.-F. Hsu, E. Khabiri, and J. Caverlee. Ranking Comments on the Social Web. In *Int Conf Computational Science and Engineering (CSE) 2009*, 2009.

[8] H. Kwak, C. Lee, H. Park, and S. Moon. What is twitter, a social network or a news media? In *Proceedings of the 19th International Conference on World Wide Web (WWW)*, Raleigh, NC, USA, 2010.

[9] S. A. Macskassy and M. Michelson. Why do people retweet? anti-homophily wins the day! In *Proceedings of the Fifth International Conference on Weblogs and Social Media (ICWSM)*, Menlo Park, CA, USA, 2011.

[10] G. Mishne and N. Glance. Leave a Reply: An Analysis of Weblog Comments. In *Third annual workshop on the Weblogging ecosystem*, 2006.

[11] O. H. Nathan and K. Lerman. How visibility and divided attention constrain social contagion. In *Proceedings of Social Computing Conference (SocialCom)*, Amsterdam, The Netherlands, 2012.

[12] N. Naveed, T. Gottron, J. Kunegis, and A. C. Alhadi. Bad news travel fast: A content-based analysis of interestingness on twitter. In *Proc. 3rd Int. Conf. on Web Science, 2011*, Bon, Germany, 2011.

[13] M. Rowe, S. Angeletou, and H. Alani. Anticipating discussion activity on community forums. In *Proc. 3rd IEEE Int. Conf. Social Computing (SocialCom2011)*, Boston, MA, USA, 2011.

[14] M. Rowe, S. Angeletou, and H. Alani. Predicting discussions on the social semantic web. In *Extended Semantic Web Conference*, Heraklion, Crete, 2011.

[15] J. Schantl, C. Wagner, R. Kaiser, and M. Strohmaier. The utility of social and topical factors in anticipating repliers in twitter conversations. In *Proceedings of ACM Web Science Conference*, Paris, France, 2013.

[16] S. Siersdorfer, S. Chelaru, W. Nejdl, and J. San Pedro. How useful are your comments?: analyzing and predicting youtube comments and comment ratings. In *19th Int WWW Conf*, NY, USA, 2010.

[17] D. Sousa, L. Sarmento, and E. M. Rodrigues. Characterization of the twitter @replies network: are user ties social or topical? In *Proceedings of the 2nd international workshop on Search and Mining User-generated Contents (SMUC)*, Toronto, Canada, 2010.

[18] B. Suh, L. Hong, P. Pirolli, and E. H. Chi. Want to be retweeted? Large scale analytics on factors impacting retweet in Twitter network. In *Proc IEEE Second Int Conf on Social Computing (SocialCom)*, 2010.

[19] G. Szabo and B. A. Huberman. Predicting the popularity of online content. *Commun. ACM*, 53(8):80–88, 2010.

[20] C. Wagner, M. Rowe, M. Strohmaier, and H. Alani. Ignorance isn't bliss: an empirical analysis of attention patterns in online communities. In *Proc. 4th IEEE International Conference on Social Computing (SocialCom)*, Amsterdam, The Netherlands, 2012.

[21] S. Wu, J. M. Hofman, W. A. Mason, and D. J. Watts. Who says what to whom on twitter. In *In Proceedings of the 20th International Conference on World Wide Web (WWW)*, Hyderabad, India, 2011.

Collaboration in the Cloud at Google

Yunting Sun
Google Inc.
111 8th Ave
New York, NY 10011
ytsun@google.com

Diane Lambert
Google Inc.
111 8th Ave
New York, NY 10011
dlambert@google.com

Makoto Uchida
Google Inc.
1600 Amphitheatre Pkwy
Mountain View, CA 94043
muchida@google.com

Nicolas Remy
Google Inc.
8 Rue de Londres
75009 Paris, France
nicolasremy@google.com

1. INTRODUCTION

Google Docs is a cloud productivity suite and it is designed to make computer-mediated collaboration easy and natural so that users can access any document they own or that has been shared with them anywhere, any time and on any device. The question is whether this enriched model of computer-mediated collaboration matters.

There have been many analyses of the effect of email, messaging and video conferencing on collaboration. For example, [3] studied what mix of video and audio is useful for small groups doing remote real-time design work. [1] studied a spatially distributed product design team and showed that mobility enhances informal interactions and awareness.

Collaboration software is relatively new compared to email, messaging and video conferencing and quantitative studies are few. Blau and Caspi [2] ran a small experiment that was designed to compare collaboration on writing documents to merely sharing documents. The authors found that only students in the collaboration group perceived the quality of their final document to be higher after receiving feedback, and students in all groups thought that collaboration improves documents.

This study looks for the effects of collaboration on a large, diverse organization with thousands of users over a much longer period of time. The first part of the study visualizes how Google Docs is used for collaboration, and the second part analyzes how collaboration has evolved over the last two years. The full paper can be found at http://research. google.com/pubs/archive/41895.pdf

2. COLLABORATION VISUALIZATION

This section introduces ways to visualize collaboration based on the view, edit and comment actions of all full-time employees on tens of thousands of documents created in April 2013.

WebSci'14, June 23–26, 2014, Bloomington, IN, USA.
ACM http://dx.doi.org/10.1145/2615569.2615637.

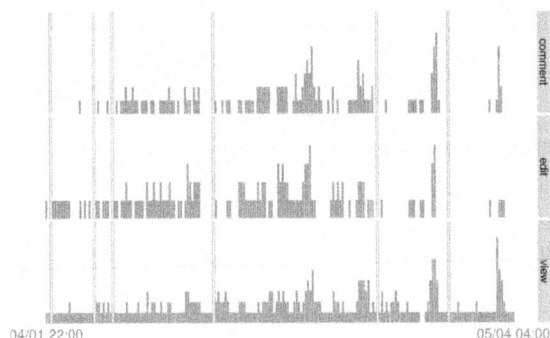

Figure 1: Collaboration activity on a design document. The X axis is time in hours and the Y axis is the number of users for each action type. The document was mainly edited by 3 employees, commented on by 18 and viewed by 50+.

Figure 1 shows the life of a design document created by engineers. The vertical axis is broken into three regions representing viewing, editing and commenting. Each contributor is assigned a color. A box with the contributor's color is drawn in any time interval in which the contributor was active, at a vertical position that indicates what the user was doing in that time interval. The X axis is time in hours and the Y axis is the number of employees working on the document for each action type. Only time intervals in which at least one contributor was active are shown, and gaps in time that are shorter than 12 hours are ignored. Gray vertical bars of fixed width are used to represent periods of no activity that are longer than the threshold. The document was mainly edited by three employees, commented on by 18 employees and viewed by more than 50 employees from three major locations. This document was completed within two weeks and viewed many times in the subsequent month.

Employees use the Docs suite to collaborate with colleagues across the world. Figure 2 shows one month of global collaborations for full-time employees using Google Docs. The blue dots show the locations of the employees and a line connects two locations if a document is created in

Figure 2: Global collaboration on Docs.

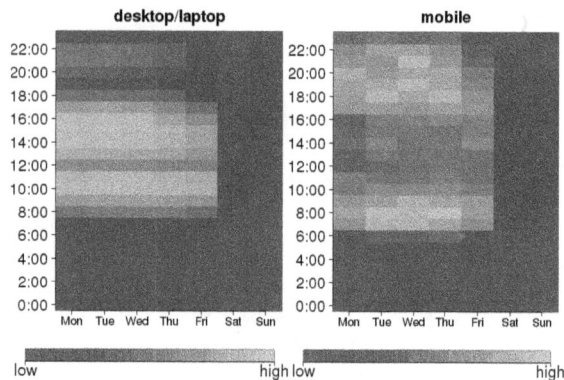

Figure 3: The average number of active users working in Google Docs in each day of week and time of day slot. The X axis is day of the week and the Y axis is time of the day in local time.

one location and viewed in the other. The warmer the color of the line, moving from green to red, the more documents shared between the two locations.

The advantage of cloud-based software and storage is that a document can be accessed from any device. Not surprisingly, the pattern of working on desktops or laptops during working hours and on mobile devices out of business hours holds generally at Google, as Figure 3 shows. Each pixel is colored according to the average number of employees working in Google Docs in a day of week and time of day slot, with brighter colors representing higher numbers. Pixel values are normalized within each plot separately.

3. THE EVOLUTION OF COLLABORATION

This section explores changes in the usage of Google Docs over time for new employees. We call two employees collaborators (or subscription collaborators to be clear) if one is a subscriber to a document owned by the other and has viewed the document at least once and the document has fewer than 20 subscribers. The owner of the document is said to have shared the document with the subscriber.

Here we define the new employees for a given month to be all the employees who joined Google no more than 90 days before the beginning of the month and started using Google Docs in the given month. Each month includes different employees. New employees are said to share a document if they own a document that someone else subscribed to,

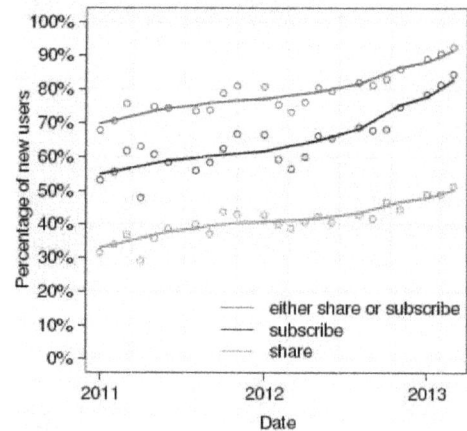

Figure 4: This figure shows the percentage of new employees who share, subscribe to others' documents and either share or subscribe in each one-month period over the last two years.

whether or not the person subscribed to the document is a new employee. Similarly, a new employee is counted as a subscriber, regardless of the tenure of the document creator.

Figure 4 shows that collaboration among new employees each month has increased since 2011. Over the last two years, subscribing has risen from 55% to 85%, sharing has risen from 30% to 50%, and the fraction of users who either share or subscribe has risen from 70% to 90%. In other words, new employees are collaborating earlier in their career, so there is a faster ramp-up and easier access to collective knowledge.

4. CONCLUSION

We have developed a visualization technique for the revision history of a document and analyzed key features in Docs such as collaborative editing, access from anywhere and on any device. Although we don't have survey results like those in [2], we find that new employees are becoming more engaged in using the Docs suite, which suggests that Docs suite is helping new employees ramp up and collaborate.

5. REFERENCES

[1] V. Bellotti and S. Bly. Walking away from the desktop computer: distributed collaboration and mobility in a product design team. *Proceeding of the ACM conference on Computer supported cooperative work*, pages 209–218, 1996.

[2] I. Blau and A. Caspi. What type of collaboration helps? psychological ownership, perceived learning and outcome quality of collaboration using google docs. *Learning in the technological era: Proceedings of the Chais conference on instructional technologies research*, pages 48–55, 2009.

[3] J. Olson, G. Olson, and D. Meader. What mix of video adn audio is useful for small groups doing remote real-time design work. *Proceedings of the SIGCHI conference on Human factors in computing systems*, pages 362–368, 1995.

Named Entity Evolution Analysis on Wikipedia

Helge Holzmann
L3S Research Center
Appelstr. 9a
30167 Hanover, Germany
holzmann@L3S.de

Thomas Risse
L3S Research Center
Appelstr. 9a
30167 Hanover, Germany
risse@L3S.de

ABSTRACT

Accessing Web archives raises a number of issues caused by their temporal characteristics. Additional knowledge is needed to find and understand older texts. Especially entities mentioned in texts are subject to change. Most severe in terms of information retrieval are name changes. In order to find entities that have changed their name over time, search engines need to be aware of this evolution. We tackle this problem by analyzing Wikipedia in terms of entity evolutions mentioned in articles. We present statistical data on excerpts covering name changes, which will be used to discover similar text passages and extract evolution knowledge in future work.

Categories and Subject Descriptors

H.3.1 [**Information Storage and Retrieval**]: Content Analysis and Indexing; H.3.6 [**Information Storage and Retrieval**]: Library Automation; H.3.7 [**Information Storage and Retrieval**]: Digital Libraries

Keywords

Named Entity Evolution; Wikipedia; Semantics

1. INTRODUCTION

With the Web as our daily source for updates and news, archiving of Web content has become important for preserving knowledge. However, due to the vast amount of data published at different times, accessing Web archives raises a number of challenges. Historical and evolution knowledge is essential to understand archived texts that were created a longer time ago. This is particularly important for finding entities as several characteristics may have changed over time. Most severe in this regard are changes of names, which are typically used as queries.

Berberich et al. [1] tackled this problem by proposing a query reformulation technique to translate terms used in a query into terms used in older texts by connecting terms

WebSci'14, June 23–26, 2014, Bloomington, IN, USA.
ACM 978-1-4503-2622-3/14/06.
http://dx.doi.org/10.1145/2615569.2615639 .

through their co-occurrence context today and in the past. Kaluarachchi et al. [2] proposed another approach for computing temporally and semantically related terms using machine learning techniques on verbs shared among them. Both approaches work on the available corpus without exploiting explicit evolution information. Tahmasebi et al. [3] proposed a similar approach that additionally considers the time of a name change. External resources have widely been neglected in this field. Even though several knowledge bases exist, most of them represent just current facts of entities. None of the popular ones, like DBpedia[1], provide evolution information. An often used resource is semi-structured information from Wikipedia, such as info boxes. While these sometimes include alternative names of entities, they do not provide further details, for instance, whether or not a name is still valid and when a name was introduced. The only evolution that has been explicitly made available on Wikipedia is its revision history. However, this shows the development of an article rather than of the corresponding entity. Kanhabua and Nørvåg [4] achieved promising results in discovering former names from anchor texts by exploiting the actual revisions of articles. In terms of evolution though, following this approach, the only time information that is available is the revision date.

Our analysis shows that most name evolution information is available in small passages within the current article of an entity. The corresponding excerpts in the texts have been identified by incorporating lists on Wikipedia, which provide semi-structured name evolution information for a limited set of entities. In future work, these findings will be used for extracting patterns and learning classifier models, which in turn can help to automatically discover more evolutions on Wikipedia as well as in other sources, like historical texts, newswire articles, social networks and blogs.

2. DATASET

The data we used for our analysis was collected from the English Wikipedia on February 13, 2014. As starting point we used list pages dealing with name changes. Due to the different formats of these lists, we focused on those that are easy and reliable to parse. We found 19 lists in an appropriate format. Each name change on these is represented as follows: *"preceding name → succeeding name (date)"*. After filtering redundant items, we ended up with 10 lists. A downside of the format constraint is that we only found lists of geographic entities: *Geographical renaming, List of city*

---

[1] http://www.DBpedia.org

name changes, List of administrative division name changes as well as lists dedicated to certain countries. The parsed lists contain 1,926 distinct entities with 2,852 name changes. For the found names, we fetched 2,782 articles. The larger number of articles compared to entities is a result of 766 entities with names that could be resolved to different articles. For 28 entities we were not able to resolve any name.

3. STATISTICAL RESULTS

Based on the dataset we gathered statistics on name evolutions of entities in their corresponding articles. First, we analyzed the lists of entity name changes in terms of completeness and their suitability for such an analysis. Afterwards, we incorporated articles to analyze the mentions of the available changes.

3.1 Lists of Entity Name Changes

Out of the 1,926 entities with 2,852 name changes that we extracted from lists, 1,898 could be resolved to corresponding articles (98.5%). As the ultimate goal is to identify excerpts that describe a full name change (i.e., consisting of preceding name, succeeding name and change date) only those that are annotated with corresponding change dates were subject of further analysis (e.g., ... → preceding → succeeding (date) → ...). Out of the remaining 2,810 changes, this holds for 918, which is 32.2% of the ones that were originally extracted. These relevant changes belong to 696 entities, which is 36.1% of all entities we started with. They constitute the subject of our research regarding excerpts that describe name evolutions.

3.2 Mentions in Wikipedia Articles

Proceeding with the entities that meet the prerequisites, we analyzed the corresponding articles for name changes mentioned in the text. For entities that were resolved to multiple articles, all articles have been taken into account. Out of the available 918 date-annotated name changes of entities with articles, we found 572 (62.3%) mentioned with all three components (preceding name, succeeding name and change date). These were used for taking a closer look at the excerpts of texts that report changes. We measured the sentence distances of the three components for each of the 572 name changes. This is the minimum distance from a sentence mentioning one of the components to next sentence that mentions the last component, while bypassing the remaining one. For instance, if one sentence contains all the components, the sentence distance for this change is 0. Overall, the average sentence distance of the extracted excerpts was 19.9. However, this is caused by a very few, very high distances and is not representative, as indicated by the median of 1. In fact, 488 excerpts out of the total 572 excerpts, which is 85.3%, have a distance less than 10. A significant majority of 79.7% of these excerpts even have a sentence distance of less than three.

4. DISCUSSION

Our analysis was driven by the question about Wikipedia's suitability as a resource for extracting name evolution knowledge. The hypothesis was, that name evolutions are described in short excerpts within texts, which can be used later to learn common patterns to discover evolutions automatically. Based on our observations, this can be affirmed.

More than 60% of the 918 name changes that were available with corresponding articles and dates are mentioned in Wikipedia articles. Out of these, more than two-thirds were found within excerpts with less than three sentences. The extraction of particular patterns in order to train classifiers for the purpose of identifying evolutions automatically remains for future work. However, a first look at some excerpts already revealed that many of them contain certain signal words, such as "became", "rename", "change".

Unfortunately, the analyzed lists only consist of geographic entities as we were not able to fully reliably parse rather unstructured lists on Wikipedia that cover entities of different domains. At this point, accuracy was most important for building a foundation to train classifiers with a high precision in order to extend the training set later on. Accordingly, we can only carefully make the assumption that our observations hold for entities of other domains, too. This needs to be verified in future work.

5. CONCLUSIONS AND FUTURE WORK

In our study we investigated how name changes are mentioned in Wikipedia articles regardless of structural elements and found that a large majority is covered by short text passages. Using lists of name changes, we were able to automatically extract the corresponding excerpts from articles. Although the name evolutions mentioned in Wikipedia articles by far cannot be called complete, they provide a respectable basis for discovering more entity evolutions. In future work, we are going to use the excerpts that we found on Wikipedia for discovering patterns and training classifiers to find similar excerpts on further Wikipedia articles as well as other sources. The first step on this will be a more detailed analysis of the extracted excerpts, followed by engineering appropriate features. Eventually, we are going to build a knowledge base dedicated to entity evolutions. Such a knowledge base can serves as a source for application that rely on evolution knowledge, like information retrieval systems, especially on Web archives. Furthermore, it constitutes a ground truth for future research in the field of entity evolution, like novel algorithms for detecting entity evolutions on Web content streams.

References

[1] K. Berberich, S. J. Bedathur, M. Sozio, and G. Weikum. Bridging the terminology gap in web archive search. In *WebDB*, 2009.

[2] A. C. Kaluarachchi, A. S. Varde, S. J. Bedathur, G. Weikum, J. Peng, and A. Feldman. Incorporating terminology evolution for query translation in text retrieval with association rules. In *CIKM*, 2010.

[3] N. Tahmasebi, G. Gossen, N. Kanhabua, H. Holzmann, and T. Risse. Neer: An unsupervised method for named entity evolution recognition. In *Coling*, Mumbai, India, 2012. URL `http://www.l3s.de/neer-dataset`.

[4] Nattiya Kanhabua and Kjetil Nørvåg. Exploiting time-based synonyms in searching document archives. In *JCDL*, 2010.

Twelve Years of Wikipedia Research

Judit Bar-Ilan
Department of Information Science, Bar-Ilan University
Ramat Gan, 5290002, Israel
Judit.Bar-Ilan@biu.ac.il

Noa Aharony
Department of Information Science, Bar-Ilan University
Ramat Gan, 5290002, Israel
Noa.Aharony@biu.ac.il

ABSTRACT

Wikipedia was formally launched in 2001, but the first research papers mentioning it appeared only in 2002. Since then it raised a huge amount of interest in the research community. At first mainly the content creation processes and the quality of the content were studied, but later on it was picked up as a valuable source for data mining and for testing. In this paper we present preliminary results that characterize the research done on and using Wikipedia since 2002.

Categories and Subject Descriptors

H.5.3 [**Information Systems**]: Group and Organization Interfaces – *Web-based interaction.*

H.3.5 [**Information Systems**]: Online Information Services – *Web-based services.*

General Terms

Measurement.

Keywords

Wikipedia, analysis, longitudinal trends

1. INTRODUCTION

Wikipedia is a unique, online, collaborative encyclopedia that was established in 2001 [5]. Since then it experienced exponential growth, and has been studied extensively. Among the studied topics related to Wikipedia are its structure, collaborative processes, reliability, content, improvements and research where Wikipedia data serve as input (e.g. data mining, semantics, and visualization). It is an attempt to create an online encyclopedia that presents the "wisdom of crowds" [1, 4]. As of December 2013 it contains 30 million articles written in more than 287 language editions [6] and more than 4.4 million articles in the English Wikipedia alone [7]. Wikipedia is one of the ten most visited sites on the web (see www.alexa.com).

This study aims to characterize research publications related to Wikipedia extracted from Elsevier's Scopus. Scopus is a multidisciplinary, citation database with extensive coverage. In particular we characterized how trends in studying Wikipedia during twelve years from 2001 to almost the end of 2013.

2. RESEARCH SETUP

2.1 Data Collection

Elsevier's Scopus (http://www.scopus.com) was searched on November 17, 2013. We searched for the occurrence of the term Wikipedia in the article title, abstract and keywords. Time span or article type were not limited. The number of retrieved records was 3582. Scopus is a multidisciplinary citation database. It was chosen over Thomson-Reuters' Web of Science (WOS, http://www.isiknowledge.com), because of its wider coverage of current publications especially of proceedings papers that constituted the majority of the retrieved documents from Scopus (2261 items, 63% of the total). The number of items retrieved from WOS was only 1,550, even though the proceedings citation databases were included in the search. Theoretically we could have used Google Scholar (GS, http://scholar.google.com), but on GS one can only search either in the text indexed by GS, which is often the full text of the article, or limit the search to title only. Looking at items that contain the term Wikipedia in the title only is too limiting (for example in the Scopus dataset only 864 out of the 3582 retrieved items contained the term Wikipedia in their title), and without any limitations the number of items reported by GS for the search Wikipedia was about 805,000 (this presumably includes papers that refer to a Wikipedia article for a definition). Thus it was not feasible to base our study on Google Scholar.

2.2 Content Categories and Reliability

The content of the items was analyzed. According to Krippendorff [2] content analysis is a "research technique for making replicable and valid inferences from texts (or other meaningful matter) to the contexts of their use" (p. 24).

The analysis was mainly based on the abstracts of the items. In case there was no abstract, or it was not possible to decide on the topic of the item based on the abstract, the full text of the item was consulted. We created a light-weight classification, which allowed us to classify the whole set of papers. Three facets were defined; the first described to which extent the item relates to Wikipedia (major, minor or unrelated). We encountered 614 cases of "unrelated" (17%) – although the Scopus records of these items included the term Wikipedia, but it was clear that the paper did not study or discuss. The second facet related to the actual topic of the item. Here we differentiated between articles that studied Wikipedia or its use (e.g. in education), and articles that used Wikipedia either as a source/resource for other research or used Wikipedia to test the feasibility and applicability of tools or methods developed for purposes not directly related to Wikipedia (e.g. the INEX initiative (https://inex.mmci.uni-saarland.de/) is using an xml collection based on Wikipedia to test the submitted outputs). The first category is called in what follows *about*, while the second is called *using*. The third facet concentrated on the item's approach: we explored if the item's focus was technological or social/theoretical. We decided to include in the social/theoretical approach analyses and visualizations of Wikipedia. The technological approach for the *about* category only included tools developed for improving Wikipedia. We named the two categories in this facet *soc* and *tech* respectively.

The reliability of the categorization was assessed on a 10% random sample of the classified items by both authors [3, p.149]. The two coders agreed on 90% of the categorizations.

3. RESULTS

As mentioned before, 641 items were categorized as unrelated. The rest were either major (2301, 64%) or minor (667, 19%). From this point onward we only discuss the set of 2968 items that were categorized either as *major* or as *minor*.

In terms of topic, there were almost an equal number of items *about* Wikipedia (1431, 48%) as there were *using* Wikipedia (1537, 52%). As for approach, the *technological* approach was considerably more popular (1856 items, 63%) compared to the *social* approach (1112 items, 37%).

Figure 1 depicts the overall growth in the number of relevant publications indexed by Scopus (with *unrelated* excluded), and the growth in the topic and approach categories. We excluded 2013 from the graph, because we did not have the full data for that year. We see that the first papers using Wikipedia appeared in 2005, but since 2009 there are more papers that *use* Wikipedia than papers that are *about* Wikipedia. In terms of *social* versus *technological*, we see that at first the social aspects were emphasized, but since 2007 papers on technological aspects are much more frequent. Thus the crossover between *social* and *technological* occurred earlier than the crossover between *about* and *using*.

There is an overall growth in the total number of relevant papers published per year, but it seems that the number of publications per year plateaued and the growth rate is starting to level off. In order to support this finding we retrieved data from WOS, from Scopus and from the ACM Digital Library on May 7, 2014, assuming that the records for 2013 are complete by then. Figure 2 depicts the number of items per year in all three databases, with unrelated included in all years, since it was impossible to check the relatedness of the newly retrieved records by submission time. It clearly shows that the growth rate is slowing this down.

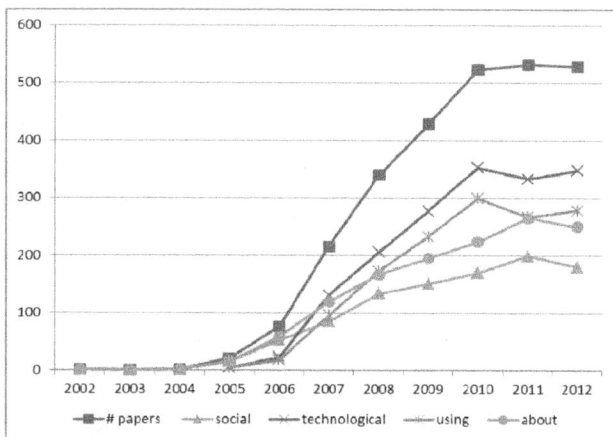

Figure 1: Number of papers per year, per topic and per approach

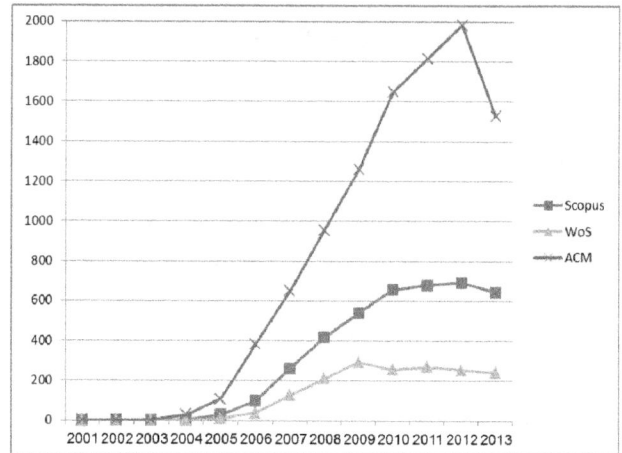

Figure 2: Number of retrieved items per year – Scopus, WOS and the ACM Digital Library

4. DISCUSSION AND CONCLUSIONS

We see that the growth rate is slowing down. This is somewhat surprising, since Wikipedia is an excellent, semi-structured, multilingual, interlinked and manually categorized data source that can and should be utilized extensively in NLP, IR, IE and ontology building. In addition, Wikipedia is a result of an unprecedented collaborative effort, and thus the social dynamics of editing, reaching consensus and creating quality encyclopedia articles should be of ongoing research interest.

This study is limited by the retrieval capabilities and the coverage of Scopus. We only considered records containing the term Wikipedia in the title, the abstract or the keywords, and thus might have missed some records. We could have possibly included the search term Wikipedians as well. The results highlight Wikipedia's importance in studying the Web and social media, and in advancing Web-based research.

5. REFERENCES

[1] Kittur, A., and Kraut, R. E. 2008. Harnessing the wisdom of crowds in Wikipedia: Quality through coordination. In *Proceedings of the ACM Conference on Computer-Supported Cooperative Work* CSCW 2008. New York: ACM Press, 37-36

[2] Krippendorff, K. 2013. *Content analysis: An introduction to its methodology*. Third Edition. Sage Publications.

[3] Neuendorf, K. A. 2002. *The content analysis guidebook*. Sage Publications.

[4] Surowiecki, J. 2004. *The Wisdom of Crowds*. Anchor Books. New York, NY.

[5] Wikipedia contributors. 2014. History of Wikipedia. http://en.wikipedia.org/w/index.php?title=History_of_Wikipedia&oldid=595511145

[6] Wikipedia contributors, 2014. Wikipedia. http://en.wikipedia.org/w/index.php?title=Wikipedia&oldid=596604227

[7] Wikipedia: Statistics. 2013. http://en.wikipedia.org/w/index.php?title=Wikipedia:Statistics&oldid=587963650

Some Challenges for the Web Observatory Vision: Field Notes from a Southampton-Tsinghua-KAIST Collaboration

Evangelia Papadaki, Abby Whitmarsh, Eamonn Walls
Web Science Doctoral Training Centre
University of Southampton, UK
ep11g12@soton.ac.uk, aw3g09@soton.ac.uk, ew1g12@soton.ac.uk

ABSTRACT

This paper outlines some challenges for the Web Observatory vision with reference to field notes from a student exchange and research collaboration in December 2013 between the University of Southampton, Tsinghua University and KAIST. These field notes outline a methodological narrative of the practical challenges that we faced in using the Web Observatory in collaborative research. It is suggested that these challenges particularly come in the form of technical, organizational and legal issues. The paper concludes with some proposals for the future of the Web Observatory vision.

Categories and Subject Descriptors

K.4.2 [Computers and Society]: Social Issues

Keywords

Web Observatory; Field Notes; Sina Weibo; Corruption

1. INTRODUCTION

The Web Observatory started under the WSTn (Web Science Trust network) and builds on open data initiatives [3, 10]. The objective is to build in bottom-up fashion a distributed environment facilitating greater access to datasets and interoperable analytic and visualisation tools [10]. The Web Observatory is still an idea in progress – there are few strictly agreed definitions or standards, and processes to move towards such standards are still ongoing. The Web Observatory has been thought of as part of the vision of the evolution of the Web in general and Web Science in particular [10]. However there are a number of difficult and ongoing questions surrounding big data management that may have an influence on the future development of the Web Observatory [2]. There have been calls in the literature for wider discussion in the Web Observatory community to begin to define relevant criteria by which data might be assessed and improved over time [1, 5, 8].

2. FIELD NOTES FROM A STUDY USING THE WEB OBSERVATORY

This paper refers to field notes of a study using the Web Observatory 'in the wild'. This study was part of a collaboration and student exchange between the University of Southampton, KAIST and Tsinghua University in December 2013. The aims and objectives of the project were chosen with guidance from professors at the University of Southampton. Using datasets from various Web Observatories and hosted at the University of Southampton Web Observatory, the project aimed to discover how political corruption was discussed and reported on social networking sites (SNS) in China, such as Sina Weibo.

A dataset from Sina Weibo which had been harvested by researchers at Tsinghua University had been made available to members of our research group. After examining the data it became apparent that the dataset we were using had been filtered to only two topics, neither of which were related to corruption. This was the first challenge to the project - not knowing what data was available in a Web Observatory nor the provenance of the data. For the research week at the University of Southampton our research group instead collated manual figures from Twitter and Sina Weibo. A list of official hashtags which were used on Sina Weibo to report corruption was supplied to University of Southampton academics. Using these hashtags we were able to produce some visualisations showing the frequency of use of the different hashtags by month.

We received access to a different dataset while taking part in the research week at Tsinghua University. However the provenance of the dataset was not discovered until after the research week was over. This appears to be a recurring issue for Web Observatories in general. Once we had access to some meaningful data we began the process of querying the database, and came upon our next challenge. The dataset is called weibo_2012 and is hosted at mdb-001.ecs.soton.ac.uk in a mongoDB database. Our team had no experience with using mongoDB and had to learn quickly how to query, view and group data to make it meaningful. This may suggest that researchers who wish to use data hosted at Web Observatories in its current form will require a relatively high level of technical skills. Querying the dataset we found the number of weibos in the dataset was 5,279,579. Such a large dataset was slow to query and our original plan of creating a visualisation which could be queried dynamically had to be abandoned and we decided to create visualisations on data that we had already filtered. Many of these decisions were influenced by purely practical considerations – limitations in computing resources, time, and labour all strongly influenced the direction of the project. Using a python script we created a smaller dataset based on ten search terms with and without hashtags.

3. CHALLENGES FOR THE WEB OBSERVATORY VISION

3.1 Technical Challenges

In order for the Web Observatory to operate as a common infrastructure for sharing data, effective research communication is required for the identification of interworking standards, which will allow datasets to be used effectively across the Web Observatory community [7]. A key concept for the design of a globally distributed Web Observatory is 'interoperability' [3]; querying across different platforms and datasets can be achieved only by addressing the challenges of data harmonization, standardization and the development of shared methodologies for facilitating data harvesting. What is more, given that the Web Observatory needs to be collaborative, it is recommended that the activities of Web Observatory researchers adhere to best practices of technology support for scientific method deriving from previous collaborative activities [8]. Issues of reusability could be addressed by documented and principled methods based on best practices such as Linked Data technologies [1].

3.2 Organizational Challenges

Given that the quality of the data is closely intertwined with the purposes of each funding project that creates it, questions arise as to whether this data could meet the needs of projects that want to reuse them [4]. Even if this first hurdle can be surmounted, accessing the datasets raises major privacy concerns imposing significant burdens on the implementation of the Web Observatory vision. Depending on the terms of service of the data source many datasets may not be entirely open; such datasets may require anonymization at source, data security, restricted access or even legal approval in order to be collected and shared [9]. Therefore, a variety of competing Internet players need to undertake the responsibility of ensuring that access to data sources is ethically controlled; it is essential that ethics processes are placed into the heart of Web Observatory governance structures instead of being managed around the edges [4, 9].

3.3 Legal Challenges

Under the terms of the Copyright, Designs and Patents Act 1998 (CDPA), databases are treated as a class of literary work and may therefore receive copyright protection; copyright protection afforded to a database as a whole should be distinguished from any protection that its individual components may attract. Copyright law aims at rewarding the author's intellectual creativity by protecting his work against copying without licence or permission; that is why, protection is limited to databases containing a sufficient degree of creativity in the selection and/or the arrangement of the data. To sum up, a body considering sharing data should consider whether the databases potentially qualify for copyright/database right protection, who is the owner of the databases, whether additional contractual protection is required with the party data is being shared, whether there are any licences to use the databases, whether it is complying with its obligations under data protection legislation etc. The borderless nature of cyberspace renders the sharing of online data even more complicated given that legal outcomes may differ between countries and thus the abovementioned rights may be enforceable in one country but not another.

4. CONCLUSION

Our experience of using the Web Observatory 'in the wild' suggests that many challenges lie ahead for the Web Observatory vision. The Web Observatory must demonstrate an ability to provide value to its stakeholders if it is to succeed in facilitating data exchange and research [1]. This point applies both on the individual and on the organizational level. "Whatever metric is used to value return on investment it need not be a financial value in itself but must be translatable into one. Otherwise, the funding of exchange systems like Observatories will remain fundamentally detached from the value created in the exchange" [1]. If the goal of Web observatories is to encourage and facilitate the sharing of data, it is essential that there is some incentive for data to be shared. It is imperative that the value of data exchanges can be framed in terms of measurable return on investment [1].

5. ACKNOWLEDGMENTS

This study was part of an ongoing collaboration between the University of Tsinghua, People's Republic of China, KAIST Advanced Institute of Science and Technology, Republic of Korea and the University of Southampton, UK.

6. REFERENCES

[1] P. Booth, P. Gaskell, and C. Hughes, "The Economics of Data: Quality, Value & Exchange in Web Observatories," in *Proceedings of the 22Nd International Conference on World Wide Web Companion*, Republic and Canton of Geneva, Switzerland, 2013, pp. 1309–1316.

[2] V. Borkar, M. J. Carey, and C. Li, "Inside 'Big Data Management': Ogres, Onions, or Parfaits?," in *Proceedings of the 15th International Conference on Extending Database Technology*, New York, NY, USA, 2012, pp. 3–14.

[3] I. Brown, W. Hall, and L. Harris, "From Search to Observation," in *Proceedings of the 22Nd International Conference on World Wide Web Companion*, Republic and Canton of Geneva, Switzerland, 2013, pp. 1317–1320.

[4] T. Davies, "Web Observatories: The Governance Dimensions", *Open Data Impacts Blog*, October 9, 2013, http://www.opendataimpacts.net/2013/10/web-observatories-the-governance-dimensions/.

[5] D. De Roure, C. Hooper, M. Meredith-Lobay, K. Page, S. Tarte, D. Cruickshank, and C. De Roure, "Observing Social Machines Part 1: What to Observe?," in *Proceedings of the 22Nd International Conference on World Wide Web Companion*, Republic and Canton of Geneva, Switzerland, 2013, pp. 901–904.

[6] E. Diaz-Aviles, "Living Analytics Methods for the Web Observatory," in *Proceedings of the 22Nd International Conference on World Wide Web Companion*, Republic and Canton of Geneva, Switzerland, 2013, pp. 1321–1324.

[7] C. Gallen, "Some Considerations for a Web Observatory", in *1st International workshop on Building Web Observatories, ACM Web Science,* May 2013.

[8] H. Glaser, "Observing Observatories: Web Observatories should use Linked Data", in *1st International workshop on Building Web Observatories, ACM Web Science,* May 2013.

[9] M. J. K. Gloria, D. L. McGuinness, J. S. Luciano, and Q. Zhang, "Exploration in Web Science: Instruments for Web Observatories," in *Proceedings of the 22Nd International Conference on World Wide Web Companion*, Republic and Canton of Geneva, Switzerland, 2013, pp. 1325–1328.

[10] W. Hall and T. Tiropanis, "Web evolution and Web Science," *Computer Networks*, vol. 56, no. 18, pp. 3859–3865, Dec. 2012.

Insights From Brands in Facebook

Kyle Taylor
University of Iowa
Iowa City
krtaylor@eng.uiowa.edu

Omar Alonso
Microsoft Corp.
Mountain View, CA
omalonso@microsoft.com

ABSTRACT

Companies are increasingly turning to social media as a way to engage with their customers and to promote their brand and products. We analyzed the content of Facebook fan pages of the top 100 brands to gain insight into how companies utilize social media. These brands span 14 different categories from fashion and apparel to computer hardware. We find that different brands use different types of posts and get varying levels of engagement from users based on their business category. Interestingly, 45.53% of posts contained a reference to a company or a person with many of the companies referencing others.

Categories and Subject Descriptors

J.4 [**Computer Applications**]: Social and Behavioral Sciences

Keywords

Social media, electronic commerce, Facebook

1. INTRODUCTION

With over 70% of the Fortune 500 companies having a Facebook presence, companies are viewing Facebook as a legitimate platform for customer engagement and brand promotion. While there has been a wide range of research published on online social networks, analyzing how social networks are being utilized by companies has received little attention.

On Facebook, users can perform three actions on each post: like, comment, and share. Out of all of these, sharing is probably the most beneficial for a company because it results in the post being displayed in the user's friends news feed. This is effectively free advertising and promotion for the company and their products. Furthermore, in 2011 Facebook introduced fan pages, which dramatically changed how content is presented to users and is different from when the majority of the prior research was done. This structural

WebSci'14, June 23–26, 2014, Bloomington, IN, USA.
ACM 978-1-4503-2622-3/14/06.
http://dx.doi.org/10.1145/2615569.2615653.

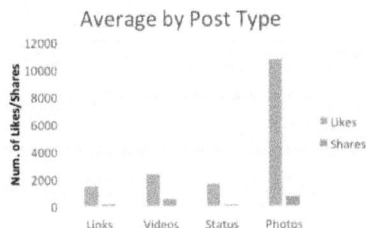

Figure 1: **The average number of likes and shares by post type, heavily skewed towards photos. Sharing is more consistent across all post types than likes.**

change minimized the appearance of comments on fan pages and confined any user posts to a single timeline item. Our research focuses on user engagement measured by likes and shares along with content analysis of the posts. Previous research on corporate fan pages have focused on post content and user engagement [2], but have not included analysis of sharing of posts by users. From a marketing perspective, a study that analyzes the influencing factors in terms of characteristics of the content communicated by the company is presented in [1].

2. DATA ANALYSIS AND FINDINGS

Wall posts from the Top 100 brands of 2012 listed by Interbrand[1] were collected from a 30-day period ending July 17, 2013 using Facebooks public API. Of the 100 companies, 94 had active pages (one notable exception was Apple), and 75 had posts that were publicly available though the Facebook API. A total of 2,650 posts were collected and analyzed. These posts consisted of only posts that were made by the companies and were publicly available.

There are four types of posts that a user could see when visiting a fan page: *status*, *links*, *photos*, and *videos*. Of those four types, photos consist of 70% of the posts and links are 26%, following by status (3%) and videos (1%). The average number of likes and shares by type is shown in Figure 1, and shows a similar bias towards photos being the most liked/shared. The other three types of post showed a similar level of engagement with themselves.

This can be further broken down into categories based on the company type, shown in Figures 2. The category that a company belongs to is self-selected from a predefined set

[1]http://www.interbrand.com/en/best-global-brands/2012/Best-Global-Brands-2012.aspx

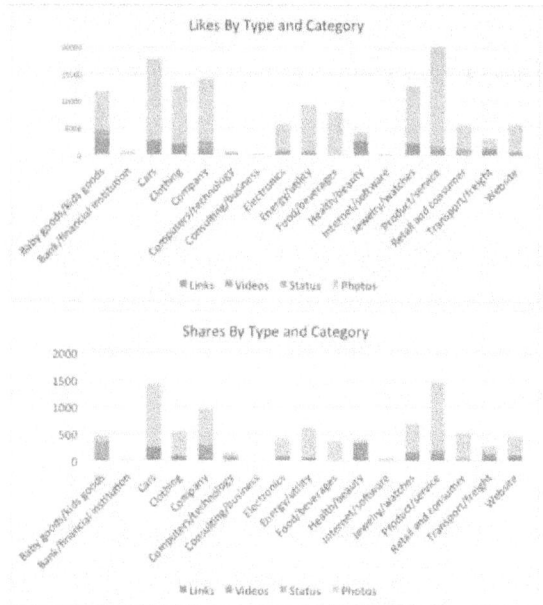

Figure 2: Likes and shares broken down by company and post type.

Brand	% Eng.	Page likes	Avg. # of likes
Allianz	11.68%	843	98
Nike	0.72%	15,169,480	109,699
Louis Vuitton	0.44%	14,599,240	64,695
Intel	0.39%	21,449,590	84,290

Table 1: Percent engagement of company pages as measured by the average number of likes divided by the number users who liked the page.

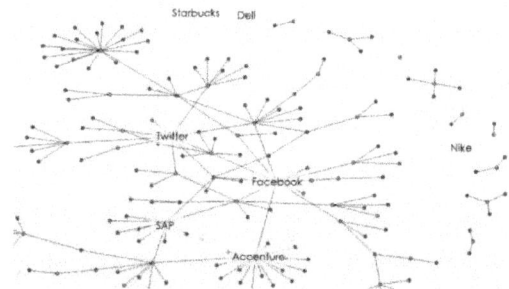

Figure 3: Graph showing the relationship between companies that mentioned others in their posts.

and are listed in the companies "about" section on the fan page. Some example categories are Clothing, Baby goods, Electronics, and Company (a generic term) – a total of 17 categories were listed in the 100 brands. If a company had multiple categories listed, then one was chosen arbitrarily. The number of shares and likes per category seemed to be similarly proportioned to the average number by type shown in Figure 1. Overall cars and products and services had the highest average likes and share, and also had a high percentage of engagement. Table 1 shows the engagement by brand for a sample of the data set.

Engagement was measure by the average likes divided by the total number of users who have liked the page. Baby goods had a high number of status updates that were shared, and upon further investigation, it was determined that a large portion of their status updates contained coupons. Allianz was considered an outlier because the because of the relatively few number of page likes compared to the rest of the companies, with an overall average engagement of 0.29%.

The likes and shares can be further broken down by post type (Figures 2). The only company that was heavily skewed by type and category was Pampers, which was the only company listed in the Baby goods and services with an overall average engagement of 0.29%. Most of the status updates were coupon offers and also consisted of fill in the blank questions that resulted in high engagement of the fans.

We are also interested in studying the presence of entities in the posts for identifying specific relationships based on entity types likes names, companies, organizations, and location to name a few. All posts were processed using an internal Named-Entity Recognizer (NER) tagger. The most frequent type of entity mentioned were company names (23.37%), followed by person (22.16%), date (18.33%), and location (15.78%). This distribution is expected because brand names are often mentioned preceding product names such as Honda CR-V or Samsung Galaxy S.

We also computed the number of times an entity was mentioned on Facebook, but does not allow us to understand the relationship between companies. To investigate this, a graph was made that maps the relationship between the entities based on the content of their posts. In the graph shown in Figure 3, red vertices are the companies in the Top 100 brands, blue veritices are other companies not in that list. Edges connect companies that were mentioned in at least one of their posts. Both Twitter and Facebook were also discussed in others' posts, but companies like Dell, Starbucks and Nike did not mention any other company. Exploring the graph of companies can be useful for determining relationships amongst companies, sectors, markets, and see how those related to other factors outside of social media such as stock price.

3. CONCLUSIONS

We conducted an exploratory study on Facebook pages from a pure electronic commerce perspective focusing on top brands. Our analysis shows that the majority of posts were photos and those were also the most liked and shared. The number of engaged fans was relatively low (0.29%), but we could not determine how consistently engaged the users were. Based on the NER analysis, we can see that a large number of the companies mentioned others (23.37%)

4. REFERENCES

[1] I. Cvijikj, F. Michahelles. Online engagement factors on Facebook brand pages. *Social Netw. Analys. Mining* 3(4), 2013, pp. 843-861.
[2] L. de Vries, S. Gensler, P. Leeflang. Popularity of Brand Posts on Brand Fan Pages: An Investigation of the Effects of Social Media Marketing. *Journal of Interactive Marketing*. 26(2), 2012, pp. 83–91.

A Web Observatory for the Machine Processability of Structured Data on the Web

Wouter Beek
VU University Amsterdam
De Boelelaan 1081a
Amsterdam, The Netherlands
w.g.j.beek@vu.nl

Paul Groth
VU University Amsterdam
De Boelelaan 1081a
Amsterdam, The Netherlands
p.t.groth@vu.nl

Stefan Schlobach
VU University Amsterdam
De Boelelaan 1081a
Amsterdam, The Netherlands
k.s.schlobach@vu.nl

Rinke Hoekstra
VU University Amsterdam
De Boelelaan 1081a
Amsterdam, The Netherlands
rinke.hoekstra@vu.nl

ABSTRACT

General human intelligence is needed in order to process content on the Web of Documents. On the Web of Data (WoD), content is intended to be machine-processable as well. But the extent to which a machine is able to navigate, access, and process the WoD has not been extensively researched. We present LOD Observer, a web observatory that studies the Web from a machine processor's point of view. We do this by reformulating the five star model of Linked Open Data (LOD) publishing in quantifiable terms. Secondly, we built an infrastructure that allows the model's criteria to be quantified over existing datasets. Thirdly, we analyze a significant snapshot of the WoD using this infrastructure and discuss the main problems a machine processor encounters.

Categories and Subject Descriptors

E.m [**Data**]: Miscellaneous; H.3.5 [**Information Systems**]: Information Storage and Retrieval—*On-line Information Services*

Keywords

Web Observatory; Machine processing; Web of Data; Linked Open Data

1. PROBLEM STATEMENT

There is an increasing amount of structured and semi-structured data available on the Web [4]. This data is made available in a variety of formats[1]. Initiatives such as the Open Knowledge Foundation (OKFN) and the Linking Open Data (LOD) community have promoted the release of data in an open fashion with the explicit goal of facilitating ease of reuse by others.

WebSci'14, June 23–26, 2014, Bloomington, IN, USA.
ACM http://dx.doi.org/10.1145/2615569.2615654.

Table 1: Five Star Linked Open Data

⋆	Make your data available on the web with an open license.
⋆⋆	Make it available as machine-readable structured data (e.g. excel instead of image scan of a table).
⋆⋆⋆	As above, plus use a non-proprietary format (e.g. CSV instead of excel).
⋆⋆⋆⋆	As above, plus use open standards from W3C to identify things, so that people can point at them.
⋆⋆⋆⋆⋆	As above, plus link your data to other people's data to provide context.

While facilitating reuse by humans is important, one of the initial aims of the Web of Data was that data be accessible and usable by machines in an *automatic fashion* [3]. Indeed, the W3C set of standards for exposing data on the Web is specifically designed to enable machine reasoning [5]. However, the data currently available is often far from machine-friendly. Even data made available using Semantic Web standards is rife with quality issues making them difficult to process by machines [6].

2. 5-STAR DATA

In 2006 Tim Berners-Lee published an opinion piece on LOD publishing [2], which became known as the "5 star model". This model (Table 1) quickly obtained the status of a manifesto for *the right way* to publish data: webby, machine readable, non-proprietary, standards conformant and linked.

Now, 7 years later, the community tends to believe that LOD publishing according to the 5-star model has become the de facto standard. There are three problems with this claim, though. First, as the manifesto is just a manifesto it is conceptual rather than operational. This means that there is no simple checklist to which datasets have to comply in order to receive the 5 star predicate. The lack of such explicit criteria implies that investigating adherence to the manifesto is impossible to automate, which then means that claims about success or failure of LOD publishing remain vague and difficult to quantify.

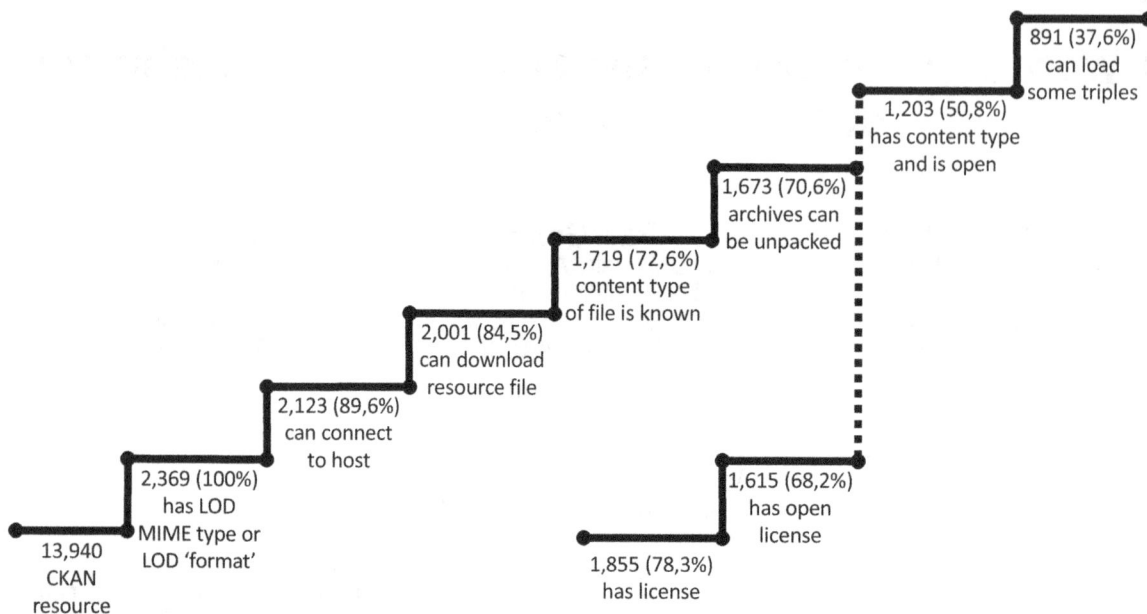

Figure 1: A 'staircase' overview of the succes rates of the various tasks a machine agent has to perform in order to retrieve LOD. The second stair from the left is the sample we have chosen to run our script on (set to 100%); the percentages that appear in the other stairs are relative to this number. The stair in the top right corner shows that 37,6% of the Datahub resources are fully machine-processsable.

3. CONTRIBUTIONS

We tackle the problem of providing an up-to-date view on the machine friendliness of the Web of Data. We address this problem in three ways: first we argue for an operationalization of the 5 criteria for LOD publishing from the manifesto. With this operationalization, checking for compliance with LOD principles can now be automated. To this end we implement a Web Observatory, called LOD Observer, which collects and analyses thousands of datasets, and measures and reports on their machine friendliness. This allows us to focus on specific aspects that prevent a dataset from being consumed and processed by a software agent. This analysis (Figure 1) gives a far more detailed and shaded picture of the state of LOD publishing than previous analyses have provided. These results show that in its current state the Web of Data is not yet machine friendly.

We have run our operationlized Web Observatory on a specific CKAN repository: Datahub (`http://datahub.io/`). It contains 13,940 descriptions of data documents, 2,369 of which can be identified as containing LOD based on MIME content type mappings. From this sample, 2,123 data documents (89,6%) have a host to which LOD Observer can connect, and 2,001 (84,5%) have a data file that can be retrieved by using the designated communications protocol (e.g. HTTP(S)). For the sample of 2,369 resources LOD Observer retrieved, 540 (22.8%) did not have a license associated with it. 240 (10.1%) resources have a closed license, and 1,615 (68.2%) resources have an open license. Not all files with an associated open license have syntactically well-formed contents. LOD Observer can load some triples (i.e. one or more) for 891 resources, or 37,6% of the original sample.

4. CONCLUSION

We conclude that in its current state, much of the LOD available on the Web is far from reaching the 5-star level. This is not just a technical issue but a social issue where the dynamics of the Web's social technical system have not reached a point where machine friendly data is widely available. By providing an observatory on the state of the machine processability of Web data, we hope to guide interventions at both the technical and social level. Additionally, this observatory will help in tracking the outcome of those interventions.

5. REFERENCES

[1] M. D. Adelfio and H. Samet. Schema extraction for tabular data on the web. *Proc. VLDB Endow.*, 6(6):421–432, Apr. 2013.

[2] T. Berners-Lee. Rdf schema 1.1. Technical report, 2006.

[3] T. Berners-Lee, J. Hendler, and O. Lassila. The semantic web. *Scientific American*, 2001.

[4] N. Dalvi, A. Machanavajjhala, and B. Pang. An analysis of structured data on the web. *Proc. VLDB Endow.*, 5(7):680–691, Mar. 2012.

[5] P. Hayes and B. McBridge. RDF semantics. Technical report, W3C, 2004.

[6] A. Hogan, A. Harth, A. Passant, S. Decker, and A. Polleres. Weaving the pedantic web. In C. Bizer, T. Heath, T. Berners-Lee, and M. Hausenblas, editors, *LDOW*, volume 628 of *CEUR Workshop Proceedings*. CEUR-WS.org, 2010.

Analysing the Duration of Trending Topics in Twitter Using Wikipedia

Tuan Tran, Mihai Georgescu, Xiaofei Zhu, Nattiya Kanhabua

L3S Research Center / Leibniz Universität Hannover, Germany

{ttran, georgescu, zhu, kanhabua}@L3S.de

ABSTRACT

The analysis of trending topics in Twitter is a goldmine for a variety of studies and applications. However, the contents of topics vary greatly from daily routines to major public events, enduring from a few hours to weeks or months. It is thus helpful to distinguish trending topics related to real-world events with those originated within virtual communities. In this paper, we analyse trending topics in Twitter using Wikipedia as reference for studying the provenance of trending topics. We show that among different factors, the duration of a trending topic characterizes exogenous Twitter trending topics better than endogenous ones.

Categories and Subject Descriptors

H.3.4 [**Systems and Software**]: [Information networks]

General Terms

Algorithms, Experimentation

Keywords

Twitter, Wikipedia, time series, temporal analysis

1. INTRODUCTION

Recently recognized as an important channel for instant updates about real-world incidents, information in Twitter often exhibits spikes during prominent events such as the Super Bowl. Existing methods detect and track real-world events reported in Twitter typically through the volume of posts [3, 2]. However, the lack of contextual information from resources other than Twitter sphere makes these methods unable to identify whether trending topics truly reflect real-world events, or just "virtual" topics that stay within Twitter only (e.g. spontaneous meme such as "#uFromLAif") . This misleads systems towards spam topics, while missing other potential events. In this work, we propose a new framework to analyse the provenance of Twitter trending topics, by exploiting background information

WebSci'14, June 23–26, 2014, Bloomington, IN, USA.

ACM 978-1-4503-2622-3/14/06..

from Wikipedia. Intuitively, information in Wikipedia is more reliable and focused as compared with Twitter. Previous work [3, 2] proposed using hashtag to predict the future behaviour of trending topics in Twitter. Unlike previous work, we predict how long it takes for a trending topic to saturate after a peak. Our exploratory analysis shows that duration is a stronger signal to indicate the long-term influence of a hashtag than peak volumes, and distinguish better endogenous and exogenous topics.

2. METHODOLOGY

Datasets. From Wikipedia, we obtain the English revision history dump on 30 Nov. 2012 (380 million updates of 4 million articles), and the Wikipedia page view log. We use the TREC Tweets2011 corpus[1], which has 16 million public tweets sampled from 23 Jan. to 8 Feb. 2011. Volumes are aggregated to daily level.

Burst and Duration. To define a trending hashtag, we employ a simplified strategy to detect bursts in a time series as follows. For each time point t with the value $n(t)$, we look back at preceding k values, and claim t a peak if the current value is l-time standard deviations higher than the mean value of the preceding window: $n(t) \geq l\sqrt{(n(t-i)-\mu)^2} + \mu, i = \overline{1,k}$ where μ is the mean of k variables $n(t-i)$. We measure the duration as the distance (number of days) from the first peak to the closest day where the hashtag volume goes under a threshold τ. If the hashtag has several peaks, the duration is the average. We observe that $k = 3, l = 3$ and $\tau = 10$ give the most intuitive peak outcomes in Tweets2011.

We get only hashtags with more than 40 tweets in at least one day, and choose 628 random hashtags, amounting for 672,580 tweets. For each hahstag, assessors are presented with the set of peak days and top 50 tweets on each day. The assessors then use keywords, mentions, abbreviations, etc. in the tweets and use the published days to query a search engine and Wikipedia. Each hashtag is annotated as whether the related information can be found on the Web (exogenous), and further whether it is found on Wikipedia (ongoing, otherwise breaking event). To prevent including future information in the Wikipedia dataset, we start with matching articles as seeds, process their revisions of the corresponding days, and include all outgoing linked articles to the study. In the end, we have 275 hashtags about endogenous topics, 353 about exogenous topics, in which 231 are breaking events (information found on the Web but not in Wikipedia in the peak day) and 122 ongoing topics.

---

[1] http://trec.nist.gov/data/tweets

	FullSet		Endo		Breaking		Ongoing	
	WM	TwiNER+AIDA	WM	TwiNER+AIDA	WM	TwiNER+AIDA	WM	TwiNER+AIDA
Baseline	0.5865	0.5865	0.4167	0.4167	**0.6333**	**0.6333**	0.5444	0.5444
wstatic	0.7242	0.6912	0.6234	0.6190	0.6292	0.5801	0.5667	0.5590
wview	0.7284	0.6976	**0.7382**	0.7146	0.6333	0.5711	0.5667	0.5616
wedit	0.7383	0.6882	0.7355	0.7192	0.6333	0.5825	0.5731	0.5684
wstatic+wview	0.7355	0.7012	0.5612	0.6018	0.6250	0.5804	0.5625	0.5718
wstatic+wedit	**0.7411**	0.7134	0.6345	0.6129	0.6250	0.5727	**0.5778**	0.5645
wview+wedit	0.7346	0.7035	0.7337	**0.7682**	0.6333	0.5705	0.5670	0.5691
wstatic+wview+wedit	0.7374	**0.7276**	0.4333	0.4212	0.6250	0.5793	0.5767	**0.5792**

Table 1: Accuracy of hashtag saturation prediction in Tweets2011

Duration Prediction. We propose a framework that, given a hashtag h peaked on day t_0, can predict the saturation length $L(t, h)$. As finding an exact value of L is difficult and often not necessary, we propose to classify the range which L falls in. For the Tweets2011 dataset (spanning 3 weeks), the range is defined as: $[1]$ (last only 1 day), $[2\text{-}3]$, $[4\text{-}7]$ (last longer than 3 days to 1 week), $[7\text{-}14]$ (last longer than 1 week to 2 weeks), $[14\text{-}21]$ (last longer than 2 but less than 3 weeks), $[0 \text{ or } 22+]$ (last more than 3 weeks or the hashtag is continuous).

Entity Linking. For each hashtag h and the peak day t_0, we concatenate all the tweets in the order of published time, and use existing tools to link to a set of Wikipedia entities. As a supervised approach, we use WikipediaMiner [2], and as an unsupervised approach, we use TwiNER [1] to identify entities in tweets, and AIDA[3] to disambiguate the entities.

Type	Features
Hashtag	(1) Hashtag length, (2) No. of segmented words in the hashtag, (3) (binary) if it has digits, (4) if it collocates with other hashtags, (5) no. of collocating hashtags, (6) fraction of capitalized characters in the hashtag
Tweets	(1)-(4) fraction of tweets having URLs/hashtags/ mentions/emoticons, (5)-(8) fraction of URLs/hashtags/ mentions/emoticons over tokens, (9) no. of distinct users, (10) average token length per tweet, (11) fraction of retweets, (12) 3-d emoticon vectors of tweets
Wiki static	(1) no. of matching Wikipedia articles, (2) no. of persons, (3) no. of locations, (4)-(5) maximal/average authority score of Wikipedia pages
Wiki Temporal	(1)-(4) if the edit/view count increase in all/any Wikipedia articles that match the hashtags, (5)-(8) minimal/maximl length of increase chains in view/edit count, (9) fraction of Wikipedia revisions that have URLs

Table 2: Features used for prediction

Model Features. We define 40 features, grouped in four categories as described in Table 2. The Hashtag and Tweets types are derived from previous work [3, 2] and used as the baseline. We propose several features extracted from matching Wikipedia entities to enhance the contextual knowledge. For instance, the authority score of an entity measures how importance it is w.r.t. to other entities: $authority(w) = \frac{|IN(w)|}{|OUT(w)|}$, with IN and OUT are incoming and outgoing link sets of the snapshot of article w on day t.

3. EXPERIMENTS

We conducted experiments on both the entire set of 48,803 hashtags (FullSet) in Tweets2011 and the annotated sample sets, each with the baseline and with Wikipedia feature types (static, view, edit) incrementally added. We used LibSVM[4] to train the classification model.

[2] http://wikipedia-miner.cms.waikato.ac.nz
[3] https://github.com/yago-naga/aida
[4] http://www.csie.ntu.edu.tw/~cjlin/libsvm

Results. Table 1 summarizes the accuracy of the classification on different feature settings. For the FullSet, using both entity-linking systems, we see a clear improvement when incorporating Wikipedia information as features. Wikipedia edit history and Wikipedia structure information contribute the most to the increase in accuracy. Moreover, the performance of TwiNER+AIDA system is lower. This is explained by the fact that TwiNER is unsupervised and has inferior quality, and that AIDA is backed by the YAGO knowledge base, which only contains a subset of Wikipedia articles. Again, this emphasizes the importance of adding more information from Wikipedia to improve the prediction.

The performance varies on different kinds of trending topics. For endogenous topics, the result is unstable with both entity linking outcomes; adding different Wikipedia features sometimes harms the performance (although it does improve in general). This is because endogenous hashtags merely diffuse information within Twitter communities, and mentioned entities in tweets will not correlate well with the main content of the Twitter topic. For breaking topics, both systems do not gain any improvements with Wikipedia features; this confirms the fact that breaking events in Twitter spread quicker than in Wikipedia. For ongoing topics, incorporating Wikipedia information does effectively improve the performance of the prediction in both entity linking settings. Methods based on WikipediaMiner perform best with Wikipedia static and edit features, and methods based on TwiNER+AIDA perform best on the full combination. Last but not least, the general prediction performance of the systems can gain significant benefit when we increase the size of our data (from sample sets to FullSet). This positively supports the idea that despite the small size of the annotated dataset, our system does not overfit and has a good generality.

Acknowledgements. This work was partially funded by the European Commission for the FP7 projects CUbRIK and ForgetIT (under grants No. 287704 and No. 600826 respectively), and the ERC Advanced Grant ALEXANDRIA under grant No. 339233.

4. REFERENCES

[1] C. Li, J. Weng, Q. He, Y. Yao, A. Datta, A. Sun, and B.-S. Lee. Twiner: named entity recognition in targeted twitter stream. In *SIGIR*, pages 721–730, 2012.

[2] Z. Ma, A. Sun, and G. Cong. On predicting the popularity of newly emerging hashtags in Twitter. *JASIST*, 64(7):1399–1410, 2013.

[3] O. Tsur and A. Rappoport. What's in a hashtag?: content based prediction of the spread of ideas in microblogging communities. In *WSDM*, pages 643–652, 2012.

Quantifying Collective Mood by Emoticon Networks

Kazutoshi Sasahara

Graduate School of Information Science, Nagoya University
Furo-cho Chikusa-ku Nagoya 464-8601, Japan
sasahara@nagoya-u.jp

ABSTRACT

Emoticon networks are proposed to quantify the nontrivial nature of collective mood in social media. The nodes represent Japanese emoticons and adjectives, and directed links represent information flows among them, which are measured by effective transfer entropy. The emoticon networks before the 2011 Japan earthquake show one-directional chains of emoticons and adjectives; in contrast, those after the earthquake exhibit a strange loop as well as uninteractive nodes.

Categories and Subject Descriptors

J.4 [**Computer Applications**]: Social and Behavioral Sciences

General Terms

Collective mood, emoticons, social media, transfer entropy

1. INTRODUCTION

Collective mood linked with real-life events often emerge in online social media, the observations of which may provide novel insights into human nature [2]. To quantify mood at the macro level, previous studies have mainly focused on linguistic expressions related to emotion in a sentiment analysis. As several studies have shown, however, online textural communication involves not only linguistic expressions but also emoticons—symbolic representations of facial expressions—in order to convey one's emotional information [4]. Simple emoticons such as ' :-) ' (a smiley face) are used in written English, whereas a wide variety of emoticons are used in written Japanese, e.g., (^_^), (^o^), \ (^ ▽ ^) ╱, (=^_^=). These express positive yet slightly different emotional information. Here, we focus on the interactions between linguistic representations and emoticons in Japanese tweets, thereby constructing "emoticon networks." With this method, we demonstrate the structural properties of the collective mood before and after the 2011 Japan earthquake.

2. METHODS

Tweet Collection

We continuously collected user timelines between April 2011 and January 2012 by snowball sampling using Twitter REST API [1]. We obtained a dataset of about 0.5 billion tweets from about 440,000 users (mostly Japanese) [5]. Each tweet data contains a text message and metadata, including the timestamp of the tweet, user name and profile.

Emoticon Networks

Emoticon networks visualize interactions between verbal and nonverbal expressions: nodes are Japanese emoticons and adjectives, and directed links represent information flows among these nodes. First, we select candidate emoticons by reference to Wikipedia[2] and a Japanese emoticon site[3], and then corresponding Japanese adjectives. While some emoticons are quite popular, others are rarely used in tweet conversation, and therefore we have to know their frequency distributions before selecting candidates. To this end, we examined 528 symbol representations of emotion, including emoticons and Kanji characters in all of the collected tweets.

Next, we analyze tweets within a period of interest, measuring the frequencies of candidate emoticons and the related adjectives as well as their time stamps, which are covered to the time-series of their relative frequencies by resampling hourly and normalizing daily. We discretize the time-series of the relative frequencies of emoticons and adjectives in the same manner of permutation entropy [1]. Let us suppose $X = \{4, 7, 9, 10, 6, 11, 3\}$ would be a time-series of tweet counts, and the window size would be set to two. We compare these data two by two with an overlap, and assign the order: e.g., 4 and 7 become 12, while 10 and 6 become 21. Consequently, the original data are discretized as $\{12, 12, 12, 21, 12, 21\}$, which are used for later computation.

From every pair of the discretized time-series of emotions and adjectives, we compute the effective transfer entropy [3, 6] as defined below.

$$ET_{Y \to X} = T_{Y \to X} - \overline{T}_{Y' \to X},$$

$$T_{Y \to X} = \sum_{x_{n+1}, x_n, y_n} p(x_{n+1}, x_n, y_n) \log_2 \frac{p(x_{n+1}|x_n, y_n)}{p(x_{n+1}|x_n)}.$$

Here, $ET_{Y \to X}$ is the effective transfer entropy from the time-series Y to X, which modifies the original transfer en-

---

[1] https://dev.twitter.com/docs/api/
[2] http://en.wikipedia.org/wiki/List_of_emoticons/
[3] http://japaneseemoticons.net

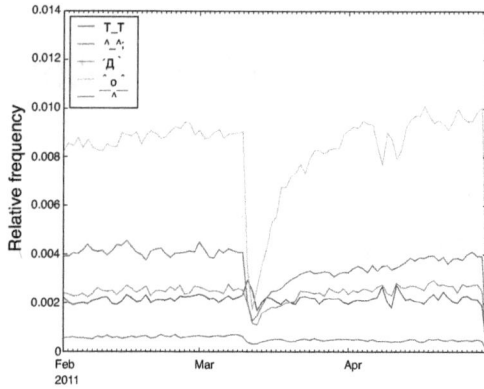

Figure 1: Time-series of emoticons before and after the 2011 Japan earthquake.

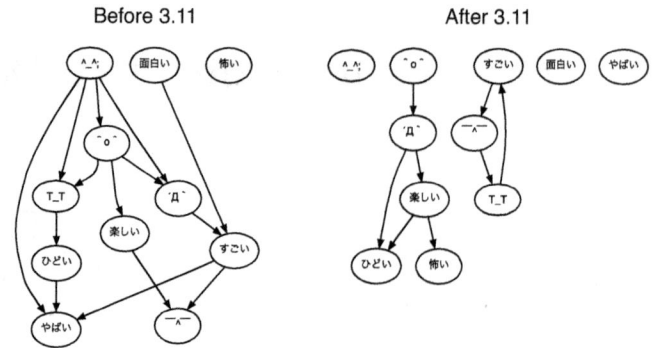

Figure 2: Emoticon networks before and after the 2011 Japan earthquake.

tropy T by subtracting the apparent T based on the 1000 times randomly-shuffled time-series Y'. Several studies have shown that transfer entropy is useful to characterize online social data in terms of information flows [7]. To construct emoticon networks, we use the selected emoticons and adjectives as nodes, and the effective transfer entropy with positive values as directed links.

3. RESULTS

For the purpose of demonstration, we use five emoticons {T_T, ˆ_ˆ;, ´Д`, ˆoˆ, ‾ˆ‾}, which are popular ones in the frequency distributions, and six related adjectives {すごい (cool), やばい (cool/bad), 怖い (scary), 楽しい (fun), ひどい (awful), 面白い (interesting)}. Figure 1 shows the time-series of the relative frequencies of these emoticons from February to April in 2011. As shown, except T_T, the frequencies of other emoticons rapidly drop after the Japan earthquake (March 11, 2011); in particular, the frequency of ˆoˆ does not return to prior levels for a few weeks. The result implies that after the earthquake, people were so depressed that they could not (or intentionally did not) use positive emoticons in tweet conversations.

Figure 2 demonstrates how these emoticons and adjectives interact during one week before and after the 2011 Japan earthquake. Before the earthquake there are specific one-directional chains in the emoticon network (left): a positive information flow such as ˆ_ˆ;→ˆoˆ→ 楽しい (fun), and a negative one such as T_T→ ひどい (awful)→ やばい (bad). It is important to note that やばい has an incoming link from すごい (cool) and ひどい (awful), since やばい can be positive and negative depending on context. There is only one node without interactions (i.e., 怖い (scary)).

In contrast, after the earthquake there is a strange loop of すごい (cool)→ ‾ˆ‾ →T_T→ すごい in the emoticon network (right), which is virtually indecipherable; there are rare connections 楽しい (fun) with ひどい (awful) and 怖い (scary), which are unlikely to happen under normal conditions. Furthermore, there are more nodes isolated from interactions, such as ˆ_ˆ; and 面白い (fun). These structural differences can reflect the public mood swing trigged by the 2011 Japan Earthquake. To address the collective mood on this event in detail, a further investigation is required with more emoticons and adjectives.

4. DISCUSSION

As demonstrated, emoticon networks can be useful in exploring collective mood in social media. It is, however, difficult to evaluate whether or not the resulting emoticon networks are appropriate. One possible way is to compare emoticon networks with co-occurrence networks where nodes denote emoticons and adjectives, and when these co-occur in the same tweets undirected links are attached. Comparison of these networks may shed lights on the nontrivial nature of collective mood for the target event.

5. ACKNOWLEDGMENTS

This research was supported by JSPS KAKENHI Grant Number 24700291 and the Grant-in-Aid from The Hori Sciences and Arts Foundation.

6. REFERENCES

[1] C. Bandt and B. Pompe. Permutation Entropy: A Natural Complexity Measure for Time Series. *Physical Review Letters*, Vol. 88, No. 17, p. 174102, 2002.

[2] P. S. Dodds, K. D. Harris, I. M. Kloumann, C. A. Bliss, and C. M. Danforth. Temporal Patterns of Happiness and Information in a Global Social Network: Hedonometrics and Twitter. *PLoS ONE*, Vol. 6, No. 12, p. e26752, 2011.

[3] R. Marschinski and H. Kantz. Analysing the Information Flow between Financial Time Series. *The European Physical Journal B*, Vol. 30, No. 2, pp. 275–281, 2002.

[4] J. Park, .V Barash, C. Fink, and M. Cha. Emoticon Style: Interpreting Differences in Emoticons Across Cultures. *Proceedings of the Seventh International AAAI Conference on Weblogs and Social Media*, 2013.

[5] K. Sasahara, Y. Hirata, M. Toyoda, M. Kitsuregawa, and K. Aihara. Quantifying Collective Attention from Tweet Stream. *PLoS ONE*, Vol. 8, No. 4, p. e61823, 2013.

[6] T. Schreiber. Measuring Information Transfer. *Physical Review Letters*, Vol. 85, pp. 461–464, 2000.

[7] G. Ver Steeg and A. Galstyan. Information Transfer in Social media. *WWW '12 Proceedings of the 21st international conference on World Wide Web*, 2012.

Towards Laws of the 3D-printable Design Web

Spiros Papadimitriou
Rutgers University
New Brunswick, NJ, USA
spapadim@business.rutgers.edu

Evangelos Papalexakis
Carnegie Mellon University
Pittsburgh, PA, USA
epapalex@cs.cmu.edu

ABSTRACT

This is a preliminary descriptive study of a new form of digital content: 3D-printable designs of physical things. We introduce a new dataset collected from one of the most popular sites for publishing and sharing physical object designs. We describe the data and its properties, and present an interactive visualization to facilitate further exploration of this space.

1. INTRODUCTION

Very recently we have witnessed an explosive growth of 3D printing, and rapid manufacturing at the consumer level in general. Almost every day we see examples of the technology and its application in the news. Even though much of this is still fraught with some hype (such as dreams of Star Trek replicators, or noble but perhaps utopian visions of "democratizing manufacturing"), the fact that 3D printing has substantially lowered barriers to entry in designing and making physical objects is undeniable (as one of the authors himself can attest). Part of the reason is that now objects can be designed and manipulated in a computer. However, like other forms of digital content (e.g., documents, software, music), this is only part of the story: digital representation also enables online sharing and collaboration [2, 3]. A prime example of the potential of all these technologies is the design of consumer-grade 3D printers themselves [1] which, perhaps unsurprisingly, was what many early adopters of the technology used it for.

However, despite hearing about 3D printing daily, very few studies have looked at the digital content of physical things, and the processes that generate it. This work is a first step towards covering this gap.

2. DATA AND OBSERVATIONS

In this work we aim to introduce the overall context and dataset to a broader audience, rather than analyze a single specific aspect of the data; this is beyond the present scope. After a general description of the domain and collected data, we then highlight some initial observations, which we believe are interesting, and perhaps surprising, from a web science perspective.

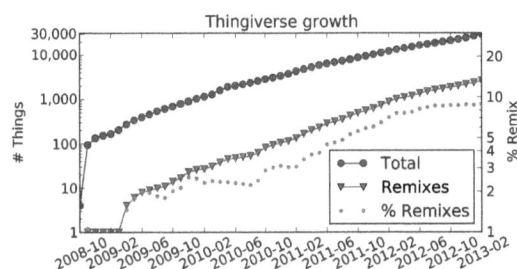

Figure 1: Thingiverse and remix growth (log).

Thingiverse is a site for publishing and sharing physical object designs, which combines aspects of a publishing platform and social network. Although many similar sites have recently appeared, Thingiverse is one of the earliest and by far the most popular, for both the designer and user communities. The data contains 36,504 public things. Although "things" can be anything, the *vast* majority (almost 90%) are designs that can be 3D printed.

The two main entities on Thingiverse are *things* and *users*. Things are *created* by one user (multiple authors are not supported) and has a fixed creation date. Each thing also has text attributes, such as title, description, and, optionally, instructions. The creator has to classify it under one category among a predefined set and may, optionally, add free-form text tags. Finally, each thing typically has a number of files associated with it; 89% of all things have a 3D mesh representation and, out of these, 18% have an algebraic representation as a constructive solid geometry (CSG) expression, typically in the OpenSCAD language.

Users can interact with things in a number of ways, which includes *comments*, *likes*, and *makes* (a stronger form of like, which requires building a thing and uploading one or more photos). Although only creators can add tags, other users can create named *collections* and add things to them.

Finally, creators can indicate that their design *remixes* another thing. This is a directed many-to-many relationship, from a *source* which is remixed into a *derived* thing. The exact semantics of a remix are up to the creator, but the relationship is typically used to indicate some form of creative affinity. The aspect of remixing has been identified in other domains as well, where it often takes a more structured form (typically indicating a direct derivative or "branch"), and has been studied in the context of, e.g., videos [5], music [4], and educational programming language communities [6].

Doubling every six months. Figure 1 shows the total number of things over time (blue) which is growing expo-

Variable	Best predictors	Worst predictors
$\#Views$	$\#Likes : 43.1\text{–}44.6, \#DLs : 0.35\text{–}0.38, \overline{\#Views}' : 0.28\text{–}0.31$	$\overline{\#Make}'(p = 0.48), \overline{\#Remix}'(p = 0.06)$
$\#D/Ls$	$\#View : 0.20\text{–}0.21, \#Like : 8.5\text{–}9.8, \#Make : 42.0\text{–}50.1$	$\#Remix(p = 0.66), \overline{\#Remix}'(p = 0.51)$
$\#Likes$	$\#Views : 0.006, \#Make : 2.72\text{–}2.83, \overline{\#Likes}' : 0.42\text{–}0.46$	$\overline{\#Remix}'(p = 0.59), \overline{\#DLs}'(p = 0.27)$
$\#Makes$	$\#Likes : 0.074\text{–}0.077, \#Files : -0.13\text{–}0.11, \overline{\#Makes}' : 0.28\text{–}0.33$	$\overline{\#Remix}'(p = 0.99), \overline{\#DLs}'(p = 0.51)$
$\#Remix$	$\#Views : 0.0003, \mathbf{\#Remix}' : 0.18\text{–}0.27, \#Sources : 0.19\text{–}0.39$	$\overline{\mathbf{\#Make}}'(p = 0.71), \#DLs(p = 0.66)$

Table 1: Best and worst predictors for various features (overbars indicate averages over *other* things by the *same* designer); see text for discussion of highlights.

nentially, with a compound doubling time of 6.1 months! Furthermore, if we consider only remixes (green), then the growth rate far outpaces the overall rate, with a compound doubling time of 4.6 months. Even though remixing is a popular feature of Thingiverse and perhaps unique among similar sites, it is far from the reason of its existence, unlike other sites [4]. Despite this, the growth rate of remixing is impressive and, although bound to abate, there is no evidence that this is happening (red)[1].

Popularity: views vs. likes vs. makes. Table 1 summarizes the results of least-squares regression on measures of user actions. The table shows the top-3 best predictive features ($p < 0.01$, ranked by t-test scores) and 95% confidence intervals of corresponding regression coefficients, as well as the bottom-2 worst features.

The relative incidence of user actions depends on the relative effort required to take those actions. Therefore, we observe that roughly (order of magnitude) 100 views "contribute" one like in our linear models, and roughly 10 likes "contribute" a make. The first is not particularly surprising. However, the fact that only 10× likes contribute a make seems to suggest that users are actively seeking things, and have the means and motivation to actually *print* things that they have liked.

Another interesting and intuitive observation is that the number of files has a *negative* effect on makes. This provides evidence for the hypothesis that simpler things (consisting of fewer parts) are more likely to be made.

Sublinearities. Similar relationship between user actions has been observed in other domains [7]. These are also present in our data (Figure 2, exponential-size bucket smoothed), where we find more specifically that $\#Likes \propto \#Makes^{0.70}$ and $\#Views \propto \#Likes^{0.85}$.

Popular vs. generative: likes do not predict remixes. A more surprising finding is that typical measures of general popularity have little relation to whether a thing is remixed or not: (i) makes are, in fact, the worst predictor of number of remixes (also Figure 2 right); and (ii) in fact, the number of remixes is a *bad* predictor of almost everything, *except* of other remixes (Table 1)! This suggests that aspects of a design that make it broadly appealing are distinct from

---

[1]In fact, after the introduction of the Thingiverse Customizer, the rate has picked up even further.

aspects that make it inspiring and, furthermore, agrees with the author's personal experience that following remix links is more useful when looking for ideas, than when looking for utilitarian or fun things to print.

Interactive visualization. We have also developed an interactive visualization of the thing corpus, accessible at http://bitquill.net/make/remix, as a step towards further exploration and understanding of the data at an aggregate level. The visualization is based the excellent D3 Javascript library, with some preprocessing on the back-end to extract relevant aspects from the data. It is under active development and currently focuses on the thing remix graph. We encourage readers to browse the visualization. For example, how is an iPhone case with customized image engravings related to a 3D scan of Stephen Colbert's head, or to the Stanford bunny 3D model?

3. DISCUSSION AND CONCLUSION

Despite the explosive growth and rising importance of 3D printing, to the best of our knowledge there are very few data-driven studies [8] that try to understand it. Our work, which originally stems from one of the authors' involvement in 3D printing, introduces the overall context and dataset to a broader audience, and we identify and highlight observations, including: (i) explosive growth with a clear doubling law, and remixes outpacing general growth; (ii) sublinearity laws in the relationship between user actions; (iii) quantitative evidence for difference between generativity and popularity.

4. REFERENCES

[1] RepRap. reprap.org.

[2] C. Anderson. *Makers: The New Industrial Revolution.* Crown Business, 2012.

[3] Y. Benkler. *The Wealth of Networks.* Yale Press, 2006.

[4] G. Cheliotis and J. Yaw. An analysis of the social structure of remix culture. In *C&T*, 2009.

[5] N. Diakopoulos, K. Luther, Y. Medynskiy, and I. Essa. The evolution of authorship in a remix society. In *ACM HT*, 2007.

[6] B. M. Hill and A. Monroy-Hernández. The cost of collaboration for code and art: Evidence from a remixing community. In *CSCW*, 2013.

[7] D. Koutra, V. Koutras, B. A. Prakash, and C. Faloutsos. Patterns amongst competing task frequencies: Super-linearities, and Almond-DG. In *PAKDD*, 2013.

[8] H. Kyriakou and J. Nickerson. Idea inheritance, originality, and collective innovation. In *WIN*, 2013.

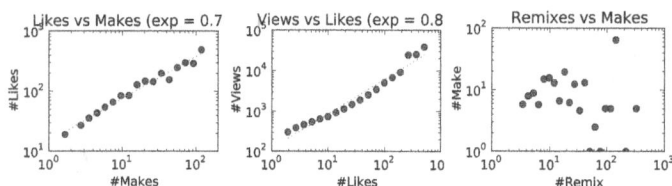

Figure 2: Likes, makes, and remixes.

A Cross-Modal Warm-Up Solution for the Cold-Start Problem in Collaborative Filtering Recommender Systems

Behnoush Abdollahi
Knowledge Discovery & Web Mining Lab,
University of Louisville
b.abdollahi@louisville.edu

Olfa Nasraoui
Knowledge Discovery & Web Mining Lab,
University of Louisville
olfa.nasraoui@louisville.edu

ABSTRACT

We present a cross-modal recommendation engine that leverages multiple domains of data while performing matrix factorization. We show how our approach has the potential to alleviate the cold-start problem for new items, one of the notorious limitations of Collaborative Filtering (CF) techniques.

Categories and Subject Descriptors

G.1.3 [**Sparse, structured, and very large systems (direct and iterative methods)**]: Numerical Linear Algebra; H.3.3 [**Information filtering**]: Information Search and Retrieval

Keywords

Collaborative Filtering; Non-negative Matrix Factorization

1. INTRODUCTION

Non-negative Matrix Factorization (NMF) [5] has recently gained popularity as a powerful technique for generating Collaborative Filtering (CF) recommendations [2]. Using matrix factorization, items, users and their attributes can be represented in a latent space and the recommendation task can be performed in this latent space. NMF has been used as a recommender system technique [3] to map both users and items to a joint latent space of k factors, where each user p_u, and item q_i, is represented as a vector of k elements. The user-item interaction can then be modeled as the dot product of their representation in the latent space, which estimates the interest of user p_u in item q_i, as follows:

$$\hat{r} = \mathbf{p}_u \mathbf{q}_i^T \qquad (1)$$

However, the rating matrix is usually very sparse, and when new users enter the system there is not enough information regarding their interest. Also, new items may have insufficient or even no ratings at all. The latter case is known

as the new item cold-start problem, which is a prevalent problem in CF recommender systems. Using multiple domains of data is one way to overcome this problem, typically within the scope of hybrid recommender systems. Combining information from multiple domains (ratings, item attributes, etc) has been used in cross-domain recommendation engines, such as [6, 8] which can transfer a learned model from the rating data to another rating domain. Koren et al. [4] used movie attributes and demographic data to build their NMF-based recommender systems. The latter model is a mixed model, that considers all data domains simultaneously. In contrast to the mixed model, our approach is based on an asymmetric multi-domain NMF-based model [1] that was recently proposed for multimodal image retrieval and annotation. Our NMF-based cross-modal CF recommender system leverages multiple domains of data to recommend even new items, thus overcoming the new item cold-start problem.

2. NON-NEGATIVE MATRIX FACTORIZATION (NMF)

Non-negative matrix factorization (NMF) is a family of algorithms where the non-negative data R is factorized into two non-negative matrices P and Q [5]

$$\mathbf{R}_{n \times m} \simeq \mathbf{P}_{n \times k} \mathbf{Q}_{m \times k}^T \qquad (2)$$

where k is the rank of matrices P and Q. In order to estimate P and Q, the Frobenius norm of the errors between the approximation PQ^T and the data matrix R is used as the cost function to be minimized

$$J_{NMF} = ||\mathbf{E}||_F^2 = || \mathbf{R} - \mathbf{P}\mathbf{Q}^{\mathbf{T}} ||_F^2 \qquad (3)$$

where $||\mathbf{E}||_F^2 = \sum_i \sum_j E_{ij}^2 = tr(\mathbf{E}^T \mathbf{E})$. This optimization problem can be solved using gradient descent algorithms.

3. PROPOSED APPROACH

3.1 Asymmetric NMF for Collaborative Filtering

In CF, the item attributes can be a valuable source of information to integrate into building a multi-domain model. In this work, we use multi-domain Asymmetric NMF to exploit multi-modal interactions between user ratings and other domains such as movie genre (for movie recommendation), and hence improve recommendations while solving the new item cold start problem. In Asymmetric NMF, the latent semantic space is first derived using the first domain, then follows an adaptation phase in which the second domain is utilized to fit the former latent space. This results in a common space where all domains co-exist.

For movie recommendation, the two domains are: Movie Genre (R_1 ($g \times m$)) and Movie Ratings (R_2 ($n \times m$)), where g is the number of genres, m is the number of movies, and n is the number of users. The two main steps of the algorithm are as follows:

1. Build a latent space model based on the Movie Genre domain: This step applies NMF to the Movie Genre matrix: $R_1 = P_1 Q^T$. In this formula, P_1 ($g \times k$) is the basis matrix for transforming the Genre data to the latent space and Q ($k \times m$) is the representation of the items (movies) in latent space.

2. Adapt the basis data in the latent space: $R_2 = P_2 Q^T$. In this step, Q is transferred as fixed latent factor coefficients from the first step and the ratings matrix is used to adapt the basis P_2 ($n \times k$) for the second domain consisting of the user-item ratings, and thus construct a combined latent space based on both the Movie Ratings and the Movie Genres. As a consequence, Q spans the semantic space of both ratings and item attributes.

4. EXPERIMENTS

We tested our approach on the MovieLens dataset [1]. The movies fall into 19 different genres, such as comedy, drama, etc. The ratings data has 100,000 ratings, on a scale of 1 to 5, for 1700 movies by 1000 users. We performed two experiments. In the first experiment, where we test the recommendation accuracy, a different percentage of the ratings data (from 5% to 50%) is selected randomly out of all ratings (1700×1000) and changed to unrated to serve as test data. The remaining percentage of data, in addition to the genre domain, are used in training. In the second experiment, we focus on the new item cold start problem. The test set is selected by sampling varying percentages from the 1700 movies (from 5% to 50%). Then the ratings of the selected test movies are changed to unrated to test the impact of new items. In addition to varying the percentage of test data, the number of factors, k, was varied. All the experiments were repeated 10 times and the average metrics are reported. We compared our method with the classical NMF as the baseline on the data used in Experiment 1. Figure 1 shows the Mean Square Error (MSE) for both experiments and the classical NMF with different percentages of test data. We also illustrate our results in Table 1 which shows the top 5 rated movies for two sample users and their top 5 recommended movies. The underlined recommended movies are new movies with no ratings available in the training data. The results show that Asymmetric NMF increases the accuracy of recommendations compared to the classical NMF. In the new movie cold-start case, our approach performed even better, while classical NMF cannot be applied for lack of any ratings.

---

[1] http://grouplens.org/datasets

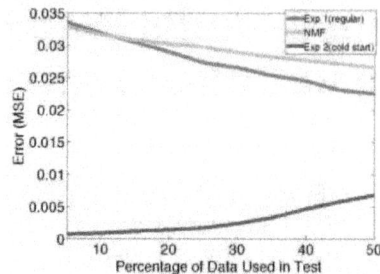

Figure 1: MSE vs. percentage of data as test

Table 1: Top 5 rated and recommended movies to 2 sample users. Underlined movies are unrated movies.

Model	Test user	Top 5 rated movies by the user	Top 5 recommended movies
Expt 1	User#1	**Braveheart (1995), Star Wars (1977), Pulp Fiction (1994)**, Stargate (1994), Crow The (1994)	**Star Wars (1977), Braveheart (1995)**, Raiders of the Lost Ark (1981), Terminator The (1984), **Pulp Fiction (1994)**
Expt 2	User#2	Star Wars (1977), Godfather The (1972), **Bottle Rocket (1996)**, Twelve Monkeys (1995), **When We Were Kings (1996)**	**Bottle Rocket (1996)**, Shallow Grave (1994), 2 Days in the Valley (1996), **When We Were Kings (1996)**, Blue in the Face (1995)

5. CONCLUSION

Cross-modal Asymmetric NMF provides an easy and accurate solution to the cold-start problem, a notorious problem plaguing traditional collaborative filtering recommender systems. We have also used this approach in other applications, such as cross-modal annotation for hashtag completion in tweets [7].

6. REFERENCES

[1] BEN-ABDALLAH, J., CAICEDO, J. C., GONZÁLEZ, F. A., AND NASRAOUI, O. Multimodal image annotation using non-negative matrix factorization. In *Web Intelligence* (2010), pp. 128–135.

[2] HERLOCKER, J. L., KONSTAN, J. A., BORCHERS, A., AND RIEDL, J. An algorithmic framework for performing collaborative filtering. In *SIGIR* (1999), pp. 230–237.

[3] KOREN, Y. Factorization meets the neighborhood: A multifaceted collaborative filtering model. *Proceedings of the 14th ACM SIGKDD* (2008), 426–434.

[4] KOREN, Y., BELL, R., AND VOLINSKY, C. Matrix factorization techniques for recommender systems. *IEEE Computer 42, 8* (2009), 30–37.

[5] LEE, D. D., AND SEUNG, H. S. Learning the parts of objects by non-negative matrix factorization. *Nature 401* (1999), 788–791.

[6] LI, B., YANG, Q., AND XUE, X. Transfer learning for collaborative filtering via a rating matrix generative model. *Proceedings of the 26th Annual International Conference on Machine Learning* (2009), 617–624.

[7] NUTAKKI, G. C., NASRAOUI, O., ABDOLLAHI, B., BADAMI, M., AND SUN, W. Distributed lda-based topic modeling and topic agglomeration in a latent space. In *SNOW 2014 Data Challenge, 23rd International World Wide Web Conference (WWW 2014)* (2014), pp. 17–24.

[8] PAN, W., XIANG, E., LIU, N., AND YANG, Q. Transfer learning in collaborative filtering for sparsity reduction. *Proceedings of the 24rd AAAI Conference on Artificial Intelligence* (2010), 425–434.

Online Sentiment-based Topic Modeling for Continuous Data Streams

Gopi Chand Nutakki
Knowledge Discovery & Web Mining Lab,
University of Louisville
g0nuta01@louisville.edu

Olfa Nasraoui
Knowledge Discovery & Web Mining Lab,
University of Louisville
olfa.nasraoui@louisville.edu

ABSTRACT

Continuous social text streams, such as tweets, provide a timeline of discussions. Topic modeling techniques such as Latent Dirichlet Allocation (LDA) have been used to extract the topics being discussed on social media streams. Recently, Online LDA has been proposed as a fast alternative for topic extraction, based on on-line stochastic optimization, while sentiment analysis is often used to track the polarity of posts. In this paper, we propose an online technique, integrating Online LDA and sentiment analysis to extract more refined polarity-aware topics within an online learning framework from continuous Twitter streams.

Categories and Subject Descriptors

H.2.8 [**Database Applications**]: Data Mining;
H.3.3 [**Information Search and Retrieval**]: Clustering

Keywords

Online LDA, sentiment analysis, social media, stream data.

1. INTRODUCTION

Among opinion mining tasks, sentiment classification [4] assigns a semantic orientation of a text as positive, negative or neutral. Sentiment classification models trained on one domain might not work well in another domain. Furthermore, in more fine-grained sentiment classification problems, such as involving sentiments on different topics, topic detection and sentiment classification are often performed in a two-stage pipeline process, by first detecting a topic/feature and then assigning a sentiment label to that particular topic [5, 6]. Continuous text streams provide a timeline of topics where new topics are created, while older topics evolve, decay or disappear over time. In this paper, we propose a hybrid technique that integrates sentiment detection with an Online LDA technique to extract refined topics from a continuous stream of tweets.

WebSci'14, June 23–26, 2014, Bloomington, IN, USA.
ACM 978-1-4503-2622-3/14/06.
http://dx.doi.org/10.1145/2615569.2615666 .

2. BACKGROUND

The Batch Variational Bayes LDA algorithm converges faster than batch collapsed Gibbs sampling LDA, but requires a full pass through the entire corpus[2, 3]. It is therefore not suited to cases where new data is constantly arriving. Hoffman, Blei et al.[3] proposed an Online Variational Inference algorithm that is even faster than the batch version, and where a stochastic optimization algorithm optimizes an objective using noisy estimates of its gradient. Variational inference replaces sampling with optimization in a manner that is analogous to the EM algorithm. Online LDA is an approximate posterior inference algorithm that can analyze massive collections of documents and converges faster [3]. Online LDA can be extended to handle an infinite vocabulary by using a generative process that is identical to LDA, except that instead of being drawn from a finite Dirichlet[7], the topics are drawn from a Dirichlet Process with base distribution G_0 over all possible words. In the LDA framework, topics are associated with documents, and words with topics. In order to model document sentiments, Joint Sentiment Topic modeling (JST) was proposed by Lin and He[4]. JST uses a lexicon based training data set containing positive, negative and neutral scores for each lexicon. JST is effectively a four layer model, where sentiment labels are associated with documents, under which topics are associated with sentiment labels and words are associated with both sentiment labels and topics.

3. ONLINE JOINT SENTIMENT BASED TOPIC MODELING (ONLINE JST)

For online variational inference, the posterior over the per-word topic assignments z is parametrized by ϕ, the posterior over the per-document topic weights θ is parametrized by γ, and the posterior over the topic β is parametrized by λ. S is the sentiment category. Symmetric priors are assumed on θ and β. A good setting of the topics λ is one for which the Evidence Lower Bound (ELBO) $\mathcal{L}$ [1] is as high as possible after fitting the per-document variational parameters γ and ϕ with the Expectation step. Let $\gamma(n_t, \lambda)$ and $\phi(n_t, \lambda)$ be the values of γ_t and ϕ_t produced by the E-step. The goal is to set λ to maximize:

$$\mathcal{L}(n, \lambda) \triangleq \sum_t \ell(n_t, \gamma(n_t, \lambda), \phi(n_t, \lambda), \lambda) \tag{1}$$

where $\ell(n_t, \gamma_t, \phi_t, \lambda)$ is the tth document's contribution to the variational bound. The Online LDA with variational

Algorithm 1 Online LDA, and Joint Sentiment based Topic Modeling Framework (Online JST).

Input: A list of documents D, α, β, sentiment lexicons
Output: Association between D×Topics, and Topics×S.

1 Define $\rho_t \triangleq (\tau_0 + t)^{-\kappa}$;   // *Weight given to* $\tilde{\lambda}$
2 Initialize λ randomly
   for $t=0 \to \infty$;   // *For each Tweet*
   do
   | ***E step:***
3 | Initialize $\gamma_{tks} = 1$ (constant 1 is arbitrary)
   | **repeat**
4 | | Set $\phi_{twks} \propto \exp\{E_q[\log\theta_{tks}] + E_q[\log\beta_{kws}]\}$
5 | | Set $\gamma_{tks} = \alpha + \sum_w \phi_{twks}n_{tw}$
   | **until** $\frac{1}{KS}\sum_{ks}|change\ in\ \gamma_{tks}| < 0.00001$;
   | ***M step*** (update after mini-batch to reduce noise):
6 | Compute $\tilde{\lambda}_{kws} = \eta + D(n_{tw})(\phi_{twks})$
7 | Set $\lambda = (1 - \rho_t)\lambda + \rho_t\tilde{\lambda}$
   end

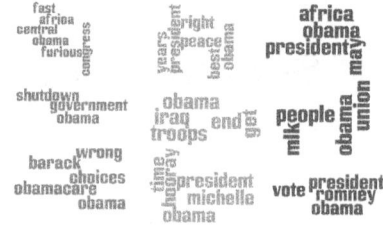

Figure 1: Word clouds of topics with different sentiments, obtained using Online JST. Red, Green and Blue denotes negative, positive, and neutral topics, respectively.

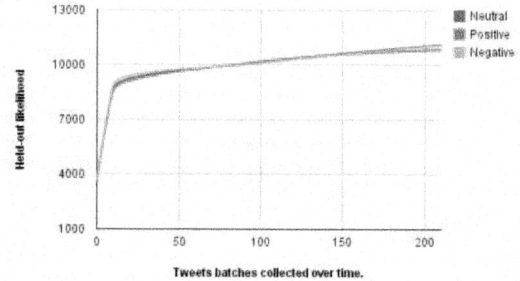

Figure 2: Held-out-likelihood measuring the topic model perplexities for the three sentiment polarities extracted using Online JST. The trend shows the perplexity improvement as new batches of tweets arrive through the stream.

Bayes, with joint sentiment prediction (Online JST), is listed in Algorithm 1. As the tth vector of word counts n_t is observed, for each sentiment category s and topic k, an E step is performed to find locally optimal values of γ_t and ϕ_t, while holding λ fixed. In the true online case, $D \to \infty$, corresponding to empirical Bayes estimation of β. λ is updated using a weighted average of its previous value and $\tilde{\lambda}$. The weight value for $\tilde{\lambda}$ is given by $\rho_t \triangleq (\tau_0 + t)^{-\kappa}$, where $\kappa \in (0.5, 1]$ controls the rate at which old values of $\tilde{\lambda}$ are forgotten, $\tau_0 \geq 0$ slows down the early iterations of the algorithm and is needed to guarantee convergence.

4. EXPERIMENTS

The experiments were performed on data consisting of over 300,000 tweets collected from Twitter's public API between October 2011 and December 2013, filtered using keyword *obama*. Stop words were retained to preserve the context information for sentiment detection. Figure 1 shows a sample of three topics per sentiment category extracted using the proposed Online JST. A common metric used to evaluate language models [2] is Perplexity, which is given by

$$perplexity\,(D') = \exp\left\{-\frac{\sum_{d=1}^T \ln p\left(\vec{w}^{(d)}|\vec{\alpha},\beta\right)}{\sum_{d=1}^T N_d}\right\},\ \text{for a test}$$

set of T documents $D' = \left\{\vec{w}^{(1)}, \cdots, \vec{w}^{(T)}\right\}$ with N_d keywords in the dth document. Since the numerator is the held-out likelihood, a lower perplexity indicates a better generalization performance of the topic model. Figure 2 shows the improvement of the held-out likelihood for the Online JST models, with more iterations. Each iteration integrates a new window[1] of data arriving through the stream. The results show that the model matures as new data arrives.

5. CONCLUSION

The proposed Online JST model provides a faster topic modeling compared to the slower Gibbs sampling based techniques such as JST. Our experiments showed that adding a sentiment layer to the Online LDA technique can produce

---

[1]window: a pool of 100 Tweets, ordered by timestamp.

good quality topics while being faster and handling an infinite stream of tweets.

6. REFERENCES

[1] BLEI, D. M., AND MCAULIFFE, J. D. Supervised topic models. *arXiv preprint arXiv:1003.0783* (2010).

[2] BLEI, D. M., NG, A. Y., AND JORDAN, M. I. Latent dirichlet allocation. *the Journal of machine Learning research 3* (2003), 993–1022.

[3] HOFFMAN, M., BLEI, D. M., AND BACH, F. Online learning for latent dirichlet allocation. *Advances in Neural Information Processing Systems 23* (2010), 856–864.

[4] LIN, C., AND HE, Y. Joint sentiment/topic model for sentiment analysis. In *Proceedings of the 18th ACM conference on Information and knowledge management* (2009), ACM, pp. 375–384.

[5] LIU, Y., HUANG, X., AN, A., AND YU, X. Arsa: a sentiment-aware model for predicting sales performance using blogs. In *Proceedings of the 30th annual international ACM SIGIR conference on Research and development in information retrieval* (2007), ACM, pp. 607–614.

[6] LU, Y., AND ZHAI, C. Opinion integration through semi-supervised topic modeling. In *Proceedings of the 17th international conference on World wide web* (2008), ACM, pp. 121–130.

[7] ZHAI, K., AND BOYD-GRABER, J. Online topic models with infinite vocabulary. In *International Conference on Machine Learning* (2013).

Enthusiasm and Support: Alternative Sentiment Classification for Social Movements on Social Media

Shubhanshu Mishra
University of Illinois
Urbana-Champaign
The iSchool
smishra8@illinois.edu

Sneha Agarwal
University of Illinois
Urbana-Champaign
The iSchool
sagarwa8@illinois.edu

Jinlong Guo
University of Illinois
Urbana-Champaign
The iSchool
jguo24@illinois.edu

Kirstin Phelps
University of Illinois
Urbana-Champaign
The iSchool
kphelps@illinois.edu

Johna Picco
University of Illinois
Urbana-Champaign
The iSchool
picco2@illinois.edu

Jana Diesner
University of Illinois
Urbana-Champaign
The iSchool
jdiesner@illinois.edu

ABSTRACT
We present a novel sentiment classifier particularly designed for modeling and analyzing social movements; capturing levels of *support* (supportive versus non-supportive) and degrees of *enthusiasm* (enthusiastic versus passive). The resulting computational solution can help organizations involved with social causes to disseminate messages in a more informed and effective fashion; potentially leading to greater impact. Our findings suggest that enthusiastic and supportive tweets are more prevalent in tweets about social causes than other types of tweets on Twitter.

ACM Classification Keywords: I.2.7; H.3.3

Author Keywords
Social Network Analysis; Data Classification; Data Corpus; Social Causes; Human Factors

1. INTRODUCTION
Common sentiment classifiers typically label statements as positive, negative or neutral. While helpful for consumer products or marketing initiatives, this simplistic scale of sentiments is of limited applicability to other real-world problems, e.g. social causes. We present a novel sentiment classifier unique to social causes which captures more nuances of sentiment along the level of *support* (supportive versus non-supportive) and degree of *enthusiasm* (enthusiastic versus passive). With this classifier, relevant types of stakeholders for social causes can be identified, and this information be further used for collective action and advocacy.

WebSci'14, June 23–26, 2014, Bloomington, IN, USA.
ACM 978-1-4503-2622-3/14/06.
http://dx.doi.org/10.1145/2615569.2615667

2. BACKGROUND
Twitter has redefined the way in which social activities are discussed, coordinated and executed. Of particular interest for social media studies is the detection of influencers on Twitter, with a focus on the understanding of influence based on the number of followers, retweets and/or mentions [1]. Identifying influencers on Twitter has a number of important real-world applications, including marketing/advertising costs [2] and consumer feedback [3]. While relying only an account's indegree (number of followers) reveals little about a user's influence[1], categorizing users by specific roles based on their dynamic communication behavior (e.g. URLs and hashtags) can improve retweetability [4].

Sentiment extracted from Twitter is found to be predictive of real-world outcomes. Yet, the majority of sentiment analysis of Twitter involves labeling tweets according to polarity, or a scale of positive-neutral-negative [6]. However, especially from a social science point of view, solutions to reliably capturing more nuanced dimensions of emotions (on social media) are lacking. Thus, we address the following research questions:

1. *How can we construct a better classification system for sentiment analysis on Twitter fine-tuned for better understanding social movements?*
2. *How can we improve the identification of influential users on Twitter via such a novel sentiment analysis approach?*

3. METHODS
3.1 Classification Schema
Digging deeper into the needs for identifying users/tweets for social causes, we identified the classification of two orthogonal classes shown in Figure 1. This schema allows us to move beyond the classic positive/ negative/ neutral categorization.

3.2 Corpus Collection
We collected over 1,500 tweets related to three social causes: "Cyberbullying", "Concussions in NFL", and "LGBT" during the 1st week of November 2013.

3.3 Codebook Generation

We created a codebook to label tweets for generating a training corpus for each of the four classes considered herein. The codebook was used to hand code the 1500 tweet corpus. We avoided using context based knowledge for the coding to limit personal opinions from the coding process. Inter-coder reliability scores were high for both classes [Table 1.]

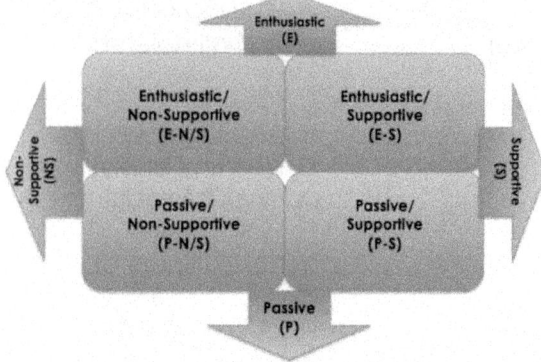

Figure 1 Orthogonal Classification Schema

For the Non-Supportive class, we considered the case where the tweets could be categorized as being either directly against the cause, or just spreading negative information about the cause. We merged these two cases to build the Non-Supportive class. The corpus contained only a very few tweets that spoke directly against a cause.

Table 1. Inter-Coder reliability for annotation

Classification Schema	Inter- coder Reliability
Enthusiastic v/s Passive	93%
Supportive v/s Non - Supportive	85%

3.4 Classifier Training

We used a Linear Support Vector Machine (SVM) based classifier, which we trained using the following features: # of Emoticons, # of URLS, # of Mentions, # of Hashtags, Word Features, # of Double Quotes Length of Tweets. Our 10 fold cross validation achieved a 77% to 79% prediction accuracy in terms of the F-measure [Table 2].

Table 2. Prediction accuracy

Classification Schema	Accuracy
Enthusiastic v/s Passive	79%
Supportive v/s Non - Supportive	77%

3.5 User Classification

The classifiers were made actionable by using them to identify particular types of influencers on Twitter, as follows: We leverage the classifier confidence scores for each tweet to calculate a sum total of sentiment shared by the users for that specific class. Then, we rank the users and construct a social network of users to identify influencers per sentiment based on a) sentiment scores and b) centrality measures like degree and betweeness. The technology (*SentiNets*) and results are made publicly available through a web-based tool (http://people.lis.illinois.edu/~smishra8/sentinets.php).

This tool allows users to search for tweets on a social topic and then share all the metrics for all the users involved.

We envision *SentiNets,* the user dashboard, to benefit organizations and individuals working with social causes by providing a way to classify tweets according to the level of support and degree of enthusiasm on Twitter.

4. DISCUSSION AND CONCLUSION

Our work contributes to ongoing research that aims to expand and leverage our understanding of language use, specifically sentiment, on social media. While still limited by sarcasm and other jargon, our work moves the conversation forward, beyond simple positive-negative scales.

Social media has the potential to build relationships, raise awareness, and support advocacy of important issues facing our communities. However, social causes are nuanced, at times controversial, and infused with opinions that are often lost when evaluated along a scale of simple positive/negative polarity. Our work provides a possible solution for this problem by creating a way to classify tweets according to the level of support and degree of enthusiasm. Even with unstructured data, our classifier was able to successfully predict sentiments on social causes with decent performance. Our classifier is limited by the use of language on social media, however, and may not be able to classify context based tweets or sarcastic tweets.

A public interface is provided with our solution. Through *SentiNets*, we are able to combine our sentiment classifier with aspects of user influence in social networks to help those working toward important social causes to make sense of social media data for desirable social outcomes.

5. REFERENCES

[1] Cha, M., Haddadi, H., Benevenuto, F., & Gummadi, P. K. (2010). Measuring User Influence in Twitter: The Million Follower Fallacy. ICWSM, 10, 10-17.

[2] Bakshy, E., Hofman, J. M., Mason, W. A., & Watts, D. J. (2011, February). Everyone's an influencer: quantifying influence on twitter. In Proceedings of the fourth ACM international conference on Web search and data mining (pp. 65-74). ACM.

[3] Jansen, B. J., Zhang, M., Sobel, K., & Chowdury, A. (2009). Twitter power: Tweets as electronic word of mouth. *Journal of the American Society for Information Science and Technology, 60*(11), 2169-2188.

[4] Tinati, R., Carr, L., Hall, W., & Bentwood, J. (2012, April). Identifying communicator roles in twitter. In *Proceedings of the 21st international conference companion on World Wide Web* (pp. 1161-1168). ACM

[5] Sannella, M. J. 1994. *Constraint Satisfaction and Debugging for Interactive User Interfaces.* Doctoral Thesis. UMI Order Number: UMI Order No. GAX95-09398., University of Washington.

[6] Pang, B., Lee, L., & Vaithyanathan, S. (2002, July). Thumbs up?: sentiment classification using machine learning techniques. In Proceedings of the ACL-02 conference on Empirical methods in natural language processing-Volume 10 (pp. 79-86). Association for Computational Linguistics.

For What it's Worth: Digital Inequalities, Attitudes and a Typology of Internet (Non-)Users

Bianca C. Reisdorf
University of Leicester
Department of Media & Communication
br86@le.ac.uk

Darja Groselj
University of Oxford, Oxford Internet Institute
darja.groselj@oii.ox.ac.uk

ABSTRACT

This paper addresses limitations of previous digital inequality research through a systematic analysis of factors that distinguish Internet non-users from low users of the Internet, and in turn low users from regular and broad Internet users. In addition to socio-demographic characteristics, we examine the role of attitudes toward technologies and the Internet in gradations of Internet (non)use. Results indicate that apart from socio-demographic characteristics attitudes play a strong role in determining who is online and offline, and also how much and how broadly Internet users engage with these technologies.

Categories and Subject Descriptors

K.4.m [**Computers & Society**]: Miscellaneous–*digital divide*

Keywords

Digital inequalities; user typologies; non-use; low use; attitudes.

1. INTRODUCTION

In an increasingly connected world, a large body of literature is concerned with digital divides[12] and digital inequalities[2,4]. The shift away from a binary divide has led to a growing number of studies conducted on different types of Internet users[1]. However, only little research focuses on non-users[9] or low users[10]. Extending the analyses of digital inequality research and in particular Helper's[4] study on the "digital underclass" this paper examines whether British low users are more similar to non-users in their socio-economic characteristics and attitudes than to those who use the Internet regularly and broadly. Based on the 2013 data from the OxIS, we characterize low use, regular use, and broad use of the Internet. Using logistic regression analysis, we compare socio-economic characteristics and attitudes of non-users to the three identified groups of users.

2. BACKGROUND

Digital inequalities research has experienced a shift away from the binary digital divide[7] and towards the examination of more detailed gradations of Internet use[7] that focuses on differences in Internet skills and different categories of Internet users[4]. Blank and Groselj[1] found that most publications differentiate between occasional users, frequent users, and broad frequent users. To construct these categories, most studies included the frequency of use and the range or variety of use[6,10]. We hence included time spent online and range

WebSci'14, June 23–26, 2014, Bloomington, IN, USA.
ACM 978-1-4503-2622-3/14/06.
http://dx.doi.org/10.1145/2615569.2615640

of different online activities in our categorization of low, regular, and broad users.

Helsper's[4] work on the "digital underclass" shows that although most Britons are now online, we find large differences in their usage patterns and their skills. These differences are mostly related to factors that influence traditional digital divides and inequalities, such as age, education, income, occupation, and disability. We thus hypothesize:

H1: The socio-economic background of low users is similar to that of non-users and hence considerably different from that of regular users and broad users.

H2: The more privileged the socio-economic background, the more and broader the Internet use.

Attitudes have been mainly looked at with regards to topics, such as mobile Internet, Internet shopping, or other specific topics. Porter and Donthu[8] extended the Technology Acceptance Model and applied it to Internet use and non-use. Ease of use and usefulness of technologies will affect an individual's attitude towards technologies, which in turn influences the intention to use them and eventually actual use or non-use. We hypothesize:

H3: Attitudes towards technologies and the Internet are a factor (at least) as significant in predicting the categories of non-users, low users, regular users, and broad users as socio-economic factors.

3. METHODOLOGY

The Oxford Internet Surveys (OxIS) is a cross-sectional, face-to-face population-based survey of Internet users and non-users in Great Britain. In our analysis, we use the main sample data which consisted of 2,053 individuals[3]. In 2013, 78% of the British population was online. Based on the analysis of their amount (time) and variety of use, we categorize Internet users into three categories: low, regular, and broad users. For each respondent, we summed the amount of time they report spending online in any location. 6% report they spend less than 90 minutes per week online. We categorize this group as 'low users'. Most spend between 1.5-19 hours per week online (66%; 'regular users'), and 28% spend more than 19 hours per week online (several hours a day; 'broad users'). Relying just on self-reported time spent online is too narrow. Thus, we combined this measure with the number of activities people engage in online[1]. Identifying breaks in the distribution, we split Internet users into: 0-2 different activities are low users; 3-7 are regular users; 8-10 are broad users. Pearson's Chi^2 test verified that time spent online is significantly and positively related to the variety of activities that people do online. We combined both variables to assign respondents to 3 categories of Internet use: low (17%), regular (34%) and broad users (28%); 18% are non-users.

The OxIS includes items measuring attitudes toward technologies. With an exploratory factor analysis, we developed 3 combined attitudinal variables: general technology, Internet efficiency, and

Internet escape. E.g., for the 'Internet escape' factor, a higher score means that respondents agree more strongly with statements related to the Internet being a good means to escaping reality.

To differentiate whether socio-economic backgrounds and attitudes vary between non-users, low users, regular users, and broad users, we conducted a set of logistic regressions that included those socio-economic variables that are traditionally related to digital inequalities[5].We ran 8 different models—2 models (socio-economic factors only, and with attitudinal variables) for each of the following: (1) prediction of being a low user vs. non-user; (2) regular user vs. low user; (3) broad user vs. regular user; and (4) broad user vs. low user.

4. RESULTS & DISCUSSION

The results only partially support our first hypothesis. While the comparison between low and regular users showed that age and educational qualifications played a large role in predicting who is a low user and who is a regular user, none of the other socio-economic factors played a significant role. Comparing low to broad users, age, education, income, and living alone played a strong role with those who are older, with lower educational qualifications, and low incomes being significantly less likely to be broad users. This confirms Helsper's[4] findings about the digital underclass. Even if they are online, those from disadvantaged socio-economic backgrounds use the Internet less and less broadly. Those who are worst off in society, however, are much more likely to be complete non-users rather than low users. There are big differences between Internet non-users and low users, which leads us to reject H1.

The second hypothesis was broadly supported in our analyses. For each step 'upward' in Internet use several socio-economic factors played a role, and always in a positive direction. Those with better educational qualifications were more likely to be regular users than low users. Those who were—on top of that—younger and had higher incomes were more likely to be broad users than regular users. In accordance with previous research[4], these results confirm H2.

Based on previous research[9] we assumed that attitudes are an important factor in predicting the categories of use and non-use. The results do not support this hypothesis. While attitudes generally play a strong role in predicting non-use and different types of use, their predictive values were not as strong as the strongest socio-economic factors: education, age, and income. Nonetheless, positive attitudes towards the Internet were a strong and significant predictor for differentiation of all types of users and for differentiating between non-users and low users. Our analyses show that attitudinal variables are a valuable asset to explaining Internet use and non-use[8].

5. CONCLUSION

This paper set out to examine the influence of socio-economic and attitudinal factors on predicting non-use and three types of Internet use: low, regular, and broad use. The findings confirm those from previous studies on digital inequalities: those who are from socio-economically disadvantaged backgrounds are less likely to be online in the first place[2,7], and among those who are online, those from less fortunate backgrounds use it less and for fewer activities[4,6]. Non-users are more likely to be worst off in comparison to low users. While this shows that those who are online in the first place are mostly socio-economically better off than complete non-users, the

comparison of low users with regular and broad users also showed that there are strong (digital) inequalities between Internet users. Additionally, there are vast differences in attitudes between non-users and low users, and between user categories themselves. This shows that tackling digital inequalities has to include various dimensions. Combined with less advantaged socio-economic backgrounds among low users, these negative attitudes increase digital inequalities, as they may prevent them from trying a wider range of online activities and spending more time online. However, research shows that both wider range of online activities and more time spent online are positively associated with Internet skills[11]. Thus, it would be worthwhile to extend our models with a measure of Internet-related skills.

Both non- and low use need to be addressed in policy interventions, which need to tackle not only traditional socio-economic inequalities and infrastructures, but also motivations and attitudes that may prevent both groups from spending (more) time online and engaging in more diverse set of Internet uses.

6. REFERENCES

[1] Blank, G., & Groselj, D. 2014. Dimensions of Internet Use: Amount, Variety and Types. *Information, Communication & Society*, 17(4), 417-435.

[2] DiMaggio, P., Hargittai, E., Celeste, C., & Shafer, S. 2004. Digital inequality: From unequal access to differentiated use. *Social Inequality*, 355-400.

[3] Dutton, W.H., & Blank, G., with Groselj, D. 2013. *Cultures of the Internet: The Internet in Britain. Oxford Internet Survey 2013.* Oxford Internet Institute, University of Oxford.

[4] Helsper, E.J. 2011. *LSE Media Policy Brief 3.*

[5] Helsper, E. J., & Reisdorf, B. C. 2013. A quantitative examination of explanations for reasons for internet nonuse. *Cyberpsychology, Behavior, and Social Networking*, 16(2), 94-99.

[6] Livingstone, S., & Helsper, E. 2007. Gradations in digital inclusion: children, young people and the digital divide. *New Media & Society*, 9(4), 671-696.

[7] Norris, P. 2001. *Digital Divide: Civic Engagement, Information Poverty, and the Internet Worldwide.* Cambridge University Press.

[8] Porter, C. E., & Donthu, N. 2006. Using the technology acceptance model to explain how attitudes determine Internet usage: The role of perceived access barriers and demographics. *Journal of Business Research*, 59(9), 999-1007.

[9] Reisdorf, B. C., Axelsson, A. S., & Maurin, H. 2012. Living Offline-A Qualitative Study of Internet Non-Use in Great Britain and Sweden. *Selected Papers of Internet Research*, 2.

[10] Selwyn, N., Gorard, S., & Furlong, J. 2005. Whose Internet is it anyway? Exploring adults' (non) use of the Internet in everyday life. *European Journal of Communication*, 20(1), 5-26.

[11] Van Deursen, A. J., & Van Dijk, J. A. 2013. The digital divide shifts to differences in usage. *New Media & Society*.

[12] Van Dijk, J. A. 2005. *The deepening divide: Inequality in the information society.* Sage.

Race, Religion or Sex: What makes a Superbowl Ad Controversial?

Rumi Ghosh
HP Labs
1501 Page Mill Road
Palo Alto
rumi.ghosh@hp.com

Sitaram Asur
HP Labs
1501 Page Mill Road
Palo Alto
sitaram.asur@hp.com

ABSTRACT

Advertisements that generate undue controversies can destroy an advertising campaign. However it is difficult to estimate the potential of controversies in advertisements through traditional methods such as customer surveys and market research. In this paper, we develop a controversy detection system based on initial comments on online advertisements posted on YouTube. We extract early YouTube comments on a collection of Superbowl advertisements and generate a comprehensive set of over 2500 semantic and linguistic features for automatically detecting controversies. Our results show good accuracy in early detection of controversies. The proposed data-driven approach can complement and greatly aid traditional approaches of market research.

Categories and Subject Descriptors

H.2.8 [**Database Applications**]: Data Mining

Keywords

Controversy, Detection, Classification

1. INTRODUCTION

Controversy in advertisements significantly affects marketing campaigns[1, 2]. Our objective is to develop an automatic mechanism for early detection of controversy in advertisements using user generated data. For this purpose, we identified a set of past Superbowl commercials and then had human judges evaluate the advertisements to get 18 controversial and 27 non-controversial (control) advertisements from Superbowl 2013. We then extracted comments on these advertisements posted on YouTube within the first 24 hours using the YouTube API. We collected more than $11K$ comments for these 45 videos. Also as an independent test set, we extracted comments on 6 advertisements that were screened during Superbowl 2014.

Figure 1(a), shows the temporal evolution of advertisements in both categories with each green (blue) dotted line

WebSci'14, June 23–26, 2014, Bloomington, IN, USA.
ACM 978-1-4503-2622-3/14/06.
http://dx.doi.org/10.1145/2615569.2615641 .

showing change in the the number of comments with time for controversial (non-controversial) advertisements and the gray (black) line showing average characteristics. We can observe that even after just 5 hours, the average rate of commenting in controversial advertisements is higher than in non-controversial advertisements and this difference becomes more pronounced with time.

In this paper, we focus on extracting semantic and linguistic features from user comments and using them to construct a classifer to automatically detect controversial comments. Our experimental results on hold-out testsets on the 2013 and 2014 Superbowl demonstrate high accuracy in detecting controversial advertisements.

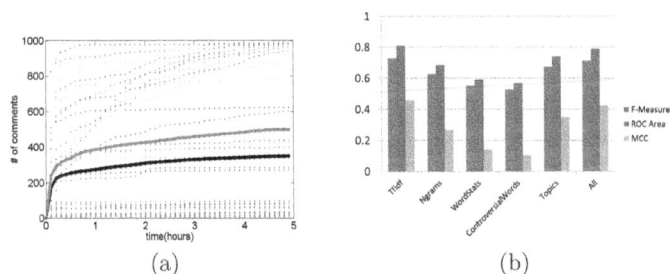

Figure 1: (a) The temporal evolution of comments over 5 hours. (b) Performance comparison of the different categories of features for the classification task.

2. CONTROVERSIAL COMMENTS

2.1 Feature Extraction

We use a wide set of content-based features. They are:
TF-IDF: Each term in the vocabulary (including emoticons) of the comments is used as a feature weighted by term frequency-inverse document frequency (TF-IDF).
Latent Topics: We used the topic modeling approach of LDA to detect latent topics. Using maximum likelihood estimate, we fix the number of topics $T = 100$. The inferred topic distributions for each comment are used as features.
Ngram: Since n-grams help to characterize additional linguistic patterns not captured by just taking single words or unigrams into account, we also extract bi-grams and tri-grams delimited by whitespaces as additional features.
Word Statistics: We include statistical features such as the number of words and the average length of words in a comment.

racist	religious	sexual	choice	negative terms	political	violent	humor	finance	abusive
tibetan	muslim	underwear	pro-choice	don't	republican	murder	funny	economy	gross
arab	bible	hot	vote	does'nt	politician	scare	mad	debt	disgust
asian	hell	homosexual	imply	protest	president	angry	joke	bailout	bullshit

Table 1: The top ranked terms associated with controversial comments

Frequency of Wikipedia controversial issues: Wikipedia[1] contains an entry on issues interpreted as controversial by the web community. We extract this list of controversial issues and for each comment, we calculate the number of controversial issues occurring in it and use it as a feature. Using this set of features, we perform supervised classification to identify controversial and non-controversial comments.

2.2 Classification

We present here the results for classification using logistic regression. We used F-measure, area under the ROC curve and the Matthews Correlation Coefficient (MCC) as evaluation metrics.

Feature Comparison: From Figure 1(b), we see that the tf-idf features seem very efficient in detecting controversial comments irrespective of the evaluation metric considered. Furthermore their performance is comparable to performance obtained on combining all features. On the other hand, the Wikipedia controversial issues and the word statistics perform very poorly.

Feature Selection: We use information gain for selecting features from this pool of over 2500 features. The best performance is obtained by using the top 700-800 features with an AUC value of 0.826.

Controversial Terms: To gain an insight on controversial terms in comments, we ranked the term features in descending order based on their odd ratios learned using logistic regression (Table 1). Our findings corroborate related research on offensiveness in advertisements [3].

3. CLASSIFYING ADVERTISEMENTS

We have shown how comments of an advertisement can be classified. To classify the advertisement, we seek to discover if there can be a threshold τ such that if the fraction of controversial comments $f \geq \tau$, then the advertisement has a very high likelihood of being controversial. We conducted a study using human annotators from CrowdFlower [2] to label a random selection of comments as controversial or non controversial. Based on the analysis, we found that if the fraction of controversial comments (C-score) of an advertisement is above 0.3 it is highly likely to be controversial i.e. if there are more than 30% controversial user comments pertaining to an advertisement, then there is a high probability (90%) that it is controversial.

Detecting a controversial advertisement is defined as a two step procedure. The first step comprises of classifying its comments as controversial or non-controversial. The next step comprises of determining if C-score > 0.3, in which case it is classified as controversial.

Predictions for Superbowl 2013: For testing our algorithm, we randomly chose 3 controversial and 5 non-controversial advertisements from the dataset as a hold-out test dataset. The rest of data is used for training. As shown in table 3, our system correctly predicts whether an advertisement is

[1] en.wikipedia.org/wiki/Wikipedia:List_of_controversial_issues
[2] www.CrowdFlower.com

Ad	Controversial Comments	Total Comments	C-score	Controversy	Predicted
ad1	92	374	0.245989305	no	no
ad2	3	68	0.044117647	no	no
ad3	2	46	0.043478261	no	no
ad4	54	464	0.11637931	no	no
ad5	45	356	0.126404494	no	no
ad6	163	458	0.355895197	yes	yes
ad7	363	686	0.529154519	yes	yes
ad8	184	600	0.306666667	yes	yes

Table 2: Superbowl 2013: C-score and Prediction Accuracy

Ad	Controversial Comments	Total Comments	C-score
Budlight	8	89	0.08988
Chevrolet	5	40	0.125
Coke	295	779	0.378691
Doritos	11	63	0.174603
Maserati	8	58	0.137931
Turbo Tax	12	76	0.157895

Table 3: Superbowl 2014: C-score detected by our classification model

controversial or not with an accuracy of 100% for the given test set.

Predictions for Superbowl 2014: We extracted comments on YouTube (for about a day) for 6 advertisements from Superbowl 2014. As shown in Table 3, our classification model predicts that most advertisements in Superbowl 2014 have a very low C-score value indicating that they have a low probability of stirring a controversy. This corroborates with the findings of newspaper analysts [3]. Though most ads had C-score below 0.3 and were predicted as non-controversial by our algorithm, we found that the Coke advertisement had a C-score value of above 0.3 raising the likelihood of it stirring a controversy and it did in fact generate a controversy [4].

4. CONCLUSIONS

In this paper, we have shown how user comments in YouTube can be mined successfully to automatically detect controversies in advertisements. We wish to extend this analysis and modeling to other types of features including visual, audio and word-ontologies.

5. REFERENCES

[1] Kim Shyan Fam and David S. Waller. Advertising Controversial Products in the Asia Pacific: What Makes Them Offensive? *Journal of Business Ethics*, 48:237–250, 2003.
[2] David S. Waller. A Proposed Response Model for Controversial Advertising. *Journal of Promotion Management*, 11:3–15, 2006.
[3] David S. Waller, Sameer Deshpande, and B. Zafer Erdogan. Offensiveness of Advertising with Violent Image Appeal: A Cross-Cultural Study. *Journal of Promotion Management*, 19(4):400–417, August 2013.

[3] http://news.yahoo.com/nothing-controversial-super-bowl-ads-050412453-finance.html
[4] http://www.latimes.com/entertainment/tv/showtracker/la-et-st-coca-cola-super-bowl-ad-stirs-controversy-20140203,0,1361331.story#axzz2sUExwosa

Crowdsourcing Knowledge-Intensive Tasks In Cultural Heritage

Jasper Oosterman*, Archana Nottamkandath†, Chris Dijkshoorn†

Alessandro Bozzon*, Geert-Jan Houben*, Lora Aroyo†

*Delft University of Technology
Mekelweg 4, 2628 CD
Delft, The Netherlands
{j.e.g.oosterman,a.bozzon,
g.j.p.m.houben}@tudelft.nl

†VU University Amsterdam
De Boelelaan 1081a, 1081 HV
Amsterdam, The Netherlands
{a.nottamkandath,c.r.dijkshoorn,
lora.aroyo}@vu.nl

ABSTRACT

Large datasets such as Cultural Heritage collections require detailed annotations when digitised and made available online. Annotating different aspects of such collections requires a variety of knowledge and expertise which is not always possessed by the collection curators. Artwork annotation is an example of a *knowledge intensive* image annotation task, i.e. a task that demands annotators to have domain-specific knowledge in order to be successfully completed. This paper describes the results of a study aimed at investigating the applicability of crowdsourcing techniques to *knowledge intensive* image annotation tasks. We observed a clear relationship between the annotation difficulty of an image, in terms of number of items to identify and annotate, and the performance of the recruited workers.

Categories and Subject Descriptors

H.4 [**Information Systems Applications**]: Miscellaneous

Keywords

Crowdsourcing; Cultural Heritage; Knowledge Intensive Tasks

1. INTRODUCTION

Some crowdsourcing tasks, referred to as *knowledge intensive tasks*[1], require specific knowledge to be successfully executed. An example is the annotation of flower images with the correct botanical names. Typically, cultural heritage institutions employ professionals, mostly art historians, who provide excellent annotations about the art-historical aspects of artworks, but lack domain expertise for other aspects such as the name of the depicted flowers. For these other aspects, people with the right domain expertise need to be found

and engaged, a process called nichesourcing [2]. How to do nichesourcing effectively is an emerging research area.

Image annotation tasks require annotators to provide tags that describe the presence of one or more instance of a given generic entity (e.g. flowers, birds, etc.). This class of tasks is typically performed on photographic images, which carefully represent the real world; they are also quickly performed, as the knowledge and skills required for their execution are commonly available in the general population (e.g. the ability to recognise a flower). We claim the annotation of artworks to be a more involved process, especially when coupled with the need for accurate, possibly domain-specific labels. It is a good example of a *knowledge intensive* image annotation task, that features *entity identification* as an important source of complexity. The correct recognition of the targeted entities in an art image might be hindered by its artistic representation; for instance, colours or details might be missing; or the depicted content might be stylised or even completely abstract. This additional complexity increases the cognitive effort for an annotator by needing to 1) have the ability to "see" the raw content trough the lens of a given style or technique; and 2) possess domain-specific knowledge.

In a previous work[1] we showed that niche sourcing can help with the creation of useful annotations in the domain of cultural heritage. In this paper, we study the performance of workers employed via crowdsourcing platforms for annotating a collection of prints depicting flowers from the Rijksmuseum Amsterdam[1]. We have created a testbed, similar to existing image annotation interfaces, where workers could tag prints with the specific names of flowers. The testbed measured the annotation behaviour of the workers and stored the annotations. In our study we try to answer the following questions: *What is the relation between entity identification difficulty and crowd annotation behaviour?*

2. EXPERIMENTAL SETUP

We manually selected 82 prints that were annotated with the *Flowers* taxonomy term, i.e. prints that were identified as containing at least one flower. A team of 3 trusted annotators inspected each print, labelling it as **Prominent (P)** (17 prints) or **Non Prominent (NP)** (65 prints), counting the number of contained **flower instances**, and counting the number of **flower types**. Despite the full focus and attention

[1] http://rijksmuseum.nl

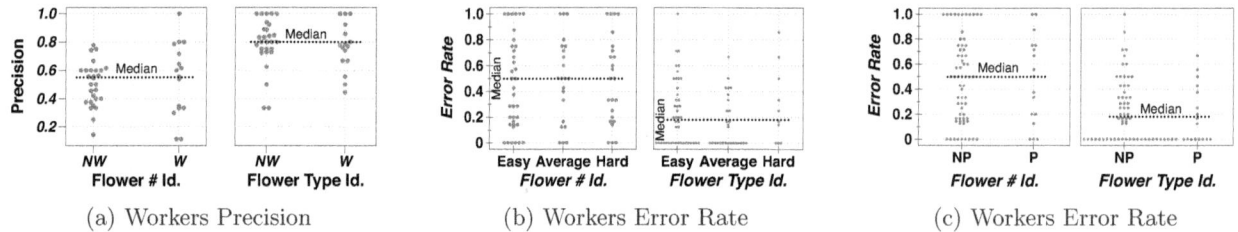

| (a) Workers Precision | (b) Workers Error Rate | (c) Workers Error Rate |

Figure 1: Distribution of worker precision w.r.t to identification difficulty and prominence

| | Flower Type | | | |
	Easy	Average	Hard	Total
Easy	30	6	0	**36**
Average	10	11	1	**22**
Hard	4	11	9	**24**
Total	**44**	**28**	**10**	**82**

Table 1: Distribution of prints in the dataset according to the assessed entity identification difficulty.

put in this annotation process, some prints proved challenging to label. To account for such difficulty, we classify prints in three categories, according to the *disagreement* shown by the trusted annotators when counting the number of identified flower instances and flower types. Respectively: **Easy**: prints where all trusted annotators agreed on the same count; **Average**: prints where trusted annotators disagreed by 1 or 2 flowers/types; **Hard**: prints where the trusted annotators disagreed by more than 3 flowers/types. Table 1 reports the distribution of number of prints according to their combined identification difficulty.

The experiment was performed in February 2014, and it involved anonymous annotators drawn from the *CrowdFlower*[2] platform, which recruits workers worldwide. Of 732 workers that inspected the published task, 151 attempted execution (abandonment rate of 80%), and only 44 passed the qualification test and the designed quality checks. An extended description of the experimental setup and the resulting data is available online[3].

Each print annotation required workers to indicate the number of flower instances, and the number of flower types they were able to identify. We compared the provided numbers with the corresponding assessment performed by our trusted annotators. With `easy` prints, we considered correct only values equal to the ground-truth ones. With `average` and `hard` prints, we considered correct values falling in the range of disagreement of the trusted annotators. Figure 1a reports the average precision of workers, aggregated according to the country of belonging (Western – Western Europe, plus USA and Canada – and non-western). Figure 1b and Figure 1c depicts the average error rate of workers according to the flower identification difficulty and to the flower prominence on the print. Flower type identification is generally performed more precisely than flower number identification, although hard and non-prominent prints generally lead to more errors. Flower type identification was also performed more precisely by Western workers, but errors affect every category of prints in a similarly distributed manner.

[2] http://crowdflower.com
[3] http://www.wis.ewi.tudelft.nl/WebScience2014

3. DISCUSSION AND CONCLUSION

Our study provided interesting insights on the nature of the annotation behaviour of crowd workers in knowledge-intensive image annotation tasks. With respect to our research question, we observed that the difficulty in flower identification clearly played a role in the performance of workers. Tasks addressing difficult prints achieved, on average, a worse flower number identification precision. This result can be explained by the nature of the flower number identification task, which is tedious and very error-prone: the very high abandonment rate at task inspection (80%) combined with the comparably relevant number of low quality workers suggests the adoption of a different task design. For instance, a more structured task decomposition (e.g. showing just a portion of the print), or more engaging and/or rewarding interactions (e.g. using a game with a purpose) could result in better performance. Studies about the adoption of such solutions are planned for future work. Flower type identification, compared to flower instance identification, generally resulted in a lower error rate, thus suggesting that anonymous crowd workers can effectively support this aspect of knowledge intensive image annotation tasks. Prints with prominent flowers received on average a slightly bigger number of tags. In future work, we will continue our investigation on the targeted dataset, including an analysis of the quality of the retrieved annotations. We also plan investigations addressing other knowledge domains (e.g. annotation of birds, castles, etc.). We will also focus on user modelling and expert finding [3] in the crowd such that given a task pre-selected contributors can be contacted (nichesourcing)[2].

Acknowledgements. This publication was supported by the Dutch national program COMMIT.

4. REFERENCES

[1] Jasper Oosterman et al. Crowd vs. experts: Nichesourcing for knowledge intensive tasks in cultural heritage. In *Proceedings of the Companion Publication of the 23rd International Conference on World Wide Web*, pages 567–568, 2014.

[2] Victor de Boer et al. Nichesourcing: Harnessing the power of crowds of experts. In *Knowledge Engineering and Knowledge Management*, volume 7603 of *Lecture Notes in Computer Science*, pages 16–20. Springer Berlin Heidelberg, 2012.

[3] Alessandro Bozzon et al. Choosing the right crowd: Expert finding in social networks. In *Proceedings of the 16th International Conference on Extending Database Technology*, pages 637–648, New York, NY, USA, 2013. ACM.

"Stop G8" – An Ethnographic Account of Web Use in Global Justice Activism

Philip Waddell
Web Science Doctoral Training Centre
University of Southampton
phil.waddell@soton.ac.uk

David Millard
Web Science Doctoral Training Centre
University of Southampton
dem@soton.ac.uk

Clare Saunders
Environmental Sustainability Institute
University of Exeter
clare.saunders@exeter.ac.uk

ABSTRACT

It is well known that the Web, as with any communications technology, has brought new opportunities for citizens around the world to transcend the physical borders of their states. Global Justice activism seeks to challenge dominant socio-political power systems and promote fairer, free and environmentally friendly political discourse on a global scale. The nature of Global Justice activism has meant that it has historically maintained a close relationship with the Web and is influenced by new Web tools and technologies. Social media in particular has been lauded as opening up a new era for Global Justice activism, providing activists with means to network and organise horizontally, circumventing hierarchical power dynamics. However, these tools and technologies are becoming ever more ubiquitous in the everyday socio-political landscape, they are not the radical tools they once were. This poster presents the findings from a week of participation in the "Stop G8" demonstrations in London in June 2013, a week of meetings, lectures and direct action designed to raise awareness regarding the contention of some citizens to dominant capitalist, neoliberal and globalising socio-economic systems.

ACM Classification

A.0 General

Keywords

Activism, Networks, Global Justice, Politics, Social Media

1. METHODOLOGY

In order to explore Web use of Global Justice activists, this research applies a methodology rooted in ethnography. By conducting ethnographic participant observation, the researcher is able to observe activists engaging with the Web in the field, and document the opportunities and challenges conflicts which arise and which the activists themselves may not be aware of. Much of the ethnography that takes place with regards to Web Science revolves around observing or recording online use, through passive observation or data mining.

WebSci'14, June 23–26, 2014, Bloomington, IN, USA.
ACM 978-1-4503-2622-3/14/06.
http://dx.doi.org/10.1145/2615569.2615647

These methods are amenable for identifying online communities and associations between particular activists, and it is partly through these kinds of research methods that the argument, that the Web has enabled communication and online community formation between activists, has come to pass. However, these methods tell us little about how activists perceive the technologies they use, as they may be engaging with these technologies reluctantly. Participant observation requires the researcher to take some role in the field and become accepted by participants, participating in events and activities as a member of the community being researched. Ethnography within Global Justice activism is common, and the work of Jeffrey Juris provides valuable insight into the subject [1]–[5]. In our methodology, the researcher attends Global Justice protests and events. Data collection is carried out primarily through video/audio recording, or if events are static (i.e.: meetings) then through field notes. Ethnography will provide the researcher with the raw data in the form of video clips, audio recordings and written notes which can then be put into a Post-Event Document (PED), a written narrative of the ethnographic research, which is then subsequently dissected for useful information. PEDs serve as collected archives of the event which can then be used to glean further information about user behaviour and interactions with technology in both a physical and ideological sense. Once ethnographic data is collected in the form of PEDs, it must then be analysed. In this study, thematic analysis is undertaken and this involves a process of codification in order to connect observed behaviour and statements regarding Web use.

2. FINDINGS

The main events of this week involved the field researcher participating in collective discussions relating to protest events centering around an occupied building in central London, subsequent participation in these events on the streets of London and a workshop which aimed to explore whether the activists present at the time were engaging with the Web. Three key findings were observed in the week of action.

5.1 The abandonment of cohesive, alternative media spaces in favour of autonomous social networking.

"How things have changed, we used to have loads of photographers, loads of videos, where are they now?"

"They're out with their phones, uploading to their private Facebook accounts".

Where once the creation and maintenance of alternative media and blogs represented the identity of a large group of activists, the story that emerged from these observations indicated that activists who were using the Web during action seemed content to engage with their own personal social network, with their friends, followers and various online connections entirely free of any overarching narrative or organization, which is at odds with historical Web engagement by social movements.

5.2 Public appropriation of protest events in the virtual space.

It appeared that there existed amongst the activists a reliance on the public for documenting protest events. As one activist put it in the run up to the day of protest;

"There will be 100 camera phones there. They won't be our camera phones."

This comment indicates the presence of at least some concern regarding the nature of contemporary, Web centric documentation of protest and the challenge that activists now face.

5.3 The growing mistrust of Web tools as representing capitalism, governments, and the establishment.

Throughout the week of participant observation, one dominant narrative amongst the activists was the (then) recent discovery of the level of surveillance that USA intelligence agencies had on members of the public around the world. The complicity of big US technology companies, Google, Facebook, Microsoft in allowing access to this data was just being understood by these activists. The knowledge of online activity being collected by nation states confirmed for many of these activists, their suspicions. Indeed, many of the conversations overheard during the planning stages of protests regarding Web use centred on what *not* to say and what *not* to share. Faced with the inability to control a virtual environment the activists in the Stop G8 space were trying to shape their physical environment so that it was hostile to a virtual one.

This suggests a growing, but perhaps still implicit, realisation within this activist community that the kinds of Web services and tools commonly used today may not have the best interests of horizontal activist networks at heart. Furthermore activists expressed a desire to re-shape the Web along the ideological lines of their cause:

"The Web is the largest P2P network in the world. It's basically anarchist. It was built by anarchists, core anarchists, the whole Web is an anarchist institution. So yeah we need to use the open internet and stop being captured by these "this is fantastic, let's use that" [narratives]. If it's owned by a corporation, they have to make money at some point. Don't go near it, we need to have

this "don't go near these sparkling toys" even though they sparkle and they're beautiful and they're given to you for free...don't go near it."

The above quote is interesting because it shows the projecting of a political philosophy onto a technology. Arguing that the Web is inherently anarchist in its ideology means that a narrative can be established which shows how modern capitalism and neoliberalism has appropriated the Web for its own ends. Rather than adhere to this appropriation and work within its boundaries, this activist wants to see a social transformation which creates an ideological narrative that draws people away from using mainstream Web tools.

3. CONCLUSIONS

The idea of a new way of doing politics, driven by non-hierarchical associations, decentralized networking and open access to software still exists, but the increasing appropriation of activism by capitalistic social media and the broadening of interaction between activists and the public may be lessening its impact, or even locking activism into a system of exploitation. This poster has explored, in a small way, how some activists now see the Web as a socio-technical construct symbolic not of change, but of the deepening entrenchment within the social, economic and political systems they seek to change. The ethnography carried out with these activists has shown that while the Web is still important to them as a tool of communication, activists struggle to marry their identity and beliefs with dominant "mainstream" technology, which appears to be representative of capitalism.

4. REFERENCES

[1]   J. S. Juris, "The New Digital Media and Activist Networking within Anti-Corporate Globalization Movements," *Ann. Am. Acad. Pol. Soc. Sci.*, vol. 597, no. 1, pp. 189–208, Jan. 2005.

[2]   J. S. Juris, "Practicing Militant Ethnography with the Movement for Global Resistance in Barcelona," 1999.

[3]   J. S. Juris, "Reflections on #Occupy Everywhere: Social media, public space, and emerging logics of aggregation," *Am. Ethnol.*, vol. 39, no. 2, pp. 259–279, May 2012.

[4]   J. S. Juris, "Performing politics: Image, embodiment, and affective solidarity during anti-corporate globalization protests," *Ethnography*, vol. 9, no. 1, pp. 61–97, Mar. 2008.

[5]   J. Juris, G. Caruso, and L. Mosca, "Freeing Software and Opening Space: Social Forums and the Cultural Politics of Technology," *Soc. Without Borders*, vol. 3, no. 1, pp. 96–117, Feb. 2008.

Taking The Relationship To The Next Level: A Comparison Of How Supporters Converse With Charities On Facebook and Twitter

Christopher Phethean
Web Science Doctoral Training Centre
University of Southampton
Southampton, UK
C.J.Phethean@soton.ac.uk

Thanassis Tiropanis
Faculty of Physical Sciences and Engineering
University of Southampton
Southampton, UK
tt2@ecs.soton.ac.uk

Lisa Harris
Faculty of Business and Law
University of Southampton
Southampton, UK
L.J.Harris@soton.ac.uk

ABSTRACT

Social media provide a unique opportunity for charities to reach a large audience with whom they can engage in productive two-way conversations. This abstract reports findings from a study that seeks to determine the extent to which these conversations occur, and whether they differ between Facebook and Twitter. Differences arise showing that Facebook receives more conversations in response to the charities' own posts. However, on Twitter more comments are made per each engaged supporter, which could represent more unsolicited discussion that provides an alternative type of value.

Categories and Subject Descriptors

K.4.0 [**COMPUTERS AND SOCIETY**]: General

Keywords

Social media, charities, marketing, communication, web science

1. INTRODUCTION

The current popularity of social media makes it easy to assume that the numbers of people interacting online provide a plentiful resource of brand advocates, supporters and critics for an organisation. There is the hope—perhaps even belief—that when analysed at scale, this will allow the organisation to determine the current perception of their product or service, respond, drive more engagement, and ultimately lead to a more devoted audience who become co-creators of a successful brand presence. The organisation would subsequently be driven towards their goals, becoming one step closer to success. For charitable organisations,

WebSci'14, June 23–26, 2014, Bloomington, IN, USA.
ACM 978-1-4503-2622-3/14/06.
http://dx.doi.org/10.1145/2615569.2615648 .

knowing that this is the case is of vital importance when allocating limited funds to maintaining a social presence. However, there is currently a lack of understanding as to how effective these sites are for developing any sort of relationship with their supporter-base. It is commonly perceived that social media provide platforms for user engagement, co-creation and activism, but equally there is also extensive research to suggest that the proportion of any online community that is actually engaging is low, and that the majority of users are lurkers or listeners [3]. If this is the case, then to what extent is this apparent for charities on social media? This paper, therefore, seeks to assess what evidence there is on social media of relationships between charity and supporter developing.

2. BACKGROUND

Social media can produce various forms of results through spreading awareness of a new product or campaign, increasing referral traffic and building relationships with audience members. Additionally, social media can be used in contrasting ways—each site offers unique features that may make one aim a more reasonable target given the engagement options available. However, sometimes the use of these sites does not match their perceived value. Twitter, for example, is often discussed as a great platform for rapid customer service and two-way engagement with customers or charitable supporters. USA-based nonprofits appear to be missing this, however, and instead a content analysis of their tweets indicates that their focus is on sending one-way messages in order to broadcast information [5], while similar studies have also suggested a reluctance to move away from primarily information spreading behaviour [2]. However, interactivity through two-way communication on social media is said to be essential in allowing productive relationships to develop with supporters, as it can increase trust [1].

Previous research by the current authors has investigated the area of social media aims for charities. Through interviewing members of charities, recurring themes about why social media was used, and what they hoped to get out of using it, were discovered [4]. Developing relationships was seen as one of the most important aspects of using social media, and that achieving 'action' through donations was seen as a side-effect of doing this. There was a slight favouring towards Facebook for achieving this [4]. Where there was less clarity was regarding the success of these sites in achieving relationship building. For the purposes of this paper, replies and mentions on both Facebook and Twitter will be used as a representation of engagement and developed relationships. We seek to answer the following question:

- Does either Twitter or Facebook show evidence of more sustained relationships between supporters and charity, and do posts by a charity on either site tend to generate more engagement than on the other?

3. METHODOLOGY

A sample of 7 UK charities was used for this study (Diabetes UK, The Dogs Trust, Help for Heroes, Jeans for Genes, The Woodland Trust, The National Trust and Wessex Heartbeat). For each charity, a dataset of 6-months worth of data was collected for each site: on Twitter, a variation of the University of Southampton Tweet Harvester[1] was used to collect tweets over the course of the study, whereas the Facebook dataset was collected retrospectively using a combination of the Facebook Graph API and Facebook FQL. For both sites, the data covered the period June–December 2013. Custom scripts were then written in Python to process each of the datasets and extract quantitative data on posts, replies and conversations, and then statistics were carried out to provide insights around the research question. Furthermore, the top 5 commented on posts from each network for each charity were extracted so that qualitative content analysis could be carried out in order to determine whether there were any charity-specific or overall themes that appeared to cause the highest levels of conversation.

4. RESULTS

For the first part of the question, it was necessary to examine the behaviours of commenters towards each charity. Calculations were made to assess how many posts each user made, and a Wilcoxon signed-rank test was then carried out on these values to determine whether one site produced significantly higher values. Twitter produced the higher scores here ($z=-2.366$, $p<0.05$, $r=-0.63$) and suggests that more interactions are made per interacting supporter on this site.

The second part of the question focused more on how the audience responded to the charities' posts. Looking at the data from the perspective of the *posts*, rather than the posters, calculations were made to find the number of replies per charity-authored post on the two networks. Again, a Wilcoxon signed-rank tests were carried out on the results. For the average number of comments per post per like (or follower), this time Facebook was consistently higher ($z=-2.366$, $p<0.05$, $r=-0.63$), meaning that per supporter on each site, Facebook produced a higher number of comments or replies on each of the charities's posts than Twitter. This was shown again when looking at the average number of *commenters* or posters per like or follower on each site, with Facebook again consistently higher ($z=-2.366$, $p<0.05$, $r=-0.63$), indicating that Facebook provides a higher proportion of interacting or engaged supporters than Twitter.

Looking qualitatively at the content of the messages that received the highest number of comments highlighted several recurring types of message. On Facebook, posts asking informal questions (12/35 posts) and promoting competitions (10/35) were common. On Twitter, informal questions (16/35) and informational messages (14/35) tended to be popular. There are indications here that these categories are more effective at generating responses from the audience.

5. DISCUSSION

This study set out to investigate conversations on social media as a method of ascertaining the extent to which supporters were engaging with charities in a way that reflected that they had a strong relationship. It is interesting to discover that for the sample of charities in this study, Twitter appeared to accomodate supporters who made more interactions each, compared to Facebook. Yet when looking at the data from the point of view of responses to the charities' own posts and in relation to the number of likes or followers each charity possessed, Facebook posts received both more comments, and more commenters than Twitter. The difference in post response rate could be down to the fact that charities don't see Twitter as a channel for relationship building and conversation in the way that they do with Facebook, supporting the views presented in the current authors' previous study [4]. However it appears from the qualitative aspects of this study that there is some evidence to suggest that tweets attempting to elicit a reaction—primarily asking informal questions—are still the most popular on Twitter in terms of replies received, and that engagement in this way is still possible on the site. Further qualitative analysis could provide much richer insights in to what it is people are actually conversing about on social media—this is seen as the main opportunity for future research.

To conclude, this paper has shown that social media does appear to facilitate relationship development, and there is a portion of charities' supporter-base that is keen to respond and communicate on social media. Twitter and Facebook each appear to contribute to this in differing ways, and it would seem that to effectively take advantage of social media as a whole, each of these sites must be mastered individually in order to achieve the best possible outcomes.

6. ACKNOWLEDGMENTS

This research was funded by the Research Councils UK Digital Economy Programme, Web Science Doctoral Training Centre, University of Southampton. EP/G036926/1.

7. REFERENCES

[1] S. Jo and Y. Kim. The effect of web characteristics on relationship building. *Journal of Public Relations Research*, 15(3):199–223, 2003.

[2] K. Lovejoy and G. D. Saxton. Information, community, and action: How nonprofit organizations use social media. *Journal of Computer-Mediated Communication*, 17(3):337–353, 2012.

[3] J. Nielsen. Participation inequality: Encouraging more users to contribute, Oct. 2006.

[4] C. Phethean, T. Tiropanis, and L. Harris. Rethinking measurements of social media use by charities: A mixed methods approach. In *Web Science 2013*, Paris, France, May 2013.

[5] R. D. Waters and J. Y. Jamal. Tweet, tweet, tweet: A content analysis of nonprofit organizations' twitter updates. *Public Relations Review*, 37(3):321–324, Sept. 2011.

---

[1] http://tweets.soton.ac.uk

Data Havens, or Privacy Sans Frontières? A Study of International Personal Data Transfers

Reuben Binns, Dr. David Millard, Dr. Lisa Harris
Web Science Doctoral Training Centre
University of Southampton
Southampton, UK
{rb5g11,D.E.Millard,l.j.harris}@soton.ac.uk

ABSTRACT

The web routinely spreads personal data from one jurisdiction to another, where levels of legal protection over such data vary. This raises the potential for some jurisdictions to become 'data havens' specialising in either strong protection of data, or allowing its unrestricted use [5],[3]. In order to promote interoperability and harmonisation, some jurisdictions with similar levels of protection may approve each others data protection regimes, lifting restrictions on international transfers[4].

This article presents a quantitative analysis of over 16,000 international data transfer arrangements made by UK organisations in 2013. Our findings support the hypothesis that one jurisdictions' approval of another's data protection regime is associated with more data transfer arrangements between them. We conclude with implications for the future of cross-border data transfers and the prospect of 'personal data havens'.

Categories and Subject Descriptors

K.4.1 [**Public Policy Issues**]: Regulation, Transborder data flow, Privacy

General Terms

Economics, Legal Aspects

Keywords

International Data Transfers; Data Protection; Data Havens.

1. INTRODUCTION

While the web is global, most of the laws which govern it are national or supranational. In the realm of data protection, this means different jurisdictions offer different types and degrees of privacy protection and rules for organisations who use personal data. To complicate matters, the individual whom the data is about, the organisation responsible for

WebSci'14, June 23–26, 2014, Bloomington, IN, USA.
ACM 978-1-4503-2622-3/14/06.
http://dx.doi.org/10.1145/2615569.2615650.

it, and the server on which it is stored may each be located in different jurisdictions.

Some providers of web services appear to be attempting to exploit this situation, using their location in a jurisdiction with strong data privacy laws to gain a competitive advantage. In August 2013, in the wake of controversy over U.S. government surveillance activity, three of Germany's largest email providers jointly launched a new service called 'Email Made in Germany' which promotes itself as protecting the inbox in accordance with German law [2]. If choice of jurisdiction becomes an important product differentiator for privacy-conscious consumers, some states may seek to boost their domestic web service industry by ensuring high privacy protections.

At the same time, in order to promote a cross-border digital market, some states have sought to harmonise their respective data protection regimes and lift restrictions on the flow of personal data between them[1]. For instance, cross-border transfers within the European Economic Area do not require additional approval. For 'third country' (non-EEA) jurisdictions, the European Commission issues decisions on the adequacy of their data protection regimes. Transfers of data to organisations located in 'adequate' jurisdictions involve less onerous responsibilities for the transferring parties [2]. If inter-jurisdictional harmonisation and/or approval is worthwhile, it ought to go hand-in-hand with data transfers between those jurisdictions. In this study we test the hypothesis that EU regulatory approval of a third country's regime is associated with more data transfer arrangements from the UK to that country.

2. DATA SOURCE AND EXTRACTION

The data source is the UK Information Commissioner's Office's register of data controllers (February 2013), which features over 350,000 UK organisations. The UK Data Protection Act states that data controllers must contact their national supervisory authority, notifying them (amongst other things) of any arrangements for transfers of personal data to third countries (Section 16, 1f, Data Protection Act 1998).

---

[1] We use the UK Data Protection Act (DPA) definition of personal data: 'data which relate to a living individual who can be identified (a) from those data, or (b) from those data and other information which is in the possession of, or is likely to come into the possession of, the data controller' (DPA 1998, s.1)

[2] Countries with adequacy status include Andorra, Argentina, Australia, Canada, Faroe Islands, Guernsey, Isle of Man, Israel, Jersey, New Zealand, Switzerland, Uruguay, and the United States [1]

Country	Transfers	Country	Transfers
USA	8060	Singapore	334
India	1627	**New Zealand**	322
Canada	1064	**Isle of Man**	293
Australia	1042	Philippines	168
Guernsey	879	Malaysia	129
Switzerland	575	Dubai	117
Japan	551	**Israel**	117
South Africa	448	Turkey	80
Hong Kong	370	Brazil	63
Jersey	353	Pakistan	63

Table 1: The 20 most common destinations for international data transfers from the UK. Jurisdictions whose data protection regimes have been approved by the European Commission are highlighted in bold.

The register is made available as XML. We first parsed the data using SAX [3], then restructured it as an SQL database which was queried to extract relevant portions of the data for further analysis.

3. RESULTS

Most instances of data collection described in the register (90.1%) claimed not to transfer data outside the European Economic Area (EEA). 8.6% were listed as 'Worldwide', with no further specificity about locations. The remaining 1.3% (16,906) reported specific jurisdictions to which the data was transferred.

We separated the recipient countries into two populations; those who have been approved by the EC as 'adequate' in their data protection regime, and those who have not. 'Adequate' countries were found to be the destination of international data transfers more often (a mean average of 961 against the general average of 457). We repeated this after excluding the USA from the results, as it accounts for nearly half of all specified transfer arrangements and therefore may be considered an outlier. Also, unlike other jurisdictions listed as 'adequate' by the Commission, the US is considered adequate for transfers only if the recipient organisation has signed up to the 'Safe Harbour' programme [4]. We still found a higher average transfer frequency for countries with approved adequacy status (463) than the general case (252).

Finally, in order to show how these numbers relate to general business relations between jurisdictions, we also calculated a new score for each country. This is expressed by the ratio of the value of the UK export market for that country (in $million), to its total number of data transfer arrangements[5]. The average score for adequate countries was 6:1, compared to 47:1 for non-adequate countries, i.e. the former had more transfer arrangements in relation to their general export market value. This indicates that even adjusting for existing trade relations, 'adequate' countries have a greater number of transfer arrangements.

---

[3]www.saxproject.org

[4]http://export.gov/safeharbor/

[5]Where data was available, based on historical figures released by the UK Office for National Statistics on UK trade, available at http://www.ons.gov.uk/ons/rel/uktrade/uk-trade/february-2014/index.html

4. DISCUSSION

These preliminary results paint a picture of the flow of personal data from the UK to countries outside Europe. Further research will be needed to establish a robust causal relationship between adequacy status and international transfers, and if so, the direction of causation. Further longitudinal analysis could provide evidence one way or the other by comparing the change in frequency of transfers to a jurisdiction before and after the EC issues a positive adequacy decision. Only two countries (New Zealand and Uruguay) were given this status during the time period for which data is available (2011-2013), for which the change in transfer volume was negligible (+2.5% and 0 respectively).

5. CONCLUSIONS

Cross-border personal data flow is much higher between jurisdictions with harmonised or 'approved' privacy laws, evidenced by the higher portion of transfers from the UK which do not leave the EEA, and the higher average number of recipients in non-EEA countries whose levels of protection have been deemed adequate by the EC. Harmonisation and its effect on international transfers has implications for those governments attempting to create 'data havens' with strong privacy protections (and for the emerging web companies who seek to benefit from locating themselves within them). Strong privacy laws may be needed in order to gain another state's approval and therefore access to foreign privacy-conscious consumer markets.

But states also have an incentive to be selective with their approvals; the privacy credentials of a given jurisdiction depend partly on the privacy credentials of *other* jurisdictions it allows personal data to be transferred to without restriction. If strong privacy laws are to become a selling point for domestic web services, governments may also need to ensure that those laws only permit personal data to be transferred to third countries if they can ensure equal levels of protection.

6. ACKNOWLEDGMENTS

This research was funded by the RCUK Digital Economy Programme, EP/G036926/1.

7. REFERENCES

[1] E. Commission. Commission decisions on the adequacy of the protection of personal data in third countries.

[2] F. R. Elizabeth Dwoskin. Nsa internet spying sparks race to create offshore havens for data privacy.

[3] J. N. Geltzer. New pirates of the caribbean: How data havens can provide safe harbors on the internet beyond governmental reach, the. *Sw. JL & Trade Am.*, 10:433, 2003.

[4] C. Kuner. The european commission's proposed data protection regulation: A copernican revolution in european data protection law. *Privacy and Security Law Report*, 11:1–15, 2012.

[5] M. U. Porat. Global implications of the information society. *Journal of Communication*, 28(1):70–80, 1978.

The Norm of Normlessness:
Structural Correlates of A Trolling Community

Hyeongseok Wi
GSCT, KAIST
trilldogg@kaist.ac.kr

Wonjae Lee
GSCT, KAIST
wnjlee@kaist.ac.kr

ABSTRACT

While online trolling is mostly committed by a small number of trolls who enjoy irritating other members in the same social space, it is also often observed that a larger number of trolls establish an online community dedicated to trolling against the public outside. Using network data from two Korean online communities, we fit a longitudinal fixed effects model to test the trolling community's network structures differ from an ordinary online community. We found that the trolling community, ILBE, had a unique reward mechanism to maintain the anonymity of trolls in order to make the illegitimate behaviors collectively sustainable.

Categories and Subject Descriptors

J.4 [**Social Behavioral Science**]: *Sociology*

Keywords

Online community; Trolling community; Eigenvector centrality; Longitudinal fixed effect model

1. INTRODUCTION

While online trolling is one of the major issues in online communities, it has rarely been the focus of attention in online community researches. Among a few exceptions is Herring' research that distinguishes the concept of trolling from flaming, and suggests strong sanctions against trolling behaviors [4]. Shachaf and Hara analyze Wikipedia trolling by categorize four types of trolling motivations in comparison to hacking [7]. Moor finds underlying motivations of flaming behavior in YouTube [6]. What these studies share in common is that they consider the trolls as social outcasts in the online communities. However, there are other online communities entirely dedicated to trolling behaviors. In the United States and Japan, 4chan and 2ch are two major examples. In South Korea, ILBE (daily best) is the most popular trolling community, of which extreme anti-social posts are incurring public indignation and even police investigation.

Given that the trolling researches focus on the ephemerality of the trolling contents [1], and ostracism against trolls, the prevalence of trolling communities is puzzling. How can the trolling communities overcome the social sanctions, and maintain the production of extremely offensive contents that leave nothing to the imagination? Two studies give a clue about the mechanism. Suh and Wagner argue that de-anonymizing technology, such as persistent labeling and deep profiling, is effective in curbing flaming [8]. Chau and Xu find that trolls are not apt to social hierarchy, because independent and spontaneous nature of trolling keeps them from forming a centralized structure [2]. From the two studies, we derive two counterfactual propositions about trolls. First, trolls would not want to expose their true identity. Second,

trolls do not want to form a social hierarchy of themselves. These two propositions are indeed interrelated, because decentralized structure of trolls would help them keep their true identity undetectable, making them feel safe being a part of the illegitimate communities.

To assess these propositions, we analyze two Korean online communities in terms of reputation mechanism. Reputation mechanism is known to be closely associated with the reputable actors' structural positions in networks as well as their individual actions. For instance, in an analysis of actors' reputation and their network centralities (betweenness and constraints), Ganely and Lampe find that users with higher reputation are located in locally constrained networks [3]. However, an actor with higher local constraints would not feel safe being a troll, because shorter distance may enable his adjacent peers to figure out his true identity. To remain anonymous, he should stay away from local peers as well as from remote observers. We suspect that this striving for anonymity is shared collectively in trolling communities. If it's the case, rewards such as reputation would go to actors who are disconnected locally as well as globally. Likewise, the actors would perform better in writing offensive posts when he is less connected with others locally and globally.

Hypothesis 1: A troll with lower standing in the community network would get more recommendations per a post.
Hypothesis 2: A troll with less local constraints in the community network would get more recommendations per a post.

2. DATA

We analyze ILBE and AGORA, Korea's two biggest online communities attracting major social attentions in recent years.

ILBE. Although it started out as a storage mirror for humor-related contents from 'DC Inside', ILBE has deviated to nurture more and more politically biased contents, and now became Korea's biggest online community. Especially during the last presidential election, ILBE gained rapid popularity by supporting an extremely conservative perspective, and developed to present substantially anti-social behaviors, such as distortion of Korean history, derogatory remarks on political foes, and hate crimes against women and minorities. Contrary to Kelly's observation that trolls reside at the periphery of online communities due to the lack of attention from peers [5], ILBE becomes a stronghold, where the anti-social and offensively immoral contents are continuously produced and widely shared by the users.

AGORA. AGORA is the first Korean online discussion community that has brought major social impacts for the last decade. In 2008, AGORA played a pivotal role in a mass protest against the FTA by provoking extremely controversial issues of the 'mad cow disease'. AGORA users were able to forge bonds, and brought together a wide range of people including politically less inclined teenagers through AGORA. Currently, AGORA users are directly discussing social issues on politics, society and economy bulletins. AGORA has established itself as a significant public representative that organizes substantial social involvements through features like online petition.

Network Data. Using Python, we crawl the activity of every user who posts in the politics thread in both communities every 2 hours for 72 hours (21:00 Dec. 26th ~ 21:00 Dec. 29th 2012). User's Activity includes the number of posts, the number of received comments and replies and the number of received recommendations. A time window is set to 2 hours because the most responses from others occur within 2 hours (ILBE: 99% comments in 111min, AGORA: 99% comments in 124min) and the author may delete the post after a while. Combining individual actors' activities for 36 time windows, we construct 36 interaction networks for ILBE and AGORA. We regard the interaction occurred when user A comments to user B's post. If user C comments to the user A's comment, we regard interaction occurred between user B and C also. From the 36 matrices of each community, we calculate constraints and eigenvector centrality scores for each and every actor in both communities (6434 actors for ILBE; 2140 for AGORA). In addition to activity and network centralities, we calculate a friend ratio. When an actor receives comments and replies on a post, some alters would have sent them multiples times. Friend ratio is the ratio of the more than once interacting alters to total alters.

3. ANALYSIS AND RESULTS

Model. We use a longitudinal fixed effects model to assess the two hypotheses:

$$Y_{it+1} = \mathbf{X}_{it}\beta + \phi Y_{it} + \mu_i + \tau_{t+1} + \varepsilon_{it+1}$$

, where Y_{it+1} is the average number of recommendations per a post that the actor i writes in the two hour time window $t+1$. Within the matrix $\mathbf{X}_{it}$ are two network covariates of substantive interests and four controls. Burt's constraints and Bonacich's eigenvector centrality represent how much an actor i is constrained within his local ego-centric network, and how high i is standing in the hierarchy of the global network. To exclude reasonable confounding factors, we include the number of comments and replies the i gives to others (outdegrees), the number of comments and replies the i receives from others (indegrees), the number of posts i writes, and the ratio of friends over those who give comments to i. All are observed during the lagged time window t.

In the regression models estimating network processes, the error terms are not independent. Known as network autocorrelation, the correlated error terms reduce the standard errors of the parameter estimates artificially. One of the several solutions for this is to include a fixed effect for each case (μ_i). The actor fixed effects also control for actors' unobserved time-constant heterogeneity such as gender, age, and attitude. To address serial correlation, which is typical of longitudinal data, we introduce time fixed effects (τ_{t+1}), and a lagged dependent variable (Y_{it}). Time fixed effects also control for unobserved time specific heterogeneity such as the time of a day and environmental influences. The lagged dependent variable, whether it is significant or not, controls for any self-promoting mechanism in reputation growth. In addition to autocorrelation and serial correlation, heteroskedasticity is inherent to cross-sectional time-series data, which we correct using heteroskedasticity-robust estimator.

Results. Consistent with our expectation, only the troll community (ILBE) exhibits negative rewards for the trolls whose global standing is higher and local presence is more constrained by interconnected peers (Table 1). A standard deviation increase in eigenvector centrality decreases the average recommendations per a post by .11 (-7.27*.016), while a standard deviation increase in constraints decreases the average recommendation by .05 (-.22*.22). Neither of two factors is significant in AGORA.

4. CONCLUSION AND DISCUSSION

For a trolling community to maintain the volume of trolling behaviors, it should be able to keep the trolls' anonymity. Unlike 4chan where anonymity is enforced at system level [1], ILBE trolls use unique nicknames by which some of them unwittingly expose their true identity. To avoid this risk, ILBE has developed social norms called *Nick-Ban* and *Chinmok-Ban*. *Nick-Ban* is a norm banning calling others' nicknames, while *Chinmok-Ban* is a norm banning hanging out with other users on the bulletin. Little is known for the origin of the two norms. However, some statements on ILBE offer a very convincing rationale. ILBE trolls believe that *Nick* and *Chinmok* would break down the community by making users hesitating to go extreme. From experiences of decades, the longtime Internet users have realized that inter-personal relationships would compromise their anonymity, and, in turn, the quality of the posts would let up. In structural level, these norms are translated into decreasing recommendations for the trolls well-connected locally and globally. It is paradoxical for the trolls to purposively developing collective norms to foster anonymity, because anonymity is a means for an individualistic value -- privacy. Therefore, trolling communities warrant further studies to see how individualistic and collective values are articulated in future online communities.

Table 1. Regressions predicting the number of recommendations per a post $_{t+1}$

	AGORA	ILBE
Constraints	0.057	-0.218*
	(0.070)	(0.109)
Eigenvector Centrality	-4.499	-7.274**
	(2.395)	(2.513)
The Number of Indegrees	0.176*	0.093*
	(0.075)	(0.036)
The Number of Outdegrees	-0.049	-0.020
	(0.031)	(0.026)
The Number of i's Posts	0.195	0.620***
	(0.179)	(0.164)
Friend Ratio	-0.304	0.042
	(0.309)	(0.357)
Recommendations per a Post t	-0.021	-0.007
	(0.034)	(0.011)
Constant	0.043*	0.370***
	(0.020)	(0.076)
N	72,760	218,756
R^2	0.015	0.004
The Number of is	2,140	6,434

*** p<0.001, ** p<0.01, * p<0.05
Robust s.e. in parentheses; Actor-/time-fixed effects omitted

5. REFERENCES

[1] Bernstein, M. S, 2011. 4chan and /b/ An Analysis of Anonymity and Ephemerality in a Large Online Community. 2011. *Proceedings of the Fifth International Conference on Weblogs and Social Media* (2011). AAAI press 50-57.

[2] Chau, M. and Xu, J. 2006. Mining communities and their relationships in blogs: A study of online hate groups. Int. J. Human-Computer studies 65 (2007) 57-70.

[3] Ganely, D. Lampe, C. 2009. The ties that bind: Social network principles in online communities. Decision Support Systems 47 (2009) 266-274.

[4] Herring S. 2002. Searching for Safety Online: Managing "Trolling" in a Feminist Forum. *The Information Society: An International Journal* 18, 5 (2002) 371-384.

[5] Kelly, J.W., 2006. Friends, Foes, and Fringe: Norms and Structure in Political Discussion Networks. ACM International Conference Proceeding 151 (2006) 412-417.

[6] Moor, P.J., Flaming on YouTube. *Computers in Human Behavior* 26 (2010) 1536-1546.

[7] Shachaf, P. and Hara, N. 2010. Beyond vandalism: Wikipedia trolls. *Journal of Information Science* 36, 3 (2010) 357-370.

[8] Suh, A. and Wagner, C. Factors Affecting Individual Flaming in Virtual Communities. 2012. *46th Hawaii International Conference on System Sciences* 2013 3282-3291.

Information Diffusion on Twitter: The Case of the 2013 Iranian Presidential Election

Azade Sanjari
School of Informatics and Computing
Indiana University Bloomington
1320 East 10th Street,
Bloomington, IN 47405-3907
812-391-9263
asanjari@indiana.edu

Emad Khazraee
Annenberg School for Communication
University of Pennsylvania
3620 Walnut St. Philadelphia, PA 19104
215-898-9727
emad@asc.upenn.edu

ABSTRACT

In this paper we analyzed information propagation on Twitter during the 2013 Iranian presidential election. We studied the most influential users based on their retweet communication network. Our results show that conversation about Iran on Twitter in Persian is mostly conducted by micro-celebrities while official media, news agencies, and journalists are the most retweeted entities when examining both English and Persian tweets.

Keywords: Social Media, Twitter, Information Diffusion, Micro-celebrities, Iran

1. INTRODUCTION

Twitter as a popular social network enables individuals to share information with their followers and get updates from those they follow. Scholars have utilized Twitter to analyze public behavior and political sentiment in the context of elections and campaigns [5][1].

In this study, we reviewed the user population participating in the discussion of Iran during the 2013 election, in which hardliner president Mahmoud Ahmadinejad was replaced by moderate Hassan Rouhani. We examined correlations between the number of tweets per day and dates of major events before, during, and after the election. Then, we identified the most retweeted users during the election period to understand the flow of information and direction of information propagation.

2. DATA SET

In this study, we collected and analyzed tweets discussed Iran broadly and specifically the presidential election, based on important keywords. We used Twitter search API for data collection. During the period of data collection from May 14 to June 29, 2013, every keyword and hashtag was collected multiple times to ensure that we collected all instances of tweets within the Twitter search index. We included both Persian and English keywords for our search to collect a more inclusive data set.

To determine which keywords were most important to cover the discussion about Iran during election, we started with the general

WebSci'14, June 23–26, 2014, Bloomington, IN, USA.
ACM 978-1-4503-2622-3/14/06.

keyword, Iran, and then added most frequently used keywords through time when a new keyword or hashtag emerged, such as the names of candidates in Persian and English (with multiple possible spellings in English). Through this process we collected tweets using 47 keyword and hashtags. After the collection period, we merged collected data for each keyword and removed duplicated tweets which were collected multiple times for different keywords. The final data set consisted of 3,006,528 tweets.

3. DISTRIBUTION OF TWEETS

The number of tweets each day during the election period corresponded with major events in this period, with peak number of tweets on days of major events.

As Figure 1 shows, from the total of 3,006,528 tweets in English and Persian that were collected, 12% of them (241,699 tweets) were posted on June 15, the day after the election, when Rouhani was officially announced as Iran's new president by Iran's Ministry of Interior. Three other dates had a high number of tweets: June 14, Election Day and the date some preliminary results were announced, had a total of 149,092 tweets. June 16, the day after Rouhani's victory was official announced saw 132,748 tweets.

Our data set contained 460,008 tweets in Persian (see Figure 1 for distribution). The peak of Persian language tweets occurred on Election Day, June 15, with 45,119 tweets. Each round of presidential debates also saw peaks in Persian tweets: May 31 with 22,415 tweets, June 5 with 28,448 tweets, and June 7 with 35,489 tweets.

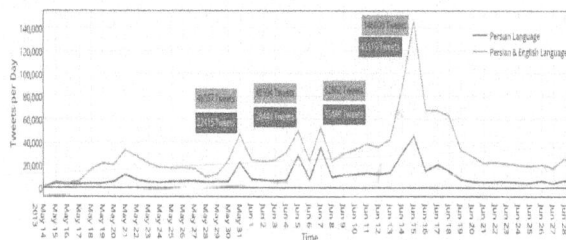

Figure 1. Distribution of Tweets per Day

4. ANALYZING RETWEET NETWORK

Retweeting has become one of the key aspects of information diffusion on Twitter [4]. By retweeting, a user extends the scope of receivers of that tweet and shares it with all her followers. Retweets are usually posted using prefix "RT" following the name of the person who originally shared the post. Since retweets can be defined as a measure of information propagation among people [2], we studied the retweet network of Twitter users to determine the main actors of information propagation who impacted the direction of the conversation and flow of information during the election period.

We classified the 100 most retweeted users in four main categories:

- Official news/media outlets: Official news agencies such as @cnnbrk (breaking news from CNN).

- Journalists: Individuals who work as a journalist for an official news agency or media or as a freelance journalist Such as @Gesfandiari (Radio Free Europe).

- Politicians: official twitter accounts of politicians.

- Social media (Twitter) celebrities: Popular users who tweet from inside or outside Iran and famous Iranian bloggers. This category is defined based on Theresa Senft's concept of micro-celebrity, a performance style on social media in which people use their account to increase their popularity among readers, viewers and those to whom they are linked online [3].

By creating these categories, we sought to determine which of these categories was most influential during the election by holding central positions in the retweet network. We analyzed two datasets to understand which groups played a significant role in information propagation, tweets only in Persian and the combination of Persian and English tweets.

First, we analyzed the retweet network of Persian tweets. Our results show that Mohammad Reza Aref (@MohamadRezaAref) one of the eight candidates who withdrew his candidacy before the election day, was the most retweeted source (1,447 retweets). Iranian Twitter celebrities had the highest presence among the top 100 most retweeted users in Persian; the second most retweeted group was journalists. There were eight official news/media outlets among the 100 most retweeted accounts. These news media sources are:

- BBC news in Persian (@bbcpersian), ranked 3rd,

- Kaleme, non-official news source of Green Movement in Iran (@kaleme), ranked 23rd,

- Deutsche Welle radio in Persian (@dw_persian), ranked 33rd,

- Manoto Persian TV from London (@ManotoNews), ranked 48th,

- Official Persian channel of US Secretary of State (@USAdarFarsi), ranked 79th,

- Mardomak, non-official news source of opposition in Iran (@mardomak), ranked 80th,

- Radio Farda, Radio Free Europe in Persian (@RadioFarda_), ranked 90th,

- IPOS: Information and Public Opinion Solutions, a survey and research consultancy (@IPOSme), ranked 98th.

In the dataset of both Persian and English tweets, the most retweeted users were from two categories, journalists and

news/media outlets. Of the top 100 retweeted users, there were 27 news/media accounts: Reuters international news agency (@Reuters), Al-Arabiya TV in English (@AlArabiya_Eng) and BBC World News (@BBCWorld) ranked fifth, sixth, and seventh respectively. Two users on this list, BBC news in Persian (@bbcpersian), based in London and Mehr News Agency, (@MehrnewsCom), in Tehran, tweet in Persian.

Our findings demonstrate a structural difference between Persian and English Twitter-spheres in discussion of Iran. Discussion about Iran in Persian on Twitter is mostly dominated by micro-celebrities whereas the English Twitter is dominated by official media, news agencies and journalists.

Table 1. Top ten retweeted users for Persian language compared with tweets in all languages

Username (Persian language)	#retweets	Username (All languages)	#retweets
MohamadRezaAref	1447	onlywaqas	4892
Vahid	1154	neverknownfacts	2237
bbcpersian	957	charlespgarcia	2144
sharifi123	739	negarmortazavi	2051
1mahraz	579	Reuters	1833
_Cafe	457	AlArabiya_Eng	1678
Sam1kia	422	BBCWorld	1580
Taiwanii	420	ThomasErdbrink	1568
ArashBahmani	418	HassanRouhani	1497
HassanRouhani	386	antijokeapple	1469

5. REFERENCES

[1] Conover, M. D., Gonçalves, B. B., Ratkiewicz, J. J., Flammini, A. A., & Menczer, F. F., Predicting the political alignment of twitter users. In *Proceedings of 2011 IEEE International Conference On Privacy, Security, Risk And Trust And IEEE International Conference On Social Computing, PASSAT/Socialcom* (Boston, MA, USA, 2011), IEEE, 192-199.

[2] Pezzoni, F., Passarella, A., Conti, M., An, J., & Crowcroft, J. *Why do I retweet it? An information propagation model for microblogs.* Springer International Publishing, 2013.

[3] Senft, T. M. *Camgirls : celebrity and community in the age of social networks.* Peter Lang Publishing Inc, New York, 2008.

[4] Suh, B. B., Hong, L. L., Pirolli, P. P., & Chi, E. H. Want to be retweeted? Large scale analytics on factors impacting retweet in twitter network. In *Proceedings of Socialcom 2010: 2Nd IEEE International Conference On Social Computing, PASSAT 2010: 2Nd IEEE International Conference On Privacy, Security, Risk And Trust* (Minneapolis, MN, USA, 2010), IEEE, 177-184.

[5] Tumasjan, A. A., Sprenger, T. O., Sandner, P. G., & Welpe, I. M., Predicting elections with Twitter: What 140 characters reveal about political sentiment. In *Proceedings of the 4th International AAAI Conference on Weblogs and Social Media*, (Washington DC, USA, 2010), the AAAI Press, 178-185.

From Media Reporting to International Relations: A Case Study of Asia-Pacific Economic Cooperation (APEC)

Chun-Hua Tsai
School of Information Sciences
University of Pittsburgh
Pittsburgh, PA 15260, USA
cht77@pitt.edu

Yu-Ru Lin
School of Information Sciences
University of Pittsburgh
Pittsburgh, PA 15260, USA
yurulin@pitt.edu

ABSTRACT

Network analysis has brought new perspectives in studying emergent structure in international relations. Prior work on networks of international relations has mostly relied on data derived from formal alliances and trade flows, which can hardly capture the rapidly evolving international relations due to globalization and recent advances in information technology. In this work, we propose a novel research design that aims at capturing "real-time" international relations through news reporting. We collect worldwide news on a daily basis, and characterize the relationship between any two countries through analyzing the similarity of their news content. Our empirical results based on news about the APEC (Asia-Pacific Economic Cooperation) CEO Summit in 2013 revealed interesting and meaningful international relations among member countries.

Categories and Subject Descriptors

H.2.8 [**Database Management**]: Database applications—*Data mining*; H.4 [**Information Systems Applications**]: Miscellaneous

General Terms

Measurement; Experimentation

Keywords

online news media, international relations, network analysis

1. INTRODUCTION

The rapid development in technologies, such as transportation and telecommunication infrastructure, has expedited the process of globalization at almost every corner in the world. This globalization process has distinguished speed and volume of integration of political, economic and cultural activities across country borders, through the exchanges of views, ideas, labors, products and other aspects

of culture, which permeates everyone's life. How can we capture such ever-changing cross-country relations in the real-time age?

Most of the prior work on networks of international relations has relied on data derived from formal alliances and trade flows [3]. These studies have provided important insights to the understanding of historic and contemporary international relations covering political and economic aspects. Nevertheless, the data employed in these studies are insufficient to capture the up-to-date, rapidly evolving international relations because of two reasons: the data are collected with considerable time lag, and the datasets often do not cover the diverse and fluid views or ideas possessed by different cultures.

In this work-in-progress paper, we present a novel research design that aims at providing a research infrastructure to capture "real-time" international relations through news reporting. Our design is inspired by the observation that news from different countries reflects different cognitive representations of the world [6]. We develop a system to collect the news articles from Google News website on a daily basis. We then apply text analysis, including matrix factorization based document clustering technique, on the news corpus. Based on the topical similarity between countries' reporting news, we construct time-varying networks among countries that capture the cross-country relations through their common or different topical interests attended in the daily news.

2. APPROACH

We propose a system to collect the news from Google News website into our database. Google News is an automatic-aggregated news website that provides news from thousands news outlets in 70 regional and countries winh 20 languages [1]. This is one of the sources that allow for collecting daily news with worldwide coverage. In our system, we implement a web spider to monitor the Google News by different countries, at an hourly basis. This system collects and parses texts from HTML source pages after downloading the news pages. In order to analyze theses the global news articles, we employ the Google Translate function to convert non-English texts into English texts [5]. We then remove the stop words and perform stemming on the translated English texts. We then create term-document matrix for further analyses.

We apply Non-negative Matrix Factorization (NMF) on the term-document matrix to discover countries' similar topical interests in news reporting as "themes" [2, 4]. NMF is a matrix factorization technique that is used to transform

WebSci'14, June 23–26, 2014, Bloomington, IN, USA.
2014 ACM 978-1-4503-2622-3/14/06 .

the term-document matrix into word-themes and theme-documents matrix. The non-negative feature provides the better interpretability from the text [4]. Based on the theme-document matrix obtained from NMF and the documents' source countries, we create two types of networks. (1) *Country-to-theme network* is a bipartite network where connecting two types of nodes, country and theme nodes, and edge weights are computed by aggregating all documents from the same countries. (2) *Country-to-country network* is a unipartite network where nodes are countries, and the weight of an edge between two countries is given by the cosine similarity of the two countries' aggregated theme distributions.

3. CASE STUDY

We use APEC CEO Summit 2013 as our case study. This meeting was held in Bali, Indonesia from 05 Oct, 2013 to 07 Oct, 2013. There were 21 member countries participated in this meeting. Four countries' news (Indonesia, Thailand, Brunei Darussalam and Papua New Guinea) are missing by Google News. Hence, we only collected 17 member countries' news articles in our dataset. The news volume peaked at Oct. 07. In our analysis, we focus on news that contains the keyword "APEC" during the two weeks centered on Oct. 07 (from Oct. 1 to 15, 2013). Figure 1(a)(b) show the news frequency of APEC.

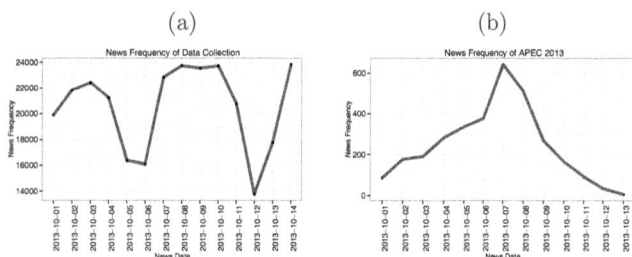

Figure 1: (a) News Frequency of Data Collection. (b) News Frequency of APEC 2013.

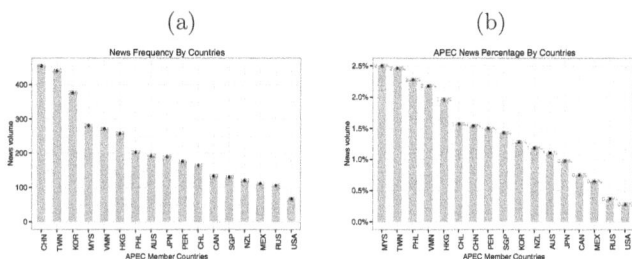

Figure 2: (a) News frequency by countires: China and US had the highest and lowest APEC news volumes, respectively. US has relative low volume of news articles due to the absence of US president.

4. RESULTS

We tested the number of themes from 2 to 10 in NMF. Six themes are selected based on manual inspection as they covers the major events well. The six themes are: C1) Trade and economic growth issues; C2) China president Xi Jin Ping; C3) the cross-strait relation between Taiwan and China; C4) United Government shutdown and President Obama absence; C5) Association of Southeast Asian

Nations and South Sea dispute; C6) The conflict between Hong Kong and Philippine.

Figure 3(a) and (b) present the networks of country-to-theme and country-to-country, respectively. In this international event, most countries mentioned about trade and growth issues. China's news reporting covered a diverse set of issues, while other countries had relatively limited interests. Taiwan is the only country focusing on the cross-strait relation. US had relatively weak connection with other countries due to lower media attention about this meeting, which was probably due to Obama's absence.

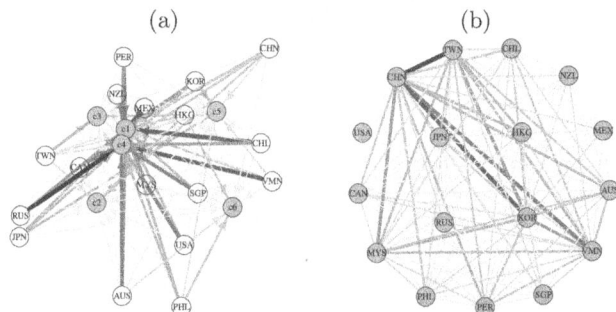

Figure 3: (a) Country-to-theme network: Theme C1 and C4 are dominant themes; (b) Country-to-country network: China, Japan and Korea have strong similarity in news reporting.

5. CONCLUSION

We have experimented our framework on news articles about the APEC CEO Summit held Indonesia 2013. Our empirical results suggested that the content similarity between the participating countries' new articles revealed the structure captured by international trade flows, but also capture emergent relationships and roles in these countries. Our initial finding also has important implications for analyzing online media corpus for understanding underlying social and political changes on a global scale.

6. REFERENCES

[1] A. S. Das, M. Datar, A. Garg, and S. Rajaram. Google news personalization: scalable online collaborative filtering. In *Proceedings of the 16th international conference on World Wide Web*, pages 271–280. ACM.
[2] R. Gaujoux and C. Seoighe. A flexible r package for nonnegative matrix factorization. 11(1):367.
[3] E. M. Hafner-Burton, M. Kahler, and A. H. Montgomery. Network analysis for international relations. 63(3):559–592.
[4] D. D. Lee and H. S. Seung. Learning the parts of objects by non-negative matrix factorization. 401(6755):788–791.
[5] J. Savoy and L. Dolamic. How effective is google's translation service in search? 52(10):139–143.
[6] E. Segev and T. Hills. When news and memory come apart: A cross-national comparison of countries mentions. 76(1):67–85.

Quantifying Cross-platform Engagement through Large-scale User Alignment

Jiejun Xu, Tsai-Ching Lu, Ryan Compton, David Allen
HRL Laboratories
3011 Malibu Canyon Road
Malibu, CA 90265
{jxu, tlu, rfcompton, dallen}@hrl.com

ABSTRACT

As online social media becomes prevalent as part of our daily life, it is increasingly common for a user to have accounts on multiple social media platforms. In this work, we present our findings on quantifying the extent of user engagement of different platforms as well as their correlations. The study is conducted based on a large-scale user alignment on 6 major social media platforms. Specifically, we identify both explicit and implicit mentions of social media accounts from the Twitter Decahose stream over a period of 22 months. During the process, we have aligned a total of $21,456,808$ Twitter users to their alternative accounts on different platforms. Subsequently, we extract the number of overlapping users between any combination of these social media platforms exhaustively.

Categories and Subject Descriptors

H.4 [**Information Systems Applications**]: Miscellaneous; J.4 [**Computer Applications**]: Social And Behavioral Sciences

General Terms

Measurement, Human Behavior

1. INTRODUCTION

Online social media has gained tremendous popularity over the past decade. Each social media platform has different characteristic and usually focuses on different aspect of the user needs. For instance, Twitter and Facebook focus more on communication, while Tumblr and Instagram focus more on photo sharing. As a results, it is common for a user to have multiple accounts on different social media platforms to accommodate his needs. In this work, we present a study on quantifying the level of user engagement on different combinations of the social media platforms. Specifically, we conduct a large-scale user alignment across 6 major social media platforms to extract the number of overlapping

WebSci'14, June 23–26, 2014, Bloomington, IN, USA.
ACM 978-1-4503-2622-3/14/06.
http://dx.doi.org/10.1145/2615569.2615662 .

users. These platforms include Twitter, Tumblr, Wordpress, Blogger, Instagram, and Facebook.

Several recent works have started to investigate the cross-platform alignment problem for user modeling, personalization and recommendation. For instance, Abisheva et al. [1] combined user data from Twitter and YouTube to provide a descriptive analysis of the demographics and behavioral features on the two online communities. Vu et al. [7] proposed a general and extensive system architecture for aggregating and integrating users' social profiles into collaborative systems. Tiroshi et al. [6] modeled online users based on features extracted from different social media sites. They showed that aggregated user profile enhanced personalization service effectively. Similar study has been conducted by Deng et al. [2] to improve personalized video recommendation. There are also studies focused on developing methodologies to accurately map users across platforms. Zafarani et al. [9] introduced a behavioral-modeling based approach to connect individual across social media sites. Other recent works on user mapping utilized network attributes [3] and a variety of content features [5] to de-anonymize users across sites.

Most prior work focused on aligning users with relatively confined datasets. In contrast, the main contribution of our effort is the cross-platform user alignment *at scale*, using a large real-world data stream to derive representative results for major social media platforms. To the best of our knowledge, this is the first attempt to quantify overlapping social media usage from a variety of platforms in such a scale.

2. USER ALIGNMENT

We take a simple extractive-based approach to identify mentions of social media user accounts from the Twitter datastream, which consists of 10% sample of public tweets

Tumblr	http://[www.]*[a-zA-Z0-9-_]+.tumblr.com http://tmblr.co/(\\S{4,20})\
Wordpress	http://[www.]*[a-zA-Z0-9-_]+.wordpress.com http://.*wp[.]me.*
Blogger	http://[www.]*[a-zA-Z0-9-_]+.blogspot.com N/A
Instagram	http://[www.]*instagram.com/[a-zA-Z0-9-_]+ http://instagr\\S{3,7}/p/\\S+?\
Facebook	http://www.facebook.com/(\\S+) N/A

Figure 1: Regex patterns used for identifying social media accounts from the Twitter data. Note that the matched Short URLs are resolved to full account address in post processing.

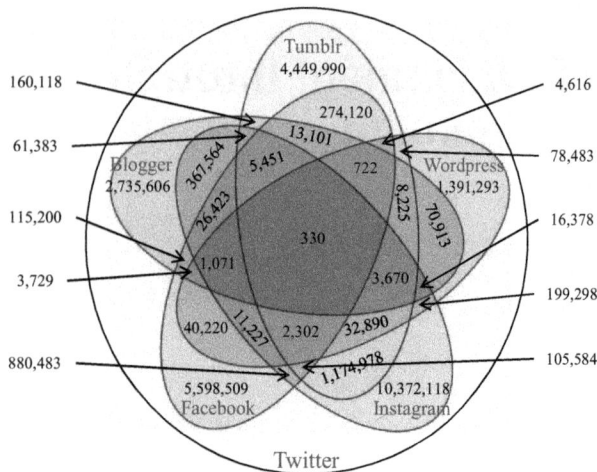

Figure 2: A Venn Diagram showing the number of aligned users from different combinations of social media platforms.

	Total Aligned Pairs	Unique Users (By Twitter ID)	Geo-coded Users
Tumblr	6,549,937	4,449,990	3,593,058
Wordpress	1,766,825	1,391,293	887,986
Blogger	3,042,319	2,735,606	1,794,895
Facebook	6,545,446	5,598,509	4,040,912
Instagram	10,372,118	10,372,118	9,605,944

Figure 3: User alignment and geocoding statistics derived from Twitter.

3. DISCUSSION

A total of 21,456,808 Twitter users have been aligned to other accounts in various social media platforms. Subsequently, we compute the number of overlapping users for different combination of social media platforms exhaustively. The Venn diagram in Figure 2 summarizes our findings. New platforms such as Instagram, Tumblr and Facebook appear to have more penetrations on the alignment, while older blogging platforms such as Blogger and Wordpress seem to have less. User alignment allows for information reuse across platforms. For instance, user geolocations are derived in [4] for the Twitter platform, and a substantial amount of this information propagates to other platforms through alignment (see Figure 3). Our future work may include user profile modeling, interest prediction, and collaborative summarization from aligned accounts in multiple social media platforms.

4. ACKNOWLEDGMENTS

Supported by the Intelligence Advanced Research Projects Activity (IARPA) via Department of Interior National Business Center (DoI / NBC) Contract Number D12PC00285. The U.S. Government is authorized to reproduce and distribute reprints for Governmental purposes notwithstanding any copyright annotation thereon. The views and conclusions contained herein are those of the author(s) and should not be interpreted as necessarily representing the official policies or endorsements, either expressed or implied, of IARPA, DoI/NBC, or the U.S. Government.

5. REFERENCES

[1] A. Abisheva, V. R. K. Garimella, D. Garcia, and I. Weber. Who watches (and shares) what on youtube? and when? using twitter to understand youtube viewership. CoRR, 2013.

[2] Z. Deng, J. Sang, and C. Xu. Personalized video recommendation based on cross-platform user modeling. In International Conference on Multimedia and Expo, 2013.

[3] P. Jain, P. Kumaraguru, and A. Joshi. @i seek 'fb.me': Identifying users across multiple online social networks. In Proceedings of the 22Nd International Conference on World Wide Web Companion, WWW '13 Companion, 2013.

[4] D. Jurgens. That's what friends are for: Inferring location in online social media platforms based on social relationships. In International Conference on Weblogs and Social Media, 2013.

[5] M. Korayem and D. J. Crandall. De-anonymizing users across heterogeneous social computing platforms. In International Conference on Weblogs and Social Media, 2013.

[6] A. Tiroshi, S. Berkovsky, M. A. Kaafar, T. Chen, and T. Kuflik. Cross social networks interests predictions based ongraph features. In Proceedings of the 7th ACM Conference on Recommender Systems, RecSys '13, 2013.

[7] X.-T. Vu, M.-H. Abel, and P. Morizet-Mahoudeaux. Integrating social network data for empowering collaborative systems. Advances in Intelligent Systems and Computing. Springer, 2013.

[8] J. Xu, R. Compton, T.-C. Lu, and D. Allen. Rolling through tumblr: Characterizing behavioral patterns of the microblogging platform. In ACM Web Science Conference, 2014.

[9] R. Zafarani and H. Liu. Connecting users across social media sites: A behavioral-modeling approach. In Proceedings of the 19th ACM SIGKDD International Conference on Knowledge Discovery and Data Mining, KDD '13, 2013.

from April 2012 to January 2014 obtained through the GNIP Decahose. The full dataset amounted to 67.2TB of uncompressed JSON records. Each record contains the content of the tweet as well as the profile information of the corresponding Twitter user. Two types of user account mentions are searched in our work. The first type is the *Explicit Self-reported* accounts. We search for every user profiles in our Twitter corpus with the regular expressions, which indicate different social media platforms. For instance, we searched for the pattern "http://[www.]*[a-zA-Z0-9-_].tumblr.com" for mentions of Tumblr user accounts. The second type of account mention is obtained through *Implicit Cross-Links*. Many existing social media sites support content synchronization in order to reduce end user effort. This allows a user to submit a post from one platform, and publish the same content to all other social media accounts under him or herself. For the case of Twitter, there is usually a URL appended at the end of a tweet to indicate its origin. For example, if a post was original published in Tumblr, and the content was synchronized to Twitter. There would be a short URL encoded at the end of the tweet referring back to the Tumblr post (e.g., http://tmblr.co/ZVxw1y15H_Go3). The original Tumblr user account can be obtained by resolving the short URL. This type of cross-referencing is very useful in terms of identifying the same user across the two platforms. This is because the short URL (with prefix pattern "tmblr.co") is automatically generated by the Tumblr server, and it would be triggered by the synchronization process between two linked accounts. Since synchronization only happens when a user owns both accounts, this is a reliable way to identify same users across platforms. A more detailed evaluation is presented in [8] to demonstrate the effectiveness and accuracy of this approach. Overall, this method results in 95% accuracy in terms of linking user across platforms. The rare cases of error are due to direct "copy-and-paste" of tweet messages. Figure 1 summarizes the Regex patterns used for both explicit and implicit identification of account mentions of different platforms. Note that we do not search the implicit cross-link patterns for Blogger and Facebook, as the short URLs generated from both platforms can't be resolved to user accounts exclusively.

Infowar on the Web: Measuring Mass Annoyance

Stéphane B. Bazan
UIR Web Science - CEMAM
Saint-Joseph University of Beirut.
stefan.bazan@usj.edu.lb

Sabrine Saad
UIR Web Science - CEMAM
Saint-Joseph University of Beirut
sabrine.saad@usj.edu.lb

Addis Tesfa
UIR Web Science - CEMAM
Saint-Joseph University of Beirut
addis.tesfa@usj.edu.lb

ABSTRACT

Research on Information Warfare on the Web is still at an early stage and the question of the true nature of Cyberwarfare actions that target the Web needs to be answered on both conceptual and methodological levels. Existing research proved that the Web is a new battlefield with specific strategic objectives, but research needs to create assessment tools to validate the impact of Cyberattacks, especially when they aim at "soft" targets like Web sites or Social Media platforms. This position paper serves as starting point of reference and discussion and wants to clarify several misunderstandings in definitions of Information Warfare and Cyberwarfare. It also offers methodological directions to identify actions and measure their impact to answer the question: Is Cyberwarfare just a weapon of mass annoyance?

Categories and Subject Descriptors

K.4.1 [**Computers and Society**]: Public Policy Issues – *Abuse and crime involving computers.*

General Terms

Measurement, Documentation, Human Factors, Theory.

Keywords

Web Science, Cyberwarfare, Information Warfare, Security, Strategy, Measurement, Definitions.

1. INTRODUCTION

The UIR Web Science at USJ Beirut answered the call for interdisciplinary research to understand the Web and its impact on society, with a specific approach: the Web is one, but the experience is quite different depending on where you are on the globe [1]. This "contextual" dimension is almost inevitable when you observe the Web from the Middle-East. Cultures, languages, history, politics create distortions and alter the global trends of Web impact and usage.

1.1 Examples of Infowar on the Web

Our previous researches on the use of the Web as a weapon to create strategic advantages in asymmetric conflicts provided the Web Science community with original insights in what War on the Web could look like from a contextual point of view. The first context was the 2006 war between Israel and Hezbollah [2] and

WebSci'14, June 23–26, 2014, Bloomington, IN, USA.
ACM 978-1-4503-2622-3/14/06.
http://dx.doi.org/10.1145/2615569.2615664

we demonstrated at the time that the Web was deliberately used by belligerents as a strategic platform to gain strategic advantage. The second study aimed at understanding the rules of engagement on the Web in the context of the Syrian civil war [3]. Considered as the first example of "civil Infowar", the Syrian war proved that the Web and Social Media platforms could easily be transformed into battlefields to make strategic gains: the regime used fake accounts and deception techniques to identify rebels, denature their claims and create confusion. We also witnessed in this context the first official recognition by a chief of state that his regular army was supported online by an "Electronic Army", the first of its kind in the region.

2. RESEARCHING WEB INFOWAR

From Sun Tzu and Clausewitz to more recent definitions of Digital Wars, Information Operations or Computer Networks Operation, Information Warfare is a catch-all concept and "scholars should improve the research agenda on CNO to include more rigorous studies and thus contribute to reversing the hype and misinformation that now surrounds such important topic". [4]

2.1 Cyberwar, a myth?

On a fundamental level and following Thomas Rid's clarion call that "Cyberwar will not take place" [5], there's a growing debate on the nature of "Electronic Wars". Erik Gartzke talks about the "myth of Cyberwar" [6] and explains that "studying what could happen in Cyberspace (or anywhere else) makes little sense without considering how Internet conflict is going to accomplish the tasks commonly addressed by terrestrial warfare. Cyberwar is much more likely to serve as an adjunct to, rather than a substitute for, existing forms of political violence. Indeed, rather than threatening existing hierarchies, cyberwar appears much more likely to augment the military advantages of status quo powers" [6]. If authors do not agree on the definition of Infowar, they all agree that most countries did have an "awakening" at some point in recent times and "are only now beginning to see attempts to deal with the inherent vulnerability in critical infrastructure and government military networks" [7].

2.2 The Web as a multiplier effect

A second level of complexity comes with the technical nature of Infowar and raises the following question: does Cyberattacks target the Web or is the Web just another collateral asset to multiply the effect of larger scope objectives? To answer this question, we need to make a clear difference between Cyberattacks and warfare actions that target the communication structure (the Internet) and Infowar tactics on the Web itself. This distinction was clearly illustrated by the famous "weapons of mass annoyance" notion phrased by Stewart Baker [8].

2.3 Identification and measure

The third level concerns methodology: how do we measure Infowar, in terms of types of actions, frequency and efficiency? A 2003 paper by Giacomello [4] suggests that it should be possible to measure Cyberwars. "In democratic countries, it should be even possible to compare different measurements and include the public in an open discussion. But research on digital wars takes place in closed laboratories and feeding public opinion with unverifiable data and the media with "ad hoc" anecdotes seem common developments in several countries".

The main questions behind Infowar research lie in the difficulty to observe and independently measure it: like any information related to strategic issues, data is scarce and most of the sources use deception techniques or amplification of assessment, in order to guarantee efficiency. Many authors [5, 6] are questioning the reality of Infowar, due to the lack of independent scientific tools to evaluate the true impact of Cyberattacks.

3. The BTKP rule and Infowar on the Web

The pivotal aspect of the nature of Infowar resides in the capability of the attack to transform the equilibrium of forces or imply destruction or killing of human beings. To define Infowar on the Web, we need to delimitate what we call "the Web": Should we just consider the Web as a set of technologies (Hypertext, HTML, URLs, browser and HTTP servers) or do we need to extend the Web to all kind of human activities created with it? A Cyberattack could indeed reduce our capacity to link, share and post, learn or be informed of a situation through web sites by denying access to a server or limiting a server's capacities. In the context of the Cyberwar in the Middle-East, official telecommunication structures are heavily controlled by public stakeholders: they control access to information through the public networks and security services-owned proxy servers [3]. But for different approaches that might consider the strict military definition of CNO (Computer Networks Operations), this type and many other types of Cyberattacks on the Web do not fall under the "break things and kill people" rule [4]. This includes psychological warfare (PSYOP), Open source intelligence, Web page defacement or hacktivism. These actions could give a strategic advantage to a belligerent that might eventually lead him to victory, but this situation is highly improbable. Infowar on the Web appears in certain contexts and seems to have different strategic objectives than the more "traditional" examples of Cyberattacks (DDOS, viruses, worms, Man in the Middle, etc.). Subnational, transnational and supranational organizations and groups [9] have a preference for Web targets: the visibility they provide and their relative harmlessness is a strategic choice for them

4. MEASURING INFOWAR

Major contributions to the subject were outlined in Giacomello's paper [4]. The author presents the example of "missions of peace" researchers that needed to provide dependable data "as counterbalance to the views expressed by national security communities and military analysts". Today, most of the data available on Infowar operations comes from two main sources: the intelligence community (mainly built around state structures or official think tanks and research centers) and hackers using specialized forums or Darknet sites to promote the technicalities of their achievements. Both sources have their own agendas and their information cannot be fully trusted. Measuring Infowar would need independent observers to validate: 1) the existence of

the action, by identifying qualitative traces or quantitative distortions in usage, 2) a clear reading of the strategic intention by following available web content, 3) the availability of technical means in the hands of the attackers and 4) a precise evaluation of the damage done. Such a dataset would of course indicate the context of the attack, if related to direct conflict on the ground, or if the attack is just another event in an ongoing Cyberwar. Existing Web Science research could also be used to shed a new light on the reality of Infowar: research methods related to trust (Metaxas 2010, O'Hara 2011, Vafopoulos 2011), gatekeepers and filtering (Jürgens et Al. 2011), cybercrime (Yip, 2011, Sugiura, Weber, 2012) and the Web observatory project [1] would eventually provide models and tools to store, analyze, "validate and interpret the data to advise industrialists, policy makers and the wider public as to its true significance".

5. CONCLUSION

To provide the scientific community with a correct assessment of how the Web might be used as a battleground or as a weapon of mass annoyance, Infowar researchers need valid and reliable data to look at, use multiple indicators and gather data from multiple sources. These preliminary steps could lead the way to the creation of resources of reference for research and real-time observation of the evolution of Infowar on the Web... far from the hype.

6. REFERENCES

[1] Bazan, S., Varin, C.(2010) Web Science in the context of the Arab Near East. In: *Proceedings of the WebSci10: Extending the Frontiers of Society On-Line*, 2010, Raleigh, NC: US.

[2] Saad, S., Bazan, S., Varin, C. (2011) Asymmetric Cyber-warfare between Israel and Hezbollah: The Web as a new strategic battlefield. pp. 1-4. In: *Proceedings of the ACM WebSci'11*, June 14-17 2011, Koblenz, Germany.

[3] El Amine, S., Bazan, S., Saad, S., Tesfa, A., Varin, C. Infowar in Syria: The Web between Liberation and Repression. In: *Proceedings of the ACM WebSci'12*, June 2012, Evanston, USA.

[4] Giacomello, G., 2003. Measuring Digital Wars: Learning from the experience of peace research and arms control. *The Information Warfare Site Infocon Magazine Issue 1.*

[5] Rid, T (2012). Cyber War Will Not Take Place in *Journal of Strategic Studies*, vol 35, no 1, 5–32.

[6] Gartzke, E. (2013). The Myth of Cyberwar. *In International Security*, Vol. 38, No. 2 (Fall 2013), pp. 41–73,

[7] Stiennon, R. (2011). There is no cyberwar the way there is no nuclear war. Forbes. November 2011.

[8] Lewis, J. A. (2002). Assessing the Risks of Cyber Terrorism, Cyber War and Other Cyber Threats. CSIS. December 2002.

[9] Kalb, M., Saivetz, C. (2007). The Israel-Hezbollah War of 2006: The Media as a Weapon in Asymmetrical Conflict. The Shorenstein Center on the Press, Politics and Public Policy at Harvard's Kennedy School of Government.

---

[1] http://wstweb1.ecs.soton.ac.uk/?page_id=1637

Scholarometer: A System for Crowdsourcing Scholarly Impact Metrics

Jasleen Kaur, Mohsen JafariAsbagh, Filippo Radicchi, and Filippo Menczer
Center for Complex Networks and Systems Research
School of Informatics and Computing, Indiana University, Bloomington, USA

ABSTRACT

Scholarometer (`scholarometer.indiana.edu`) is a social tool developed to facilitate citation analysis and help evaluate the impact of authors. The Scholarometer service allows scholars to compute various citation-based impact measures. In exchange, users provide disciplinary annotations of authors, which allow for the computation of discipline-specific statistics and discipline-neutral impact metrics. We present here two improvements of our system. First, we integrated a new universal impact metric h_s that uses crowdsourced data to calculate the global rank of a scholar across disciplinary boundaries. Second, improvements made in ambiguous name classification have increased the accuracy from 80% to 87%.

1. SCHOLAROMETER

Scholarly classifications systems like Web of Science, MeSH for life sciences, and ACM CCS for computing, are based on a top-down approach in which the ontology is maintained by curators. As a result, these disciplinary categories do not accommodate the trend toward interdisciplinary scholarship and the continual emergence of new areas at disciplinary boundaries. Disciplinary boundaries create similar hurdles for measuring scholarly impact.

Crowdsourcing approaches can empower scholars to annotate each other's work. The crowdsourcing model has the added advantage that when combined with citation information, it can enable the collection of statistical data necessary for the computation of cross-disciplinary impact metrics. *Scholarometer* (`scholarometer.indiana.edu`) is a social tool for scholarly services developed in our lab with the dual aim of exploring the crowdsourcing of disciplinary annotations and developing cross-disciplinary impact metrics [4, 5]. These two aims are closely related and mutually reinforcing. The annotations enable the collection of discipline-specific statistics and therefore the computation of universal impact metrics. In turn, the service provided

WebSci'14, June 23–26, 2014, Bloomington, IN, USA.
ACM 978-1-4503-2622-3/14/06.
http://dx.doi.org/10.1145/2615569.2615669 .

by computing these metrics works as an incentive for the users to provide the annotations.

Tools exist for both citation analysis (e.g., Publish or Perish [2]) and social management of bibliographic records (e.g., Mendeley). To our knowledge, Scholarometer is the first system that attempts to couple these two functions with the goal of achieving a synergy between disciplinary annotations and universal impact metrics [4, 5]. Social tagging of scholarly work has already been adopted in popular systems such as Bibsonomy [1] and many others. In the folksonomies that result from these social tagging systems, tags are assigned to papers. Tags have also been used to describe journals [3]. In Scholarometer, users tag authors instead. Recently, similar skill endorsements have been introduced by systems such as LinkedIn and ResearchGate. Currently, our system is the only one that makes these annotations publicly available.

The Scholarometer interface (Figure 1) lets users query and tag authors. The tagging interface implements a compromise between the use of a controlled vocabulary and free tagging; the user must enter at least one subject category from the Thomson-Reuters/ISI citation indices and can enter any free tags without additional constraints. Facilities are available for sorting, filtering, deleting, merging, and exporting records. Finally, a citation analysis panel reports on various impact measures.

As of March 2014, the queries submitted to Scholarometer resulted in a collection of citation data about 39,000 authors of 2.8 million articles in 2,400 disciplines. Further statistics for authors and disciplines are available on the Scholarometer website.

Scholarometer provides ways to share the crowdsourced data with the research community via an API and to explore the data through interactive visualizations of discipline networks and author networks. These visualizations can help identify potential referees, members of program committees and grant panels, collaborators, and so on.

2. GLOBAL RANKING BY IMPACT

Our tool has been used to evaluate many proposed impact metrics with the goal of providing "universal" metrics that allow for the comparison of author impact across disciplines [5, 6]. One of these metrics, h_s, has been shown to be able to remove discipline bias [6]. We defined h_s as the h-index of an author normalized by the average h of the author's discipline. We have integrated this universal impact metric in Scholarometer. However, it is not trivial to compute the global ranking of scholars who are annotated with multiple disciplines. A multi-disciplinary author will have

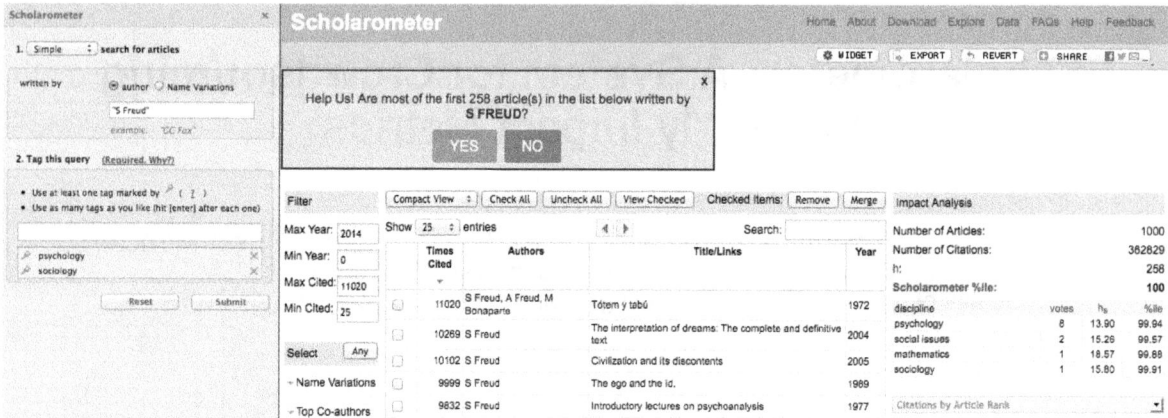

Figure 1: Illustration of the Scholarometer interface. The box at the top allows the user to provide binary feedback about whether the queried name is ambiguous.

multiple h_s values. To obtain a single Scholarometer rank (see Figure 1), we considered the following methods:

$$rank_s = rank(\sum_{d \in D} w_d.rank_d(h)) \qquad (1)$$

$$rank_s = rank(h/\sum w_d.\langle h \rangle_d) \qquad (2)$$

$$rank_s = rank(\sum_{d \in D} w_d.h/\langle h \rangle_d) \qquad (3)$$

where d is a discipline in the set D of disciplines, $\langle h \rangle_d$ is the average h of the authors annotated with discipline d, w_d corresponds to the number of times an author is tagged with discipline d, and, finally, $rank_d$ is the rank of an author within discipline d.

We computed the ranks of all scholars based on all three methods. We rejected method (1) as it is sensitive to the local rank of the author, especially in those disciplines with few authors. Methods (2) and (3) produce the same author rankings, except when authors are tagged with more than one discipline, some of which are unreliable. Method (2) tends to penalize authors who are tagged with unreliable disciplines. Let us consider the example of an author with $h = 10$ who is tagged once with "computer science (cs)" ($\langle h_{cs} \rangle = 2$). Both methods (2) and (3) would produce the same value of $h_s(cs) = 5$: this implies that the author is 5 times above the average of authors in "cs"; this value will be used to obtain her/his global rank. Now, let us imagine that the author is also tagged once with the unreliable discipline "underwater basket weaving (ubw)", that has only this one author; the discipline's $\langle h_{ubw} \rangle$ would be 10 and the author's $h_s(ubw) = 1$. According to the two methods, the combined h_s value would be 1.67 (method (2)) and 3 (method (3)). To avoid such penalizations, we adopted method (3) to generate the global Scholarometer rank.

3. NAME DISAMBIGUATION

The name ambiguity problem is especially challenging in the field of bibliographic digital libraries. The problem is amplified when names are collected from heterogeneous sources and leads to computation of biased impact metrics. This is the case in the Scholarometer system, which performs bibliometric analysis by cross-correlating author names in user queries with those retrieved from digital libraries. The uncontrolled nature of user-generated annotations is very valuable but creates the need to detect ambiguous names. We obtained promising results in the scholar name disambiguation problem by employing three kinds of heuristic features based on citations, publications, and crowdsourced topics [7]. However, ambiguous names remain a serious challenge for bibliometric analysis.

Here we report on improvements in the ambiguous name detection, achieved by integrating feedback from users. We added a button in the results window (see Figure 1) to obtain feedback about whether the query is ambiguous or not. This is the only feedback we collect from users, who cannot modify our database. We used the collected feedback to retrain the classifier. This way, the training set increased from approximately 500 manually labeled authors to 3,350 authors at the time of this writing. We used the same four features based on citations, crowdsourced topics, and publication metadata with the random forest algorithm, as it outperformed the previous logistic regression algorithm [7]. Our modified approach can detect ambiguous author names in crowdsourced scholarly data with an improved accuracy of 87% compared to the previously reported accuracy of 80%.

Acknowledgements. We thank Xiaoling Sun, Diep Thi Hoang, and Lino Possamai for their contributions to the Scholarometer project. This work is partly supported by the Lilly Endowment and NSF (award IIS-0811994).

4. REFERENCES

[1] D. Benz, A. Hotho, R. Jäschke, B. Krause, F. Mitzlaff, C. Schmitz, and G. Stumme. The social bookmark and publication management system bibsonomy. *The VLDB Journal*, 19(6):849–875, 2010.

[2] A.-W. Harzing. *The publish or perish book*. Tarma Software Research, 2010.

[3] S. Haustein and I. Peters. Using social bookmarks and tags as alternative indicators of journal content description. *First Monday*, 17(11), 2012.

[4] D. T. Hoang, J. Kaur, and F. Menczer. Crowdsourcing scholarly data. In *Proc. Web Science Conference: Extending the Frontiers of Society On-Line (WebSci)*, 2010.

[5] J. Kaur, D. T. Hoang, X. Sun, L. Possamai, M. JafariAsbagh, S. Patil, and F. Menczer. Scholarometer: A social framework for analyzing impact across disciplines. *PloS one*, 7(9):e43235, 2012.

[6] J. Kaur, F. Radicchi, and F. Menczer. Universality of scholarly impact metrics. *Journal of Informetrics*, 7(4):924—932, 2013.

[7] X. Sun, J. Kaur, L. Possamai, and F. Menczer. Ambiguous author query detection using crowdsourced digital library annotations. *Information Processing and Management*, 49(2):454–464, 2013.

Analyzing the Climate Change Debate on Twitter – Content and Differences between Genders

Kim Holmberg
Department of Organization Sciences
VU University Amsterdam
The Netherlands
kim.holmberg@abo.fi

Iina Hellsten
Department of Organization Sciences
VU University Amsterdam
The Netherlands
i.r.hellsten@vu.nl

ABSTRACT

We present a study about gender differences towards anthropogenic impact on climate change, as discovered from the climate change debate on Twitter. Our dataset consists of about 250,000 tweets and retweets for which the authors' gender was identified. We researched the hashtags and usernames that were proportionately more frequently mentioned by either male or female tweeters. Our results show significant differences between female and male tweeters, with female tweeters mentioning significantly more campaigns and organizations with a convinced attitude towards anthropogenic impact on climate change, and male tweeters mentioning significantly more private persons and usernames with a sceptical stance.

Keywords

Climate change, Twitter, gender differences, male, female

1. INTRODUCTION

Social media and Twitter in particularly provide new venues and research opportunities for computational social sciences as researchers can mine tweets for public opinions and attitudes, social activities and networks, and trends in conversations and information sharing patterns. Social media may even have an important role in creating public opinions about different issues as it has been discovered to be a very efficient medium to spread ideas and news [1] and to engage people in environmental activism [2]. Environmental issues, climate change and global warming are hotly debated topics on many forums, social media none the least. In this paper, we focus on Tweets about climate change and in particular gender differences in the climate change debate between male and female tweeters.

2. LITERATURE REVIEW

In general, women have been found to be more concerned about climate change than men and possessing greater scientific knowledge about the issue, in the context of American public [3]. This is related to a more general tendency of women being more concerned about local environmental issues than males. In addition, women tend to be more willing to take voluntary actions to mitigate climate change, such as trying to reduce greenhouse emissions, while men *are more willing to support government policies to impose public sacrifices in order to reduce greenhouse gas emissions* [4]. Gender differences in online context have not

WebSci'14, June 23–26, 2014, Bloomington, IN, USA.
ACM 978-1-4503-2622-3/14/06.
http://dx.doi.org/10.1145/2615569.2615638

been widely researched before. Bamman et al. [5] focused on linguistic gender differences and contrasted 'female' and 'male' linguistic styles in Twitter to the social networks of these tweeters. Cunha et al [6] focused on gender differences in the use of hashtags on Twitter and found that while hashtags used by women show a personal involvement (e.g. I vote for…), hashtags used by men show a persuasive strategy, for instance by expressing a command (e.g. Vote for…). It has also been discovered that men opt for more overt ways of persuasion in their "political hashtags", while women opt for more indirect ways in their hashtags [7]. These topics, climate change debate, gender differences, and social media, have not to the best of our knowledge been combined in a research before. Our aim is to study what kind of differences in the use of hashtags and mentioning of other usernames there are in tweets about climate change from male and female tweeters.

3. DATA AND METHODS

Tweets containing the words "climate change" were collected between October 26, 2013, and January 10, 2014, via Twitter's API with Webometric Analyst [8]. We used Mozdeh (http://mozdeh.wlv.ac.uk/) to identify the gender of the authors of these tweets by comparing tweeters' first names (as written in their Twitter profiles) to common US first names by gender. A total of 94,579 (17.0%) tweets were identified as sent by female tweeters and 145,275 (26.1%) tweets were identified as sent by male tweeters. For 56.9% of the tweets the tweeters' gender could not be determined. For the hashtags and the usernames mentioned in the tweets we calculated the differences in proportions from normal distribution between the two groups of tweeters, i.e., hashtags and usernames that were proportionately more frequently used by either male or female tweeters in comparison to the other. We analyzed usernames and hashtags that scored highest on the z value, i.e. indicating largest proportionate differences. Usernames were coded according to the users' stance in the climate change debate (convinced that the climate change is caused by humans, neutral, sceptic, unclear) and categorized by type of account as: campaign, climate scientist, news sharing, organization, private person, other, and unclear. Type of user was determined based on information from Twitter profile pages and by following links to other webpages. The coding was done by the authors and inter-coder agreement was measured with Cohen's Kappa.

4. RESULTS

We chose to focus on the 15 hashtags with the highest proportionate differences in how female and male tweeters used them. While female tweeters mentioned proportionately more frequently hashtags that were connected to different campaigns and online movements related to climate change (e.g., #thisisreal, #climatenamechange), male tweeters used proportionately more frequently hashtags related to politics (e.g., #policy, #tcot, #gop) or to climate change and environmental issues on a general level (e.g. #agw, #eco, #sustainable). Male tweeters also used hashtags that were on a more general level and that were more descriptive, while female tweeters used more specific hashtags related for instance to a specific event, campaign or person.

The results indicate that both male and female tweeters frequently mention usernames of private persons in their tweets, although men do so much more frequently (male: 51.4%, female: 29.9%). Usernames related to news or news sharing were also frequently mentioned by both groups (male: 18.9%, female: 15.6%). While female tweeters mention organizations frequently in their tweets, men do not so much (male: 2.7%, female: 27.3%). Female tweeters also mentioned usernames related to different campaigns in their tweets, while none of the usernames mentioned more frequently by male tweeters were related to campaigns or online movements (male: 0%, female: 14.3%). Some male tweeters on the other hand mentioned usernames of climate scientists, while none of the usernames mentioned more frequently by female tweeters belonged to climate scientists (male: 8.1%, female: 0%). The inter-coder agreement between the two researchers was calculated using Cohen's kappa, which gave an agreement of 0.765 (81.6% agreement), which constitutes as good agreement.

The results from the coding of the usernames based on the users' stance in the climate change debate showed that female tweeters mentioned significantly more convinced users in their tweets and retweets, and that the male tweeters mentioned significantly more sceptics, while among the usernames mentioned more frequently by female tweeters there were no sceptics at all (Table 1).

Table 1. Usernames mentioned more frequently by male and more frequently by female tweeters according to the username's stance in the climate change debate.

	Mentioned by male tweeters	Mentioned by female tweeters
Convinced	9 (24.3%)	47 (61.0%)
Neutral	9 (24.3%)	11 (14.3%)
Sceptic	11 (29.7%)	0 (0.0%)
Unclear	8 (21.6%)	19 (24.7%)
Total	37 (100.0%)	77 (100.0%)

These differences were also tested for statistical significance by running a chi-square test which confirmed that the proportion of female tweeters mentioning convinced tweeters and the proportion of male tweeters mentioning sceptic tweeters are higher than expected from random tweeting (chi-square=31.28, p=0.000001). The inter-coder agreement was 0.522 on Cohen's kappa (68.4% agreement). The results do however not mean that female tweeters would not mention sceptic usernames at all in their tweets. The results show that among those usernames that women mentioned proportionately more frequently than men there were no sceptics and that among the usernames mentioned proportionately more frequently by male tweeters there were significantly more sceptics. A closer look at the tweets revealed however that some of the usernames mentioned proportionately more frequently by either group were due to frequent retweeting.

5. DISCUSSION

We set out to study differences in the climate change debate between female and male tweeters. The results indicate that while female tweeters tend to show more interest and belief in the anthropogenic impact on climate change and towards campaigns and organizations involved in the debate, male tweeters are more concerned with politics related to climate change and connect more with those that have a sceptic stance in the climate change debate. It is however unclear whether these differences are due to more fundamental differences in the way men and women use social media or whether the differences reflect male and female opinions about anthropogenic impact on climate change. The latter is however supported by some earlier findings [e.g. 3, 4].

The present study is not without limitations. The tweets represent only those tweeters whose gender could be determined. This however still means that about 250,000 tweets were included in the study, which should constitute for large enough sample for detection of reliable trends. Another concern that one might raise is that because we calculated large numbers of proportional differences in the frequencies hashtags and usernames were used there is a possibility that some of the results were gained by chance, however, the z values are still useful to indicate trends in the proportional differences between the two groups. In addition, any anomalies should have been detected when the data was analyzed and coded into categories, which was not the case.

6. ACKNOWLEDGMENTS

The authors acknowledge the support of the Dutch Scientific Organization in the Netherlands (NWO-ORA grant 464-10-077).

7. REFERENCES

[1] Jansen, B.J. et al. (2009). Twitter power: tweets as electronic word of mouth. *Journal of the American Society for Information Science and Technology*, 60, 11, 2169-2188.

[2] Cheong, M. & Lee, V. (2010). Twittering for earth: A study on the impact of microblogging activism on Earth Hour 2009 in Australia. *Lecture Notes in Computer Science*, 5991, 114-123.

[3] McCright, A. M. (2010) The effects of gender on climate change knowledge and concern in the American public, *Population and Environment*, 32, 66-87.

[4] O'Connor, R. E., Bord, R. J & Fisher, A. (1999) Risk perceptions, general environmental beliefs, and willingness to address climate change. *Risk Analysis*, 19, 3, 461-471.

[5] Bamman, D., Eisenstein, J. & Scnoebelen, T. (2012). Gender in Twitter: Styles, stances, and social networks. *arXiv:1210.4567 [cs.CL]*.

[6] Cunha, E., Magno, G., Almeida, V., Goncalves, M. A. & Benevenuto, F. (2012). A gender based study of tagging behavior in Twitter. Proceedings of the 23rd ACM Conference on Hypertext and Social Media, 323-324. Retrieved on February 15, 2014, from http://www.decom.ufop.br/fabricio/download/ht-evandro.pdf.

[7] Cunha, E., Magno, G., Goncalves, M.A., Cambraia, C. & Almeida, V. (2014). He votes or she votes? Female and male discursive strategies in Twitter political hashtags. PLoS ONE, 9, 1: e87041. doi:10.1371/journal.pone.0087041.

[8] Thelwall, M. (2009). *Introduction to webometrics: Quantitative web research for the social sciences*. Synthesis Lectures on Information Concepts, Retrieval, and Services, 2009, 1, 1. San Rafael, CA: Morgan & Claypool.

Are Mobile Users More Vigilant?

M. Giles Phillips
Subforum HCI
PO Box 130451, Boston, MA 02113
+1 617 447 5568
giles@subforum.org

ABSTRACT

As mobile device usage continues to grow, active mobile users frequently interact with mobile devices while doing other things, dividing their attention between the real world and the mediated world. We may infer that these users are highly engaged within a mobile experience or unfulfilled by their real world experience, or maybe they're simply addicted to their social network. But in many cases their frequent usage may be compelled instinctually, by a form of vigilant behavior. This research seeks to understand whether or not mobile usage leads to an increased prevalence of user vigilance, first by establishing criteria that can be used to determine if a specific session of use is vigilant, and then applying these criteria to analyze observed sessions of use for two distinct cohorts: mobile users and situated users. In the analysis, it was found that everyday vigilant usage scenarios are fairly prevalent, and also that mobile users were 3 times more vigilant than situated users. These initial findings need further validation, but may prove significant to interaction design: optimizing a software interface to better support vigilant usage requires an opposing set of considerations when compared to traditional consumer product design. These design considerations are discussed, in addition to the limitations of the study, and guidance for future work.

Categories and Subject Descriptors

H.1.2 [**Information Systems**]: User/Machine Systems – *human factors, human information processing, software psychology.*
H.4.0 [**Information Systems Applications**]: General
H.5.m [**Information Interfaces and Presentation**]: Miscellaneous

Keywords

Vigilance; Social Media; Mobile; Interaction Design.

1. INTRODUCTION

Vigilance is a state of watchfulness, the compulsion for which maps directly to the perceived consequence of missing out on possible observations. Most prior research into vigilance in the realm of HCI has focused exclusively on situated usage with specific tasks that involve watchfulness, in order to understand the physiological impact of a sustained vigilance state when interacting with machines [3-5]. This narrow focus seems to

imply that vigilant scenarios only exist within a small subset of human-computer interactions, namely, situated tasks performed by trained professionals or operators. However, in our interactions with computers, just as with our interactions in the physical world, vigilance is inclusive of, but is not limited to, specific and situated tasks [6]. The true measure of vigilance is not that usage is sustained, but that attention is sustained.

The instinctual basis for entering into a vigilant state is the preservation of self or society [2]. It's easy to see how this applies to a radar operator huddled over the radar screen in a WW2 aircraft. But it's a little more difficult to see how vigilance might relate to everyday device usage by normal users. To understand everyday vigilance, consider teenage social networking behaviors:

For many teens, social network usage is associated with self-preservation because their interactions within that system are a basis for socialization and, partially, the formation and preservation of their identity, their sense of self [7]. In developing these social interactions, a teenager must break her natural methods for real-time communication into the discrete unidirectional communiques that these technologies enable: things like messages, status updates, and photo uploads. These communiques are signals that the teen uses for social encoding, impression management, and identity performance [1]. In so doing, the teen extrapolates socialization from her natural and immediate embodied experience, and pushes it into exogenous and persistent media that she must then watch over. The resultant compulsion to be watchful forces the teenager to be vigilant.

2. STUDY

Are mobile devices, with their nagging, their beeping, and their omnipresence, creating more vigilance scenarios than earlier technologies did? This research seeks to answer this question.

Two user groups were established and their device usage was monitored for vigilance. One user group was comprised of situated users, and the other group was comprised of mobile users. 8 participants were selected for each of the two user groups.

The study consisted of two distinct phases. The first phase was a phone interview within which users were asked to describe their technology usage patterns and their relationship to their devices.

The second phase was a longitudinal study. Participants were asked to maintain an online daily journal, where they described a specific session of use that occurred on that day.

Because of the diversity of users and their relationship to computing devices and software, it is difficult to describe any general usage scenario as categorically vigilant or not. For a user who is deeply engaged in a social network, monitoring that network might become an important aspect of socialization -

important enough to trigger vigilant attention. However, a casual user of that same social network may feel no need to monitor things – their usage may be entirely non-vigilant. In order to observe the prevalence of vigilance among day-to-day computer usage scenarios, we must establish a set of criteria against which an individual observed session of use can be evaluated as vigilant or not. For this study, the following criteria were used:

1. High Task Importance
2. Endogenous or Exogenous Cueing
3. Dire Consequences for Failure to Complete Task

3. ANALYSIS

A total of 224 journal entries were recorded: 14 entries for each of the 16 participants. Each journal entry described a single session of device usage for the day the entry was submitted; as such, the journal captured user descriptions of 224 distinct sessions of use. Users were not directly asked if they were being vigilant or not; rather, they were asked a number of questions related to the type of tasks they were doing, the relative importance of these tasks, and what events prompted their session of use. The responses within each journal entry were then analyzed according to the vigilance criteria in order to determine whether the corresponding session of use appeared to be vigilant or not. For the mobile group, 43.8% of the recorded sessions were vigilant. For the situated group, 14.3% of the recorded sessions were vigilant. Thus, it was observed that mobile users are about 3 times more likely to be vigilant than situated users.

Users were also asked to speculate about the consequences if they had not completed the tasks involved. This was accomplished through a pair of questions that were together included in 144 of the 224 journal entries, the first asking if failure to complete the task would have been a problem, the other asking for speculation about what would have happened if they'd failed to complete the task. Users associated negative or dire consequences with failure to complete their task for 95.2% of the vigilant sessions captured. This high correlation may validate that the usage was vigilant.

Mobile users had a higher standard deviation of 2.6 vigilant sessions per user compared to 1.5 for the situated users, indicating greater variance in the vigilance of mobile users. This could be because mobile devices support a greater diversity of usage scenarios, whereas situated usage was more often correlated with planned work. There may also be more variation among mobile users in the perceived importance of monitoring the device.

Mobile users reported that they felt the need to be watchful over their device on 78% of the days observed, while situated users felt the same need on 44% of the days observed. Watchfulness was established by directly asking users whether they felt the need to be watchful or not, each day. Measuring watchfulness was useful a number of ways. First, to account for unobserved usage sessions that may have been vigilant. Because each daily journal asked users only to describe their most recent, or most notable session of use on a particular day, it captured only a subset of all sessions that the user actually conducted each day. Self-reported watchfulness was much more commonly observed than vigilance was: the ratio of watchfulness to vigilance was 78:43.8 (57%) for mobile users and 44:14.3 (32.5%) for situated users. This may suggest that a significant number of vigilant sessions occurred outside of the sessions described in the journal entries. Secondly, self-described watchfulness was used as a measure of quality

control of the vigilance criteria: vigilant sessions should always correlate to days where the user described a need to be watchful. This was found to be the case: across both mobile and situated user groups, it was observed that 95.5% of the sessions that were found to be vigilant occurred on days where the user described a need to be watchful over his or her device.

4. CONCLUSION

This study had several limitations requiring additional research in order to validate the findings. With a small population size of 16 participants, the results are not statistically reliable. A similar study should be performed with an increased population size, increasing the total number of journal entries for analysis. With a larger population, distinct cohorts could also be defined, enabling analysis of vigilance behavior based upon age range or other demographic criteria. Another key limitation of this work was that it relied upon self-reporting rather than instrumentation or direct observation.

This study suggests that vigilance is an important and common usage motivator for everyday consumers, and also that mobile devices have increased the prevalence of vigilant use. This research further supports the observation that everyday users might be quite vigilant in their device usage. Vigilance in HCI is not limited to specific situated tasks performed by trained professionals or operators; rather, vigilant use applies to a broad spectrum of tasks performed by consumers. In short, it is more important to support vigilance in a world full of mobile users. This has profound implications for software, because optimizing the interaction design of a software product to better support vigilant usage requires a different, and at times opposing, set of considerations than traditional consumer product design does.

5. REFERENCES

[1] Boyd, D.: Why Youth (Heart) Social Network Sites: The Role of Networked Publics in Teenage Social Life. In: Buckingham, D. (ed.) MacArthur Foundation Series on Digital Learning - Youth, Identity, and Digital Media Volume, pp. 119-142. MIT Press, Cambridge MA (2007)

[2] Edmunds, M.: Defense In Animals: a Survey of Anti-predator Defenses. Longman, New York NY (1974)

[3] Mackworth, N.H.: The breakdown of vigilance during prolonged visual search. Quarterly Journal of Experimental Psychology 1, 6-21 (1948)

[4] Parasuraman, R.: Sustained attention: a multifactorial approach. In: Posner M., Marin, O. (eds.) Attention and performance XI, pp. 493-511. Lawrence Erlbaum, Hillsdale NJ (1985)

[5] Parasuraman, R. & Caggiano, G.: Neural and genetic assays of mental workload. In: McBride, D., Schmorrow, D. (eds.) Quantifying Human Information Processing, pp. 123–155. Rowman and Littlefield, Lanham MD (2005)

[6] Phillips, M.G.: Designing for Vigilance during Intermittent Use. In: 3rd Annual ACM Web Science Conference, pp. 243-246. ACM, New York, NY (2012)

[7] Turkle, S.: Alone Together. Basic Books, New York NY (2011)

Open Educational Resource based Information Understanding via PDF Document Interaction

Xiaozhong Liu, Noriko Hara
School of Informatics and Computing
Indiana University Bloomington
Telephone number, incl. country code

liu237, nhara@indiana.edu

Liangcai Gao
Institute of Computer Science &
Technology

Peking University, Beijing China
gaoliangcai@pku.edu.cn

Yizhou Sun
College of Computer and Information
Science

Northeastern University
yi.sun@neu.edu

ABSTRACT

While classical information retrieval and recommendation can provide users effective information access, for scientific documents, i.e., scientific publications, however, understanding the content of scientific publications remains daunting, i.e., *Information Access ≠ Information Understanding*. In order to help students and junior scholars better understand the essence of scientific topics discussed in scholarly papers, we propose an innovative approach to recommend high-quality open educational resources (OER), such as presentation slides, tutorials, video lectures, project source code, and Wikipedia pages, collected from a number of social media systems. The proposed new system – OER-based Collaborative PDF Reader (OCPR) – captures students' emerging implicit/explicit information needs when reading a scientific paper, while recommending OERs to assist them better understand the target paper.

Keywords
Cyberlearning; Information Understanding; OER; Meta-search

1. INTRODUCTION AND MOTIVATION

Access to digital scientific publications provides convenience and rapid distribution of research, which may result in accelerated research. However, reading and understanding scientific publications remain problematic [2], while most existing reading systems limit learning possibilities and are proving to be increasingly inadequate as the complexity and volume of scholarly output grows: *Information Access ≠ Information Understanding*. Students need innovative scaffolding methods [4] to assist them better understand scientific publications.

Although the content of scientific publications is becoming challenging and difficult for students, a large number of open educational resources (OERs) are increasingly available to help students better comprehend the essence of these publications. For example, scholars, organizations and institutions commonly share conference slides, video lectures, tutorials, Wikipedia pages, datasets and source codes generated from research. As these OERs are often seamlessly blended or integrated with other scholarly publications or research topics students can, we surmise, better understand the papers by leveraging those OERs. In this paper, we define it as OER-based Scaffolding.

A number of studies have presented empirical evidence that social annotation can enhance learning. For example, students were found to have positive perceptions of usefulness, ease of use, learning satisfaction, and willingness for future use towards the Personalized Annotation Management Software (PAMS) 2.0 system. We believe that a specialized educational scaffolding system is necessary to help students better navigate published scientific research. In a study by Liu [2], students expect that a blend of OER-based learning objects could significantly improve learning. Unfortunately, not all OERs exist in a publication as cited references; some may be scattered across different social media (e.g., *TED, SlideShare, GitHub,* and *Wikipedia*). As another use of OER-based learning objects [3], the algorithm can recommend high-quality resources by using a language model to answer students' textual questions related to a specific paper.

Motivated by these observations and preliminary results, we propose a new solution as well as an innovative system framework to help students and scholars understand and learn from scientific publications in a course environment by leveraging OERs, a.k.a. OER-based scaffolding. A new learning system, called the **OER-based Collaborative PDF Reader (OCPR)**, is to be implemented as a first step towards this effort. Theoretically speaking, the system is also designed to accommodate the needs of students in MOOC (massive open online courses) in addition to those in physical classrooms with varied backgrounds. As Figure 2 shows, the system will provide the following key features:

1. *Capture evidence of students' emerging implicit/explicit information needs when reading a scientific paper.*
2. *Automatically recommend high quality OERs to resolve students' information needs.*
3. *Other students and instructors can actively contribute to this auto-learning process by recommending, changing, annotating, or removing certain resources given an information need. Meanwhile, user feedback can effectively enhance the recommendation algorithm accuracy.*

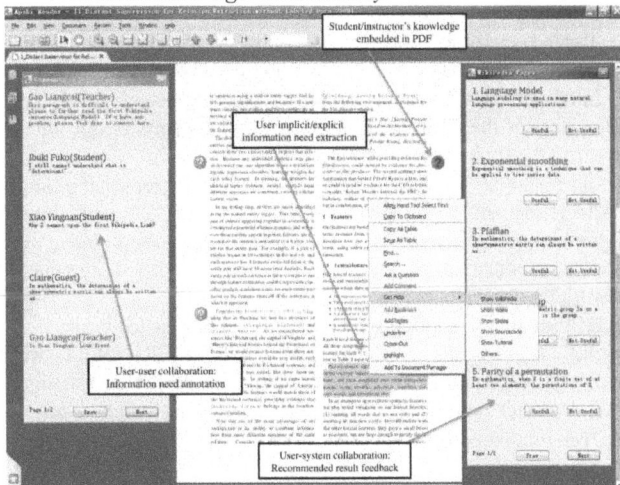

Figure 1. OER-based Collaborative PDF Reader System

WebSci'14, June 23–26, 2014, Bloomington, IN, USA.
ACM 978-1-4503-2622-3/14/06.

2. OER-based Collaborative PDF Reader

To validate the new scaffolding hypothesis and help students better understand the scientific publications in a course environment, we design and implement the novel learning and reading system, OER-based Collaborative PDF Reader (OCPR). The candidate OERs are collected in our prior study [2] with meta-search algorithm. At the backend, the Collaborative PDF Reader has access to OERs and the class reading index and algorithm package, which guarantees efficient OER recommendations and different scaffolding methods.

1) Course Information Management: managing class readings and students information. By using the OCPR, the class instructor can easily manage the class reading list by uploading the class syllabus (in a pre-defined format).

2) OER-based Scaffolding: capturing evidence of students' emerging implicit or explicit information needs when reading a scientific paper and recommending high OERs to address their information needs. As Figure 1 shows, by using the OCPR, students could ask a specific question given a piece of text, which serves as evidence of an explicit information need, or highlight part of a text in the paper, as evidence of an implicit information need. In either case, the OCPR is able to capture the selected or inputted question, and its reading context, from a student in the PDF document. Meanwhile, students can also provide relevance and usefulness feedback for system recommended OERs. The judgment and student click information will be saved as system logs, which will be important for OER recommendation.

3) Collaborative Scaffolding and Instructional Collaborative Scaffolding: enabling students and instructors to asynchronously annotate PDF documents or provide feedback and comments to each existing information need from other students.

3. Recommending OER based on implicit/ explicit information need

This study offers an innovative method to address users explicit or implicit information needs by recommending a variety of OERs. The implicit information need means students cannot propose a specific question when they need help to understand the selected portions. Alternatively, students could ask a specific question, an explicit information need. In either case the algorithm will recommend OER resources based on the following hypotheses.

(1) Keyword hypothesis: Any resource closely related to the target paper topics (keywords) may help the student solve their questions about the paper.

(2) Paper hypothesis: Any resource closely related to the target paper may help the student solve their questions about the paper.

(3) Information need hypothesis: Any resource content that matches the content of the information need (highlighted parts or question) may help the student solve their questions.

To formulate a high quality query for this system, take into consideration all three hypotheses, "Keyword", "Paper", and "Information need", to optimize the OER results. In this study, we used a combination of the language model and the inference network model [1] to address this problem.

As OCPR can also capture students' OER usefulness feedback, i.e., "useful" (POS_OER) or "not useful" (NEG_OER) OERs, we employed relevance feedback method to enhance the information need characterization, θ_{IN}, where the updated information need, θ'_{IN}, can by written by:

$$\theta'_{IN} = \alpha \cdot \theta_{IN} + \frac{1}{|POS\_OER|} \sum_{POS\_OER} \frac{OER_i}{|OER_i|} - \frac{1}{|NEG-OER|} \sum_{NEG-OER} \frac{OER_j}{|OER_j|}$$

4. OER Recommendation Evaluation

In order to validate the system, and automatic OER recommendation algorithm performance, we designed a preliminary evaluation by using a prototype system, where the user can ask any specific question for a target publication, and the system can recommend OERs to answer their questions. A total number of 334 recommended OERs were judged by participants, and participates joined this evaluation were required to read the paper and OERs. We used Mean Reciprocal Rank (MRR), the multiplicative inverse of the rank of the first correct answer, and normalized Discount Cumulative Gain (nDCG), the cumulative relevance gain a user receives by examining retrieval results up to a given rank on the list, as the evaluation metrics for this study.

The MRR score for this evaluation is **0.499**, which means, on average, that the first correct answer (OER) appeared in the second position on the recommendation ranking list given a question from student, which is quite positive. For the ranking performance, we test the NDCG@5. The NDCG@5 score for this evaluation is **0.8350**, which means the ranking method by integrating three different hypotheses is effective for OER recommendation ranking.

5. Conclusion and Future Work

In this study, we proposed a new method for recommending high quality OERs to help students better understand the essence of scientific publications given an implicit/explicit information need. We also proposed a new system – OER-based Collaborative PDF Reader – to capture students' information needs, which enables them to interact with system generated OERs. The preliminary evaluation shows that the fully automatic OER recommendation is effective to assist students better understand a given paper.

The evaluation employed for this study is in the preliminary stage, as we do not yet have sufficient data for parameter tuning and model training, i.e., relevance feedback and smoothing. Another critical piece of the future work is personalization. For instance, different users may have varying kinds of information needs, even though they proposed the same question or selected the same part of text in a paper. Some students may prefer to watch a video, while others may want to read a Wikipedia page. In order to tailor the recommendation results for each student, we will use users' feedback to improve the results. In conclusion, we believe that the proposed new system will provide innovative scaffolding for students to improve general understanding of scientific publications with the use of relevant OERs.

REFERENCES

[1] Croft, W. B., Turtle, H. R., & Lewis, D. D. (1991). The use of phrases and structured queries in information retrieval. Paper presented at the Proceedings of the 14th annual international ACM SIGIR conference on Research and development in information retrieval.

[2] Liu, X., (2013). Generating Metadata for Cyberlearning Resource through Information Retrieval and Meta-search, Journal of the American Society for Information Science and Technology, 64(4), 771-786.

[3] Liu, X., & Jia, H. (2013). Answering academic questions for education by recommending Cyberlearning resources. Journal of the American Society for Information Science and Technology, 64(8), 1707–1722.

[4] Wood, D., Bruner, J., & Ross, G. (1976). The role of tutoring in problem solving. Journal of Child Psychology and Psychiatry, 17(2), 89-100

Data-Driven Web Entertainment: The Data Collection and Analysis Practices of Fantasy Sports Players

Gabriel S. Dzodom
Department of Computer Science
Texas A&M University
College Station, TX 77843-3112
gabriel.dzodom@tamu.edu

Frank M. Shipman
Department of Computer Science
Texas A&M University
College Station, TX 77843-3112
shipman@cse.tamu.edu

ABSTRACT
More and more data is available on the Internet. This data can provide the context for new forms of entertainment and edutainment. Here we study fantasy sports as an example of how this happens and how users bound their data-oriented activities. Fantasy sports are enjoyed by many tens of millions of players around the world. But how engaged are these players and how do they manage the information-rich nature of the game? To start to answer these questions, we are investigating players' fantasy sports practices. How much time do they spend playing? What information do they use to make decisions? How do they interact with other players? In this paper, we report on 160 responses to a questionnaire of US-based Amazon Mechanical Turk workers who are self-identified fantasy sports players.

Categories and Subject Descriptors
K.8.0 [**Personal Computing**]: General– *games.*

Author Keywords
Fantasy sports; gaming practices.

1. INTRODUCTION
The Web is not just a provider of content aimed at human consumption. Whether provided by organizations intending to add their content to the "Web of Data" or by institutions viewing the Web as a delivery mechanism for the data they collect, more and more data streams are being captured and made available in near real time. These datasets enable new forms of engagement and entertainment. We are interested in encouraging engagement with data through new on-line activity. To gain insight into how this can be accomplished, we explore fantasy sports as a success model for motivating people to analyze large data sets.

Fantasy sports are interactive games where players act as if they are the manager of a team of athletes. The player competes against other fantasy team managers. Similar to real team management, players decide which athletes start, substitute for injured athletes, and trade athletes with other fantasy players. Each player's score is based on statistics about the performance of their athletes, generated by a single athlete or a team during a real sport event. Up-to-date knowledge of the sport is valuable for these games [2].

*WebSci'14,*June 23–26, 2014, Bloomington, IN, USA.
ACM 978-1-4503-2622-3/14/06.
http://dx.doi.org/10.1145/2615569.2615649

Fantasy Sports are very successful. According to the fantasy sports trade association (FSTA), 33.5 million people played fantasy sports in the United States in 2013 and this number is expected to rise in subsequent years[1].

While there has been a variety of research into the demographics and motivations of fantasy sports players, our focus is on how players collect and use information to make decisions. To explore this topic, we asked self-identified fantasy sports players about their gameplay and experiences. The five main research questions we were trying to answer:

Q1: *How do players select athletes for their teams?* Do players collect and analyze data or rely on their existing knowledge and tools provided by the game site (e.g. autodraft)?

Q2: *What are players' data collection and analysis practices?* For players that include data collection and research as part of athlete selection,(a) What resources are they using for data gathering? (b) What tools are they using for data analysis?

Q3: *How do players scope the data they include in their decision process?* Do players find the volume and velocity of athletes' statistics overwhelming? How many data types are included in their data analysis and decision making process?

Q4: *What is the time commitment and activities of players?* What are users' habits after the constitution of their team? Is there activity during the off-season?

Q5: *What aspects of fantasy sports are problematic?* What are constraints or issues perceived by users that impede their gameplay? What are recommendations for improvement?

2. METHOD AND RESULTS
A questionnaire was administered on Amazon's Mechanical Turk to help answer our five research questions. 160 responses were received to the 57 questions about respondent demographics, fantasy sports experiences and practices, and suggestions. Due to space constraints, we limit the discussion here to a few questions of engagement with the game and game data.

Participants were limited to Mechanical Turk users from the United States that had achieved a 95% or higher acceptance rate on past Human Intelligence Tasks. The 160 participants included 136 males (85%) and 24 females (15%). In terms of age, 71 (44%) were 18 to 25, 80 (50%) were 26 to 40, and 9 (5%) were over 40. The time commitment of players is quite high with almost all respondents reporting at least two interactions a week and slightly more than half reporting at least five interactions per week. (See Figure 1.) When asked about the average length of these interactions, 87.5%

of the respondents reported at least 15 minutes. This is shown in Figure 2.

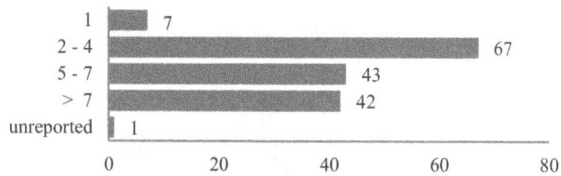

Figure 1. Interactions per week

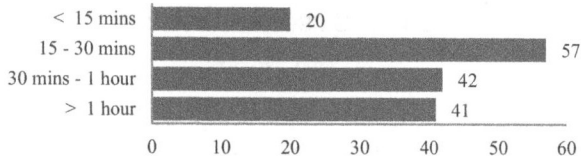

Figure 2. Length of average interaction during last season

In terms of data gathering and analysis during decision making, they reported most often using data provided by on-line sources with slightly more reporting use of external data/information sources than those that primarily used in-game data/information.

When asked about the number of variables or data streams used in making decisions, exactly half of the respondents reported using at least five data streams, as shown in Figure 3. The tools used to analyze this data were varied; most respondents reported using a combination of in-game tools for searching and sorting players and external tools, e.g.MS Excel for more complex analyses.

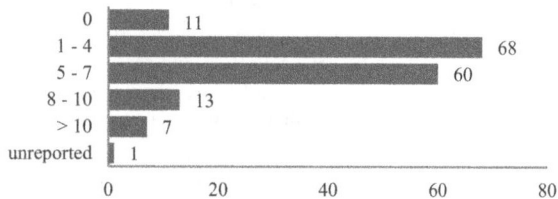

Figure 3. The number of data fields employed during the athlete selection process.

Comments from respondents indicated that the availability of data and tools in the game engine increased the likelihood of its use. This points towards the need for prediction game engines to support more than just the basic prediction and scoring functions. To encourage learners to increase their data interpretation skills, the data and the analysis tools need to be provided within the game engine.

Our survey also asked about motivations for playing fantasy sports. As found in other surveys on this topic, sports engagement, entertainment, socializing, and intellectual challenge are common to many players. Social reasons were discussed in open-ended responses more than any of the other factors. This is important for the design of prediction games in non-entertainment domains. It confirms that communication channels provided in the game (e.g. player-to-group forums and player-to-player direct messaging) are components that keep people engaged.

3. DISCUSSION AND CONCLUSION

This study provides insight into the data gathering and analysis practices of fantasy sports users, their time commitment to the game, and their motivations to their efforts.

During the athlete selection process to build their team, fantasy sports players prefer online resources like sports sites, social networks or discussion forums. They often employ strategies that involve analyzing the athletes' statistical data using a combination of tools built in to the game and external tools (excel or paper). Most of our respondents consider seven or fewer data fields during their analysis. Once their team is complete, they at least occasionally frequent the fantasy sports site to either get the latest updates on athletes, monitor their team scores, their rank and status in the league or to interact with other players.

Social interaction is a major factor for motivating our participants to play fantasy sports in the first place. Fantasy sports are considered important by many for maintaining family, friends, and workplace relationships. Other significant motivations include the engagement with sports, intellectual challenge and competition, and pure entertainment. Prizes were less commonly viewed as an important motivator.

The main complaints about fantasy sports concerned user interface issues and data limitations. The user interface issues included frustration over the inability to control data presentation and organization, e.g. the inability to sort or filter data. Participants also indicated that a simpler user interface would be welcome for novice players. Second, participants report that missing historical data and slow data updates undermine their data analysis activities. Finally, some players wanted better data analysis support, such as tools enabling data comparison/visualization and data export capabilities.

Our results have implications for improving fantasy sports systems and the design of data-driven web entertainment systems in other domains. First given the different responses regarding the volume of data and data analysis practices, future systems should consider enabling different levels of complexity to accommodate different classes of users. Systems for more advanced players should support the ability to filter data sets and compare/visualize subsets of data. They should also enable exporting data in an open format so that the user can transfer data to the tools of his/her choice and importing results that rank potential decisions.

Social interaction is an important factor for many forms of web entertainment. As such, design of data-driven entertainment should foster community building through competition or challenges to be overcome collaboratively. Game design should sustain communication at multiple levels. This includes forums for general discourse about the data domain, other forums at the contest level to discuss and set the rules or voice and resolve concerns of the members, and a chat system to facilitate user-to-user conversation.

As ever more data streams are made available via the Web, there are more opportunities for developing entertaining activities that motivate people to learn about this data. System developers can design activities that provide an intellectual challenge, generate opportunities to show one's knowledge or abilities, and foster social engagement and competition. The results here provide insight into such data-driven web entertainment systems.

4. ACKNOWLEDGEMENTS
This work was supported in part by NSF grant DUE-0938074.

5. REFERENCES
[1] FSTA. 2014. Industry Demographics. November 26, 2013. Retrieved from http://www.fsta.org/industry_demographics

[2] Shipman, F. "Blending the Real and Virtual in Games: The Model of Fantasy Sports", *Proc. ICFDG*, 2009, 169-17

Motivations of Citizen Scientists – A Quantitative Investigation of Forum Participation

Ramine Tinati
University of Southampton
Web and Internet Science
rt506@ecs.soton.ac.uk

Markus Luczak-Roesch
University of Southampton
Web and Internet Science
mlr1m12@soton.ac.uk

Elena Simperl
University of Southampton
Web and Internet Science
e.simperl@soton.ac.uk

Nigel Shadbolt
University of Southampton
Web and Internet Science
nrs@soton.ac.uk

Categories and Subject Descriptors

H.4.m [**Information Systems Applications**]: Miscellaneous

Keywords

Citizen science; online communities; discussion forums

1. INTRODUCTION

In recent years, the Web has fostered an emergent activity which has enabled individuals to take part and contribute to scientific discovery without the need for specific knowledge or expertise. These activities, which have been labelled as *Citizen Science* [1, 3, 4], use crowdsourcing and human-computation techniques[6] as a means to complete scientific tasks. Whilst the primary focus of citizen science is to achieve computationally complex tasks there has been growth of online citizen science community activity[5]. Online discussion forums and other forms of communication mechanisms such as social media are offering citizen scientists to talk, engage, share knowledge, and in several cases, achieve citizen-led scientific discovery [1].

In this paper we build upon previous qualitative studies of investigating the motivations of citizen science volunteers [8, 7] and analyse the Galaxy Zoo discussion forum[1]. We explore the motivations of citizen scientists participation and develop a model based on a number of features extracted from an individual's participation within the discussion forum. The purpose of this study is to further develop our current understanding of the characteristics of citizen science participation the factors that affect their participation and help better understand the engagement of citizen scientists.

In summary, we identified 9 clusters of participants which reflect the different features of forum interaction. By contextualising the features, we show that the interactions of the clustered participants may represent the motivations identified in previous studies.

---

[1]Galaxy Zoo Forums http://www.galaxyzooforum.org

Feature	Feature viable	Feature selected
# of posts created by a user	x	x
# of boards a user posted to	x	x
# of threads a user posted to	x	x
active lifetime of user account	x	
average length of a user's posts	x	
Frequency of user posts	x	x
# of personal messages sent	x	x
# of personal messages received	x	
# of voting polls created by a user	x	
# of votes cast by a user	x	x
# of sticky threads created by a user	x	
# of views received for user threads	x	x
# of responses received user threads	x	x
# of thread update notifications	x	x
# of board update notifications	x	
median position of a user's first posts in threads	x	
median position of a user's last posts in threads	x	
# of threads created by a user	x	x
# of threads that the user has provided the first reply	x	x
median # of posts a user contributes a thread	x	
# of questions asked by a user		
# of questions answered by a user		
# of quality posts created		

Table 1: **Overview of our extension of the user contribution model and the final set of features selected.**

2. RESULTS AND ANALYSIS

The analysis in this paper uses a dataset containing a snapshot of the Galaxy Zoo forum, containing all the posts made between 25th July 2007 (the first entry on the forum) to 31st January 2012. In order to investigate the relationship between the activity of a participant and the motivations of citizen scientists identified in previous studies within the Galaxy Zoo forum [8, 7], we propose a set of features that relate to a participant's activity within a forum based on 'user contribution management' literature [9, 2]. Table 1 lists the user contribution features which we use in this analysis.

We applying the Expectation Maximisation (EM) method as a model-based clustering approach which does not assume a fixed set of clusters and also allows for the detection of over fitting. By refining the feature set and fitting the best suited model to be applied we also gain insight into how many clusters represent the best partitioning of our data. We also apply a k-means approach iteratively for a minimum k=2 up to a maximum of k=15 (k is incremented by 1 in each iteration). This allows for estimating the optimal number of clusters for a given data set by determining significant drops in within groups sum of squares plotted against k.

The first iteration of the EM clustering method indicated that the 20 features result in overfitting. We iteratively eliminated features which did not perform well in terms of differentiating participant types until overfitting was reduced. The model-based approach and the k-means clustering suggest that good results can be achieved by 9 clusters. This result is the first indicator that not all of the 12 motivation categories of citizen scientists can be mapped to participant participation profiles in the Galaxy Zoo forum. Based on the results, we analyse the characteristics of each of the nine clusters and summarise the nine different participant types as follows:

Cluster 1: This group of highly active participants contributes a significantly high proportion of first replies to other participants' posts in a wide variety of threads. Since the amount of thread update notifications is rather low, we suggest that this represents question answering participants.

Cluster 2: The most active forum participants; they produce a very high number of posts in a wider variety of boards and threads, start threads and also provide initial replies. This seems to be the core group of participants, which feature a domestic behaviour on the Galaxy Zoo forum, so that they do not tend to exploit the thread notification feature for example.

Cluster 3: Similar feature characteristics as those in cluster 1 but differentiate from the by the high amount of thread notifications and low amount of first replies. These participants are likely to start new threads and show a significant interest in ongoing discussions without the motivation to contribute answers. Hence, they can be regarded as the followers asking new questions occasionally driven by a learning motivation.

Cluster 4: Participants who produce a high number of initial replies in the widest variety of boards. Since thread notifications are not used by this group, we suggest that these participants answer questions as the participants in cluster 1 but which are typically more trivial and do not result into real community discourse.

Cluster 5: Showing a very similar feature characteristic as cluster 3, this cluster is bordered by the lower personal message activity and amount of thread notifications. Both features indicate that these participants are also followers (as those in cluster 3) but with a lower involvement into the community and most likely also not driven by the motivation to learn from experienced participants and particular contents.

Cluster 6: This largest group of participants can be described as typical forum reader being active over a longer period of time due to a general interest in the forum thread. No feature shows significant peaks or dales.

Cluster 7: Characterised by kicking of a majority of threads in a wide variety of boards, participants in this cluster represent the long tail of only few participants contributing the majority of the content to a forum.

Cluster 8: People classified into this group participate in polls fairly frequent and spread a high number of posts across a wide variety of threads and boards. Also the low number of thread notifications and the high amount of initial replies stick out but most noteworthy is the number of responses the threads created by these participants obtain. We suggest, that these participants are highly engaged in real discussions and dispose fair domain knowledge they share with the community.

Cluster 9: Participants asking individual questions only, with a small number of posts, almost no personal message and poll activity and a low number of first replies to posts of other participants. The latter may indicate that participants within this group ask for help in the forum but do not have any other recognisable motivation for contributing forum content.

3. CONCLUDING REMARKS

The findings in this paper have show how there are several groups of individuals which are highly active, posting multiple times, within many different boards, and are eager respond. Alongside these highly motivated individuals are the the 'lurkers' on the forums that do not engage much. From a citizen science perspective the clusters identified support previous studies of citizen science motivations and relate interaction characteristics to these motivations [8, 7]. These findings provide further insight regarding the motivations of citizen scientists, as well as the study of online communities.

Future work in this area involves taking the features identified in this study and applying it to other citizen science discussion systems as well as communities using social media platforms. By applying the feature model developed in this paper to these systems, we wish to compare the characteristics of participation, and whether the same clusters, thus motivations can be identified.

4. ACKNOWLEDGEMENTS

This work is supported under SOCIAM: The Theory and Practice of Social Machines. The SOCIAM Project is funded by the UK Engineering and Physical Sciences Research Council (EPSRC) under grant number EP/J017728/1 and comprises the Universities of Southampton, Oxford and Edinburgh.

5. REFERENCES

[1] R. Bonney, C. B. Cooper, J. Dickinson, S. Kelling, T. Phillips, K. V. Rosenberg, and J. Shirk. Citizen science: a developing tool for expanding science knowledge and scientific literacy. *BioScience*, 59(11):977–984, 2009.

[2] K. Chai, V. Potdar, and E. Chang. User contribution measurement model for web-based discussion forums. *2009 3rd IEEE International Conference on Digital Ecosystems and Technologies*, pages 347–352, June 2009.

[3] S. A. Gray, K. Nicosia, and R. C. Jordan. Lessons learned from citizen science in the classroom. a response to" the future of citizen science.". *Democracy and Education*, 20(2):14, 2012.

[4] A. Irwin. *Citizen science: A study of people, expertise and sustainable development*. Psychology Press, 1995.

[5] G. Mugar, C. Ø sterlund, and K. Hassman. Planet Hunters and Seafloor Explorers: Legitimate Peripheral Participation Through Practice Proxies in Online Citizen Science. *CSCW'14*, 2014.

[6] A. J. Quinn and B. B. Bederson. Human computation: a survey and taxonomy of a growing field. In *Proceedings of the SIGCHI Conference on Human Factors in Computing Systems*, pages 1403–1412, 2011.

[7] J. Raddick, C. Lintott, and S. Bamford. Galaxy Zoo: Motivations of Citizen Scientists. *Astronomy Education Review*, pages 1–41, 2013.

[8] M. J. Raddick, G. Bracey, P. L. Gay, C. J. Lintott, P. Murray, K. Schawinski, A. S. Szalay, and J. Vandenberg. Galaxy zoo: Exploring the motivations of citizen science volunteers. *Astronomy Education Review*, 9:010103, 2010.

[9] Y. Wang and D. Fesenmaier. Understanding the motivation of contribution in online communities: An empirical investigation of an online travel community. *TTRA Annual Conference*, (2000), 2003.

Assisting Coordination during Crisis: A Domain Ontology based Approach to Infer Resource Needs from Tweets

Shreyansh Bhatt[1], Hemant Purohit[1], Andrew Hampton[2],
Valerie Shalin[1], Amit Sheth[1], John Flach[3]
Kno.e.sis Center, Wright State University, Dayton, OH, USA
[1] {shreyansh,hemant,amit,valerie}@knoesis.org,
[2,3] {hampton.14, john.flach}@wright.edu

ABSTRACT

Ubiquitous social media during crises provides citizen reports on the situation, needs and supplies. Previous research extracts resource needs directly from the text (e.g. *"Power cut to Coney Island and Brighton beach"* indicates a power need). This approach assumes that citizens derive and write about specific needs from their observations, properly specified for the emergency response system, an assumption that is not consistent with general conversational behavior. In our study, Twitter messages (tweets) from Hurricane Sandy in 2012 clearly indicate power blackouts, but not their probable implications (e.g. loss of power to hospital life support systems). We use a domain model to capture such interdependencies between resources and needs. We represent these dependencies in an ontology that specifies the functional association between resources. Accurate interpretation of resource need/supply also depends on the location of a message. We show how inference based on a domain model combined with location detection and interpretation in the social data can enhance situational awareness, e.g., predicting a medical emergency before it is reported as critical.

Categories and Subject Descriptors

H.1.2 User/Machine Systems

Keywords

Crisis Response, Crisis Response Co-ordination, Domain Model, Semantic Inference, Social Media for Emergency Management (SMEM).

1. INTRODUCTION

Use of social media during crises promises to revolutionize situational awareness in the emergency response community. Prior research applies information filtering and extraction techniques directly to the reported observation content to identify those that may assist the response activities [1]. However, explicit content is often incomplete due to unstated common ground among participants. According to established conversational maxims, explicit content appropriately provides only new information. For

example, while many tweets identify power blackouts, citizens do not identify the implications of power blackouts for each hospital. Newspapers however, document the resulting hospital compromise during Hurricane Sandy: http://j.mp/2Hospitals. Limitation of explicit tweet content is recognized and vocabulary tags are recommended in [2] for message creation but this can burden citizens. Role of ontology is acknowledged in [4] but they do not mine the implications of resource inter-dependencies. There have been several studies for using location to assist co-ordination e.g. [3]. However, these solutions considers only geo-location metadata while most of the tweets do not have geo-location metadata e.g. out of 4 million tweets we collected during first week of Hurricane Sandy, only 20% of the tweets had location metadata (location from source device sensor or author profile). Consistent with [7] we found that location information might appear in text. However, interpretation of location has not discussed.

The main contributions of this study are, (1) Use of domain knowledge to annotate and capture the inter-dependencies between resources (section 2), (2) Identification and annotation of text location (section 2).

2. APPROACH

We use the Twitter Streaming API to collect tweets and further process them for resource detection and location detection. We spot the entities in tweet text for the entity set of concepts in the domain model. Tweets are annotated with the crisis ontology (available at http://goo.gl/mm2qK8) that includes the relationship between power, medical, and food/water resources.

Next, we identify text location. Consider the resource identification in the tweet *"American Red Cross & City of Nashua Have Opened Shelter In Response to Hurricane Sandy"*. Understanding "Nashua" is critical to the utility of this tweet. In addition to sensor geo-location information provided from Twitter API and author profile location, we consider location from tweet text. Our aim is to locate resources, a problem that is more directly related to assisting responders than identifying the location of a person. Responders need to know whether a named location is country, state, county, or a specific street in a city. We used a twofold approach to identify and interpret text locations. First we use the Stanford NER [6] to detect location content from tweet text. Next we query DBpedia ontology [5] to determine whether the identified location is part of the locations list in DBpedia. DBpedia includes both global locations as well as information for well-known hospitals, parks, buildings, etc., that people often mention while tweeting and that may not otherwise be covered by a geo-location ontology. For example, the following tweet is annotated with two locations:

Evacuation in progress at Bellevue Hospital in New York City has begun. Their power generator has 1 hour left. #hurricane #sandy #nyc #nypd

http://dbpedia.org/resource/New_York_City,
http://dbpedia.org/resource/Bellevue_Hospital_Center

3. RESULTS AND DISCUSSION

Here we review some of the key findings for our full corpus of 4 million hurricane Sandy related tweets crawled during the period of 27th Oct to 4th Nov, 2012. The frequency of power related tweets is much greater than the frequency of medical tweets, or even food and water related tweets. Moreover, people rarely (less than 1% of the time) make the explicit link between compromise to the power grid and the consequences to medical, food, and water resources. From a sample of 1.4 million tweets collected between the 29th and 30th of October 2012, we found 50 tweets that reported a blackout well before the 21 tweets that reported hospital evacuation. Table 2 illustrates the trend from general power-related comments to specific comments about the compromised hospital. Tweets confirm the power outage at midnight, yet the report of hospital compromise appears three hours later, at 3:00 a.m. the next day.

Table 1: Tweets related to specific resource and location types

Type	Total	Text Location	Metadata Location	Text w/o metadata	Text and Metadata	Metadata w/o Text
Power	103102	14969	24361	10974	3995	20366
Medical	16002	3243	6015	2057	1186	4829
Food/water	38952	5046	9152	3574	1472	7680
Power & medical	948	231	377	134	97	280
Power & food	2908	382	839	260	122	717
Power, food & medical	44	39	30	13	26	17

Table 2: Medical/power tweets about http://j.mp/2Hospitals

Time (2012)	Message text	Text Location identified
Oct. 29, 21:30:02	Lots of wind and some rain but still running and no power outage in Clinton Hill, Brooklyn. #Sandy #Hurricane	http://dbpedia.org/resource/Brooklyn
Oct. 29, 23:56:57	Power cut to coney island and Brighton beach #HurricaneSandy #NYC	http://dbpedia.org/resource/Coney_Island
Oct. 30, 01:30:36	Power may be cut off soon in south bklyn. Coney, Gravesend Sheedshed Bay etc #Sandy #Frankenstorm	http://dbpedia.org/resource/Coney_Island
Oct. 30, 03:15:08	@911BUFF: BREAKING CONEY ISLAND HOSPITAL ON FIRE. NYU HOSP. EVACUATED, BELLEVUE HOSPITAL ALSO LOSING BACKUP POWER #SANDY #NYC #frankenstorm	http://dbpedia.org/resource/Bellevue_Hospital_Center
Oct. 30, 20:20:42	SANDY: Bellevue Hospital is on backup power, trying to evacuate as much as possible, 2 young boys missing from SI since beginning of Hurricane	http://dbpedia.org/resource/Bellevue_Hospital_Center

As shown in the Table 1, the ability to infer location from text increases location information over tweet metadata information by approximately 50%. To study this location dynamics we considered the sample of 1000 tweets having either metadata or text location from the above categories (food/water, medical, power and shelter) and manually labeled each tweet with whether identified text location is semantically relevant or not. We obtained 88% accuracy (agreement) for identifying location from text. That is, in 88 cases out of 100 human labelers considered the text location semantically relevant. The following example illustrates the potential for error: *"Hurricane Sandy projected to slam into New England coast... binders of woman seek shelter"*. This tweet was identified as having the location New_England, Australia. This happens because of location name ambiguity (New England exists in USA and Australia), which is not addressed in this paper. As we have used dbpedia to annotate locations, we could differentiate tweets having location of affected region and location which doesn't have affected region. Based on which table 3 suggests that in almost 66% of cases, when text location was mentioned in a tweet, it was mentioning a location from the affected crisis region. However only 43% of time, were tweets with tweet metadata location consistent with the crisis affected region. This suggests that mention of text location is more reliable than the tweet metadata location to locate a resource need/supply in the affected region. This observation is somewhat unexpected, and emphasizes the need for text interpretation.

Table 3: Text and tweet metadata location comparison

Location source	Total tweets	Total tweets with location in affected region	Tweets with location not in affected region
Text	517	340 (66%)	177 (34%)
Metadata	313	238 (43%)	323 (57%)

CONCLUSION AND ACKNOWLEDGEMENT

We present an approach using a domain knowledge model for understanding contextually interdependent resource needs reported via social media during crisis response. We also present an approach to identify location from text with relatively high accuracy and importance of text location. This work supported by NSF (IIS-1111182, 09/01/2011 - 08/31/2014) SoCS program.

4. REFERENCES

[1] Varga, I.; Sano, M.; Torisawa, K.; Hashimoto, C.; Ohtake, K.; Kawai, T.; Jong-Hoon, O.; & De Saeger, S. (2013). Aid is out there: Looking for help from tweets during a large scale disaster. In Proceedings of the 51st Annual Meeting of the Association for Computational Linguistics Vol. 1, pp. 1619-1629.

[2] Starbird, K.; & Stamberger, J. 2010. Tweak the tweet: Leveraging microblogging proliferation with a prescriptive syntax to support citizen reporting. ISCRAM '10.

[3] Cameron, M.A.; Power, R.; Robinson, B.; & Yin, J. 2012. Emergency situation awareness from twitter for crisis management. Proceedings of the 21st International Conference Companion on World Wide Web, pp. 695–698.

[4] Jihan, S.H.; & Segev, A. Context Ontology for Humanitarian Assistance in Crisis response. Proceedings of the 10th International ISCRAM Conference.

[5] Auer, S., Bizer, C., Kobilarov, G., Lehmann, J., Cyganiak, R., & Ives, Z. (2007). Dbpedia: A nucleus for a web of open data. The Semantic Web (pp. 722-735). Springer Berlin Heidelberg.

[6] Marie-Catherine de Marneffe, Bill MacCartney and Christopher D. Manning, Generating Typed Dependency Parses from Phrase Structure Parses, LREC-2006

[7] D. Pohl, A. Bouchachia, H. Hellwagner. Supporting Crisis Management via Detection of Sub-Events in Social Networks. International Journal of Information Systems for Crisis Response and Management. In Press (2013)

Data-Driven Web Entertainment: The Data Collection and Analysis Practices of Fantasy Sports Players

Gabriel S. Dzodom
Department of Computer Science
Texas A&M University
College Station, TX 77843-3112
gabriel.dzodom@tamu.edu

Frank M. Shipman
Department of Computer Science
Texas A&M University
College Station, TX 77843-3112
shipman@cse.tamu.edu

ABSTRACT

More and more data is available on the Internet. This data can provide the context for new forms of entertainment and edutainment. Here we study fantasy sports as an example of how this happens and how users bound their data-oriented activities. Fantasy sports are enjoyed by many tens of millions of players around the world. But how engaged are these players and how do they manage the information-rich nature of the game? To start to answer these questions, we are investigating players' fantasy sports practices. How much time do they spend playing? What information do they use to make decisions? How do they interact with other players? In this paper, we report on 160 responses to a questionnaire of US-based Amazon Mechanical Turk workers who are self-identified fantasy sports players.

Categories and Subject Descriptors

K.8.0 [**Personal Computing**]: General– *games.*

Author Keywords

Fantasy sports; gaming practices.

1. INTRODUCTION

The Web is not just a provider of content aimed at human consumption. Whether provided by organizations intending to add their content to the "Web of Data" or by institutions viewing the Web as a delivery mechanism for the data they collect, more and more data streams are being captured and made available in near real time. These datasets enable new forms of engagement and entertainment. We are interested in encouraging engagement with data through new on-line activity. To gain insight into how this can be accomplished, we explore fantasy sports as a success model for motivating people to analyze large data sets.

Fantasy sports are interactive games where players act as if they are the manager of a team of athletes. The player competes against other fantasy team managers. Similar to real team management, players decide which athletes start, substitute for injured athletes, and trade athletes with other fantasy players. Each player's score is based on statistics about the performance of their athletes, generated by a single athlete or a team during a real sport event. Up-to-date knowledge of the sport is valuable for these games [2].

*WebSci'14,*June 23–26, 2014, Bloomington, IN, USA.
ACM 978-1-4503-2622-3/14/06.
http://dx.doi.org/10.1145/2615569.2615649

Fantasy Sports are very successful. According to the fantasy sports trade association (FSTA), 33.5 million people played fantasy sports in the United States in 2013 and this number is expected to rise in subsequent years[1].

While there has been a variety of research into the demographics and motivations of fantasy sports players, our focus is on how players collect and use information to make decisions. To explore this topic, we asked self-identified fantasy sports players about their gameplay and experiences. The five main research questions we were trying to answer:

Q1: *How do players select athletes for their teams?* Do players collect and analyze data or rely on their existing knowledge and tools provided by the game site (e.g. autodraft)?

Q2: *What are players' data collection and analysis practices?* For players that include data collection and research as part of athlete selection,(a) What resources are they using for data gathering? (b) What tools are they using for data analysis?

Q3: *How do players scope the data they include in their decision process?* Do players find the volume and velocity of athletes' statistics overwhelming? How many data types are included in their data analysis and decision making process?

Q4: *What is the time commitment and activities of players?* What are users' habits after the constitution of their team? Is there activity during the off-season?

Q5: *What aspects of fantasy sports are problematic?* What are constraints or issues perceived by users that impede their gameplay? What are recommendations for improvement?

2. METHOD AND RESULTS

A questionnaire was administered on Amazon's Mechanical Turk to help answer our five research questions. 160 responses were received to the 57 questions about respondent demographics, fantasy sports experiences and practices, and suggestions. Due to space constraints, we limit the discussion here to a few questions of engagement with the game and game data.

Participants were limited to Mechanical Turk users from the United States that had achieved a 95% or higher acceptance rate on past Human Intelligence Tasks. The 160 participants included 136 males (85%) and 24 females (15%). In terms of age, 71 (44%) were 18 to 25, 80 (50%) were 26 to 40, and 9 (5%) were over 40. The time commitment of players is quite high with almost all respondents reporting at least two interactions a week and slightly more than half reporting at least five interactions per week. (See Figure 1.) When asked about the average length of these interactions, 87.5%

of the respondents reported at least 15 minutes. This is shown in Figure 2.

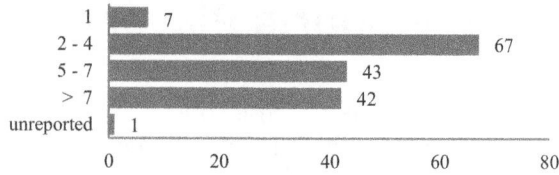

Figure 1. Interactions per week

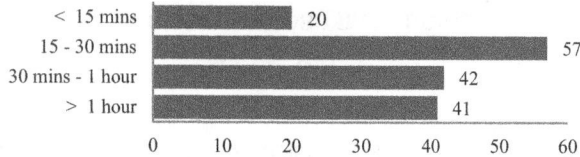

Figure 2. Length of average interaction during last season

In terms of data gathering and analysis during decision making, they reported most often using data provided by on-line sources with slightly more reporting use of external data/information sources than those that primarily used in-game data/information.

When asked about the number of variables or data streams used in making decisions, exactly half of the respondents reported using at least five data streams, as shown in Figure 3. The tools used to analyze this data were varied; most respondents reported using a combination of in-game tools for searching and sorting players and external tools, e.g.MS Excel for more complex analyses.

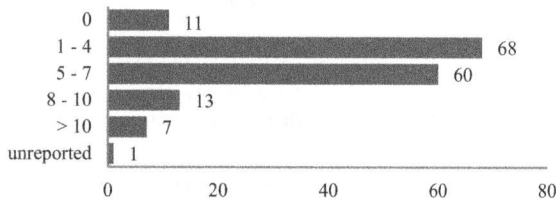

Figure 3. The number of data fields employed during the athlete selection process.

Comments from respondents indicated that the availability of data and tools in the game engine increased the likelihood of its use. This points towards the need for prediction game engines to support more than just the basic prediction and scoring functions. To encourage learners to increase their data interpretation skills, the data and the analysis tools need to be provided within the game engine.

Our survey also asked about motivations for playing fantasy sports. As found in other surveys on this topic, sports engagement, entertainment, socializing, and intellectual challenge are common to many players. Social reasons were discussed in open-ended responses more than any of the other factors. This is important for the design of prediction games in non-entertainment domains. It confirms that communication channels provided in the game (e.g. player-to-group forums and player-to-player direct messaging) are components that keep people engaged.

3. DISCUSSION AND CONCLUSION

This study provides insight into the data gathering and analysis practices of fantasy sports users, their time commitment to the game, and their motivations to their efforts.

During the athlete selection process to build their team, fantasy sports players prefer online resources like sports sites, social networks or discussion forums. They often employ strategies that involve analyzing the athletes' statistical data using a combination of tools built in to the game and external tools (excel or paper). Most of our respondents consider seven or fewer data fields during their analysis. Once their team is complete, they at least occasionally frequent the fantasy sports site to either get the latest updates on athletes, monitor their team scores, their rank and status in the league or to interact with other players.

Social interaction is a major factor for motivating our participants to play fantasy sports in the first place. Fantasy sports are considered important by many for maintaining family, friends, and workplace relationships. Other significant motivations include the engagement with sports, intellectual challenge and competition, and pure entertainment. Prizes were less commonly viewed as an important motivator.

The main complaints about fantasy sports concerned user interface issues and data limitations. The user interface issues included frustration over the inability to control data presentation and organization, e.g. the inability to sort or filter data. Participants also indicated that a simpler user interface would be welcome for novice players. Second, participants report that missing historical data and slow data updates undermine their data analysis activities. Finally, some players wanted better data analysis support, such as tools enabling data comparison/visualization and data export capabilities.

Our results have implications for improving fantasy sports systems and the design of data-driven web entertainment systems in other domains. First given the different responses regarding the volume of data and data analysis practices, future systems should consider enabling different levels of complexity to accommodate different classes of users. Systems for more advanced players should support the ability to filter data sets and compare/visualize subsets of data. They should also enable exporting data in an open format so that the user can transfer data to the tools of his/her choice and importing results that rank potential decisions.

Social interaction is an important factor for many forms of web entertainment. As such, design of data-driven entertainment should foster community building through competition or challenges to be overcome collaboratively. Game design should sustain communication at multiple levels. This includes forums for general discourse about the data domain, other forums at the contest level to discuss and set the rules or voice and resolve concerns of the members, and a chat system to facilitate user-to-user conversation.

As ever more data streams are made available via the Web, there are more opportunities for developing entertaining activities that motivate people to learn about this data. System developers can design activities that provide an intellectual challenge, generate opportunities to show one's knowledge or abilities, and foster social engagement and competition. The results here provide insight into such data-driven web entertainment systems.

4. ACKNOWLEDGEMENTS

This work was supported in part by NSF grant DUE-0938074.

5. REFERENCES

[1] FSTA. 2014. Industry Demographics. November 26, 2013. Retrieved from http://www.fsta.org/industry_demographics

[2] Shipman, F. "Blending the Real and Virtual in Games: The Model of Fantasy Sports", *Proc. ICFDG*, 2009, 169-17

Regular Behavior Measure for Location Based Services

Aki Hayashi, Tatsushi Matsubayashi, Hiroshi Sawada
NTT Service Evolution Laboratories, NTT Corporation
1-1 Hikari-no-oka Yokosuka-Shi, Kanagawa, Japan
{hayashi.aki, matsubayashi.tatsushi, sawada.hiroshi}@lab.ntt.co.jp

ABSTRACT

We introduce a method that can measure the degree of regularity or irregularity of the behavior for enhancing the performance of location-based services (LBSs) such as *check-in*. It is still challenging for LBSs to determine the places to recommend that best suits the user's needs. Our aim is to identify the user's status (regular or irregular) of each check-in. Most previous studies approached this problem by acquiring usual locations (e.g., home or office) or assessing check-in frequency. We propose more effective measure by using a multinomial-distribution-based method that considers the periodic check-ins of the user on various time-scales. Our method can accurately identify irregular check-ins even in usual locations and we find that the users tend to continue irregular check-ins in a certain range of time.

Categories and Subject Descriptors

H.4.m [**Information system applications**]: Miscellaneous

Keywords

Location Based Social Networks; Recommendation system; Probabilistic model; Next location prediction

1. INTRODUCTION

The growth of mobile devices and social networking services has led to a rapid increase in the importance of LBSs. Most existing services based their recommendations on the present location and log frequency. They tend to recommend the user's favorite shops in a usual situation such as being near home. However, in unusual circumstances the user might desire something new. In those circumstances, they tend to recommend shops that are popular with local residents, though the user would prefer to find restaurants unique to the area that are popular with travelers. LBSs still have great difficulty in determining the most suitable timing and locations that will satisfy the user's needs because two aspects of the user's information needs must be considered. One is *daily-life information*; this is related to the user's regular behaviors and includes information such as weather information and traffic jams around the office. The other is *novelty*; this is related to irregular behaviors and tends to consist of information on local restaurants and shops.

WebSci'14, June 23–26, 2014, Bloomington, IN, USA.
ACM 978-1-4503-2622-3/14/06.
http://dx.doi.org/10.1145/2615569.2615657.

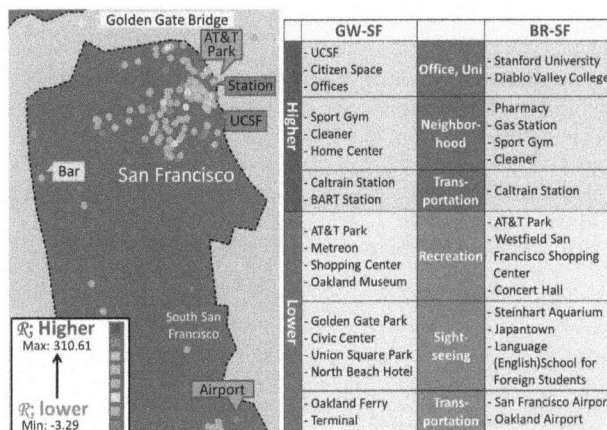

Figure 1: (Left) Averaged regularity of visits to the places around San Francisco. (Right) Places that is likely to be visited in particularly regular/irregular situation.

An LBS that can emphasize daily-life information during regular actions and novel information during irregular actions stands a greater chance of user acceptance. To create such an LBS, we need to identify the user's status; how regular or irregular each action (check-in) is. Many conventional methods consider the user's behavior patterns. Some rule-based methods [1, 2] distinguish irregular situations according to the distance from the home or office, while another method [3] considers log entries made within a period of time. However, these methods fail to distinguish kinds of irregular actions such as "back home late" and "go shopping close to the office with family on weekend." Our solution is to take account of the check-in timing by using multinomial-based distributions with four time scales: hour (for restaurants whose opening hours are fixed), day of the week (out-of-office workers), hour and day simultaneously (in-house staff) and without time consideration (railway stations and convenience stores). The best time scale in terms of regularity/irregularity measurement depends on the user, place and time. Thus we combine these four distributions.

As an example of the proposal, Figure 1(left) shows the averaged regularity of visits around San Francisco(SF) colored by our measure. The value is higher if the place is visited regularly (e.g., every week), and lower if it is visited irregularly (e.g., occasionally, for the first time). Figure 1(right) shows the places in San Francisco whose averaged value is particularly higher or lower using two LBS datasets (GW-SF and BR-SF) we explain in Section 3. We can distinguish the places that are popular in irregular situations (airport, AT&T park) and those popular in regular situation (universities, stations). We can also find Golden gate bridge (whose regularity is relatively low) to be a nice place for travelers to enjoy sightseeing.

Table 1: Sample data and accuracy of each model

DATA	L	U	$M_{ut}^{(1)}$	$M_{ut}^{(2)}$	$M_{ut}^{(3)}$	$M_{ut}^{(4)}$	M_{ut}
GW-JP	50,785	1,164	29.6	28.8	28.0	32.4	**33.2**
GW-SF	258,355	7,044	21.0	19.9	19.5	22.0	**22.4**
BR-JP	332,716	3,194	40.6	35.1	38.0	40.1	**40.8**
BR-SF	118,323	4,552	66.8	63.7	65.5	66.0	**67.6**

2. REGULAR BEHAVIOR MEASURE

First, the proposed method combines four probabilistic models to consider periodic behavior formulated by $\mathcal{M} = \{\{\{M_{ut}^{(i)}(l)\}_{t=1}^{T_i}\}_{u=1}^{U}\}_{i=1}^{4}$ where $M_{ut}^{(i)}$ represents multinomial distribution and where $\sum_{l=1}^{L} M_{ut}^{(i)}(l) = 1$. Here, u =user ID, l =location ID (L stands for the number of locations) and t =time obtained from check-in logs. when i=1, t indicates hour[1-24] h, when i=2, it indicates day of the week d, when i=3, it indicates both h and d, and when i=4, it does not consider either. Thus, $T_1 = 24, T_2 = 7, T_3 = 168, T_4 = 1$.

Next, we define *regular behavior measure* $\mathcal{R}$ as follows:

$$\mathcal{R} = \{\mathcal{R}_{lut}\}, \quad \mathcal{R}_{lut} = \sum_{i=1}^{4} w_{ut}^{(i)} \mathcal{R}_{lut}^{(i)}, \quad (1)$$

where $\mathcal{R}_{lut}^{(i)} = \frac{M_{ut}^{(i)}(l) - \mu}{\sigma_{ut}^{(i)}}$. μ stands for the average probability for all locations, which is constant value $(1/L)$, and $\sigma_{ut}^{(i)}$ is the variance of $M_{ut}^{(i)}$. $\mathcal{R}_{lut}^{(i)}$ is high if the probability for the current location is outstanding in the distribution. Thus its value is high if the check-in is considered to be a regular action. When the user visits a place for the first time in t, $\mathcal{R}_{lut}^{(i)}$ is a negative value: $-1 < \mathcal{R}_{lut}^{(i)} \leq 0$. Here, if $\mathcal{R}_{lut}^{(i)}$ is close to 0, the check-in is considered to be more irregular. Therefore, it replaces $\mathcal{R}_{lut}^{(i)}$ with $-\mathcal{R}_{lut}^{(i)} - 1$ to reverse the magnitude correlation. $w_{ut}^{(i)}$ is the weight of $\mathcal{R}_{lut}^{(i)}$ that considers the check-in count stored in t divided by the maximum count of all time period of each time-scale: $w_{ut}^{(i)} = C_{ut}^{(i)} / \max_j C_{uj}^{(i)}$, where C stands for the check-in count and $C_u^{(i)} = \{C_{u1}^{(i)}, C_{u2}^{(i)}, ..., C_{uT_i}^{(i)}\}$.

3. EVALUATION AND DISCUSSION

We obtained four check-in data sets taken from two LBSs, Gowalla(GW) and Brightkite(BR) for each location, Japan (JP) and San Francisco(SF) from SNAP[1]. The number of locations L and users U are shown in column 2-3 of Table 1.

Before discussing the results of $\mathcal{R}$, to evaluate the accuracy of the probabilistic model, we divided the data into training data (80%) and test data (20%) then calculate the predicted next location and choose the top 5 places. The results are shown in column 4-8 of Table 1. Column 8 shows the results of the combination model defined as $M_{ut} = \sum_{i=1}^{4} \hat{w}_{ut}^{(i)} M_{ut}^{(i)}$, where $\hat{w}_{ut}^{(i)}$ is the normalization of $w_{ut}^{(i)}$ defined in equation (1). M_{ut} achieves the highest accuracy among all models. We can see the effectiveness of time-scale combination that is also considered in definition of $\mathcal{R}$.

Figure 2(top) shows the map(latitude and longitude) of several user's personal $\mathcal{R}$ averaged over his all check-ins to the place. We can find some irregularly visited places even near regularly visited places as indicated by circles. Figure 2(bottom) shows the transition of a specific user's $\mathcal{R}$ of each check-in. It is clear that the user's behavior status exhibits continuity. We can capture subtle changes in the

[1]http://snap.stanford.edu/data/#locnet

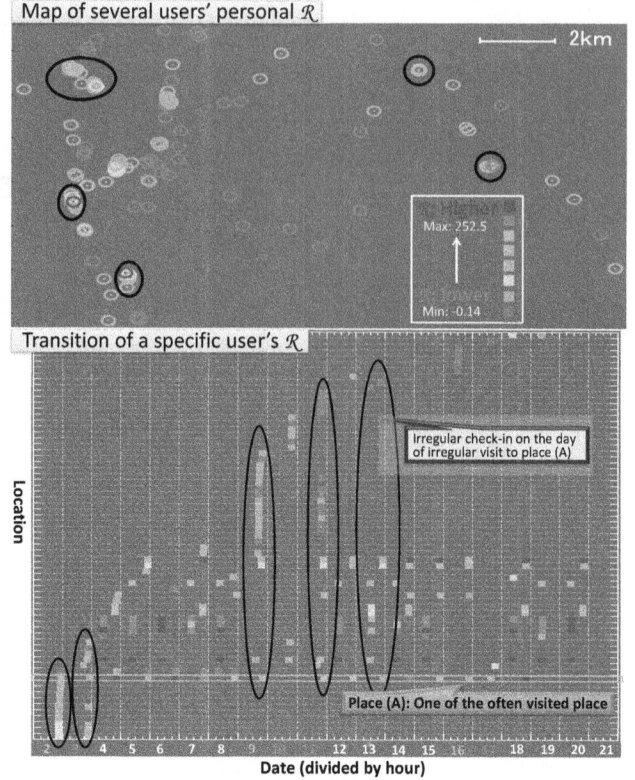

Figure 2: (Top) $\mathcal{R}$ map of several users. (Bottom) Transition of a specific user's $\mathcal{R}$ of each check-in.

degree of irregularity even in often visited place (A) surrounded by the pink rectangle. This is an attribute that cannot be matched by conventional methods. When the user visited (A) later or earlier than usual, $\mathcal{R}$ became lower. On the days surrounded by the black ellipse, the user visited (A) a little bit irregularly, and around the time of such visit, the user visited other places irregularly. We can assume that the user will welcome recommendation of unknown places in such an irregular situation.

4. CONCLUSION

We presented *regular behavior measure* $\mathcal{R}$, that offers good performance in terms of scoring the degree of regularity / irregularity of check-ins to yield more effective LBS. Using $\mathcal{R}$, we can even identify how irregular a check-in is and we show the continuousness of irregular check-ins. Moreover we find that the variation of $\mathcal{R}$ for the identical place is small enough. Therefore, according to $\mathcal{R}$, LBS can find the timing of irregular check-ins and recommend new places often visited by other users in a similar situation using the map of $\mathcal{R}$ (e.g., more detailed version of Figure 1(left)). We expect that the proposed measure will play an active role in many applications.

5. REFERENCES

[1] Cho. et al. Friendship and Mobility: User Movement in Location-based Social Networks. *SIGKDD*, pages 1082–1090, 2011.

[2] Kurashima. et al. Geo Topic Model: Joint Modeling of User's Activity Area and Interests for Location Recommendation. *WSDM*, pages 375–384, 2013.

[3] Leung. et al. CLR: A Collaborative Location Recommendation Framework Based on Co-clustering. *SIGIR*, pages 305–314, 2011.

Female Semantic Web Researchers: Does Collaboration with Male Researchers Influence their Network Status?

Tamy Chambers, Staša Milojević, Ying Ding
School of Informatics & Computing, Department of Information & Library Science
Indiana University, Bloomington, Indiana
tischt@indiana.edu, smilojev@indiana.edu, dingying@indiana.edu

ABSTRACT

The movement to increase gender diversity in computing and computer science is a well-funded and well researched mission. However, despite this, female representation within the field tends to lag behind that of other disciplines within the academy, both among students and faculty. This study sets out to correlate bibliometric and network measures to identify successful and influential women in the computer science subdomain of semantic web research and identify the impact of their collaboration with both men and other women as part of the their success.

Categories and Subject Descriptors

K.7 THE COMPUTING PROFESSION

1. INTRODUCTION

Gender diversity in computing has been addressed by the highest of organizations though both research and financial support. Since 2001, The United States National Science Foundation (NSF) has funded more than $130M in ADVANCE grant projects to increase the representation of women in the STEM sciences, of which Computer Science is one. The Association of Computing Machinery (ACM), the largest and most influential scientific computing society in the world, maintains a *"Women in Computing"* committee (ACM-W) to advocate on behalf of women in all computing fields. Based on findings form a European Commission report by the ETAN Expert Working Group on Women and Science (2002), the European Union has initiated "gender mainstreaming" to increase female participation in all activities relating to science and technology.

Research in the area of gender diversity in computing is considerably broad as it addresses female representation both within the educational and employment process [2]. The current study however, focuses on academic faculty in the computer sciences; in particular the collaboration patterns of female researchers within the Semantic Web area. Given that collaboration and co-authorship is very prevalent in this domain, this study seeks to understand how gender impacts collaboration. The study first identifies the most successful and influential female Semantic Web researchers based on the co-authorship network centrality measures (degree, betweeness, and Eigenvector), and second analyzes their collaboration patterns

based on gender to see if those who are most influential have more collaborations with men than women.

Other studies of gender in academic publishing have included, a survey study in 2002 [4] that concluded "rank, years since PhD, type of university, discipline and department, amount of research time, and marital status are better associated with publication than gender" (p.172), a more recent study in 2013, where researchers assigned *h-indices* to faculty based on their publication record, noted that "men had significantly higher h-indices than women" [1] (p.215), and a study that analyzed paper counts and citation counts in a far reaching study of all women in science across the world, to conclude that "despite many good intentions and initiatives, gender inequality is still rife in science" [3] (p. 211).

2. METHODOLOGY

Bibliographic data for this study was obtained from Arnetminer and supplemented with data mined to identify gender in a process described below. Arnetminer (arnetminer.org) is search and mining service which automatically creates semantic based researcher profiles by extracting information distributed throughout the Web. The data captured by this system is primarily from the computer science domain and includes more than 6000 conferences and 3,200,000 publications integrated into 700,000 researcher profiles from more than 200 countries. Our dataset included 8,193 publications from 11,290 authors published between 1983 and 2009.

Identification of the gender of each author was based on analysis of their first name. This means of gender identification has been used in other studies including a study commissioned by the European Commission [5] which created a database from multiple sources including dictionaries, name lists from foreign consulates, academies, and government organizations. More recently a study analyzing gender disparities in scholarly publishing also used a similar gender assignment method from sources such as the US census, WikiName, and Wikipedia [3].

In this study we used the US census list and lists from two international baby name websites (Baby Names Wizard and Babynames World) to obtain gender. The US census list of first names is drawn from the 2010 census and each name is identified with the percentage of its use as either a male or female. This, however, identified only 20% of the names used in our study. Lists of names and gender identification for European, Indian, African, and Asian names were run against the remaining names, after which the gender of less than 30% of the authors remained unknown.

A co-authorship network was created and analyzed based on the following three centrality measures: degree centrality, which identifies those nodes most connected to the community and which are thus the most influential, betweeness centrality which identifies nodes which serve as bridges in the network, and Eigenvector centrality which identifies nodes most connected to influential nodes.

The collaboration patterns of the top female authors for each centrality measure were identified based on the gender of all their co-authorship connections. The percentage of both male and female collaboration for each was found by dividing each by the total collaborations for that author. The average collaboration and standard deviation are based on the totals of the top 24 women identified using the three centrality measures.

3. RESULTS

The first goal of this study was to identify the most successful and influential female researchers in the Semantic Web domain given co-authorship. Table 1 lists the top researchers identified by each centrality measure. The following three tables identify the collaboration percentage of each researcher by centrality measure.

Table 1: Top 5 ranked women by centrality measure

Degree Centrality	Betweeness Centrality	Eigenvector Centrality
C Goble	C Goble	C Goble
A Gomez-Perez	K Sycara	M Sabou
D McGuinness	A Gomez-Perez	A Gomez-Perez
M Sabou	D McGuinness	T Catarci
Y Gil	M Sabou	A Illarramendi

Table 2: Female researchers ranked by degree centrality and compared by collaboration percentages

Degree	Male Coll.	SD	Female Coll.	SD
C Goble	69.5%	0.77	18.9%	-0.31
A Gomez-Perez	64.5%	0.30	22.4%	0.41
D McGuinness	64.0%	0.26	22.7%	0.47
M Sabou	59.2%	-0.19	30.6%	2.14
Y Gil	56.3%	-0.46	20.8%	0.08

Avg. male collaboration = .61 (σ =.107784). Avg. female collaboration = .20 (σ =.047582)

Table 3: Female researchers ranked by betweeness centrality and compared by collaboration percentages.

Betweeness	Male Coll.	SD	Female Coll.	SD
C Goble	69.5%	0.77	18.9%	-0.31
K Sycara	55.8%	-0.50	16.3%	-0.87
A Gomez-Perez	64.5%	0.30	22.4%	0.41
D McGuinness	64.0%	0.26	22.7%	0.47
M Sabou	59.2%	-0.19	30.6%	2.14

Avg. male collaboration = .61 (σ =.107784). Avg. female collaboration = .20 (σ =.047582)

Table 4: Female researchers ranked by Eigenvector centrality and compared by collaboration percentages.

Eigenvector	Male Coll.	SD	Female Coll.	SD
C Goble	69.5%	0.77	18.9%	-0.31
M Sabou	59.2%	-0.19	30.6%	2.14
A Gomez-Perez	64.5%	0.30	22.4%	0.41
T Catarci	68.3%	0.66	22.0%	0.32
A Illarramendi	69.2%	0.74	17.9%	-0.52

Avg. male collaboration =. 61 (σ =.107784). Avg. female collaboration = .20 (σ =.047582)

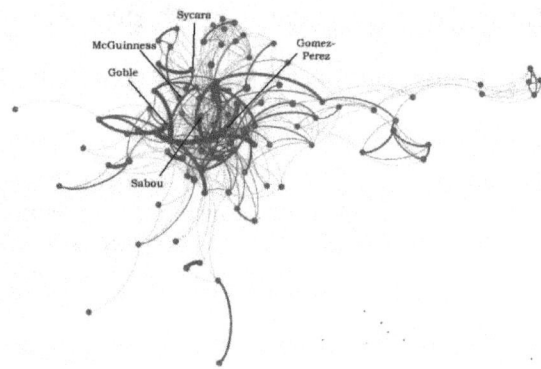

Figure 1: Top 99 researchers based on degree centrality

4. CONCLUSIONS

The results of the current study, show a small correlation between the network measures of women in the Semantic Web domain and their higher than average collaboration with male researchers. Figure 1 shows that most collaboration is either between men (blue line) or men and women (purple line), but that there is little collaboration between women (red line).

C. Goble ranked first in all three network measures, she also had a higher than average collaboration rate with male researchers and a lower than average collaboration rate with female researchers. **A Illarramendi** shows a similar collaboration pattern. **A. Gomez-Perez, T Catarci,** and **D.McGuinness** have similar higher than average collaboration with men, but all also have a higher than average collaboration with women. The collaboration pattern of **M Sabou and Y Gil** are complete opposite to both **C. Goble** and **A Illarramendi** in that they both have lower than average collaboration with men and higher than average collaboration with women.

Later stages of this research will review results past the top five women for each measure and increase the gender identification process to identify the gender of more researchers.

5. ACKNOWLEDGEMENTS

We would like to thank the NSF for the funding support made possible through the grant named "Incubators of knowledge: Predicting protégé productivity and impact in the social sciences"

6. REFERENCES

[1] Eloy, J.A. et al. 2013. Gender disparities in scholarly productivity within academic otolaryngology departments. *OTOLARYNG HEAD NECK* 148, 2 (Feb. 2013), 215–22.

[2] Franklin, D. 2013. *A Practical Guide to Gender Diversity for Computer Science Faculty.* Morgan Claypool.

[3] Lariviere, V. et al. 2013. Bibliometrics: Global gender disparities in science. *Nature.* 504, 7479 (2013), 211–213.

[4] Nakhaie, M.R. 2002. Gender Differences in Publication among University Professors in Canada. *CAN REV SOCIOL* 39, 2 (2002), 151–179.

[5] The ETAN Expert Working Group on Women in Science 2002. *Science policies in the European Union: Promoting excellence through mainstreaming gender equity.* European Commission.

Author Index